Equity and Trusts

D1556105

Equity and Trusts

Emma Warner-Reed, LLB (Hons), LLM

Solicitor
Senior Lecturer in Law, Leeds Metropolitan University

Longman
is an imprint of

Harlow, England • London • New York • Boston • San Francisco • Toronto
Sydney • Tokyo • Singapore • Hong Kong • Seoul • Taipei • New Delhi
Cape Town • Madrid • Mexico City • Amsterdam • Munich • Paris • Milan

Pearson Education Limited
Edinburgh Gate
Harlow
Essex CM20 2JE
England

and Associated Companies throughout the world

Visit us on the World Wide Web at:
www.pearsoned.co.uk

First published 2011

© Pearson Education Limited 2011

ISBN: 978-1-4082-2456-4

British Library Cataloguing-in-Publication Data
A catalogue record for this book is available from the British Library

Library of Congress Cataloging-in-Publication Data
Warner-Reed, Emma.
    Equity and trusts / Emma Warner-Reed.
        p. cm.
    Includes index.
    ISBN 978-1-4082-2456-4 (pbk.)
    1. Equity--England--Outlines, syllabi, etc.   2. Trusts and trustees--England--
Outlines, syllabi, etc.   I. Title.
    KD674.W37 2011
    346.42'004--dc22

                                                        2010053157

10 9 8 7 6 5 4 3 2 1
15 14 13 12 11

Typeset in 10.5/13pt Minion by 35
Printed by Ashford Colour Press Ltd., Gosport

Brief contents

Contents

Your complete learning package

Visit **www.mylawchamber.co.uk/warner-reed** to access a wealth of resources to support your studies and teaching.

 All our premium sites provide access to **an interactive Pearson eText**, an electronic version of *Equity and Trusts* which is fully **searchable**. You can **personalise** your Pearson eText with your own notes and bookmarks and extensive **links are provided to all of the resources** below. The eText page presentation mirrors that of your textbook.

Use the eText to link to **Case Navigator** for help and practise with case reading and analysis in *Equity and Trusts*.

In addition access:

✦ Practice exam questions with guidance to hone your exam technique

✦ Interactive 'You be the judge' multiple choice questions

✦ Annotated weblinks to help you read more widely around the subject and really impress your lecturers

✦ Glossary and key case flashcards to test yourself on legal terms, principles and definitions

✦ Audio legal updates to help you stay up to date with the law and impress examiners

Use the access card at the back of the book to activate mylawchamber premium. Online purchase is also available at **www.mylawchamber.co.uk/register**.

Teaching support materials

✦ **Case Navigator** is easy to integrate into any course where case reading and analysis skills are required

✦ The **Equity and Trusts MyTest testbank** can be used to create print tests or to create tests to **download into your learning environment**. It gives you access to a wide variety of questions designed to be used in formal assessments or to check students' progress throughout the course and includes over **350** questions

✦ **Instructor's Manual** including ideas for seminars and assessment with handouts for use in class

✦ **Downloadable documents from the law** and **diagrams** for use in seminars.

Also: The regularly maintained mylawchamber premium site provides the following features:

✦ Search tool to help locate specific items of content.

✦ Online help and support to assist with website usage and troubleshooting.

Use the access card at the back of the book to activate mylawchamber premium. Online purchase is also available at **www.mylawchamber.co.uk/register**.

Case Navigator access is included with your mylawchamber premium registration. The LexisNexis element of Case Navigator is only available to those who currently subscribe to LexisNexis Butterworths online.

Guided tour

Key points
Identify the essential elements of each chapter, aiding your core understanding of the chapter.

Key points In this chapter we will be looking

- ◆ The historical development of equity and the Court of Chancery
- ◆ The maxims of equity
- ◆ The development of the trust and why we need trusts
- ◆ The anatomy of a trust
- ◆ The terminology of trusts
- ◆ The terminology of wills
- ◆ Different types of trust
- ◆ Trusts distinguished from other c
- ◆ Modern uses for trusts

People in the law
Read the interviews from people affected by Equity and Trusts law and gain insight from their first-hand experiences.

People in the law
Tracing heirs: difficulties in evidential uncertainty

One of the best-known cases of evidential uncertainty is the famous Hall/Edwards Estate, which is purported to own some 77 acres of downtown Manhattan, New York, including such New York City landmarks as Trinity Church, the Woolworth Building, New York University, Washington Square Park and the ill-fated World Trade Center, the site having been valued at up to $680 billion before 9/11. Canadian-born Bob Sterne tells us all about it.

So, Bob, what is your connection with the story? I am a descendant of the Edwards line and a keen genealogist, and so I have become interested in the 'Edwards Estate' legend.

What is it all about? There are several versions of this story, all of which have probably become

Source: Photodisc/Life File/Andrew Ward

over 5,000 claimants to a share in the Hall/Edw fortune.

Law in action
Learn how the system works in practice through examples and problem scenarios found in the news.

Law in action The Gillingham Bus Disaster

At three minutes to six on the evening of the 4 December 1951 a double-decker bus careered into a company of Royal Marine cadets who were marching en route to attend a boxing tournament. Of the cadets, who were all between the ages of 10 and 13, 24 were killed and a further 18 were injured. At the time, the accident was reported to be the highest loss of life in any road accident in British history.

The mayors of three local parishes set up a memorial fund, asking for donations:

to be devoted, among other things, to defraying the funeral expenses, caring for the boys who may be disabled, and then to such worthy cause or causes in memory of the

boys who lost their lives, as the mayors determine.

The fund received almost £9,000 in donations. event, the bus company admitted liability fo accident and paid out £10,000 in compensati the families of the boys. Only a small proporti the mayors' fund was therefore ever used. To thi the Chatham Marine Cadet Unit still holds an a memorial parade at the cemetery in which the ca were buried to commemorate the tragic loss many young lives.

For more information about the disaster, g http://www.historicmedway.co.uk/disast gillingham_bus_disaster.htm.

Case summary

Learn the essential facts, details of the case and the decision, all in these concise summaries, integrated into the text yet pulled out in the margins for easy reference.

both of which date back to the 1800s. In the case of *Pettinghall* v. *Pettinghall* (1842) 176, a testator left a gift to his favourite black mare in the following terms:

y **bequeath**, that at my death, £50 per annum be paid for her keep in some park in d or Wales; her shoes to be taken off, and she never to be ridden or put in harness; at my executor consider himself in honour bound to fulfil my wish, and see that she well provided for, and removable at his will. At her death all payment to cease.

was upheld by the court, albeit with very strict requirements imposed on the as to the maintenance of the horse, and with the right reserved to the bene- of the remainder of the testator's **estate** to claim the trust money if it transpired horse was not being properly cared for.

ilar result was achieved in the later case of *Re Dean* (1889) 41 Ch D 552, in which purported to leave sufficient money in trust to allow a sum of £750 per year to or the maintenance of his horses, ponies and hounds over a period of 50 years, ny of them live that long'.

Documenting the law

Documents are reproduced throughout to give you a sense of how the law looks and feels in practice through real examples.

Documenting the law

The form shown here is that which employees of Air Jamaica were asked to complete to make a c respect of the fund following the closure of the pension scheme.

Note the wording at the bottom authorising payment of the trust funds into a nominated bank acc

Key stats

Information about what is happening in the real world helps you to relate to the practical side of the law.

Key stats

In November 2007, the Directory of Social Change ('DSC'), a charity focused on providing information and training to the voluntary sectors, ran a survey aimed at gauging public opinion on whether the position of trustee should come with a wage attached. The DSC posed the following to a total of 932 people:

> The DSC has long maintained that unpaid trus-teeship is a fundamental characteristic of the voluntary sector, and that trustees should not receive remuneration either for their contribution as trustees, or for other services delivered to the charities they govern. Do you agree with us?

Source: Imagestate/John Foxx Collection

Diagrams and flowcharts

These visual aids make complex legal processes easier to follow and understand.

Figure 14.2 Proposed division of the trust fund

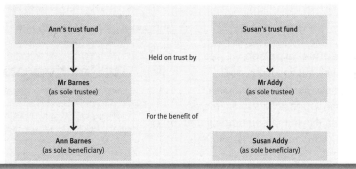

You be the judge
Use your knowledge and apply it as you go to real-life scenarios to fully test your understanding.

You be the judge

Q: Which of the following are public trusts?

(a) £10,000 towards the education of the nephews and nieces of Mathilda and Edward Jones.

(b) £10,000 towards the education of the children of employees of Leeds Metropolitan University.

(c) £10,000 towards the education of children from impoverished backgrounds in th county of North Yorkshire.

A: Only (c) is a public trust, being directed at a section of the public. The others are all private being for the benefit only of a private group of people, albeit a potentially large group in the c the university.

Writing and drafting
Practise your drafting and writing to enhance your practical legal skills and employability.

Writing and drafting

Bearing in mind the types of things listed in the text, now have a go at writing your own simple will. You should not need to spend more than 30 minutes on this.

Don't worry if you are not a member of any sports or social clubs, or if you don't own a pet; you can use these as examples, or have a bit of fun and simply use your imagination. Just think about who or what you would like your money to benefit and go from there.

Remember, the aim of this exercise is not to create the perfect legal document, but only to get you thinking about the types of gifts you may wish to incorporate in it. Your will therefore does not have to be technically correct: it is the thought that counts!

 Handy tip: Not sure where to start? Most lawyers use precedents, or templates, to help them when they are creating a new document: it saves them from having to write the whole thing from scratch every time. There are many will precedents available online which vary in length and quality. Alternatively, if you prefer to use a more tradi-

Out and about
Venture out and visit the suggested places or stay in and visit the websites to improve your understanding of the areas covered in each chapter.

Out and about

Are you a member of an unincorporated association? Think about clubs which you may have joined: a sport or social club, perhaps the working men's club or tennis club; or maybe you belong to a choir or an amateur dramatics society.

Now pick one of these clubs or associations to use as the basis for this exercise. If you are not a member of any group, ask your family or friends for help: there is bound to be somebody who belongs to a club near you. Failing this, just choose a local club, a golf or cricket club would be a good choice, one you can easily contact.

Your next task is to get hold of the rules and

Reflective practice
How well did you really do? Use these sections to critically analyse your answers to exercises, deepening your understanding and raising your marks in assessments.

Reflective practice

As you can see the policy statement is really quite comprehensive. How does it compare with the one you created for Bernie Madoff? Is there anything you missed from your statement that you think you should have included? Are there things that you thought of from which you think this policy statement would benefit?

Summaries

Identify and recall the important cases and legal principles you need to aid revision and guarantee you go into assessments with confidence.

Summary

◆ In order for a trust to be created, the parties must be of the requisite age and mental capacity.

◆ It is not possible for anyone under the age of 18 to create a trust of land, or to create a trust by will, with the exception of members of the armed forces, who can create a will at the age of 17. There is no age requirement for creating trusts of personal property.

◆ The formalities for the creation of a trust differ depending on whether the trust is made during

◆ Conveying the trust property to the trustee can be done simply by physical delivery o property in the case of all personal posses but the conveyance of land, shares and ce other property requires a formal deed of tr plus registration with the relevant bodies.

◆ A transfer of a beneficial interest under a t generally require writing under section 53 Law of Property Act 1925, subject to the t exceptions set out in the *Vandervell* cases

Question and answer

Test and apply your knowledge by doing the exercises. Use the guidance to help structure your answers.

Question and answer*

Problem: Neesha's father, Saleem, made the following bequests in his will:

1. I give to my trustees, Neesha and Aslam, my house and contents in Shoreditch, London, to hold my grandsons, Adesh and Khalil, until they reach the age of 21, on the condition that they each of the Hindu faith on or before his twenty-first birthday.

2. I give to my trustees, Neesha and Aslam, the collection of gold jewellery which belonged to my m in safety deposit box number 43569 at the Shoreditch branch of the Amicable Bank plc. The jewell held on trust for my granddaughter, Harika, until her marriage to a man of the Hindu faith. Shou marry by the age of 21, the jewellery should be given to any daughter of Adesh and Khalil's marri

Aslam is Neesha's husband. Neesha and Aslam wish to vary the trusts, to account for the following:

Further reading

Annotated references to journals and websites point you to that extra reading necessary to ensure you hit the higher marks.

Further reading and references

Buckley, C. (2008) 'The Charities Act 2006: consolidation or reform?', *Charity Law and Practice Review*, 11(1), 1–42.
This is a pretty long article, but worth reading if you want an in-depth review of the Charities Act 2006. In particular, the article reviews the case law on the public benefit requirement and discusses changes to the law in this area.

Quint, F. (2009) 'Recent developments in the cy près principle', *Charity Law and Practice Review*, 11(2), 49–57.

existing charities set up for 'poor relations' and 'poor employees' can withstand the change.

Warburton, J. (2009) 'Charities, gran campaigning', *Charity Law and Prac Review*, 11(2), 1–17.
Excellent article on the dangers of using ch funds for political purposes, discussing in the consequences of a charity becoming in with funding a non-charitable political pur including being held in breach of trust and

Lawyer's brief

Become an executor and trustee by completing the tasks in chapter 17, giving you the opportunity to apply the law and skills you have learnt practically.

Document 8

INTERNAL MEMORANDUM

To:	Nathan Soames
From:	Adrian Wardell
File Reference:	LOUDEN/LOU01458
Date:	22 February 2010

Nathan,

I have been called away from th able to make the first trust trust my ex

Chapter 17 Lawyer's brief

Introduction

So you have reached the end of Chapter 16 and the substantive part of the textbook has finished – now for something a little different! This final chapter of the book gives you the opportunity to put into practice many of the skills and much of the knowledge that you have learned throughout the rest of the book.

of a working solicitor. In addition to these do there are a number of questions and task have been designed both to test your under of the law of trusts and to give you a real f how the law is applied in practice. We hope will find this a valuable and worthwhile lear

premium
mylawchamber
unrivalled support for legal education

Your complete learning package

Visit **www.mylawchamber.co.uk/warner-reed** to access **an interactive Pearson eText**, an electronic version of *Equity and Trusts* which is fully **searchable**. You can **personalise** your Pearson eText with your own notes and bookmarks and extensive **links are provided to all of the self-study resources:**

✦ Case Navigator to help improve your case reading and analysis skills

✦ Practice exam questions with guidance to hone your exam technique

✦ Interactive 'You be the judge' questions

✦ Annotated weblinks to help you read more widely around the subject and really impress your lecturers

✦ Glossary and key case flashcards to test yourself on legal terms, principles and definitions

✦ Audio legal updates to help you stay up to date with the law and impress examiners

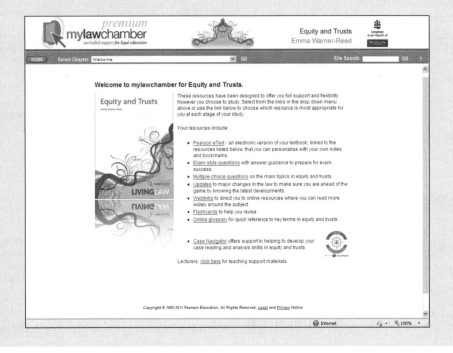

Preface

This is the first title in the Living Law series, the aim of which is to breathe a little bit of life into the core areas of undergraduate legal study by illustrating them in a more practical context than is the case in other textbooks currently available on the market. The topic of equity and trusts is one of the subjects with which, traditionally, students have the most difficulty. In this book I have sought to show the reader, by giving practical illustrations and examples of the law in action in a contemporary setting, that trusts are not only highly relevant in very many personal and business scenarios, but also that the subject can actually be quite interesting and, at times, controversial.

As both an experienced practitioner of law and as an academic, I have always been very keen to teach my students the law in a practical context. I believe quite strongly that students learn more effectively and their understanding of legal concepts is both deeper and more permanent if given a practical grounding on which to base those concepts. It is so easy for students to write off a topic (equity and trusts in particular!) as dry, dull or irrelevant if they do not appreciate it as a current, living and wholly applicable area of the law. It is for this reason that I am really quite excited about authoring one in a new and, hopefully, quite groundbreaking series of core textbooks for Pearson Longman.

This text is an introductory one and thus assumes no prior knowledge of the law of equity and trusts. In order to achieve the practical focus required for such a book, in covering the black letter law I have sought to draw out the more topical and socially relevant issues and minimise the discussion of drier and more archaic areas of the law. Nevertheless, I've sought to include all of the topics that are covered on a typical undergraduate course. In addition, the book contains more practical exercises than those typically found in an undergraduate law textbook. These exercises, whilst being carefully tied to the book's content, seek to highlight not only an application of the legal principles set out in each chapter, but also to hone the variety of skills that a law student needs to have in practice and in employment more generally, from legal research to organisational skills.

An outline of the book

The book is divided into two parts. In Part 1, Chapters 1 to 8 centre on the creation of trusts in their various forms and the difficulties inherent in the formation of certain types of trust. In Part 2, Chapters 9 to 16 consider how those trusts are administered and what should happen if the trust is not administered properly or correctly.

As stated above, the book includes a number of 'in chapter' features. I've tried to make all of these as interesting and relevant as possible. It is hoped that by reading the features and undertaking some of the tasks the student will gain a broader understanding of how the legal principles are applied in practice and how they affect the everyday world, the result being a deeper understanding of the principles themselves. Where possible I've provided feedback or hints to the tasks in the book and there is also more guidance available on the accompanying **mylawchamber** site.

I hope you enjoy reading this book as much as I have enjoyed writing it. If you would like to comment on anything contained within the book or with the approach of the series in general, I would encourage you to contact me via the **mylawchamber** site. The law is as stated on 16 August 2010, although some minor updates may have been possible at proof stage. Whilst I am grateful to reviewers and colleagues for the valuable advice provided to me in earlier drafts, any oversights or errors do of course remain my responsibility.

Wishing you all the best of luck with your study of equity and trusts.

Emma Warner-Reed

Senior Lecturer in Law
Leeds Metropolitan University
March 2011

Acknowledgements

Author's acknowledgements

There are many people who have helped to make this book happen, especially the editorial team at Pearson Longman who have worked tirelessly to turn my scribblings into print. However, there are a number of people to whom I owe my particular thanks:

To my editor Zoe Botterill, for her time, her patience and her support. As a first-time author, I have found her an absolute joy to work with and I look forward very much to working with her on future projects.

To my friend and colleague Bridget Walker, for giving me the confidence to embark on this project, for checking my proposal, and for being a constant source of both moral and academic support throughout the book-writing process. I quite simply could not have done this without her.

To my friend and colleague Jane Taylor, for her valuable input and discussion on the chapters on the laws of resulting and constructive trusts (my personal *bête noir*).

To my reviewers, for their useful insight and comments.

To my 'People in the law', who allowed me to interview them, and to all those who gave me their permission to use documents and statistics to illustrate the text and bring it to life.

To Jonathan, my long-suffering husband, who has acted alternately as reviewer, proofreader, emotional crutch, tea-maker and weekend babysitter, and to whom I am eternally grateful.

And finally to our baby son Harry, to whom this book is dedicated, who has suffered my absence uncomplainingly (for the most part!) and who spent the first ten months of his life asleep on my left knee, whilst I balanced a computer and typed one-handed on my right.

Publisher's acknowledgements

We are grateful to the following for permission to reproduce copyright material:

Text

Interview on pages 28–29 from Duncan Milwain, Director and Head of Trusts, Wills & Probate Department, Lupton Fawcett Solicitors, Leeds; Interview on page 42 from Fay Copeland, Partner at Wedlake Bell Solicitors, London; Interview on page 134 from Krystyna McGrath, Dogs Trust, Photo by Pete Rooney; Interview on pages 165–6 from Sharon Pallagi, Clarion Solicitors, Leeds; Table on page 173 reproduced from the Office for National Statistics Licensed under the Open Government Licence v.1.0; Interview on pages 215–6 from Caroline Wigin, Park Court Chambers, Leeds; Extract on pages 241–2 from Charity Trustee Network, The Results of this survey have been reproduced with the kind permission of Charity Trustee Networks; Interview on pages 242–3 from Sam de Silva, Terence Higgins Trust; Interview on page 266 from Ben Wittenberg, Ben Wittenberg, Director of Policy & Research, Directory of Social Change; Director of Policy & Research, Directory of Social Change; Interview on pages 309–10 from Jonathan Sapier, Independent Financial Adviser, Leeds; Interview on pages 356–7 from Bajul Shah Barrister, XXIV Old Buildings, London; Interview on pages 365–6 from David Sowden, Director in Forensic & Investigation Services, Grant Thornton, Leeds; Interview on page 401 from Ian Coupland, Lupton Fawcett, Leeds; Box on pages 404–5 from Freezing Injunction, http://www.justice.gov.uk/civil/procrules_fin/contents/practice_directions/pd_part25a.htm#IDANPKTB., Ministry of Justice

Picture Credits

The publisher would like to thank the following for their kind permission to reproduce their photographs:

Corel Corporation Limited: 96, 275; **Ingram Publishing**: 284; **Pearson Education Ltd**: Alamy/MedioImages 162, Digital Vision 245, Eyewire 223, Imagestate/John Foxx Collection 264, Jules Selmes/Patrick Gardner & Co 185, Photodisc 347, Photodisc/Life File/ Andrew Ward 85, Photodisc/Photolink 30, 128, 321, 376, 406, Photodisc/Spike Mafford 75, Photodisc/Steve Cole 49, 311; **PhotoDisc**: Photodisc/Getty Images 109.

In some instances we have been unable to trace the owners of copyright material, and we would appreciate any information that would enable us to do so.

Table of cases

Visit **www.mylawchamber.co.uk/warner-reed** to access unique online support to improve your case reading and analysis skills.

Case Navigator cases are highlighted in **bold colour** and **with a symbol** in the margin.

Case Navigator provides:

✦ **Direct deep links** to the core cases in criminal law.

✦ **Short introductions** provide guidance on what you should look out for while reading the case.

✦ **Questions** help you to test your understanding of the case, and provide feedback on what you should have grasped.

✦ **Summaries** contextualise the case and point you to further reading so that you are fully prepared for seminars and discussions.

Please note that access to Case Navigator is free with the purchase of this book, but you must register with us for access. Full registration instructions are available on the website. The LexisNexis element of Case Navigator is only available to those who currently subscribe to LexisNexis Butterworths online.

Case Navigator cases are highlighted in **bold**.

Table of statutes

Table of statutory instruments

Part 1 Creation of Trusts

Chapter 1
Introduction to trusts

Key points In this chapter we will be looking at:

- ✦ The historical development of equity and the Court of Chancery
- ✦ The maxims of equity
- ✦ The development of the trust and why we need trusts
- ✦ The anatomy of a trust

- ✦ The terminology of trusts
- ✦ The terminology of wills
- ✦ Different types of trust
- ✦ Trusts distinguished from other concepts
- ✦ Modern uses for trusts

Introduction

Imagine a young man, let us call him Alec, is a member of the armed forces. He is about to embark upon an extended tour of duty in Afghanistan. Theirs is a peace-keeping mission but the country is in a state of political turmoil and the relationship between the soldiers and civilians is volatile at best. He knows he will be gone for a long and uncertain period of time and that there is a possibility he may not return. He leaves a wife, Claudia, and two young children, Charlie and Cecile, behind him.

Concerned for the financial welfare of his young family in the event of his prolonged absence, Alec asks his brother, Brendan, to look after his affairs whilst he is gone. Brendan agrees and, in order to allow him to manage Alec's assets effectively whilst he is away, Alec transfers all of his property into Brendan's name.

Five years on, Alec returns home to find his house has been sold, his savings spent and Claudia and the children living with Claudia's mother. When he confronts his brother about the situation, Brendan simply says

'sorry' but he needed the money to pay off a gambling debt. He has no way of returning the money and property to Alec and, in the eyes of the law, Alec gave Brendan his money and property anyway: from the time Alec transferred the property into Brendan's name, Brendan became the legal owner of that property and any obligation Brendan might have towards Alec's family was a moral one at best. Legally, there is nothing Alec can do to protect his family's rights.

Clearly this situation is unjust. And it is the very situation described above that the concept of the **trust** was designed to protect. Throughout the course of this chapter we will be considering what is meant by the term 'trust' and considering how trusts work on a practical level. We will also be looking at some of the basic terminology appertaining to trusts and trust law which you will come across throughout the course of this book. And finally we will be considering some examples of the everyday uses of trusts. But first it is necessary to spend a little time giving the trust a bit of historical context.

The development of the court of equity

In medieval times the only court was the court of the **common law**, in which the king's judges enforced the law of the realm. The common law was developed on the basis of previously set **precedent**, judges adhering to judgments made in the cases that went before them. This provided a strict body of law for the courts to follow. If the decisions of the judges were regarded as unfair, or if the rules laid down by precedent were too slow to change where change was required, the parties to the claim had the option to appeal directly to the king, 'throwing themselves upon the king's conscience', for his ultimate judgment in the matter. The king soon became inundated with applications, however, and so he began to delegate his powers to his secretarial department, under the supervision of the Lord Chancellor. The secretariat of the king, which was commonly known as 'the **Chancery**', soon began to resemble a judicial body, and by the fifteenth century the Chancery was formally recognised as having judicial power. It was at this time that it became known as the 'Court of Chancery'.

The Court of Chancery was not without its flaws, however. Unlike the court of the common law, which was administered by lawyers and guided by precedent, the Court of Chancery had at its head the chancellor, who was traditionally a member of the clergy and had no formal legal training. Neither was the chancellor guided by precedent. This naturally led to a wide disparity between the judgments of different chancellors. In contrast to the rigid and unbending application of the common law, the law of **equity**, called such because of its basis on the principles of impartiality and fairness, seemed to be almost entirely dictated by the chancellor's own personal moral code. This highly unsatisfactory state of affairs continued right up until the end of the sixteenth century, when a lawyer, Sir Thomas More, was appointed Lord Chancellor and a new precedent was set. Sir Thomas strove to provide the Court of Chancery with a more ordered, legal framework, and records of proceedings started to be kept. This in turn led to the development of a number of equitable rules, or **doctrines**, and to the formation of the **maxims of equity**. As a result, the Court of Chancery also began to base its equitable judgments on precedent, as the court of the common law did.

This new development of the laws of equity within the Court of Chancery was not without its problems, however. There were now two fully fledged but completely separate legal systems in England, each with their own courts: the common law, which dealt with strict matters of law in the common law courts, and equity, which dealt with matters of fairness, or conscience in the Court of Chancery. This lack of cohesion was a problem: as the two systems were autonomous the developing law of equity, as enforced by the Chancery, soon began to conflict with the rules of the common law, and even to rival them. Tensions broke out between the rival jurisdictions and it became clear that something needed to be done. Eventually, the matter was referred to the Attorney-General of the time, Sir Francis Bacon. Sir Francis, on the authority of King James I, held that, in the event of any conflict between the common law and equity, equity would prevail. Thus, the law of equity was held to override the common law in the event of a conflict between the two courts.

Unification of the courts

Once equity had became a fully recognised body of law, rather than an arbitrary exercise of the king's (or chancellor's) conscience, the need for a separate court system to run it became obsolete. In fact, the running of two entirely separate legal systems was rather unwieldy and often inconvenient, parties having to use both courts simultaneously in the resolution of a single dispute. The advent of the Judicature Acts in the 1870s changed all this. The new body of legislation swept away the previous system of separate courts and created one single Supreme Court in their stead. This meant that whilst the two systems of common law and equity still operated under very different rules they could now be administered from one single court, with a single judge (or panel of judges, as appropriate) giving judgment on both legal and equitable matters in the course of a single case. **Claimants** would no longer have to bring two separate actions in order to resolve issues arising under one claim. It is worth stressing that this fusion of the common law and equity was only an administrative advance in the law: it was not a melting together of the two systems. The rules of equity and the common law are still entirely separate and distinct; it is simply that they can now both be administered under the same roof. This system still forms the basis of our courts today.

> this fusion of the common law and equity was only administrative

The equitable maxims

It was mentioned above that the development of the Court of Chancery into a fully-fledged legal system entailed the developments of a series of equitable maxims. These maxims of equity are, in effect, a set of guidelines or standards devised by the court of equity as an aid to deciding cases which come before them. The equitable maxims are therefore not a strict set of rules, such as those which might be used in the courts of the common law, but rather they serve as an aid or a set of 'moral markers' for the court in making its decisions. This means that the court is not bound to follow the maxims (although they usually will), but they can draw upon them as and when required in order to justify their decisions on something more than simply the judge's personal moral compass.

There are quite a number of equitable maxims and you do not need to know them all by heart. However, it will certainly be useful in your study of the law of trusts to be familiar with the most commonly used of the maxims, and to understand their meanings, which are outlined below. As you will see from the various examples given in the following text, there is no shortage of evidence of the maxims in use. The examples given here are not the only examples you will find within the book, though: keep an eye out for the use of equitable maxims as you read through the rest of the text.

Equity will not suffer a wrong without a remedy

This first equitable maxim is linked to the very origins of equity. The maxim alludes to the fact that equity was devised specifically with the intention that it should act as a supplementary, or alternative, court of justice where the common law is not able to provide a remedy. So as we shall shortly see in the case of the trust, an invention of equity, the legal owner of the property will be prevented from asserting their rights in respect of that property because they are deemed, in equity, to hold the **beneficial**, or **equitable**, **interest** in the property on trust for the beneficiary.

He who comes to equity must come with clean hands

This is probably the best known of all the equitable maxims. The idea behind the maxim is that a person who has acted wrongly cannot then seek to rely on the court for assistance in the bringing of a claim. The most extreme and obvious example of this would be in the case of murder, as in *Cleaver* v. *Mutual Reserve Fund Life Association* [1892] 1 QB 147. Here a woman who had murdered her husband was denied the right to claim the payout under a life insurance policy underwritten in her favour, on the basis that she should not be allowed to profit from her crime.

Case Summary

However, examples can be far more ordinary and involve only a moral, and not necessarily a legal, wrong. Perhaps the most wide-ranging example of the maxim comes in the form of the doctrine of **proprietary estoppel**. The doctrine itself is designed to prevent a legal owner of property from asserting their legal rights against a third party where it would be **unconscionable**, or unjust, for them to do so because they have misled that third party in some way, encouraging them to act to their detriment as a result. An example of this might be the situation where a claimant allows the defendant to build a house on their land but then, once the house is built, makes an application to the court to have the defendant evicted from the house on the basis that the claimant is the strict legal owner of the land. In such a situation the claimant would be viewed by the court as having '**unclean hands**' and their action would fail.

The requirement of clean hands does not mean that someone of generally morally reprehensible character will be barred from using the courts of equity at all, however. The maxim will only apply if there is a genuine link between the claimant's wrongful act and the rights they wish to enforce. A good example of this is the case of *Tinsley* v. *Milligan* [1994] 1 AC 340 (HL). The case concerned a couple who had bought a house together but registered it in the name of just one of them so that the other could claim to be a lodger in the house and continue to claim housing benefit. However, when the couple separated the House of Lords nevertheless allowed Miss Milligan's claim of an interest in the house because her fraudulent behaviour had no bearing on the fact that she had contributed to the purchase of the house. It should be noted that the outcome of this case has been heavily criticised as condoning Miss Milligan's fraudulent behaviour. For a more detailed insight into this case see Chapter 7, on resulting trusts.

Case Summary

He who seeks equity must do equity

This maxim is closely related to the maxim which states that 'he who comes to equity must come with clean hands'. In essence, it means that, if a person wishes to make a claim in equity, they must be prepared to submit to the judgment of the court in respect of the rights of the other party to the action as well. So a person who wishes to claim the equitable remedy of **specific performance**, for example, thus forcing the defendant to complete the terms of a contract in accordance with their agreement, must also be willing to complete all of their own obligations under that same contract.

Equity regards as done that which ought to be done

This equitable maxim is significant because it means that two parties contracting to perform certain legal actions will, in the eyes of equity, be considered to have carried out those actions from the moment of contracting to do them, rather than when the contract is actually performed. The best example of such a situation would be in the context of a house purchase. From the moment of **exchange of contracts** (when the seller and buyer enter into a legally binding contract to sell and purchase the property) the buyer will acquire an equitable interest in the house, albeit that they do not become the legal owners until after the formal legal transfer of the house is completed. This means that if either party fails to go ahead with the sale or purchase, the injured party not only has the option of claiming **damages** at common law for the **breach of contract**, but they also have the option (albeit at the discretion of the court) of claiming the equitable remedy of specific performance, thereby forcing the defaulting party to complete the sale or purchase. This is on the basis that 'equity regards as done that which ought to be done': in this case, the completion of the sale.

Equity follows the law

As the wording of this maxim suggests, in divining an answer to a problem in equity, the court of equity will always look to the legal position first and, where appropriate, take their lead from the common law. The best example of this might be where two people share ownership of a piece of land. In the absence of a declaration to the contrary, at law the two people will automatically own the property as **joint tenants**, meaning they both hold the property together as one 'joint owner' and have no individual shares in that property. If the two people approach the court of equity for clarification as to their beneficial, or equitable, ownership of that property, the court's starting point will be that they own the property as joint tenants in equity too. It will only be on the provision of evidence from either party that the position should be different in equity that the court will depart from the common law position.

The maxim 'equity follows the law' also serves as confirmation of the fact that equity will not allow a remedy that is contrary to law; in other words, the court of equity will not seek to override the law. The common law is very much the governing body for English law and it is only where the court of equity is met with an issue which the common law rules do not account for that equity will step in. As we have seen from the maxim 'equity will not suffer a wrong without a remedy', therefore, equity's role is to work as a supplement to the common law, and not as an alternative form of justice where the law already exists to cover a particular issue.

> equity will not seek to override the law

Equity will not permit a statute to be used as an instrument of fraud

This equitable maxim serves to prevent a person from relying on the absence of statutory provision if to do so would result in unfairness to a third party. Evidence of this maxim in practice can be seen in the chapters on resulting and constructive trusts. In Chapter 7 on resulting trusts you will see that, under section 37 of the Matrimonial Proceedings and Property Act 1970, where a spouse makes a substantial financial contribution to improve a property they will be treated as having then acquired a share in the beneficial interest of that property, regardless of whether or not they have a legal interest in it. However, the Act only applies to married couples, and not to cohabitees. The law of equity has therefore stepped in and provided that, under such circumstances the contributing party may be entitled to an interest in the property under a constructive trust instead. As you can see, this is also an example of equity 'plugging the gap' where the law makes no provision for a particular set of circumstances, as opposed to overriding the law as it already exists ('equity follows the law'). For a more in-depth look at the law relating to constructive trusts as it relates to the rights of cohabitees, go to Chapter 8.

Equity looks to substance not form

This maxim describes an important feature of the court of equity, which is that it is able to look beyond the external appearance of any state of affairs that exists between the parties and make its judgment based on the position of the parties as they genuinely intended it. In other words, it will not simply adhere t[...] [...]e strict legal position as might be dictated [...] [...]e facts of the case that the real position is [...]ayed to the outside world. The most famous [...]v. *Mountford* [1985] 1 AC 809, which con-[...]greement between the parties was given the [...]ted to avoid the tenant acquiring a right to [...]statutory provisions applicable to residential [...]ough the pretence and held that, regardless [...]t was nevertheless a lease and therefore the [...]law under the statutory provisions. In giving [...]nously said:

Case Summary

[...]t for manual digging results in a fork even if [...] language, insists that he intended to make

[...]on between the two courts of the common [...] the court of equity was developing, one [...] common law was that, whereas the courts of the common law made judgments over the property in dispute, an action being brought *in rem* (that is, over 'the thing'), the court of equity made its judgments *in personam*: in other words, judgment was made against the individual. The practical effect of this was that the courts of the common law had the ability to adjust ownership rights in property, giving all or part of the property in dispute to the claimant. The courts of equity, on the other hand, had the ability instead to require an individual to obey their judgments, in default of which they could take away that person's liberty (by putting them in prison) or issue fines until such time as they obeyed their edict.

Even today, and despite the **fusion** of the two courts **of common law and equity**, the ability of equity to act *in personam* retains some very specific benefits. For example, in Chapter 16 on remedies, you will come across a type of injunctive remedy called a '**freezing injunction**'. The purpose of a freezing injunction is to prevent the defendant from moving property or assets out of the reach of the claimant before the matter gets to court, either by moving them out of the UK, or from one jurisdiction to another. The making of such an **injunction** is possible because equity acts *in personam*, and therefore the injunction is made by the court against the person, not against their assets. This means that the location of the assets is irrelevant to the proceedings and that the remedy is, effectively, worldwide.

Equality is equity

The equitable maxim 'equality is equity' ensures that, where there is a dispute over property in which more than one party has a beneficial interest, that property will be divided equally, unless there is evidence showing that the property should be divided in some other way. So, in the case of *Midland Bank* v. *Cooke* [1995] 4 All ER 562, which concerned a dispute between husband and wife over the ownership of a matrimonial home, Lord Justice Waite said that:

Case Summary

> In such a case the court must first do its best to discover from the conduct of the spouses whether any inference can reasonably be drawn as to the probable common understanding about the amount of the share of the contributing spouse upon which each must have acted in doing what each did . . . if no such inference can be drawn . . . the court is driven to apply . . . the maxim 'equality is equity', and to hold that the beneficial interest belongs to the spouses in equal shares.

You can find the full facts of this case in Chapter 8 on constructive trusts.

Delay defeats equity

If a person wishes to bring a claim in equity they must do so without delay or otherwise risk their claim being rejected. This means that a person who delays unnecessarily in making a claim in equity could be found guilty of acquiescing to the conduct complained of by their failure to do anything about it. Alternatively, their claim could fail under the **doctrine of laches**, where there has been a delay in bringing an action. The maxim 'delay defeats equity' is often not required because of statutory limitations imposed on bringing an action by the Limitation Act 1980. You can find out more about both the Act and the doctrine of laches in Chapter 13 on breach of trust.

Equity will not assist a volunteer

A '**volunteer**' in this context is not the person who helps out on the cake stall at the local village fête. In equity the term 'volunteer' has a rather different meaning, which is that a volunteer is someone who receives a benefit without **consideration**; in other words, that person does not give anything in return for the benefit: they are the recipient of a gift. Generally speaking, persons in receipt of gifts of property cannot rely on the court of equity to enforce the promise of that gift because, having done nothing in return for it, the volunteer has nothing to enforce against. Put simply, there is no bargain. To give an example of how this might work, if Sannia were to give her old laptop to Nicola, Nicola cannot then make a claim against Sannia if the laptop runs slowly, or is difficult to use, because it was the subject of a gift.

Equity will not perfect an imperfect gift

This maxim of equity is closely related to the maxim which states that 'equity will not assist a volunteer'. If a person makes an '**imperfect gift**', that is a gift which lacks the formalities required at common law, the maxim says that equity will not assist the intended recipient of that gift. This equitable maxim is particularly relevant in cases of gifts of land or shares, which require a process of formal transfer rather than mere physical delivery of the object in question. The courts' application of this maxim has suffered a significant amount of criticism in recent years, primarily because of a tendency of the courts to waive, or 'soften', the rule wherever it would seem equitable on the facts of the case to do so. This is particularly evident since the handing down of the Court of Appeal decision in *Pennington* v. *Waine (No. 1)* [2002] EWCA Civ 227, in which an aunt's botched attempt to give 400 shares in a company to her nephew was considered to have been sufficient to tranfser the equitable interest across to him. The full facts of this case are discussed in Chapter 2, on formalities.

Case Summary

It should also be noted that an alleged exception to the maxim is the rule in **Strong v. Bird** (1874) LR 18 Eq 315. The rule says that if a person appoints the intended recipient of a gift as the executor of their will, on that person's death the gift will be perfected. However, the facts of the case applied to the cancellation of a debt and, although the rule has subsequently been applied to outright gifts, it has never been tested in the context of transfers of trust property. This issue is discussed in more detail in Chapter 2.

Equity abhors a vacuum

The idea behind this maxim is that it goes against the principle of the court of equity for a piece of property to be left with no beneficial owner. This maxim is most commonly seen in the context of resulting trusts. As we shall see in Chapter 7, one of the scenarios in which a resulting trust will arise is where property has not been properly disposed of. This might be because a trust has failed due to the identity of the beneficiaries not being ascertainable, or in situations where there is surplus property left over after the trust has come to an end. In such circumstances, the trustees are unable to keep the property for their own benefit, and so the property in the trust 'results' or returns (in most cases) to the original owner of the property, leaving the trustees holding the property on trust for them. This solves the problem of the property being left with no one to benefit from it. A further example might be seen in the case of a charitable gift which has failed because the charity has ceased to exist before the gift to that charity was completed. In such circumstances, the doctrine of **cy près** will be applied, and the property will go to another charity with similar aims. We will be looking in more detail at the equitable doctrine of cy près in Chapter 5, on charities.

Equity will not want for a trustee

The court of equity will not allow a trust to fail simply because the person creating the trust has failed to appoint a trustee or, in the case of a trust created by will, if the trustee has died before the testator (that is, the person writing the will). The court of equity therefore has the power to appoint a trustee where there is no valid trustee appointed. It should be noted that in many circumstances statutory provision has been made for the appointment of trustees and so there will be no need for the court to have to rely on their general power to appoint. To read more about the appointment of trustees, go to Chapter 9.

Equity imputes an intention to fulfil an obligation

This maxim dictates that, where a person is under an obligation to do one thing but they do something slightly different instead, their actions may be treated as a close enough approximation of the required act to have fulfilled that person's obligation in equity. This is better explained by way of an example. The case in which the maxim was first set out is that of *Sowden* v. *Sowden* (1785) 1 Bro CC 582, which concerned a **marriage settlement**. A marriage settlement is a legally binding agreement made between the parties to the marriage under which the husband and wife agree to put certain property, including property acquired after the marriage, into trust for the benefit of themselves and any children they might have. In *Sowden* v. *Sowden* a husband, as part of his marriage settlement, had promised to pay the trustees under the settlement a total sum of £2,000 with which they were to buy property to provide an income for his wife in the event of his death. The money was never paid to the trustees but, shortly after his marriage, the husband bought a property in Devon called 'Pound', for £2,150. The husband subsequently died and the wife sought to claim the property as part of the marriage settlement. The court of equity found in her favour, on the basis that the husband was assumed to have bought the property in the performance of his obligations under the marriage settlement.

A more modern example of how this maxim might work would be the example of a person who owed money to a creditor. Say Alec owes £100 to Rani. Alec dies without paying his debt to Rani, but he leaves Rani a gift in his will of £100. The £100 will be construed by the court as representing the payment of Alec's debt and Rani will therefore achieve the repayment of the debt. Of course, this would also prevent Rani from making a separate claim for the debt under the rules of the common law.

Where the equities are equal the law prevails

This equitable maxim overlaps with the maxim 'equity follows the law' which was mentioned previously. The meaning of the maxim simply is that the person in possession of the legal estate will get priority over any prior or subsequent equitable interests. So when both parties in a dispute are equally entitled to obtain help from courts of equity because their equitable rights are equal, the party who has the law in his favour will succeed. In essence, therefore, this maxim provides confirmation of the fact that an equitable interest is not as strong as a legal interest. Thus, according to the maxim, 'the law shall prevail'.

Where the equities are equal the first in time prevails

This final maxim simply states what may seem obvious, which is that in the case of competing equitable interests the interest which was created first will take precedence over the others. The best example of this in practice is in the case of someone who takes out second and third mortgages over their house. It is only possible for the first mortgage over a property to be legal; therefore any subsequent mortgage will be an equitable mortgage. In deciding which equitable mortgage has priority over the others, the one which was entered into first will take priority. Thus, the 'first in time prevails'. Further discussion of mortgages is outside the scope of this book.

The development of the trust

We have so far looked at the development of the court of equity and at some of the equitable maxims by which the court is guided. Now it is time to turn our attention to one of the greatest creations of equity: the trust. The development of the trust as a basic concept began during the time of the Crusades, which were a series of holy wars spanning two centuries between 1095 and 1291. The wars were waged by much of Christian Europe, including England, against the Muslim-occupied countries of the near East including the city of Jerusalem, which the Crusaders had the goal of recapturing and restoring to Christian rule. The long series of protracted military campaigns overseas meant that English households were frequently deprived of their male heads for years, and in some cases even decades. In order to facilitate the management of their land in their absence, knights going away to battle would frequently transfer the ownership of their property into the hands of a trusted relative or friend so that they could act in their place, managing the estate until their return. To do this was a risky business, however. Under the strict rules of the common law once the knight had transferred the legal ownership of his property to a third party, all his rights in that property ceased. There was therefore no *legal* way for the knight to protect his family from an unscrupulous friend or family member. This left the knight completely at the mercy of the friend or relative; he had no other choice than to rely on the honour and good conscience of the person he trusted to do the right thing by his family. Unfortunately, it was too often the case that crusaders would return from abroad to find their wife and family gone and their fortune dissipated. Something clearly had to be done to protect such persons; what was needed was a new concept.

> he had to rely on the honour and good conscience of the person he trusted

Equity came to the rescue. In response to the crusaders' plight, a new concept began to be formulated. This concept, unique to English law, was the '**use**'. Put in basic terms, the use was the earliest and most primitive form of what we today call the trust. Its effect was that one person owned the land under the common law, but a second person had a right to use the land under the law of equity. Thus, two separate rights in one property could now exist at the same time. In the case of our knight, let us call him Cyril, this meant that Cyril would be able to transfer his land 'to the use' of a third party, let us call him Balthazar, for the duration of his absence abroad. Under the terms of the use, Cyril could do this safe in the knowledge that he had an equitable remedy if Balthazar did not manage the land in accordance with his wishes. Whilst technically the legal ownership would still be with Balthazar, under the terms of the use equity would be able to step in and enforce Cyril's equitable rights, forcing Balthazar to act in accordance with the terms of his promise. This ensured that whilst Cyril's family, for whom his property had been left to benefit, had no *legal* claim on his lands once they had been given over into 'use', they nevertheless had the force of equity behind them. In equity's eyes, Balthazar would be the

Figure 1.1 Property ownership under the 'use'

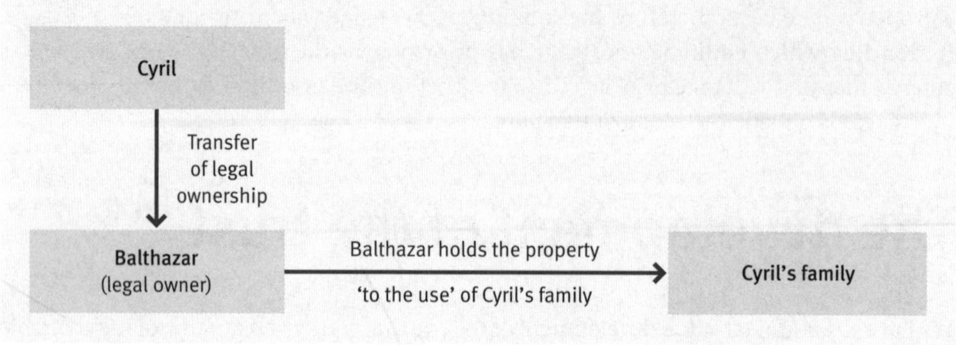

legal owner of the property in name and nothing more. The right to benefit from the property belonged to Cyril's family. Diagramatically, the use might look as shown in Figure 1.1 above.

To put the use into a modern context, we can look at the example of our soldier, Alec, from the beginning of the chapter. If you think about the story of Cyril, it is remarkably similar to the story of Alec going off on his tour of duty in Afghanistan. The only difference is that, in the original scenario, the soldier in question is a knight and the war he would have been leaving his family behind for would have been the Crusades. We will be considering the modern uses of the trust in more detail later in the chapter.

Whilst the use was created very much with equity, or fairness, in mind, by the sixteenth century a very different application had been found for the concept which was not nearly so noble. This was as a method of tax avoidance. Under the laws of the time, by transferring the legal ownership of property to the use of a third party the original property owner could avoid the payment of feudal dues (or taxes). In an attempt to quash such practices, Henry VIII enacted the Statute of Uses in 1535. The Act effectively ignored the legal owner of the property and, for taxation purposes, recognised only the beneficial owner of the land. However, lawyers soon got around this by creating the 'double use'. Land would be given to Harold 'to the use' of Jakob 'to the use' of Charlotte. The Statute recognised only the first use, and so the second use remained untaxed. Over a period of time the terminology shifted so that Harold was seen to be giving the property 'to the use' of Jakob 'on trust' for Charlotte, and the modern trust was born.

What is a trust?

You should already have an idea of how the modern trust is formulated from our look at its ancestor the use, above. Let us take some time to look at the anatomy of the modern trust in a little more detail, however. A good place to start might be by defining, in legal terms, exactly what is meant by a 'trust'. Lawyers and academics have striven over several centuries to come up with a clear definition of the legal term 'trust', some with rather less success than others. However, the simple fact of the matter is that it is easier to explain how a trust works or, one might say, what a trust looks like, than to give it a definitive explanation. Put in its simplest terms, as with its ancestor the use, a trust is where one

Figure 1.2 Format of a basic trust

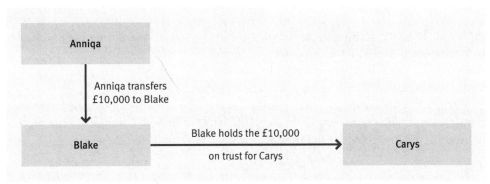

person transfers the legal ownership of property to another to hold that property for the benefit of somebody else. Historically the property transferred was usually land, but in the modern trust such property can take the form of money, land, jewellery or other personal items. So, using cash as an example, in the most basic form of our modern trust a woman, Anniqa, might give £10,000 to her brother, Blake, to hold for the benefit of her daughter, Carys.

Diagrammatically, the situation might look as shown in Figure 1.2 above. And so we have the anatomy of a basic trust: Anniqa transferring property to Blake to hold on trust for Carys. The effect of this 'trust' is that, in legal terms, Blake becomes the owner of the property: we might say that Blake holds the 'legal title' to the property. In the eyes of the law, Blake has the right to use that property or dispose of it as anyone with absolute ownership of property could do. However, because in giving the property to Blake to hold for the benefit of Carys Anniqa has created a trust, whilst Blake is technically the legal owner it is Carys who is actually entitled to the benefit of that property: she is the beneficial, or equitable, owner and has the benefit in equity. It is this separation of the legal or formal 'paper' ownership of property, and the beneficial or equitable ownership of the same which is fundamental to the anatomy of any trust; without it, trusts could not exist.

But why is there a need for Anniqa to give the property to Blake to hold on behalf of Carys in the first place? Why does not Anniqa just give the property directly to Carys? Of course, times have changed dramatically since the eleventh century, and the use of trusts is far more wide-ranging in a modern context, as we shall see later on in the chapter. But the concept of the trust as an instrument of equity remains the same. Its function is to allow a person to give their property over to another for the benefit of a third party and yet still to protect that third party, the beneficiary of the trust, from abuse by the legal owner. It is a simple method of protection and control, enabling the person creating the trust to hand property over for someone else's benefit, whilst still retaining control of that property through the medium of the trustees.

You should now have some idea of what trusts are and why they exist, and of the historical development of equity and its maxims. For the rest of this chapter we will be taking a look at some of the terminology used in the law of trusts and which we will be using throughout the remainder of the text; and we will also be looking at the different types of trusts and exploring some of the other modern uses of the trust. This should help to deepen your understanding of the concept and crystallise the idea of the trust in your mind.

The terminology of trusts

First of all, let us think about the terminology of trusts. You can use this part of the chapter to refer back to until you are completely comfortable with the terms referred to or, alternatively, you may prefer once you have read this to use the glossary which you will find at the back of the book as a quick reference guide.

The description was given earlier in the chapter of a trust being created by Anniqa transferring property to Blake to hold on behalf of Carys. In legal terminology, the process of creating this trust and all the persons involved in it are given their own labels, and these are as follows:

The person transferring their property over for the benefit of the third party is known as the '**settlor**'. The settlor, in our example Anniqa, can be described as 'settling' her property on Blake, for the benefit of Carys. She can also be described as 'giving her property over into trust'.

The person in receipt of the property, in our scenario Blake, is the person to whom the settlor, Anniqa, entrusts the property. He is known as the '**trustee**'. So the trustee (Blake) is the person the settlor (Anniqa) trusts to look after the property for the benefit of Carys. The trustee is the *legal* owner of the property. It is worth noting here that there is usually more than one trustee appointed by the settlor for administrative reasons (for further explanation see Chapter 9 on the appointment and retirement of trustees).

> The trustee is the *legal* owner of the property

The person whom the property is to benefit, Carys in our scenario, is known as the '**beneficiary**'. The beneficiary holds the beneficial, or equitable, title to the property. The beneficiary can be an individual who will be identified by name, as in our example, or by description: for example 'my daughter'. Alternatively the beneficiary can be a specified group of persons, such as 'children', 'nephews' or 'relatives'. It might also include the settlor's '**heirs**', meaning anyone who is entitled to inherit on the settlor's death, or '**issue**', meaning any descendants of the settlor. These groups of persons are often referred to as a '**class of beneficiaries**'. The beneficiary (or class of beneficiaries) is commonly described as the '**object**' of the trust because he or she is the object of the settlor's wishes: the person the settlor intends to benefit.

So if we were to revisit our earlier diagram it will now look as shown in Figure 1.3. The three parties to the trust will be referred to throughout the remainder of the book as the settlor, trustees and beneficiaries.

Figure 1.3 Parties to the trust

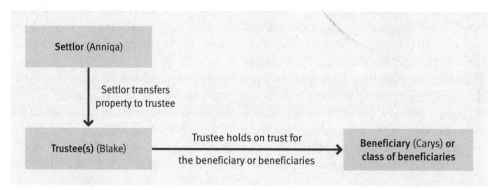

The beneficiary's interest under the trust can be vested or contingent. A '**vested interest**' means that the beneficiary has an interest which is either already in the hands of the beneficiary, or will definitely come to them in the future. If the beneficiary's interest is dependent on the happening of a future event, that event must be certain to happen: for example, the death of another person. The fact that no one can say when the death will occur is irrelevant. This will be the scenario where someone is the ultimate beneficiary under a '**lifetime trust**', where property is put into trust for the benefit of one person for the duration of their life, and is then given to a third party on their death. If, on the other hand, the interest of the beneficiary is dependent on an event which is *not* certain to occur, the beneficiary's interest will be a '**contingent interest**', and not a vested one. Such a contingent event might be the beneficiary reaching the age of 25 or 30. In this scenario, the beneficiary might die before reaching the required age and there is therefore no certainty in them attaining their interest. This is in contrast to the vested interest, which is dependent on the death of another person: as everyone dies sooner or later, the beneficiary's interest in that event is based on a certainty, not a contingency.

The final part of the trust which needs to be considered is the actual content of the trust; that is the property given over into trust by the settlor. This can be referred to simply as the 'trust property' or, alternatively, as the '**subject matter**' of the trust. As mentioned above, the subject matter of the trust is often land or property, but it may also consist of money, stocks and shares, or any other kind of personal property.

The terminology of wills

It would be sensible as we consider the terminology of trusts also to give some thought to the terminology of wills. The reason for this is that, as we shall see later on in the text, many trusts are created by will. The following 'whistle-stop' tour of will terminology should therefore be helpful as you progress through the book:

In a will, the person writing the will, that is the person whose last wishes the will portrays, is known as the '**testator**' (masculine) or '**testatrix**' (feminine). As testators and testatrixes often create trusts within their wills you will frequently see the settlor referred to in context as a testator or testatrix. This is particularly the case when the facts of cases are being described, as many of these came about because of an ambiguity or dispute over a will. Throughout the course of the text, therefore, when you see reference to a testator or testatrix you should be aware that this refers not only to the person creating the will, but also in most cases the settlor as well, settlor and testator/testatrix usually being one and the same person. So, for example, you may read the following:

> A testator gave £100,000 to his trustees to hold on trust for his children until they reach the age of 18.

It is clear to see that the testator in this instance was also the settlor of the trust.

Another term you will come across relating to wills is '**executor**' (masculine) or '**executrix**' (feminine). The executors of a will are the person or persons who are in charge of carrying out the testator's wishes. On the death of the testator, they will gather together his possessions, pay any debts of the testator and be responsible for the division of his assets. The executors named in a will are often also named as the trustees of any trusts which may be created under it and so take on a dual role as executors and trustees under the will.

These are the people you will come across when we look at wills. In terms of the subject matter of the will, this is given its own special label as well, depending on what part of the testator's property is being referred to.

The assets of the testator as a whole are collectively referred to as his '**estate**'. So the testator's estate will include everything he owns, including money, personal possessions and land or property.

A gift of a personal possession of the testator or a share in the testator's estate made to a specific person in the will is termed a '**legacy**' or '**bequest**'. Legacies or bequests can be made either of money or of personal, moveable property, or '**chattels**'. An example of a legacy or bequest of a chattel might be a gift of a treasured piece of jewellery made by a testatrix to her favourite niece, or a more substantial gift such as the family home, to be shared between the testatrix's children. Gifts of money are known as '**pecuniary legacies**'. You should note that legacies or bequests need not necessarily be made to individuals; a charitable donation of £10,000 to a testator's favoured charity would also come under this heading.

Once all of the testator's debts and funeral expenses have been paid by the executors and any legacies have been given out, whatever is left in the testator's estate is termed the '**residue**' or '**remainder**'. It is usual for the testator to specify to whom he wishes the residue to be given. This may be to friends or family members or to a named charity. In many cases the residue is divided into shares and given to a mixture of two or more persons or charities.

A person who dies without leaving a will is referred to as dying '**intestate**'. The person who administers the deceased's estate on intestacy is called the '**administrator**' (masculine) or '**administratrix**' (feminine).

The excerpt in Documenting the law from the will of a very famous testatrix, the late Diana, Princess of Wales, shows much of this terminology in use. It can be seen from the terms of the will that the Princess of Wales appointed two executors to administer her estate: her mother and her personal private secretary, Commander Patrick Jephson. The main beneficiaries under the will were her two children, the Princes William and Henry (Prince 'Harry'). The money comprised in the estate (totalling in excess of £21 million) was held on trust for them until they inherited at the age of 25.

Documenting the law

Excerpt from the will of Diana, Princess of Wales

I DIANA PRINCESS OF WALES of Kensington Palace London W8 HEREBY REVOKE all former Wills and testamentary dispositions made by me AND DECLARE this to be my last Will which I make this first day of June one thousand nine hundred and ninety-three

1. I APPOINT my mother THE HONOURABLE MRS FRANCES RUTH SHAND KYDD of . . . and COMMANDER PATRICK DESMOND CHRISTIAN JEREMY JEPHSON of . . . to be the Executors and Trustees of this my Will

2. I WISH to be buried

3. SHOULD any child of mine be under age at the date of the death of the survivor of myself and my husband I APPOINT my mother and my brother EARL SPENCER to be the guardians of that child and I express the wish that

should I predecease my husband he will consult with my mother with regard to the upbringing in education and welfare of our children

4.   (a) I GIVE free of inheritance tax all my chattels to my Executors jointly (or if only one of them shall prove my Will to her or him) (b) I DESIRE them (or if only one shall prove her or him) (i) To give effect as soon as possible but not later than two years following my death to any written memorandum or notes of wishes of mine with regard to any of my chattels (ii) Subject to any such wishes to hold my chattels (or the balance thereof) in accordance with Clause 5 of this my Will . . .

5.   SUBJECT to the payment or discharge of my funeral testamentary and administration expenses and debts and other liabilities I GIVE all my property and assets of every kind and wherever situate to my Executors and Trustees upon trust either to retain (if they think fit without being liable for loss) all or any part in the same state as they are at the time of my death or to sell whatever and wherever they decide with power when they consider it proper to invest trust monies and to vary investments in accordance with the powers contained in the Schedule to this my Will and to hold the same UPON TRUST for such of my children PRINCE WILLIAM and PRINCE HENRY as are living three months after my death and attain the age of twenty five years if more than one in equal share PROVIDED THAT if either child of mine dies before me or within three months after my death and issue of the child are living three months after my death and attain the age of twenty one years such issue shall take by substitution if more than one in equal shares *per stirpes** and the share that the deceased child of mine would have taken had he been living three months after my death but so that no issue shall take whose parent is then living and so capable of taking

. . .

IN WITNESS whereof I have hereunto set my hand the day and year first above written

SIGNED by HER ROYAL HIGHNESS in our joint presence and then by us in her presence

[*Source*: **http://edition.cnn.com/WORLD/9803/04/diana.will/index.html**. See also news article **http://news.bbc.co.uk/1/hi/uk/61285.stm** for further detail.]

*Note: **Per stirpes** is a Latin legal term meaning that the children of the deceased princes would take the amount representing their father's share of the estate between them in equal shares.

Types of trust

There are many different types of trust, all of which you will come across throughout the course of this book, and which the following section aims briefly to introduce you to. As with the section above on the terminology of trusts, you may wish to use this section as a quick reference guide as you navigate your way around the text, or you may prefer instead to use the glossary at the back of the book, which contains brief definitions of all the terms described here, as well as many more.

Private and public trusts

We have discussed the scenario of a basic trust whereby a settlor gives money or property to their trustees to hold on trust for their beneficiaries. This most basic type of trust, where money is given over into trust for the benefit of one or more named individuals, is a '**private trust**'. In other words, the trust has been created by the settlor for the benefit of a private individual or individuals. In such a scenario these private individuals are likely to be close family members or friends, or people who have some kind of personal relationship with the settlor.

A '**public trust**', on the other hand, is a trust in which the settlor has given money or property over to their trustees to be used for some public use or benefit. All charitable trusts would therefore come under this heading.

You be the judge

Q: Which of the following are public trusts?

(a) £10,000 towards the education of the nephews and nieces of Mathilda and Edward Jones.

(b) £10,000 towards the education of the children of employees of Leeds Metropolitan University.

(c) £10,000 towards the education of children from impoverished backgrounds in the county of North Yorkshire.

A: Only (c) is a public trust, being directed at a section of the public. The others are all private trusts, being for the benefit only of a private group of people, albeit a potentially large group in the case of the university.

Fixed and discretionary trusts

The terms of a trust may be either fixed or discretionary. If the terms of a trust are fixed, this means that the trustees are given very specific instructions as to how and to whom the subject matter of the trust is to be distributed; the trustees do not have any power to vary the amounts given to the different beneficiaries named, or to decide whether or not to benefit one particular beneficiary over the others. A **fixed trust** might look as follows:

I give £10,000 to my trustees to divide equally between my children, Jacob and Frances.

You will see here that the trustees have no discretion as to how to divide the £10,000: they must divide the money equally. Neither are the trustees given any discretion as to whom the money is to be given. The settlor is clear that the money is to be divided equally between Jacob and Frances; they are each to be given a half-share of the money and so will each receive the sum of £5,000. To give a further example of a fixed trust, the following would also come within this category:

I give £10,000 to my trustees to hold for my children, Jacob and Frances.

Despite the fact that there is no express stipulation as to how the money is to be divided, the trust will still be fixed. In the absence of a direction as to how the trustees are to divide the money, the equitable maxim 'equity is equality' will apply, and the money will be divided equally between the two children, as with the first example.

With a **discretionary trust**, on the other hand, the trustees are given discretion, either to decide the shares into which the trust fund will be divided, or to decide who will benefit under the terms of the trust, or sometimes both. A discretionary trust might look like this:

> I give £10,000 to my trustees to divide between those of my children they consider most deserving in their absolute discretion.

In this scenario, the trustees have discretion as to how the money is divided. They also have discretion as to whom the money is given. The settlor has allowed them to choose which of the children they consider most deserving and divide the money between them. No shares are specified and so the trustees are free to decide in what proportions the money is to be divided. Thus, the trustees could decide to split the money between Jacob and Frances, £7,000 to Jacob and the remaining £3,000 to Frances. Alternatively, if they considered Jacob undeserving of a share of the trust fund, they could decide to benefit Frances with the whole £10,000. Such is the nature of their discretion. The Writing and drafting exercise will help you to test your understanding of the nature of fixed and discretionary trusts.

> trustees are free to decide in what proportions the money is to be divided

Writing and drafting

You are Nasreen Aqeel, a trainee solicitor at the firm of Irash & Co. Solicitors. You are dealing with the estate of the late Mrs Elda Myers. The following is a section of her will:

I make the following bequests:

(a) I give my collection of vintage port to be shared between my friends Danyl Shah and Enid Carlton at the Carleon Amateur Dramatics Association in memory of all the good times we had together.

(b) I give £10,000 to be divided between the following charities:
   (i)   St Luke's Hospice
   (ii) Candlelighters, the children's charity
   (iii) Rainbow Days Donkey Sanctuary
   in such shares as my trustees shall in their wisdom determine.

(c) I leave the residue of my estate to be divided equally between those of my grandchildren as my trustees shall consider deserving.

Mrs Myers's trustees are coming in to see your training principal this afternoon. They would like advice on what discretion they have (if any) in distributing the various gifts listed in the will. Your training principal, Mr Irash, is out of the office all morning and will not have time to look through the file. He has asked you to write him a memo detailing what the trustees are allowed to do under the terms of the will. Your memo should be no more than one side of an A4 sheet in length so you will need to be succinct. You have another appointment in 40 minutes so you have until then to complete the memo.

 Handy tip: Look at each clause of the will separately. What are the trustees allowed to do? Are they given discretion as to how to divide the fund or who to give it to? If so, how wide is that discretion?

Reflective practice

How did you find explaining the difference between fixed and discretionary trusts? When you read back through what you have written have you explained the difference between the two clearly? Do you think you would be able to write your own discretionary trusts now? Is there any way you could improve on what you have written?

Remember that this is a practical exercise as well as an academic one, so the layout of your memo is important. The training principal will not be impressed if, as a trainee in a law firm, you hand him a hastily-scribbled answer on a scrap of paper! Did you find out how to set out a business memorandum before starting this exercise? Would you know how to write one in the future?

 Handy tip: It may be helpful to keep a template business memorandum for your future use. You can download a free example of a standard office memo on the web at: http://www.8ov.org/memo.htm.

For a more in-depth look at fixed and discretionary trusts, go to Chapter 3 on certainties.

Purpose trusts

Purpose trusts are trusts which are set up by the settlor to carry out an abstract purpose, rather than to benefit a specific person. Purpose trusts can be private or public. All charitable trusts are **public purpose trusts**, because they are trusts which have been put into effect for a purpose which benefits the public. An example of a **private purpose trust**, on the other hand, would be a trust set up to build a tomb or monument in memory of the settlor after their death. Subject to a couple of exceptions, private purpose trusts are not a valid form of trust in English law. We will be looking at the topic of private purpose trusts in detail in Chapter 4.

Charitable trusts

As outlined above, charitable trusts are public trusts which are set up for charitable purposes as opposed to purely private purposes. Charitable trusts are the biggest exception to the 'no purpose trusts' rule. Chapter 5 examines the role of charitable trusts and how they work in detail.

Express trusts

The majority of trusts are **express trusts**. These are trusts which the settlor has specifically and purposefully taken steps to create, either by way of a verbal declaration that they wish to form a trust or, as is the case in most instances, by some form of writing. The formalities required for the creation of express trusts are discussed in Chapter 2.

Resulting and constructive trusts

Unlike express trusts, resulting and constructive trusts are created without the need for any express declaration of trust or writing of any kind. They are therefore completely informal in their creation. A **resulting trust** will arise in one of two situations:

1. Where the settlor has tried to create a trust but has, for one reason or another, failed to transfer the beneficial interest in the property effectively. This is an '**automatic resulting trust**'.

2. Where contributions are made to the purchase price of property by more than one person but the legal title is held by one of the parties only, in which case the intention of the settlor is presumed to have been that they intended to create a trust. This is a '**presumed resulting trust**'.

A **constructive trust**, on the other hand, will be imposed by the court in any situation where the conduct of one party is so unconscionable, or morally reprehensible, that to allow any other outcome would be unjust, or inequitable. With a resulting trust therefore (regardless of type), the intentions of the parties to the trust are implied. With a constructive trust, on the other hand, the intentions of the parties to the trust are irrelevant and the constructive trust is said to be imposed by operation of the law.

The law relating to resulting and constructive trusts is discussed in detail in Chapters 7 and 8.

Statutory trusts

Unlike express trusts, which are created by individuals, **statutory trusts** are created or implied under the provisions of a statute. There are many examples of statutory trusts, one of the most common being the trust which is imposed on any person who purchases property jointly with another under sections 34(2) and 36 of the Law of Property Act 1925 (as amended by Schedule 2 of the Trusts of Land and Appointment of Trustees Act 1996). The sections state that where land is owned by two or more people, it will be held on a trust, each party holding the beneficial, or equitable, interest in the land on trust for the other. This creates a rather unusual trust situation because it means that the property owners become both trustees and beneficiaries of the land. Figure 1.4 may help to explain.

You should note that there is no need to understand the concept of **co-ownership** any more fully for the purposes of this book, although you may have already come across this example of a statutory trust in your study of land law.

Figure 1.4 Division of legal and equitable ownership of property

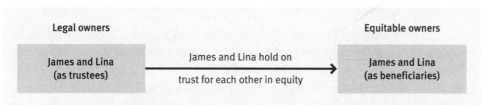

Perhaps a rather simpler example is that of the statutory trust imposed under section 46 of the Administration of Estates Act 1925, in respect of intestacy. When a person dies intestate (you will remember this means without leaving a will) leaving a widow and children, a statutory trust is imposed on that person's assets wherever their assets exceed a fixed sum set by statute (currently £125,000). The widow is entitled to the fixed sum outright. Half of the remainder of the estate is then held on trust for the widow's lifetime, during which the widow receives the income from the trust. After her death this sum goes to her children, unless they have not yet reached the age of 18, in which case the money will be held on trust until they do so. The other half of the remainder is held on trust for the children until they reach the age of 18, or on marriage if that is earlier.

Lifetime trusts

A lifetime trust is a trust created to benefit one person during that person's lifetime, and another person or persons after their death. So, for example, Victor might leave in his will his house at 1 Ingfield Avenue on trust for his wife, Jenny, during her lifetime, and then to his son, Jonathan, after Jenny's death. In this scenario, Jenny would be described as having a '**life interest**' in 1 Ingfield Avenue and would be termed a '**life tenant**' of the property. As we saw earlier in our terminology of trusts, Jonathan would have a vested interest in the house, because Jenny's death is a certainty, albeit that we do not know when she is going to die. He would be termed the '**remainderman**', because he is entitled to the remainder of the interest after his mother's death. The function of such lifetime trusts is usually to ensure that a spouse is provided for during their lifetime, but that the children of the marriage are the ultimate beneficiaries of the trust property. Such a provision would, for example, prevent Jenny cutting Jonathan out of her will in the event of her remarriage.

Trusts compared with other concepts

We have taken some time to get to grips with the meaning of trusts and the terminology which surrounds them. However, there may be situations in which a trust may appear, on the face of it, to be very similar to another legal concept. As a final consolidation of your understanding of the meaning of the trust, let us now consider the trust as compared with a selection of other legal devices.

Trusts and contract

Trusts are often cited as being virtually synonymous with contracts, but the differences between them are in fact quite marked. If you have studied the law of contract before, you will know that the fundamental requirement for any contract is that of consideration: put simply, a bargain must be struck between the parties, one party giving consideration for something provided by the other. With trusts there is no consideration, and there is no bargain or agreement. The creation of a trust is a unilateral event, the settlor transferring property to another for the benefit of a third party and gaining nothing in return. One could argue that a contract made for the benefit of a third party would have the same result. This may be so, but the two concepts would still be founded on an entirely different basis: the trustee having given no consideration for the transfer, whereas in a contract to provide services for a third party, the contracting party would be given consideration for their services. An additional difference between the creation of a trust and a contract is that, with a trust, the settlor has no power to enforce the trust once it has been created. The beneficiaries will have the power to do so, of course, but not the settlor. With a contract the person transferring their property under the contract would have a contractual right, on the basis of the consideration paid by them for the service rendered or goods supplied, to seek redress if the other party to the contract did not keep to their side of the bargain.

One final, fundamental difference between the two concepts lies in their origin: whereas a contract is a creation of the common law, the trust is an invention of equity. The remedies available to the two concepts are therefore different. In the case of a breach of contract, the injured party will be entitled to the remedy of damages at common law, their remedy being a **personal remedy** against the party in breach. If the trustee is bankrupt, therefore, the party to the contract who is making the claim may end up with nothing. In the case of a breach of trust, on the other hand, the beneficiaries will be entitled to a **proprietary remedy** as against the trustees, meaning that they can claim the return of the trust property to the trust, in priority over and above any other claim which may exist against the trustees' assets. For a more detailed explanation of personal and proprietary remedies, see Chapter 16 on remedies.

Trusts and agency

Again, the trust relationship is often described as being indistinguishable from that of agency. However, this is far from being the case. Although there are similarities between the two concepts, they act very differently from one another on a practical, as well as a legal level. In thinking about the concept of agency, it may be helpful to bear in mind the role of an estate agent. The respective roles of the estate agent and the trustee are similar in that both carry with them a fiduciary duty: in other words, they require the trustee or agent to act in good faith in the best interests either of the beneficiaries, in the case of a trustee or, in the case of an **agent**, of their **principal**. But here already we can see a difference between the two because, whereas an agent acts on behalf of their principal as the person who instructed them, a trustee acts on behalf of the beneficiaries and not on behalf of the settlor who sets up the trust. The basis of the relationship between principal and agent and settlor and trustee is also different. If you think about our estate agent, he will be instructed to act on behalf of the seller of a property, the principal, and the two will enter into a contract for the agent's services, in return for an agency fee. As we have already seen, a settlor receives nothing in return for their transfer of the property to the trustees, not even a right to enforce the terms of the trust.

One final difference between agency and trusteeship is in the ownership of the property concerned. In an agency agreement, whilst the agent may have physical control of the property they are dealing with they do not have legal ownership of it: this remains at all times with the principal. All the agent is doing is brokering, or dealing with, the property on their principal's behalf. A trustee, on the other hand, will always be the legal owner of the property, the transfer of the legal title to the property into the trustees' hands being fundamental to the creation of the trust.

Trusts and bailment

Bailment is an agreement under which the legal owner of the property (the '**bailor**'), usually under contract and for the payment of a fee, places property under the physical control (and usually possession) of another, in return for which the holder of the property ('**bailee**') assumes responsibility for the property's safe keeping and return. Examples of bailment are safety deposit boxes and storage facilities (but not 'lock ups', as the goods must be under the actual physical control of the bailee, not the bailor), automobile garaging services and animal boarding kennels. There are instances of bailment in which there is no contract or payment involved, such as when a person finds a diamond ring in the street and takes it to the local police station for their safe keeping, pending finding the real owner. This is perhaps what causes difficulty in distinguishing between the concepts of bailment and trusts. But there always remains a fundamental difference between the two, which is the issue of legal ownership. Whilst a bailee will be in physical control of the subject matter of the bailment for a limited period of time, and may even take physical possession of it, they never take legal ownership of the goods. As we know with a trust, on the other hand, the trustees will always be the legal owners of the trust property.

Trusts and powers

A **power** is a form of official authority, given by the owner of property, or '**donor**', to a second person, or '**donee**', to deal with property, usually on behalf of a third person. As such, the power is the concept which most closely resembles that of the trust and it is therefore the distinction between trusts and powers which is perhaps the most difficult to make. There are two types of power: those which give the donee power to dispose of property, which are known as **powers of appointment**, and those which give the donee a more limited power to deal with property. You will most often come across the power to deal with property in the context of trusts, trustees being given powers to invest trust property, or the power of maintenance and advancement. For a further insight into what these powers entail, go to Chapters 11 and 12 of this book.

However, there are instances of powers to deal with property outside of the trust arena, such as a power of attorney, which gives the donee power to sell the donor's property, sign legal papers on the donor's behalf or otherwise carry out their affairs whilst the donor is perhaps out of the country, or during a period of illness.

It is powers of appointment, however, that bear the greatest resemblance to the trust. To make matters more complicated, powers of appointment will often be found mixed in with trusts created under the same document or will. Take a look at the following clauses from a will:

1. I give £200,000 to my niece Ursula on trust for life with remainder to whomsoever she shall appoint.
2. I give £200,000 to my niece Ursula on trust for life with remainder to my grandson Eric.
3. I give £200,000 to my niece Ursula on trust for life with remainder to her children in such shares as my trustees shall in their discretion decide.

How do you tell the difference between the clauses? Which are trusts and which are powers? It would seem on the face of it to be impossible, but in actual fact there is a fundamental difference between a power and a trust which clearly distinguishes them, and this is the element of choice. Whereas a power gives the donee of the power discretion as to whether or not they use the power they are given, a trustee has no choice in carrying out their duties. The trustee may be given a choice as to *how* they are to carry out their duties as trustees (for a reminder of this, see fixed and discretionary trusts, above), but they have no discretion as to whether or not they wish to carry out those duties. The creation of a trust carries with it an imperative element: the trustees are required by the settlor to carry out their duties as trustees; they are not given a choice as to whether to do so or not. The only way in which a trustee could refrain from carrying out their duties would be by retiring from the trust, thereby ending their trusteeship. A donee under a power, on the other hand, could simply choose to do nothing with their power and they would not be accountable to the donor for their lack of action.

Taking another look at the three will clauses above, then, we can see that clause 1 is a power, whereas the other two are trusts. In clause 1, there is a life interest in favour of Ursula with a power given to her to give the remainder to 'whomsoever she shall appoint'. Ursula is therefore under no duty to transfer the property to a specific person: rather she has the power to appoint any person of her choosing to receive the property in the event of her death. Clauses 2 and 3 are trusts because, in both cases, the trustees are instructed to distribute the trust property to a specific beneficiary, or class of beneficiaries, on Ursula's death. The fact that the trustees are given discretion in clause 3 as to how the money is to be divided is irrelevant: their discretion relates only to the division of the money; their obligation to distribute is absolute. To give another slightly different example of a trust and a power of appointment together, take a look at the following:

4. I give £5,000 to my good friend Sadiq to distribute between his children as he shall decide.
5. I give £5,000 to my good friend Sadiq to distribute between his children if he shall decide.

Clauses 4 and 5 are almost identical, save for one small word, but the word makes all the difference. In clause 4, Sadiq is given money to distribute between his children '*as* he shall decide'. This is a trust, because the discretion is as to the method of distribution: the instruction to distribute itself is imperative. In the case of clause 5, however, the wording is that Sadiq should distribute the money between his children '*if* he shall decide'. There is therefore no imperative here: Sadiq can choose whether he wishes to distribute the money between his children or not. This is clearly a power of appointment. It can be seen, then, that the difference between powers of appointment and trusts can rest on a simple matter of construction. The difference, however, is quite significant.

One last point to mention about powers of appointment is that they can be put into three sub-categories. These are:

✦ **general powers**;

✦ **special powers**; and

✦ **hybrid powers**.

With a general power, the donee is not subject to any restrictions as to who they exercise their power in favour of. An example of a general power would be clause 1, above. Here, Ursula is given the power to appoint to whomsoever she chooses, including herself theoretically (although in this particular instance this would be pointless as the money would simply go into Ursula's estate on her death). In a different example, this would result in the donor having made, to all intents and purposes, an outright gift to the donee: it would be like saying 'I am giving you my CD collection; do with it whatever you want.'

A special power is more restrictive in that it limits the donee to distributing the subject matter of the power between a specified class of persons. An example of a special power would be clause 5, above, where Sadiq is given the power to distribute amongst any of his children.

A hybrid power is similar to a special power, except that it works exclusively, meaning that, using our example of Sadiq above, he would be able to distribute the money amongst anyone *except for* a specified class of beneficiaries: in this case, say, his children.

Modern uses for trusts

We looked earlier in the chapter at the historical reasons for the creation of the trust by the court of equity. However, the use of the trust in modern times has expanded far beyond protecting the families of absentee landowners, and the modern trust now covers a whole range of different situations. The following is intended to give you a flavour of just some of the uses of the modern-day trust. By way of introduction, take a look at what solicitor Duncan Milwain has to say, in the People in the law feature, about how he uses trusts on a day-to-day basis.

People in the law

Name and position: Duncan Milwain, Director and Head of Trusts, Wills & Probate Department, Lupton Fawcett, Leeds.

What is your role? To advise clients on estate planning matters including on wills, inheritance tax and planning through the use of trusts.

How long have you been working as a wills and probate lawyer? I started my articles [or what would now be termed 'training contract'] in March 1993, qualified in mid-1995 and have been practising since then.

What made you choose this area of the law? I would like to say that I always had a keen desire to be a private client lawyer from an early age. This would, however, be untrue. I was fortunate to obtain a training contract at one of the Magic Circle firms in London and was even more fortunate that they, unusually, continued to do private client work. My seat in that department was sufficient for me to realise this was what I most enjoyed.

Source: Duncan Milwain, Lupton Fawcett Solicitors (*text and photo*)

How much do trusts feature in your work on a day-to-day basis? Trusts in all their guises form a central part of the work which I carry out. This may be advising on the establishment of new trusts or the administration of pre-existing trusts. The latter may be trusts either created during a person's lifetime or established under a will.

How important are trusts to your work as a lawyer? Trusts are a fundamental part of the work of a private client lawyer. They are a time-proven effective means of protecting and preserving assets over several generations. There are nuances to trusts over time, primarily as tax legislation changes, but the underlying theme of asset preservation remains unchanged.

What are the most common uses of trusts in your business? There has been a concerted attack on the use of trusts by the former Labour administration over recent years. This has undermined the ability of families to use trusts as a means of preserving wealth. This attack has arisen based on a mistaken assumption that trusts are solely the preserve of the rich and used only for tax avoidance. Neither of these assumptions is correct and it is to be hoped that some of the recent legislative changes are repealed or amended in due course.

Many of my clients are the owners of family businesses. A common and increasingly used purpose for trusts is for business assets (usually company shares) to be transferred to a trust. Such business assets should attract inheritance tax relief so that the transfer into trust can be achieved without triggering inheritance tax charges. The assets are then in a trust environment where they can be used to provide for the following generation or generations. This is a classic use of trusts.

Would you be able to do your job without them? In short, probably no. However, the law and lawyers are nothing if not inventive and alternative structures to trusts have been proposed over the last few years, most notably the use of limited partnerships for family assets. Whilst these have gained some small degree of popularity the associated costs are for the most part prohibitive. More importantly, partnerships do not have the natural fit that trusts have with asset preservation. Ultimately, notwithstanding the recent attack on them, trusts will continue to survive and flourish. [A limited partnership is a special kind of partnership in which the partners' liability extends only to the amount of their original investment to the partnership. For more information about limited liability partnerships go to: **http://www.companieshouse.gov. uk/infoAndGuide/faq/llpFAQ.shtml**.]

What is the most unusual or interesting trust you have ever come across? There are at least three different ways of looking at this: to the interesting and unusual technical aspects of trusts, to the assets held by the trust and to the people who have settled or are trustees of the trust. I am fortunate to have noteworthy representatives of each. Some of the most interesting deals which I have been involved with have included a transfer of a large country estate down to the next generation of the family, and dealing with the trust aspects of a re-categorisation of shares in a business held by a series of family trusts. From one extreme to the other: I have on two occasions been involved with establishing trusts to make provision for a family pet!

Trusts for the family

As we saw from Duncan Milwain's interview in the People in the law feature, a large proportion of trusts are still dedicated to the protection of the family and its assets. A prime example is where a settlor wishes to ensure that both their spouse and their children are adequately provided for in the event of their death. In such a scenario, the settlor might create a lifetime trust, giving their spouse the right to live out their days in the family home and thus ensuring a roof over their head for the remainder of their lifetime, whilst at the same time ensuring that the house will go to their children on the death of the spouse. In doing this, the settlor would prevent the spouse from cutting the children out of their will, say, in the event of their remarriage, and thus depriving the children of their inheritance. This use of a trust to restrict the spouse's use of the property is not something which the testator would be able to do if the house was made to the spouse as an outright gift.

Another family situation in which a trust might be used is where a parent or guardian wishes to set up a trust to provide for the specific needs of one or more of their children. Such needs might include the children's education or perhaps the maintenance of a child with disabilities. Alternatively, a settlor may wish, in the event of their death, to put inheritance money into the hands of trustees to prevent an immature or irresponsible child from needlessly dissipating the fund. The Law in action feature gives an interesting insight into some of the problems child trust funds can be used to solve.

Law in action Child actors: protected by their trust funds?

Many people envy the glamorous life of the child actor: travelling the world and working with famous actors; and then, of course, there is the money. But is it as good as it sounds? There have been many stories told over the years, of the fortunes of child actors being squandered by unscrupulous parents and guardians. So what can be done to protect them?

The status of child actors has led to a whole raft of recent controversy over the protection of the children who starred in British director Danny Boyle's Oscar-winning movie, *Slumdog Millionaire*. The controversy stems from the alleged underpayment of the child stars, Rubina Ali and Azharuddin Ismail, who were taken from the slums of Mumbai in India in order to lend authenticity to the film, which was set in the area. The children initially received under £2,500 between them for a whole year's work. Despite claims by the film-makers that the children were well paid for their roles in the film, earning three times the average annual salary for their work, the public outcry forced them to re-evaluate the plight of the slum actors. However, film director Boyle soon realised that further cash payments would not be the best way to serve the children's interests in the long term. Boyle therefore set up trust funds for the children's education, with a lump sum payable on completion of their studies.

This still did not relieve the children from the immediate poverty they faced living in their makeshift homes in the slums of Mumbai though. Amid further criticism of the film-makers, stemming from the publication of photographs showing the continuation of the children's squalid existence, Boyle has vowed to take further action, this time providing better housing for the children's families. Each child has been bought a flat on the outskirts of the area in which they live, which has

Source: Photodisc/Photolink

been put into trust until the children turn 18. 'It would have been pointless giving them the flats outright,' said Boyle, 'because their families would have sold them.' This way the children will have better homes to live in, with electricity and running water, whilst still remaining within their own community, close to friends and extended family.

Reportedly, the film's investors and distributors have also set up a fund for the slum and street children of Mumbai, setting an initial £500,000 aside for the task. Have the film-makers done enough for the stars of a film that has grossed over £70 million worldwide? That is a question which remains to be answered.

For a more detailed look at the story of the Mumbai child actors, go to: **http://www.dailymail.co.uk/tvshowbiz/article-1154667/Boyle-takes-Slumdog-children-film-bosses-pledge-buy-poverty-stricken-families-new-homes.html**.

Another way in which the vehicle of a trust was used until recently within a family setting was in inheritance tax planning. By putting certain assets of the family into trust, parents were able to save their children from a large proportion of their inheritance tax bill in the event of their death. In brief, the idea behind a basic inheritance tax-saving scheme was as follows: one parent acting as settlor put a sum of money, say £100,000, into trust. The trust was a discretionary trust, allowing the trustees to pay some or all of the fund to one or more of the settlor's spouse or children. The trustees were given complete discretion as to who was to be paid out of the trust fund. The theory was that, because the trust was discretionary, the spouse contained in the list of beneficiaries had no actual *right* to the fund (they would have no entitlement until they were actually chosen by the trustees to become a beneficiary of it). This meant that the fund could not be classed as an asset of the spouse's estate when they died and as a consequence of this the money held in trust would not be included in any inheritance tax calculation, thus significantly reducing or even negating the children's inheritance tax bill, which would usually be payable at 40 per cent over and above assets amounting to £325,000. Since October 2007, however, the surviving spouse can now carry forward the deceased spouse's unused nil rate band and hence the discretionary trust does not have the same inheritance tax-saving effect that it used to have. The Key stats feature provides a useful overview of the current inheritance tax position in the UK.

Key stats Increases in inheritance tax liability set to continue

The payment of inheritance tax by homeowners is on the increase and a move by the government to freeze the inheritance threshold until 2014 is estimated to raise in excess of £254 billion for the Treasury over the next four years. But exactly how can a freeze on the tax threshold amount to such a huge source of additional revenue for the government? It all comes down to inflation. Take a look at the figures.

Inheritance tax is calculated at 40 per cent on the value of a person's total assets, including their family home, after the deduction of a tax-free allowance which is currently set at £325,000. This means that on an estate totalling £425,000 the tax liability would be £40,000: that is 40 per cent of the taxable £100,000.

The inheritance tax threshold usually rises in line with inflation, meaning that at current inflation rates, which stand at over 3 per cent, the £325,000 threshold should have been increased to about £350,000 by 2014.

But even if a rise in line with inflation were instigated, this still goes nowhere near the level of increase in house prices in the UK, which has seen the cost of property rising by an incredible 89 per cent in the last decade. Keeping the inheritance tax threshold in line with the increase in house prices would mean that the threshold should actually now stand at over £500,000: significantly more than the current tax threshold.

According to a recent Office of National Statistics report called *Wealth in Great Britain*, because of the rise in house prices around one in five households in the UK now has a net worth of over £325,000, making their owners liable to inheritance tax.

The effect is that more than 4 million people in the UK face having to pay an extra £10,000 in death taxes, making the total potential liability under the tax in excess of £250 billion.

During the 2010 electoral campaign the Conservatives pledged to scrap the levy for anyone leaving less than £1 million, but in the emergency budget of 22 June 2010, no further changes to the inheritance tax threshold were unveiled. It would appear that trust lawyers countrywide are going to be kept busy drafting and implementing tax avoidance schemes for some while to come.

To see the Office of National Statistics report in full, go to: **http://www.statistics.gov.uk/downloads/ theme_economy/wealth-assets-2006-2008/Wealth_in_GB_2006_2008.pdf.** A full copy of the 2010 Budget can be viewed at: **http://www.hm-treasury.gov.uk/d/junebudget_complete.pdf.**]

A more detailed discussion of inheritance tax is outside the scope of this book.

Trusts for the protection of creditors

We have seen trusts used to protect vulnerable children or family members either from others or from themselves. Another common use of the trust as a scheme for the protection of the more vulnerable can be seen in its use as a vehicle for the protection of people to whom money is owed: in particular customers of an ailing business. When an individual is made bankrupt or a company goes into liquidation a **trustee in bankruptcy** (or, in the case of a company, an administrator) is appointed. (The trustee in bankruptcy should not be confused with the trustees we have come across so far in the context of an ordinary trust. The trustee in bankruptcy is simply the name given to the person who is appointed by the court to administer the bankrupt's assets. They are in no way similar to trustees of an ordinary trust as we would understand them in the context of this book.)

Case Summary

The trustee in bankruptcy then takes over the management of the bankrupt's affairs, using the remaining assets of the bankrupt to pay off the creditors in order of priority. Priority will depend on a number of factors, including the age of the debt, and whether the debt was secured against any property of the debtor. In such circumstances, if the debtor is aware that they are in financial difficulty before their bankruptcy is declared, they can set up a trust account into which customer money is placed pending their orders being dispatched. In this way, the customers' money is protected from being claimed by the trustee in bankruptcy in the event of the debtor being declared bankrupt before the customers' orders have been processed. This was what happened in the case of *Re Kayford Ltd* [1975] 1 WLR 279, the full facts of which appear in Chapter 3 on certainties. The process of creating a trust account to protect customers of an ailing business in this manner is known as '**ring-fencing**' assets.

Case Summary

Another similar, but subtly different, method of using trusts to protect the assets of creditors is by the creation of what is known as a '**Quistclose trust**'. This type of trust takes its name from the leading case in the area, *Barclays Bank Ltd* v. *Quistclose Investments Ltd* [1970] AC 567 HL. In this case, a company in trouble, Rolls-Razor, approached a loan company, Quistclose Investments, for money to make payments to its shareholders. Aware that the company was in trouble, Quistclose gave Rolls-Razor the money, but on specific instructions that the money was only to be used for the purpose of paying the shareholders. The money was placed in a designated bank account and separated from the general funds of the company. Rolls-Razor subsequently went into liquidation and the court held that Quistclose, in directing the money be used only for a specific purpose, had successfully created a trust, with the ailing company as trustee, and the shareholders as its beneficiaries.

When Rolls-Razor went under, the purpose of the trust had been frustrated and so the monies were returned to the settlor (Quistclose) on a resulting trust. The issue of resulting trusts is dealt with in detail at Chapter 7. The subtle difference between a Quistclose trust and a *Re Kayford* type trust is that, in *Re Kayford*, the monies were received from customers and subsequently set aside by the company in an attempt to protect them from creditors, whereas in Quistclose, the trust was created, not by the struggling company but by the creditor prior to the money being handed over. In Quistclose, therefore, the company was never the legal owner of the property – it was only ever the trustee of the money. Conversely in *Re Kayford*, it was the company who acted as settlor, setting money aside in trust for its creditors.

There is an interesting article showing the practical implications of using trusts to protect creditors in the Law in action feature in Chapter 3.

Trusts as property-holding vehicles

Whilst trusts can be used as a method of keeping property safe from a spendthrift beneficiary or even from the trustee in bankruptcy, they can also be used as a method of holding property on behalf of those who, through no fault of their own, do not have the required capacity to hold property by themselves. Obvious examples of this might be children under the age of 18, who do not have the legal capacity to own land and therefore would need to do so under the protection of a trust, and those who do not have the required mental capacity to hold property. We will be exploring the issue of capacity further in Chapter 2.

There are other equally common situations in which the use of a trust is necessary in the holding of property. Whilst a company which has been formally **incorporated** has its own legal identity and is therefore able to hold company funds and land in its own right, **unincorporated** bodies which are not organised and maintained as a legal corporation, such as clubs, societies and political parties, do not share the same privilege and are therefore unable to hold property of any kind in their own name. In order to get around this, these unincorporated bodies have to nominate trustees who will safeguard their funds and property on their behalf. This scenario would also apply to unincorporated business partnerships, such as solicitors' practices or accountancy firms. It should be noted that the holding of property on behalf of unincorporated associations can raise particular difficulties. This will form the subject of further discussion in Chapter 4.

Trusts to carry out a purpose

As has already been described in the section of this chapter concerning the terminology of trusts, it is possible for trusts to be used for the carrying out of a particular purpose as opposed to for the benefit of a person. Examples of this might be a trust set up to ensure a pet was looked after in the event of the owner's death, or a trust set up to carry out some abstract purpose such as to help the employees of a company suffering financial hardship or to provide scholarships or financial assistance towards tuition fees at a school or university. As previously mentioned, there are difficulties incumbent with trust funds set up for private purposes such as these (as opposed to trusts for public purposes, such as charitable trusts). These will be explored in further detail in Chapter 4.

Pension schemes and investment trusts

The final example of uses to which a trust can be put is that of money held on trust as part of an investment or savings strategy. With both pension schemes and investment trusts, money is paid into a fund which is then managed by trustees on behalf of the investor or persons nominated by them with a view to achieving an increase in value in the fund that is to be paid out to the beneficiaries at some future point in time. The responsibility of trustees to invest such funds responsibly and, in particular, not to lose that money, is a notable point of interest and one which will be discussed in further detail in Chapter 12 on trustee powers of investment.

Out and about

You have been given many examples of trusts in practice. But how many different types of trusts can you find which affect the daily life of you or your family? You may not be lucky enough to have your own trust fund, but what other trusts do you come across as part of your daily life? Take some time to think about it. Consider all of the daily activities of you and your family. You will be surprised to find how many trusts you come across.

You should take no longer than 40 minutes on this task.

 Handy tip: Are you a member of a college or university? What trusts can you find there?

Summary

- The Court of Chancery developed equity as an alternative form of justice to the harsh unbending rules of the common law.

- The administration of equity and the common law was fused together in the Judicature Acts of the 1870s.

- The Court of Chancery developed a series of equitable maxims, which served as a set of guidelines or standards in deciding cases which came before them.

- The trust derives from the 'use', which allowed two separate rights in one property to exist at the same time, one in law and one in equity.

- A trust is where one person (the settlor) gives property to another (the trustee) to look after for a third person (the beneficiary).

- The trustees are the legal owners of the trust property. The beneficial, or equitable, interest belongs to the beneficiaries.

- When trusts are created by will, the person writing the will is called the testator or testatrix, and the people who administer the will are known as the executors. The executors are often also named as the trustees of any trust created by the will.

- There are many different types of trust. Trusts can be created expressly, or implied by law or statute; they can be fixed in nature, so that the trustees have no say as to how the trust fund is administered, or discretionary, giving the trustees the ability to decide who to benefit and in what amounts.

- Trusts share similarities with other concepts, including contract, agency and bailment. However, they are fundamentally different from all of them in nature.

Trusts and powers can be seen as sharing the most in common, a power being an authority given by the owner of property to a second person to deal with property on behalf of a third. However, whereas a trust carries with it an imperative element, the use of a power is discretionary.

 Trusts were originally created by the court of equity to protect the families of absentee landowners. However, their use has been expanded to cover a wide variety of situations.

 Examples of uses for modern-day trusts include provision for the family, tax planning, the protection of creditors, as a vehicle to hold property on behalf of charities, clubs, societies and partnerships, and in pension schemes and investment trusts.

Question and answer*

Problem: Take a look at the following scenarios. In each case, say which equitable maxim or maxims you think would apply, giving reasons for your answer:

1. Jude transfers his house into the name of his brother, Xavier, in order fraudulently to gain Xavier access to the country under immigration law. Jude then seeks to evict Xavier on the basis that Jude has bought and paid for the house, but Xavier claims legal ownership of the property.

2. Lola and Zidi buy a house together in their joint names. They both pay equal amounts towards the purchase of the property, but Lola uses an inheritance to build a substantial extension to the property, doubling its value. Lola's money also pays for the house to be rewired and a new central heating system to be put in. When the couple later separate and the house is sold, Zidi claims that the proceeds of sale of the house should be split equally between them, but Lola does not agree. Lola and Zidi are not married.

3. Hayley wins a hot air balloon flight across the Yorkshire Dales in a crossword competition. Unfortunately, on the day the flight is due to take place, the weather conditions are not favourable and they are unable to take off. Hayley demands that the balloon company take her on another day instead.

4. Chester is the beneficiary under a large trust fund to which he will become entitled when he is 30. For the last 10 years one of the trustees has been 'borrowing' money from the trust fund. Chester was aware of this, but chose to do nothing about it as the sums were small and 'he could spare the money anyway'. However, after a furious row with the trustee, Chester is now threatening to take the trustee to court to demand the return of the money to the fund.

You should allow yourself no more than 40 minutes to complete this task.

Essay: If we were asked what is the greatest and most distinctive achievement performed by Englishmen in the field of jurisprudence I cannot think that we should have any better answer to give than this, namely the development from century to century of the trust idea.

(F.W. Maitland, *Selected Essays* (Cambridge University Press, 1936), p. 129.)

Discuss the use of trusts today with reference to this statement.

This question should be answered in 40 minutes.

✱ Answer guidance is provided at the end of the chapter.

Further reading

Baker, J.H. (2002) *An Introduction to English Legal History*, **3rd edn, London: Butterworths.**
Whilst the present book has, for the sake of conciseness, skipped over much of the more detailed historical background relating to the development of the trust, those of you who are interested in the historical development of the law in this area should find a wealth of information on both the development of equity (including trusts) and the courts of equity in any good textbook on legal history. Baker's is one such book although, of course, there are others.

Groves, C. and Tee, C. (2009) 'Where there's a will', *Legal Week* **11(2), 32, 34.**
A useful article discussing the use of trusts for inheritance tax planning, dealing with funds held on trust for children, lifetime trusts and discretionary trusts.

Hayton, D. (2006) 'Pension trusts and traditional trusts: dramatically different species of trusts', Conv 229.
This article gives a thorough and in-depth analysis of the practical workings of a pension trust in contrast to ordinary trusts and gives arguments for reform of the law in this area.

Leech, T. (2001) 'The use of trusts and constructive trusts in lawyers' claims', 20 October, http://www.maitlandchambers. com/articles.
This is an excellent article written by a barrister specialising in trust law, which talks through the various different uses for trusts by lawyers. Brilliantly practical and really puts the area of trust law into context.

Martin, J.E. (1994) 'Fusion, fallacy and confusion: a comparative study', Conv 13.
This article provides an intelligent and in-depth analysis of the modern effects of the fusion of the courts of law and equity in England, in contrast with other Commonwealth systems.

Pettit, P.H. (1990) 'He who comes to equity must come with clean hands', Conv 416.
This article provides an interesting discussion on the continued relevance of the maxim in the modern law of equity.

Yeo, T.M. and Tjio, H. (2003) 'The Quistclose trust', 119 LQR 8–13.
A short article which gives a thorough analysis and explanation of the working of the Quistclose trust, in the light of Lord Millett's judgment in the House of Lords case of *Twinsectra* v. *Yardley* [2002] 2 AC 164.

Question and answer guidance

Problem:

1. '*He who comes to equity must come with clean hands*.' Jude has transferred the property into his brother's name to allow him to enter the country illegally. He should not therefore expect the court to recognise his beneficial interest in the property under the rules of equity.

2. '*Equity will not permit a statute to be used as an instrument of fraud*.' Lola has no entitlement to be compensated for the work she has carried out at the property under the Matrimonial Homes Act 1970 because the couple were not married. However, she should be entitled to make a claim under the rules of constructive trusts, based on the size of her contribution.

3. *'Equity will not assist a volunteer.'* Hayley won the balloon flight in a competition and did not therefore pay for it. She is not in a position to demand a second flight when the first is unsuccessful.

4. *'Delay defeats equity.'* Chester has had 10 years to take action against the rogue trustee, but has chosen not to do so. He is therefore unlikely to be allowed to bring a claim in equity for the lost money.

Essay:

A good answer to this question would introduce the reader to the concept of the trust, perhaps with a little historical context, and then take them briefly through all the modern uses of trusts today, with comment on the adaptability of the trust to modern uses over the course of the centuries, in accordance with the quotation. Modern uses would include:

✦ trusts for the protection of family assets;

✦ trusts to make provision for family members and other dependants;

✦ trusts for inheritance tax-planning purposes;

✦ trusts for the protection of creditors;

✦ trusts as a method of holding property;

✦ private and public purpose trusts;

✦ trusts for pensions and investments.

Reference could be made to Duncan Milwain's article which gives some really useful comment on the use of trusts in day-to-day practice and would give the essay currency.

Your conclusion should agree or disagree with the quotation, summarising the usefulness of the trust in the modern context and confirming its necessity in legal practice today.

Chapter 2
Capacity and formalities

Key points In this chapter we will be looking at:

✦ Who can create a trust

✦ What formal steps need to be taken to create a trust

✦ The creation of trusts by will

✦ Transferring the trust property to the trustees

✦ What happens when trust property has not been properly transferred

Introduction

The aim of Chapter 1 was to introduce you to the concept of the trust and to get you thinking a little bit about why they exist, how they work and what they are used for. In this second chapter we will be starting to look at the creation of trusts, so that by the end of the chapter you should understand not only who has the power to create a trust but also what, in real terms, the **settlor** actually needs to do in order for that trust to be created.

Capacity requirements

So, first of all, we need to answer the question: 'Who can create a trust?' Essentially, anybody capable of owning property is capable of creating a trust of that property. What we need to know, then, is who is capable of owning property. The answer depends on the kind of property that is going to form the subject matter of the trust. Different rules apply to property ownership depending on whether the property is **personal property** or **real property**.

Personal property

Personal property can be categorised as any property owned by an individual that is not or does not form part of the land: in other words, any property which is not 'real' property (for a further definition of real property, see below). Personal property would therefore include all of an individual's personal possessions, money, stocks and shares, bonds, investments, pensions, insurance policies, and larger assets such as furniture, cars, boats, caravans and so on (but not land or buildings). It would even include a person's pets. Personal property such as this is also often referred to in a legal context as '**chattels**'.

Anyone with the required mental capacity, regardless of age, can own personal property. There is therefore no *theoretical* reason why anyone of any age cannot create a trust of personal property during their lifetime. In theory, even a child could create a trust of the toys contained in their toy-box, although it is difficult to think of a situation in which the child would wish to do so! Of course, in reality the idea of the creation of a trust by a child brings with it a number of difficulties, of which free will and understanding are but two. Despite the theoretical ability to create a trust, therefore, the court has the ability to declare the trust to be **void**, in other words that it is without legal force or binding effect, in cases where a child has created a trust and it is clearly not in their interests to do so. This is also the case in respect of the still more extreme situation in which the child is proved to be too young to understand what they have done. Wherever the court declares the trust void the **subject matter** of the trust will be held on a **resulting trust** for the child themselves, rather than for whoever the child has named as beneficiaries under the trust. (You will remember that in Chapter 1 we said that a resulting trust enabled the **beneficial interest** in the trust property to revert back to the settlor in cases where the beneficial interest had not been properly disposed of. This would be such a case.) In cases where there has been no such intervention on behalf of the child, that child still has the option of 'revoking', or cancelling, the trust on or shortly after reaching the age of **majority** (that is when they have reached legal adulthood, currently the age of 18) should they choose to do so. The upshot of all this is of course that whilst anyone, including a child, has the theoretical ability to create a trust of personal property, it would be most unwise to rely too heavily on the creation of a trust by a **minor** and situations in which such trusts exist are few and far between.

One situation in which someone under the age of 18 might create a trust is in the case of a member of the armed forces making a will. Under section 9 of the Wills Act 1837 children under the age of 18 cannot make a valid will. As a consequence, it therefore follows that a child would be unable to create a trust by this method. However, there is an exception to the rule in the case of members of the armed forces who are carrying out military duties or whilst at sea, for whom an exception is made to the age requirement. It would be possible for a 17-year-old soldier to make a will which incorporated trusts, therefore. The rather poignant document featured in Documenting the law gives us an example of this.

Documenting the law

Last will and testament of a soldier

For generations of service personnel Army Book 64 was a vital piece of kit. A serviceman or woman had to keep the book on their person at all times and failure to produce it was a punishable offence. The book contained the person's service number, personal ID, training records, employment history (including details of all pay advanced to them), medical data, next of kin identification and a blank page at the back for the soldier's last will and testament. The following image shows the will written in the back of the service book of William Illingworth, who fought in the First World War. William enlisted in the army on 14 December 1914, at the age of 17, joining the 3/6th Battalion Cheshire Regiment.

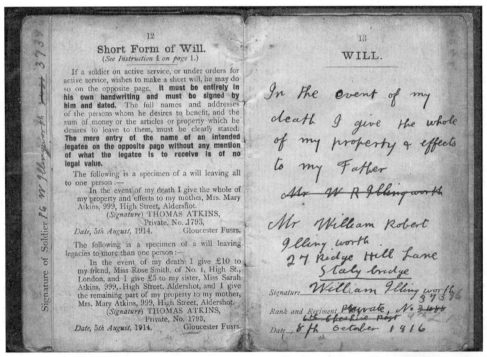

Source: http://www.ypressalient.co.uk/

William was posted to France in 1916, where he was transferred to the 9th Battalion Lancashire Fusiliers and saw military action at the Battle of Broodseinde. Luckily there was no need for the will, however, and William returned home from the war decorated with the Military Medal, victory and war medals. William was discharged from the army in February 1919 and died in 1979, aged 82, in Stalybridge, Cheshire.

Although Army Book 64 has long been replaced, it serves as a reminder of the very real threat of danger under which servicemen and women work.

To read the full story of William Illingworth, go to: **http://www.ypressalient.co.uk/** and click on 'William Illingworth, MM'.

Regarding the ability to become a **trustee** of personal property, section 20 of the Law of Property Act 1925 states that a minor cannot be a trustee and that any attempt to create a child trustee will be invalid. However, it would appear that this restriction does not extend to the trustees of resulting trusts. In the 1935 case of *Re Vinogradoff* [1935] WN 68, a grandmother, Mrs Vinogradoff, transferred an investment valued at £800 into the joint names of herself and her granddaughter, who was 4 years old at the time. When Mrs Vinogradoff died the question arose as to whether the granddaughter was entitled to the investment outright, or whether she was deemed to be holding it on a resulting trust for her grandmother's estate. The court held that the child should hold the investment on a trust for her grandmother's estate, with the effect that the granddaughter became a trustee of the investment, despite her young age. In spite of this decision it is suggested that this was a rare case and that in the vast majority of instances the courts would strive to avoid such an impractical outcome. For the full facts of this case and a discussion of the reasoning behind the judgments, see Chapter 7 on resulting trusts.

Case Summary

Real property

Real property can be defined as any property which includes land and buildings, or anything fixed to the land. So, for the most part in the context of trusts this would mean people's houses or other buildings or land owned by them. Throughout the rest of this book trusts of real property will be referred to as 'trusts of land'. Trusts of real property, or land, are treated somewhat differently from trusts of personal property. According to section 1(6) of the Law of Property Act 1925, it is not possible for anyone under the age of 18 to own land. As we have already seen, therefore, it is not possible for someone under the age of 18 to create a trust of land because one has to have ownership of the land in order to create a trust of it. Neither can a person under the age of 18 be a trustee of land. Thus, only those who have reached the age of majority can either create trusts of land or act as trustees of land.

Mental capacity

The above text discusses the age requirements for the creation of trusts but, as one might expect, there are also **mental capacity** requirements. The law has recently changed in relation to the requirement for mental capacity and is now dealt with under the provisions of the Mental Capacity Act 2005. Section 2(1) of the Act states that a person lacks the required mental capacity to dispose of property and thereby to create a trust if, at the relevant time, 'he is unable to make a decision himself in relation to the matter because of an impairment of, or a disturbance in the functioning of, the mind or brain'. The burden of proving that the settlor does not have the required mental capacity lies with the person wishing to have the settlement declared invalid.

In the case of a person who has been admitted to hospital against their will, or 'sectioned' under the Mental Health Act 1983, a person called a **receiver** will have been appointed to manage that person's affairs. This means that the mentally ill person no longer has any legal control over their property with the result that any attempt to dispose of that property, including any attempt to create a trust of it, will be void. It is worth noting that the appointment of a **trustee in bankruptcy** will have the same legal effect in the case of a person who has been declared bankrupt.

The interview with Fay Copeland, in the People in the law feature, puts claims of mental incapacity into the context of wills as she talks about the increase in will disputes over recent years.

People in the law

Name and position: Fay Copeland, Partner at Wedlake Bell Solicitors, London.

Fay, why do you think disputes of this kind are on the up? We are seeing more and more cases where disputes arise from spouses from first, second or even third marriages. Things get even more complicated when it comes to provisions for the children of each marriage. People can end up very displeased with the size of the slice of the estate they receive and have fewer qualms about taking matters to court if they feel they have been treated unfairly under the will. Long-term cohabitation also creates many will disputes. The family of a deceased may object to will provisions for a cohabiting partner if the couple was never officially married. Likewise, a cohabiting partner might contest a will that does not include provisions for them.

On what grounds are these challenges made? A higher number of people are now challenging wills on the grounds of the mental incapacity of the will-maker, partly as people now live long into their old age when their mental state may start to deteriorate. People left out of wills may think that the deceased was no longer of sound mind at the time of drafting their will or may have been vulnerable to pressure to favour one beneficiary over another and so the will should be set aside.

And are the families of the will-makers really being left less? To a point, yes. Many older people feel disconnected to their children nowadays, as families are increasingly dispersed across the UK and worldwide, and in many cases have no communication at all. We have seen an increase in the number of people who decide to leave their sizeable estates to charitable institutions, as they feel closer to these than to their own children. These can range

Source: Fay Copeland, Wedlake Bell Solicitors (*text and photo*)

from the legendary local cat shelter through to medical research charities.

In other cases, parents who have paid for a good education for their children or helped them buy their first home feel they have done enough for their children and want to see them stand on their own two feet. In these cases it can be harder to successfully challenge a will leaving sizeable charitable legacies, but some children will still try.

Is there anything will-makers can do to protect their will from being challenged? If an individual wants to leave a significant portion of their estate to a charity, or leave someone out of a will, it is a good idea to leave a supporting letter that explains that this is what they intend to do and why. This kind of additional supporting documentation can help if a will is disputed. It can also help a beneficiary who is being left out of a will to understand that it is not a reflection of their parents' feelings for them.

DIY wills are becoming more popular, primarily because they are cheaper, and that means that individuals are more likely to leave behind a poorly drafted and even contradictory will. In the long term, this can turn out to be a false economy. Better to get it right the first time around.

Key stats 315 per cent increase in High Court battles over wills

Research from the Ministry of Justice shows an alarming rise in legal disputes over wills over the last three years:

✦ In London alone the number of High Court cases involving disputes over wills and inheritance rose by 315 per cent, from 83 in 2006 to 262 in 2009.

✦ Will disputes leading to court action rose by 208 per cent, from 73 in 2006 to 152 in 2009.

✦ Inheritance disputes rose by 1,100 per cent, from 10 in 2006 to 110 in 2009.

The actual number of legal disputes over wills is likely to be far higher as only a fraction of cases end up in the courts, with most settled out of court. For a full copy of the report go to: **http://www.justice.gov.uk/publications/docs/judicial-court-statistics-2009.pdf**

Clearly **capacity** issues are a focus in legal arguments over wills. However, perhaps the real issue here is the difficulty caused by modern living and the ensuing problems where second marriages and cohabitation are becoming ever more the norm in society.

Companies

It should be noted that an **incorporated association**, or company, has its own legal personality and is therefore capable of holding both personal property and land, provided the company's constitution gives it the authority to do so. In practice, companies are structured so as to be given very wide powers for the holding of both real and personal property as a matter of course, so there is rarely any difficulty with a company being able to act either as settlor or trustee.

Unincorporated associations

Conversely **unincorporated associations**, which you will remember from Chapter 1 are informally created clubs, groups, societies and partnerships, do not have a separate legal identity and so are unable to own property in their own right. An unincorporated association is therefore unable to create a trust: if it does not own any property it has nothing with which it can form the subject matter of the trust. For the same reason unincorporated associations are also unable to become trustees, although the individual members of the association can, of course, fulfil this role in their personal capacities.

It is worth mentioning here that, on a basic level, this inability of unincorporated associations to own property creates fundamental problems in the practical running of the associations altogether. For example, in the case of a football club, how does the club go about maintaining ownership of the training ground? In most cases the association will be forced to nominate members of the club's committee or other senior or highly regarded and trusted persons within the club to hold property as trustees on the club's behalf. However, this in turn can create its own problems as a club or association cannot technically be a beneficiary in its own right either. If you think about it this makes sense: an unincorporated association is not an entity to which property can be given; it is simply a common name given to a group of people gathered together in the pursuit of a common interest. How can such a fluid group become the beneficiaries under a trust? This particular issue is given further discussion in Chapter 4 on purpose trusts.

Beneficiaries under a trust

There is no capacity requirement in relation to beneficiaries and therefore the prerequisites relating to the ability to own property do not apply to them. This makes absolute sense, given that the reason for the creation and existence of many trusts is to provide for or otherwise protect the interests of minors or those incapable of looking after themselves. If capacity requirement existed for beneficiaries, many beneficiaries would be prevented from benefiting under trusts which have been set up for the very purpose of protecting them.

The only requirement for a beneficiary to benefit under a trust is that they are human. This is what is known as the '**beneficiary principle**', which requires that all trusts must have a human beneficiary on whose behalf the terms of the trust can be enforced. Animals and inanimate objects are thus generally not capable of being the recipients of benefits under the terms of a trust (although it is possible for an animal to benefit from a trust set up for the purpose of maintaining that animal, as will be seen in Chapter 4 of the book). It is also for this reason that, as we have seen above, unincorporated associations cannot become beneficiaries under a trust. Nor can abstract ideals or purposes. Thus, a trust set up to promote world peace in general would not be valid, as the promotion of world peace is an abstract ideal with no personal focus. Neither would a trust for the maintenance of the local village hall be valid, as this is a purely private purpose with no human beneficiary (albeit that the local residents would undoubtedly benefit indirectly from its continued use). The issues and difficulties with trusts set up for private purposes are discussed in detail in Chapter 4.

> all trusts must have a human beneficiary

Formalities required for the creation of trusts

We have considered who is capable of creating a trust; now let us move on to think about the formalities for the creation of trusts. So, first of all, when we consider the 'formalities' of trusts, what do we mean by this? Furthermore, why do we need such **formality**? The formalities of a trust are those requirements which dictate the way in which the trust must be set up or created. For the most part, the formalities required for the setting up of a trust relate to trusts of land. This is probably on account of land's value and the consequent need to formalise its transfer. However, in the case of all formalities relating to the creation of trusts, there is a greater principal issue, and that is the prevention of fraud. If you think about it, without any formal or written evidence of the existence of a trust any person wishing to prove a trust's existence would have to rely solely on their recollection of the trust being declared verbally by the settlor, corroborated by any witnesses there may have been to the event. In the absence of reliable witnesses, the court's belief in the existence of the trust would be reduced to one person's word against another and the more persuasive party would win.

The legal requirement for certain formalities to be adhered to in the creation of trust instruments (that is, the document creating the trust) was originally put into place with the Statute of Frauds in 1677. This early statute required the parties to trusts of certain kinds of property to provide documentary evidence of their existence in order to prove their validity. Today, the requirements for the creation of valid trusts are contained in two separate statutes, depending on the manner of creation of the trust. For trusts created by the settlor during their lifetime, the formalities are set out in section 53 of the Law of Property Act 1925. For trusts created by will the requirements are contained in section 9 of the Wills Act 1837. The requirements or formalities for the creation of trust under both sets of circumstances will be dealt with in this chapter in turn.

Lifetime trusts

Lifetime trusts, or **inter vivos trusts**, are trusts which the settlor creates during their lifetime. Take the example of Harun, who wishes to set up a trust for the benefit of his daughter, Suri. He wishes to ensure that she has a pot of money to set her up in life in whichever way she chooses, whether it is for the deposit on her first home, to set her up in business, or to pay towards her wedding ceremony. However, Harun also wishes to ensure that Suri has the maturity to spend the money wisely when it comes to her, and so he puts the money into trust for her until she reaches the age of 21. How does Harun go about setting up the trust? What does he have to do in order to formalise it? For guidance on this issue we must look to statute, in the form of section 53 of the Law of Property Act 1925.

Section 53(1)(b) of the Act states that:

> A declaration of trust respecting any land or any interest therein must be manifested and proved by some writing signed by some person who is able to declare such trust or by his will.

The first thing to note here, then, is that section 53(1)(b) applies only to trusts of land; it does not apply to trusts of personal property. So, there is a requirement of writing in the case of trusts of land, but a trust of personal property does not require the same formality. Therefore if Harun wishes to create a lifetime trust of personal property, such as cash, for Suri this can be made quite informally: even orally, provided his intention to create the trust is made sufficiently clear. Theoretically Harun need simply say to his daughter:

> This £10,000 is for you, Suri; I will hold it on trust for you until you reach the age of 21.

and the trust would be created. Of course there are obvious evidential difficulties in the making of such a declaration. In the event of a later dispute, a court might well be unwilling to take Suri's word as the beneficiary of the trust to the oral declaration, if she was the only witness to the declaration. Nevertheless, in theory this is all that would be needed to create the trust.

The second thing to note about the wording of section 53(1)(b) is that it requires the trust to be 'manifested and proved by some writing'. This is extremely significant because it means not that the declaration of a trust in land must in itself be in writing but only that the trust be 'manifested or proved' by some writing. Like a trust of personal property, then, there actually is no need for writing in order to *create* a trust of land: the only

Case
Summary

requirement is that there is something in writing to *prove that the trust exists*. An example will make the distinction plainer. In the case of *Childers* v. *Childers* (1857) 1 De G & J 482, a trust had not been created in writing but the beneficiaries were able to provide evidence of the trust's existence by producing a letter from the settlor the contents of which made reference to the trust. This was held by the court as sufficient to prove the existence of the trust. A further example is that of *McBlain* v. *Cross* (1871) 25 LT 804. In this case a telegram which made mention of a trust was also held to be sufficient evidence of its existence. A perhaps still more significant factor in the interpretation of section 53(1)(b) in these cases is the fact that the written evidence of the trust need not have been created at the time the trust was declared. To the contrary, by virtue of its very nature it is quite possible that the written evidence could have been created at a significantly later date.

Case
Summary

A third and final point to note is that the writing evidencing the existence of the trust, in order for it to satisfy section 53(1)(b), must be signed by the 'person who is able to declare such trust'; in other words, it must be signed by the settlor. The signature of any other person on the settlor's behalf will not suffice. The You be the judge feature illustrates this.

You be the judge

Q: On the twins' tenth birthday, their grandmother, Margery, says to them 'I am giving you my plot of land at Greyfriars Lane. It is for you. I will keep it for you until you are eighteen.' A week or so later Margery writes to the twins' mother, making mention of the gift in her letter, which she signs. Margery then dies without having ever made a formal declaration of trust. Are the twins entitled to the land?

A: Yes. The wording of the statute requires only signed evidence in writing of the trust, not that the declaration of trust itself be in writing.

On the facts of the You be the judge feature, therefore, had Margery not signed the letter, it would not have been sufficient to evidence the existence of the trust and the trust would have failed.

This deals with the creation of express trusts during the lifetime of the settlor. Of course, resulting and **constructive trusts**, as we saw in Chapter 1, will not be bound by the same rules as those of expressly created trusts, as these are either created informally through the actions of the parties to the trust or imposed by order of the court. Section 53(2) of the Law of Property Act 1925 specifically excludes the operation of resulting and constructive trusts from the provisions of the section.

Trusts created by will

As we have seen above, a will can only be made by a person who has reached the age of 18, with the exception of members of the armed forces on active duty, who are allowed to make their valid wills under the age of 18 in accordance with section 3 of the Wills (Soldiers and Sailors) Act 1918, as amended. The minimum recruitment age into the armed forces is currently 16 in the UK.

Section 9 of the Wills Act 1837 requires that a will is made in writing and signed by the **testator** in the presence of two witnesses. The witnesses must be **independent persons**, meaning that they must not have any interest at stake in the will. For example, a relative or any person who stands to inherit under the terms of the will would not be a valid independent witness. Provided these requirements are met, any person with the required age and mental capacity (as discussed above) can create a valid will. Equally, any trusts contained within that will, having complied with all the formalities necessary for their creation, will also be valid.

Of course, the fact that a trust has been created in the proper manner, either during the settlor's lifetime or by will, does not in itself mean that the trust will not fail for a number of other reasons, such as ambiguity or uncertainty about who is to benefit from the trust, or about the property the trust is to contain. Such matters will be considered in Chapter 3. Nor does it mean that the terms of the trust can be implemented straightaway. In order to do this, the settlor (or their **executors** in the case of a trust created by will) will need to transfer the legal ownership of the trust property over to the trustees. This is unless, of course, the settlor is declaring themselves as trustee, in which case no transfer of the trust property is necessary. However, one might instead say that following the correct procedures for the creation of the trust will get the settlor over the first hurdle in the creation of a valid trust. The transfer of trust property over into trust will be discussed in more detail below.

Conveying trust property to the trustees

The next aspect we are going to look at in the creation of a trust is an extremely practical one: the **conveyance**, or transfer, of the trust property into the hands of the trustees. If you think about it, it is all well and good for a settlor to declare a trust of his property, but until that property is delivered into the hands of his trustees, the trustees will be unable to get on with managing that property on the beneficiaries' behalf or distributing it, if that is what they are required to do under the terms of the trust. Furthermore, until the trust property is conveyed into the hands of the trustees, the beneficiaries will be unable to enforce the terms of the trust against the trustees. Until the trustees have ownership of the trust property there can be no relationship of trust between the settlor and the beneficiaries upon which they can take action.

So what does the settlor need to do to transfer the trust property to their trustees? In the case of lifetime trusts, let us first of all consider the scenario in which the settlor has declared themselves as trustee of the property. You will remember that this was the case in our example of Harun, whose trust for his daughter Suri we looked at earlier in the chapter. Harun created a trust verbally, by saying:

This £10,000 is for you, Suri; I will hold it on trust for you until you reach the age of 21.

In this situation the settlor, Harun, has declared himself the trustee of the trust. He has not introduced any third parties into the trust to act in the position of trustees: he has merely said 'I will keep the money on trust for my daughter.' There is therefore no need for him to do anything to transfer the trust property, because he already owns the **legal title** (or legal ownership) of the property of which he is the trustee. There is nothing further for him to do to formalise the trust. A diagram of the position would look as shown in Figure 2.1.

This rule also applies if the settlor has declared a trust in which he is going to be a trustee together with other people. So, for example, this would be the case if Harun were to declare a trust in favour of his daughter, Suri, with himself and his wife Geeta to become trustees.

Figure 2.1 Declaration of self as trustee

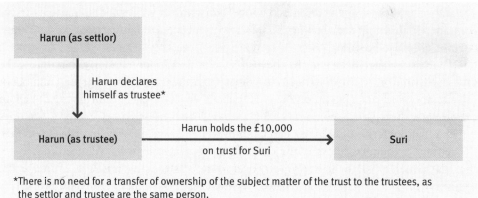

*There is no need for a transfer of ownership of the subject matter of the trust to the trustees, as the settlor and trustee are the same person.

The fact that Geeta may not yet be in receipt of the trust property is deemed to be irrelevant because the trust property is already **vested** in one of the trustees (the settlor), and the settlor is deemed to be bound by his declaration to carry out the terms of the trust and transfer the trust property to all the trustees in due course. This was the decision in the case of *T. Choithram International SA* v. *Pagarani* [2001] 2 All ER 492, which concerned the transfer of property owned by the settlor into a charitable foundation of which he was a trustee.

If the settlor has named others (not including the settlor themselves) to be the trustees under the trust, the settlor will need to do whatever is necessary to transfer the legal title to the trust property to them. The action they need to take will differ depending on the type of property the settlor is putting into trust.

Personal property

If the settlor is creating a trust of personal property, in theory all that is necessary for the settlor to transfer the legal ownership of the property to the trustees is the physical delivery of the property in question. So if the subject matter of the trust was jewellery or furniture, for example, the settlor would simply hand it over to the trustees for their safe keeping. If the trust contained money, the settlor could either give the trustees the cash or write a cheque to be invested or paid into a trust account to be set up by the trustees. We will be dealing with the duties of trustees to invest or otherwise maintain trust property in Chapter 12. In order to provide clarity and prevent any dispute at a later date, it would always be advisable for the settlor to have a **deed of gift** (which is a legal document transferring ownership without the requirement of a purchase or other consideration) drawn up to formalise the transfer of the property to the trustees, but this is not at all necessary.

But is the actual physical delivery of personal property always strictly necessary? It would appear not, according to the case *of Jaffa and Others* v. *Taylor Gallery Ltd*; *Jaffa and Others* v. *Harris* (1990) *The Times* 21 March. In this case it was held that the written declaration of trust was in itself enough to constitute the transfer of the trust property, a painting, to the trustees, without the need for physical delivery of the item itself. What should be noted here, however, is that in such circumstances the intention of the settlor to give the items over into trust must be unequivocal. The facts of *Jaffa*, in which there was a written declaration of trust, can therefore be distinguished from the case of

Re Cole [1964] Ch 175, in which a wife claimed that her husband had created a trust of the contents of the family home by gesturing towards the house and saying to his wife, 'it's all yours'. In this case the court did not consider it sufficiently unequivocal and a valid trust was not found to have been created. A particularly unusual and, one might even say, unique case in which the issue of physical delivery in the case of a gift is considered, is that of *Thomas* v. *Times Book Company* [1966] 1 WLR 911, which is discussed in the Law in action feature.

Case Summary

Law in action The case of the missing manuscript

In the case of *Thomas* v. *Time Book Company*, writer Dylan Thomas's statement to a friend that he could have the original manuscript of his most famous work, *Under Milk Wood*, if he could find it in one of a number of pubs where Thomas said he might have left it, was held by the court as sufficient to give the friend ownership of the manuscript.

On Monday 19 October 1953, legendary playwright Dylan Thomas famously told BBC producer Donald Cleverdon that he could keep the original manuscript of the play *Under Milk Wood* if he could find it. Thomas had given the manuscript to Cleverdon a few days earlier for copies to be made, as Thomas was due to fly to America three days later to promote the play. Cleverdon had returned the manuscript to Thomas a day later but Thomas had managed to lose it in the interim. Reportedly, this was not the first time Thomas had lost a manuscript.

Cleverdon took three copies to the airport to give to Thomas before his departure to the States. Thomas thanked Cleverdon, saying that he had 'saved his life', confiding in Cleverdon that he believed the play, on which he had been working tirelessly for the past seven years, was by far and away the most interesting work he had done. He then reputedly told Cleverdon that if the producer could find the manuscript, he could keep it. Thomas suggested a number of likely locations where the manuscript might be found, including a dozen public houses in the Soho area of London, or he said that he might have left it in the back of a taxi. The manuscript, which contained the play, handwritten by Thomas, together with his notes and musings on the work, was potentially quite valuable.

Later that day, Cleverdon told his secretary that Dylan Thomas had given him the manuscript of *Under Milk Wood* if he could find it, and that he was going

Source: Photodisc/Steve Cole

to try to locate the missing document. A few days later Cleverdon did in fact manage to find the manuscript in one of the public houses in Soho. Cleverdon kept the manuscript until 1961, when he sold it for £1,620 to an antiquarian book dealer, Mr Cox, who in turn sold it to the defendant, Times Books, for £2,000.

Learning that the manuscript was still in existence, Dylan Thomas's widow, acting as his **administratrix** (Dylan died intestate), sued Times Books for possession of the manuscript as part of Thomas's estate, claiming that there had been no gift of the manuscript to Cleverdon and that Thomas had meant only that Cleverdon could keep the manuscript in safe keeping until such time as it could be returned to the writer. The court, however, found in favour of Times Books, stating that the act of obtaining possession, with the donor's consent, of a chattel which a donor intends to give to a donee, is sufficient delivery to complete a gift.

A full transcript of the case can be found at *Thomas* v. *Times Book Company* [1966] 1 WLR 911.

In some cases physical transfer may be less easy to achieve due to the nature of the property. This would be the case for the transfer of **intangible property** that has no physical form, such as stocks and shares. Typically in such cases, the transfer of the property will require an additional layer of formality. For example, if the trust property consists of shares, under the terms of the Stock Transfer Act 1963 the settlor will have to complete a **stock transfer form** and the change of ownership of the shares noted on the company's share register before the trustees can go ahead with managing those shares on behalf of the beneficiaries. Special rules also apply to the transfer of copyright under the Copyright, Designs and Patents Act 1988.

Some other forms of personal property will also require additional formalities to be undertaken in order to complete their transfer. One such example is motor vehicles. Take a look at the Out and about feature to find out what would be required.

Out and about Putting a motor vehicle into trust

Your great uncle has told you that he is going to give you his prized Harley-Davidson motorbike, but not until you have passed your bike test. Until then, he is going to give it to your father to keep on trust for you. He wants to do things properly, but isn't sure what he needs to do (if anything) to put the bike into trust for you.

It is time for you to do a little bit of research! You must find out what steps he needs to take to transfer the trust property into the hands of your father. Using any resources available to you, make a note of exactly what needs to be done to complete the transfer. Good luck with your research.

This task should take you no more than 35 minutes.

 Handy tip: The DVLA would perhaps be a good place to start. Don't forget to make a note of *all* the necessary steps.

Reflective practice

How did you find the above task? Did you find it pretty straightforward? Have you made sure that you collected all the necessary information? For example, what form(s) might you have required and where could you get them from? Do you have all the relevant website and/or email addresses, postal addresses and telephone numbers?

At what point do you think that a court of law would consider the transfer complete?

Equitable interests: section 53(1)(c)

Special rules also apply to the transfer of existing **equitable interests** under section 53(1(c) of the Law of Property Act 1925. The wording of the section is as follows:

(c) a disposition of an equitable interest or trust subsisting at the time of the disposition, must be in writing signed by the person disposing of the same, or by his agent thereunto lawfully authorised in writing or by will.

So exactly what dispositions will this section include? In a trust scenario, the 'disposition of an equitable interest' would include the situation in which a beneficiary wishes to dispose of their beneficial interest under the terms of a trust. But why would a beneficiary wish to do this? There are many reasons why a beneficiary might wish to dispose of their beneficial interest: one might be that they wish that interest to be used for the benefit of a child, instead of for them. Take the example of a father, David. He is entitled to the rental income received from a half-share in a large commercial office building, known as Langman's Wharf. The income in the building is quite substantial, but David has made his own way in life and has plenty of his own disposable income. He therefore decides to transfer the benefit of his interest to his son, Reuben, who has just started his own business and would benefit from an additional injection of income at this time. It is this type of transfer, or gift, of David's beneficial interest which would qualify as a disposition under the wording of section 53(1)(c). As we can see from the wording of the section, David could leave the interest to his son by will and satisfy the terms of the section in that way; but if he wants to make the transfer more immediate, he will be required to do so in writing, which he must sign, as the person disposing of the interest. Only then will David have fully complied with the requirements of the section and successfully disposed of his beneficial interest under the trust.

This all sounds fairly straightforward, but the wording and use of section 53(1)(c) has been the subject of a significant amount of judicial and academic wrangling over the years. Let us take a look at the reasons why.

First of all, the section creates some interesting anomalies. As we have already seen, except in the case of land and a few other exceptions, a beneficial interest can be created quite informally, even orally. But the strict wording of section 53(1)(c) means that to transfer that same beneficial interest would require writing and a signature. Even in the case of land, you will remember that section 53(1)(b) only requires that the **declaration of trust** (creating the beneficial interest) be *proved* by some writing, not that writing is actually needed to create the trust. The requirement for writing therefore seems disproportionate to the interest involved, given the lesser requirements of its creation.

So why take such a heavy-handed approach in respect of the transfer of beneficial interests, specifically? One reason is to prevent fraud. Owing to the intangible nature of beneficial interests, it is seen as a more sensible approach to keep their transfer visible, by way of documentation, to prevent those interests being disposed of without the knowledge of the beneficiaries, or even of the other trustees. It is also considered a good idea to keep a paper trail showing with whom the ownership of a beneficial interest lies at any one time, in order to make the job of the trustees in administering the terms of the trust more manageable.

Another reason why section 53(1)(c) has found itself in the judicial spotlight on a number of occasions is because of the number of cases that have come to court through people trying to get around the requirement in the section for writing in order to avoid payment of **ad valorem stamp duty**. *Ad valorem* stamp duty was a kind of tax which preceded the current Stamp Duty Land Tax regime, and which made tax payable on deeds of transfer. This meant that, with every transfer of a beneficial interest under section 53(1)(c), the recipient of the interest would have to pay stamp duty at the current rate (which would be a percentage of the value of the beneficial interest). In order to avoid such payments, owners of beneficial interests wishing to dispose of their share often came up with quite complex schemes for their transfer.

One of the ways in which owners of beneficial interests initially tried to get around this rule was by declaring not that they had transferred their beneficial interest but that they

Figure 2.2 Comparison between transfer of the beneficial interest and creation of a sub-trust

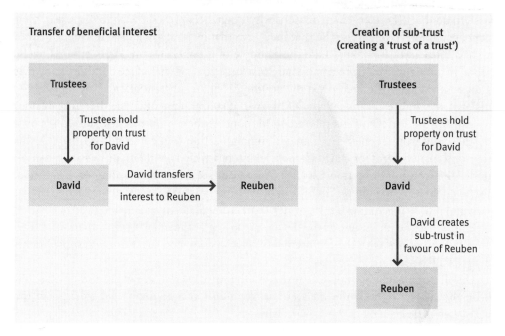

had created a new beneficial interest, thereby creating a **sub-trust**, in favour of the recipient. So how would this work? To go back to our example of David and Reuben: let us imagine that David, rather than wanting to transfer his equitable interest to Reuben altogether, wanted to create a sub-trust out of his equitable interest. Visually, the two different scenarios might look as shown in Figure 2.2.

As can be seen from Figure 2.2, whereas in the first situation David is making an outright transfer of his beneficial interest to Reuben, in the second situation David is retaining his beneficial interest, and merely creating a new interest out of his own. There are logical reasons for doing this. For example, creating a sub-trust would enable David to retain control over the interest and prevent Reuben from frittering the money away. However, when the reason for creating such a sub-trust was in order to prevent the payment of money to the Inland Revenue, the courts were faced with having to make a decision on the grounds of **public policy**.

Case
Navigator

Case
Summary

The House of Lords case of ***Grey*** **v.** ***IRC*** [1960] AC 1 concerned an example of one such scheme. Mr Hunter established six trust funds, one in favour of each of his grandchildren. He then transferred 18,000 shares to the trustees of the trust funds, which he directed the trustees should hold for Mr Hunter's own benefit. In doing this, Mr Hunter had created a new trust of the 18,000 shares in his own favour. This newly created trust did not attract payment of stamp duty under section 53(1)(c), which only applies to dispositions of *existing* equitable interests. Mr Hunter then later instructed the trustees that his beneficial interest in the 18,000, shares which the trustees were holding on trust for him, should now be held in favour of his six grandchildren. In doing this, he was creating a sub-trust of his interest in the shares. The Inland Revenue claimed that stamp duty should be payable on the transaction because it was a disposition of an equitable interest under section 53(1)(c). Mr Hunter's lawyers argued that there had been no disposition of Mr Hunter's equitable interest in the shares at all: he had not disposed of his interest, only created a further trust out of it.

The outcome of the case was that the House of Lords held that the term 'disposition' under the wording of section 53(1)(c) included the creation of a new equitable interest out of an existing one: in other words it included the declaration of a sub-trust. It is arguable that this reasoning is somewhat tenuous, but the policy reasons behind the decision explain the court's judgment clearly enough. In defending the Lords' decision, Lord Radcliffe said:

> Whether we describe what happened in technical or more general terms, the full equitable interest in the eighteen thousand shares concerned, which at that time was his, was . . . diverted by his direction from his ownership into the beneficial ownership of the various equitable owners, present and future, entitled under his six existing settlements.

In other words, in the Lords' view, it does not matter how Mr Hunter described the transaction, the outcome was that he disposed of his interest in the shares in favour of his grandchildren and that he should pay tax on that disposal. Perhaps it could be said that, in the wider context, this is a good example of **equity** 'looking to substance and not form', in accordance with its **equitable maxim**.

Another clever attempt to circumvent the rule in section 53(1)(c), again for the purposes of tax avoidance, was brought to light in the very same year, in the case of *Oughtred* v. *IRC* [1960]AC 206. Once more the case reached the House of Lords. This was a more complicated transaction with which the Lords found greater difficulty, however. The facts of the case were as follows: Mrs Oughtred held shares in a private company for life, with the remainder going to her son, Peter. If Peter inherited under the terms of the trust as it stood, this would mean that Peter would pay a considerable amount of inheritance tax on receipt of the shares. In order to try to avoid this, Mrs Oughtred agreed with Peter that he would give his interest in the shares to his mother, so that he no longer had an interest in the trust, and that she would then transfer to Peter some other shares, which she owned independently of the trust. This agreement was oral, but subsequently documents were drawn up, first declaring that the shares contained within the trust were now for the sole benefit of Mrs Oughtred and, secondly, transferring the new shares to Peter. The transfer of the shares to Peter was a simple gift and therefore was not in issue. However, in respect of the surrender to his mother of Peter's beneficial interest in the trust, the Inland Revenue claimed that this was a disposition of Peter's equitable interest and that therefore stamp duty should be payable on the transfer. Mrs Oughtred claimed that the agreement which had taken place between her and her son amounted to an oral contract and that, from the time of the agreement, this meant that Peter held his beneficial interest in the shares on constructive trust for his mother.

Case Summary

If you are beginning to get a bit lost at this point, remember the explanation contained in Chapter 1 on the equitable maxim of 'equity sees as done that which ought to be done'. The example was given of the effect of **exchange of contracts** in a house purchase. You will remember that from the time the contract is entered into, because 'equity sees as done that which ought to be done' the person buying the house is seen by equity as owning the beneficial, or equitable, interest in the house. The seller simply remains the holder of the property in name only, until such time as the transfer of the legal ownership of the property is completed. So, from the time of the contract the legal owner of the property effectively holds the beneficial interest in that property on a trust for the buyer (that trust being a constructive trust by nature due to its informal creation), retaining the legal interest as a trustee until completion of the transfer. Now applying this reasoning to Mrs Oughtred and her son, what they were saying was that they had entered into a contract to transfer Peter's equitable interest to his mother, and that from the time of the contract this had in turn created a constructive trust of the interest in favour of his mother. On this basis, as Mrs Oughtred was already in receipt of the equitable interest in the shares via the constructive trust when the declaration was made, there was therefore no transfer to be taxed.

section 53 does not apply to resulting or constructive trusts

Why would the mother and son go to all the trouble of saying that a constructive trust had been created? The answer is simple: because under section 53(2) of the Law of Property Act 1925 there is an exception which states that section 53 in its entirety does not apply to resulting or constructive trusts. It was a brilliant, albeit complicated, attempt to get around the requirement that the transfer be in writing, and thus the payment of stamp duty under the terms of section 53(1)(c). The House of Lords found this a difficult argument to counter, and in fact the decision in the case was eventually reached on a 3:2 majority. The two **dissenting** judges agreed that the contract had created a constructive trust in favour of Mrs Oughtred, and thereby removed any need for a formal transfer for stamp duty purposes. Lord Jenkins, however, leading the majority vote, said that this could not be the case:

> This interest under the contract is no doubt a proprietary interest of a sort . . . But its existence has never (so far as I know) been held to prevent a subsequent transfer, in performance of the contract, of the property contracted to be sold from constituting for stamp duty purposes a transfer on sale of the property in question.
>
> In truth, the title secured by a purchaser by means of an actual transfer is different in kind from, and may well be superior to, the special form of proprietary interest which equity confers on a purchase in anticipation of such transfer.

Lord Jenkins's suggestion is therefore that, whilst he concedes to the contract creating an equitable interest in favour of Mrs Oughtred, such an interest can never be sufficient to prevent the need for a formal transfer under section 53(1)(c), to the extent that it renders the payment of stamp duty unnecessary.

Again, the reasoning in *Oughtred* v. *IRC* very much suggests that the decision was reached on grounds of policy, rather than on the strict application of legal principle. In any event, two further decisions in this area have served to muddy the waters still further. The first of the two cases, which were heard on a related set of facts, is that of **Vandervell v. IRC** [1967] 2 AC 291. The case concerned a very wealthy man named Mr Vandervell, who was the owner of an engineering company CAV Ltd and founder of the famous Vanwall Formula One racing team during the 1950s. Mr Vandervell wished to reduce his income tax liability and so his advisers invented a complex tax avoidance scheme for him. The scheme involved Mr Vandervell transferring £150,000 worth of shares in his company, Vandervell Products Ltd, to the Royal College of Surgeons (the 'RCS'), in order to establish and fund a 'chair', which is a type of academic post such as a professorship. The shares, which were held on trust for Mr Vandervell by his bank, were transferred at Mr Vandervell's instruction. In return, the RCS granted Mr Vandervell an **option to purchase** the shares for the nominal sum of £5,000 (an option to purchase is a contract that gives a person the right to buy a property within an agreed time period, upon service of written notice). During the RCS's ownership of the shares, substantial **dividends**, which are payments out of the company's profits, were declared in favour of the sole shareholder (Mr Vandervell) by the company's board of directors. Mr Vandervell then exercised his option and repurchased the shares, in this way hoping to avoid paying

Case Navigator

Case Summary

tax on the dividends. He believed he could do this as the dividends had been declared at a time when the RCS owned them, and the RCS was a charity which was therefore not subject to income tax.

The scheme was a brilliant one but, unfortunately for Mr Vandervell, it was unsuccessful. The Inland Revenue charged Mr Vandervell tax on the dividends on the grounds that Mr Vandervell had not absolutely divested himself of the shares. They said that, whilst his oral instruction had been sufficient to transfer the legal ownership of the shares by the bank, the transfer of his beneficial interest required writing under section 53(1)(c), which he had not provided. In addition, the Inland Revenue argued that the option to repurchase the shares at a future date retained by Mr Vandervell in effect gave him a beneficial interest in those shares. According to the Inland Revenue, this not only meant that he would be liable to pay income tax on the value of that beneficial interest but also that he would have to pay tax on the value of the option.

The court agreed with the Inland Revenue, but only as to part of their claim. In respect of the transfer of ownership of the shares to the RCS, the court found that Mr Vandervell had done everything required of him to divest himself of his ownership, both legal and equitable, and that writing under section 53(1)(c) was not required in this case. This was because the legal and equitable ownership in the property were being transferred together and therefore constituted a consummate whole, not two separate interests, one legal and one equitable. If the court had found that the transfer of the equitable interest required writing, they would have been saying, in effect, that *any* transfer of property required writing, because there was a requirement of writing in respect of the equitable interest in it. This could not be correct. The House of Lords nevertheless held, by a 3:2 majority (Lords Reid and Donovan dissenting) that Mr Vandervell was liable for tax, because of his beneficial interest in the shares under the option to purchase.

The Lords' reasoning for this is not relevant here, although it is discussed later in the book, in Chapter 7. The essential point we need to take from this very complicated case is that, if the whole ownership in property is transferred, there is no need to comply with the requirement for transfer of the beneficial interest in that property under section 53(1)(c). The transfer of the property will be considered in its entirety and not as two separate entities, one legal and one equitable, or beneficial.

In the second Vandervell case, *Re Vandervell's Trusts (No. 2)* [1974] Ch 269, Mr Vandervell again attempted a tax avoidance scheme in relation to the same shares and the same option to purchase. This time, he instructed repurchase of the shares using money from a trust, the beneficiaries of which were Mr Vandervell's children. The scheme was successful. The court held that Mr Vandervell's beneficial interest under the option to purchase ceased to exist as soon as it was exercised. The purchase of the shares by the bank using trust monies instead created a new and separate equitable interest in favour of the children. Mr Vandervell had, in exercising the option, therefore successfully divested himself of the equitable ownership of the shares, without a 'disposition' under the terms of section 53(1)(c) and thus without the need for writing. Consequently, there was no liability to pay tax.

The four cases discussed in this section represent a particularly complex area of the law that has been the subject of much legal argument. There is certainly plenty of scope for students of the law to do a great deal of additional reading in this area and to explore in detail the rationale behind the decisions. However, for the basic purpose of applying the rules as they currently exist in respect of transfers of equitable interests under section 53(1)(c), the quick reference guide outlined in Table 2.1 provides a no-nonsense statement of the law as it stands.

Case
Summary

Table 2.1 Dispositions of equitable interests under section 53(1)(c) of the Law of Property Act 1925

Type of disposition	Writing required?	Authority/interpretation
A transfer or gift of a beneficial interest under a trust	Yes	53(1)(c) Law of Property Act 1925
Creation of a 'sub-trust' (a trust of a trust)	Yes	*Grey* v. *IRC*
Contract to dispose of an equitable interest	Yes	*Oughtred* v. *IRC*
Transfer of whole of legal and equitable interests together	No	*Vandervell* v. *IRC*
Exercise of an option to purchase	No	*Re Vandervell's Trusts (No. 2)*

Land

The formalities required for the transfer of land are perhaps the most stringent of all the different types of property. If the trust property is land, the settlor must transfer that property into the names of the trustees by **deed** (a deed is a legal document, signed by the transferor, in this case the settlor, and witnessed). This is because, under section 52(1) of the Law of Property Act 1925, it is not possible to transfer the legal ownership of land without the completion of a deed of transfer. In addition to completing the transfer, the trustees will also then have to **register** the change of ownership of that property at the Land Registry to finalise the transfer into their names. An example of what a typical transfer of land looks like can be found at: **http://www1.landregistry.gov.uk/forms2009/pdf/TR1.pdf**.

Trusts under wills

The position with wills is different from that of trusts created during the settlor's lifetime. In the case of a will, any trusts that arise under that will are considered to be completely constituted by the death of the testator, all the property of the testator immediately **vesting** in the executors. 'Vesting' means that the executors have an immediate irrevocable right to that property, albeit that they may not yet be in physical possession of it. There is therefore no need for the beneficiaries to wait for formal transfer of trust property over into the names of the trustees to be completed, before they can enforce the terms of the trust, as it is already the property of the trustees by right. It should be noted that it is common for the executors of the deceased person's estate also to act as the trustees of any trusts which arise under the terms of the will. Trustees and executors are therefore often one and the same, in this context.

Once the settlor has carried out any additional formalities required for the transfer of the legal ownership of the trust property into the hands of the trustees, the trust will be **completely constituted**, or finalised, and the trust can be enforced. But what happens if the settlor does not complete these steps, so that the creation of the trust is not complete?

Incompletely constituted trusts

A trust can be **incompletely constituted** either because the settlor fails to follow the correct procedures to transfer the trust property into the hands of the trustees or, in extreme circumstances, because the settlor simply changes his mind and refuses to transfer the property over to the trust. In either case, what the trustees and, more particularly, the beneficiaries need to know is whether the trust can still be administered and, if necessary, enforced against the settlor.

Procedural failure by settlor

Let us first deal with failed attempts by the settlor to transfer property to the trustees. Both shares and land are particularly vulnerable here because of the two-part nature of their transfer to a third party, first by completing the relevant deed of transfer and secondly by their subsequent registration. Take the example of a trust of shares. If a settlor were to attempt to transfer shares to his trustees by completing a stock transfer form (which is currently the correct method of transferring shares) and then handing it over to his trustees to complete the registration of the transfer, but the trustees never dealt with the registration of the change of ownership by the company, would that trust be fully constituted and therefore enforceable by the beneficiaries? According to the case of *Milroy* v. *Lord* (1862) 4 De GF & J 264, the answer is no: the transfer has not been properly completed and therefore the trust is not completely constituted and cannot be enforced. The facts of the case were that the settlor, Thomas Medley, executed a deed by which he meant to transfer 50 shares in the Bank of Louisiana to Samuel Lord, to be held on trust for Milroy. Mr Medley later gave the share certificates to Mr Lord, but the transfer of the shares was never registered with the bank, which was necessary to complete the legal change in ownership of the shares. The court held that the shares had never been properly transferred to the trustee and therefore there could be no trust in favour of Milroy. Lord Justice Turner made it quite clear in giving his judgment that, in order for a trust to be deemed completely constituted, the settlor must have done 'everything necessary' to transfer the property to the trustees and thereby render the trust binding.

Case Summary

Case Navigator

In contrast to the rather harsh result in *Milroy* v. *Lord*, later cases have tended to take a slightly softer approach, and it would now appear to be accepted practice that the trust will be considered to have been completely constituted provided the settlor has done everything *in his power* (as opposed to 'everything necessary', as required by *Milroy* v. *Lord*) to transfer the property to the trustees. If the delay or non-completion of the transfer is due to circumstances beyond the settlor's control, therefore, the trust is likely to be deemed completely constituted in any event. This was the decision in the 1952 case of **Re Rose** 1 All ER 1217, which also concerned the attempted transfer of shares. It was held in this case that, for the purposes of fully constituting the trust, the transfer of the trust property had taken effect on completion of the share transfer document. The registration of change of ownership of the shares in the company's books was therefore considered by the court to be no more than a formality.

The same reasoning has more recently been applied to attempted transfers of land by the settlor, as in the case of *Mascall* v. *Mascall* (1984) 50 P & CR 119. Here a father had given the completed transfer deed to his son for submission to the Land Registry, but registration had never taken place. However, it was found by the court that a trust requiring the transfer of **registered land** which had not been completed by registration at the Land Registry was nevertheless fully constituted and therefore enforceable: the father had done all in his power to complete, or '**perfect**' the gift.

One final case which should be mentioned here is the recent decision in *Pennington* v. *Waine* [2002] 1 WLR 2075. The case again concerned the purported transfer of shares, this time shares in the family business, from a woman named Ada Crampton to her nephew, Harold. Ada signed a stock transfer form in order to make the transfer of the shares to Harold, but then passed the form on to her agent, Pennington, who worked for the company's firm of auditors. She should have passed the form to the company secretary to register the transfer and so she had given the form to the wrong person. Pennington did nothing with the form, other than place it on file, so the transfer was never completed. On Ada's death, Harold claimed ownership of the shares. The Court of Appeal upheld Harold's claim, stating that the gift was completely constituted on the basis not of the fact that Ada had done everything in her power to complete the transfer but because it would have been **unconscionable** for Ada to have recalled the gift. This outcome conflicts with *Re Rose* because Ada had not done everything in her power to perfect the gift. She had merely given the stock transfer form to her agent and was therefore free at any point to request return of the form or otherwise instruct him not to register the transfer. As it is, the decision of the court to uphold the gift on the basis of unconscionability alone has left the law on this point uncertain. For a detailed critique of the decision in *Pennington* v. *Waine*, see Morris 2003.

Change of mind by settlor

Moving on, then, to the rather more serious situation where the settlor has declared their intention to create the trust, but subsequently changes their mind and refuses to transfer the trust property over to the trustees. Is there anything the beneficiaries can do to force the settlor to complete the transfer?

If the settlor has simply told the beneficiaries that they are going to create a trust of certain property, then no, there is nothing the beneficiaries can do about it. There is clearly no legal foundation upon which to enforce the promise and if the courts were to intervene to enforce what amounts to nothing more than a moral obligation this would clearly be overstepping the mark from a legal standpoint. The court of equity can be of no greater help in these circumstances either, as the beneficiaries have no beneficial claim to the property, it having not been transferred to the trustees yet. But what if the settlor has gone further than making a blind promise to enter into a trust arrangement? What if they have signed a deed promising to create that trust?

Covenants to settle

A formal promise, or covenant, to create a trust, which has been made by deed, is known as a '**covenant to settle**'. Covenants to settle are usually entered into because the settlor intends to bring the trust into being at some point in the future, usually on the happening of a future event. An example of this would be a divorce settlement, such as in the case of *Cannon* v. *Hartley* [1949] 1 Ch 213. Here, Mr Hartley had entered into a deed of separation with his wife, which detailed how the couple's finances would be divided on the couple's pending divorce. The deed contained a covenant to settle, which promised that Mr Hartley would give half of any inheritance he received on the death of either of his parents to his wife and daughter. Another example of a covenant to settle would be in the case of a **marriage settlement**, which you came across in Chapter 1. So, for example, under the terms of the marriage settlement a wife might covenant to settle property (in other words to put it into trust) for the benefit of herself, her husband and their children, on the event of the couple's marriage.

Case Summary

So how does a covenant to settle give a beneficiary the ability to enforce a trust? Finding an answer to this question is fraught with difficulty. One particular problem with the enforcement of trusts by beneficiaries under a covenant to settle is that the legal basis of covenants to settle lies not in equity but in the law of contract. As a type of contract, a covenant to settle is uniquely placed in that it is enforceable by law even if there has been no **consideration**, or payment, given in exchange for the promise. However, seeking a contractual remedy in the context of a trust scenario clearly has its limitations. This is not least because, when looking for a contractual remedy, it is only the parties to the contract who are actually able to sue under it. If the beneficiaries were not party to the covenant to settle, therefore, they would clearly be in no position to make a claim for a breach of its terms. Of course, if the trustees were party to the covenant they could make a claim against the settlor on behalf of the beneficiaries. However, their claim would have to be quantified

> seeking a contractual remedy in a trust scenario has its limitations

on the basis of the trustees' own loss. This would be difficult to quantify, given that the trustees are merely the holders of the **bare legal title**, or ownership, of the trust property and derive no benefit from it. It would be arguable, therefore, that there was no real loss to the trustees and that they are not in need of compensation.

Another difficulty in applying contract law to a trust scenario is that the remedy for breaching the law of contract is limited to **damages**. Even if the beneficiary is able to make a claim for a breach of the covenant to settle, financial compensation may not be what they want. This would be particularly the case if the trust property the settlor has promised to transfer into trust was the family home or a family heirloom, such as a piece of jewellery, which carries some sentimental value.

So what use to the beneficiaries is a covenant to settle in enforcing a trust? Clearly, the law of contract will be of little help to beneficiaries in this scenario. But is it possible to find a solution in equity? The answer is yes, but in a very limited fashion. Somewhat ironically, whilst a covenant to settle is enforceable in contract law despite there being no consideration for the covenant, the court of equity will not assist the parties in this situation, on the basis of the equitable maxim that 'equity will not assist a **volunteer**'. Quite simply, the court of equity will not help the beneficiaries in this scenario as no consideration has been given by them in exchange for the settlor's promise. The only situation in which equity will provide assistance to a beneficiary seeking to enforce the transfer of property over into trust, therefore, is where the beneficiary has provided consideration to the settlor in exchange for the trust property. It may seem an unlikely scenario where a beneficiary pays for the trust from which they are to benefit, but such situations are not altogether uncommon. Take, for example, the creation of a lifetime interest in property. It is not completely out of the question to envisage a relative or dependant of a family paying a sum of money to convert part of the family home into an annexe, in exchange for a lifetime interest allowing them to live in the house or the relevant part of it.

It should be noted that whilst under contract law marriage is not a valid form of consideration, the court of equity *will* accept marriage as sufficient consideration to warrant the enforcement of a trust. Thus, a husband who is to benefit under the terms of a marriage settlement upon his marriage to the wife will be able, by virtue of the marriage itself, to enforce the terms of the settlement in equity, if the settlor does not subsequently transfer the subject matter of the settlement into trust. Perhaps rather more interestingly, under a marriage settlement the children of the marriage are also held to be 'within the consideration' of the marriage settlement, and are therefore also able to make a claim in equity to enforce the terms of a marriage settlement. This was the case in *Pullan* v. *Koe* [1913] 1 Ch 9, which concerned the marriage settlement of a husband and wife. The terms of the settlement specified that the wife would add any property acquired by her throughout her lifetime to the marriage settlement for benefit of the husband, wife and any children of the marriage. On later receiving a gift of £285 from her mother, the wife placed the money in her husband's bank account, to which she had access. However, the husband later died and the children argued that the money should have been placed in the marriage settlement for their benefit, and not in the bank account. The court agreed and ordered that the money should be added to the marriage settlement. Such an outcome was only achievable because the children were held to be within the consideration of the marriage and were therefore entitled in the eyes of equity to make a claim for non-performance under the settlement. It should be noted that children of previous marriages and illegitimate children are not held to be within the consideration of the marriage; neither are the next of kin of the husband and wife.

Of course, marriage settlements are now less common than they were almost a century ago when this case came to the attention of the Court of Chancery. Nevertheless, the outcome in the case of *Pullan* v. *Koe* is important to note. This is not only because it illustrates the acceptance by equity of **marriage consideration** as valid consideration in a covenant to settle, but also because it sets the precedent for the type of remedy that equity is willing to give would-be beneficiaries where the settlor does not abide by their promise to transfer property into trust: that of **specific performance** (you will remember from Chapter 1 that specific performance is an equitable remedy which forces a person to carry out the terms of their promise to do something in accordance with the agreement they have entered into). This ability of equity to grant the remedy of specific performance disposes of all the difficulties encountered by parties seeking the legal remedy of damages described above. Under the doctrine of specific performance the settlor can be required to transfer into trust the actual property which was the subject of the promise, thereby putting the beneficiaries in the position they should have been in if the trust was properly constituted in the first place. Despite the court of equity's unwillingness to assist volunteers, then, by granting the remedy of specific performance to beneficiaries who have provided consideration for the settlor's covenant to settle, equity can be seen as instead adhering to another of its maxims or principles: 'equity regards as done that which ought to be done'.

Case Summary

Writing and drafting

You are a trainee at the firm of Ward Peake solicitors. You are currently working in the private client department. There is a departmental meeting tomorrow at 9.00 am and the head of department has asked you to give a short PowerPoint presentation to the rest of the department on covenants to settle. The meeting is running to a tight schedule so your presentation should be no longer than 5 minutes in length.

It is now 4.00 pm and you have to leave the office on time as you have an appointment at 5.00 pm, so you have only an hour to prepare.

Handy tip: Most employers will expect you to be able to put together presentations quickly and efficiently. Remember to keep your PowerPoint slides to a minimum: they should form only the skeleton of your speech. Use bullet points where you can (but not too many) and remain focused!

So to recap, a simple promise to create a trust is unenforceable; but a promise made by deed in the form of a covenant to settle can be enforced in equity, provided there has been consideration given for that promise by the trustees. If no consideration has been given, the trustees can sue the settlor for damages as parties to the deed, but quantifying their actual loss may be difficult. The beneficiaries will be unable to sue under the deed unless they were parties to it. As you can see, the remedies available to would-be beneficiaries if a settlor chooses not to carry out his promise to create a trust are extremely limited. However, it is arguable, looking at it from the settlor's point of view that, as what they are doing in essence is making a gift of their own property, it is a simple matter of human rights that they should have complete and unfettered freedom to do as they wish, even if that includes retracting any promise they may have made to complete the gift.

Are there then any exceptions to the strict rules applied by the courts in this situation? There are three scenarios in which the beneficiaries will be able to force the settlor or his representatives to transfer the trust property to the trustees:

✦ the rule in *Strong* v. *Bird*;

✦ gifts made in contemplation of death, or '*donatio mortis causa*'; and

✦ the equitable remedy of proprietary estoppel.

Let us look at each of these in turn.

The rule in *Strong* v. *Bird*

The rule in **Strong** v. **Bird** applies on its facts to the release of a debt, and the cases which follow it concern gifts of property; however, it has been argued that the rule could apply equally to the creation of a trust. This issue will be considered in more detail after the working of the rule has been explained. The facts of the case of *Strong* v. *Bird* (1874) LR 18 Eq 315 took place in the late 1860s. Mr Bird had borrowed £1,100 from his stepmother; quite a substantial sum of money in those days. At the time of the loan, Mr Bird's stepmother lived as a lodger in Mr Bird's house, paying him the sum of £212.50 per quarter (that is, four times a year) in rent. The agreement was that Mr Bird would repay the loan by way of deduction from the rent in the sum of £100 per quarter. However, after the payment of the first two instalments on the loan, the stepmother insisted on

Case Summary

paying the full rent and she continued to do this until her subsequent death some four years later. The stepmother's next of kin then claimed that Mr Bird owed the estate £900, which was the amount outstanding on the loan. The court held that, by the stepmother's actions, Mr Bird had been released from his debt and that Mr Bird's appointment as executor to his stepmother's estate served to complete her intended gift to him of the release of the debt. This was, of course, a fiction invented by the court to take advantage of the fact that all the property of a testator or **testatrix** vests immediately in the executors on their death. By virtue of Mr Bird's position as his stepmother's executor, he was given a special advantage which he would not otherwise have had. Put simply, had Mr Bird not been the executor of his stepmother's will, the gift would not have been formally completed by the transfer of her property to him, and the debt would not have been released.

So why did the court go to so much trouble to create this complicated fiction and thereby protect Mr Bird from the claims of his stepmother's next of kin? It is suggested that the reasons are actually practical, rather than moral. As the sole executor to his stepmother's estate, it would have been extremely difficult from a practical viewpoint for Mr Bird, as executor, to sue himself as a debtor to the estate. There may also have been an element of wishing to preserve the equity of the situation, given that the intentions of the stepmother were clearly to erase Mr Bird's debt to her. The difficulty still remains, however, that executors are not supposed to benefit from their position and, clearly, such a scenario enables them to do so.

> ## it would have been extremely difficult for Mr Bird to sue himself

Despite the difficulties posed by the judgment, the rule in *Strong* v. *Bird* continued to be applied on its facts, initially to the release of debts but subsequently also to claims relating to alleged gifts of property. In the case of *Re Stewart* [1908] 2 Ch 251, a testator bought three bearer bonds several days prior to his death. (Bonds are a type of investment under which the person who purchases the bond gives money to the bond issuer in return for a certificate. The certificate guarantees the purchaser payments of interest, together with the return of their capital investment at a stated future date. Bearer bonds are different from other bonds because they have no registered owner. The issuer is required to make payment under the terms of the bond to whoever presents the physical bond to them. In this way, bearer bonds can be traded like cash.) Following his purchase of the bonds, Dr Stewart gave his wife a letter from his brokers together with a receipt for the bonds, saying 'I have bought these bonds for you.' At the date of Dr Stewart's death, the bonds had not yet been delivered to the wife by the brokers and, despite the contents of her husband's letter, she therefore had no legal right to them. However, she claimed ownership of the bonds as **executrix** to her husband's estate. Mr Justice Neville held that the wife was entitled to the bonds under the rule in *Strong* v. *Bird*, all the necessary steps to complete the gift of the bonds to her by her husband having been made automatically on her becoming executor to his estate. Thus, it could be said that the gift of the bonds was 'perfected' on Dr Stewart's death.

Whether the act in question is a gift, the release of a debt or transfer of property into trust, for the rule in *Strong* v. *Bird* to work it is very important that the intention of the person making the transfer, gift or release is not negated in any way between the initial act of giving and the donor's death. In *Strong* v. *Bird* the court was happy to conclude that Mrs Bird's intention was to release the debt because she was consistent in her decision not to deduct any payment from the rent until the date of her death. Equally, in *Re Stewart*, the court was happy to accept the letter as evidence of the husband's intention to make a gift. However, there are cases which have failed on the basis that the intention of the party making the transfer was disrupted in some way. Take, for example, the Court of Appeal

Case Summary

Case
Summary

...aim to enforce a gift under the rule in *Strong*
...land had promised to give to the executrix of
...Freeland to a third person who was still in
...ourt held that, by loaning the car to someone
...ll being her own property to do with as she
...ved it as a gift to her executrix.

Case
Summary

...ell at the same hurdle. Here, a daughter had
...after her parents on the understanding that
...tents. When her parents died, the daughter
...le in *Strong* v. *Bird*. However, whilst she was
...held that she was not entitled to the house
...various parts of the garden of the house as
...hat the mother had negated her intention to
...wever, it should be noted that there was an
...own to the daughter, the mother had written
...he had placed in an envelope and put away.
...h she believed she was unable to leave to the
...'s illegitimacy. It was likely to have been the
writing of the cheque that swayed the court to believe that the mother's intention to make a
gift of the house had been negated, rather than the selling off of plots of land; particularly
in light of the fact that the daughter had refused to accept the proceeds of sale of the plots
from her mother, believing she would receive the main house at a future date.

The above sets out in brief the rule in *Strong* v. *Bird* but there are a couple of points
which should be noted about it. First, the rule in *Strong* v. *Bird* is commonly included in
textbooks as an exception to the equitable maxim that 'equity will not assist a volunteer',
in the context of incompletely constituted trusts, hence its inclusion here in this chapter.
However, whilst we have seen that the rule in *Strong* v. *Bird*, which originally applied only
to the release of a debt by a person who subsequently died, was later applied to incomplete
gifts, the exception has never been tested in the context of a transfer of property from a
settlor to their trustees (although arguably the court in *Re Gonin* would have been willing
to give the house to the daughter had it not been for the writing of the cheque). It therefore
remains to be seen whether or not *Strong* v. *Bird* would actually apply to the scenario of
an incompletely constituted trust and whether the rule in *Strong* v. *Bird* truly provides an
exception to the equitable maxim that 'equity will not perfect an imperfect gift'.

In addition, it could be said that both the initial reasoning behind
the judgment in *Strong* v. *Bird* and the subsequent extension of the
rule to gifts as well as debts are seriously flawed in any event. As we
have seen, in the original case of *Strong* v. *Bird* there were good practical reasons for supporting the release of the debt, not least because of
the difficulty Mr Bird would have faced as executor to the estate in
suing himself for payment of that debt. However, there is surely a
moral contradiction here: the role of an executor is to administer the
estate in the interests of the deceased and not for their own financial

> there were good
> practical reasons for
> supporting the
> release of the debt

gain. It is highly unlikely that the stepmother's intention, in appointing Mr Bird in the role
of executor, was that Mr Bird should use his position for his own benefit in seeking the
completion of an otherwise imperfect gift, regardless of her intention to cancel the debt
as evidenced by her refusal to pay a reduced rent in payment of the loan. This clear abuse
of position being condoned by the courts is something that will continue to be difficult to
reconcile.

Donatio mortis causa

Donatio mortis causa is the latin term for a gift ('*donatio*') conditional ('*causa*') on death ('*mortis*') and, as one might guess from its name, has its foundations in Roman law. Gifts conditional on death are gifts which are made by a person in contemplation of their death but which are not intended to take effect until that person has actually passed away. Take, by way of example, our young soldier Alec from the previous chapter who was going off to war in Afghanistan. He may have said to his best friend before he left: 'Here, you have my iPhone. If I die out there, I want you to keep it.' If Alec survived his tour of duty he would expect his friend to give the iPhone back to him on his return; however, if Alec died, the friend could keep the iPhone on the basis of *donatio mortis causa.*

Case Summary

The rules applicable to the making of gifts in *donatio mortis causa* were first set out in the case of *Cain* v. *Moon* [1896] 2 QB 283. The case concerned a claim by a Mr Cain, acting as the administrator of his deceased wife. Mr Cain wished to recover a deposit note for £50, which was in the possession of his mother-in-law, Mrs Moon, which Mrs Moon said was a gift to her from her daughter. The £50 in question had been deposited at the bank by the daughter, Mrs Cain, in 1890, in return for which she was given a deposit note. Mrs Cain placed the deposit note in a small cashbox, which was kept locked, and to which she retained the key. In the early part of 1893 Mrs Cain became very ill. After her recovery her mother, Mrs Moon, paid her a visit. Mrs Cain handed the deposit note to her mother, saying that she was never to part with it, and that it was a gift for the kindness her mother had shown her during her recent illness. From that day the deposit note had remained in the possession of Mrs Moon with the full knowledge of her daughter, who frequently spoke about it and asked if it was safe. In September 1895 Mrs Moon paid a visit to her daughter, who was by then seriously ill. Mrs Cain said that she believed she was going to die and, referring to the deposit note, said, 'Everything I possess and the bank-note is for you if I die.' Mrs Cain died on 5 October 1895 and, Mrs Moon having refused to give up the deposit note to the husband, Mr Cain, an action was brought. However, the judge found in favour of Mrs Moon on the grounds that there had been an effectual *donatio mortis causa*. In making his judgment in the case, Lord Chief Justice Russell of Killowen set out three requirements for a *donatio mortis causa* to be valid. These are that:

1. the gift or donation must have been in contemplation, though not necessarily in expectation, of death;

2. there must have been delivery to the recipient of the subject matter of the gift; and

3. the gift must be made under such circumstances as to show that the thing is to revert to the donor in the event that they recover.

One interesting point to note about *donatio mortis causa* is that, although the gift must be made in contemplation of the death of the **donor** (that is, the giver), if the donor subsequently dies for a reason other than that which they had contemplated, in other words, if they die in a totally unexpected way, this will not invalidate the gift. These were the facts of the case in *Wilkes* v. *Allington* [1931] 2 Ch 104, where a man made a conditional gift of property thinking he was dying of cancer but in actual fact died from pneumonia contracted whilst riding on an open-topped bus in the rain.

Case Summary

All kinds of personal property can be transferred by way of *donatio mortis causa*. If the property in question requires any further formality to be carried out to complete its transfer to the recipient of the gift, such as in the case of shares or land, then the executors or administrators of the deceased's estate can be required to do this. It was previously questionable whether land could be transferred in this way but the decision in *Sen* v. *Headley* [1991] Ch 425 confirmed that it could. In this case the donor, who was dying, gave to Mrs Sen, with whom he had lived for several years, the keys to a strong box in which the title deeds to his house were kept, stating that she was to have the house when he died. At first instance, the decision was that Mrs Sen could not have the house on the basis of *donatio mortis causa* because the donor had not, and could not, deliver the physical object of the house to Mrs Sen. However, on appeal the Court of Appeal held that this was indeed *donatio mortis causa*, and that the delivery of the title deeds to Mrs Sen was sufficient in terms of physical delivery to satisfy the requirements of the doctrine. It should be noted that this was a case based on the **unregistered** system of conveyancing, where delivery of the title deeds was sufficient. *Sen* v. *Headley* is not authority that the **registered** system of conveyancing, which does not rely on the production of title deeds to prove ownership (instead ownership is proved by reference to entries on a central register), can be transferred by way of a *donatio mortis causa*. A more detailed discussion of the systems of registered and unregistered property is outside the scope of this book.

Proprietary estoppel

You have already come across the equitable doctrine of **proprietary estoppel** in Chapter 1. As you may remember, the doctrine provides that where a person expends money on a property or otherwise acts to their detriment in the mistaken belief that they have an interest in that property, and the legal owner of the property encourages them in their mistaken belief, then the legal owner will be prevented, or 'estopped', from enforcing their legal rights against the person who has acted to their detriment. In Chapter 1 the example was given of a man allowing a person to build a house on his land but then, once the house is built, making an application to the court to have that person evicted from the house on the basis that the man is the strict legal owner of the land. But why is proprietary estoppel included here as a method of enforcing an incomplete trust? The reason is on account of one remedy which may be given by the court of equity in cases of proprietary estoppel, and that is the direction that an incomplete transfer of trust property over to the trustees be perfected, or completed.

The most prominent proprietary estoppel case concerning a transfer of trust property is that of *Dillwyn* v. *Llewelyn* (1862) 4 De GF & J 517. In this case, a father said that he would give his son a piece of land on which to build a house. The father allowed his son to enter into possession of the land and also handed him a signed memorandum which was intended to be, but which was not in fact, a deed of gift of the land. The son then spent £14,000 building a house on the land, all the while being encouraged by his father to do so. On the death of the father, the son sought to require a conveyance of the land to him, on the basis of their agreement. The court ordered that the conveyance to the son should go ahead on the basis of proprietary estoppel because the father had, by his conduct, promised to convey the land to the son if he built a house on it and the son had spent a considerable amount of money, thereby acting to his detriment in reliance on the father's promise.

It should be noted that, as an equitable remedy, the use of the doctrine of proprietary estoppel comes with no guarantees: the transfer of the property is entirely at the discretion of the court. If the court feels that damages, or indeed some other remedy is more appropriate, then the claimant may end up with one of these lesser alternatives. The doctrine of proprietary estoppel is considered in further detail in Chapter 8.

Summary

◆ In order for a trust to be created, the parties must be of the requisite age and mental capacity.

◆ It is not possible for anyone under the age of 18 to create a trust of land, or to create a trust by will, with the exception of members of the armed forces, who can create a will at the age of 17. There is no age requirement for creating trusts of personal property.

◆ The formalities for the creation of a trust differ depending on whether the trust is made during the settlor's lifetime ('inter vivos') or by will.

◆ Trusts of land created inter vivos must be made in writing (section 53 Law of Property Act 1925).

◆ Trusts of personal property do not require any formality.

◆ Trusts created by will must be in writing, signed and witnessed by two independent witnesses (section 9 Wills Act 1837).

◆ Conveying the trust property to the trustees can be done simply by physical delivery of the property in the case of all personal possessions, but the conveyance of land, shares and certain other property requires a formal deed of transfer plus registration with the relevant bodies.

◆ A transfer of a beneficial interest under a trust will generally require writing under section 53(1)(c) Law of Property Act 1925, subject to the two exceptions set out in the *Vandervell* cases.

◆ If the conveyance of the trust property to the trustees has not been properly completed, there is little the beneficiaries can do at law to enforce the transfer. However, if they have given consideration for the trust property, they can instead claim damages in respect of their loss.

◆ In equity, the beneficiaries may be able to require the transfer of the trust property to the trustees under the rule in *Strong* v. *Bird*, *donatio mortis causa* or the doctrine of proprietary estoppel.

Question and answer*

Problem: Wesley Simpkin-Bale is an eccentric old bachelor and owner of the Vinery Manor estate. Welsey's pride and joy is his collection of vintage motor vehicles, which he keeps on display in the converted coach house at the Manor. Wesley likes to spend his days tinkering with the old vehicles, with the help of his chauffeur, Cedric. Cedric spends all of his spare time working on the cars, and Wesley can be very demanding but, despite Wesley's protestations, Cedric refuses to take any additional payment for his mechanical expertise as he enjoys helping the old boy and, besides, Wesley has told Cedric on many occasions that one day the collection will be his. He even lets Cedric have use of one of the cars as and when he wishes to take his lady-friend out on day trips to the seaside.

One afternoon when Wesley is being particularly demanding, Wesley and Cedric enter into a blazing row, ending in Cedric storming out of the coach house, slamming the door behind him. Unfortunately, the slamming door causes one of the car jacks under which Wesley is working to collapse, crushing him beneath it. The housekeeper, on hearing the commotion, rushes to the coach house and, seeing Wesley caught beneath the car, calls the emergency services.

As the ambulance arrives to take him away, Wesley hands over the keys of the house to his housekeeper, saying 'Here Aggie. It looks as if I shall never see the old place again. Look after the Manor for me. It's your home now.'

Sadly, Wesley dies in hospital a few days later. Wesley has left no will but his nephew, Timothy, is appointed to administer his estate. Cedric tells Timothy about Wesley's intention to give his car collection to him, Cedric, but Timothy claims that Wesley meant the collection to go to him, having promised the cars to him as a boy. Timothy even claims Wesley gave him a set of keys to the coach house, which he has kept ever since and now produces.

In the meantime, Aggie is claiming that she is entitled to the entire estate, including the house contents and the coach house car collection. What are the respective entitlements of Aggie, Cedric and Timothy?

You should allow yourself no more than 40 minutes to complete this task.

Essay: 'The rule in *Strong* v. *Bird* was never designed for the purpose for which it is now used. Any attempt to extend it still further would be to open the floodgates to unscrupulous executors.' Discuss.

This question should be answered in 40 minutes.

✱ Answer guidance is provided at the end of the chapter.

Further reading and references

Green, B. (1984) '*Grey*, *Oughtred* and *Vandervell*: a contextual reappraisal', 47 MLR 385.

Interesting article detailing the decisions in the three section 53(1)(c) cases, suggesting the minority in *Oughtred* were correct and that it is simply policy considerations that influenced the majority. Worth taking a look at for a more detailed analysis of the law in this area.

Jaconelli, J. (2006) 'Problems in the rule in *Strong* v. *Bird*', Conv 432.

Article with good practical focus, discussing the development of the doctrine and talking about how it works today, with practical advice for laywers on how to avoid liability in negligence under the rule.

MacMillan, M. (2008) 'Disputed wills', *Private Client Business*, 3, 159–66.

An excellent article. Very practical in its focus. Considers the main grounds for challenging the validity of wills, outlining the key issues relating to execution, testamentary capacity, forgery, lack of knowledge of the will and undue influence. Particularly interesting are the notes on precautions which practitioners can take to minimise the risks of a will being challenged.

Morris, J. (2003) 'Questions: when is an invalid gift a valid gift? When is an incompletely constituted trust a completely constituted trust? Answer: after the decisions in *Choithram* and *Pennington*', *Private Client Business*, 6, 393–403.

This article provides an excellent critique of the decisions in *Choithram* v. *Pagarani* and *Pennington* v. *Waine*, focusing on the apparent judicial softening of the approach towards the legal maxim 'equity will not assist a volunteer' in the context of incompletely constituted trusts. Essential reading on this topic.

Neenan, L. and Welsh, P. (2001) 'Is the *donatio mortis causa* of land dead or alive?', *Trusts and Estates Law Journal*, 28 Supp (Back to basics), 1–3.

This article gives the background to the doctrine of *donatio mortis causa* and talks about the difficulties with the passing of land under the doctrine.

Tham, C.H. (2006) 'Careless share giving', Conv 411.

An interesting article examining the problems which can occur with lifetime gifts of certificated shares where the correct formalities for the declaration of trust have not been observed.

Question and answer guidance

Problem:

Rights of Aggie, Cedric and Timothy

The cars, and the garage they were housed in, were never formally transferred to any of the three claimants. Neither was the house formally transferred to Aggie. In order for a formal transfer to take place, in respect of the house and garage, there should have been a deed under section 52 Law of Property Act 1925 (because both are transfers of land); as regards the cars, they should have been transferred in accordance with the requirements of the DVLA (see the Out and about feature, earlier in the chapter). The gifts are therefore not completely constituted. There is nothing the three claimants can do to enforce the gifts at law, as they are based on informal promises (so covenants to settle do not apply here). But will one of the exceptions to the equitable doctrine that 'equity will not assist a volunteer' apply?

Aggie

The gift to Aggie may be successful under *donatio mortis causa*, as a gift made in contemplation of death – *Cain* v. *Moon*: the gift must have been made in contemplation of death; there must have been delivery of the subject matter of the gift; the gift must revert to the donor if they should recover. Wesley said to Aggie as he was on his way to the hospital: 'Here Aggie. It looks as if I shall never see the old place again. Look after the Manor for me. It's your home now.' He also hands over the keys to the house to Aggie. This would suggest compliance with *Cain* v. *Moon* in the first instance. However, it is questionable whether a gift can be made *donatio mortis causa* in respect of land: note *Sen* v. *Headley* in which the key to a strong box containing title deeds was given to the donee (we do not know whether the land in this instance is registered or unregistered). Is simply giving Aggie the keys to the house sufficient delivery of the house itself? Unlikely, given *Sen* v. *Headley*. Even if Aggie's claim was successful, there is a question as to whether she would just be entitled to the house, or the whole of Wesley's land, including the garage and cars. He asked her to look after 'the Manor' for him, so this is unclear.

Cedric

Cedric may have a claim under the doctrine of proprietary estoppel. He has worked on the cars for no additional payment, believing he will own them one day. He has therefore acted to his detriment in reliance on Wesley's promise (see *Dillwyn* v. *Llewelyn*). There may be a question as to whether Wesley has encouraged Cedric in his belief that he will inherit the car collection. We are told that Wesley tried to pay Cedric but he would not take the additional money. Wesley also 'paid' Cedric by allowing him use of one of the cars to take his lady-friend out on trips to the seaside. If proprietary estoppel is found, the remedy is discretionary, but could include a requirement for Wesley's estate to perfect the gift to Cedric, thus transferring the garage and contents to him. The court may also decide on a lesser remedy, however, or even decide that the periodic loan of one of the cars was sufficient payment for Cedric's services. We will be taking a more detailed look at the doctrine of proprietary estoppel in Chapter 8.

Timothy

Could the rule in *Strong* v. *Bird* apply here? Unlikely: Timothy wasn't appointed executor to the estate, he was simply appointed an administrator on intestacy. There is arguably a difference between the motivations of a testator in appointing him, and in his simply being appointed administrator as next of kin. In any event, for the rule in *Strong* v. *Bird* to work, the intention of the donor, in this case Wesley, must not be disrupted in any way. Wesley gave the keys to the garage to Timothy and said it was his, but his later promises to Cedric, and the fact that he allowed Cedric to use one of the cars, suggest that Wesley has since revoked his promise (see *Re Freeland*). Wesley's subsequent giving of the keys to the house to Aggie may also serve as evidence against the alleged gift to Timothy.

Essay:

A good answer to this question would briefly introduce the reader to the issue of incompletely constituted trusts, and then describe the rule in *Strong* v. *Bird* as an exception to the general rule, giving an explanation of the context in which it was originally used (i.e. the settlement of an outstanding debt).

The student could then move on to discuss the adaptation and widening of the rule to cover gifts of property, mentioning the key cases of *Re Stewart* and *Re Gonin*.

The remainder of the essay should concentrate on the reasoning behind the original decision in *Strong* v. *Bird*, and whether this has been lost in translation with the cases that followed (i.e. given the policy behind the original decision, should it ever have been extended to gifts?). Mention could also be made of the fact that the rule has never actually been tested in the context of trusts.

In conclusion: the question is asking for a moral judgement or comment on the use of the rule to benefit executors, and whether this should be allowed, so the conclusion should address this, based on the information set out in the remainder of the essay.

Visit **www.mylawchamber.co.uk/warner-reed** to access study support resources including practice exam questions with guidance, interactive 'You be the judge' multiple choice questions, annotated weblinks, glossary and key case flashcards and audio legal updates all linked to the **Pearson eText** version of *Equity and Trusts* which you can **search**, **highlight** and **personalise** with your **own notes** and **bookmarks**.

Use Case Navigator to read in full some of the key cases referenced in this chapter with commentary and questions:

Grey **v. *IRC*** [1959] 3 All ER 603
Milroy **v. *Lord*** (1862) De GF & J 264
Re Rose [1952] 1 All ER 1217
Vandervell **v. *IRC*** [1967] 1 All ER 1

Chapter 3
Certainty

Key points In this chapter we will be looking at:

✦ The need for certainty in the creation of express trusts

✦ Certainty of intention, subject matter and object

✦ What is conceptual uncertainty?

✦ What is evidential uncertainty?

✦ Trusts which are administratively unworkable

Introduction

In the previous chapter we looked at the **formalities** involved in the creation of an **express trust**. In this chapter we will be focusing in more detail on the content of the instrument which creates the trust, whether it is a will or a trust deed, and what informa-tion or wording is needed to create a valid trust. So, in essence, what we will be thinking about here is what information the **settlor** needs to give their **trustees** to enable the trustees to carry out the settlor's wishes effectively.

The need for certainty in trusts

In order to carry out the terms of a trust the trustees need to be clear about what exactly it is that they are required to do. First of all they must be certain of the intentions of the settlor: that is, the settlor's intention to create the trust. Secondly, they must know exactly what is the **subject matter** of the trust: in other words, they need to know the precise extent of the property for which they are to be responsible. And thirdly, they have to be able to ascertain who it is who will benefit from that trust and in what shares. Without this vital information trustees could easily give the wrong property to the wrong person and find themselves in breach of their trustee duties, possibly with quite serious con-sequences. For further information on the duties of trustees and the penalties for breach see Chapter 10.

It is also important from the point of view of the judiciary that there is clarity in the creation of the **trust instrument**. If the settlor has not made his intentions clear, it becomes very difficult for the courts to intercede should the trustees run into difficulties or have some disagreement over the management of the trust. And it is for both of these very practical reasons that it has become a requirement of any express trust that it must be sufficiently certain in its construction in order to be valid.

The three certainties

As we have seen above, certainty is vital to the administration of any trust: but how to define it? The official benchmark for certainty in trusts was set by Lord Langdale, Master of the Rolls, in the case of *Knight* v. *Knight* in 1840 (3 Beav 148). The case concerned the will of Richard Knight which purported to tie up his estate in trust for future generations of the Knight family, following the male line. Commenting on the wording of the will, Lord Langdale said that a trust will only be created:

> when property is given absolutely to any person, and the same person is, by the giver who has the power to command, recommended, or entreated or wished, to dispose of that property in favour of another . . . [f]irst, if the words were so used, that upon the whole, they ought to be construed as imperative; secondly, if the subject of the recommendation or wish be certain; and thirdly, if the object or persons intended to have the benefit of the recommendation or wish also be certain.

If we break down the dictum of Lord Langdale we can see that the requirement for certainty in the creation of express trusts can be divided into three separate elements:

1. The wording of the trust must be imperative, or compulsory (this is 'certainty of intention').
2. The property which is the subject of the recommendation or wish must be certain (this is 'certainty of subject matter').
3. The **object** or persons intended to have the benefit of the recommendation or wish must be certain (this is 'certainty of object').

So there are three types of certainty for the purpose of creating an express trust: certainty of intention, certainty of subject matter and certainty of object; and all three of these certainties must be proved in order for an express trust to be valid. Let us now spend a little time considering these three elements in turn.

Certainty of intention

You may be wondering how Lord Langdale's reference to the need for the wording of the trust to be imperative translates into the phrase 'certainty of intention'. In order to be certain that the settlor *intended* to create a trust, we must look to their words or actions. One of the key indicators of intention in the context of trusts is that the settlor is imposing his wishes upon the trustees. If the settlor intends to create a trust, they will not give the trustees a choice as to whether or not the trust property is used for the benefit of the **beneficiaries**; rather, they will instruct the trustees to act on the beneficiaries' behalf. This instruction is imperative: any discretion on the part of the trustees, if it exists at all, will be limited only to the management of the trust property. It will not extend to whether or not the trustees choose to act. It is this imperative, or compulsory, element to which Lord Langdale was referring in his judgment. Certainty of intention is proved by the existence of a compulsory element in the creation of the trust.

The importance of proving certainty of intention, in other words that it was truly the settlor's intention to create a trust, is easily demonstrated when put into context. In a real life trust scenario if certainty of intention cannot be proved, it will be assumed by the court that the settlor must have intended instead to make an absolute gift to the trustees. The simple consequence of this assumption is that the supposed beneficiaries of the trust will receive nothing, and the trustees will receive a gift of property the settlor never intended to make. This was what happened in the case of *Lassence* v. *Tierney* (1849) 1 Mac & G 551, which concerned a failed attempt to create a trust of property under the terms of a will.

Case Summary

Take, by way of example, an attempt by a settlor, Bob, to put money into trust for his children, with his brother and sister, Michael and Julia, as the named trustees. If Bob gives £500,000 to Michael and Julia and it cannot be proved that his intention was that they retain this money on trust for the children, the £500,000 will be construed by the courts as an absolute gift to Michael and Julia and the children will get nothing. As you might imagine, such an outcome would not only be grossly unfair to Bob's children but it would also be completely at odds with his wishes as settlor that his children should benefit from the trust. This is why the ability to prove certainty of intention is such a critical element of any purported trust.

Despite the devastating effect the law has on a trust which cannot prove certainty of intention, the courts are nevertheless quite strict about the wording which must be used to create a valid trust. Whilst the use of the actual word 'trust' is not essential, the need for clarity is paramount and the settlor must make his intentions absolutely plain in order for the trust to succeed. The You be the judge feature illustrates this.

You be the judge

Q: Shirley makes the following gifts in her will. Consider the wording of the gifts. Which, if any, do you think Shirley intended to give over into trust?

1. I give £50,000 to my friend Elizabeth, which I desire should be divided equally between my children and grandchildren.

2. I leave the cottage to my cousin John, wishing that he should give it to the most deserving of my sons.

3. I give my favourite diamond earrings to my sister Dorothy, in the hope that she will pass them on to my eldest daughter on her coming of age.

4. I give the rest of my estate to be divided equally between the current members of the Alderton Flower Arrangers' Guild in memory of the many happy hours I spent there.

A: Clause 4 is a trust; the others are not. Whilst clause 4 has the necessary certainty of intention, there being a clear imperative to divide the funds equally between the members of the guild, none of the other gifts would be viewed by the courts as showing a sufficiently clear intention to create a valid trust. Shirley's use of the words 'desire', 'wish' and 'hope' are seen by the courts merely as an indicator of her preferences for the use of the money and not as imposing a legal obligation on the trustees to use the gifts in the ways specified by her.

Early case law on the issue shows that the judiciary had previously taken a rather more lenient approach to the subject of certainty of intention, the courts being keen to find that a settlor had intended to create a trust wherever the construction of the settlement would sensibly allow them to do so. The result of this was that **precatory words** used in the body of the trust instrument (these are words expressing a hope or desire, such as those used in the examples below) were often held sufficient evidence of intention to create a trust.

However, this perhaps understandable leaning in favour of any purported beneficiaries in the trust scenario was quashed in the 1871 case of _Lamb_ v. _Eames_ (6 Ch App 597). The case concerned the will of a man who had left all of his property to his wife 'to be at her disposal in any way she may think best, for the benefit of herself and her family'. The court was quite clear in stating their belief that the testator had not intended to impose a trust upon his widow; rather he had made an outright gift of his estate to her to use at her discretion.

Case Summary

This case was to form the basis of the current view on the use of precatory words in trust instruments, as was confirmed by the Court of Appeal in the 1881 case of _Re Adams and the Kensington Vestry_ (27 Ch D 394). This later case once more concerned the will of a husband leaving property to his wife 'in full confidence that she will do what is right as to the disposal thereof between my children, either in her lifetime or by will after her decease'. The court again held the wording used in the will constituted an absolute gift to the widow and not a trust in favour of his children, Lord Justice Cotton stating that some of the older cases had taken the law too far in favour of precatory words and that any such words in future should be considered only in the light of the document as a whole with a view to helping to determine the true intentions of the settlor.

Case Summary

The result of the ruling in _Re Adams and the Kensington Vestry_ is that in the majority of cases the use of precatory words will not on its own be sufficient to show an intention on the part of the settlor to create a trust. Words which have since been held precatory in nature, and therefore insufficient to create a trust, include:

+ '_it is my desire_ that she allows [. . .] an annuity of £25 during her life' (_Re Diggles_ (1888) 39 Ch D 253).

+ '_I wish_ them to bequeath the same between the families of [. . .] and [. . .]' (_Re Hamilton_ [1895] 2 Ch 370).

+ '_in the fullest trust and confidence that_ she will carry out my _wishes_ in the following particulars' (_Re Williams_ [1897] 2 Ch 12).

+ '_for the benefit of_ themselves and their respective families' (_Re Hill_ [1923] 2 Ch 259).

In contrast to these cases is the matter of _Comiskey_ v. _Bowring Hanbury_ [1905] AC 84. Here a testator left his estate to his widow:

Case Summary

> in full confidence that she will make such use of it as I should have made myself and that at her death she will devise it to such one or more of my nieces as she may think fit and in default of any disposition by her thereof in her will . . . I hereby direct that all my estate and property acquired by her under this my will shall at her death be equally divided among the surviving said nieces.

This is one of the rare cases in which, based on the construction of the gift in its entirety, a gift containing precatory words has been held to constitute a trust. In this case the husband had made provision for the money to be divided equally between his nieces should his wife not make any decision as to which of them should benefit during her lifetime. This provision of an alternative in the event of non-distribution of the funds clearly imposes the necessary imperative element on the trust. The wife's discretion extended

it is important to view the entire wording of the gift

only to how the monies were to be divided, not as to whether they were divided. This effectively made her a trustee of the monies, and not the recipient of an absolute gift. We can therefore see that it is important to view the entire wording of the gift when seeking to prove certainty of intention. Looking at the precatory words in isolation could be misleading.

Case Summary

The only exception to the rule that the use of precatory words will be insufficient to show certainty of intention is where a settlor has specifically copied the wording of a trust which has previously been tried in the courts and which has been held to create a trust. In such cases the use of identical wording by the settlor is considered sufficient evidence of their intention to create a trust. This is what happened in the case of *Re Steele's Will Trust* [1948] Ch 603 in which a will used wording identical to that which had been held to create a trust in the 1868 case of *Shelley* v. *Shelley* (1868) LR 6 Eq 540. Presumably the assumption here is that the solicitor drafting the will had used the wording from the earlier document as a precedent (or template) intending that it will create a trust, that specific wording having successfully been shown to do so in the earlier case. However, the finding in this case opens up a number of questions: How close must the wording of the new will be to the original case? Must the wording be an exact copy, or can there be some differences? If there can be differences, how different can they be? Unless the matter is given fresh judicial consideration, these questions seem likely to remain unanswered.

Must there always be writing to evidence certainty of intention?

Case Summary

Not necessarily. The words or conduct of a party alone can create a trust if they are sufficiently clear. The case of *Paul* v. *Constance* [1977] 1 All ER 195 concerned a couple who lived together as husband and wife, although they were both married to other people. Mr Constance put £950 of his own money into a bank account in his sole name, telling his partner, Mrs Paul, that the money was 'as much yours as it is mine'. The fund was subsequently topped up from time to time with the joint bingo winnings of the couple. On the death of Mr Constance his estranged wife, Mrs Constance, claimed the contents of the account as constituting part of Mr Constance's estate. However, Mrs Paul claimed that it had always been the intention of Mr Constance to hold the money in the account on trust for himself and Mrs Paul, and that she should therefore be entitled to a half share in the account. The courts agreed, splitting the contents of the account between the two women.

Case Summary

The case of *Re Kayford Ltd* [1975] 1 WLR 279, which also concerns money placed in bank accounts, is particularly pertinent in the current financial climate. The case concerned a mail order company which had run into financial difficulty. Wishing to protect their customers from losing money paid for orders should the company go into liquidation they put all their customer money into a bank account separate from their own company funds pending their orders being processed, naming the account the 'customers' trust deposit account'. When the company went into liquidation the question arose as to whether the money held in the account formed part of the assets of the company and could be claimed by the liquidator. The court held that it was the intention of the company to hold the monies on trust for their clients and therefore the liquidator was not entitled to the fund.

Clearly this was morally the right thing to do in this particular instance, in order to safeguard the customers of the failing company. It should be noted, however, that, irrespective of any moral arguments which may apply to a particular set of facts, the intention to create a trust must nevertheless be a genuine one in order for the courts to rule in favour of a trust being created. This is illustrated by the outcome of the earlier case of

Jones v. *Lock* (1865) LR 1 Ch App 25. The case concerned a father who, on his return from a business trip, was chastised by his child's nurse for not bringing his infant son a gift. In order to appease the nurse, the father placed a cheque made payable to himself (which was, in fact, the proceeds of his business dealings) into his son's hands, declaring 'this cheque is for baby; it is for himself, and I am going to put it away for him'. The cheque was then placed in the family safe. When the father died less than a week later it was found that the cheque had unfortunately not been endorsed by him and therefore that the gift to his son was invalid (to endorse a cheque simply means for the payee to authorise its payment to a third party by inserting the third party's name on the cheque and signing it). The question then arose as to whether the failed gift could instead be construed as a declaration of trust on the part of the father, declaring himself trustee of the money for the infant's benefit. The court held, however, that the father's intention was clearly to make a gift of the money to his son and the fact that the gift had failed was not sufficient reason to find intention to create a trust. We can see from this that the court is unlikely to consider vague promises or comments made on the spur of the moment to constitute sufficient evidence of an intention to create a trust. The Law in action feature further illustrate this.

Case Summary

Law in action The 'Farepak Fiasco': could a trust have saved customers' money?

Farepak Food and Gifts Ltd ran a Christmas savings scheme. Savers would give money to the company each month, in exchange for hampers and gift vouchers which would be distributed to them by Farepak at the end of the year. However in 2006, disaster struck when Farepak collapsed, taking a staggering £38 million in savers' money with it.

How is this relevant to the law of trusts? Knowing that they were in financial difficulty, in the three days leading up to the administration the directors of Farepak had sought to 'ring-fence' any money received from their customers, so that it could be returned to the savers if necessary and would not be swallowed up by the liquidators in paying off the company's creditors. The directors even signed a deed of trust to this effect and set up a 'trust account' for this purpose. Unfortunately, however, the directors' attempt to protect their customers for the most part failed. The majority of customer monies had been received prior to the setting up of the fund, which meant that, in the eyes of the court, they were viewed not as beneficiaries under the terms of the trust, but rather they were existing creditors of the company. This also meant that the customers could not claim that the money was held under a **Quistclose trust**, which would have required that the trust was set up by the customers prior to handing it over to

Source: Photodisc/Spike Mafford

Farepak (Quistclose trusts are dealt with in further detail in Chapter 1). There was an additional complication as to the trust fund itself, as it transpired that the directors had made a mistake as to the bank account identified by it, and the trust therefore failed. This meant that almost 150,000 savers would have to wait in turn with all the other company creditors and would receive nothing from the failed trust fund. This was the result of the case of *Re Farepak Food and Gifts Ltd (In Administration)* [2008] BCC 22.

The administrators dealing with Farepak initially estimated that these unlucky savers would get something back but, as the money raised from the liquidation of the company had to be shared between all of Farepak's creditors, the amount they were likely to receive would amount to less than four pence in the pound for each saver. Following the recent securing of a further £4 million from directors of the company by its liquidators, the dividend payable to creditors is now estimated to be nearer to 15 pence in the pound, but this still falls significantly short of the amount lost. In the recent court case of *Re Farepak Food and Gifts Ltd* [2009] EWHC 2580, an order was made for the distribution of these funds to savers, so they should be receiving this money shortly.

But what about the rest of the savers' money? Will they ever see its return? The short answer is no. The Farepak Response Fund, which was set up in support of those who lost money through the scheme, has raised the amazing sum of £6 million in charitable donations to help the out-of-pocket savers. This still only represents an additional 17 per cent of savers' funds, however.

The worst thing about the situation is that, with the right legislation, this disaster could have been avoided. Most companies who operate savings schemes are regulated by the Financial Services Authority ('FSA'), and are required to put savers' money in a separate account, or give it to a third party to protect it. But Christmas savings scheme firms are not regulated by the FSA and thus have never had to abide by this rule. Consequently, Farepak was able to continue to take its customers' money up until only two days before they went into administration.

For full details of the court case on which the validity of the Farepak customer trust scheme was decided, see *Re Farepak Food and Gifts Ltd (In Administration)* [2008] BCC 22.

Certainty of subject matter

Even if the intention of the settlor to create a trust is made abundantly clear, the trust will still fail if the subject matter of the trust, that is the money or other property which the settlor is putting into trust, is not certain. It may seem on the face of it quite difficult for a settlor to be *uncertain* about what property he is going to give to his trustees; after all, a gift of £50,000 cannot easily be construed as anything other than what it is: a gift of money for a certain sum. However, when one starts to talk about gifts of other types of property it is surprisingly easy to fall into the trap of uncertainty of subject matter if sufficient thought is not given to the wording of the gift.

Take, for example, the gifts made by Shirley in the You be the judge exercise, earlier in the chapter. With the first gift of £50,000 the subject matter of the trust is perfectly clear: £50,000 cash. However, what about the purported gift at clause 2 of 'the cottage'? If Shirley owns a house named 'The Cottage', or if she has a house which she commonly refers to as 'the cottage', it may be possible to deduce from this the house to which she is referring. But what if Shirley owns more than one property: her main house, a cottage property in the country, and a smaller seaside property? Which one is 'the cottage' referred to in the will? If there is no other information available about which cottage Shirley intended to give her gift will fail as neither the courts nor the trustees have the authority to decide which of Shirley's houses should be included; after all, the houses are likely to be very different, in size, location and value. The outcome of this uncertainty as to what comprises the subject matter of the gift is that 'the cottage' will remain in Shirley's estate and the 'most deserving son' will get nothing.

A second example is clause 3 of Shirley's will and her gift of her favourite diamond earrings. Again, this is all very well if Shirley owns only one pair of diamond earrings; but what if she has more than one? Who is to say which of the earrings was her favourite? It will not be possible to ask her as the will only comes into operation on her death, by which time it will be too late to ask.

A similar problem was encountered in the case of *Boyce* v. *Boyce* (1849) 16 Sim 476, in which a father made a gift in his will to his daughter Maria of her choice of any one of his houses, the remaining houses to be given to Maria's sister, Charlotte. Sadly, Maria died before her father and therefore never made a choice of house. This had the unfortunate, and seemingly rather harsh, outcome that Charlotte received nothing either. As Maria had not chosen which of the houses she was going to take, there was no way of determining which were 'the remaining houses' that constituted the subject matter of the gift to Charlotte. The houses were therefore returned to Charlotte's father's estate on a resulting trust, and were eventually inherited by her father's grandson. It is worth noting that the result might have been quite different if Maria had died after her father. It is likely that, in this event, Maria's right to choose one of the houses would have fallen to her own representatives to make, and the gift to Charlotte would not then have failed.

The problems encountered with certainty of subject matter in cases such as *Boyce* v. *Boyce*, above, where a gift is dependent upon the discretion or choice of a beneficiary, do not occur where the trustees are given a similar discretion. On the contrary, a discretion given to trustees over a choice of gift can save a gift that would otherwise fail for uncertainty of subject matter. A good illustration of this is the case of *Re Golay* [1965] 1WLR 969. Here, a father left a will entitling his daughter, whom he fondly referred to as 'Tossy', to 'enjoy one of my flats during her lifetime' and further instructing that she should be allowed a 'reasonable income' from the others. As to the lifetime gift of the flat, despite a particular flat not being specified, the court interpreted the wording of the gift to allow the trustees the discretion to choose a flat for her to live in, thus saving the gift from failing for uncertainty of subject matter. The court also held that a 'reasonable income' was something which the trustees or, in their default, the court, could measure and determine.

The above examples illustrate on a basic level the difficulties which can result from the simplest of things not being properly described by the settlor. One particular problem which can arise is when a settlor wishes to make a gift of a share in something. This is illustrated by the case of *Sprange* v. *Barnard* (1789) 2 Bro CC 585 in which a wife left £300 in her will to her husband for his sole use:

> at his death, the remaining part of what is left, and he does not want for his own wants and use, to be divided between my brother . . . and my sister . . . equally.

With such vague wording, how could the husband know what part of the £300 he was supposed to give to his wife's brother and sister? The court held in this instance that the wording of the gift was not certain enough to support the notion that the wife had intended a trust to be created. This was an outright gift to the husband to spend as he pleased and he was under no obligation to save any part of the fund for the benefit of his brother- and sister-in-law at all.

Another case in point is that of *Palmer* v. *Simmonds* (1854) 2 Drew 221 in which the testator purported to make a gift of 'the bulk' of his estate. Again, the gift failed as there was no way for the trustees or ultimately the court to determine exactly what part of the **testator**'s property 'the bulk' did or did not include.

It is not too difficult to see from the wording in these cases that a court of law might struggle to determine exactly what, if anything, was going to be the entitlement of the purported beneficiaries. Less obvious, however, are the cases where the settlor purports to give a specified share in a collection of items. Take the example of a case of wine. If the settlor makes a gift of half of that case of wine to a friend it would be simple to divide the wine in two, giving six bottles to the named friend and retaining the other six. However, what if the case of wine was mixed? Rather than comprising 12 identical bottles it might now contain different coloured wines of different vintages with different qualities and very different values. How then would it be possible to ascertain which of those very individual bottles the settlor intended his friend to have? Taking the example a step further, even if the case of wine consisted of 12 bottles of the same wine, who is to say that one bottle may not be spoiled, or the label damaged, thus affecting its value?

Case Summary

A similar difficulty was encountered in the case of *Re London Wine Co. (Shippers) Ltd* [1986] PCC 121 which concerned the stocks of a wine merchant. The argument put forward in that instance was that once an order was placed with the company the wine which had been ordered would be held on trust by the company until such time as it was delivered to the purchaser. However, the court held that unless the subject matter of the order had been specifically removed from the general stock of the company and placed on one side, it would be impossible to say exactly which cases of wine were held on trust and which belonged to the company. The trust argument therefore failed in that case. The same outcome was also

Case Summary

reached in the later case of *Re Goldcorp Exchange Ltd* [1994] 2 All ER 806, which involved orders for the purchase of gold bullion from the reserves of a New Zealand mining company.

Case Summary

The outcome of these cases should be contrasted with the case of *Hunter* v. *Moss* [1994] 3 All ER 215, which concerned the transfer of 50 shares by Mr Moss to Mr Hunter from his stock of a total of 950 shares. The court held in this instance that, as the shares were identical, it did not matter which of the 950 shares were allotted to Mr Hunter, and thus the gift did not fail for uncertainty. The distinction between the cases is that the shares were **intangible property**, whereas wine and gold bullion is tangible. A share of intangible property can be carved out of a bulk, whereas with **tangible property** the share must be physically separated from the remainder in order to be recognisable as such under the terms of a gift. It should also be noted that both *Re Goldcorp* and *Re London Wine* were purely commercial cases, where the buyers were trying to 'jump the queue' of other creditors by declaring a trust. *Hunter* v. *Moss*, on the other hand, was merely an attempted gift of shares under the terms of a will. It is therefore likely that the court was willing to be more lenient in this case. Following the outcome of *Hunter* v. *Moss*, gifts of shares should therefore be treated as an exceptional case.

Writing and drafting

You are a trainee solicitor at the firm of Ward Peake. Your client has sent you a letter giving her instructions in respect of her will, which are as follows:

> The desk is a family heirloom. I wish it to go to my daughter, Cecile, and I hope that in turn she will pass it on to her own daughter on her death.
>
> I wish to share my premium bonds between my best friends, Chloe and Adeline, who are each to be given a half share, hoping that their numbers come up.
>
> I wish the remainder of my estate to be divided between my three children, Owen, Claude and Cecile.

You should consider the instructions given and write a letter in response to your client, outlining the difficulties (if any) you foresee in carrying out her instructions. You should aim to spend no more than 40 minutes on this task.

 Handy tip: Don't forget to begin and end your letter correctly. Remember, you are writing this letter on behalf of your employer and part of giving your client the right impression is to show that you know how to address a letter properly.

Certainty of object

The last of the three certainties, certainty of object, relates to the object, or beneficiary, of the trust. It stands to reason that the trustees must be able to ascertain to whom the subject matter of the trust is to be given. In the case of *Morice* v. *Bishop of Durham* [1805] 10 Ves 522, a testatrix, Ann Cracherode, left the whole of her estate: 'to such objects of benevolence and liberality as the Bishop of Durham in his own discretion shall most approve of . . '. The trust was held to be void for lack of certainty as to its objects. No one could determine who the beneficiaries under the trust might be.

The above case is a rarity. In the majority of circumstances, the beneficiary of the trust will be easy to determine as they will be referred to by name in the trust instrument. It is when the object of the trust is not a named individual, but rather is a class of individuals, that more care must be taken by the settlor to avoid ambiguity and thus uncertainty of object. If the trust fails for uncertainty of object, the trustees will be unable to distribute to the beneficiaries and the subject matter of the trust will revert to the settlor (or to their estate, if they have died).

The rules for certainty of object differ depending on whether the trust is a fixed or a discretionary trust. You will remember from the discussion of different types of trust in Chapter 1 that **fixed trusts** are those which leave the trustees with no discretion as to how or to whom the trust fund is to be distributed, whereas **discretionary trusts** give the trustees the power to choose either in what shares the subject matter of the trust is to be divided, or to whom it is to be given (or in some cases both of these things). So, as a brief reminder, a fixed trust might read as follows:

> I give £10,000 to my trustees to be divided equally between my four children, Jake, Myriam, Aidan and Isobella.

And a discretionary trust might differ thus:

> I give £10,000 to my trustees to be divided in their absolute discretion amongst those of my children they consider most deserving.

With these examples in mind, let us now deal in turn with certainty of object as it appertains to each type of trust.

Fixed trusts

With a fixed trust, the trustees are given no discretion as to who will benefit from the trust. It is therefore essential that they know exactly to whom they should distribute the fund if they are to carry out their duties as trustees effectively. In the example given above, this will not be a problem: we have been given the names of all four children of the settlor so there can be no question as to whom the trustees should distribute the £10,000. Even if the settlor had not named his children specifically, it would be a simple matter to ascertain their identities and distribute the fund in accordance with his wishes.

The trustees will run into difficulty with a fixed trust, however, if they are unable to determine the names of each and every person who is to benefit under the trust. Thinking about it logically, if the trustees are given instructions to divide the £10,000 between a **class of beneficiaries**, but it is not possible to ascertain from the wording of the trust exactly how many people that class contains, then they will be unable to calculate the amount of each person's share and thus distribution will become impossible. This is what is known as the 'complete list' principle: if the trustees are not able to draw up a complete list of all the intended beneficiaries of the trust, the trust will fail for uncertainty of object.

Case Summary

The principle was first noted in the case of *IRC* v. *Broadway Cottages Trust* [1955] Ch 20, which concerned an £80,000 trust fund set up by a Mr Alan Timpson, the income from which was to be distributed between a very large class of persons, including family members, employees of the family business and their wives and families, various named persons and two charities. The inclusion of employees of the business within the class of beneficiaries caused particular difficulty. The trust specified that the class should include:

In paragraph 1
Persons employed in the past or at the date of the settlement or at any time thereafter during the period until December 31, 1980, not only by the settlor and his wife but by:

+ the settlor's father who died in 1929,
+ his mother who died in 1940,
+ the company, William Timpson Ltd, which was a public company formed in 1929 to take over the business of a private company of the same name formed in 1912 to take over the business founded in 1870 by the settlor's father,
+ any other limited company succeeding the business of William Timpson Ltd,
+ any other limited company of which the settlor was a director at the date of the settlement.

In paragraph 2
The wives and widows of any of the persons specified in paragraph 1.

The trust failed for uncertainty of object. It was simply impossible to divine who the persons were who should benefit under the terms of the trust at any one time. In giving judgment in the case, Lord Justice Jenkins said:

In view of the wide scope of paragraphs 1 and 2 of the schedule it is conceded . . . that the persons who . . . constitute 'the beneficiaries' for the purposes of the settlement, comprise an aggregate of objects which is incapable of ascertainment, in the sense that it would be impossible at any given time to achieve a complete and exhaustive enumeration of all the persons then qualified for inclusion in the class of 'beneficiaries' under the terms of the schedule . . . It must . . . follow . . . that the class of 'beneficiaries' is incapable of ascertainment, and . . . that the trust . . . must be void for uncertainty, inasmuch as there can be no division in equal shares amongst a class of persons unless all the members of the class are known.

The result of the case was that the trustees held the income of the fund on **resulting trust** for the settlor.

Discretionary trusts

With a discretionary trust, you will remember from Chapter 1 that the trustees are given discretion, either as to whom out of the class of beneficiaries named in the trust fund they are to benefit, or as to the shares in which the trust fund is divided. So in the example given earlier, which said:

> I give £10,000 to my trustees to be divided in their absolute discretion amongst those of my children they consider most deserving.

we can see that the trustees are not required to benefit every single one of the settlor's children; rather the discretion allows the trustees to give money to any of the settlor's children they consider deserving. This could be all of the settlor's children, or conversely it could be only one of them. Because the trustees in a discretionary trust are not required to divide the trust fund between every single member of a given class, there is no need for the trustees to draw up a complete list of those beneficiaries. Instead, unlike the situation with fixed trusts, the trustees simply need to know whether any given beneficiary falls within the relevant class. Let us take the following example:

> I give £500,000 to my trustees to divide between those of my fellow employees at Leeds Metropolitan University who my trustees consider may be suffering financial hardship.

Here we have a trust fund set up for the benefit of employees of the university, discretion being given to the trustees as to whom they should benefit. Any employee who believes that they are suffering financial hardship may approach the trustees and ask for financial assistance, to be provided out of the trust fund. As long as the would-be beneficiary can show that they are a member of the class of beneficiaries, that is, that they are an employee of Leeds Metropolitan University, the trustees can give them money from the fund, safe in the knowledge that they are entitled to do so (it will, of course, also be at the discretion

Any employee who believes that they are suffering financial hardship may approach the trustees

of the trustees as to whether the applicant is actually suffering financial hardship in the first place!). Alternatively, if it should become apparent that the person in question is not an employee of the university, the trustees can refuse to make payment to them. The point here is that the trustees do not have to draw up a list of all Leeds Metropolitan University employees in order to benefit the few who need assistance from the fund; proof of the beneficiary's standing on an individual basis, as and when required, will be sufficient.

This test to determine whether someone 'is or is not' a member of a particular class was held to be the definitive test for certainty of object in discretionary trusts in the case of **McPhail v. Doulton** [1971] AC 424 (also known as *Re Baden's Deed Trusts (No. 1)*). The need to take another look at the law relating to certainty of object in discretionary trusts had come about because of the consistent failure of discretionary trusts under the complete list requirement set out in *IRC* v. *Broadway Cottages*, which had originally applied to all kinds of trusts: both fixed and discretionary alike. The facts of *McPhail* v. *Doulton* were similar to those given in the example of Leeds Metropolitan University, above, in that the case concerned a fund set up by a settlor, Mr Bertram Baden, to benefit the employees of a company, Matthew Hall & Co. Ltd. Discretion was given to the trustees of the fund to use it for the benefit of: 'any of the officers and employees or ex-officers and ex-employees of the Company or to any relatives or dependants of any such persons'. The direction by Mr Baden that the fund should be applied not only to employees of the company but also to former employees and any relatives or dependants of those persons provided the trustees with quite an extensive class of potential beneficiaries from which to choose. As with the trust in *IRC* v. *Broadway Cottages*, this meant that it would have been difficult in the extreme to draw up a complete list of potential beneficiaries, with the result that, under the 'complete list' principle, the trust would have failed. However, in allowing the trust to survive under the 'is or is not' test (also termed the 'any given postulant'

Case
Navigator

Case
Summary

test), the House of Lords sensibly chose to give cases of this sort a wider practical application. It should be noted that the finding in *McPhail* v. *Doulton* was simply the widened application of a test which had previously been applied, not to trusts, but to powers, as set out in the earlier case of *Re Gulbenkian's Settlement Trusts* [1970] AC 508. For a reminder on the difference between trusts and powers see the comparison given in Chapter 1.

Following the House of Lords decision in *McPhail* v. *Doulton*, the Court of Appeal was once again given the opportunity to consider how the 'is or is not' test should be interpreted in the case of *Re Baden's Deed Trusts (No. 2)* [1973] Ch 9, when the executors of Mr Baden made a further attempt to claim that the trust should fail, this time on the basis that the words used to describe the objects of the trust, 'relative' and 'dependant', were uncertain. The three judges in the case, Lords Justice Sachs, Megaw and Stamp, agreed unanimously that the term 'dependant' was quite certain, each interpreting the common meaning of the word as being a person who relied on the financial support of an employee of the company. Thus, the 'is or is not' test could be applied in the case of 'dependants' quite simply: if a person was financially dependant on an employee of the company then they would be entitled to apply to the fund for benefits. On the other hand, if they could not prove their financial dependency, they would not be classed as a potential beneficiary to the fund and their claim would fail.

The word 'relatives' gave the judges rather more difficulty. All three judges held that the term could be valid under the 'is or is not' test; however, they each gave different reasons for saying so.

Lord Justice Sachs gave the term a very wide meaning, saying that 'relative' simply meant the descendant of a common ancestor. In applying this to the 'is or is not' test, his view was that, as long as the term was certain, it was for the purported beneficiary to prove they were in the class and should therefore benefit under the terms of the trust.

Lord Justice Stamp agreed with Lord Justice Sachs, albeit that he interpreted the term 'relative' much more narrowly, saying it meant '**next of kin**' (an often used legal term meaning near blood relatives), rather than 'descendants of a common ancestor'. In applying the term to the 'is or is not' test, Lord Justice Stamp said any object described under the terms of the trust had to be certain enough so that it could be shown that any given person was definitely in or out of the class, before the trust could work.

Lord Justice Megaw agreed with Lord Justice Sachs's definition, but his interpretation of the 'is or is not' test was quite different from that of the other two judges. In Lord Justice Megaw's opinion, in order for a class of beneficiaries to be valid it was necessary to show not that any given person was definitely in or out of the class but rather that a substantial number of persons would fall within it. His concern was that, whilst it is usually possible to tell whether or not someone is, for example, a relative, there would undoubtedly be cases which caused difficulty: what about adopted children of the employees, for example, or foster children, or perhaps step-children? Which would be included? Equally, in the case of dependants, how financially dependant is 'dependant'? It would be a matter of fact and degree in each particular case. It is not clear which one of the judge's interpretations represents the law.

So, to conclude, there are two different tests or principles to determine whether there is certainty of object:

✦ the 'complete list' principle, which applies to fixed trusts; or

✦ the 'is or is not' test, which applies to discretionary trusts.

We have seen from the case of *Re Baden's Deed Trusts (No. 2)*, that the 'is or is not' test can pose potential difficulty where the objects listed under the terms of the trust are not absolutely certain. If the terms 'relative' or 'dependant' had been held by the judges to be uncertain, the trust would have failed. Let us now look in a little more detail at exactly the type of difficulties with the wording of a trust which might be sufficient to cause the issue of uncertainty of object to arise in the first place.

Conceptual uncertainty

Conceptual uncertainty is the most likely cause of uncertainty of object. This is when the description of the object of the trust quite simply isn't clear enough and it is impossible to determine with certainty to what, or in this case to whom, the settlor is referring. We have already seen examples of conceptual uncertainty when we were talking about certainty of subject matter earlier in the chapter. Both the descriptions given by Shirley of 'the cottage' and her 'favourite diamond earrings' were conceptually uncertain because the descriptions given by her were not sufficiently precise to enable the trustees to determine exactly which were the cottage and earrings in question.

As we have also seen in the case of *Re Baden's Deed Trusts (No. 2)*, this same rule can be applied to the object of the trust: if the settlor does not describe with sufficient clarity who is to benefit from the trust, the trust will again fail for uncertainty of object. Let us consider again our previous examples of fixed and discretionary trusts. You will remember that these were as follows:

> I give £10,000 to my trustees to be divided equally between my four children, Jake, Myriam, Aidan and Isobella.

> I give £10,000 to my trustees to be divided in their absolute discretion amongst those of my children they consider most deserving.

In the first trust, the fixed trust, the settlor's children are specifically named and so there is no problem in terms of certainty. Equally, with the second, discretionary trust, we can say that the object of the trust is certain because the description of 'my children' has a definite meaning: it is conceptually certain. The same would apply to a gift to brothers and sisters, or nephews and nieces. This is because there is a common understanding of the terms 'nephew', 'niece', 'brother' and 'sister'. They mean the same thing to all people; there is no room for debate as to what the description means.

the description of 'my children' has a definite meaning

Now consider a gift to fellow employees. Arguably, again, the term 'employees' is conceptually certain: it means the people who work for the company or organisation named. However, what if, rather than use the term 'fellow employees', the settlor had used the term 'colleagues'? Who would this include? Would it include the people in the settlor's team, or the whole department? Would it include the whole company or only those within the company that the settlor knew or liked? Would it include the settlor's boss? And so it goes on. This is the issue with conceptual uncertainty: if a term means different things to different people it becomes impossible for the trustees to say with certainty who should be included within a list of possible objects or who is or is not a member of a class of beneficiaries. Unfortunately, as we have seen from the discussion in *Re Baden's Deed Trusts (No. 2)*, this means that, if any part of the trust is conceptually uncertain, the trust will fail: conceptual uncertainty is not something over which it is possible for the courts to intervene and fix.

Out and about

Let us imagine you have won the National Lottery: an amazing £14 million (it was a rollover week). You have decided to set up a fixed trust fund with part of your winnings to benefit the whole of your extended family in equal shares. As you have decided to benefit your whole family, you will need to draw up a list of every family member. You are to call the trust the 'Family Fund'.

Now spend around 40 minutes creating a comprehensive list of all the living members of your extended family to include within the fund.

 Handy tip: You may find it easier to track all the members of your family by creating a family tree. If you are struggling to do this and want some help, you could try going to http://www.genesreunited.co.uk. The site has a useful family tree builder and registration is free.

Reflective practice

Now take some time to review the list (or tree) that you have created. Who did you include on the list? Remember, the instructions were to include the whole of your extended family on the list. Who did you take this to include? Did you include cousins, or second cousins? Did you include the husbands or wives of family members? Did you include godparents as part of your family? What does the term 'extended family' mean to you?

And finally, what could you have done to avoid having to draw up the list?

Evidential uncertainty

Unlike conceptual uncertainty, **evidential uncertainty**, whilst it can certainly be problematic, *is* something which can often be fixed, usually with a bit of research by either the trustees or by the beneficiary claiming an interest in the trust. If an object of the trust is evidentially uncertain, it means that it is difficult to prove that the beneficiary in question is a member of the class of objects specified by the settlor. Such a difficulty might occur, for example, where an employee of the company was working 'cash in hand' and he therefore did not appear on the official list of employees of the company. Alternatively, if the person worked for the named company a number of years ago, there might no longer be records in existence of his period of employment at the company. This evidential uncertainty is not always insurmountable, however. A person's record of employment can be proved in any number of ways: through a sworn statement from a colleague who remembers them; from an old employment contract or payslip; and so on. So whilst evidential uncertainty can amount to the failure of the trust for lack of certainty of object, it can often be overcome. The People in the law interview shows just how difficult a problem the issue of evidential uncertainty can be, in the context of tracing heirs.

> evidential uncertainty is not always insurmountable

People in the law

Tracing heirs: difficulties in evidential uncertainty

One of the best-known cases of evidential uncertainty is the famous Hall/Edwards Estate, which is purported to own some 77 acres of downtown Manhattan, New York, including such New York City landmarks as Trinity Church, the Woolworth Building, New York University, Washington Square Park and the ill-fated World Trade Center, the site having been valued at up to $680 billion before 9/11. Canadian-born Bob Sterne tells us all about it.

So, Bob, what is your connection with the story? I am a descendant of the Edwards line and a keen genealogist, and so I have become interested in the 'Edwards Estate' legend.

What is it all about? There are several versions of this story, all of which have probably become embellished with the passage of time. The source of the fortune, depending on which version you follow, is either Thomas Hall (1611–99), or his great-grandson Robert Edwards (1716–88).

One version has it that Thomas Hall was given land by the Dutch of 'New Amsterdam' (now New York) for warning them so that they could evacuate the women and children before he shelled the city with his British gunboat. The second story, which relates to Hall's great-grandson, Robert Edwards, is that he was in fact a pirate, and was rewarded by Queen Anne for the raiding of Spanish ships, by the grant of land in New York.

Either way, Edwards apparently leased out 77 acres of this land to a John and George Cruger in 1778 for a period of 99 years. When the lease expired, the land was to revert to Edwards's lawful heirs, the descendants of his seven siblings (since he was unmarried). Immediately after signing the lease, Edwards was said to have embarked for England, and the ship and all passengers were lost in a terrible storm.

When the lease expired in 1877, the search for the rightful heirs started, and the controversy over who owns the land continues to this day. Trinity Church, with whom the title to the land now rests, maintains that the land was granted to them directly by Queen Anne in 1705; however, there is apparently no deed available. Trinity Church once said there had been

Source: Photodisc/Life File/Andrew Ward (photo); Bob Sterne (text)

over 5,000 claimants to a share in the Hall/Edwards fortune.

So what's the problem? Evidence. The records are incomplete and those which exist are contradictory and confusing. A lack of baptismal records or marriage records does not help matters, but there is also evidence that some or even all of the land may have been sold off in previous generations.

Will the heirs ever gain their fortune? Unlikely. In 1933, Trinity Church was successful in obtaining a court victory that stated that any further applications would fail under the doctrine of 'laches', which basically means that they didn't act soon enough on their claim. I suppose that there is a remote possibility that this could be overturned if someone could prove that there was fraud or other illegal acts involved in covering up the facts surrounding the existence of the lease, but it's a long shot.

So are you a potential heir to the fortune? I admit that the thought of descending from an eighteenth-century Welsh pirate who owned a trillion dollars (Canadian) worth of Manhattan real estate is pretty tempting! I myself have no documentation previous to my great, great, great-grandparents though and, if my lineage is correct, the split between the Edwards line which allegedly ended up with the land in New York and my branch of the family was seven generations before them. I therefore have only a casual interest in this whole affair.

It should be noted that evidential uncertainty, the difficulty in proving that a person comes within a specified class of objects, is quite different from the situation where the trustees are having trouble in locating a beneficiary from a particular class who has gone missing. If the trustees are unable to find a particular beneficiary they can request what is known as a '**Benjamin order**' from the court, which will allow them to pay out the trust fund, reserving the missing person's share for a period of time after which the money can be distributed amongst the remaining beneficiaries. This is what happened in the case of *Re Benjamin* [1902] 1 Ch 723, from which the order takes its name. The facts of the case were as follows: David Benjamin had made a will ten years previously, in 1891, leaving his fortune to be divided between any of his children still living at the date of his death. When Mr Benjamin died in 1893 he had thirteen children. Twelve of the children were still living; however one of them, Philip David Benjamin, had disappeared under mysterious circumstances in the previous year and it was therefore not known whether he had pre-deceased his father or not. In September 1892, Philip had been holidaying in France with a friend, when he received an urgent communication from his employers requiring his return. Philip took the train immediately for London, promising his friend that he would return in a few days. Since that day nothing had been heard of him, although extensive enquiries had been made and advertisements published all over the world requesting information as to his whereabouts. An examination of Philip's accounts showed that he had embezzled money from his employers, but their communication to him had contained no threat or suggestion of prosecution, and the amount he had taken was at once made good to the firm by Philip's father. The executors under the will asked the court for an order to distribute the estate as if Philip Benjamin had predeceased the testator. But the court held that there was no evidence that this was the case. On the contrary, the presumption of the court was that he was still living.

The court said that just because there was a good motive for Philip's disappearance (his embezzlement from the firm) this did not equate to a presumption of death. The presumption of death could only arise where it could be shown that, if the person were living, they would probably have communicated with friends or relatives. In Philip's case there was sufficient reason for his disappearance and for his not communicating with his relatives. There should therefore be no presumption of the court that he had died. Having said all this, Mr Justice Joyce was keen that the other siblings should not be prevented from benefiting under the terms of the will. He therefore made an order allowing for the executors to distribute the estate of David Benjamin as if his son had died, provided that no evidence was forthcoming which pointed to Philip's survival.

The number of unclaimed inheritances is surprisingly high. The Key stats feature shows just how much unclaimed money there is in the UK alone.

Key stats Unclaimed inheritances: the statistics

Estimates are that one person in twelve forgets to inform their bank and other financial institutions when they move, so it is not so difficult to believe that people would forget entire accounts over the years and with a UK population of in excess of 60 million, you can imagine how those forgotten pennies could soon add up. Take a look at the figures:

Experts estimate that there is at least £15 billion in unclaimed money in the UK. Some even believe that the figure may be in excess of £20 billion.

Experts claim that there's some £5 billion sitting in dormant bank and building society accounts, with another £3 billion each in National Savings, pensions, and shares and dividends. They also think there's a billion in unclaimed life policies, and around £300 million of unclaimed lottery winnings.

So where have these missing people gone and why haven't they claimed their money? Much of it comes down to sheer forgetfulness, but in the end, many of these people will simply have died either without making a will or informing relatives of the existence of certain accounts. This means solicitors dealing with their estates don't know to look for or claim the money.

[*Source*: This information has been reproduced from **www.UnclaimedFinances.co.uk** – 'tracing and claiming your unclaimed money'.]

Administrative unworkability

As with conceptual uncertainty, if a trust is **administratively unworkable** the trust will fail and the trust fund will revert to the settlor. Essentially, a trust will usually become administratively unworkable if the class of objects is too large and unwieldy for the trustees to sensibly manage. This was the case in *Ex parte West Yorkshire County Council* (1985) *The Times* 25 July in which the County Council tried to set up a trust for the benefit of 'any or all or some of the inhabitants of West Yorkshire'. It was held in this case that the class provided for was far too wide for the trustees to realistically deal with, given that 'all' of the inhabitants of West Yorkshire could potentially amount to as many as 2.5 million people.

Case Summary

Documenting the law
Getting it right . . .

The examples given above deal with difficulties encountered when describing more complex divisions of property or large classes of persons. However, let us not forget the possibility of simple human error. The implications of making a mistake in your will can be serious. On the wills services website, 'The Will Site', we are given the following anecdotal evidence of two significant errors made in wills purporting to leave gifts to two well-known charities.

✦ The will of Frank Clifford, we are told, included a legacy to:
   'The Royal Society for the Protection of Cruelty to Animals';

✦ whilst the will of another tried to leave a fortune to:
   'The Royal Society for the Prevention of Birds'.

For these, and other amusing will quotes, go to: **http://www.thewillsite.co.uk/wills.php**

Summary

◆ In order for a trust to be valid the three certainties must be present. These are: certainty of intention, subject and object.

◆ Certainty of intention will be proved where it is certain that it was the intention of the settlor to create a trust. Precatory words will usually not be sufficient evidence of certainty of intention.

◆ There will be certainty of subject matter so long as the settlor has given an adequate description of the subject matter of the trust. Extra care should be taken when describing shares of property.

◆ The test for certainty of object will depend on whether the trust is fixed or discretionary. With a fixed trust, a 'complete list' of beneficiaries must be drawn up; with a discretionary trust, the trustees have only to determine whether a proposed beneficiary 'is or is not' a member of the class of objects.

◆ There are three areas of difficulty with the wording of a trust which may lead to uncertainty. These are: conceptual uncertainty; evidential uncertainty and administrative unworkability. Whilst evidential uncertainty can often be overcome, both conceptual uncertainty and administrative unworkability will inevitably lead to the failure of the trust.

Question and answer*

Problem: Take another look at the will of Shirley from You be the judge, earlier in the chapter. Now, using the knowledge you have acquired from reading this chapter, comment on the validity of all four clauses, citing the relevant authorities to support your argument. You may assume for the purpose of this question that Shirley owns only one cottage and one pair of diamond earrings.

You should allow yourself no more than 40 minutes to complete this task.

Essay: 'Any lay person seeking to write their own will is stumbling upon a minefield of uncertainty. This is one task which should definitely be left to the professionals.' Comment on this statement with reference to the three certainties.

This question should be answered in 40 minutes.

✱ Answer guidance is provided at the end of the chapter.

Further reading

Ellis, M. and Verrill, L. (2007) 'Twilight trusts', _Insolvency Intelligence_, 20(10), 151–9.
A really useful and interesting article detailing the practical implications of companies trading on the verge of insolvency and the use of trusts to ring-fence customer monies.

Hardcastle, I.M. (1990) 'Administrative unworkability – a reassessment of an abiding problem', Conv (Jan/Feb), 24–33.
This article, whilst not very recent, still gives a good overview of administrative unworkability, putting

forward an interesting argument that it is just an extension of evidential uncertainty.

Parkinson, P. (2002) 'Reconceptualising the express trust', CLJ, 61(3), 657–83.
This article gives an in-depth discussion of the meaning of the trust in a modern context, with particular emphasis given to the issue of certainty of subject matter.

Thomas, G. (2001) 'A test of (un)certainty', _Trusts and Estates Law Journal_, 26, 11–14.
A nice, concise article dealing with discretionary trusts and the issue of conceptual uncertainty.

Question and answer guidance

Problem:

1. I give £50,000 to my friend Elizabeth, which I desire should be divided equally between my children and grandchildren.

Subject and object are both certain: subject matter being the £50,000, and objects being the children and grandchildren. The class of objects 'children and grandchildren' is conceptually certain: the terms mean the same thing to all people. Intention to create a trust is uncertain, however. Use of the precatory words 'I desire' does not impose a sufficiently imperative element on the trust, suggesting that Shirley is making an outright gift to Elizabeth, with only an expression of desire – imposing a moral, but not a legal obligation on Elizabeth to pass the money on to the children and grandchildren (_Re Diggles_).

2. I leave the cottage to my cousin John, wishing that he should give it to the most deserving of my sons.

As we have seen above, the subject matter of 'the cottage' could cause difficulty if Shirley had more than one cottage. However, we are told that she has only one, so subject matter can be said to be certain. Again, the use of precatory words 'wishing that' preclude the creation of a trust (_Re Hamilton_), the result being that the cottage will be construed as an outright gift to cousin John (we assume there is only one cousin called 'John'). Even if the trust had not failed for certainty of intention, it would certainly fail for certainty of object. Who is to say who Shirley considers to be 'the most deserving' of her sons? If discretion had been given to John to decide which of Shirley's sons were the most deserving, this would have saved the trust.

3. I give my favourite diamond earrings to my sister Dorothy, in the hope that she will pass them on to my eldest daughter on her coming of age.

Certainty of subject matter may have been a problem if Shirley had more than one pair of diamond earrings – who is to say which were her favourites? However, we are told she has only one pair of diamond earrings. Again, the trust would fail on the basis of the precatory words 'in the hope that', resulting in an outright gift of the earrings to Dorothy. However, there may have been difficulty with the object, in any event. The term 'eldest daughter' is conceptually certain, even though she is not specifically named. However, there is a question as to whether

Shirley was referring to the gift being given to her daughter on her legal or traditional coming of age (18 or 21), or did she simply mean when she was old enough to be responsible for them. In all likelihood the court would construe this as meaning Shirley's daughter's legal coming of age, 18, on the basis that the common interpretation of the term for most people would be the age of 18.

4. *I give the rest of my estate to be divided equally between the current members of the Alderton Flower Arrangers' Guild in memory of the many happy hours I spent there.*

Subject matter' 'the rest of my estate', should not pose a problem as it is an exclusive description, referring to everything in Shirley's estate other than the other gifts made under the terms of the will. The term 'estate' is a legal term referring to the whole of a person's assets on death. This is an outright gift so intention is not an issue. The object of the trust are the current members of the Alderton Flower Arrangers' Guild. The gift is to be shared equally between the members so a complete list will need to be drawn up of the current members (*IRC* v. *Broadway*). This may cause evidential difficulties if there are not accurate records of who the current members are, but there should be a list of current members which would get around any problem here.

Essay: This essay title is looking for an explanation of why will-writing should be left to the professionals (if you agree with the statement).

As the question is asking for the student to refer to the three certainties a good answer would introduce the reader to the three certainties of intention, subject matter and object, and then take them briefly through the difficulties and pitfalls which may be encountered by a lay person in attempting to draft each one. For example, the student might say that certainty of subject matter can be problematic if the testator is trying to leave shares in something. They might then go on to explain what the difficulty is with shares and why careful drafting is essential to avoid failure of the gift.

One point which it would be particularly important for the student to make would be the effect on a purported gift in the event that it failed for uncertainty. Remember that the effect will be different dependent upon the grounds for the failure for the gift: in the event that the gift fails for uncertainty of intention, the effect will be that of an outright gift to the trustees. With a failure for uncertainty of subject matter or object, however, the gift will either revert into the residue of the will and will be divided with the rest of the estate, or if the failure is of a gift of residue, this might result in the gift being distributed in accordance with the rules on intestacy. Either way, the testator's gift will be unlikely to reach its intended recipient.

For additional marks, reference could be made to Fay Copeland's People in the law article above (see p. 42), which gives some really useful comment on the problems encountered by the writers of wills and would give the essay currency. (see p. 42)

In conclusion, the student should agree or disagree with the quotation, perhaps summarising or referring very briefly to the dangers encountered in drafting wills.

Visit **www.mylawchamber.co.uk/warner-reed** to access study support resources including practice exam questions with guidance, interactive 'You be the judge' multiple choice questions, annotated weblinks, glossary and key case flashcards and audio legal updates all linked to the **Pearson eText** version of *Equity and Trusts* which you can **search**, **highlight** and **personalise** with your **own notes** and **bookmarks**.

Use Case Navigator to read in full some of the key cases referenced in this chapter with commentary and questions:

McPhail* v. *Doulton [1970] 2 All ER 228

Chapter 4
Purpose trusts

Key points In this chapter we will be looking at:

- ✦ The nature of purpose trusts
- ✦ Difficulties with the validity of purpose trusts
- ✦ Exceptions to the general rule against purpose trusts
- ✦ Avoiding purpose trusts
- ✦ Gifts to unincorporated associations

Introduction

So far we have been concerned purely with the **settlor** putting money or property into **trust** for the benefit of a person or specified group of persons. But a settlor may not always want to benefit a person: he may want his money to be used for some other purpose instead. This chapter is concerned with such circumstances.

What is a purpose trust?

A **purpose trust**, as its name would suggest, is a trust which exists in order to carry out a specific purpose, as opposed to the usual form of trust which exists for the benefit of a person or group of persons. There are any number of purposes for which you may wish to set up a trust, but the following example may help to put the subject into context:

Let us imagine that you are writing your will. Think about what you would like it to contain. Apart from the usual gifts to family and friends and any charitable donations you may wish to make, is there anything else you wish to consider? You may own a pet you want to ensure is cared for after you are gone; or maybe you would like to leave behind some kind of memorial by which you will be remembered. This might be a plaque in your local place of worship or at a favourite old haunt; something more practical such as a bench or bandstand; or you may have even grander plans: perhaps you would like to have an elaborate tomb built to house your remains, for example. You may also wish to leave something to the sports or social club of which you are a member. Is there anything they particularly need money for: a new sports pitch, perhaps, or even a new club house?

The Writing and drafting feature is designed to get you thinking about the types of purposes you may wish to put your own money to in the future. Why not have a go?

Writing and drafting

Bearing in mind the types of things listed in the text, now have a go at writing your own simple will. You should not need to spend more than 30 minutes on this.

Don't worry if you are not a member of any sports or social clubs, or if you don't own a pet; you can use these as examples, or have a bit of fun and simply use your imagination. Just think about who or what you would like your money to benefit and go from there.

Remember, the aim of this exercise is not to create the perfect legal document, but only to get you thinking about the types of gifts you may wish to incorporate in it. Your will therefore does not have to be technically correct: it is the thought that counts!

 Handy tip: Not sure where to start? Most lawyers use precedents, or templates, to help them when they are creating a new document: it saves them from having to write the whole thing from scratch every time. There are many will precedents available online which vary in length and quality. Alternatively, if you prefer to use a more traditional method to find your will template, the library should have plenty to choose from; the *Encyclopaedia of Forms and Precedents* is a good place to look in the first instance.

If you are really stuck, take a look at the will of Helen Tabor in the extract below. You can use this as the basis for your own will.

Now, take a moment to read through the will you have drafted. It may look something like this:

THIS IS THE LAST WILL AND TESTAMENT of me, Helen Constance Tabor of 17 The Mount, Long Marton, Sinderfield, which I make this   day of   2010

1. I hereby revoke all former wills.

2. I appoint as my **executors** and **trustees** (hereinafter called 'my Trustees') my best friend Nicola Jane Saxby and my cousin Harry Neil Jensen.

3. I give £20,000 to my Trustees to hold a party for my family and friends in memory of all the good times we had together.

4. I give £500 to my Trustees to pay for a course of French lessons for my silver macaw, Gloria.

5. I give £10,000 for the maintenance of my tortoise, Clarence, whom I direct should be fed on a diet of freshly shelled garden peas for the rest of his days.

6. I give £10,000 to my Trustees for the erection of six drinking water fountains at strategic points in Sinderfield Park, where I liked to go jogging. Each fountain should be inscribed in my memory.

7. I give £20,000 for the continued maintenance of the trees, shrubs and flower beds at Sinderfield Park.

8. I give my house at 17 The Mount, Long Marton, Sinderfield to the Monster Raving Loony Party to use as their campaign headquarters.

9. I give the land and gardens to the rear of the aforementioned 17 The Mount to the Sinderfield Gardeners' Association for use as allotments by their members.

10. I give the residue of my estate to my trustees on the following trusts:
    a. To pay debts funeral and **executorship** expenses
    b. To divide what remains in their absolute discretion between:
       i. Long Marton Tennis Association
       ii. Sinderfield and District Cricket Club

Signed by the above-named
HELEN CONSTANCE TABOR
in our joint presence
and then by us in hers

If you examine the various clauses in the will, what you will see is that you have actually created a number of trusts, not for the benefit of people, but for purposes. In the example will above, these purposes include to teach a parrot French, to care for a pet tortoise, to provide drinking fountains in the park, and so on. It is purposes like these that we will be considering throughout the course of this chapter.

Problems with purpose trusts

The will of Helen Tabor may look fairly straightforward. She is simply attempting to provide for those causes dearest to her heart. It is perhaps surprising, then, that attempts by settlors to leave money in trust for a specified use or purpose have always given the English judiciary a certain amount of difficulty. The primary reason for this is that, whilst at first glance common sense would seem to dictate that a settlor should be able to dispose of his fortune however he wishes, purpose trusts are in reality a particularly vulnerable form of trust and open to abuse by their trustees. This is so much the case that the courts have traditionally been reluctant to accept the validity of purpose trusts in England and Wales and, to this day, purpose trusts are actually considered to be an invalid form of trust in English law, save for a few hand-picked exceptions.

> purpose trusts are a particularly vulnerable form of trust

The beneficiary principle

Why so vulnerable? It all comes down to the ability of the **beneficiary** of the trust fund to protect their interest. With an ordinary trust there is always a human beneficiary, a person for whose benefit the trust exists, whereas with a purpose trust there is merely the purpose for which it has been created. This is, at best, an abstract entity which has no champion or enforcer. In practical terms this means that if the trustees do not act in the best interests of an ordinary trust there is always someone on whose behalf the trust can be enforced: that is, the beneficiary or their representatives. However, with a purpose trust, if the trust fund monies are not used for their proper purpose, or if the trustees are not running the trust properly, there may be no one who is willing or, indeed, who has the authority to take the necessary court action to enforce it. So, for example, Gloria the parrot from our sample will above has no legal standing to enforce her rights as the beneficiary of a trust; equally, if the trustees do not use money left by Helen under the terms of the will to erect the six drinking fountains in Sinderfield Park, there is no one else who has authority to ensure that her wishes are carried out. On the other hand, if Helen had left the money to her old French teacher rather than to her parrot, provided the teacher was adequately described, there would be no difficulty in enforcing the trust for the teacher's benefit.

In order to counter the sheer difficulty of enforcing purpose trusts, the courts established a rule that any trust must have a human beneficiary in order to be valid. This rule, which is often referred to as the '**beneficiary principle**', had the sweeping effect of rendering all purpose trusts **void**. The rule was first set out in the case of *Morice* v. *Bishop of Durham* [1805] 10 Ves 522, which we came across previously in Chapter 3 in the section on certainty of objects. You may remember that the case concerned an attempt by a **testatrix** to create a trust of money to be used in favour of: 'such objects of benevolence and liberality as the Bishop of Durham in his own discretion shall most approve of . . .' The court held that the trust was void for uncertainty of **object**. Sir William Grant, Master of the Rolls, in justifying the court's position, stated that the very nature of a trust was that it should be enforceable. Without the ability to enforce the trust, it would simply become 'a gift to the trustees to keep or dispose of at will'. This is the essence of the beneficiary principle: in order for the trust to be valid, there must be somebody in whose favour the court can decree performance.

Now take a look at the You be the judge feature to test your understanding of the beneficiary principle.

Case Summary

You be the judge

Q: Take another look at clause 3 of Helen Tabor's will, above. You may remember that it reads as follows:

I give £20,000 to my Trustees to hold a party for my family and friends in memory of all the good times we had together.

On the basis of the beneficiary principle, would this be a valid clause?

A: No. The trust is for an abstract purpose (the purpose being to throw a party) and not for the benefit of an individual and so, in accordance with the beneficiary principle, will fail.

The beneficiary principle has been more recently addressed in the case of *Re Astor's Settlement Trusts* [1952] Ch 534, which involved a **lifetime trust** created by Viscount Astor in 1945. The trust directed that all the issued shares of his company, The Observer Limited (which owned *The Observer* newspaper), should be put into trust and their income used for, amongst other things, 'the maintenance of good understanding, sympathy and cooperation between the nations' and 'the preservation of the independence and integrity of newspapers', purposes which were particularly pertinent in 1945, in the context of post-war Britain. Following the beneficiary principle, Mr Justice Roxburgh was clear in stating that the trust should fail. In spite of Lord Astor's noble intentions, the trust had been set up for specified purposes and not for the benefit of human individuals. It is perhaps worth noting that these very wide abstract ideals would have proved very difficult to maintain in any event.

Case Summary

Exceptions to the rule

We have established that, as a general rule, purpose trusts are invalid and that any purported trust for a purpose will fail. But the courts have on rare occasion made an exception and allowed a purpose trust to stand. These few exceptional cases in which the general principle has been waived can be categorised broadly as:

✦ the 'animals' cases;

✦ the 'tombs and monuments' cases; and

✦ 'trusts for the saying of masses'.

The 'animals' cases

Working on the basis of the beneficiary principle set out above, it follows that if a trust without a human beneficiary cannot be valid, a trust with an animal beneficiary must automatically fail. Thus, as we have seen in our example will, the gift to Gloria the silver macaw would fail and the pampered parrot would not get her French lessons. However, whilst a direct gift to an animal will fail under the beneficiary principle, the courts have chosen to make an exception in the case of purpose trusts which are made for the *maintenance* of a specific animal, or animals.

What is the reason for this? Probably quite simply because the United Kingdom is a nation of animal lovers and it would go against the grain if the courts were to disallow a person's wish to provide for a much-loved pet in the event of their death. Indeed, Mr Justice Roxburgh, in *Re Astor's Settlement Trusts* famously quoted such cases as being nothing more than 'concessions to human weakness or sentiment'. The Law in action feature gives some interesting examples of the kind of gifts people have made to benefit pets in their wills.

Law in action

In 2007 New York's notorious property billionairess and celebrated 'Queen of Mean' Leona Helmsley made the headlines of newspapers worldwide when she died leaving a mammoth $12 million fortune to her Maltese bitch, Trouble. Trouble shared a home with Mrs Helmsley in the penthouse of a Manhattan hotel, feasting daily on a diet of gourmet foods prepared by the hotel chefs and hand-fed to her by the staff.

But Leona's decision to favour her beloved dog above all others was not as unusual as you might think. A substantial number of animal lovers every

Source: Corel Corporation

year make often quite generous allowances in their wills to provide for their pets in the event of their death. In 2002, the actress Drew Barrymore placed her £3 million Beverly Hills home in trust for her dog, Flossie, after she claimed the animal saved her and her husband from a house fire.

Pop icon Dusty Springfield also left her pet a **legacy**. Dusty's cat, Nicholas, was left a lifetime supply of his favourite brand of baby food. The singer also directed that her old dressing gown should be used to line the animal's basket and a medley of her songs played to him at night to help him to sleep.

And it is not just rich and famous Americans who give their pets inheritances. In 2002, childless widow Margaret Layne left her three-bedroomed house in the London Borough of Harrow, worth an estimated £350,000, to her favourite cat Tinker, together with £100,000 for his care. Tinker's designated carers, a Mr and Mrs Wheatley, will inherit the house and any remaining money on Tinker's death, or if Tinker goes missing for a 'reasonable time'.

For the latest information on the world's richest pets, go to: http://www.petplan.co.uk/contactus/press/affluent_pets.asp.

So what is included in the maintenance of an animal? One can assume that it includes feeding and watering the animal, and providing it with a home or shelter; it may also include veterinary bills for that animal. Does it, though, include allowing that animal the opportunity to breed and, if so, who makes the decision for it as to how many times it breeds and what happens to its offspring? The trust, after all, has been set up to provide for the care of only one animal.

There is also the question of how much money is required to maintain a specific animal. If the **testator** requires that a dog should live out its days in a penthouse apartment in Beverly Hills, or that a cat should be fed exclusively on a diet of wild salmon freshly caught in the Scottish Highlands, who is to say that this is excessive and at what point, if any, will the courts intervene? We have seen that there are an increasing number of cases of this kind, not just in England and Wales, but across the globe, and this raises the question, exactly where should the English legal system draw the line? Alternatively, one might ask whether the judiciary should be allowed to interfere with the wishes of the testator at all.

There are two main legal authorities for purpose trusts for the maintenance of specific animals, both of which date back to the 1800s. In the case of *Pettinghall* v. *Pettinghall* (1842) 11 LJ Ch 176, a testator left a gift to his favourite black mare in the following terms:

Case Summary

I hereby **bequeath**, that at my death, £50 per annum be paid for her keep in some park in England or Wales; her shoes to be taken off, and she never to be ridden or put in harness; and that my executor consider himself in honour bound to fulfil my wish, and see that she will be well provided for, and removable at his will. At her death all payment to cease.

The gift was upheld by the court, albeit with very strict requirements imposed on the executor as to the maintenance of the horse, and with the right reserved to the beneficiaries of the remainder of the testator's **estate** to claim the trust money if it transpired that the horse was not being properly cared for.

A similar result was achieved in the later case of *Re Dean* (1889) 41 Ch D 552, in which a testator purported to leave sufficient money in trust to allow a sum of £750 per year to be used for the maintenance of his horses, ponies and hounds over a period of 50 years, 'should any of them live that long'.

Case Summary

It should be noted that there is a subtle difference between actually giving money to an animal, and the setting up of a purpose trust the purpose of which is to maintain that animal during its lifetime. Whilst the latter is possible under the above exception, the former is of course not possible in English law, animals not possessing the legal capacity to own property of any kind.

It is also important to recognise the difference between a trust for private purposes and public or charitable purposes. A trust which might fail as a **private purpose trust** might still be a valid **public purpose trust**, or charitable trust, if, for example, the trust is for the benefit of animals in general and not one specific animal. Charitable trusts will be discussed in more detail in Chapter 5.

The rule against perpetuities

Despite allowing purpose trusts for the maintenance of specific animals, the courts have been careful to construe the exception fairly narrowly and without offending other equitable principles. One such principle is the **rule against perpetuities**. The rule against perpetuities is a **common law** rule which prevents a person from putting provisions into effect which will continue to control or affect the distribution of assets long after they have died. As a matter of **public policy**, the courts do not like to see money tied up in trust indefinitely. To allow large sums of money to be out of circulation for long periods of time restricts the free flow of the economy and so goes against the public interest. The rule against perpetuities therefore states that, even if a purpose trust falls within one of the rare exceptions allowed by the courts, the trust will still fail if it purports to tie up money in the trust fund for a period exceeding the '**perpetuity period**'. In relation to trusts, the perpetuity period is the longest period the courts will allow a trust to remain in existence.

> the courts do not like to see money tied up in trust indefinitely

Rather than being limited to a fixed term of years, the perpetuity period is traditionally limited to 21 years after the death of the last identifiable individual living at the time the interest was created. This is known as the '**life in being**'. The life in being will usually be the beneficiary of the interest. However, in the case of a purpose trust, there is no human beneficiary against whom the length of the trust can be measured. This means that the longest period of time for which a purpose trust can be allowed to continue is just 21 years.

As perpetuity is measured against human lives, the life of an animal will not apply. In the Irish case of *Re Kelly* [1932] IR 255, when a hopeful barrister tried to put forward the life of a greyhound as representing a life in being, Mr Justice Meredith made the opinion of the judiciary abundantly clear, famously stating that: 'There can be no doubt that "lives" means lives of human beings, not animals or trees in California.'

In order not to fall foul of the perpetuity rule, the perpetuity period must either be stated expressly in the **trust instrument** (by saying 'this trust shall expire at the end of 21 years', for example) or, by virtue of careful wording, limited to the maximum period the law will allow. Wording which has been accepted by the courts as creating a valid purpose trust include the following:

✦ 'so long as the law for the time being permitted.' (*Pirbright* v. *Salwey* [1896] WN 86)

✦ 'so far as they can legally do so and . . . for as long as may be practicable.' (*Re Hooper* [1932] 1 Ch 38)

The requirement for explicit wording in respect of the perpetuity period is generally interpreted strictly by the courts. It is clear from the case of *Re Compton* [1946] 1 All ER 117, in which a testatrix attempted to create a trust to continue 'for ever' in favour of certain children, that the courts will not be willing to allow a longer stated period in a

Case Summary

Case Summary

trust instrument to be reduced to 21 years, simply to allow a gift to remain valid. This means that a trust for 30 years would simply be held invalid, rather than the courts reducing the period of the trust to 21 years so that it could continue. Equally, a trust instrument which is silent as to the length of its duration may be viewed as an attempt to create a trust in perpetuity and thus fail. This was what happened in the case of *Mussett* v. *Bingle* (1876) WN 170, which concerned an attempt to create a trust for the maintenance of a family tomb. The full details of this case can be seen below.

If this is the case, how is it then that North J, in *Re Dean*, held as valid a purported 50-year purpose trust for the care of horses and hounds? Some would say that North J took **judicial notice** of the fact that the trust could not possibly last beyond the end of the perpetuity period ('judicial notice' meaning the court's acceptance of a well-known fact without the necessity of proof). This was the case in *Re Haines*, which was reported in *The Times* on 7 November 1952 and in which a woman's gift to her cats was held valid on the basis that cats do not live past the age of 21. But, as it is a fact that horses commonly live into their thirties, considerably longer on average than the 21-year period allowed by the perpetuity rule, it is arguable that *Re Dean* was a wayward decision, particularly in the light of *Re Compton*, above. Either way, this is clearly a matter which should be approached with caution and considered carefully on the facts of each case. A settlor wishing to set up a trust for the maintenance of an animal would be advised to take care to limit the length of the trust to no longer than 21 years.

This strict interpretation of the perpetuity period also brings up another issue in relation to trusts for the maintenance of animals. A gift by a testator for the maintenance of a specific animal, for example '£5,000 for the care of my beloved Persian cat, Esmerelda', is perfectly straightforward. The money is put into trust for that animal's care and that animal alone. However, what if the gift was for 'the working dogs of Hill Beck Farm'? The gift would have to be limited to all those dogs working on the farm at the time of the testator's death. If the gift included any dogs working on the farm at any time in the future, this would have the effect of rendering the gift void on the basis that it offended the perpetuity rule. A gift for the 'working dogs of Hill Beck Farm and their offspring' would also have the effect of rendering the gift invalid for perpetuity purposes, as there would be no way of telling when the trust would end.

The rule against perpetuities at common law has been much amended by statute. Major alterations to the common law rule in England and Wales came into effect on 6 April 2010, under the new Perpetuities and Accumulations Act 2009. However, section 18 provides that the provisions of the Act do not extend to private purpose trusts and therefore the perpetuity period in respect of all such cases continues to be limited to a life or lives in being plus 21 years. Further discussion of the Perpetuities and Accumulations Act 2009 is beyond the scope of this book

The 'tombs and monuments' cases

As with the animal cases, the courts have allowed certain exceptions in the case of the erection and maintenance of tombs and monuments.

Erection of tombs and monuments

The exception which allows a testator to leave money for the erection of a tomb or monument is a settled area of the law, and appears to be a relatively straightforward exception.

This can be shown in two cases: that of *Trimmer* v. *Danby* (1856) 25 LJ Ch 424 and *Mussett* v. *Bingle* (1876) WN 170, which we came across earlier in the chapter. In the case of *Trimmer* v. *Danby*, the courts upheld a purpose trust for the erection of a monument in St Paul's Cathedral in memory of the testator. Similarly, twenty years later, in the case of *Mussett* v. *Bingle*, a testator who made a gift of £300 for the erection of a monument in memory of his wife's first husband was held to be valid.

An initial point which can be noted from these cases is that it is irrelevant whether the tomb or monument is for the testator themselves or for some other person, the gift in *Trimmer* v. *Danby* being in memory of the testator, and the gift in *Mussett* v. *Bingle* being in memory of the first husband of the testator's wife. It should also be noted that the monument to be erected does not necessarily have to be in a church or churchyard. There are considerably fewer cases on the issue but, in the 1889 case of *Re Dean*, which concerned a purported gift for the maintenance of animals, as we have seen above, Mr Justice North remarked that a trust to build a memorial on unconsecrated ground would be valid. Presumably on this basis money left for the placing of a park bench or bandstand in a public park would be an acceptable form of purpose trust, subject to the necessary consents from the local authority. Indeed, in a small village in south Devon, one of its parishioners recently left a sum of money to the local church for the building of a public convenience in his memory 'so that he would continue to be of daily use to his parish'.

Having said this, the courts are nevertheless keen to adhere to public policy when allowing the existence of such purpose trusts, and if they have, in the past, considered a purported memorial to be little more than the lavish whim of a wealthy testator they have been quick to strike it down. This was so in the Scottish cases of *McCaig* v. *University of Glasgow* (1904) 41 SLR 700 and *McCaig's Trustees* v. *Kirk-Session etc.* (1915) SC 426 which concerned the wills of John Stuart McCaig and his unmarried sister, Catherine. In the first will, Mr McCaig left the whole of his fortune to be used in the building of various towers and statues of himself, his parents, brothers and sisters in various locations on his estate in Oban, Scotland; and, in the second will, Miss McCaig purported to leave a substantial amount of money for the erection of bronze statues in memory of her mother and father and their nine children, not costing less than £1,000 each. In both cases the courts held the trusts to be invalid, Lord Kyllachy in the first case likening the purported trust to '[turning] the income of the estate into money, and throw[ing] the money yearly into the sea'.

One can, perhaps, understand Lord Kyllachy's sentiment, but one could question whether a man's decision as to how he chooses to distribute his own wealth can be a matter of public policy at all. Surely, as a man is entitled during the course of his lifetime to dwindle away his fortune at the gambling tables or to back a poor investment, then he should be able, essentially, to spend his money as he chooses on his death. In any event, the decisions remain controversial.

Maintenance of tombs and monuments

Purpose trusts for the *maintenance* of tombs and monuments prove a little more problematic than trusts for the building of them. The reason for this is, again, the issue of perpetuity. As with the animal cases, a monument can only be maintained under a purpose trust for a maximum period of 21 years without offending the perpetuity rule.

In the case of *Pirbright* v. *Salwey* [1896], £800 was given to the rector of the parish to use the income for the upkeep of a grave. A trust to maintain the grave for an unlimited period would have been invalid on grounds of perpetuity. However, the trusts were saved by the stipulation in the will that the money should be used by the trustees for such purposes only for 'so long as the law for the time being permitted'. This allowed the court to put a positive interpretation on the wording of the trust and hold that it should continue for the duration of the 21-year perpetuity period allowed by law.

A similar outcome was reached in the case of *Re Hooper* [1932] 1 Ch 38. Mr Hooper had left £1,000 to the trustees of his will for the upkeep of, amongst other things, a grave and monument in Torquay cemetery; a vault containing the remains of his wife and daughter and a grave and monument to his son at Shotley churchyard near Ipswich. Again, there was a stipulation in the will, this time that the money should be used 'only so far as they can legally do so and . . . for as long as may be practicable'. The court accepted this as creating a valid 21-year purpose trust.

Case Summary

Conversely in the 1876 case of *Mussett* v. *Bingle*, whereas we have seen above that the gift of £300 for the *erection* of a monument in the testator's memory was allowed, a further gift of £200 left in the will for its *maintenance* was held to be invalid, because no finite time period for its maintenance had been stated.

Whilst a 21-year perpetuity period is long enough to ensure the continued maintenance of most domestic animals during their lifetimes, when the purpose in question is the maintenance of a tomb or monument in a person's memory, this might not seem very long. So is there anything else testators can do to ensure the upkeep of their grave or memorial for as long a period as possible?

Royal lives clauses

One way of doing it would be to specify within the trust instrument a human life, or life in being, against which the length of the trust was to be measured. In the case of *Re Khoo Cheng Teow* (1932) Straits Settlements Reports 226, a purpose trust stated to continue for the duration of the longest to survive of 'Her Majesty Queen Victoria and her descendents now living . . . and [for] the period of twenty-one years after the death of such survivor' was held to be valid on this basis. This kind of clause is aptly known as a '**royal lives clause**'. The later case of *Re Astor*, which we came across earlier in the chapter, also contained a royal lives clause, this time specifying as the duration of the trust 20 years after the death of the last descendant of the late King George V who had been living at the date of the settlement. Had the outcome of the case been that the trusts were valid (you will remember they failed for not having a human beneficiary), this in fact means that the trusts would have continued until 20 years after the death of the King's granddaughter, the current Queen Elizabeth II, who was 19 years old at the date of the settlement. The trust would therefore still be in existence.

Case Summary

Case Summary

Charitable purposes

Alternatively it may be possible to use a *charitable* purpose trust to ensure the continued upkeep of your tomb or monument. On the basis of the beneficiary principle described above, one might think that trusts for charitable purposes would also fall foul of the principle, as they too are for the benefit of a purpose and not a person. However, this is not the case. Charitable trusts *do* have someone to ensure that the trust is administered correctly on their behalf and that is the Attorney-General, who acts as the 'enforcer' of all charitable trusts (for more information on charitable trusts see Chapter 5 on charities).

But how can a private purpose gain the protection of a charitable trust? There are two methods.

First, under some circumstances a trust for the maintenance of a tomb or monument may be seen as charitable. In the case of *Re Hooper* [1932], a gift of money to trustees for the care and upkeep of a tablet and window in a church, to the memory of various members of Mr Hooper's family, was held to be charitable because it enhanced the fabric of the church. Under the current law, the maintenance of religious buildings is included under the heading 'advancement of religion' under section 2(2)(c) of the Charities Act 2006 (again, for more detail on this point see Chapter 5 on charities).

Equally, if a testator were to leave money to maintain the whole of the churchyard where he is to be buried, rather than just leaving money for the maintenance of his own grave, this would come under the same charitable head. These were the facts in the case of *Re Vaughan* (1886) 33 Ch D 187. Thus, if the gift will help to maintain the whole or part of the religious site which houses the tomb or monument, the purpose trust may be allowed to exist indefinitely on charitable grounds.

The second method by which a testator could ensure the long-term maintenance of his tomb is by making a gift to charity conditional on its upkeep. This is exactly what happened in the nineteenth-century case of *Re Tyler* [1891] 3 Ch 252, in which Mr Tyler left the quite substantial sum of £42,000 to the London Missionary Society on the condition that, should they fail to keep his family vault in good repair, the money should go instead to another named charity.

Note, however, that a testator must word his gift carefully so as not to invalidate it. If the condition could be construed by the courts as putting a *positive* obligation on the charity to maintain the tomb, this would amount to an attempt to create a perpetual purpose trust and would in consequence fail. In *Re Tyler*, the will merely stated that the London Missionary Society would lose the gift if it *failed* to maintain the tomb. Here the gift was upheld: there was no positive obligation for the tomb's upkeep. However, in the contrasting case of *Re Dalziel* [1943] Ch 277, where a testatrix gave £20,000 to St Bart's Hospital in London subject to the condition that the income from the trust be used to maintain a mausoleum in Highgate Cemetery, the gift was held to be void. The testatrix had required the income to be used for the upkeep of the mausoleum and in doing so had created a purpose trust for its maintenance. As there was no time limit put on the obligation to maintain, the trust offended the perpetuity rule and failed.

Parish Councils and Burial Authorities (Miscellaneous Provisions) Act 1970

Finally, there is one method of ensuring the upkeep of a tomb for a substantial period of time without resorting to the use of purpose trusts at all. This is under the Parish Councils and Burial Authorities (Miscellaneous Provisions) Act 1970. Section 1 of this Act enables a person during their lifetime to enter into a contract with their local council or the relevant authority in return for the payment of a sum of money to maintain a grave, memorial or monument for a period of not greater than 99 years.

Other exceptions to the rule

There are two other instances where trusts for private purposes have been held valid by the courts, and these are trusts for the saying of private masses and the singular case of *Re Thompson* [1934] 1 Ch 342.

Trusts for the saying of private masses

It is a tradition of the Catholic Church, as it is with many other faiths, to honour their dead by saying prayers, or masses, for them. It is therefore not uncommon for testators to stipulate in their wills that masses be said either for them on their death, or for some other member of their family. As with trusts for the maintenance of tombs and monuments, provided that a purpose trust for the saying of private masses for the dead is limited in duration to the perpetuity period, it will be valid. This was the case in *Bourne* v. *Keane* [1919] AC 815 in which an Irish Roman Catholic testator left substantial sums of money to both Westminster Cathedral and the Jesuit Fathers for the saying of masses for his soul. Whilst the Court of Appeal in this case had ruled that the gifts should be void as gifts for 'superstitious uses', the House of Lords overturned the ruling and held both gifts to be valid. The case of *Re Khoo Cheng Teow*, which we came across in the context of royal lives clauses earlier in the chapter, also concerned a gift for the performance of religious ceremonies: this time a form of ancestor worship called Sin Chew to perpetuate the testator's memory. Again, the gift was upheld by the Supreme Court of the Straits Settlement as it had been properly limited to the perpetuity period.

It should be noted that both the saying of masses and the celebration of any other religious services in public will come under the heading of purposes for the 'advancement of religion' under section 2(2)(c) of the Charities Act 2006 and thus be valid charitable purposes. There is therefore no need to limit the duration of a purpose trust for the conduct of religious services for the general public. The exception will still apply to the saying of masses in private, however. For more detail on charitable purposes students should refer to the following chapter on charities.

Re Thompson [1934]

In the case of *Re Thompson* [1934] 1 Ch 342, a gift 'for the furtherance and promotion of fox-hunting' was held to be valid. Fox-hunting was of course legal in 1934; today, such a purpose trust would almost certainly fail as its purpose would be illegal under the Hunting Act 2004. For further discussion on this point see the discussion on purpose trusts which offend public policy, below.

Expanding the list of exceptions

As we have seen, the list of exceptions to the general rule that purpose trusts are invalid is a small one, limited only to trusts for the maintenance of specific animals, trusts for the erection and maintenance of tombs and monuments and trusts for the saying of religious masses in private. Arguably the fourth exception, of trusts for the promotion of fox-hunting, would no longer stand for public policy reasons (see below).

Is there any likelihood of this list ever being expanded, however? The short answer is no: Lord Justice Harman made the view of the judiciary on this point quite clear in *Re Endacott* [1960] Ch 232. The case concerned the will of Albert Endacott. Mr Endacott had tried to leave a gift of his **residuary estate** to North Tawton Devon Parish Council 'for the purpose of providing some useful memorial to myself'. The court did not allow Mr Endacott's memorial on the basis that it offended the beneficiary principle, being for a purpose and having no human beneficiary. Clearly, the court did not feel that 'some useful memorial to myself' was certain enough in its terms to allow the gift to fall within the exception of trusts for the creation of tombs and monuments. The case has particular relevance here because, in making his judgment in the case, Lord Justice Harman commented on the position regarding the exceptions to the rule against purpose trusts. He stated that:

> these cases stand by themselves and ought not be increased in number, nor indeed followed, except where one is exactly like another.

Case Summary

Such is the dislike of the courts of purpose trusts that Lord Justice Harman even went on to suggest, referring to the existing exceptions, that it would be better if 'some authority should now say those cases were wrong'. Certainly attempts to create trusts for purposes which fall outside the three categories of valid purpose trust have been struck down by the courts without hesitation. See, in this respect, the case of *Re Shaw* [1957] 1 All ER 745, in which a gift for the creation of a 40-letter alphabet was denied on the basis that it did not form a valid exception to the rule against purpose trusts; and also the case of *Re Astor*, in which the court confirmed that any gift made outside the existing categories of exception would fail.

Key stats

Despite the courts' dislike of purpose trusts as a vehicle for the giving of money to abstract purposes, they nevertheless continue to be popular with the general public.

During April 2006 James Brown, senior lecturer in property law at London Metropolitan University, carried out a survey across 100 firms of solicitors in England and Wales, asking a number of questions in order to ascertain the extent to which purpose trusts are used and employed on a day-to-day basis by probate practitioners. The results, as published in his article entitled 'What are we to do with testamentary trusts of imperfect obligation?' (Brown 2007), were as follows:

Percentage of clients wishing to make a provision in their wills:

✦ for the purpose of maintaining an animal	53.00
✦ for the erection and maintenance of tombs and monuments	37.25
✦ for the saying of prayers or other religious ceremony or ritual in private	7.80
✦ for the promotion and furtherance of fox-hunting	0.00

The trusts, Mr Brown reports, were made for varying amounts of money, ranging from £100 to substantially larger sums of more than £10,000.

Other potential problems with purpose trusts

We have already seen that the issue of perpetuity is a potential source of difficulty when seeking to validate a purpose trust, even where it falls comfortably within one of the anomalous exceptions the courts will allow. However, there are certain other issues which we must briefly address as possible problem areas when looking at a purported trust for an abstract purpose.

Certainty

Over the course of the previous chapters we have looked in some detail at the creation of trusts and, in particular, the necessity that the three certainties of intention, **subject matter** and object, be present in order to form a valid trust. It is important for us to remember here that the issue of certainty must not be forgotten simply because we are dealing with purpose trusts and not ordinary

> the issue of certainty must not be forgotten

trusts. Thus, in the case of *Re Endacott*, considered above, a purported trust to build 'some useful memorial to myself' failed for lack of certainty of object. The same would apply to the animals cases: taking the example of the 'working dogs of Hill Beck Farm' we looked at earlier, it is necessary to ask what exactly 'working dogs' means. Does it include all the dogs that work on the farm; or is the reference to 'working dogs' merely a method of describing the class, or breed, of dog which will be included? One could also ask whether the phrase 'working dogs' should or would include a dog kept at the farm which had been retired from working due to old age or ill health.

Trusts which offend public policy

We have already seen in our discussion of the beneficiary principle that the courts are keen not to offend matters of public policy in allowing certain trusts to exist, but the taking of money out of general circulation is not the only public policy issue with which the courts are concerned.

The term 'public policy' can be described as the generally accepted public opinion concerning certain matters in the common interest. As such, it is something which may change in line with the social and moral norms or indeed the economic climate of the time. In relation to purpose trusts, any purported trust for purposes which were either illegal or which were considered immoral or capricious at the time of their creation would be struck down as being contrary to public policy.

Thus, in the case of *Re Thompson* [1934], whilst at the time the judgment was made fox-hunting was a perfectly acceptable pastime, in the current social climate fox-hunting for sport is banned under the Hunting Act 2004. An attempt to create a purpose trust for the furtherance of fox-hunting, hare coursing or any other kind of illegal hunt would today be an attempt to create a trust for illegal purposes and would therefore fail.

There is some question as to whether under the wording of the Act certain types of cull remain legal and that therefore purpose trusts under the *Re Thompson* umbrella should still be considered valid as purpose trusts. However, it is argued that, in the light of Lord Justice Harman's keenness to construe such cases narrowly and, given that current public opinion goes against hunting, any such purported trust would in any event fail were it to go before the courts.

As regards trusts for immoral purposes, this could be broadly interpreted to include any trust for a purpose which was considered unethical at the time of its making or which, in effect, pricked the public conscience. A good example of this is the case of *Brown* v. *Burdett* (1881) 21 Ch D 667 in which an attempt to create a trust to board up a house for 20 years was held by the courts to be invalid for public policy reasons. As well as serving no logical purpose, the trust offended the sensibilities of the public in general by purporting to lessen available housing stock for a substantial period of time.

Case Summary

Trusts for capricious purposes, or purposes which have no useful meaning, will also be viewed unfavourably. We have already seen an example of the courts striking down such trusts in the somewhat contentious *McCaig* cases, discussed above. However, the most infamous case rejected by the courts on the basis of its sheer capriciousness is that of *Re Shaw* [1957] 1 WLR 729. In this case George Bernard Shaw left money in his will to set up a trust to undertake research into the benefit of a new 40-letter phonetic alphabet which he hoped would, in due course, replace the standard 26-letter alphabet. The trust was, however, held to be void as a purpose trust on the basis that it was purely a whim of the playwright and of no meaningful use to anybody.

Avoiding purpose trusts: creative interpretation

The judiciary has been keen not to open the floodgates to an infinite number of private purpose trusts by allowing new categories of purpose trust to exist in exception to the general rule. However, there have been instances instead where, by creatively interpreting the wording of the trust, certain trusts for purposes have been allowed to continue under the guise of a trust for human benefit.

Gifts to a specified group of persons

If, looking at the wording of the trust, the courts can interpret the meaning of that trust as being for the benefit of a particular group of individuals, rather than for abstract purposes, it will be held valid. This is perhaps better explained by way of example. In the case of **Re Denley's Trust Deed** [1968] 3 All ER 65, an employer set up a trust to provide his employees with a sports ground. Construed as a trust for the purpose of providing recreational facilities the gift would have failed. The provision of a sports ground is an abstract purpose and would thus fall foul of the beneficiary principle. However, by choosing instead to interpret the gift not as a trust for an abstract purpose but rather as an outright gift to the employees of the company in existence at the time the trust was created, the court was able to allow the employer's gift to his employees to stand. And this is what they did.

But there are obvious problems with such a construction. It is clear from the wording of the trust instrument that the employer's intention was to create a purpose trust: the purpose being to provide a sports ground for the benefit of his employees. If the purported trust is instead construed as an outright gift to his employees, there is nothing to force the employees to use the money in the way in which the employer had envisaged. They could instead simply all decide to divide the money up between them and spend their individual shares on a new car or a holiday or whatever took their fancy. Surely, then, any decision to allow a purported purpose trust to stand on the basis of *Re Denley* puts the trust at serious risk of going against the true intention of the settlor; effectively relying on nothing other than the good conscience of the beneficiaries to use the money as the settlor had wanted. In the case of a gift to family members or close friends, there is perhaps some chance that the beneficiaries will decide to use the money in accordance with the settlor's wishes, but the likelihood of a diverse group of employees all sharing the same ideas and interests and all together wanting to use the money to buy a sports ground is slim.

This was not a line of reasoning taken in *Re Denley*, however, and the case has since been approved and followed in the later case of *Re Lipinski's Will Trusts* [1976] Ch 235, which concerned a gift by a testator of half of his residuary estate to the Hull Judeans (Maccabi) Association (a non-charitable **unincorporated association**), 'to be used solely in the work of constructing new buildings for the association and/or improvements in the said buildings'. The gift was held valid as a gift to the members of the time being of that association.

Case Summary

A further example of where a *Re Denley* type construction has been used to save a trust for a purpose is in the case of **Quistclose trusts**, which you will remember from Chapter 1 are created where money is loaned to a company for a specific purpose. It could be argued that, in directing that money be used for a specified purpose, Quistclose Investments were creating a trust for a purpose and not a trust for the benefit of human beneficiaries at all. However, this problem was avoided by construing the trust as a trust set up not for a purpose but for the benefit of the shareholders who were ultimately to receive the money. It should be noted that this reasoning may not always work in a Quistclose type scenario, however. What if the money has been loaned to the company to buy equipment, for example? Here the purpose of the loan would be an abstract purpose and a *Re Denley* type construction could not be used to save it. These were the facts of *Re EVTR* [1987] BCLC 646, which concerned a man who gave money he had won on the Premium Bonds to his employers, EVTR, to buy new equipment. The man deposited £60,000 with his solicitors, authorising them to release the money to EVTR for that purpose. The money was handed over to EVTR and the equipment ordered, but the company went into liquidation before the equipment arrived.

Case Summary

It should be noted that, on the facts of the case, despite the abstract purpose of the trust, the court nevertheless held that a trust had been successfully created by the employee. This meant that, when the purpose of the trust was frustrated, the monies were able to be returned to him on a resulting trust. It is arguable, therefore, that Quistclose trusts stand alone as a case in which, due to their special circumstances, the settlor appears to be exempt in the eyes of the court from the difficulties caused by the purpose trust issue. The difficulties arising in Quistclose type trusts were given more recent discussion by Lord Millett in the House of Lords case of **Twinsectra Ltd v. Yardley** [2002] 2 AC 164. The judgment is well worth a read for a detailed analysis of the problems which can arise in this area.

Case Navigator

One other difficulty in interpreting the purported purpose trust as a gift to a group of individuals is the ever-present issue of perpetuity. In both *Re Denley* and *Re Lipinski*, the court had to construe the gift so as to include only the *current* employees of the company and members of the association, as a gift to both present and future employees or members would have offended the perpetuity rule and rendered the gifts invalid. The same would, of course, apply to any other class of individuals named by a settlor.

The nature of the gift itself could also make it impossible to interpret it as a simple gift to be divided between a **class of beneficiaries**. Whereas a gift of money is easily divided, with a gift of land or other property it becomes less easy to infer that the settlor intended that the parcel of land be broken up and the pieces given to the individual members of the class. This whole issue came under discussion in the Commonwealth case of *Leahy* v. *Attorney-General for New South Wales* [1959] 2 All ER 300. The case concerned a purported gift by the testator of a sheep station in Australia to an order of nuns or monks of the trustees' choosing. The **Privy Council** held the gift as invalid as offending the perpetuity rule on two counts:

Case Summary

1. The fact that the gift was to be made to an order of nuns or monks suggested that the gift was not limited to the current members of that order only, but to present and future members (it thus offended the rule against perpetuities).

2. It was highly unlikely that the testator intended that each individual member of an order of, for the sake of argument, a hundred or so nuns should be given a personal interest in the property, the value of which they could retrieve at any given time by demanding either monetary payment or the sale of the property.

It is worth remembering here that the testator's gift was of a 730-acre sheep station, presumably to be farmed by the order well into the future to allow it to continue as a self-sufficient organisation and possibly to earn money for the order for the furtherance of its work. Given the nature of the gift and the intended beneficiaries, it is less likely that the testator intended that the farm be broken up into individual allotments and each nun or monk given a sheep to farm by themselves.

Gifts to unincorporated associations

We looked briefly at the definition of an unincorporated association in Chapter 1, where it was defined as any group of individuals not formally incorporated to form a corporation, or company. Thus, you will remember that an unincorporated association would include sporting or social clubs or associations like a local golf or tennis club, members' clubs such as the Rotary Club or Women's Institute, and political groups and associations, for example the Liberal Democrats or the Labour Party. This is the ordinary meaning of the term. However, 'unincorporated association' also has a more strict legal meaning, which was set out in the case of *Conservative and Unionist Central Office* v. *Burrell* [1982] 2 All ER 1. The case actually concerned an appeal against a demand for the payment of corporation tax received by the central office of the Conservative and Unionist political party. The office contended that it was not an unincorporated association and therefore that it was not liable to tax under the Income and Corporation Taxes Act 1970. The Court of Appeal held that, by its nature, the office did indeed lack the characteristics of an unincorporated association and that it did not therefore fall within the remit of the statute for the purposes of tax assessment.

Case Summary

In making his judgment Lord Justice Lawton set out the definition of an unincorporated association as meaning:

(i) two or more persons;
(ii) bound together for a common purpose (not being business purposes);
(iii) each person having mutual duties and obligations with each other;
(iv) which has rules which identify who controls the association and its funds and on what terms; and
(v) which can be joined or left at will.

If we consider once again the examples of unincorporated associations given above, we can see that all these groups and associations tend to share certain common elements: they all have members who join the club, usually through payment of an annual subscription fee, and who agree on joining to be bound by the club rules and regulations. Unlike a company, however, which exists independently of its members, what an unincorporated association does not have is a legal identity of its own. This causes problems when testators want to leave gifts of money to sporting or social clubs in their wills because, technically, there is nothing to leave their money to: the name of the club or association is just a descriptive term for this group of individuals who share a common interest, it is not an entity in its own right and, as such, cannot own or transfer property of any kind.

Furthermore, as the purported beneficiary under the terms of a will, a club or association has no legal authority under which it can enforce the gift.

Out and about

Are you a member of an unincorporated association? Think about clubs which you may have joined: a sport or social club, perhaps the working men's club or tennis club; or maybe you belong to a choir or an amateur dramatics society.

Now pick one of these clubs or associations to use as the basis for this exercise. If you are not a member of any group, ask your family or friends for help: there is bound to be somebody who belongs to a club near you. Failing this, just choose a local club, a golf or cricket club would be a good choice, one you can easily contact.

Your next task is to get hold of the rules and regulations of membership of your chosen association. You should be able to get a copy of this from the club secretary if you did not receive one on joining, or if you no longer have it. If it is a larger organisation with a website, you may be able to bring up their membership rules online.

Source: Ingram Publishing

Take some time to look through the club rules. Depending on your choice of association, these may be quite extensive, or fairly short and succinct. Either way, you should find that whatever rules you look at they comprise all of the basic elements listed in *Re Burrell*, above. Now, try to answer the following questions:

1. What is the purpose of the club? What are its aims and objectives?

2. Who can be a member of the club?

3. What are the duties and obligations of club members?

4. Are there regular meetings and are you obliged to attend them?

5. Is there a joining fee? How much is it?

6. Who controls the club funds? What are funds used for?

7. Who makes decisions about the club? Is the club autonomous or is it bound to another branch or 'head office'?

8. Are you part of the decision-making process?

9. How do you leave the club?

10. Are the club rules missing anything – is there anything you would add?

Try to spend no more than 40 minutes on this exercise.

 Handy tip: Do you think you are not a member of an unincorporated association? What about your university or college students' union? Are you a member of that?

If you really are unable to find a suitable set of club rules, you can always use the club rules of the Bredon Lawn Tennis Club which you will find in the Documenting the law feature further on in the chapter.

Reflective practice

Spend a little time, if you can, reflecting on how the exercise went. Did it take longer than you thought, or was it fairly quick to find what you were looking for? Did you manage to answer all the questions? If you couldn't find an answer, was the information simply not contained in the rules and regulations of your chosen club? Is there anything you would do differently if you were undertaking this exercise again?

You should now have a good grasp of what unincorporated associations are and how they work in practice. But what does any of this have to do with purpose trusts? The reason we include unincorporated associations in a chapter on purpose trusts is that commonly gifts by testators to clubs and associations are worded, whether intentionally or not, as purpose trusts. For example, a testator might leave money to his local sports club 'for the purchase of new equipment', or to the social club of which he was a member 'in order that they might acquire new premises'. As we have seen above, trusts for purposes rather than people are invalid and so a gift for such a purpose would fail. But it is in the interest of the testator and the association to allow the gift to stand: after all, it does not make sense that on your death you are unable to benefit an association which you can freely patronise during your lifetime.

We have seen how the court in *Re Denley* used constructive interpretation to allow gifts to ascertainable groups of individuals to stand as valid trusts. In the same way, and for the reasons given above, the courts have also seen fit to find ways to get around the problem of gifts to unincorporated associations. The case of *Neville Estates* v. *Madden* [1961] 3 All ER 769 concerned land held by a Jewish synagogue. The purposes of the synagogue were held to be charitable and therefore there was no problem with the trustees of the synagogue holding the property. However, Mr Justice Cross took the opportunity in the case to discuss what would have been the position, had the synagogue been held to be an unincorporated association. As with *Re Denley*, Mr Justice Cross said that the interpretation of gifts to unincorporated associations should be made on the basis of their construction. In order to succeed, the gift would either have to be interpreted as:

Case Summary

✦ an absolute gift to the club members themselves; or

✦ a gift to the members subject to the rules and regulations of the club.

An absolute gift to the club members

The idea behind interpreting a gift to an unincorporated association as a gift for the benefit of the club members themselves (also commonly referred to as making a gift to the members 'as **joint tenants**') is that, rather than the gift being used for the association's own purposes, any member of the association can decide at any time to claim their share in the gift for their own personal use. However, this method of interpretation creates similar difficulties to the *Re Denley* type cases, in that a gift to members of an association, which in no way restricts the members' use of that gift, gives the settlor no guarantee that his gift will be used in the manner and for the purpose he intended.

Case Summary

Unlike *Re Denley*, however, the courts have given consideration to this issue in the context of unincorporated associations. In the case of *Bowman* v. *Secular Society* [1917] AC 406, which again concerned a claim of charitable status by the recipients of a gift (contrary to the decision in *Neville Estates* v. *Madden*, the claim in this instance failed), Lord Parker stated that a gift could only be construed as a straightforward gift to the club members if 'neither the circumstances of the gift nor the directions given nor the objects expressed impose on the **donee** the character of a trustee'. In other words, a gift could only be construed as an outright gift to the club members if there was nothing in the wording of the gift, or in the way the gift was given, to suggest that the members should act as trustees of that gift on behalf of the club. Exactly what kind of circumstance then, following Lord Parker's judgment, might this entail?

The first thing to look at would be the nature of the club to which the gift was being made. It becomes obvious when looking at different types of club, whether sporting, political or social, that most have been set up for the furtherance of a particular purpose or aim, which is clearly not to benefit the members of that club as individuals. In fact, it would be most unusual to read a statement of aims and objectives within a club's rules of association that sets out their purposes as being to benefit the members personally. By way of example, take a look at the constitution of Bredon Lawn Tennis Club in Gloucestershire, reproduced in the Documenting the law feature. You will see from the 'objects' clause (Part I, clause 2), that the purpose of the club is for 'the provision of lawn tennis, social and other facilities for its members, together with the promotion of lawn tennis for the benefit of the community'.

Documenting the law

Bredon Lawn Tennis Club

Rules & Constitution

On-Court Rules

1. Tennis shoes must be worn.

2. Shoe tags must be worn by members.

3. Sports clothing must be worn.

4. Four (4) players per court is the maximum allowable and spectators must be outside the fencing.

5. Chewing gum must not be deposited on the court surface, nor the nets, net posts or fencing.

6. Nets must not be over tensioned and must be wound down at the conclusion of play.

7. A mandatory ball fee will be levied on all participants on club nights and mornings.

The committee reserves the right to invoke clause II(4) of the constitution if any member or visitor is in contravention of any of these on-court rules.

The Constitution

I. Description

1. **Name** . . . The Club shall be called the Bredon Lawn Tennis Club.

2. **Objects** . . . The Club shall have as its objects the provision of lawn tennis, social and other facilities for its members, together with the promotion of lawn tennis for the benefit of the community.

3. **Constitution** . . . The Club is a non-profit-making, unincorporated members' club, which shall be governed by this Constitution.

4. **Dissolution** . . . On dissolution of the Club, the assets must only be used for local sporting or charitable purposes, i.e. the assets must be given or transferred to another CASC, a registered charity or the Sports Governing Body.

II. Membership

1. **Qualification for Membership** . . . Any person shall be eligible for full membership provided that they are sixteen years of age or over. Children below the age of sixteen may be elected as junior members without the right to vote or hold office.

2. **Subscriptions** . . . All annual subscriptions shall be payable on or after the date of the Annual General Meeting. If subscriptions are not paid by April 30th then the late payment rate will apply.

3. **Number of Members** . . . In the event of the membership being in excess of a number ensuring the comfort and convenience of existing members, the committee shall have the power to restrict membership until such times as extended facilities are available.

4. **Suspension or Expulsion** . . . The committee shall have the power to terminate or suspend the membership of any member, or to exclude any member or visitor whom it considers guilty of a breach of this Constitution or the On-Court Rules or of misconduct or offensive behaviour to any other member, visitor or employee, whether on the Club's premises or elsewhere.

   The member has the right of appeal. This must be made in writing to the secretary giving the grounds for the appeal within 14 days of the expulsion or suspension. It will be considered by the committee within 14 days of receipt, and the decision made after due consideration of the written details presented.

5. **Visitors** . . . Every member shall have the right to introduce visitors subject to such regulations as shall be made from time to time by the committee. Every visitor shall be the guest of, and be accompanied by, the member introducing him or her.

III. Committee

1. **Committee** . . . The entire management of the Club (except as otherwise provided by this Constitution) shall be deputed to a committee consisting of the three elected officers (Chairman, Secretary, and Treasurer) and not less than six other members.

2. **Quorum** . . . A quorum shall consist of five committee members.

3. **Election of Committee** . . . At the Annual General Meeting members of the committee shall retire, but shall be eligible for re-election. Any two members of the Club may propose any other candidate or candidates at such times and the proposal shall be put to the meeting. A majority vote shall decide. In the case of two candidates receiving the same number of votes the proposal shall be put to the meeting for a second time and in the event of a tie, the chairman shall have a second or casting vote.

   In the event of a vacancy on the committee, the committee shall have the power to elect any members of the Club to fill such a vacancy. The committee shall also have the power to co-opt additional members should the need arise.

4. **Sub-Committee** . . . The Committee may from time to time appoint a sub-committee, which shall conduct its business in accordance with the direction of the committee.

5. **Committee's Powers** . . . The committee shall from time to time make, repeal, and amend all such regulations (not inconsistent with this Constitution) as they shall think expedient for the internal management, use of courts and well-being of the Club. All such regulations shall be binding upon members until repealed by the committee, or set aside by a resolution of a General Meeting of the Club.

   The committee shall have the power to make arrangements for holding matches, tournaments, or other like competitions, including the imposition of a charge for the admission of non-members to the grounds, to provide cups and other prizes, and to reserve courts as may be required.

IV. General Meetings

1. **Annual General Meeting** . . . The Annual General Meeting (AGM) of the Club shall be held prior to the 1st May in each year upon a date and at a time to be fixed by the committee, for the following purposes.

   a. To receive from the committee a report, balance sheet and statement of account for the preceding year, and details of the income and expenditure expected during the current financial year.

   b. To elect the officers and committee, and appoint one auditor for the ensuing year.

   c. To fix the annual subscriptions.

   d. To decide upon any resolution which may be duly submitted to the meeting.

2. **Special General Meeting** . . . The Chairman and/or committee may at times for any special purpose call a Special General Meeting (SGM), and they shall do so forthwith upon the requisition in writing of any ten members stating the purpose for which the meeting is required.

3. **Notice** . . . Ten days at least before the AGM or any SGM, a printed or written notice of such meeting and of the business to be transacted thereat shall be sent to every member.

4. **Chair and Voting** . . . At General Meetings of the Club the Chairman, and in his/her absence a member of the committee, shall take the chair. Every member present entitled to vote shall have one vote upon every motion, and in the case of an equality of votes, the chairman shall have a second or casting vote.

V. Finance

1. **Trustees** . . . The trustees of the Club shall be the elected officers of the Club.

2. **Financial Year** . . . The financial year of the Club shall end on March 31st each year, to which day the accounts of the year shall be balanced.

3. **Loans** . . . The committee has the authority to borrow monies up to the value of £12,000 to assist with the financing of capital projects provided that it is a unanimous decision of the committee. Any loan in excess of this must be approved by members at an AGM or SGM.

4. **Surplus Funds** . . . All surplus income or profits are re-invested in the club. No surpluses or assets will be distributed to members or third parties.

5. **Payment of Members** . . . No member, except for services rendered at the request of the committee, shall receive any profit or emolument from the funds of the Club.

VI. Other

1. **Power to Vary the Constitution** . . . This Constitution may only be amended by resolution at a General Meeting of the Club. No such resolution shall be deemed to have been passed unless it be carried by a majority of at least two thirds of the members voting thereon.

[*Source*: Bredon Lawn Tennis Club. For more information on the club, go to: http://www.bredon-tennis.org.uk.]

So what circumstances would lead to a valid gift to the club members as individuals? Clubs which might allow a gift to their members as individuals are few and far between but by way of example perhaps a small social group, such as a mother and toddler group with only half a dozen members and no formal rules of association, might be included here. In such an instance, a simple gift by a settlor of £600 to the members of the club for no stated purpose could only sensibly be construed as for the benefit of its members in their individual capacities. To give another example, Mr Justice Vinelot in *Re Grant's Wills Trust* [1979] 3 All ER 359, the facts of which are given below, suggested that this category might include a legacy given to a small dining club of which the testator had been a member during his lifetime.

The nature of the club aside, it is also possible that the club's rules might contain specific provisions preventing the members from acquiring personal rights to such gifts; and so an examination of the club rules would always be necessary when making a decision as to the validity of a gift on this basis.

As with the *Re Denley* type cases, the issue of perpetuity and thus the subject matter of the gift would also be relevant here. So a gift of money is always going to be viewed in a more favourable light when seeking to divide it between individual members than something more permanent such as a piece of land.

The other issue with which Lord Parker was concerned relates to the wording of the purported gift. If a settlor directs that a gift to his golf club is to be used to refurbish the club house, it is clear that his intention was not to benefit the members as individuals but rather that it was to achieve a particular purpose, that of restoring its premises: presumably for the benefit of the club as a whole. It therefore follows that any gift to an unincorporated association for which the settlor has specified a particular use could never be construed as a gift to the individual members of that association as joint tenants because the wording of the gift negates this.

> any gift to an unincorporated association would have to be examined on its individual facts

Considered as a whole, Lord Parker's judgment essentially means that any purported gift to an unincorporated association would have to be examined on its individual facts and both the intentions of the settlor and the nature of the gift taken into account. If the court then decided that, on its proper construction, the gift was for an abstract, non-charitable purpose and not for the benefit of its members individually, it would be held invalid. The consequence of this ruling is that to find a valid gift to individual members of an unincorporated association is quite rare.

A gift to the members subject to the rules and regulations of the club

This is by far the more common interpretation of a purported gift to an unincorporated association. Instead of construing the gift as being given to the members as individuals, in this scenario the gift is seen to have been given to the members to hold as part of the association's funds and to be used strictly in accordance with their club rules. Held in this way, any single club member would be unable to take their share of the gift and put it to their own personal use; rather, as part of the club funds, the money (or other property) would remain with that club, accruing to the remaining members should that member choose to leave.

The only problem with this construction is that, in terms of the perpetuity, if the gift was to be held indefinitely as part of the club funds and could not be spent in any way other than as specified by the club rules, the money would effectively be tied up in the club funds forever and would therefore breach the perpetuity rules. With this in mind, the courts specified in *Neville Estates* v. *Madden* that such an interpretation would only be valid on the proviso that either the club rules could at any time be changed to allow the money to be spent in some other way or the association wound up and the funds divided between the individual members of the club at that time. This approach was confirmed and followed in subsequent cases, including that of *Re Grant's Wills Trust* [1979] 3 All ER 359. The case concerned a purported gift to a local Labour Party. The gift was held to be invalid because the local branch was unable to act independently of the national Labour Party, who ultimately made all decisions in respect of party funds. In consequence, money left to any branch of an association which does not have authority to act autonomously of the main association or club headquarters could not be construed in this way and would therefore fail as a gift on grounds of perpetuity.

If the club could be wound up or the rules of association amended to allow the funds to be used for some other purpose, however, making a gift to the members of the association even on this basis still carries with it no guarantee that the money will be used in accordance with the giver's wishes. The only small comfort for a testator in leaving their money to a club or association rather than a class of individuals, then, is that the members of a club are likely to share the same ideals and interests as they do. As such, club members might be more inclined to use the money in accordance with the testator's wishes than a class of individuals who are grouped together through something as arbitrary as a bloodline or their employer, and who may have nothing more than that simple fact in common. Nevertheless, the court in **Re Recher's Will Trusts** [1972] Ch 526, which concerned a gift in the will of Eva Recher to the Anti-Vivisection Society, has since held that, whenever a gift is made to an unincorporated association, the presumption should now be that it is a gift made under this category.

Case
Summary

Case
Summary

Case
Navigator

Summary

◆ Purpose trusts are trusts set up for the carrying out of an abstract purpose rather than for the benefit of an individual.

◆ As a general rule, purpose trusts are invalid. This is because of the beneficiary principle, which states that a trust must have a human beneficiary in order to be valid.

◆ There are three exceptions to the general rule. These are purpose trusts

1. for the maintenance of specific animals;
2. for the erection and maintenance of tombs and monuments, and
3. for the saying of private masses.

The fourth exception, purpose trusts for the promotion of fox-hunting, would arguably be invalid today for public policy reasons.

◆ Even if a trust falls within one of the named exceptions, it will still fail if it offends perpetuity or principles of certainty or public policy.

◆ Some purpose trusts may be construed as valid trusts for persons if they can be interpreted as trusts for the benefit of an ascertainable group of individuals (*Re Denley* type cases).

◆ Gifts to unincorporated associations are difficult because an unincorporated association has no legal identity and is therefore unable to hold property.

◆ Gifts to unincorporated associations may be saved if they can be interpreted either as a gift to the members between themselves as joint tenants, or as a gift to the members subject to the rules of the association. In the latter case, there must be nothing to prevent the club from disbanding and dividing up the club funds at any given time.

Question and answer*

Problem: Take another look at the will of Helen Tabor earlier in the chapter. Now, using the knowledge you have acquired from reading this chapter, comment on the validity of clauses 5, 6 and 9.

You should allow yourself no more than 40 minutes to complete this task.

Problem: Eccentric businessman Eric van Hoogstraten has reportedly converted the east wing of his £40 million Sussex home into a gargantuan mausoleum, where he plans to be sealed up with his collection of priceless arts and treasures for a term of no less than 5,000 years. When asked why he wishes to do this, Mr Hoogstraten said: 'It's the nearest I can get to taking all my wealth with me and ensuring that nobody else benefits from it.'

What measures will Mr van Hoogstraten have to take in order to achieve this? Do you think he would be successful in achieving his aim and, if not, why not?

This question should be answered in 40 minutes.

✱ Answer guidance is provided at the end of the chapter.

Further reading and references

Brown, J. (2007) 'What are we to do with testamentary trusts of imperfect obligation?', Conv (Mar/Apr), 148–60.
Survey and article on the use of purpose trusts by solicitors in England and Wales and comment on how the law could be amended.

Gardner, S. (1998) 'A detail in the construction of gifts to unincorporated associations', Conv (Jan/Feb), 8–12.
A useful discussion of gifts to unincorporated associations, focusing on gifts to the members subject to their contractual rights and obligations.

Luxton, P. (2007) 'Gifts to clubs: contract holding is trumps', Conv (May/Jun), 274–81.
This article considers the different methods of making gifts to unincorporated associations in the light of the recent decision in *Re Horley Town Football Club* [2006] EWHC 2386 (Ch).

Pawlowski, M. and Summers, J. (2007) 'Private purpose trusts – a reform proposal', Conv (Sept/Oct), 440–55.
An interesting discussion of the difficulty of enforcement with purpose trusts with suggestions for possible reform.

***Re Astor's Settlement Trusts* [1952] Ch 534.**
If you are going to read any case on purpose trusts, this is the one to read. In particular, Mr Justice Roxburgh's judgment sets out the law and opinion on the purpose trusts in a clear and easy to read way.

***Twinsectra Ltd* v. *Yardley* [2002] AC 164, Lord Millett's judgment.**
The judgment is well worth a read for a detailed analysis of the difficulties which can arise with trusts for purposes in the context of Quistclose type trusts. Lord Millett's analysis of the situation is singular in that there has as yet been no other attempt to surmount the problem.

Question and answer guidance

Problem: *5. I give £10,000 for the maintenance of my tortoise, Clarence, whom I direct should be fed on a diet of freshly shelled garden peas for the rest of his days.*

Trusts for purposes are generally void, because they do not have a human beneficiary (*Morice* v. *Bishop of Durham*). However, this case falls within one of the exceptions to the rule against purpose trusts, being a trust for the maintenance of a specific animal: Clarence the tortoise (*Dean* v. *Dean*; *Pettinghall* v. *Pettinghall*). Issues:

✦ Perpetuity: tortoises tend to live for longer than the perpetuity period (21 years in the case of a trust for the maintenance of an animal), and so it would be void for this reason.

✦ There is also a question as to whether £10,000 is sufficient for his needs or whether the amount might be considered excessive and therefore capricious.

✦ Who will look after Clarence and what will happen to any excess in the fund on his death?

6. I give £10,000 to my Trustees for the erection of six drinking water fountains at strategic points in Sinderfield Park, where I liked to go jogging. Each fountain should be inscribed in my memory.

Could this be construed as a gift for the erection of a tomb or monument? If so, it would come within one of the exceptions to the rule against purpose trusts (*Trimmer* v. *Danby*; *Mussett* v. *Bingle*). *Re Dean* says that a monument need not be on consecrated ground. Issues:

✦ Could it be construed as capricious? See *McCaig's Trustees* for comment.

✦ Is there enough detail in the wording of the trust? What kind of fountains? What are they to be made of? Is £10,000 enough/too much?

9. I give the land and gardens to the rear of the aforementioned 17 The Mount to the Sinderfield Gardeners' Association for use as allotments by their members

As a trust for a purpose (to use the land as allotments) the gift would fail. As a gift to an unincorporated association, it would also fail, unless it can be construed either as a gift to the individual members or as a gift to members subject to rules of the association (*Neville Estates* v. *Madden*). Issues:

✦ Note the difficulty with the second type of construction, if the association is a branch (no evidence of that here).

✦ Could it be given a *Re Denley* type construction? Note problems that there are difficulties in construing a gift of land to the individual members of the group, though: *Leahy* v. *AG for New South Wales*. But this case can be distinguished on its facts from *Leahy*, because of the nature of the gift as allotments, which assumes the land is going to be split up into, and worked as, individual plots.

✦ Note the perpetuity issue: must be the current members of the association in order not to offend the perpetuity rule.

Problem: Presuming the building of the mausoleum had been completed at the time of van Hoogstraten's death (the building currently remains unfinished), he could attempt to create a trust for the maintenance of a tomb or monument, thereby avoiding the rule against trusts for private purposes (see *Trimmer* v. *Danby*; *Mussett* v. *Bingle*). However, there are a number of difficulties with his objectives:

1. He wants the trust to continue for no less than 5,000 years. A trust for this long would offend the rule against perpetuities and render the trust void. The maximum period of time he could make the trust for would be a

life in being plus 21 years. As this is a purpose trust, the maximum period for the continuation of the trust would be 21 years (as there is no life in being to measure against). He could extend this period by using a royal lives clause (*Re Khoo Cheng Teow*), although this would still go nowhere near his preferred 5,000 year period. He could also possibly ensure the maintenance of the mausoleum by making a conditional gift to charity, such as in *Re Tyler*, but note the difficulty with the wording of such gifts (*Re Dalziel*). To make the trust charitable would require an element of public benefit and therefore probably mean opening the mausoleum up to the public, which van Hoogstraten is unlikely to want to do.

2. The trust is likely to be void on grounds of public policy. Compare with *Brown* v. *Burdett*, in which instructions to seal up a house for 20 years were held void. A trust to seal up a collection of priceless arts and treasures for this period would undoubtedly be void for the same reasons.

3. The trust is likely to be viewed by the courts as capricious. Compare with *McCaig's Trustees*. A £40 million mausoleum is hugely extravagant, as is the idea of locking up van Hoogstraten's treasures in it.

Students could conclude by raising the issue of a man's freedom to do what he wishes with his own money and commenting on the suggestion that a man should have the same ability in death to do what he can in life.

Visit **www.mylawchamber.co.uk/warner-reed** to access study support resources including practice exam questions with guidance, interactive 'You be the judge' multiple choice questions, annotated weblinks, glossary and key case flashcards and audio legal updates all linked to the **Pearson eText** version of *Equity and Trusts* which you can **search**, **highlight** and **personalise** with your **own notes** and **bookmarks**.

Use Case Navigator to read in full some of the key cases referenced in this chapter with commentary and questions:

Re Denley's Trust Deed [1969] ch 373
Re Recher's Will Trusts [1971] 3 All ER 401
Twinsectra Ltd v. *Yardley* [2002] 2 All ER 377

Chapter 5
Charities

Key points In this chapter we will be looking at:

✦ The definition of charity
✦ The different heads of charity under the Charities Act 2006
✦ The need for public benefit
✦ Charities and political purposes
✦ Trusts for mixed purposes
✦ Failure of charitable trusts and the doctrine of cy près

Introduction

In Chapter 4 we started to talk about **trusts** being created not for the benefit of a specific person or persons but for some other abstract purpose, such as the erection of a tomb or monument. And we saw in that chapter that the law will only allow the existence of such **purpose trusts** in very limited circumstances. One such circumstance is where the trust is created not for some purpose which is personal or private to the **settlor** but where it is created instead for a charitable purpose. Table 5.1 shows this and a number of other differences between charitable and **private purpose trusts**.

Table 5.1 Differences between private and charitable (or public) purpose trusts

Private purpose trusts	Charitable (public) trusts
Most purpose trusts are **void** for having no human beneficiary	Charitable trusts do not need a specified human beneficiary in order to be valid
Purpose trusts can only last for the length of the **perpetuity period**	Charitable trusts can exist in perpetuity
Purpose trusts can exist for the personal benefit of the settlor	Charitable trusts must carry some element of public benefit
The list of purpose trusts is closed and can never be expanded	The concept of charity is constantly evolving and new charitable purposes are specifically provided for in the Charities Act 2006

We can see here that charities are treated more favourably than private purpose trusts in a number of key areas. Not only do they have no requirement for a specified human beneficiary, but they do not carry the same perpetuity issues as private purpose trusts.

So why are charitable purposes treated so differently from all other purpose trusts? In order to help us answer this question let us turn, first of all, to the meaning of charity.

What is a charity?

The concept of charity is well known. If you were asked to give an example of a charity you would be able to come up with the names of several without giving it too much thought. Neither is the idea of charity a new one; there have been charities in existence, and people have been giving to charitable causes, for many hundreds of years.

Law in action Charity begins at home?

Multimillionaire and philanthropist Brian Burnie is selling his multimillion pound estate in Northumberland and says he will use the proceeds in the fight against cancer. It is all part of the 64-year-old's vow to devote the rest of his life and his fortune to charity.

Burnie purchased the historic 191-year-old Doxford Hall from the council in a dilapidated state for £500,000 and has since ploughed a staggering £16 million, and more than fourteen years, into transforming the house and 10-acre estate into one of the country's most luxurious spa hotels. Burnie says that he had always planned to use income from the property to help in the fight against cancer, but he brought his plans forward following his wife's recent battle with breast cancer. Mrs Burnie has thankfully now made a full recovery from the illness.

'You come into the world with nothing, and you should go out with nothing,' says Burnie. According to property experts, Doxford Hall and the surrounding 10-acre estate is likely to be sold for at least £10 million.

Proceeds from the sale will be used to establish and fund a cancer nurse for north Northumberland, and vehicles to take cancer patients to hospital.

[Source: http://www.timesonline.co.uk/tol/news/uk/article6289653.ece]

Charities are commonplace in today's society; you have only to switch on the television to see reference to the National Lottery Fund, or BBC's Children in Need, or to watch an advertisement for one of the many other worthwhile charities: the British Heart Foundation, Cancer Research, the Dogs Trust, the list is endless. As can be seen from the Law in action feature, you can even create a charity yourself. Take a look at the list of interesting figures on charities in the Key stats box.

Key stats

1 UK's oldest charity: The King's School, Canterbury, founded AD 597

2 UK's biggest charity: The Wellcome Trust (a charity supporting medical research)

3 Number of UK charities currently registered: 162,164 (as at 30 June 2010)

4 Amount donated to charity in 2010: £52.514 billion

5 Most popular charity (in terms of donations given): Cancer Research

[Source: I am grateful to Eleanor Tew at the Charity Commission for supplying me with most of this information. For further statistics on charities go to the Charity Commission website at **http://www.charity-commission.gov.uk**.]

So charity is certainly not a new concept, neither is it a rare one. But if you had to put into words the meaning of 'charity', if you had to define it, what would you say? What makes a charity a charity? What makes some purposes charitable, and others not? Despite the longevity of the charitable cause as a concept in English law the term 'charity' has only very recently been given a statutory definition. Prior to the Charities Act 2006, in fact, the legal profession had only a wholly archaic list of charitable purposes conceived in the time of Elizabeth I (believe it or not!) as amended, updated and expanded by some 400 years of case law, on which to rely in determining whether any particular clause was charitable.

Writing and drafting

Imagine you are one of the legislators behind the Charities Act. It is your job to come up with a definitive meaning for the term 'charity'. Take some time to think about what defines a charity. Now try putting your definition down on paper. This task should take you no more than 30 minutes.

 Handy tip: Remember, you are drafting a legal definition for charity; it may not be as easy as you think! Try thinking about what qualities a charity should have to begin with, and go from there.

This original list of charitable purposes drawn up by Elizabeth I was contained in the preamble to the Statute of Charitable Uses (1601) 43 Eliz. I, c. 4. The list details a number of charitable uses to which money could (at that time) be put:

some for Relief of aged, impotent and poor People, some for Maintenance of sick and maimed Soldiers and Mariners, Schools of Learning, Free Schools, and Scholars at Universities, some for Repair of Bridges, Ports, Havens, Causeways, Churches, Sea-Banks and Highways, some for Education and Preferment of Orphans, some for or towards Relief,

Stock or Maintenance for Houses of Correction, some for Marriages of poor Maids, some for Supportation, Aid and Help of young Tradesmen, Handicraftsmen and Persons decayed, and others for Relief or Redemption of Prisoners or Captives, and for Aid or Ease of any poor Inhabitants concerning Payment of Fifteens,* setting out of Soldiers and other Taxes.

* Fifteens were a kind of tax on personal property

Whilst many of the uses contained in the list and a large proportion of the case law which follows it is still relevant today (we will cover this point in more detail later in the chapter), the updated statutory definition contained in section 2 of the Charities Act 2006 is altogether more modern in its ambit and wording. The section reads as follows:

(1) For the purposes of the law of England and Wales, a charitable purpose is a purpose which –

    (a) falls within subsection (2), and

    (b) is for the public benefit (see section 3).

(2) A purpose falls within this subsection if it falls within any of the following descriptions of purposes –

    (a) the prevention or relief of poverty;

    (b) the advancement of education;

    (c) the advancement of religion;

    (d) the advancement of health or the saving of lives;

    (e) the advancement of citizenship or community development;

    (f) the advancement of arts, culture, heritage or science;

    (g) the advancement of amateur sport;

    (h) the advancement of human rights, conflict resolution or reconciliation or the promotion of religious or racial harmony or equality and diversity;

    (i) the advancement of environmental protection or improvement;

    (j) the relief of those in need, by reason of youth, age, ill-health, disability, financial hardship or other disadvantage;

    (k) the advancement of animal welfare;

    (l) the promotion of the efficiency of the armed forces of the Crown or of the efficiency of the police, fire and rescue services or the ambulance services;

    (m) any other purposes within subsection (4).

Nevertheless, there are remarkable similarities between Elizabeth's preamble and the new statutory definition. In particular, you will notice that the statutory definition is still nothing more than a list of charitable purposes, as opposed to a definition in the strict sense of the word. The new statutory list may appear to be in altogether more modern form, now including a number of new purposes, but in actual fact these are nothing more than those purposes not originally listed in the Statute of Elizabeth I but which have been held to be charitable in subsequent case law.

> the statutory definition is nothing more than a list of charitable purposes

So the point to note here is that the statutory definition contained in the Charities Act 2006 has not changed the law; it has consolidated it, taking Elizabeth I's original list of charitable uses and amending it to include all those instances where the definition of charities has been expanded and clarified over the years. Indeed, from an academic viewpoint, the Charities Act 2006 has not, for the greater part, effected a change in the law, but rather the codification of it.

The 'heads' of charity under the Charities Act 2006

Having introduced you briefly to the notion of charity as described by reference to a statutory list of charitable causes, let us now look in a little more detail at each type of charity, and see what comes within each definition. The Charity Commission has issued a substantial amount of helpful guidance on what is and is not included under each charitable heading of the new Act. Much of this guidance is replicated or referred to in the detail that follows, but for a complete description of what is contained within each definition you can go to **http://www.charity-commission.gov.uk**.

(a) The prevention or relief of poverty

This first charitable heading may seem pretty straightforward but there are a couple of points to be aware of here. First of all, there is the issue of exactly how poor is 'poor'.

What is meant by 'poor'?

Case Summary

For the purposes of our statutory definition, to be poor certainly does not go as far as to be destitute. This was made clear in the case of *Re Coulthurst* [1951] Ch 661, which concerned an attempt by John William Coulthurst to set up a charitable trust in favour of:

> the . . . widows and orphaned children of deceased officers and deceased ex-officers [of the bank] as the bank shall in its absolute discretion consider by reason of his, her or their financial circumstances to be most deserving of such assistance . . .

The court held that the trust was charitable, in that the intention of Mr Coulthurst was to help the poor, within the meaning of the Statute of Elizabeth (as was the law at that time). In making his judgment in the case, Sir Raymond Evershed, Master of the Rolls, said:

> It is quite clearly established that poverty does not mean destitution . . . it may . . . be paraphrased for present purposes as meaning persons who have to 'go short' in the ordinary sense of that term, due regard being had to their status in life.

We can see from this that the courts acknowledge that the concept of poverty is a relative one, meaning different things to different people, dependent on their circumstances and social status. The effect of this is that the meaning of the word 'poor' will vary from case to case. Therefore, in the case of *Re Young (Deceased)* [1951] 1 Ch 344 a gift by **testator** Roger Pilkington Young 'for the permanent aid of distressed gentlefolk' was held to be charitable, as was a gift to 'persons of moderate means' in *Re Clarke* [1923] 2 Ch 407.

More recently, in *Re Segelman* [1996] Ch 171 Mr Justice Chadwick held that **minors** who became students would be likely to experience 'relative poverty' when money received from parents and any grants for which they might be eligible fell short of 'their actual or perceived needs' and thus a charity in support was allowed under this charitable heading.

The Charity Commission issued guidance on the issue in 2001, stating that:

> generally speaking anyone who cannot afford the normal things in life which most people take for granted would probably qualify for help.

It also commented that people in receipt of state benefits may qualify as needing additional help. There is no further guidance given, however, as to what would qualify as 'the normal things in life' and whether this might include food, shelter, heating, or even ownership of a telephone or television. This leaves the test for poverty as very much a **subjective** one, the things that people take for granted in life being bound to differ substantially in each individual case.

The benefit must be exclusively for the poor

The second point to note as regards charities for the poor is that for a trust under this heading to be charitable it must be for the benefit of the poor *exclusively*. If anyone who could not be considered poor will benefit, whether incidentally or otherwise, the trust cannot be charitable. Thus in the Welsh case of *Re Gwyon* [1930] 1 Ch 255, a gift for the provision of 'knickers' (which were a type of short trouser) for boys resident in a particular location was not held to be charitable as it could benefit children from more wealthy families as well as those coming from impoverished backgrounds.

Following the same line of reasoning, the court in the later case of *Re Sanders Will Trusts* [1954] Ch 265 held that money given to provide dwellings for 'the working classes and their families' was not charitable because the term 'working class' was not exclusively reserved for the poor. However, care should be taken to construe the wording of the trust in its full context. In *Re Niyazi's Will Trusts* [1978] 1 WLR 910, a trust to build a working men's hostel was held to be charitable on the basis that the very nature of a hostel was to provide temporary accommodation for those who could not afford lodgings elsewhere. In addition, the amount of money which had been left for the construction of the hostel dictated that the nature of the building would be modest and not suitable for more affluent members of society.

(b) The advancement of education

As with the meaning of poverty, the law takes a generous approach to the meaning of 'education', construing the term very broadly. The case of *IRC v. McMullen* [1981] AC 1 concerned an attempt by the Football Association to set up a charitable trust to enable pupils at schools and universities to play football and other sports. The House of Lords held that it was a valid charitable trust for the advancement of education, Lord Hailsham defining education as:

> a balanced and systematic process of instruction, training and practice containing . . . spiritual, moral, mental and physical elements.

So what might this include? As one might expect, the advancement of education includes education both in schools and in places of higher education, including universities. Even trusts for fee-paying schools are charitable providing they are non-profit-making. The term 'education' can also cover the act of teaching itself: thus a trust for the payment of teachers would be charitable.

It should be noted that education also includes anything ancillary to education, such as in the case of *AG* v. *Ross and others* [1985] 3 All ER 334 where the students' union at a polytechnic was held to be charitable as its function was to further the educational function of the polytechnic as a whole. This means that certain associations, such as the Royal College of Surgeons and the Royal College of Nursing, could be regarded as charitable under this heading, provided that their objectives were educational and not political. For this reason, trade unions such as the National Union of Teachers could not be seen as charitable. The difficulties encountered with charities and political purposes are dealt with in further detail below.

Is research 'education'?

Research is included within the definition of the advancement of education, provided the research has some genuine value to those other than the researchers themselves. The case of *Re Besterman (deceased)* [1984] Ch 458 helpfully sets out three basic requirements to determine when a trust for research will be charitable. These are:

1. the subject matter of the research must be a useful subject of study;
2. the knowledge acquired by the research must be disseminated (i.e. distributed) to others; and
3. the trust must be for public benefit or for a sufficiently important section of the public.

To give two contrasting examples of research we can look at the *Re Besterman (deceased)* case itself, which involved research into the works of the French playwrights Voltaire and Rousseau and which was held to be charitable, and a case we looked at previously in Chapter 4 on purpose trusts of *Re Shaw* [1957] 1 All ER 745, where creating a 40-letter alphabet and translating one of Shaw's plays into it was regarded as having no value to the public and therefore was held as not charitable.

(c) The advancement of religion

The idea that religious purposes can be charitable may at first glance seem a strange one. After all, in a society which is predominantly Christian, how can a charity promoting another religion benefit the public? The answer to this question is given in the case of *Neville Estates* v. *Madden* [1961] 3 All ER 769, in which the charitable status of a Jewish synagogue in Catford, London, was questioned. Mr Justice Cross said that:

> as between different religions the law stands neutral, but it assumes that any religion is at least as likely to be better than none.

And so one can conclude from this that religion is included in the definition of charity because in the eyes of the judiciary, regardless of the religion being promoted, it will be in the interests of the general public because religion as a general rule teaches people to behave better. The fact that religion has been seen to have prompted plenty of bad behaviour too, when interpreted wrongly, is not something which the courts have chosen to address or even acknowledge in this context.

> because religion as a general rule teaches people to behave better

Despite this positive approach towards religion as the promoter of a better standard of behaviour, however, prior to the Charities Act 2006 the definition of religion required belief in one God. This was the judgment of the House of Lords (as per Lord Parker) in the case of *Bowman* v. *Secular Society* [1917] AC 406. The case concerned an attempt by a testator to establish a charitable gift for the Secular Society Ltd, a company whose **objects** were:

Case Summary

> to promote . . . the principle that human conduct should be based upon natural knowledge, and not upon super-natural belief, and that human welfare in this world is the proper end of all thought and action.

Lord Parker's judgment in the case had the rather bizarre outcome that an organisation which promoted good behaviour and high morals but which did not believe in the worship of one God could not be charitable. An even more nonsensical outcome of the pre-2006 definition was that the requirement to believe in a divine being would rule out Buddhism (Buddhists do not believe in a deity, just in the good in people); and that the requirement to worship a single deity would rule out Hinduism (as there are several deities in the Hindu religion).

Although clearly the Charity Commission recognised the obvious nonsense in this and did in fact register Buddhist and Hindu organisations as charitable prior to 2006, the Charities Act 2006 has now formally removed the difficulty posed by these anomalies by stating at section 2(3)(a) that for the purposes of the Act the definition of religion includes both a religion which involves the belief in more than one god and a religion which does not involve a belief in a god. Nevertheless, it is unclear as to whether some of the less mainstream religions would qualify under this heading. Presumably fringe religions such as 'Jedi' or 'Pastafarianism' (an American religion which follows the Gospel of the Flying Spaghetti Monster) would still have to prove that they genuinely promoted a better standard of behaviour in their followers and therefore were of some benefit to the public in general, before they could be classed by the Charity Commission as charitable.

> it is unclear as to whether some of the less mainstream religions would qualify

As with trusts for the advancement of education, one final point to note is that a trust for the advancement of religion can include ancillary purposes such as the erection or maintenance of religious buildings.

(d) The advancement of health or the saving of lives

We are told in section 2(3)(b) of the Charities Act 2006 that 'the advancement of health' includes the prevention or relief of sickness, disease or human suffering. Hospital trusts, trusts for the provision of medical treatments and hospices would therefore all come under this heading. As with the first three types of trust, the concept of a trust to assist those in poor health or for the saving of lives is by no means new, reference having been made in the 1601 Statute of Charitable Uses to the relief of the 'aged, impotent or poor', impotent in this context meaning with disability or illness.

As with the provision of private schooling, whilst one would have thought private hospitals could not be charitable because they charge fees and therefore benefit only the relatively rich, the case law suggests that gifts to private hospitals will still be charitable, since they help to ease the pressure on public services. This was the outcome in the 1969 case of *Re Resch's Will Trusts* 1 AC 514, in which a trust set up to support the provision of private beds in a general hospital was held charitable on the basis that there would be a benefit 'to the standard of medical care in the general hospital . . . aris[ing] from the juxtaposition of the two institutions'.

Case Summary

You be the judge

Q: Could a trust set up to promote faith healing be charitable under this heading?

A: Theoretically, yes. The Charity Commission has certainly suggested that the promotion of alternative medicine could be charitable, and methods which are widely recognised such as acupuncture and osteopathy will undoubtedly be included. However, one would need to provide evidence of the efficacy of less well-established or 'fringe' methods of healing and this could be difficult to prove in the case of faith healers. Irrespective of this, however, it could be argued that the art of faith healing is nonetheless valuable on the basis of the hope and spiritual well-being it provides to those who believe in it; or alternatively, it could be charitable under the 'promotion of religion' heading. There are, in fact, currently 19 different faith healing charities registered on this basis.

Source: Photodisc/Photolink

It should be noted that, as with education and religion, ancillary purposes may be regarded as charitable under this heading. This would include, for example, the provision of hospital buildings, the care of nurses or even a students' union at a medical school. In addition, the inclusion of ancillary purposes within this heading means that the saving of lives and property combined could also be charitable. This would encompass charities such as the Royal National Lifeboat Institution (RNLI). The fire service comes under its own separate heading (see below).

(e) The advancement of citizenship or community development

You may be wondering what on earth comes within this heading. Fortunately we have been given a little bit of help in deciphering the meaning of 'the advancement of citizenship or community development' from the statute itself, at section 2(3)(c), in which we are told that it includes:

(i) rural or urban regeneration; and

(ii) the promotion of civic responsibility, volunteering, the voluntary sector or the effectiveness or efficiency of charities.

So, in essence, what this heading really covers is anything which could amount to acts of good citizenship: the Guides and the Scouts would be charitable under this category, for example. The Charity Commission has also given us further assistance by issuing some additional guidance on what may be included under these expanded headings:

Rural and urban regeneration

Trusts set up for rural and urban regeneration projects would be covered provided, according to the Charity Commission, that the aim of the project is to improve 'the physical, social and economic infrastructure' of the area in order to assist people who are disadvantaged by 'their social and economic circumstances'. Naturally, this would rule out profit-making regeneration schemes run by developers.

Volunteering

And we can see from the statutory guidance that volunteer work, that is, action taken for the benefit of others or for the benefit of society in general and which is either unpaid or which is not undertaken purely for financial gain, will come under this head, so long as that action is not politically motivated.

Community capacity building

We are also told in the Charity Commission guidance that promoting 'community capacity building' will be covered under this charitable heading. And we are told that this means 'developing the capacity and skills of the members of a community in such a way that they are better able to identify and help meet their needs and to participate more fully in society'. So the setting up and running of skills workshops would be covered here, for example.

Promoting ethical standards in business and corporate responsibility

And finally, it should be noted that the Charity Commission, despite there being no direct judicial authority on this point, has indicated that charitable organisations which promote the incorporation of ethics into business practice will also be recognised as valid, provided that their aims are not political. A further discussion of the difficulties with charities and political purposes can be seen below.

(f) The advancement of arts, culture, heritage or science

Again, the Charity Commission has issued guidance here as to what is covered under this heading.

Advancement of the arts

The term 'art' includes not just fine art but also abstract, conceptual and performance art and representational and figurative art. As one might expect, the advancement of art covers the promotion of the various forms of art, but it also covers the provision of arts facilities and charities set up to encourage high standards of art. This might encompass a trust set up for the provision of prizes for talented young artists, for example.

One interesting point to note here is that, despite the category of advancement of the arts being open to a wide number of different artistic genres, there is a requirement that the genre being advanced or promoted by any particular charity has genuine artistic merit. Perhaps surprisingly, merit will initially be decided by the Commission, albeit that it reserves the right to seek expert evidence should there be any doubt in the matter.

Case Summary

One rather amusing case in which a trust did not meet the level of artistic merit required under this head is that of *Re Pinion* [1964] 1 All ER 890. The case concerned a testator who had left his artist's studio and its contents, which included the testator's lifetime collection of art, to be turned into a museum and exhibited to the general public. Lord Justice Harman, however, refused to give the trust charitable status on the basis that the collection was practically worthless and of no artistic merit. The judge commented that it was surprising that the unfortunate testator had not managed throughout his lifetime of collecting to acquire one single piece of artistic value, even accidentally, and was famously quoted as saying of the collection, 'I can conceive of no useful object to be served by foisting on the public this mass of junk.'

Advancement of heritage

The Charity Commission describes 'heritage' as anything which might be regarded as part of the country's local or national history, including any traditions passed down through successive generations, such as Morris dancing, cheese rolling, the wearing or making of traditional costumes, and any number of other village traditions or pastimes. Any charity which has as its purpose the carrying out or promotion of any activities which aim to preserve or maintain a particular tradition will be included here, provided a benefit to the public in preserving it can be shown. The issue of public benefit is discussed in further detail below. Advancing heritage also rather importantly includes charities for the preservation of historic land and buildings, such as the National Trust.

It should be noted that the broad term 'culture' is one which is often used in the context of advancing art or heritage.

The Charity Commission has given a number of useful examples of the sorts of charities which would come within the heading of advancement of the arts, culture and heritage:

✦ Art galleries and festivals, theatres, cinemas, choirs, orchestras, music, operatic and dramatic societies.

✦ The promotion of crafts and craftsmanship.

✦ Local art or history societies.

✦ The preservation of historic buildings.

✦ The preservation of historical traditions, such as carnivals, country/folk dancing societies, Scottish country dancing and Highland dancing societies, Eisteddfods (that is a Welsh festival of literature, music and the performing arts), folk clubs, etc.

Advancement of science

It should be noted that charitable trusts for the advancement of science are also included within this heading. The Charity Commission guidance states that the advancement of science includes the undertaking of scientific research and charities connected with various learned scientific societies and institutions.

(g) The advancement of amateur sport

This new heading has been a great help to many local sports associations who could not previously hold property under the rules for purpose trusts (see Chapter 4) as any amateur sports club would now be included within this heading and thus could apply for charitable status, should they so wish.

Another interesting point to note about the advancement of amateur sport is that this new heading is not just limited to sports which require physical exertion. In section 2(3)(d) of the Charities Act 2006 we are told that 'sport' includes sports or games which promote health by involving either physical *or mental* skill or exertion. This removes any of the difficulties that may have been encountered with games of a less physical nature, such as chess, draughts or even tiddlywinks, which previously could not be included under the heading of 'sport'.

> 'sport' includes sports or games involving either physical *or mental* skill or exertion

It should be noted that any amateur sports club seeking charitable status must be able to benefit a wide range of people from all walks of life; so very expensive sports such as skydiving, or ocean yacht racing, a sport famously described by cynics as 'a sport for those who enjoy standing under an ice-cold cold shower tearing up five pound notes', are unlikely to be considered charitable under this heading.

(h) The advancement of human rights, conflict resolution or reconciliation or the promotion of religious or racial harmony or equality and diversity

This category is not without its difficulties as a charitable purpose, as the advancement of human rights may often require advocating a change in the law and will therefore be held to be political in nature. Political purposes cannot be charitable, as we shall see later on in the chapter.

Because of this difficulty, the Charity Commission has been careful to define human rights charities and so has produced a model set of objects listing all the things a human rights charity could engage in without falling foul of the rule against charities for political purposes. These objects include such activities as raising awareness, commenting on proposed human rights legislation (but not campaigning for changes in the law), and so on.

The following list produced by the Charity Commission should give you a flavour of the sorts of charities that might come under this heading:

✦ Charities concerned with the promotion of human rights at home or abroad.

✦ Mediation charities.

✦ Charities promoting good relations between persons of different racial groups.

✦ Charities promoting the elimination of discrimination on the grounds of age, sex or sexual orientation.

✦ Charities enabling people of one faith to understand the religious beliefs of others.

For a more detailed discussion of the rule against charities with political purposes, see below.

(i) The advancement of environmental protection or improvement

According to the Charity Commission, this heading includes both the preservation and conservation of the natural environment and also the 'promotion of sustainable development' (in other words, the use of resources in a way that aims to preserve the environment so that those resources will be available to future generations as well as our own). Conservation of the environment includes the conservation of animals, birds or other wildlife, plants and their habitats. It also includes the preservation of areas of natural beauty and of special scientific interest, and the preservation of flora, fauna and the environment in general.

It should be noted, however, that charities concerned with the protection or improvement of the environment may be required by the Charity Commission to produce independent expert evidence to show that the species of wildlife in question or the habitat they wish to conserve is worthy of conservation.

The Charity Commission has given the following examples as the sorts of charitable purposes that will fall within the description of the advancement of environmental protection or improvement:

✦ Conservation charities.

✦ Zoos.

✦ The promotion of recycling and sustainable waste management.

✦ Research projects into the use of renewable energy sources.

(j) The relief of those in need, by reason of youth, age, ill-health, disability, financial hardship or other disadvantage

Again, the sorts of charitable purposes which might come under this heading are by no means new, reference having been made to 'Relief of aged, impotent and poor People' in the 1601 Statute of Charitable Uses. We have already seen two very similar categories, providing for the advancement of health or the saving of lives and the prevention or relief of poverty. So why do we need this additional heading?

It is really a much wider category than the two seen previously, aiming to cater for those charities set up to provide relief for those people who might need assistance not simply because they are poor, but because they might have other needs based on their current position in life. The category is of particular assistance to those who are vulnerable due to their age (young or old), or to those who are mentally or physically disabled. It should be noted that under section 2(3)(e) of the Act this includes relief given by the provision of accommodation and care to such persons.

Examples have been given by the Charity Commission of the sorts of charities that might fall within this description:

✦ Charities concerned with the care, upbringing or establishment in life of children or young people; for example, children's care homes; apprenticing; and so on.

✦ Charities concerned with the relief of the effects of old age, such as those providing specialist advice, equipment or accommodation and drop-in centres.

✦ Charities concerned with the relief of disability, such as those providing specialist advice, equipment or accommodation or providing access for the disabled.

✦ Charities concerned with the provision of housing, such as almshouses and housing associations.

Out and about

This task seeks to introduce you to the Charity Commission website, if you have not already seen it, and in particular to familiarise you with the Register of Charities and the information contained within it.

Your client would like to leave a substantial **legacy** to a charity he knows only as 'Candlelighters'. He wants you to make a few checks before he does so, however. Please answer the following:

(a) Are they a current registered charity?

(b) What is their full name and charity number?

(c) When was the charity registered?

(d) What are their objects (i.e. what do they do)?

(e) Where are they based and what area do they cover?

(f) Who is their patron?

(g) What was the charity's income for the last financial year?

(h) What are their three log cabins at Bridlington used for?

(i) What are their plans for the coming year?

You should take no more than 40 minutes on this task.

 Handy tip: Getting stuck? Try looking at the charity accounts . . .

(k) The advancement of animal welfare

This heading will include any charity the aim of which is to relieve animal suffering or to prevent cruelty to animals. The heading covers both domesticated and wild animals in their natural habitats or in captivity.

The Charity Commission gives the following as examples of the sorts of charitable purposes that would fall within this description:

✦ Charities promoting kindness and to prevent or suppress cruelty to animals.

✦ Animal sanctuaries.

✦ The provision of veterinary care and treatment.

✦ Charities concerned with the care and rehoming of animals that are abandoned, mistreated or lost.

✦ Feral animal control: for example, the neutering of wild animals.

Dogs Trust is one of the more famous animal welfare charities. In the People in the law feature, Krystyna McGrath tells us a little bit about their work.

People in the law

Name and position: Krystyna McGrath, Press Officer, Dogs Trust.

What does Dogs Trust do? Dogs Trust is the UK's largest dog welfare charity, and is dedicated to ensuring the welfare of dogs everywhere. As well as rehoming dogs, we invest in campaigns to reduce the number of stray, unwanted and abandoned dogs by promoting neutering and microchipping, and we also invest in education programmes to reach the dog owners of tomorrow.

Ruby, at Dogs Trust
Source: Pete Rooney (*photo*); Krystyna McGrath, Dogs Trust (*text*)

Where are you based? Our head office is in London, but we have a network of 17 Rehoming Centres across the UK, including centres in Scotland, Wales and Northern Ireland. In 2009 we opened our first international Rehoming Centre in Dublin.

How many dogs do you help each year? The charity cares for on average over 16,000 stray, unwanted and abandoned dogs each year. In 2009 we successfully rehomed 13,909 dogs and reunited a further 178 with their owners. We had 1,573 dogs in our care at the year's end.

Do you ever have to have a dog put to sleep? Dogs Trust has a non-destruction policy, and will *never* put a healthy dog to sleep. Dogs that cannot for some reason be rehomed can be sponsored and become permanent residents at our centres.

How reliant are you on donations from the general public? Completely. Of our total income of £60,702,000 in 2009, £36,735,000 was from donations and a further £20,121,000 from legacies.

Why do you think animal charities are so popular in the UK? I think it can definitely be said that we are a nation of animal lovers. The kind actions of the majority far outweigh the cruelty and selfish behaviour of the few.

Where can we find out more? You can go to our website, at http://www.dogstrust.org.uk, or why not visit one of our Rehoming Centres? Details can be found online, or by telephoning us on 0207 837 0006.

(l) The promotion of efficiency of the armed forces of the Crown or of the efficiency of the police, fire and rescue services or ambulance services

It may seem logical that organisations which promote the fire or ambulance services or which provide mountain, sea or air rescue should be charitable, but what brings the armed forces within the scope of charity work? The reason for their inclusion in this heading is simple: the armed forces exist for the defence and security of our country and, as such, it is in the public interest for us to maintain them. Such support of the armed forces would necessarily include ensuring that those forces are properly trained and equipped and ready for battle during times of conflict, and that they have proper facilities. Similarly it is also charitable to promote the efficiency of the police force as the purpose of its existence is to protect the public by preventing and detecting crime and preserving public order. It is therefore in the public interest to maintain a police force.

Charitable purposes that might fall within this description include the following:

✦ Increasing technical knowledge of members of the services through the provision of educational resources, competitions and prizes.

✦ The provision of sporting facilities, equipment and sporting competitions.

✦ Providing memorials to commemorate the fallen or victories.

✦ Providing facilities for services training and/or recreational use.

✦ The provision of exhibitions or displays to encourage recruitment to the services.

✦ Benevolent funds for members of the services or their families.

✦ Provision of an emergency air or sea rescue service and equipment.

(m) Any other purposes within subsection (4)

The purposes contained within Section 2(4) of the Act are:

(a) any purposes which are not listed in the Act but which are recognised as charitable purposes under existing charity law; and

(b) any purposes which could reasonably be regarded as analogous to, or within the spirit of, either any of the purposes listed in the Act or those already recognised as charitable purposes under existing charity law.

The purpose of Section 2(3)(m) is therefore twofold: first, it is a 'catch all' to deal with any purposes already recognised as existing under charity law which may have been missed from the list; in other words, the new Charities Act 2006 does not replace the old law, rather it complements it. The following list represents just some of the charitable purposes which have been held valid under existing case law:

✦ Purposes considered charitable under the Recreational Charities Act 1958, which are charities that seek to provide recreational facilities in the interests of social welfare.

✦ The provision of public works and services, such as the repair of roads and bridges; the provision of public amenities, such as the provision of water, lighting and public cemeteries and crematoriums; and the provision of public facilities such as libraries and public conveniences.

- ✦ The relief of unemployment.
- ✦ Disaster funds.
- ✦ The promotion of industry and commerce.
- ✦ The promotion of agriculture and horticulture.
- ✦ Gifts for the benefit of the inhabitants of a particular locality.
- ✦ The promotion of the moral or spiritual welfare of the community.
- ✦ The rehabilitation of ex-offenders.

Secondly, this section allows room for new categories of charitable purpose to be recognised as charitable in the future, provided they are similar to another charitable purpose already existing. This second point is important because it allows charity law to continue evolving in line with changing social trends and practices.

How do we decide whether a purpose is charitable?

As a general rule of thumb, try using the following:

1. The Charities Act provides a list of purposes which are **prima facie** to be considered charitable. So our first point of call is the list – does our purpose match one of those listed in section 2(2)?

2. Any purposes which don't fall within the specific categories in the list will still be recognised as charitable if they are already recognised as charitable under the existing law (section 2(4)(a)). (So the statutory definition adds to but doesn't replace existing law.)

3. In addition, sections 2(4)(a) and (b) of the Act state that charitable purposes will also include 'any purposes that may reasonably be regarded as analogous to, or within the spirit of, any purposes falling within any' of the matters either included in the list or already recognised as charitable under the existing law.

So, in effect, we are being given examples in the Act of things which will be charitable – but it is not an exclusive and closed list: new charities not previously recognised can be added.

The need for public benefit

We have considered the issue of 'what is a charity?' and looked in some detail at the various types of charity listed in the Charities Act 2006. But in considering whether a particular purpose is or is not charitable in nature, being able to fit that purpose within one of the headings listed in the Act is only the first step. If you remember right back to the beginning of the chapter when we were looking at section 2 of the Charities Act 2006, there was not one but two prerequisites for a purpose to be charitable. Here is a reminder of the wording of section 2(1):

For the purposes of the law of England and Wales, a charitable purpose is a purpose which –

(a) falls within subsection (2), and

(b) is for the public benefit. *

* Emphasis added

So, the requirements for a charitable purpose are, first, that it falls within one of the purposes listed within the Act and, secondly, that the purpose is for the public benefit.

This requirement that public benefit must be demonstrated in the case of every proposed charitable purpose is the one part of the definition of charities which the 2006 Act has changed. The law had previously required proof of benefit to the public only for certain types of charitable purpose; the remainder carried a presumption that the benefit existed without the need for proof.

How do we measure benefit to the public? The Charity Commission guidance indicates that public benefit has two elements:

1. It must be an identifiable benefit of a kind which is recognised by law.

2. It must be provided for or available to the public at large or a sufficient section of the public.

In addition, the Charity Commission provides us with further guidance:

✦ Public benefit will be assessed in the light of modern conditions.

✦ The benefit may be practical or moral in helping the human condition.

✦ The benefit can be direct or indirect (an example of an indirect benefit would be the provision of a hospice: hospices help not only the individual, but also their families and the NHS, in that they relieve pressure on the health service).

✦ Any private benefit must be incidental.

✦ Those who are less well off must not be entirely excluded from the benefit.

This is helpful but making a decision as to whether or not there is an identifiable benefit to the public in any particular given cause can still be problematic. One of the main difficulties the courts have in deciding on the issue of public benefit is whether an **objective** or subjective test should be applied. An objective test would require the Commission to make an objective value judgement as to benefit; this would mean valuing their ideals more highly than the person trying to create the charity and therefore potentially restricting the freedom of the individual. But a subjective test, in other words, 'did the donor genuinely believe there would be public benefit?', could allow charitable trusts to exist when, far from being of public benefit, the majority view might see the purpose as harmful to the public.

There will always be difficulty in achieving an objective approach to certain topics on which public opinion is strong on both sides. An example of this would be pro- and anti-abortion groups (although note the possible difficulties which would be encountered by pressure groups because of their political agendas in any event).

A subjective approach with objective limitations perhaps provides the best alternative and is now considered the preferred basis for assessing public benefit. The two-centred approach has the benefit of allowing many apparently contradictory trusts to exist as charities alongside each other whilst still giving the courts the power to quash a wayward objective where the reality behind any given donor's vision of public benefit is that it is clearly harmful or dangerous. This subjective/objective approach was approved by the

House of Lords case of *National Anti-Vivisection Society* v. *IRC* [1948] AC 31, which concerned a claim for charitable status by the National Anti-Vivisection Society. Lord Simmonds said that:

> Where on the evidence before it the court concludes that, however well intentioned the donor, the achievement of his object will be greatly to the public disadvantage, there can be no justification for saying that it is a charitable object.

The outcome in this case was that the Society was denied charitable status, on the basis that their main object was to obtain an alteration of the law. It was therefore political, and not charitable, in its aims.

The personal nexus test

In spite of the above, in the majority of cases making a decision as to public benefit will actually be quite straightforward. Perhaps the most difficult area in which to make a decision is where a private trust (or a trust of significant private benefit) is trying to gain the advantages of charitable status by claiming it is of benefit to a section of the public.

To overcome this, the courts developed what is known as the '**personal nexus test**'. The leading case in the development of this test was *Oppenheim* v. *Tobacco Securities Trust Co. Ltd* [1951] AC 297. The case concerned a trust established by a man who owned a large stake in the British American Tobacco company. He established a trust to provide for the education of the children of employees or ex-employees of the company. Despite the considerable size of the class (the members of the group amounted to around 110,000 people at that time), the court held (Lord McDermott dissenting) that the trust could not be charitable on the basis that it was not of public benefit. In Lord Simmonds's view, in order to show public benefit, the identity of the members of the class must not be defined by means of a 'personal nexus'. He explained:

> the quality which distinguishes [the beneficiary] from other members of the community . . . must be a quality which does not depend on their relationship to a particular individual.

He went on:

> A group of persons may be numerous but, if the nexus between them is their relationship to a single [donor or organisation] they are neither the community nor a section of the community for charitable purposes.

Thus, regardless of the size of the group, if the thing that binds that group is an individual, the trust in question cannot be charitable. This test was criticised by Lord McDermott in his **dissenting judgment** in *Oppenheim* as being artificial and illogical. A trust for railway workers in the north of London would pass the test; but a trust for people working for a particular railway company expressly identified in the gift would not. He stated that the test should be one of fact and degree. Lord Cross, in the subsequent House of Lords

decision of *Dingle* v. *Turner* [1972] AC 601, which involved a trust set up to pay pensions to the poor employees of a limited company, expressly approved Lord McDermott's dissenting judgment. Whether or not a future Supreme Court case will follow this remains to be seen.

And finally, on the issue of public benefit, there are one or two interesting points to note about the following types of charity:

Public benefit and religious charities

As we have already seen in the section on charities for the advancement of religion, above, the courts see a clear benefit to the public in the promotion of any religion above the promotion of none. However, care needs to be taken in the case of private religious orders that they can be seen to be providing a genuine public service, or benefit.

In the case of *Gilmour* v. *Coates* [1949] AC 426, the income from a trust was to be used for the maintenance of an order of Carmelite nuns. The nuns lived in a cloistered community, devoting themselves to prayer and meditation and maintaining minimal contact with the outside world. The order believed their prayers and meditation were of benefit to the public because they caused the intervention of God. However, the House of Lords held that the order did not benefit the public and was therefore not charitable.

Public benefit and animal charities

Trusts for the benefit of animals can encounter similar difficulties. In asking the question 'how is a charity for the benefit of animals of benefit to the public?', it helps to take a very brief look at the historical development of this type of charitable trust. Animal trusts were originally brought about to prevent cruelty to animals and they were accepted as being charitable on the basis that they tended to improve the morality of the human race, cruelty to animals being considered 'degrading to man'. This was the judgment of Mr Justice Chitty in the case of *Re Foveaux* [1895] 2 Ch 501, which questioned the charitable status of two anti-vivisection societies. (Interestingly, in this case the societies *were* granted charitable status. As we have seen above, however, the political nature of such societies means that the judgment has not been followed in subsequent cases.)

Of course, the list of animal charities was long ago extended beyond this limited field, to include gifts in favour of animals generally. One explanation for this was given in the case of *Re Wedgewood* [1915] 1 Ch 113. A **testatrix** left her **residuary estate** on trust to be used for the protection and benefit of animals and, in particular, for seeking more humane ways of slaughter. The Court of Appeal held that the gift was charitable as such gifts tended 'to promote public morality by checking the innate tendency to cruelty, ameliorating the condition of the brute creation and stimulating humane sentiments in men towards lower animals, thereby elevating the human race'. Put simply, animal charities benefit the public because we have a feeling of altruistic well-being when we are kind to animals.

Note that there must still be a genuine benefit to mankind in making a gift to animals in order for that gift to be charitable, however. In the case of *Re Grove-Grady* [1929] 1 Ch 557, a testatrix left her residuary estate upon trust to found an animal society whose objects included the acquisition of land:

> for the purpose of providing a refuge or refuges for the preservation of all animals, birds or other creatures not human . . . and so that all such animals, birds and other creatures not human shall there be safe from molestation or destruction by man.

Her trust failed on the basis that it did not involve any benefit to the public. In explaining the reasoning behind the judgment, Lord Hanworth, Master of the Rolls, said of the trust:

It is not a sanctuary for any animals of a timid nature whose species is in danger of dying out: nor is it a sanctuary for birds which have almost entirely left our shores and may be attracted once more by a safe seclusion to nest and rear their young. No such purpose is indicated, nor indeed possible. The one characteristic of the refuge is that it is free from the molestation of man, while all the fauna within it are to be free to molest and harry one another.

Such a purpose does not, in my opinion, afford any advantage to animals that are useful to mankind in particular, or any protection from cruelty to animals generally. It does not denote any elevating lesson to mankind.

Lord Hanworth's suggestion, therefore, is that a sanctuary for endangered species would have been deemed charitable. In this case, however, there was no such purpose. It should be noted that Lord Justice Lawrence gave a dissenting judgment in this case, believing the other Lords to be making too fine a distinction between one form of sanctuary and another.

Charities and political purposes

Case Summary

As we have seen earlier in the chapter, political purposes cannot be charitable. In the case of *McGovern* v. *Attorney-General* [1982] Ch 321, in which a trust set up by the human rights group, Amnesty International, was seeking charitable status, Mr Justice Slade gave a number of reasons why it was necessary for trusts with political purposes to be vetoed in this way. He said that, as a matter of prime importance, the court could not risk prejudicing its reputation for political impartiality if it was seen to be allowing the promotion of political causes. Additionally, where the purposes of a trust were to secure a change in foreign law, as was the issue in *McGovern* v. *Attorney-General*, as a matter of public policy the court could not be seen to be advocating its purpose as this would carry with it a real risk of prejudicing the relations of this country with the foreign country in question.

> the court could not
> risk prejudicing
> its reputation for
> political impartiality

The most important reason, however, for not allowing charities with political aims was the simple fact that the courts are bound to consider the law to be correct as it stands; to do otherwise would be to undermine the very foundations on which the law is based.

So what purposes will be considered by the courts as political? Political campaigning will certainly not be seen as charitable, as a students' union was to find out in the case of *Webb* v. *O'Doherty and Others* (1991) *The Times* 11 February, where it was held that the funds of a students' union, albeit that the union was in itself an educational charity, could not be used in connection with a 'Stop the Gulf War' campaign. Nor will gifts to political parties be seen as charitable, as was seen in the case of *Re Hopkinson* [1949] 1 All ER 346, in which a gift to the Labour Party was refused charitable status. As for other political purposes, Mr Justice Slade in *McGovern* v. *Attorney-General* provided a helpful list of purposes which would be considered political, stating that trusts whose principal purpose is to:

Case Summary

Case Summary

✦ further the interests of a political party; or

✦ procure changes in the law of this or a foreign country; or

✦ procure a reversal of government policy or of particular decisions of governmental authorities in this or a foreign country

will all be considered political and thus fail as charitable purposes.

Of course, we have seen a solution to certain issues in the human rights category in the Charity Commission's production of a model set of objects for human rights charities. Nevertheless, great care must be taken by charities not to do anything which crosses the line between advocating a review of the current legal framework and campaigning for change.

The trust must be exclusively charitable

It is imperative that a purpose falls within one of the charitable purposes listed under the act in order to be granted charitable status. Therefore where a settlor creates a trust for a mixture of purposes, some of which are charitable and some of which are not, that trust will necessarily fail as not being for exclusively charitable purposes. Thus, in the case of *IRC* v. *Baddeley* [1955] 1 All ER 525, in which many of the objects of the trust were charitable but some were simply for the promotion of social activities, the trust was denied charitable status.

Case Summary

The outcome will depend, ultimately, on the exact wording of the trust and each case will be considered individually. As a general rule of construction, however, the word 'and' between listed purposes will be interpreted as conjunctive and therefore succeed as charitable, whereas the word 'or' will be interpreted disjunctively and therefore fail. To give an example of how this would work, we can take a look at the case of *Re Sutton* (1885) 28 Ch D 464. Here, a gift to 'charitable *and* deserving purposes' was held exclusively charitable because the word 'and' was interpreted as meaning that only deserving objects which were *also* charitable would benefit. If the gift had been to 'charitable *or* deserving purposes', it would have failed on the basis that a purpose can be deserving, but it is not necessarily charitable.

Case Summary

Failure of charitable trusts and the doctrine of cy près

One final matter which needs to be considered in the context of charitable trusts is what happens where the testator leaves a gift in their will to a charity but, on that person's death, it transpires that the charity named in the will has either amalgamated with another charity or is no longer in existence.

You will remember from earlier chapters that, ordinarily, if a trust fails, the money or property which would have formed the basis of that trust will instead revert to the testator, forming part of the **residue** of his estate. In the case of charities, however, there are special rules governed by the ancient doctrine of '**cy près**', a term that comes from the French, meaning 'as near as possible'. In essence, it allows the **executors** or **administrators** of the estate, where a testator leaves a gift to a charity which has ceased to exist, to apply those funds to be used instead for charitable purposes which are similar to those named by the testator rather than having to return the funds to the residue of the estate. This enables the testator's representatives to keep as closely as is reasonably possible to the wishes of the deceased in administering his estate, even where a strict interpretation of the law would, under other circumstances, prevent this.

Amalgamation

Before we turn to the rules which govern the doctrine of cy près let us first deal briefly with the position where the charity named by the testator has amalgamated, or merged, with another. Where such a situation arises, the original charities will simply be regarded as having continued in a new form. There is therefore no need to apply the doctrine of cy près as this is only necessary where the charity has actually ceased to exist. The authority for this is the case of *Re Faraker* [1912] 2 Ch 488. In this case a testatrix left a legacy to Hannah Bayly's Charity, which was a charity founded for the benefit of poor widows in Rotherhithe, London. By the time of the testatrix's death, the charity had amalgamated with another charity to create one single charity for the benefit of the poor in Rotherhithe. The court held that the gift to the original charity had not failed as the charity had continued in the form of a second amalgamated charity which encompassed the objects of the first.

Case Summary

Subsequent failure of the charity

Where a charity which forms the subject of a legacy has ceased to exist, the application of the doctrine of cy près turns on whether the charity in question ceased to exist subsequent to or prior to the testator's death.

Where the charity was still in existence when the testator died but ceases to exist before the gift is handed over the money which forms the gift will instead be applied to a charity the objects of which are as close as possible or 'cy près' to the original charity. This is allowed to happen under the doctrine of cy près on the basis that the **subject matter** of the gift was dedicated to charity at the moment of the testator's death and so the funds are no longer available to be returned to the testator's estate for distribution along with the residue.

Initial failure of the charity

Where a charity named in the will of a testator has ceased to exist *before* that person's death, however, the position is slightly more complicated. In this situation, the subject matter of the gift can only be applied cy près if it can be shown that the testator, in making the gift, did so with 'general charitable intention'. In other words, the testator must be shown not to have been so wholly committed to the particular charity named by him in the will that if that charity failed he would prefer the funds to revert back to his residuary estate rather than to go to some other similar charitable cause.

So, how do we determine whether or not the testator had a 'general charitable intention'? In the case of *Re Spence* [1978] 3 All ER 92, the facts of which are to follow, Sir Robert Megarry said that: 'the essence of the distinction is in the difference between particularity and generality'. Thus, it would appear that, basically, it depends on how specific the testator was about the gift and whether the wording of that gift left any room for a more general interpretation of it to serve a wider charitable purpose. In *Re Spence*, Mrs Spence had left half her residuary estate to the 'the Old Folks Home at Hillworth Lodge, Keighley'. The home had closed a year before she died and so it had become impossible to make the gift to them. On approaching the courts for a ruling on the matter, it was held

Case Summary

that the testatrix had clearly intended to make a gift to a specific institution and that there was no general charitable intention. Thus, the gift reverted to Mrs Spence's estate for distribution with the residue.

A contrasting case is that of *Biscoe* v. *Jackson* (1887) 35 Ch D 460. Here, a legacy was left to provide for the establishment of a soup kitchen and cottage hospital in Shoreditch. It was not possible to do this but the court nevertheless said that the testator had demonstrated in making the gift a wider underlying general intention to help the poor of Shoreditch which went beyond the specific wording of the gift. Cy près was therefore applied and the monies diverted to the more general cause.

It would appear, then, that there is quite a fine line between those charitable gifts to which cy près will be applied and those to which it will not. The case law does give us a certain amount of help here, however, depending on the wording of the gift. First of all, where the testator has made a number of gifts to charity the court will find it easier to imply a general charitable intent and apply cy près. For example, in the case of *Re Knox* [1937] Ch 109, the testatrix had directed that the residue of her estate should be divided equally between two hospitals, the Newcastle-upon-Tyne Nursing Home and the children's charity, Dr Barnardo's. At the time of her death no nursing home fitting the description of the Newcastle-upon-Tyne nursing home could be found, and so the gift would have failed. However, the court said the fact that the gift to the nursing home formed part of a wider range of charitable gifts showed a general charitable intent on the part of the testatrix. They therefore directed that the gift should be applied cy près. The money was shared equally between the Northumberland County Nursing Association and the Cathedral Nursing Society for the Sick Poor of Newcastle-upon-Tyne, these being the two institutions which seemed most nearly to correspond to the particular institution referred to in the will.

Another case in point is that of *Re Satterthwaite's Will Trusts* [1966] 1 WLR 277, in which a testatrix who hated human beings had left the residue of her estate to be divided between nine animal charities which she had apparently chosen at random from a telephone directory. It transpired that one of the purported beneficiaries, the 'London Animal Hospital', had never been a registered charity, but a London vet came forward to claim the money on the grounds that 'London Animal Hospital' was a former trading name of his. The vet was not able to provide any evidence that the testatrix knew of his business, however, either under its former guise as the London Animal Hospital or otherwise, and the court rejected his claim. The money was applied cy près instead on the basis of the testatrix's other gifts which, they said, evidenced not a desire to benefit the business of an individual but rather a more general charitable intention to help animals.

And finally, where a testator has left a gift to a charity which has never existed, the courts will find it easier to infer a general charitable intention than where a specific institution has been chosen and has since ceased to exist. This was evidenced in the 1936 case of *Re Harwood* [1936] Ch 285, in which a testatrix purported to leave legacies to two charities in her will: the Wisbech Peace Society and the Peace Society of Belfast. Unfortunately, the Wisbech Peace Society had ceased to exist before the testatrix's death, and the Peace Society of Belfast was found never to have existed. The court held that, whilst the former gift to the Wisbech Peace Society could not be applied cy près as the society had lapsed, the purported gift to the Peace Society of Belfast showed a general charitable intention to promote peace. The latter gift was therefore to be applied to charity cy près.

The flow chart in Figure 5.1 should help you in applying the rules of cy près in a problem question scenario.

Figure 5.1 Cy près flow chart

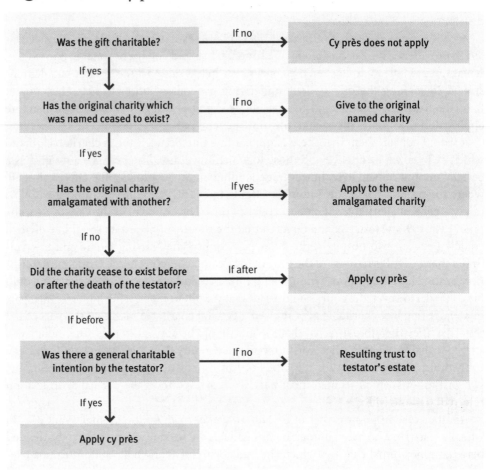

Summary

✦ The Charities Act 2006 provides a list of purposes which are prima facie to be considered charitable (section 2(2)).

✦ Any purposes not on the list will still be recognised as charitable if they are already recognised as charitable under the existing law (section 2(4)(a)).

✦ Any purposes that may reasonably be regarded as analogous to, or within the spirit of, any purposes falling within any of the matters either included in the list or already recognised as charitable under the existing law will also be considered charitable (section 2(4)(a) and (b)).

◆ In order to be charitable, the purpose must also be for the public benefit. The benefit must be an identifiable benefit of a kind recognised by law and must be for the public or a sufficient section of the public.

◆ In order to show public benefit, the identity of the members of the class must not be defined by means of a 'personal nexus' (*Oppenheim* v. *Tobacco Securities Trust Co. Ltd*).

◆ Political purposes cannot be charitable for policy reasons.

◆ Trusts which are not exclusively for charitable purposes cannot be classed as charitable.

◆ Where a testator leaves a gift to a charity which has ceased to exist, the doctrine of cy près allows those funds to be used instead for charitable purposes similar to those named by the testator.

◆ Where the charity has amalgamated, original charities will simply be regarded as having continued in a new form and there is no need to apply cy près.

◆ Where the charity still existed when the testator died but ceases to exist before the gift is handed over, the money will be applied to a charity the objects of which are as close as possible to the original charity.

◆ Where the charity has ceased to exist before the testator's death, the gift can only be applied cy près if it can be shown that the testator made it with a 'general charitable intention' in mind.

Question and answer*

Problem: Explain why each of the following purposes is or is not charitable, giving reasons for your answers:

1. A trust for the provision of land to create and maintain a sanctuary for the preservation of wildlife, into which the general public are allowed.

2. A trust for the provision of land to create and maintain a sanctuary for the preservation of wildlife, into which man is not allowed.

3. A trust for the provision of land to create and maintain a sanctuary for the preservation of wildlife, into which only a small group of researchers is allowed.

You should allow yourself no more than 40 minutes to complete this task.

Essay: Describe the difficulties which may be encountered by charities wishing to campaign for a change in the law and comment on the effect of any restrictions placed on their ability to do so.

This question should be answered in 40 minutes.

✱ Answer guidance is provided at the end of the chapter.

Further reading and references

Buckley, C. (2008) 'The Charities Act 2006: consolidation or reform?', *Charity Law and Practice Review*, **11(1), 1–42.**
This is a pretty long article, but worth reading if you want an in-depth review of the Charities Act 2006. In particular, the article reviews the case law on the public benefit requirement and discusses changes to the law in this area.

Quint, F. (2009) 'Recent developments in the cy près principle', *Charity Law and Practice Review*, **11(2), 49–57.**
This article looks at the historical development of the doctrine of cy près and talks about the changes introduced by the Charities Act 2006. Interesting comment on the application of the cy-près principle in Scotland and the possible move to develop the doctrine further for the variation of trust purposes.

Rahmatian, A. (2009) 'The continued relevance of the "poor relations" and the "poor employees" cases under the Charities Act 2006', **Conv 1, 12–20.**
This article examines the abolition of the presumption of public benefit under the Charities Act 2006 and discusses whether the previously existing charities set up for 'poor relations' and 'poor employees' can withstand the change.

Warburton, J. (2009) 'Charities, grants and campaigning', *Charity Law and Practice Review*, **11(2), 1–17.**
Excellent article on the dangers of using charity funds for political purposes, discussing in detail the consequences of a charity becoming involved with funding a non-charitable political purpose, including being held in breach of trust and loss of charitable status.

Website

The Charity Commission: http://www.charity-commission.gov.uk
The Charity Commission website is user-friendly and full of useful information about charities. In particular, there is a wealth of information on public benefit, including what is expected of charities in terms of public benefit and the law underlying the principles of public benefit. Well worth a look at.

Question and answer guidance

Problem:

1. *A trust for the provision of land to create and maintain a sanctuary for the preservation of wildlife, into which the general public are allowed.*

In order to be charitable, a trust must come under one of the heads of charity in section 2(2) Charities Act 2006, and be of public benefit. Arguably, a sanctuary for the preservation of wildlife would come under the heading of charities for the advancement of animal welfare. However, care must be taken that such a charity would also benefit the public. Presumably a wildlife sanctuary into which members of the public are allowed would be considered of benefit to the public and therefore be allowable (see *Re Grove-Grady*).

2. *A trust for the provision of land to create and maintain a sanctuary for the preservation of wildlife, into which man is not allowed.*

Because man is not allowed into the sanctuary, this raises the question whether the sanctuary is of public benefit. Again, see *Re Grove-Grady*. However, note Lord Hanworth's comments about sanctuaries for the preservation of endangered species. It may depend on what wildlife is to be preserved by the existence of the sanctuary. Consider whether it could instead be classed as a charity for environmental improvement.

3. *A trust for the provision of land to create and maintain a sanctuary for the preservation of wildlife, into which only a small group of researchers is allowed.*

Again, there is an issue of public benefit here. Would a small group of researchers be enough to constitute a public benefit? The Charity Commission says that, in order to be of benefit to the public, the charity must be provided for or available to the public at large or a sufficient section of the public. The sanctuary may therefore fail on this basis unless some other form of public benefit can be shown. What about classing the charity not as one for the advancement of animal welfare but for education (research being included in the definition of education)? See *Re Besterman* for details of what constitutes charitable research.

Essay:

This essay is asking the student to comment on difficulties encountered with trusts for political purposes. Political purposes prima facie cannot be charitable (*McGovern* v. *Attorney-General*). The courts are bound to consider the law to be correct as it stands; therefore to allow a charity that campaigns for a change in the law would undermine the foundations of the court system. It would also prejudice the courts' reputation for impartiality. For examples of cases in which the aims of a group have been held to be political, see *Webb* v. *O'Doherty* (the 'Stop the Gulf War' campaign), as well as *McGovern*, above. A good answer would also discuss the anti-vivisection cases, and what prevented them from being charitable.

Reference could be made to Warburton 2009, which comments on the practical implications of a charity being held non-charitable and the financial effects of loss of charitable status.

To conclude, the student should comment on the restrictions placed on charities wishing to campaign for change and whether they think the restrictions are acceptable. A good answer would balance any comment against the effects of the new section 2(2) charitable heading of charities 'for the advancement of human rights, conflict resolution or reconciliation or the promotion of religious or racial harmony or equality and diversity'.

Chapter 6
Variation of trusts

Key points In this chapter we will be looking at:

- ✦ Reasons for wanting to change the terms of a trust
- ✦ The jurisdiction of the court to vary trusts
- ✦ Variation of trusts under statute

- ✦ Rectification of wills under the Administration of Justice Act 1982
- ✦ 'Exporting' a trust to another jurisdiction
- ✦ The rule in *Saunders* v. *Vautier*

Introduction

With the knowledge we have acquired so far we now have the wherewithal to set up a **trust**:

- ✦ we know what the requirements are for the creation of a valid trust;
- ✦ we know what **formalities** are needed to bring our trust to life;
- ✦ we also know what the pitfalls and difficulties are in creating a trust, through our study of certainties and **purpose trusts**.

But what do we do if we want to alter a trust which is already in existence? There are many reasons for wanting to vary the terms of a trust. The most common of these is that the tax position of the trust has changed through the introduction of new legislation and it has therefore become disadvantageous to the beneficiaries for the trust to continue to be run in its present form. One example of this might be the changes in the law relating to **discretionary trusts** affecting the payment of inheritance tax that we touched upon in the 'trusts for the family' section in Chapter 1. Remember, a trust lasts for a relatively

long period of time and the likelihood of changes in the law taking place during its existence is great. If there is no flexibility written into the terms of the trust, therefore, the ability to change may have to be imposed by other means.

You may be thinking that, regardless of the reasons for wanting to change the terms of the trust, it would go against the fundamental principles of the creation of trusts to alter what has been put into place in good faith by the **settlor**. At the end of the day, the settlor has given their property to a third party in trust for them to manage on behalf of a specific person and in a specific way. Are we not then entering rather a morally grey area in starting to think about changing the terms of a trust which the settlor has put into place? It is a clear and fundamental duty of the trustees under a trust to adhere to the terms of that trust and to administer it in accordance with those terms. Indeed, any deviation from the terms of the trust on the part of the **trustees** would amount to a breach of trust. However, there are a multitude of reasons for wanting to make a change to the terms of a trust, and for the most part the changes effected will either benefit the **beneficiaries** or at least put them out of harm's way. In many cases we can therefore conclude that this is what the settlor would have done, had they been possessed of the knowledge that those making the change now have. Nevertheless, this is a sensitive area and the courts will be particularly cautious in allowing variations to a trust, even where the change will be of genuine benefit of the beneficiaries.

There are a number of ways in which a variation of trust can be effected, falling broadly into two categories. These are:

✦ variation under the court's inherent jurisdiction; and

✦ variation under statute.

We will look at each of these methods of variation in turn.

The court's inherent jurisdiction

We have already seen that the trustees under a trust have a fundamental duty to administer that trust in accordance with the terms set out by the settlor. It is therefore not within the power of the trustees to vary the terms of the trust, regardless of whether it would be in the best interests of the beneficiaries to do so. Neither do the beneficiaries have the right to vary the terms of an existing trust, even if they are all of full age and **capacity** and in agreement to the change (although they can bring the trust to an end and set up a new trust on different terms, under the rule in *Saunders* v. *Vautier*. This is dealt with later in the chapter). What is open to the trustees, however, is to make an application to the court to vary the trust if they are unable to administer the trust effectively without a change being made. In such emergency circumstances the courts have an **inherent**, or overriding, **jurisdiction** to make variations to the terms of the trust, albeit within closely defined parameters.

The ability of the court to allow variations in the terms of the trust in this way was originally set out in the case of *Re New* [1901] 2 Ch 534. The case concerned three trusts which all held shares in Wollaton Colliery Co. Ltd, a mining company. The company was undergoing a restructure, which meant that the old shares would be revoked and a greater number of new shares would be issued in the company at a lower value. Unfortunately the trustees did not have the authority under the terms of their trust deed to invest in the new shares, which left them in an impossible position as regards their investment. In authorising the variation, Lord Justice Romer commented on the need for an ability to deviate from the terms of trusts under exceptional circumstances. He said:

Case Summary

in the management of a trust . . . it not infrequently happens that some peculiar state of circumstances arises for which provision is not expressly made by the trust instrument, and which renders it most desirable, and it may even be essential, for the benefit of the estate and in the interests of all the [beneficiaries], that certain acts should be done by the trustees which in ordinary circumstances they have no power to do. In a case of this kind, which may reasonably be supposed to be one not foreseen or anticipated by the author of the trust, where the trustees are embarrassed by the emergency which has arisen and the duty cast upon them to do what is best for the estate, and the consent of all the beneficiaries cannot be obtained by reason of some of them not being *sui juris* [that is, that they have reached the age of majority] or in existence, then it may be right for the Court, and the Court in a proper case would have jurisdiction, to sanction on behalf of all concerned such acts on behalf of the trustees . . .

Despite the outcome in this case, which allowed the variation of the trust to sanction the reinvestment in the Wollaton Colliery Company, it is important to note that the court's inherent jurisdiction is not available to trustees to use as a tool wherever a change in the terms of the trust would be desirable or convenient. The power of the court to alter the terms of a trust is strictly limited to instances where the proper administration of the trust is compromised and a change in its provisions is therefore rendered necessary. Only two years later, in the case of *Re Tollemache* [1903] 1 Ch 547, which concerned an application to the court to vary the terms of a trust to allow for the life interest of a beneficiary to be mortgaged in order to provide them with a greater income, Mr Justice Kekewich was keen to stress that the facts presented in *Re New* represented the 'furthest extent to which this jurisdiction will stretch'. He refused the application to vary the Tollemache trust because he said that, although the proposed mortgage would have been of benefit to the beneficiary, there was no real 'emergency' justifying the change and so the court would be acting outside of its jurisdiction if it went ahead and authorised the change.

The Court of Appeal case of *Chapman v. Chapman* [1954] AC 429 fifty years later (the facts of which are below) sought to clarify the position further by setting out four possible situations in which the court could use its inherent jurisdiction to sanction the variation of a trust's terms. One of these situations is now only of historical interest due to changes in the law; however, the remaining three are as follows:

1. To allow trustees to enter into some business transaction which was not authorised by the settlement

This would cover situations such as the investment authorised in the case of *Re New*, mentioned above. As we have already seen, this arm of the court's jurisdiction can be used only in cases of genuine emergency, and a variation requested purely on the basis that it will be of benefit to the beneficiaries will not suffice (see the facts of *Re Tollemache*, above). To give a slightly different example of where this first type of discretion might be used we can look at the case of *Re Jackson* (1882) 21 Ch D 786, in which the trustees were given permission by the court to take out a mortgage over trust property in order to pay for vital repairs to be carried out to the building and thereby save it from imminent collapse.

2. To allow maintenance out of income which the settlor has directed to be accumulated

This allows the trustees to advance all or part of the income made by the trust fund to the beneficiaries in order to maintain them (for a more detailed discussion on trustees' powers of maintenance see Chapter 11). The courts may do this even where the settlor has directed that any income on the trust fund is paid back into the fund and accumulated until some later date. A good example of this use of the court's jurisdiction can be seen in the case of *Re Collins* (1886) 32 Ch D 229. The case concerned a **settlement** made under a will, in which the **testator** had directed that the income from his **estate** should be accumulated for a period of 21 years and then given to his sister for life and then to her three sons and their children. The court allowed for a variation in the terms of the trust allowing the trustees to make payments to the sister for the maintenance of her children during the 21 year period. In making his judgment Mr Justice Farwell said:

> Where a testator has made a provision for a family . . . it is assumed that he did not intend that these children should be left unprovided for or in a state of such moderate means that they should not be educated properly for the position and fortune which he designs them to have . . .

We can see from the facts of this case that this is one situation where the trustees are allowed to go against the clearly stated wishes of the settlor, in order the better to serve the needs of the beneficiaries. It is also interesting to note that the 'emergency' element appears to have been removed from this arm of the court's jurisdiction, the judge being more concerned about the children being maintained in the manner to which they are to be accustomed on receipt of the fund.

3. To allow a compromise on behalf of infants and beneficiaries yet to be born

This third situation was originally designed to allow the court to use their inherent jurisdiction to agree to variations in the trust in the event of a dispute as to the meaning of its terms. In its original form, therefore, it could be used by the courts wherever they needed to resolve a dispute between the parties to a trust, allowing them to intervene and provide their own interpretation of the trust wording as they felt appropriate. So, for example, if the trustees approached the court because a dispute had arisen as to how trust monies were to be invested, the court could use their jurisdiction under this heading to vary the trust, allowing for a change in its terms to reflect the outcome of the dispute. What is important here is that this does not give the courts a licence to make blanket amendments to the terms of a trust; rather it allows them to give clarity, or define the terms of the trust where there is a disagreement as to their meaning.

> this does not give the courts a licence to make blanket amendments

The case of *Chapman* v. *Chapman* was a defining case in this area because the court really used the case to crack down on what was becoming an increasing tendency of the courts to use this arm of their jurisdiction as an excuse to agree amendments to trusts wherever they saw fit, rather than specifically to solve cases of genuine dispute between the parties. In *Chapman* v. *Chapman* the trustees had made an application to the court to authorise a variation of the trust which would have the effect of reducing the risk to the beneficiaries of the payment of inheritance tax. The House of Lords did not allow the variation of the trust for this purpose, however, Lord Evershed saying that:

Case Summary

> it was not part of the function of Her Majesty's court to recast settlements from time to time, merely with a view to tax avoidance, even if they had the power to do so, which, in our opinion, they have not.

The judgment in this case served to restrict the application of the court's jurisdiction to cases of genuine dispute and prevent any further widening of the court's powers to vary trust terms. However, not everyone was happy with the decision. In giving his **dissenting judgment** in the case, Lord Cohen said that he felt the word 'compromise' should not be restricted just to compromises made between the parties in the event of a dispute. In his view, the term meant compromise in the wider sense of the word. It should include any case in which the parties were in agreement over their wish to vary the terms of the trust but were unable do so without the court's intervention, either because one or more of the beneficiaries had not yet reached the age of **majority** or because they otherwise lacked the necessary capacity to consent to the change. Lord Cohen believed that the narrowing of this area of the court's jurisdiction was an unnecessary restriction of the court's powers and that the court should continue to be able to intervene wherever adjudication was necessary. Whether there was agreement between the parties or whether the matter was a case of dispute was an irrelevance. In his own words: 'The High Court is a superior court and the control of trustees is a matter within its jurisdiction.'

A later Law Commission report (1957) shared Lord Cohen's views. It was in response to this report by the Law Commission that the Variation of Trusts Act 1958 was enacted. This gives the court much wider powers of variation and will be considered in detail below. Before we move on to look at statutory provisions, however, it may be useful to look at a couple of more recent contrasting cases in which the inherent jurisdiction to vary under a compromise has been used. The first is the case of *Allen* v. *Distillers Co. (Biochemicals) Ltd* [1974] QB 384, which concerned a beneficiary who had been a victim of the thalidomide drug, which caused widespread deformities in unborn babies of mothers who had taken the anti-sickness tablet. In that case the court used their inherent jurisdiction to order the postponement of a compensation payment to the beneficiary beyond the age of majority. The matter had been the subject of some debate between the parties to the action.

Case Summary

The second case of note is that of *Mason* v. *Farbrother* [1983] 2 All ER 1078. Here a variation was requested in respect of a pension fund to allow for wider powers of invest-ment in order to enable greater profits to be provided to its members. The court refused to make the variation under its inherent jurisdiction, despite the fact that the case had stemmed from a genuine uncertainty as to the meaning of the investment clause as stated in the pension fund documentation. The court stated that the variation which the trustees had requested took the alteration beyond a mere request for a definition of the clause's meaning and instead sought the approval of an entirely new investment clause which, under the court's inherent jurisdiction, they did not have the power to approve.

Variation of Trusts Act 1958

Whereas the inherent jurisdiction of the court, following *Chapman* v. *Chapman*, only allowed the judiciary to make variations to a trust in the event of a dispute (with the limited exceptions of variations to allow for payments of maintenance or in the case of genuine emergency), the Variation of Trusts Act 1958 is altogether wider in its scope. Broadly speaking, section 1(1) of the Act provides that the court can agree variations to trusts on behalf of anyone who is unable to consent by themselves, by reason either of age or of incapacity, provided that the variation will benefit the person on behalf of whom the consent is given. The section reads as follows:

(1) Where property, whether real or personal, is held on trusts arising, whether before or after the passing of this Act, under any will, settlement or other disposition, the court may if it thinks fit by order approve on behalf of –

(a) any person having, directly or indirectly, an interest, whether **vested** or **contingent**, under the trusts who by reason of infancy or other incapacity is incapable of assenting, or

(b) any person (whether ascertained or not) who may become entitled, directly or indirectly, to an interest under the trusts as being at a future date or on the happening of a future event a person of any specified description or a member of any specified class of persons, so however that this paragraph shall not include any person who would be of that description, or a member of that class, as the case may be, if the said date had fallen or the said event had happened at the date of the application to the court, or

(c) any person unborn, or

(d) any person in respect of any discretionary interest of his under protective trusts where the interest of the principal beneficiary has not failed or determined

any arrangement (by whomsoever proposed, and whether or not there is any other person beneficially interested who is capable of assenting thereto) varying or revoking all or any of the trusts, or enlarging the powers of the trustees of managing or administering any of the property subject to the trusts:

Provided that except by virtue of paragraph (d) of this subsection the court shall not approve an arrangement on behalf of any person unless the carrying out thereof would be for the benefit of that person.

Contingent interests under section 1(1)(b)

It has already been mentioned above that the Act gives the court authority to make variations on behalf of those who are unable to consent to amendments to the trust instrument on account of their age or incapacity. The section also gives the court the authority to make such changes on behalf of people who are yet to become entitled under the terms of the trust, either because they are the subject of trustee discretion, or because they have not yet been born. In addition the section makes provision, at 1(1)(b), for those whose interests are contingent upon the happening of some future event, such as marriage, or the death of a higher-ranking beneficiary.

What the Act does *not* authorise the court to do is to make variations on behalf of adult beneficiaries, who are deemed able to give consent personally to any change proposed by the trustees. This would include both those under section 1(1)(b) for whom the contingency in question had arisen, and those whose right under the terms of the trust had come into being. The court would be unable to give consent on behalf of such persons, as they would be in a position to give consent on their own account. To give an example of how this might work in practice, try imagining the following scenario:

Sanjeet has a **life interest** under a trust, with a **gift over** to any member of her family who is working in the healthcare industry at the date of her death. If Sanjeet or her trustees wish to vary the terms of the trust, it will be impossible to obtain the consent to the variation of those named in the gift over, as it is not possible to predict which members of Sanjeet's family will be working in the healthcare industry on the date of her death.

On the other hand, if any person is already working in the healthcare industry at the date of her application to vary the trust, the court will be unable to consent on their behalf and the direct consent of that person will have to be obtained. This is because, whilst they may no longer be working in the healthcare industry at the time when Sanjeet actually dies and they therefore may not be entitled under the terms of the trust, for the purposes of making the variation it will be assumed that Sanjeet has died at the date of the application. The trust is therefore taken as being 'set' at the date of the application and not some yet to be predicted date in the future. Figure 6.1 (overleaf) shows how this would work.

Figure 6.1 Contingent interests under section 1(1)(b)

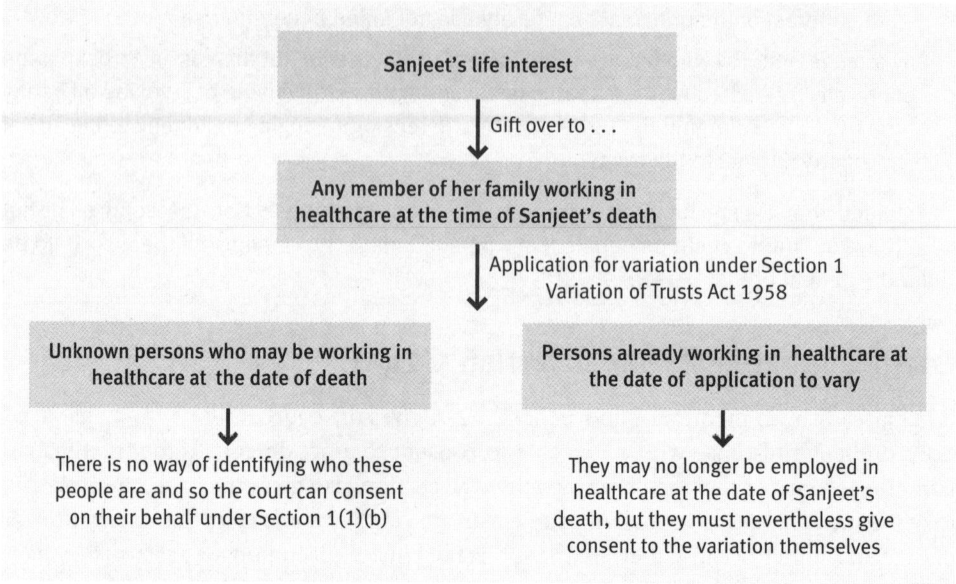

```
                    ┌─────────────────────────────┐
                    │    Sanjeet's life interest   │
                    └─────────────────────────────┘
                                │ Gift over to . . .
                                ▼
                    ┌─────────────────────────────┐
                    │ Any member of her family working in │
                    │ healthcare at the time of Sanjeet's death │
                    └─────────────────────────────┘
                                │ Application for variation under Section 1
                                │ Variation of Trusts Act 1958
                                ▼
    ┌─────────────────────────────┐      ┌─────────────────────────────┐
    │ Unknown persons who may be working in │  │ Persons already working in healthcare at │
    │ healthcare at the date of death │  │ the date of application to vary │
    └─────────────────────────────┘      └─────────────────────────────┘
                │                                       │
                ▼                                       ▼
    There is no way of identifying who these      They may no longer be employed in
    people are and so the court can consent       healthcare at the date of Sanjeet's
    on their behalf under Section 1(1)(b)         death, but they must nevertheless give
                                                  consent to the variation themselves
```

Now, using Figure 6.1, see if you can answer the question in the You be the judge feature.

You be the judge

Q: Miss Suffert holds a life interest under a trust. On her death, the capital in the trust fund is to be passed either to those appointed by Miss Suffert in her will or, if she does not make a will, to her **next of kin** under the rules of intestacy. Miss Suffert has applied to the court to vary the terms of the trust. At the time of her application, her only ascertainable next of kin are three adult cousins. Can the court consent to the variation on behalf of the cousins under section 1(1)(b)?

A: No, the court cannot give its consent under section 1(1)(b). These were the facts in the case of *Re Suffert* [1961] Ch 1. As in the example of Sanjeet, given above, the court asked themselves who would have an interest if, at the time of the application, Miss Suffert had died. As Miss Suffert had no valid will at the date of the application, the court looked to the next of kin. At the date of the application, the only ascertainable next of kin were three adult cousins. The court held that it could not provide consent for the cousins as they were adults and able to consent on their own behalf. There was therefore no place for section 1(1)(b) in this situation. However, they were able to give consent on behalf of any member of Miss Suffert's family yet to be ascertained under the terms of the will.

Case Summary

One final example of section 1(1)(b) in action can be seen in the case of *Knocker* v. *Youle* [1986] 2 All ER 914. The case concerned an application to vary a life interest under a trust, held by a daughter of the settlor, Augusta Youle. The wording of the trust was quite comprehensive, in that the settlor seemed to cover every possible eventuality following his daughter's death. The fund was to be given, in the first instance, to whomever Augusta should appoint as beneficiary of the fund under the terms of her will. If she failed to make a will, the money should go to her brother or whomever he should appoint under the terms of his will. If both children died without leaving wills, the money would go to their mother,

Mildred, or, in the event of her predeceasing them, to their mother's four sisters, or to their children should the sisters have already died. At the time of the application to vary the will, both Augusta and her brother had valid wills. Augusta's mother and all of her aunts had already died, but the aunts had left between them no less than 17 children, living in Australia. The court held that, despite the fact that both Augusta and her brother had appointed beneficiaries in their wills and therefore that the chances of their Australian cousins inheriting were extremely slim, nevertheless the cousins' consent to the variation was required because they had been identified under the terms of the trust settlement. As all the cousins had reached the age of majority the court could not use section 1(1)(b) to consent on their behalf and so the cousins would need to give their personal consent to the variation. Going back to our example of Sanjeet above, then, this means that even if Sanjeet had written a valid will at the time of her application to vary the trust, she would nevertheless need the consent of any family member working in the healthcare industry at the date of the application, by reason of the fact that such consent could not be given by the court under section 1(1)(b).

It would appear, then, that it does not matter how remote the chance of inheriting is, the fact that a person is named in the will means section 1(1)(b) cannot be used to give consent on their behalf (unless they are a **minor**, in which case section 1(1)(a) would apply). Section 1(1)(b) can therefore only be used in the case of a **class of beneficiaries** yet to be ascertained, such as 'next of kin' at the time of death of the beneficiary, or 'spouse', where the beneficiary has not yet married. This area of the law is complex and detailed and has been the subject of much comment. If you would like to gain further insight into the workings of the section there are a couple of useful articles listed at the end of the chapter to which you may wish to refer.

This inability of the court to give consent on behalf of those with the capacity to do so themselves has an additional effect. It means that trustees are unable to use the section to push through an amendment to the trust of which the adult beneficiaries do not approve. This is the case even if the trustees believe that it will work in the beneficiaries' favour as a whole. This is not quite as limiting for the trustees as it might at first appear, however. Consider the situation where trustees wish to make maintenance payments out of the fund to infant beneficiaries, but the adult beneficiaries are in disagreement with their wish. The trustees always have the option of applying to the court for the monies under its inherent jurisdiction. In addition, remember that the section does not take away from trustees any discretion they already hold under the terms of the trust: it is only in respect of changes to the terms of the trust that they must have the adult beneficiaries' consent.

> The trustees always have the option of applying to the court

'Arrangements' under section 1(1)

It is interesting to note that, rather than using the term 'variation' of the trust, section 1(1) authorises the court instead to make any 'arrangement' which varies or revokes all or part of the trust, or which serves to enlarge the administrative powers of the trustees. By putting the wording of the Act in these broad terms the legislature has given the judiciary the widest possible scope to make variatons to the trust, subject to the requirement that the variation is of genuine benefit to the beneficiaries (for more on the requirement for benefit, see below). It has nevertheless to be stressed that the wording of the act, although wide in its application, will *not* stretch to cover any change so wide in its scope as to effect in reality a wholesale change to, or **resettlement** of, the trust so as to put it on different terms from those envisaged or set out by the settlor. This was the outcome of *Re T's Settlement Trusts* [1964] Ch 158. The case concerned an application made by the mother of an **infant** beneficiary under a trust. The mother, believing her daughter to be immature and irresponsible with money, wished the terms of the trust to be amended so that her daughter would not become entitled to the trust fund on reaching her twenty-first birthday only eighteen days after the case was heard. Instead, she asked the court to agree to the daughter's share of the trust fund being transferred into a new **protective trust** for the duration of her lifetime, with the trustees being given extensive powers to advance capital when the daughter attained specified ages. The court held that the proposed arrangement was not a variation of the trust but that it was a resettlement which the court had no jurisdiction to approve. Mr Justice Wilberforce went on to say that, even if the resettlement had been within the court's jurisdiction, they still would be unable to approve the change because it was not for the 'benefit' of the daughter within the meaning of section 1 of the Act. The court did, however, in the end approve a variation of the existing trust, which postponed the vesting of the daughter's interest until a specified age, on the basis that this would be for the benefit of the daughter until she had matured sufficiently to accept the responsibility of the money that was to be given to her. So we can see that, whilst a resettlement of the trust on new terms will *not* be authorised by section 1 of the Act, a variation, even a very significant one, will be acceptable.

Case Summary

The outcome of *Re T's Settlement Trusts* may appear to send out mixed messages about what the wording of the Act will allow. In the case of *Re Holt's Settlement* [1969] 1 Ch 100, which was heard only five years after *Re T's*, Mr Justice Megarry attempted to provide some clarity, by introducing a test of substance over form into the equation. The case concerned a family settlement which consisted of a life interest for the wife and trusts for the children on their attaining the age of 21. The wife wished to surrender half of her life interest for the benefit of her children but in return to have the children's trusts rearranged so that their interests should vest at the age of 30, rather than 21 and that half the income of their respective shares should be accumulated until the age of 25. The wife proposed that, in order to achieve this, the settlement should be revoked and that new trusts should be declared in their place. Mr Justice Megarry held that such a revocation and resettlement of the existing trusts could still be classed as 'an arrangement' within section 1(1) of the Act provided that the outcome of the change amounted to a variation of the terms of the trust and not an altogether new settlement. In making his judgment, Mr Justice Megarry said he was satisfied that the outcome of the case had been no more than to effect a variation of the terms of the trust in this instance. He said:

> In my judgment, the old trusts may fairly be said to have been varied by the arrangement whether the variation is effected directly, by leaving some of the old words standing and altering others, or indirectly, by revoking all the old words and then setting up new trusts partly, though not wholly, in the likeness of the old. One must not confuse machinery with substance; and it is the substance that matters. Comparing the position before and after the arrangement takes effect, I am satisfied that the result is a variation of the old trusts, even though effected by the machinery of revocation and resettlement.

The effect of this judgment is that the proposed variation should be considered as a whole and, if the effect of the variation is to vary the existing trusts, rather than to resettle, or place, the trust fund on entirely new terms, the variation will come within section 1(1), even if the means of achieving the variation is by a resettlement of the fund. So, for example, this would mean that a variation which postponed the beneficiaries' entitlement to the trust fund would be acceptable, even if it was achieved through the resettlement of the fund; whereas a variation which altered the beneficiaries' shares would not.

The 'benefit' requirement under section 1(1)

The final point to note about section 1(1) is that, with the exception of protective trusts (which are a special kind of trust set up to protect the assets of the settlor, usually against bankruptcy), the court can only agree to a variation of trust if it would benefit the person on whose behalf the amendment is being agreed. The term 'benefit' is construed extremely widely for the purposes of the section, and need

> The term 'benefit' is construed extremely widely

not be limited to financial benefit, albeit that in the majority of situations applications to vary the terms of trusts are made because they will benefit the beneficiaries financially. In the case of *Re Holt's Settlement*, referred to above, Mr Justice Megarry said that the word benefit should not be confined to purely financial benefit, but that it may extend to 'moral and social' benefit. An interesting example of how the benefit requirement might be used by the courts can be seen in the case of *Re Remnant's Settlement Trusts* [1970] 1 Ch 560. The trust in question was for the benefit of two sisters, Dawn and Merrial, subject to a proviso that the daughters would forfeit their right to the trust fund should they either convert to the Roman Catholic faith or marry a Roman Catholic. In this event, the offending daughter's share of the trust fund would go to the children of the other daughter. Merrial married a Roman Catholic man and was thus subject to forfeiture under the terms of the trust. Both Dawn and Merrial together made an application to vary the trust to remove the forfeiture clause, in spite of the fact that this meant that Dawn's own children would suffer financially on account of the variation (because they would not inherit Merrial's share). The court allowed the variation, Mr Justice Pennycuick saying that such a clause 'might well cause very serious dissension between the families of the two sisters' and that it was therefore in the interests of all the beneficiaries to approve the variation. In this case, therefore, the variation to the trust was considered to be to the benefit of all the parties involved because the change promoted harmony between the two families where there might otherwise have been a rift.

One question this case raises is the fact that the variation so clearly goes against the wishes of the settlor. Surely the court should not allow this to happen? Mr Justice Pennycuick explained his reasoning in allowing the variation:

> It remains to consider whether the arrangement is a fair and proper one. As far as I can see, there is no reason for saying otherwise, except that the arrangement defeats this testator's intention. That is a serious but by no means conclusive consideration. I have reached the clear conclusion that these forfeiture provisions are undesirable in themselves in the circumstances of this case and that an arrangement involving their deletion is a fair and proper one.

In the judge's view, therefore, whilst the intentions of the settlor are important, they should not be considered over and above the benefit that any change may provide for the beneficiaries and the continued well-being in the administration of the trust.

In the more recent case of *Goulding* v. *James* [1997] 2 All ER 239 the court again considered the issue of the settlor's intentions. The case concerned the will of Mrs Violet Froud. Violet made a will leaving the bulk of her estate to her daughter, June Goulding, for life, with the remainder going to June's son, Marcus, on his attaining the age of 40 or, if he died before this, to Marcus's children. The terms of the will would have looked as shown in Figure 6.2.

Violet disapproved of her grandson's lifestyle and was keen to prevent him from getting hold of any inheritance money until he was older. Marcus lived in an artistic

157

Figure 6.2 Terms of Violet Froud's will

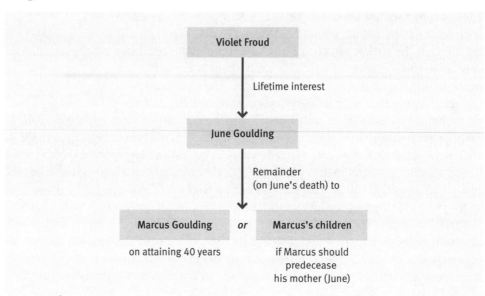

community in Nantucket in the United States. On Violet's death her daughter June was still alive and Marcus was 32. Marcus had no children. Amid fears over inheritance tax, Marcus made an application to the court, with his mother's consent, to vary the trust so that he and his mother would each receive 45 per cent of the fund straightaway, with the remaining 10 per cent being reserved for any grandchildren yet to be born. The applicants needed the court to consent to the change on behalf of the unborn grandchildren, under section 1(1)(c) of the Variation of Trusts Act 1958. The new settlement would have looked as shown in Figure 6.3.

At first instance, the judge declined their request on the basis that it would go so completely against the wishes of Marcus's grandmother. However, the Court of Appeal disagreed and, on allowing the appeal, gave their consent to the variation. The Court of Appeal said that the wishes of the settlor in respect of her grandson were irrelevant. The court had been asked to consent on behalf of the unborn children of Marcus. As the variation would be of benefit to those children in that it would give them a quantified share of the estate, this was sufficient to satisfy the terms of the Act. In the light of this and the decision in *Re Remnant's Settlement Trusts*, however, it still remains unclear as to

Figure 6.3 Proposed resettlement of Violet Froud's will

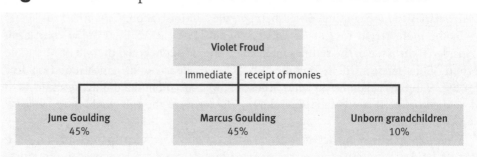

exactly how much weight the court will attribute to the settlor's intention if it relates to the interest of the beneficiary on whose behalf the court is being asked to give its consent.

A final point to make about the requirement of benefit in section 1(1) is that the court may consider that a variation is to the benefit of the beneficiary even where the effect is that the variation will in actual fact be to the beneficiary's financial detriment. As we saw earlier in the case of *Re T's Settlement Trusts*, a variation to a trust was approved which postponed the beneficiary's entitlement to the trust fund, on the basis that the beneficiary was immature and irresponsible and her mother feared that the fund would be squandered if she were given access to it at too young an age. Another case in point is that of *Re CL* [1969] 1 Ch 587. Here, the court approved a variation to a trust fund in which an elderly psychiatric patient held a life interest. The proposed variation gave the income from the fund to the beneficiary's daughter. This was justified on the basis:

Case Summary

+ first, that the court considered it to have been the action the beneficiary would have taken if she had been of sound mind; and

+ secondly, that the beneficiary was deriving very little benefit from the fund in any case, £6,500 of the £7,000 annual income that she was receiving from the fund being swallowed up in payments of tax.

In the case of *Cowan* v. *Scargill* [1985] Ch 270, which concerned a pension scheme set up for the National Union of Mineworkers, Vice-Chancellor Megarry commented on the interpretation of the term 'benefit' under section 1(1), stating that:

> 'benefit' is a word with a very wide meaning, and there are circumstances in which arrangements which work to the financial disadvantage of a beneficiary may yet be to his benefit . . . But I would emphasise that such cases are likely to be very rare and there will be a heavy burden of proof on the person arguing that there would be a benefit if the result of the proposal would be financially to disadvantage the beneficiary.

We will be looking at the facts of this case in more detail in Chapter 12.

Writing and drafting

You are a trainee in the firm of Yale Harding Solicitors, currently sitting in the trusts department. All trainees within the firm are required to give a brief talk to the rest of their department during the monthly team meeting, apprising the team of a particular area of law. The next team meeting is on Friday and it is your turn! Your training principal has asked you to prepare a short presentation summarising the provisions of section 1(1) of the Variation of Trusts Act 1958, using PowerPoint slides. You have a very busy schedule and only a small window of opportunity to write your talk. Better get writing!

You should spend no more than an hour on this task.

 Handy tip: you may find it helpful to summarise first the provisions of the Act in bullet-point form, and then flesh out the detail from there. Remember that with PowerPoint presentations less is often more, so don't get carried away with flashy animation and sound effects. Instead ensure that you communicate clearly the main provisions of the Act.

Other statutes permitting a variation of trust

So far we have seen that the court has an inherent jurisdiction to agree variations of trust in cases of emergency, or where it is necessary for the continued administration of the trust; and we have seen that the court has a statutory ability under section 1(1) of the Variation of Trusts Act 1958 to approve amendments to trusts on behalf of those unable to consent to the amendments themselves. In addition to these two main powers of the court, there are a number of other statutory provisions which allow for amendments under specific circumstances. These can be found in the following two Acts.

Trustee Act 1925

The Trustee Act 1925 contains two provisions which allow variations to be made to the terms of a trust in order to benefit child beneficiaries, and these are under sections 53 and 57(1) of the Act.

Section 53 gives the court the authority to order the sale of trust property so that the proceeds of sale of the property may be used to provide for the maintenance, education or benefit of the child beneficiary. This is an extension of the inherent jurisdiction which the court has to approve variations to the trust to allow for payments of maintenance out of trust income. The provision was used in the case of *Re Gower's Settlement* [1934] Ch 365 to authorise the mortgage of trust property to provide for the maintenance and education of a child beneficiary under the trust.

Case Summary

Section 57(1) again widens the court's inherent jurisdiction to vary trusts, this time in order to allow for the better administration of the trust. The wording of section 57(1) is as follows:

> Where in the management or administration of any property vested in trustees, any sale, lease, mortgage, surrender, release, or other disposition, or any purchase, investment, acquisition, expenditure, or other transaction, is in the opinion of the court expedient, but the same cannot be effected by reason of the absence of any power for that purpose vested in the trustees by the trust instrument, if any, or by law, the court may by order confer upon the trustees, either generally or in any particular instance, the necessary power for the purpose . . .

We can see from the wording of the section that, whereas the inherent jurisdiction of the court only allows the court to go as far as to vary the trust where it would be otherwise impossible for the trust to continue, the statutory provision allows the court to agree amendments wherever it would be 'expedient' to do so. However, as with the court's inherent jurisdiction, this extends only to variations affecting the administration of the trust, and not to variations to the beneficial interests held under its terms, which can only be effected under the Variation of Trusts Act 1958. Thus in the case of *Re Downshire Settled Estates* [1953] 2 WLR 94, which concerned an application to resettle a trust fund in such a way as to avoid the beneficiaries' tax liability, Lord Evershed, Master of the Rolls, said that the purpose of section 57(1) was to:

Case
Summary

> secure that trust property should be managed as advantageously as possible in the inter-
> ests of the beneficiaries, and with that object in view, to authorise specific dealings with
> the property which the court might have felt itself unable to sanction under the inherent
> jurisdiction, either because no actual emergency had arisen or because of inability to
> show that the position which called for intervention was one which the creator of the trust
> could not reasonably have foreseen, but it was no part of the legislative aim to disturb the
> rule that the court will not rewrite a trust.

The application was consequently turned down on the basis that the purpose of the proposed variation was to vary the beneficial interests and not to improve the administration of the trust.

Matrimonial Causes Act 1973

Under section 24 of the Matrimonial Causes Act 1973 the court has the power to vary the trusts of couples who are going through the process of divorce, by making what is known as a '**property adjustment order**'. The same power also applies to civil partners under section 72 of the Civil Partnerships Act 2004. The provisions will most commonly be applied to vary trusts of the family home in favour of one party or the other to the divorce. However, they can also be used to vary the terms of pension schemes and life policies as part of the terms of the separation.

Key stats

The provisions of the Matrimonial Causes Act 1973 are widely used in matrimonial proceedings. Table 6.1 shows the number of applications for property adjustment orders made in the County Courts in 2009.

Table 6.1 Applications for property adjustment orders, 2009

Uncontested	Initially contested, subsequently consented	Contested	Total
18,499	5,705	1,390	25,594

Source: Statistics taken from *Judicial and Court Statistics 2009*, published by the Ministry of Justice in October 2010. Full details of the report can be seen at: http://www.justice.gov.uk/publications/docs/jcs-stats-2009-211010.pdf.

An example of how such orders are used can be seen in the case of *Ulrich* v. *Ulrich* [1968] 1 WLR 180. Here, a husband and wife held the family home in equal shares. However, the court used their power under section 24 to make a property adjustment order altering the trust so that the wife's share of the house should be split between the wife and the couple's only child. A more recent and controversial case in point is that of *Charalambous* v. *Charalambous* [2004] EWCA Civ 1030, detailed in the Law in action feature.

Law in action *Charalambous* v. *Charalambous*: an attempt to escape the long arm of the law

In 2004 the case of *Charalambous* v. *Charalambous* hit legal headlines around the country.

Mr and Mrs Charalambous had married in 1984 and had two children between them, who were aged 12 and 8 at the time of the hearing. Before the birth of the couple's second child, Mr Charalambous' mother created an offshore trust in Jersey, known as 'The Hickory Trust'. The trust was a discretionary trust in favour of Mrs Charalambous senior, her son and daughter-in-law, their eldest child (the younger had not been born at the time the settlement was made) and any other persons the trustees might subsequently choose to add.

Mr Charalambous had previously been a man of some considerable wealth, his estimated net worth totalling somewhere in the region of £43 million in early 2000. However, by 1 October of the same year bankruptcy petitions had been issued against both husband and wife, and there was said to be around £5 million of debt owed between them. In an attempt to protect the trust assets from the hands of their creditors, both husband and wife were removed as beneficiaries under the Hickory Trust in January 2001. By 2002, the marriage had broken down and the couple petitioned for divorce.

Mrs Charalambous made an application under section 24 of the Matrimonial Causes Act 1973 for the Hickory Trust to be varied as part of the marriage settlement. Her husband challenged the court's ability to make an order under section 24, however. He claimed that the trust document contained a clause which stated that the trust was subject to the

Source: Alamy/MedioImages

exclusive jurisdiction of the Royal Courts of Jersey and that therefore English law did not apply. But the court rejected Mr Charalambous' claims.

The Court of Appeal held that the law which should apply in that instance was not that named in the trust deed, but rather was the jurisdiction under which the marriage was being dissolved: the court of England and Wales. The husband's attempt to prevent the application was therefore thwarted by the courts and an order was made in the wife's favour.

The full transcript of the case can be read at: *Charalambous* v. *Charalambous* [2004] EWCA Civ 1030.

It can be seen, then, that the courts take very seriously their jurisdiction to make allowances for divorcing couples. Attempts at avoidance on tax or other grounds are likely to fail.

Rectification of wills

Section 20(1) of the Administration of Justice Act 1982 allows the beneficiaries under a will to make an application to court for a will to be rectified wherever it has failed to carry out the testator's intentions, because of either (a) a clerical error, or (b) a failure to understand the testator's instructions.

In the case of *Wordingham* v. *Royal Exchange Trust Company Limited* 1992 Ch 412 the court held that, for the purposes of section 20(1)(a), 'clerical error' meant an error made in the physical process of recording the intended words of the testator either in the drafting of the transcript or in the will itself. This was in contrast to a section 20(1)(b) situation, where the draftsman made a wrong choice of words because of a misunderstanding in what the testator was trying to achieve.

Case Summary

Applications for an order under section 20 must be made within six months of the date of **grant of probate** (this is the legal document which authorises the executors under the will to administer the deceased person's estate), unless the applicants have the explicit permission of the court to apply out of that time. The application must be supported with evidence of the testator's true intentions and an explanation of how they have not been met. Notice of the application must be given to every person who has an interest under the will which might be affected by the application. If the application is unopposed the court registrar may order that the will be rectified accordingly. However, if the application for **rectification** is opposed by one of the parties to the will then proceedings must be commenced in the High Court. The following case illustrates how applications under section 20 of the Administration of Justice Act 1982 work in practice.

> Notice must be given to every person who has an interest

In *Clarke* v. *Brothwood and others* [2006] EWHC 2939 (Ch) the will of a Miss Constance Martin contained gifts of one tenth of Miss Martin's residuary estate to the Trinity Foundation Trust (a charity), one tenth to the Holy Trinity Church in Eastbourne and one twentieth to each of four godchildren. As the will was set out, this effectively disposed of only 40 per cent of the residue, leaving 60 per cent undisposed of. However if instead of fractions the figures used had been percentages (10 and 20 per cent), the whole of the residue would have been disposed of. Table 6.2 helps to illustrate this.

Case Summary

Table 6.2 Disposal of Constance Martin's assets

	Fraction	Percentage
Trinity Foundation Trust	1/10	10%
Holy Trinity Church	1/10	10%
Godchild 1	1/20	20%
Godchild 2	1/20	20%
Godchild 3	1/20	20%
Godchild 4	1/20	20%
Total	**4/10**	**100%**

The beneficiaries made an application under section 20 to rectify the will to this effect. The court found on examination of the evidence that it was clearly the intention of Miss Martin to give her godchildren 20 per cent each of her residuary estate, and thus rectification of the will was granted.

Documenting the law

The following is an extract from the contemporaneous attendance note taken by Miss Martin's solicitor, Mr Clarke, recording Miss Martin's instructions as to the disposal of assets under her will:

Residue
1/10 Trinity Foundation Trust (details to follow)
1/10 Trinity Church [Holy] E/B
1/20 to each godchild (names + addresses to follow) if they pred. then to children at 21. if not to other godchildren

The mistake of the solicitor can clearly be seen from the note taken.
A full transcript of the case can be viewed at: *Clarke* v. *Brothwood and others* [2006] EWHC 2939 (Ch).

An alternative method of making amendments to a will following the death of the testator is by way of a **deed of family arrangement**. This is wider in its application than rectification under the Administration of Justice Act 1982, because it allows for changes to the terms of the will beyond the correction of simple clerical errors. In fact, a deed of family arrangement can be used to change the distribution of the deceased's assets entirely. Most commonly, deeds of family arrangement are used to avoid the payment of inheritance tax. However, they can also be used to rearrange the distribution of the estate to distribute the assets more evenly or fairly between family members. For example, a deceased person may have given their entire estate to their husband or wife under the terms of their will, but the surviving spouse may wish to give a proportion of the estate directly to their children.

There are only a couple of provisos to the creation of a deed of family arrangment:

1. first, all of the beneficiaries under the will must be in agreement to the change in order for the deed of family arrangement to be established; and

2. secondly, the deed of family arrangement must be made within two years of the testator's death in order to be valid.

A deed of family arrangement can also be used to create a will on behalf of someone who has died intestate. In the People in the law feature, Sharon Pallagi from Clarion Solicitors in Leeds comments on the differing processes used to make amendments to wills in practice.

People in the law

Name and position: Sharon Pallagi, senior associate at Clarion Solicitors, Leeds.

What kind of work do you do at Clarion?
I do traditional private client work, which involves a varied caseload and providing advice relating to wills, trusts, the administration of estates and advice regarding inheritance tax planning.

Do you get many requests from beneficiaries to make changes to wills? Only the testator or **testatrix** can make changes to their own will during their lifetime. On death it is possible for the beneficiaries under a will to vary the terms of the deceased's will by a deed of variation (otherwise known as a deed of family arrangement) and these are frequently entered into provided all beneficiaries interested and affected are in agreement. In terms of rectification of wills, these cases are less common as it is quite difficult to establish evidence for a beneficiary to prove that the true intention of someone who makes a will has not been recorded in his or her will, when the main party to the proceedings has died.

Are you always able to comply with your client's requests? I am only able to advise my clients on an individual basis. At Clarion we have a dedicated probate team, which consists of me and a colleague who deals with litigation matters. As a team we advise our clients both on the potential of their claim, how to make an application and any applicable case law so that the client can make an informed decision as to whether to proceed with a claim.

Is the procedure for the rectification of wills under section 20 Administration of Justice Act 1982 quite simple to follow? An application may be made to a district judge or registrar together with supporting evidence as to the testator's intentions. It is also necessary to state in the application in what respect the testator's intentions were not understood or the nature of any alleged clerical error.

Notice of the application is to be given to every person having an interest under the will whose interest might be affected as a result of the application for rectification. If the registrar is satisfied that all necessary notices

have been given and the application is unopposed then he may order that the will be rectified accordingly. If the application for rectification is opposed then proceedings must be commenced by a claim in the Chancery Division of the High Court.

The difficulty is that, although procedures now exist to help beneficiaries who can prove that the testator's true intentions have not been recorded in his or her will, the battle may still be in proving what the testator's intentions were and being able to file the necessary evidence.

How were changes made to a will before the commencement of the Act? Prior to the Act there was no power to rectify a will by inserting provisions that the testator/testatrix had intended to include but which did not already appear. The only power available to the court was to strike out words that the testator/testatrix did not know of and approve of or, if necessary, the whole will.

How does the rectification procedure differ from changes made to a Will under a deed of family arrangement? The rectification procedure helps beneficiaries who can prove that the true intention of someone who makes a will has not been recorded in his or her will, and section 20 of the Administration of Justice Act 1982 has introduced a right of action enabling a disappointed potential beneficiary under a will to claim rectification. Usually the rectification procedure is used where there has been some sort of clerical error or an error made in the process of recording the intended words of the testator/testatrix.

A deed of variation is a document that is agreed after the death of the testator/testatrix to vary the terms of the will as if the deceased had made the provisions as determined by the deed in their will. Only a beneficiary of the will can enter into a deed of variation and the parties affected by the deed of variation must agree to the terms of the deed. Deeds of variation are therefore entered into by consent of all parties to the deed and there is agreement to vary the terms of the deceased's will.

What is the most interesting/strangest change you have been asked to make to a will? On a person's death it is surprising the

number of family secrets one can uncover. I have drafted many deeds of variation in order to deal with illegitimacy, children who were not in fact siblings and spouses who were not in fact married.

Is there anything else you would like to add? I chose private client work as my area of specialism as I enjoy the variety of the work and the fact that I have client contact on a daily basis. My day can be one of extremes, from advising elderly clients on documents such as wills to presenting complex inheritance tax strategies to a board of directors. I am delighted to see through Clarion's own graduate recruitment scheme that the enthusiasm for private client work is back and it is a practising area to highlight as it is very rewarding.

Exporting the trust

The term '**exporting the trust**' refers to the situation where a trust is moved, or relocated, to a foreign jurisdiction and new trustees are appointed within that jurisdiction to continue the management of the trust. The court will usually allow a trust to be exported in this way, so long as the move is made for the benefit of the beneficiaries. In the case of *Re Seale's Marriage Settlements* [1961] Ch 574, a family who were beneficiaries under a trust had emigrated to Canada. The court allowed the exportation of the trust on the grounds that the move to Canada was clearly a permanent one and that to continue to administer the trust from the UK would cause administrative difficulties.

The court has been more reticent in allowing moves to other jurisdictions purely on grounds of tax avoidance, however. In the case of *Re Weston* [1969] 1 Ch 223, two brothers sought to move their families to the tax haven of Jersey to avoid high taxes in the UK, and applied to the court to appoint Jersey trustees to the family trusts. Lord Denning, however, refused their request, on the grounds that he did not believe such a move had been made for the genuine benefit of the children to the trust or, indeed, for any other reason than tax avoidance. In making the point that benefit must extend to more than financial considerations, Lord Denning said:

> The court should not consider merely the financial benefit to the infants . . . but also their educational and social benefit. There are many things in life more worthwhile than money. One of these things is to be brought up in this our England, which is still 'the envy of less happier lands'. I do not believe it is for the benefit of children to be uprooted from England and transported to another country simply to avoid tax . . . I cannot help wondering how long these young people will stay in Jersey. It may be to their financial interest at present to make their home there permanently. But will they remain there once the capital gain is

safely in hand, clear of tax? They may well change their minds and come back to enjoy their untaxed gains. Is such a prospect really for the benefit of the children? Are they to be wanderers over the face of the earth, moving from this country to that, according to where they can best avoid tax? I cannot believe that to be right. Children are like trees: they grow stronger with firm roots.

The lesson to be learnt here therefore is that the courts will take into account the reasons for the move and whether it is for the overall well-being of the beneficiaries and not just for their financial benefit.

Cy près

Variations of trust under the doctrine of **Cy près** are dealt with in Chapter 5 on charities. You may remember that the doctrine allows for monies left in trust for a charity to be applied to another charity with similar purposes to the one named in the trust instrument, in circumstances where the named charity has ceased to exist.

The rule in *Saunders* v. *Vautier*

The rule in **Saunders v. Vautier** is not really a method of varying trusts: rather it is a way of calling the trust to an end. The rule says that if all the beneficiaries are over the age of 18 they can together agree to bring an end to the trust and either walk away with their separate shares of the trust fund or reinvest the trust monies in a new trust on terms which they agree. The facts of the case of *Saunders* v. *Vautier* [1841] Cr & Ph 240 are as follows: The case concerned a trust of property in favour of a sole beneficiary. The property was to be accumulated until the beneficiary reached the age of 25, the beneficiary receiving nothing before this time. However, when the beneficiary reached the age of 21 (which was at that time the age of majority), he applied to the court to end the trust and take the trust property. The court allowed the beneficiary's claim and the trust was brought to an end. Of course, with only one beneficiary to the trust the decision of the court was made simple. In other cases the rule will be more difficult to apply, such as when there are other beneficiaries who have not yet reached the age of majority. In such a case, those beneficiaries who are over the age of 18 may demand their share of the trust property, provided it is possible to separate their share from the rest of the trust fund (this may not be possible where the fund consists of land or buildings, for example), but will be unable to bring the trust to an end on behalf of the other beneficiaries, as the trust can only be brought to an end if all the beneficiaries together agree to this.

Case Summary

As mentioned above, the rule in *Saunders* v. *Vautier* can be used only to bring the trust to an end, and not actually to vary the terms of the trust; this would have to be achieved by a resettlement of the trust monies. The case of *Stephenson* v. *Barclays Bank Trust Co. Ltd* [1975] 1 WLR 882 illustrates this. The case concerned two adult beneficiaries, Richard and Charles Stephenson. The beneficiaries applied to the court to make changes to the way in which the trust was administered. The court, however, held that the beneficiaries did not have the right under *Saunders* v. *Vautier* to tell the trustees how to carry out their

Case Summary

duties; neither were they allowed to use the rule to override the terms of the trust. Their only course of action as adult beneficiaries if they wished to make changes to the terms of the trust was to bring the trust to an end and then set up an altogether new trust under new terms in accordance with their own wishes.

Summary

* The courts have an inherent jurisdiction to make variations to the terms of a trust where the trustees are unable to administer the trust effectively. This jurisdiction can be used only in cases of genuine emergency and not simply where it will be of benefit to the beneficiaries.

* The court's power allows them to make changes in the investment powers of the trustees, to advance monies for the maintenance of a minor, and to allow a compromise to be made where there has been a dispute over the meaning of the trust (*Chapman* v. *Chapman*).

* The courts can also allow a variation under section 1(1) of the Variation of Trusts Act 1958, which provides that the court can agree variations on behalf of anyone who is unable to consent by themselves, by reason either of age or of incapacity, provided that the variation will benefit the person on behalf of whom the consent is given.

* Section 53 of the Trustee Act 1925 gives the court the authority to order the sale of trust property to provide for the maintenance, education or benefit of a child beneficiary.

* Section 57(1) of the Trustee Act 1925 allows the court to make variations to a trust in order to allow for its better administration.

* Under section 24 of the Matrimonial Causes Act 1973 the court has the power to vary the trusts of divorcing couples by making a property adjustment order. The same power applies also to civil partners under section 72 of the Civil Partnerships Act 2004.

* The court will usually allow a trust to be exported to a foreign jurisdiction, so long as the move is made for the genuine benefit of the beneficiaries.

* The rule in *Saunders* v. *Vautier* allows beneficiaries over the age of 18 to bring an end to the trust and either walk away with their separate shares or to reinvest the trust monies in a new trust. The rule is therefore not a method of variation, but rather a means of bringing an undesirable trust to an end.

Question and answer*

Problem: Neesha's father, Saleem, made the following bequests in his will:

1. I give to my trustees, Neesha and Aslam, my house and contents in Shoreditch, London, to hold on trust for my grandsons, Adesh and Khalil, until they reach the age of 21, on the condition that they each marry a girl of the Hindu faith on or before his twenty-first birthday.

2. I give to my trustees, Neesha and Aslam, the collection of gold jewellery which belonged to my mother, kept in safety deposit box number 43569 at the Shoreditch branch of the Amicable Bank plc. The jewellery is to be held on trust for my granddaughter, Harika, until her marriage to a man of the Hindu faith. Should she not marry by the age of 21, the jewellery should be given to any daughter of Adesh and Khalil's marriages.

Aslam is Neesha's husband. Neesha and Aslam wish to vary the trusts, to account for the following:

+ Adesh is 20. His twenty-first birthday is in three months' time. He is currently studying medical ethics at university in Leicester. He is in a relationship with a girl called Sara, who is not of the Hindu faith. The relationship appears serious and Adesh has made it clear that he does not intend to marry anyone else at this time. Sara does not wish to convert to the Hindu faith.

+ Khalil is 18. He is very religious and is quite happy to comply with his grandfather's request. He does not approve of Adesh's association with Sara.

+ Harika is 15 and a promising ballet dancer. She has been offered a place at the Bolshoi school of ballet in Moscow but her parents are unable to afford the fees. She would like the jewellery to be sold to fund her place at the school. She is not religious and has no wish to marry as she believes this will impede her career as a ballerina.

+ Aslam and Neesha would like to relocate to Moscow to be closer to Harika and believe that the trust would be better administered from there. Adesh and Khalil will stay in London with their uncle, Varinder.

Can Neesha and Aslam vary the terms of the trusts and on what grounds can they do so?

You should allow yourself no more than 50 minutes to complete this task.

Essay: How relevant to the court is the settlor's intention in deciding whether to approve variations under the Variation of Trusts Act 1958?

This question should be answered in 40 minutes.

✱ Answer guidance is provided at the end of the chapter.

Further reading and references

Law Reform Committee (1957) Sixth Report, 'Court's Power to Sanction Variation of Trusts', Cmnd 310, para 13.
This is the report which led to the enactment of the Variation of Trusts Act 1958. Provides invaluable background and insight into the creation of the statute.

Luxton, P. (1997) 'Variation of trusts: settlor's intentions and the consent principle in *Saunders* v. *Vautier*', 60 MLR 719.
This article compares the provisions of the Variation of Trusts Act 1958 with the rule in *Saunders* v. *Vautier*, and suggests that the settlor's intention has

been rendered effectively irrelevant by the provisions of section1(1). Worth reading for a different view on the problems encountered in interpreting the section.

McCall, C. (1996) 'Variation of trusts: some observations', *Private Client Business* 6, 389–98.

Really clear, useful article giving some background on the enactment of the Variation of Trusts Act 1958 and taking the reader through the provisions of the Act with examples.

Riddal, J.G. (1987) 'Does it or doesn't it? – contingent interests and the Variation of Trusts Act 1958', Conv (Mar/Apr), 144–7.

A short but useful article which takes the readers through the provisions of section 1(1)(b) of the Variation of Trusts Act 1958, commenting in particular on the outcome in *Knocker* v. *Youle* and its implications.

Summers, J. and Brice, R (2007) 'What constitutes benefit?', *Trust and Estates Law & Tax Journal*, 87(Jun), 15–16.

Really interesting exploration of the meaning of benefit under the Variation of Trusts Act 1958, comparing the recent Chancery Division ruling in *S* v. *T* [2006] WTLR 1461 (Ch D) with the ruling in *Re Weston's Settlements* [1969] 1 Ch 223 (CA) (Civ Div)) and discussing whether the meaning of 'benefit' has changed over time.

Question and answer guidance

Problem: The court can use its inherent jurisdiction to give consent to a variation of trust in cases of genuine emergency, where circumstances have prevented the trustees from administering the trust effectively, or to allow for payment of maintenance for a child. In the case of Harika, there is no emergency but, as Harika is under the age of 18, this jurisdiction could possibly be used to sell the jewellery to provide for Harika's maintenance (in the form of her schooling), although the conditional nature of the trust may make this difficult to justify. Question whether some money would need to be put aside for the eventuality of her not marrying. However, the court could also use section 53 of the Trustee Act 1925 to allow for a sale of trust property to provide for Harika's maintenance in this event.

The religious condition would appear to be a bone of contention with two of the three beneficiaries. Under the Variation of Trusts Act 1958, section 1(1), the court can give consent to a variation of trust on behalf of anyone unable to consent by themselves. This would include Harika, and so it is possible that the trustees could have the condition of marriage removed, but it may be necessary to make an allowance for any children of Adesh and Khalil, given their contingent interest, should Harika not marry, under section 1(1)(b), as above. See *Goulding* v. *James*. Note that variations under section 1(1) are described within the Act as 'arrangements'. This allows for a wider scope to vary the trust; however, they must not amount to resettlement of the terms of the trust altogether. Deletion of a religious condition was agreed *in Re Remnant's Settlement Trusts*, although all members of the family were agreed to the change, unlike here.

In any event, in respect of the boys' trust, both Adesh and Khalil are over the age of 18, so the Variation of Truts Act 1958 is of no use here, as they must both give consent to any variations proposed by the trustees themselves (*Knocker* v. *Youle*). This may be difficult as Khalil opposes the amendments.

The courts will usually allow a trust to be exported to another jurisdiction, provided the reason for doing so is genuine, and not for tax evasion purposes (*Re Seale's*; *Re Weston*). Is there a genuine need for Aslam and Neesha to move to Moscow? Harika will be there, but the other two beneficiaries will remain in London, so will this be to their benefit to do this? The interests of the boys' trust may be better served in London.

Essay:

A good answer to this question would first of all set out the basis upon which the court can allow variations of trust under section 1(1) the Variation of Trusts Act 1958, stating briefly on whose behalf the court could agree variations to a trust and setting out the general requirement that the variation should be for the benefit of the beneficiaries. A short definition of benefit could follow, as per Mr Justice Megarry in *Re Holt's Settlement*, who said that the word benefit should not be confined to purely financial benefit, but that it may extend to 'moral and social' benefit.

The settlor's intention is usually considered when the court is deciding whether or not a variation will benefit the beneficiary under section 1. However, the question is not simply asking *whether* the settlor's intention is relevant: it is asking just *how* relevant that intention is. In order to answer this question, the student should discuss the cases of *Re Remnant's Settlement Trusts* and *Goulding* v. *James*.

Both cases suggest that the settlor's intentions are only a factor to be taken into account, not that they will be the deciding factor in any case. In *Re Remnant's Settlement Trusts*, the judgment clearly went against the wishes of the settlor, but was justified by the court on the basis that it promoted harmony between the two families and was therefore for the overall benefit of the beneficiaries on behalf of whom the change was made. The court was therefore willing to override the wishes of the settlor in favour of the well-being of the trust. Mr Justice Pennycuick said that the settlor's intention was 'a serious but by no means conclusive consideration'.

The facts in *Goulding* v. *James* were distinguished from *Re Remnant's Settlement Trusts* in that the known intentions of the settlor related to her daughter and grandson, but it was on behalf of the grandson's unborn children that the court had been asked to consent to the variation. The court therefore said that the intentions of the settlor in respect of her child and grandchild were irrelevant to the claim.

It thus remains unclear exactly how much weight the court would give to the settlor's intention if it relates to the interest of a relevant beneficiary. Mention could be made at this point of Luxton 1997, in which he suggests that the settlor's intentions are effectively rendered irrelevant by the provisions of the Act.

Conclude by stating whether or not you think this is the correct approach, or whether you feel the settlor's intentions should be given more sway.

Visit **www.mylawchamber.co.uk/warner-reed** to access study support resources including practice exam questions with guidance, interactive 'You be the judge' multiple choice questions, annotated weblinks, glossary and key case flashcards and audio legal updates all linked to the **Pearson eText** version of *Equity and Trusts* which you can **search**, **highlight** and **personalise** with your **own notes** and **bookmarks**.

premium
mylawchamber
unrivalled support for legal education

Chapter 7
Resulting trusts

Key points In this chapter we will be looking at:

✦ The need for informally created trusts and their use

✦ The definition of resulting trusts

✦ What is required to create a resulting trust

✦ Different types of resulting trust

✦ Gifts and transfers to third parties

✦ Failure to create a trust

✦ Surplus trust funds

Introduction

Up until this point we have considered only those **trusts** which have been created intentionally by the **settlor**, and we have looked at what **formalities** are required in order to do so correctly. In these next two chapters we are going to consider not only what happens to the trust property when the settlor fails to set up a trust successfully, but also those situations in which a settlor creates a trust without intending to do so at all. This is the area of informally created or **implied trusts**.

The concept of implied trusts is a relatively complex one, which has been subject to a great deal of change over recent years. As we shall see, much of the case law relating to informally created trusts relates to the division of the family home or co-owned assets in the event of a family break-up. As a result of this, changes in the law in this area have often happened by way of reaction to changes in social norms and the increase in cohabiting couples that have rendered much of the surrounding law out of date. The most recently available statistics from the National Office of Statistics show this.

Key stats National Office of Statistics confirm cohabiting is the fastest growing family type

According to the National Office of Statistics, the proportion of married couple families has decreased over the last ten years (from 76 per cent of families in 1996 to 71 per cent in 2006). Over the same period, the proportion of cohabiting couple families increased from 9 per cent to 14 per cent. The proportion of lone parent families increased by less than 1 per cent over this period.

All families: by family type, 1996 and 2006, United Kingdom

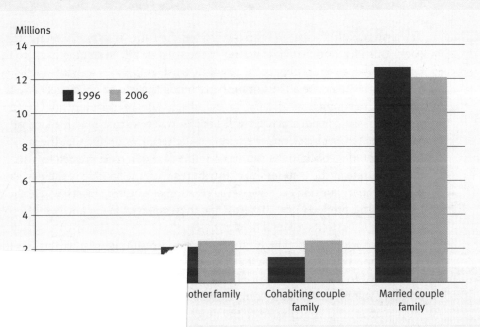

Millions

1996   2006

...other family   Cohabiting couple family   Married couple family

Office for National Statistics licensed under the Open Government Licence v.1.0.

...ounger families cohabiting, with older families being married. In ...couple families in the UK were headed by a person aged under 35, ...ried couple families. In single parent families, lone mothers tend ...ge of ten years.

...rvey data for 2005 shows that 39 per cent of single individuals ...biting, with 30 per cent of individuals between the ages of 35 and

...bitation between younger couples does not fully account for the ...rtion of younger women choosing to delay forming either married ...ge of 25.

...p://www.statistics.gov.uk/cci/nugget.asp?id=1865.

...14 October 2007 at 9:30 am. Sources taken from: Census 2001, Labour Force Survey ...rvey (GHS), Office for National Statistics; Census 2001, General Register Office for ...Research Agency.]

This means the law in this area is constantly evolving and, whilst there has been significant change over recent years, as we shall see throughout the course of the chapter, there are still plenty of areas for improvement.

As the law currently stands, informally created trusts fall broadly into two categories:

✦ **resulting trusts**; and

✦ **constructive trusts**.

We will be looking at constructive trusts in Chapter 8. This chapter will concentrate on resulting trusts.

What is a resulting trust?

The term resulting trust comes directly from the Latin '*resultare*', which means to 'spring back'. This idea of the **subject matter** of the trust or gift 'springing back' to the settlor is fundamental to the concept of the resulting trust, as this is exactly what will happen when a settlor tries to create a trust of property but fails to do so adequately. We have, in fact, seen this phenomenon already, in our discussion of certainty in Chapter 3. If you remember, we considered what will happen when a trust fails for lack of certainty of subject matter or **object**, and we said that the result would be that the subject matter of the gift would go back to the settlor or, in the case of a trust created by will, it would fall into the **estate** of the **testator** to be distributed with the **residue** of their estate. This is the first and most common example of the creation of resulting trusts: where the settlor fails to transfer his property over into trust and the property, having nowhere else to go, results, or springs back, to its original owner.

Another, slightly different, example of where a resulting trust will arise is the situation where property is purchased in the name of one person, but two people have in actual fact contributed to the purchase price of the property. In this situation the legal owner of the property will be viewed as holding the property on trust for themselves and also for the other person who contributed to the purchase price. In this second scenario, therefore, there is a less obvious 'springing back' of the trust property, but nevertheless the beneficial interest in the property can be seen to revert to the persons who contributed to its purchase. This second example of a resulting trust will be discussed in further detail later in the chapter.

The lack of formality in resulting trusts

Naturally, trusts created under such informal circumstances do not need to fulfil the usual formalities for the creation of **express trusts**. On the contrary, in the case of resulting trusts it is because of a failure on the part of the settlor in creating the trust adequately or properly that the trust comes into being. All those trusts of the type dealt with in this chapter and the next are therefore completely informal in their creation. In relation to resulting trusts in particular, in the case of *Re Vandervell's Trusts No. 2* [1974] Ch 269, the facts of which we shall consider shortly, Lord Denning stated that:

> A resulting trust for the settlor is born and dies without any writing at all. It comes into existence whenever there is a gap in **beneficial ownership**. It ceases to exist whenever the gap is filled by someone becoming beneficially entitled. As soon as the gap is filled by the creation or declaration of a valid trust, the resulting trust comes to an end.

Essentially, then, Lord Denning is saying that resulting trusts are a temporary measure that arises wherever the settlor has missed or overlooked one of the formal requirements in the transfer of beneficial ownership.

Different types of resulting trusts

It has long been held that resulting trusts fall into two different categories. According to Lord Hardwicke in the early case of *Lloyd* v. *Spillet* (1740) 2 ATK 148, which concerned a dispute over the terms of a will, these could be described as follows:

1. Where an estate is purchased in the name of one person, but the money or **consideration** is given by another.

2. Where a trust is only partially declared, in which case the part which has not been properly disposed of results back to the settlor.

These two basic categories of resulting trusts have not changed, in essence. However, the categories have more recently been given names, or descriptions. Mr Justice Megarry in the leading case of *Re Vandervell's Trusts (No. 2)* [1974] Ch 269, the facts of which are below, defined the first type of trust as '**presumed resulting trusts**' and the second type as '**automatic resulting trusts**'. But why did he feel the need to do this? Mr Justice Megarry said that he felt the two should be categorised in this way because:

> the two categories of resulting trusts . . . operate in different ways. Putting it shortly, in the first category . . . the matter is one of intention, with the rebuttable presumption of a resulting trust applying if the intention is not made manifest. For the second category, there is no mention of any expression of intention in any instrument, or of any presumption of a resulting trust: the resulting trust takes effect by operation of law, and so appears to be automatic. What a man fails effectually to dispose of remains automatically vested in him, and no question of any mere presumption can arise. The two categories are thus of presumed resulting trusts and automatic resulting trusts.

In Mr Justice Megarry's view, therefore, the two differing types of resulting trust arise out of a difference in intention: whereas the automatic resulting trust, which arises in the event of property being purchased in the name of one person but paid for by another, is based on a presumed intention of the settlor to create a trust, the automatic resulting trust depends not on the intention of the settlor, rather it reflects the return of the property automatically to the settlor where the property has been ineffectively disposed of and the beneficial interest has nowhere else to go but back to its original owner.

The somewhat complicated facts of *Re Vandervell's* are as follows: the case concerned a failed attempt at tax avoidance by Mr Vandervell. In a bid to reduce his tax bill, Mr Vandervell decided to give a number of shares in his company, Vandervell Products Ltd, to the Royal College of Surgeons. However, he wanted to ensure that he could get the shares back if he wished, and so he asked the Royal College of Surgeons to enter into a formal agreement stating that they would sell the shares back to Vandervell Trustees Ltd, at the Trustees' request. Vandervell Trustees Ltd comprised the acting **trustees** of a number of trusts operated by the Vandervell family. The Inland Revenue found out about the arrangement and took Mr Vandervell to court, arguing that the agreement with the Royal College of Surgeons equated to a beneficial interest in the shares which was therefore taxable. Mr Vandervell tried to argue that the benefit of the agreement lay with Vandervell Trustees Ltd, and not with him personally. However, the court found that Vandervell Trustees Ltd, as a trust corporation, were not able to hold the benefit of the agreement for themselves. As Mr Vandervell had failed to instruct the company for whose benefit the agreement was to be held, it would automatically result back to the settlor, in this case Mr Vandervell. So the outcome of the case was that Mr Vandervell did not manage to get out of paying that rather large tax bill!

We can see from the facts of the case that, in this instance, based on Mr Justice Megarry's categorisation, the situation arising was that Mr Vandervell was subject to an automatic resulting trust. This is because Mr Vandervell had failed to instruct the trust company as to whom the trust was to benefit, and the beneficial interest in the trust property (in this case shares) therefore had nowhere else to go but back to Mr Vandervell. Automatic resulting trusts will be considered in further detail later in the chapter. However, first, let us take a look at Mr Justice Megarry's first category: presumed resulting trusts.

Presumed resulting trusts

According to Mr Justice Megarry in *Re Vandervell's*, a presumed resulting trust will arise wherever property is purchased in the name of one person, but either all or part of the money or consideration for the purchase is provided by a third party. So if Tim buys a property in his sole name but Anna has provided some or all of the money for the purchase, then a resulting trust will be created in favour of Anna, in line with her contribution towards the purchase price. Unlike automatic resulting trusts, which, as we shall see shortly, arise automatically in situations where the trust has failed and there is nowhere else for the money to go other than back to the settlor, presumed resulting trusts are based on a presumption that the settlor gave the money fully intending that it should be held on trust for their benefit. So the thinking behind presumed resulting trusts is that Anna, in putting money towards the purchase price of the house, intended that by virtue of her contribution she would receive a beneficial interest in the property.

Presumed resulting trusts will not solely operate in situations such as Anna's. In fact, the presumption of a resulting trust will be made in all of the following situations:

✦ Where Tim has made an outright gift of property to Anna (in which case there will be a presumed resulting trust in favour of Tim).

✦ Where Tim has purchased property with his own money, but has put that property in Anna's sole name (in which case, again, there will be a presumed resulting trust in favour of Tim).

✦ Where Tim and Anna have both contributed to the purchase of a property, but the property is put into Tim's sole name, as above (in which case there will be a presumed resulting trust in favour of Anna).

Outright gifts of property

Wherever a gift of personal property is made, the presumption will be made in **equity** that the gift is to be held on resulting trust for the person making that gift, in the absence of clear evidence to the contrary. The idea may seem a little strange, that a person cannot simply make a gift of their own free will without a presumption arising, but the rule was put into place by the courts in a bid to protect the more vulnerable against those who would take advantage of them. In the words of Sir George Jessel, Master of the Rolls, in the case of *Fowkes* v. *Pascoe* [1874–75] LR 10 Ch App 343:

> the rule was put into place by the courts to protect the more vulnerable

Those that allege that other people, especially in this position, give them large sums of money, must prove it, and prove it to the satisfaction of a Court of Justice that they are entitled to that sum of money.

The case of *Fowkes* v. *Pascoe* concerned a transfer in the sum of £7,000 made by an elderly woman, Sarah Baker, to her daughter-in-law's son from an earlier marriage. The son, who was named John Pascoe, claimed that the money was meant to be a gift to him. On evidence provided to the court it was held that the money was indeed a gift, and the presumption of a resulting trust was rebutted. However, had there been no substantial evidence to prove this, a resulting trust would certainly have been imposed.

Another case in which a presumed resulting trust was found to exist was that of *Re Vinogradoff* [1935] WN 68. The case concerned the transfer of a war loan. (War loans were a sort of government investment scheme set up towards the end of the First World War. Loans were made by the general public to the government, in return for which the government promised a 5 per cent annual income, plus a guarantee that investors would receive their original savings back by 1947. In reality, the loans have to this day never been repaid.) Mrs Vinogradoff had transferred an £800 war loan into the joint names of herself and her granddaughter, who was 4 years old at the time. On the death of Mrs Vinogradoff, the granddaughter's parents claimed that the £800 was an outright gift to the granddaughter. However, the court held that the money should be held on resulting trust for the estate of Mrs Vinogradoff, there being no evidence of a gift to rebut the presumption of a resulting trust.

Transfers of land

This same presumption does not apply in the case of transfers of land, however. This is because of the provisions of section 60 of the Law of Property Act 1925, which states that:

> In a voluntary conveyance a resulting trust for the **grantor** shall not be implied merely by reason that the property is not expressed to be conveyed for the use or benefit of the **grantee**.

In other words, if someone gives land to a third party, the fact that they do *not* expressly state that the transfer is intended to be a gift will not be, by itself, sufficient to impose a resulting trust on the property in favour of the giver. This is merely removing the presumption that the giver intends to retain an interest in the property, however. It does not mean that a presumed resulting trust will never arise in the case of transfers of land.

A case in point is that of *Hodgson* v. *Marks* [1971] 1 QB 234 (CA). In this case an elderly homeowner, Mrs Hodgson, decided to take in a lodger for company and to help out with payment of the household bills. Mr Evans moved in and had soon found his way into Mrs Hodgson's confidence, making himself useful around the house and looking after her financial affairs for her. Mrs Hodgson's relatives were suspicious of Mr Evans's motives and tried to persuade Mrs Hodgson to ask Mr Evans to leave the house. Mrs Hodgson paid no attention to their advice, however, and eventually, under continual pressure from her relatives and fearing that they would find a means of removing Mr Evans from the property, took the rather drastic step of conveying the property into Mr Evans's name on the understanding that she would remain the beneficial owner of the property. Unfortunately the relatives' suspicions were well founded and Mr Evans subsequently purported to sell the property to a third party, Mr Marks, without Mrs Hodgson's knowledge. The court

held that there was a clear resulting trust in favour of Mrs Hodgson. Under the circumstances the transfer had clearly never been intended as a gift to her lodger. We can therefore see from this case that the court was willing to impose a presumed resulting trust in this instance because the facts of the case clearly showed Mrs Hodgson's intention to retain a beneficial interest in the property. Although the provisions of section 60 remove the *presumption* that Mrs Hodgson intended to retain an interest in the house, the facts of the case nevertheless show that this was her genuine intent.

The point to remember here is that presumed resulting trusts are based on just that: a presumption, and nothing more. This means that, taking our example of Tim and Anna, above, where Anna has contributed to the purchase of a property in Tim's name, if it can be shown that money provided by Anna was intended to be a gift or a loan to Tim, the presumption that Anna intended to receive a beneficial interest in the property will be rebutted, and no resulting trust will be inferred. Equally, in purchasing the property, had Tim and Anna had the foresight to make express declarations as to what they intended to be the extent of their beneficial interests in the property, then these too will be given effect over and above any presumed interest. This was confirmed in the case of **Gissing v. Gissing** [1971] AC 886, the facts of which will be considered later in the chapter. Lord Diplock said:

Case Navigator

> An express agreement between spouses as to their respective beneficial interests in land conveyed into the name of one of them obviates the need for showing . . . that the other spouse so acted with the intention of acquiring that beneficial interest . . .

Unfortunately such cases are rare and in most situations there will have been no formal agreement made. The result is that there will usually be no hard evidence existing to show what was intended between the parties at the time the property was purchased. In such circumstances, the courts will therefore have no choice but to rely on the presumed intention of the parties at the time the property was acquired, based on the contributions made and the manner in which the parties conducted themselves at the time of purchase. This is particularly the case where property is purchased in the name of another, as we will see below.

> there will usually be no hard evidence existing to show what was intended

The 'presumption of advancement'

The presumed intention of the parties is usually in favour of a resulting trust. But in certain situations, there will instead be what is known as a '**presumption of advancement**'. This presumption, which runs contrary to the presumption of a resulting trust, is that people who share certain relationships will be presumed, subject to the presentation of evidence to the contrary, to have made an outright gift to the receiving party. In such situations there will therefore be no presumption of a resulting trust created in favour of the person making the gift. The presumption of advancement runs in favour of a husband who is making a gift to his wife and a father making a gift to his child, as was the case in *Dyer* v. *Dyer* [1788] 2 Cox Eq Cases 92. The case concerned a man named Simon Dyer who had bought property in Wiltshire jointly in the names of himself, his wife and younger son. Mr Dyer had paid the whole of the purchase price for the property. On the death of Mr Dyer, his elder son argued that the property should be held on resulting trust for the estate of the father, because he had put forward the whole of the purchase price for it. This would have meant that the son would have benefited from the property as one of

Case Summary

the **heirs** to his father's estate. However, the court found that the purchase had been a gift in favour of the wife and younger son and that there was therefore no resulting trust in the father's favour. This was on the basis of the presumption of advancement in favour of the father's wife and child. In the eyes of the court the fact that, in making the gift, the father had decided that his other son should not benefit from the property was irrelevant to the raising of the presumption.

The presumption of advancement also applies to gifts made in contemplation of marriage (that is, between a man and his fiancée). Rather interestingly, there is a statutory presumption of advancement in the case of the gift of an engagement ring, under section 3(2) of the Law Reform (Miscellaneous Provisions) Act 1970, which states that:

> The gift of an engagement ring shall be presumed to be an absolute gift; this presumption may be rebutted by proving that the ring was given on the condition, express or implied, that it should be returned if the marriage did not take place for any reason.

This provision was put to the test in the 2004 case of *Cox* v. *Jones* [2004] 3 FCR 693 (Ch), in which Lawrence Jones's claim to the ring, said to be worth £10,000 or more, that he had given to his girlfriend, Kerry Cox, on their engagement, was not established because he had failed to provide the court with proof that the ring had been given on the basis that he would want it back if the engagement ended.

The basis of the presumption comes from the traditional view that it is a husband's legal duty to provide financial support for his wife and children. Therefore if he makes a gift to either wife or child his intention is not that he expects to see the return of that property, but rather that he is making an outright gift to the wife or child in the exercise of his financial obligation to them. But the presumption is very old-fashioned in that it does not apply to wives making gifts to their husbands (or prospective husbands) or children. In the case of *Bennet* v. *Bennet* (1879) 10 Ch D 474, a mother, Ann Bennet, transferred the sum of £3,000 to her son, Philip Bennet, who was in financial difficulty. Philip subsequently went bankrupt, and the **trustee in bankruptcy** claimed what was left of the money. Mrs Bennet's lawyers claimed that there was no presumption of advancement in this case, it being a case of gift between mother and son, and that the money should be returned to her as it was held by her son for her on a resulting trust. The court upheld the mother's claim, although it should be noted that, in any event, there was evidence in this case that the mother had intended the money as a loan. Nor does it apply to transfers between unmarried couples who are living together. The presumption does apply to a gift made between a man and a child where that person has taken on parental responsibility for that child, however: see *Ebrand* v. *Dancer* (1860) 2 Ch App 26, in which the presumption was held to apply between a grandchild and its grandfather, where the child's father was dead and the grandfather was raising the child.

The presumption of advancement has been increasingly criticised because of its old-fashioned nature. In the leading case of *Pettitt* v. *Pettitt* [1970] AC 777, which concerned a disagreement over the beneficial ownership of the family home, Lord Diplock commented that the presumption of advancement between husband and wife was outdated and based on the values of earlier generations. The Out and about feature gives you an opportunity to consider Lord Diplock's claim.

Out and about

Do you think the presumption of advancement is outdated? Perhaps it is time for you to carry out a little bit of empirical research. Try asking the following questions to friends, neighbours and family members:

1. What is your age?

2. Are you married or cohabiting?

3. What is the age of your partner?

4. Do you or did you, as a couple, own your own home (including with the aid of a mortgage)?

5. Have you both contributed towards the payment for the house?

6. In whose name is the property registered?

7. What is the reason for this?

Try to get answers from as many people as you can, over as wide an age range as you can. Can you see any trends in your answers? What can you learn from this? Do you think attitudes towards property ownership have changed over the last 20, 30 or 40 years?

Handy tip: You may find that your answers carry more value if you pool them with others in your tutor or seminar group. However you decide to collect the information, go carefully – remember that these are questions of a personal nature and not everyone may be happy to answer them.

In 2002 the Law Commission published a discussion paper, *Sharing Homes*, in which it was said that 'The presumption of advancement is now viewed as being somewhat anachronistic.' The outcome of the report which is due to follow the discussion paper remains to be seen.

Transfers of property for improper or illegal purposes

As with all presumptions, the presumption of a resulting trust can be rebutted. In particular, a donor will be unable to rely on the presumption of a resulting trust where there is evidence to show that the gift made by the donor was for an improper or illegal purpose. This is perfectly logical: if a person transfers property into another person's name in order to avoid the payment of taxes or creditors, they should not subsequently be able to claim a beneficial interest in the property which they have transferred in order to avoid their liabilities. So we can see that in the case of *Curtis* v. *Perry* (1802) 6 Ves Jr 739 two business partners, Mr Nantes and Mr Chiswell, owned a shipping business. The ships were registered under Mr Nantes's sole name because Mr Chiswell was a Member of Parliament and it was the law at that time that ships could not be used for the carrying out of lucrative government contracts if they were owned by a Member of Parliament. It was held by the court that the ships were owned outright by Mr Nantes. Mr Chiswell was unable to assert the presumption of a resulting trust in his favour based on his transfer of the ships into his business partner's name, because he had transferred the property in order fraudulently to conceal his interest in it.

Case
Summary

Another case in point is that of *Gascoigne* v. *Gascoigne* [1918] 1 KB 223. Here a husband put the bungalow he had built into his wife's name in order to protect the property from creditors. This was not held as sufficient evidence to rebut the presumption of advancement. Lord Justice Lush said in this case that a claimant should not be permitted to rebut a presumption raised by the law 'by setting up his own illegality and fraud, and to obtain relief in equity because he has succeeded in proving it . . .'. In other words, Mr Gascoigne should not be allowed to benefit from the laws of equity and claim an **equitable interest** in the property, when the whole reason for his transfer of that property into his wife's name in the first place, and thus the giving up of his *legal* entitlement to the property, was in order to avoid the payment of his debts.

There are, of course, more modern examples of the rule in practice. In the case of *Tinker* v. *Tinker* [1970] P 136, a husband transferred his property into his wife's name in order to protect the house from creditors in the event of his new business venture failing. However, the couple later divorced and the husband claimed the return of his property on the basis that the wife was holding it on a resulting trust for him. Lord Denning remarked, rather dryly, that the husband:

> found himself on the horns of a dilemma in that, as between himself and his wife, he wished to say that the property belonged to him, whereas, as between himself and his creditors, he wished to say that it belonged to her.

In any event, the presumption of advancement of a gift from husband to wife was applied and the wife was allowed to keep the property.

A still more recent case dealing with this point is that of *Lavelle* v. *Lavelle* [2004] EWCA Civ 223. In this case George Lavelle, the father of Tracey, bought a flat in 1997, which he subsequently transferred into Tracey's name. Tracey argued that it had always been her father's intention to make a gift of the flat to her and produced a letter which it was alleged George had signed in support of this, but George claimed that the letter was a forgery. The court found that, because of the relationship between the parties, there was a presumption of advancement. However, this was rebutted by the overall evidence which pointed not towards the transfer of the flat to Tracey as a gift but towards a transfer simply for the purpose of avoiding inheritance tax. The judge therefore found that Tracey held the flat on trust for her father.

One other interesting point to be taken from this case is the issue of timing of the evidence. The court made it clear in this case that they will consider evidence of the conduct of the parties at the time of the transaction, or gift, to carry much more weight than the actions or conduct of the parties at a later date. In the words of Lord Phillips, Master of the Rolls:

> Plainly, self-serving statements or conduct of a transferor, who may long after the transaction be regretting earlier generosity, carry little or no weight. But words or conduct more proximate to the transaction itself should be given the significance that they naturally bear as part of the overall picture.

In other words, the conduct of the person who has made the alleged gift will be taken a lot less seriously after the event than at the time when the gift was made. This is to prevent situations where the person making the gift either falls out with the beneficiary of the gift, or otherwise regrets their decision to make that gift for other reasons, and later changes their mind.

The Writing and drafting exercise should help you to consolidate your understanding of the presumption of advancement and transfers of property for illegal purposes.

Writing and drafting

You are a trainee solicitor at the firm of Tai & Co. You have just attended an interview together with your training principal with a woman, Mrs Sekhon. She tells you that she bought a house together with her daughter some years ago, for £36,000. Her daughter contributed £16,000 towards the purchase price and Mrs Sekhon contributed the rest. The house purchase was a joint commercial venture, the idea being to rent the property out and sell it at a later date for a profit. On advice from a friend, the house had been registered in the daughter's sole name in order to avoid the payment of capital gains tax on the sale of the property. The daughter had now decided to sell the house but was arguing that the £20,000 from her mother had been a gift and that the mother had no right to reclaim the money. Mrs Sekhon is distraught because the money represented her entire life savings and she needed it for her retirement.

Your training principal has asked you to write a letter of advice in response to your client's query. Write a letter advising your client as to the possible outcome of her claim.

You should spend no more than 40 minutes on this task.

◆ **Handy tip:** Do not forget to start and end your letter correctly. Remember that, as a trainee solicitor, you are representing your firm as a whole and the professionalism of the letter is almost as important to the client as the quality of the advice you give!

Despite the general rule against claiming the benefit of a resulting trust where the transfer has been made for illegal or immoral purposes, it is important to appreciate that the rule will not necessarily always prevent an interest under a resulting trust from being asserted altogether, provided the claimant does not rely on the illegal action itself to assert their interest. This can be understood more clearly by taking a look at the facts of the controversial case of *Tinsley* v. *Milligan* [1994] 1 AC 340 (HL). Kathleen Milligan bought a house together with Stella Tinsley, from which they ran the business of a boarding house. The house was paid for out of the profits of the business, which they ran in partnership with one another. However, the couple registered the house in Stella's sole name specifically so that Kathleen could claim that she was merely a lodger in the house paying rent and thus continue to claim housing benefit on this basis. When the couple split up four years later, despite the fraud which had taken place against the Department of Social Security, Kathleen was still able to claim a share in the house under a presumed resulting trust, based on her contribution to the purchase of the property as a partner of the business.

The decision in *Tinsley* v. *Milligan* was based on a 3:2 majority in the House of Lords. Lord Goff, dissenting, said that the decision in favour of Miss Milligan was effectively condoning her illegal behaviour and that the courts should take a more moral stance and refuse to uphold her claim on the basis of the equitable doctrine of 'he who comes to equity must come with clean hands'. He went on to call for a review of the law in this area by the Law Commission. Notwithstanding Lord Goff's **dissenting judgment** and the widespread criticism of the decision in *Tinsley* v. *Milligan* which followed, a year later in the case of *Tribe* v. *Tribe* [1995] 4 All ER 236, CA, the Court of Appeal followed the decision and a father, Kim Tribe, also benefited under a resulting trust despite having made a fraudulent transfer. Mr Tribe had transferred shares in his company worth £78,000 to his son in order to prevent a claim for maintenance of his leased shop properties

Case Summary

Case Summary

in South Wales. In the event, no maintenance claim was made by his landlords and Mr Tribe made a claim through the courts for the return of the shares, which his son had refused to give back to him. The Court of Appeal held that there was a resulting trust in favour of Mr Tribe. Although he had made the transfer to his son with a view to defrauding his landlords, he had never carried out the fraud and therefore could rely on evidence of the transaction to prove that he had not intended to make an outright gift to his son.

And still more recently in *Lowson* v. *Coombes* [1999] Ch 373 (CA) Douglas Lowson bought a house in the name of his mistress, Rebecca Coombes, in order to prevent his wife from claiming a share of the house under their divorce proceedings. However, the court held that Mr Lowson was entitled to claim a half share in the property under a resulting trust, despite his motives for making the transfer. His intention in putting the house into the sole name of his mistress was irrelevant: the resulting trust was based on the initial contributions to the purchase of the property and not the couple's motives, whether illegal or otherwise. It would therefore appear that, despite the criticism of the case, instances of cases following the line of *Tinsley* v. *Milligan* are unlikely to stop here.

The Law Commission has recommended reform in this area of the law in their Consultation Paper 154 (1999), entitled *Illegal Transactions: The Effect of Illegality on Contracts and Trusts*. Their recommendation is to give the judiciary discretion to decide when illegality should prevent a resulting trust from being asserted. The suggestion is that the discretion would take into account, amongst other things, the seriousness of the illegal act and the knowledge and intention of the parties involved. However, the Law Commission's recommendations have so far proved unpopular, with a significant proportion of those responding to the consultation paper believing that to give the courts such discretion would only lead to greater uncertainty in the law. The Law Commission is now looking at alternatives to judicial discretion as a means of improving this area of trusts.

Purchase of property in another's name

It is a well-established principle of equity that, in the absence of evidence of a contrary intention, where property is purchased in the name of some other person it will be held on a resulting trust for the person who has paid for the purchase. As far back as 1788 in the well-known case of *Dyer* v. *Dyer*, the facts of which we have seen above, the judge confirmed that:

> the trust of a legal estate . . . whether taken in the names of the purchasers and others jointly, or in the name of others without that of the purchaser; whether in one name or several; whether jointly or successive, results to the man who advances the purchase money.

An example of how presumed resulting trusts can work in the case of property purchased in the name of another is the case of *Bull* v. *Bull* [1955] 1 QB 234 (CA). The case concerned a disagreement which had arisen between mother and son following the son's marriage. Mrs Bull and her son bought a property at 101 Rishden Gardens, Ilford, Essex in 1949. Both mother and son contributed towards the purchase price for the property, but the son provided the greater part of the money and the property was conveyed into his sole name. In April 1953, the son married and it was arranged that his mother should keep two rooms in the house whilst he and his wife would have the rest. Soon afterwards, however, differences arose between the mother and her daughter-in-law and the son told his mother to leave the house. The mother contended that, despite the house being in her son's sole name, she had a right to live in the property by virtue of her contribution towards the purchase of it. The court agreed, finding that she had not intended to make a gift of the purchase money to her son and that there was therefore no presumption of advancement, but rather that there should be a resulting trust imposed in her favour. In making his judgment Lord Justice Denning confirmed that, whilst the son was undoubtedly the legal owner of the house, the mother and son owned the house together in equity. The mother was therefore entitled to a share of the house proportionate to her contribution to the purchase price.

Case Summary

A slightly different twist on the imposition of presumed resulting trusts is provided in the case of *Springette* v. *Defoe* [1992] 2 FLR 388 (CA). In this case, the property in question was in fact purchased in the joint names of the contributing parties; the disagreement extended only to what should be the extent of the parties' entitlement to the property in equity: in other words, in what proportion should the property be divided? The facts of the case were that Mrs Springette and Mr Defoe lived together in Mrs Springette's council flat. The council subsequently offered the couple a council house, which they moved into as joint tenants in 1982. In the same year, the council offered to sell the council house to Mrs Springette and Mr Defoe for £14,445. This included a discount of 41 per cent of the purchase price on the basis that Mrs Springette had been a council tenant for more than 11 years. The couple took out a mortgage in their joint names for £12,000, Mrs Springette paying the balance of the purchase monies from her savings. The couple agreed that they would contribute equally towards the repayment of the mortgage. On the couple's subsequent break-up, Mr Defoe claimed that he was entitled to a 50 per cent share in the house. However, the court found that the property was held on a presumed resulting trust, Mrs Springette being entitled to a 75 per cent cent share in the property by virtue of the contribution she had made out of her savings to the purchase price, and the council discount from which the couple had benefited. The court held that Mrs Springette should benefit from the full amount of the discount, which would not have been available to them had Mrs Springette not been a council tenant for 11 years and without which the couple would not have been able to afford to buy the property.

Clearly this is an instance in which the courts were prepared to construe a discount on the purchase of a property as having an equivalent cash value in determining proportionate shares under a resulting trust. But was this just a singular decision of the courts? Let us take a look at what else, then, can be included in the purchase price for the purposes of calculating contribution.

What is included in the purchase price?

We have seen above that whoever provides the purchase money for the property will be viewed in equity as having an interest in that property, in the form of a resulting trust in their favour.

The timing of the creation of the interest is crucial

The timing of the creation of the interest is crucial in the resulting trust scenario: resulting trusts are based on the presumed intention of the parties at the time the property is acquired and the courts are really quite strict in construing this. So it is only those contributions made towards the actual purchase of the property, and not any subsequent payments, which will go to form the interest of the contributing party.

You be the judge

Q: Which of the following contributions do you think would gain the payer a beneficial interest in the property under a resulting trust?

(a) payment of the deposit on the property;
(b) payment of estate agents and legal fees;
(c) making mortgage payments on the property;
(d) paying the household bills;
(e) paying for an extension to the property.

Source: Pearson Education Ltd/Jules Selmes with kind permission of Patrick Gardner & Co

A: (a), (b) and (c) would all gain the payer a beneficial interest in the property under a resulting trust because they all relate to the payment of the initial purchase price of the property; this is the case even in the case of the mortgage payments, which are considered to be payment of the purchase price, albeit paid in instalments over a period of time. Categories (d) and (e) will not be sufficient to create a resulting trust because these are payments which do not relate to the purchase price of the property, even though (e) could be substantial.

The following cases further illustrate the point made in the You be the judge feature. As we have already seen, payments towards mortgage instalments will be construed as payments towards part of the purchase price of the property, although they are paid over a period of time and not just at the time of purchase. So, in the most straightforward example of this, in the case of *Cowcher* v. *Cowcher* [1972] 1 WLR 425 (CA), Mr and Mrs Cowcher bought a house with the aid of a mortgage, the house being put into Mr Cowcher's sole name. The mortgage was subsequently paid off by Mr and Mrs Cowcher together, and the courts held that Mr Cowcher would hold an interest in the property on a resulting trust for the wife on account of this.

Case Summary

The facts of *Harwood* v. *Harwood* [1991] Fam Law 418 present a slightly more unusual scenario involving mortgage payments. The case, amongst other things, concerned an argument over the ownership of a house purchased in the joint names of Mr and Mrs Harwood but paid for partly out of the funds of Mr Harwood's business, which he ran in partnership with a third person. On Mr and Mrs Harwood's divorce, the business partner claimed an interest in the house by virtue of the contribution the partnership had made to its purchase. The court found that there was a resulting trust in favour of the partnership equivalent to the proportion of the partnership's contribution to the purchase price of the house.

The payment of mortgage instalments would appear to be straightforward, therefore. But what about such smaller items as legal fees and removal expenses? The more recent case of *Curley* v. *Parkes* [2004] 1 P & CR DG 15 deals with a claim in respect of these matters. Mr Curley and Miss Parkes had been living together in a house in Richmond, London, bought by Miss Parks and registered in her sole name. Mr Curley's employer subsequently asked him to relocate to the company's offices in Luton, offering in return a relocation package which consisted of money to help with the moving costs and with the purchase of a new property in the locality. The company also agreed to buy Miss Parkes's property from her as part of the relocation. Miss Parkes then purchased another property in Luton, again in her sole name, and with her own money. Mr Curley paid no proportion

Case Summary

of the purchase price of the new property. Over the course of the following six months, Mr Curley did pay Miss Parkes a total of £9,000, however, which he later said was to compensate her for the deposit paid by her on the new house and for legal and removal expenses. When the couple separated, Mr Curley claimed an 8.5 per cent share of the property on resulting trust on the basis of money contributed towards the purchase price. However, the court dismissed his claim, as there was no evidence that the payments made to Miss Parkes had been designed to contribute to the purchase price of the property.

Curley v. *Parkes* shows us that contributions to the purchase price must be both specific and contemporary to the purchase. In addition, in order to raise the presumption under a resulting trust, the courts must be able to attribute to such payments a genuine intention to contribute to the purchase price of the house: general contributions towards rent or household expenses will not be sufficient. In *Savage* v. *Dunningham* [1974] Ch 181 three men shared a **leasehold** furnished flat together, the lease for which was in the name of only one of them. All three parties made equal payments towards the rent and other outgoings. Mark Dunningham, who was the leaseholder, was offered the chance by the landlord to purchase the flat for himself. He agreed to buy the flat but did not tell his flatmates about the opportunity or give them the option to purchase the flat along with him. Shortly after buying the flat he served notice on his flatmates to vacate the property. The flatmates argued that Dunningham held the property on resulting trust for all three of them. However, it was held that there was no resulting trust. The contributions which had been made to the rent and household expenses did not equate to any payment towards the purchase price of the property.

From the cases above we can see that the courts take quite a strict approach as to what payments will and will not be included as contributing to the purchase of a property, particularly in the case of payments made some time after the date of purchase. In the case of subsequent payments, these are unlikely to amount to a beneficial interest under a resulting trust, regardless of the amount of the payments or the period of time over which they were made. Certainly payments of a more trivial nature will not be sufficient. The case of *Gissing* v. *Gissing* [1971] AC 886 illustrates this. The case concerned a husband and wife, Violet and Raymond Gissing. Violet and Raymond lived together in a house which was registered in Raymond's sole name. He had paid for the house partly with a mortgage and partly with a loan from his employers. When Raymond left Violet for a younger woman, Violet claimed an interest in the house, claiming that she had contributed £220 from her savings to pay for a new lawn and furniture for the house. She said that she had later contributed from her earnings to the housekeeping and paid for her own and her son's clothes. However, Violet's claim was dismissed by the Court of Appeal: her limited contributions had not been enough to earn her a beneficial interest in the house.

A similar outcome was achieved in the House of Lords case of *Pettitt* v. *Pettitt* [1970] AC 777. The case concerned an argument over the family home of Harold and Hilda Pettitt. Hilda had inherited a house, which she and her husband lived in for a number of years. Hilda then sold the house, using the proceeds to buy a plot of land on which to build a bungalow for her and Harold to live in. The bungalow was again bought in Hilda's sole name. Hilda subsequently left Harold, taking their two children with her, and made an application for divorce on grounds of cruelty. Harold claimed a share of the bungalow on the grounds that he had spent money and effort in redecorating and improving it; but the House of Lords rejected Harold's claim. The improvements Harold was claiming to have made bore no relation to the purchase of the house and could therefore not amount to a beneficial interest under a resulting trust.

Case Summary

Case Summary

Case Summary

Both of the above cases give us an important insight in the thinking of the courts regarding the interpretation of claims for resulting trusts at that time. However, perhaps one of the most influential decisions relating to contributions in respect of the family home is the Court of Appeal case of *Burns* v. *Burns* [1984] Ch 317. The case concerned a couple, Valerie and Patrick Burns, who had lived together for almost 20 years and who had children together, although they were not actually married. The house they lived in was paid for by Patrick with part cash and part mortgage. The mortgage was paid off with Patrick's earnings while Valerie stayed at home to look after the house and children. When Valerie returned to work she used her own earnings to buy furniture, fixtures and fittings for the house and did some painting and redecoration, although her money was not needed to pay for any of the household expenses. The relationship broke down and Patrick sought a declaration as to whether Valerie had a beneficial interest in the house. The Court of Appeal held that Valerie had no interest in the house: she had made no contributions referable to the acquisition of an interest in the property. The fact that the relationship had lasted 19 years was irrelevant in claiming an interest in the property under a resulting trust.

Case Summary

This case is particularly useful in the study of resulting trusts because of Lord Justice May's really detailed summary of the position in equity, depending on whether the house is purchased in the joint names of the contributors or in the sole name of one party only. In the case of a purchase in joint names, he said:

> both the man and the woman are entitled to a share in the beneficial interest. Where the house is bought outright and not on mortgage, then the extent of their respective shares will depend on a more or less arithmetical calculation of the extent of their contributions to the purchase price. Where, on the other hand, as is more usual nowadays, the house is bought with the aid of a mortgage, then the court has to assess each party's respective contributions in a broad sense; nevertheless, the court is only entitled to look at the financial contributions, or their real or substantial equivalent, to the acquisition of the house; that the husband may spend his weekends redecorating or laying a patio is neither here nor there, nor is the fact that the woman has spent so much of her time looking after the house, doing the cooking and bringing up the family.

On the other hand, if the house is purchased in the sole name of one party:

> then if the woman [assuming the property is bought in the man's sole name] pays or contributes to the initial deposit this points to a common intention that she should have some beneficial interest in the house. If thereafter she makes direct contributions to the instalments, then the case is [strengthened] and her rightful share is likely to be greater. If the woman, having contributed to the deposit, but although not making direct contributions to the instalments, nevertheless uses her money for other joint household expenses so as to enable the man more easily to pay the mortgage instalments out of his own money, then her position is the same. Where a woman has made no contribution to the initial deposit, but makes regular and substantial contributions to the mortgage instalments, it may still be reasonable to infer a common intention that she should share a beneficial interest from the outset . . . Finally, where the house is taken in the man's name alone, if the woman makes no 'real' or 'substantial' financial contribution towards either the purchase price, deposit or mortgage instalments by means of which the family home was acquired, then she is not entitled to any share in the beneficial interest in that home even though over a very substantial number of years she may have worked just as hard as the man in maintaining the family, in the sense of keeping house, giving birth to and looking after and helping to bring up the children of the union.

Lord Justice May's judgment is interesting because it suggests that the contributions made to the purchase of a house may be broadly divided into two categories: direct or indirect. **Direct contributions** include such payments as those which are made specifically towards the deposit or the purchase price and the payment of mortgage instalments. On the other hand, **indirect contributions**, he suggests, may include payments towards household expenses that the legal owner of the property would otherwise be unable to meet, in addition to making the mortgage payments. There was some initial concern on the part of the judiciary following Lord Justice May's judgment that this second category of indirect contributions might cause confusion as to what exactly could be included in defining the resulting trust. The fear was that an inaccurate interpretation of the wording of the judgment might lead to an opening of the floodgates for claimants making applications for resulting trusts on the basis of contributions which bore no relation to the purchase of the property whatever. However, it is arguable that Lord Justice May was quite clear in his statement that any indirect contribution must be directly related to the acquisition of an interest in the house, which the other party could not otherwise have made (in other words, they could not have made the mortgage payments without help in paying the other household bills from their partner).

> inaccurate interpretation of the judgment might lead to an opening of the floodgates

One point which does remain unaffected by the judgment in *Burns* v. *Burns* is that any beneficial share of property acquired under a resulting trust will be established at the time the property is purchased and will be unaffected by any later payments for improvements to the house or contributions to its upkeep. As we have seen, unfortunately this can result in a rather harsh outcome for those who have either made no contribution or paid only a small amount towards the purchase of property, but who have then spent a great deal of money adding an extension to the house or maintaining the family home over a period of years, for example. In respect of married couples, the position has been somewhat alleviated by section 37 of the Matrimonial Proceedings and Property Act 1970, which states that:

> where a husband or wife contributes in money or money's worth to the improvement of real or personal property in which or in the proceeds of sale of which either or both of them has or have a beneficial interest, the husband or wife so contributing shall, if the contribution is of a substantial nature and subject to any agreement to the contrary express or implied, be treated as having then acquired by virtue of his or her contribution a share or an enlarged share, as the case may be, in that beneficial interest.

It should be noted that the wording of the Act states that the work must be of a substantial nature. So the erection of a conservatory or the installation of a central heating system will count, but repainting and keeping the house will not.

Section 37 is helpful to a point, but it is inherently flawed in that it does not assist unmarried couples. Thus, in *Burns* v. *Burns*, Valerie was not entitled to bring proceedings under the matrimonial legislation because they were unmarried. Given the increased trend for cohabitation (shown in the National Office of Statistics data in the Key stats feature at the beginning of the chapter), the courts tend to favour, as we shall see in Chapter 8, the mechanism of the constructive trust over resulting trusts when it comes to dividing the property of separating couples.

Automatic resulting trusts

There are any number of situations in which a trust can fail, necessitating the return of the trust property to its original owners. All such failures will come within the category of the automatic resulting trust, because there can be no presumed intention that the settlor intended to hold the property on trust for themselves. On the contrary, the situation has arisen because they intended the property to benefit some other person but that trust has failed. It is only because of that failure that the property, being unable to stay with the trustees and having nowhere else to go, automatically reverts to them as the original owner of the property. The following deal with two of the more common scenarios in which an automatic resulting trust will arise.

Failure of the trust

We have already seen in the case of *Re Vandervell's* an example of a failed trust, where a settlor has tried to set up a trust, transferring the property to the trustees successfully, but has failed adequately to express exactly whom the trust property is to benefit. However, the facts of *Re Vandervell's* are somewhat unusual; so let us now turn to a rather more common example of a flawed will. Let us imagine that Delores has, under the terms of her will, made the following gift:

> I give £10,000 to my trustees on trust to be divided between all of my closest friends in such shares as the trustees may think fit.

You will remember from Chapter 3 on certainties that the intention (to make a gift) and the subject matter (£10,000) of the gift are clear. However, there is a problem with the object of the gift: only Delores was able to say who her closest friends were and without the existence of a list of closest friends drawn up by her and attached to the will, it is impossible for the trustees to judge to whom the gift should go. The trustees therefore find themselves in a dilemma. The gift will certainly fail for lack of certainty of object; but what should the trustees do with the money? As trustees, they have no right to keep the money for their own benefit, albeit that they are the legal owners of it. Their only logical choice therefore is to hold the money on a resulting trust for its original owner, Delores. The practical result of this, as Delores is dead, is that the money will be held on trust for her estate.

Another example of the working of automatic resulting trusts of this kind in practice can be seen in the case of *Re Boyes* [1884] 26 Ch D 531. The case concerned the will of George Boyes. George had made a will leaving everything on trust to his solicitor, Frederick Carritt, directing him that the money was to be held for the benefit of certain persons, details of whom George would furnish his solicitor with at a later date. After George's death a letter was found instructing Mr Carritt that the money should go to George's mistress, Nell Brown, and their illegitimate child. However, the receipt of this information after the event was not considered sufficient to create a valid trust and the will was declared void for uncertainty of object. In the view of the court, it was not enough for Mr Carritt to have been told by Mr Boyes that he was a trustee; Mr Carritt also needed to be told the terms of the trust. The court therefore held that the money must be held on a resulting trust by Mr Carritt for the benefit of George's **next of kin** under the rules of **intestacy**.

Case Summary

Of course, failure of the trust need not always be on account of a failure by the settlor to describe adequately the objects of the trust. There can be other reasons for a trust's ultimate breakdown. Take, for example, the case of *Re Ames' Settlement* [1946] Ch 217, which concerned a failed **marriage settlement**. In 1908 a father, Louis Ames, on the marriage of his son John, put £10,000 into trust for his son and daughter-in-law by way of marriage settlement. The settlement stated that the money should go to John and his wife for life, and then to their children and finally to any next of kin. Unfortunately, however, John Ames was unable to consummate the marriage and eventually, in 1926, the marriage was annulled on grounds of non-consummation. The lady renounced all claims under the trust and married another man. John Ames subsequently died. John's next of kin tried to claim the trust monies for themselves, but the **executors** of Louis Ames, who had also by that time died, claimed that the money should be returned to his estate. The court found in favour of the father's estate. It was a condition of the **settlement** that the parties should be married. As their marriage was annulled and was therefore legally held never to have existed, the condition of the settlement had not been fulfilled and so the trust property should be returned to its original owner: the settlor, Louis Ames. As Mr Ames had died the money would go into his estate and be distributed in accordance with the terms of his will.

One final example of where an automatic resulting trust will arise is in the case of a **Quistclose trust**. In the case of *Barclays Bank* v. *Quistclose Investments*, you will remember from Chapter 1, Quistclose Investments lent money to Rolls-Razor, which was in financial difficulty, to make payments to its shareholders. The money was put into a specially designated bank account for the purpose, but when the company subsequently went into liquidation, the purpose of the trust was frustrated and the shareholders could not be paid. The money was therefore held to result back automatically to the settlor, Quistclose, on a resulting trust.

Surplus trust monies

The other situation in which an automatic resulting trust will commonly arise is where there are surplus trust monies left over after the purpose of the trust has been completed. The most obvious example of such a situation arising is where money has been put into trust for the maintenance of a specific animal, as we saw in Chapter 4 on **purpose trusts**, and that animal subsequently dies, leaving money still in the trust fund. The trustees of the trust cannot keep the money, so where should it go? In the absence of any direction from the settlor, the obvious answer would be that the money would result back to the settlor or to their estate if the settlor has died.

In the case of *Re The Trusts of the Abbott Fund* [1900] 2 Ch 326, Dr Abbott had left ample money in his will in trust to support his two daughters, Frederica and Katherine Abbott, who were both deaf and dumb. Dr Abbott died in 1844 and all seemed well until the death of the last remaining trustee in 1889, when the shocking discovery was made that the whole of the trust fund, amounting to several thousand pounds, had mysteriously disappeared. All attempts to trace the fund were fruitless. A friend of the doctor, Rowland Fawcett, started up a support fund into which friends of the family contributed, in order to continue to support the daughters. The daughters both died in 1899, within two months of one another. Upon the death of the daughters there was a surplus left over in the support fund. The court held that the money should be held on resulting trust for the benefit of the subscribers to the fund (in other words, those who had originally given the money).

190

At first sight it may seem both obvious and logical that the surplus from a trust fund should go back to the settlors once the purpose of the trust has been completed. However, beware! There are many situations in which it would be either impractical or illogical for such an outcome to be determined. Take the example of disaster funds. Trust funds are very often set up in the wake of terrible disasters to raise money to support those affected by them. But what happens to any money left over once the disaster has been alleviated? With a big natural disaster, such as an earthquake appeal, there could be many thousands, or even tens of thousands, of benefactors. It would be both impractical and, in the case of money raised in street collections, impossible, to identify all those who gave money to the fund. In such a case it would make no sense to try to find all of those people to return the money to them. So what should be done? Mr Justice Harman tried to find an answer in the wake of the *Gillingham Bus Disaster Fund* [1958] Ch 300, in which monies had been raised for the benefit of families affected by the Gillingham bus disaster. The court case concerned an application by the mayors for adjudication as to what they should do with the remaining balance of the fund monies. The judge held that, as with *Re Abbott*, any surplus funds should be returned to the donors under a resulting trust. But what were the practical implications of this? Unlike in *Trusts of the Abbott Fund*, where the subscribers to the fund were small in number and all known to the trustees, the Gillingam Bus Disaster Fund attracted donations from thousands of people all over the country, many of whom were anonymous donors. It would therefore be impossible for the balance of trust monies to be returned. In actual fact the money was paid into court where it remained until 1991, when the money was finally released for the building of a memorial to the boys who had died. The full facts of the incident can be seen in the Law in action feature.

Case Summary

Law in action The Gillingham Bus Disaster

At three minutes to six on the evening of the 4 December 1951 a double-decker bus careered into a company of Royal Marine cadets who were marching en route to attend a boxing tournament. Of the cadets, who were all between the ages of 10 and 13, 24 were killed and a further 18 were injured. At the time, the accident was reported to be the highest loss of life in any road accident in British history.

The mayors of three local parishes set up a memorial fund, asking for donations:

to be devoted, among other things, to defraying the funeral expenses, caring for the boys who may be disabled, and then to such worthy cause or causes in memory of the boys who lost their lives, as the mayors may determine.

The fund received almost £9,000 in donations. In the event, the bus company admitted liability for the accident and paid out £10,000 in compensation to the families of the boys. Only a small proportion of the mayors' fund was therefore ever used. To this day the Chatham Marine Cadet Unit still holds an annual memorial parade at the cemetery in which the cadets were buried to commemorate the tragic loss of so many young lives.

For more information about the disaster, go to: http://www.historicmedway.co.uk/disasters/gillingham_bus_disaster.htm.

Reflective practice

Do you think the outcome in the 'Law in action' case was the right one? Can you think of a better solution to the problem of distributing surplus funds?

The altogether different outcome in the case of *Re Osoba* [1978] 1 WLR 791 sits in sharp contrast to the previous two. Mr Osoba left money in his will for the maintenance of his wife, his mother, and 'for the training of my daughter Abiola up to university grade'. Mr Osoba's wife and mother had both died and his daughter had finished university; so the question arose as to what should become of the surplus monies in the trust fund. The court found not that the money should revert to the estate of Mr Osoba, but that it should be given outright to the daughter, Abiola. In giving reasons for his judgment, Vice-Chancellor Megarry (as he had by now become) said:

> If a trust is constituted for the assistance of certain persons by certain stated means there is a sharp distinction between the cases where the beneficiaries have died and cases where they are still living. If they are dead, the court is willing to hold that there is a result-ing trust for the donors; for the major purpose of the trust, that of providing help and benefit for the beneficiaries, comes to an end when the beneficiaries are all dead and so are beyond earthly help whether by the stated means or otherwise. But if the beneficiaries are still living, the major purpose of providing help and benefit for the beneficiaries can still be carried out even after the stated means have all been accomplished, and so the court will be ready to treat the stated means as being indicative and not restrictive.

In Vice-Chancellor Megarry's view, then, in cases of surplus funds the trust will only be considered to have fulfilled its purpose and therefore come to an end where the beneficiaries have died. In cases where the beneficiaries are still alive the purpose will be construed as being altogether broader than the purpose stated if this means the funds will continue to be of use or benefit to the beneficiaries. It would appear that this in effect gives the court a huge discretion to choose whether to apply the doctrine of automatic resulting trusts or to claim that an outright gift has been made by the settlor, depending on the circumstances of the case and what the court considers to be an equitable outcome.

Criticisms of Megarry's classification of resulting trusts

Mr Justice Megarry's categorisation of resulting trusts in *Re Vandervell's*, as either presumed or automatic, has come under a certain amount of judicial criticism; par-ticularly from Lord Browne-Wilkinson in his judgment in *Westdeutsche Landesbank Girozentrale* v. *Islington London Borough Council* [1996] 2 WLR 802, which concerned an argument over interest rates payable to the bank under certain agreements. Whilst Lord Browne-Wilkinson has no problem with the division of resulting trusts into two categor-ies, he seems to take particular issue with Mr Justice Megarry's description of the second category of resulting trusts as being 'automatic'. In Lord Browne-Wilkinson's opinion, there must always be an element of intention, whether presumed or otherwise, and it is simply not possible to infer the existence of a resulting trust on the basis of an automatic entitlement. Thus, in Lord Browne-Wilkinson's view:

under existing law a resulting trust arises in two sets of circumstances:

(a) where A makes a voluntary payment to B or pays (wholly or in part) for the purchase of property which is vested either in B alone or in the joint names of A and B there is a presumption that A did not intend to make a gift to B: the money or property is held on trust for A (if he is the sole provider of the money) or in the case of a joint purchase by A and B in shares proportionate to their contributions . . .

(b) where A transfers property to B on express trusts, but the trusts declared do not exhaust the whole beneficial interest . . .

Both types of resulting trust are traditionally regarded as examples of trust giving effect to the common intention of the parties. A resulting trust is not imposed by law against the intentions of the trustee . . . but gives effect to his presumed intention. Megarry J in *Re Vandervell's Trusts (No. 2)* suggests that a resulting trust of type (B) does not depend on intention but operates automatically. I am not convinced that this is right. If the settlor has expressly, or by necessary implication, abandoned any beneficial interest in the trust property, there is in my view no resulting trust: the undisposed-of equitable interest vests in the Crown as *bona vacantia* . . .

The Latin term **bona vacantia** means property which has no legal owner. As a matter of long-standing tradition, all such ownerless property will be claimed by the Crown. (See the government website at **http://www.bonavacantia.gov.uk** for further information.) Lord Browne-Wilkinson's interpretation of the second category of resulting trusts, therefore, is that the intention of the settlor should be taken into account when making a decision as to where the money or property should ultimately reside: if it was the intention of the settlor to divest of his interest in the property completely it should not be returned to him automatically; rather, that property should result to the Crown.

Lord Browne-Wilkinson's assessment of the second category of resulting trusts deals efficiently with the situation where there are surplus monies in a fund, such as in the case of the Gillingham Bus Disaster. In fact, the whole legal case was based on a claim by the Crown that the contents of the fund should be declared *bona vacantia*, as it would be impossible to locate all the owners of the money donated. It could be argued that this is a more practical way of dealing with surplus trust funds than declaring the return of that money to owners who can never be found. However, Lord Browne-Wilkinson's theory sits less well with cases of failed trust. For example, in the case of *Re Vandervell's* itself, whilst Mr Vandervell's intention was undoubtedly

> It could be argued that this is more practical

to rid himself of his beneficial interest in the shares in order to avoid tax, it is highly unlikely that he would have wanted the money to go to the Crown in the event of the shares not being effectively disposed of: even if their return into his beneficial ownership would mean the payment of a large tax bill.

Even in cases of surplus funds, a declaration of the surplus as *bona vacantia* may not always be the logical choice. In the case of *Air Jamaica* v. *Joy Charlton* [1999] 1 WLR 1399, the surplus in question was a surplus in an employee pension scheme. The pension fund documentation contained a clause which stated that under no circumstances was any of the pension fund monies to be returned to the company, Air Jamaica. However, when the scheme was brought to an end, this raised the question 'what should happen to the surplus in the fund?' The court of the **Privy Council** made the decision that the monies should be distributed pro rata amongst the employees of the company, in proportion to their individual contributions to the scheme. In other words, a resulting trust was declared in favour of the original owners of the trust property: the employees.

Case Summary

Documenting the law

The form shown here is that which employees of Air Jamaica were asked to complete to make a claim in respect of the fund following the closure of the pension scheme.

Note the wording at the bottom authorising payment of the trust funds into a nominated bank account.

DEFUNCT AIR JAMAICA PENSION FUND

REGISTRATION INFORMATION

This form is required to ensure an accurate registration of contributors and to help process your information. Please complete and drop in the box marked " TRUSTEES – DEFUNCT AIR JAMAICA PENSION FUND" available at the CIBC JAMAICA branch nearest you or mail to: - "THE TRUSTEES – DEFUNCT AIR JAMAICA PENSION FUND", C/O CIBC JAMAICA LIMITED, 23 KNUTSFORD BOULEVARD, KINGSTON 5, no later than the 20th day of July, 2001.

If this form is returned after the above date or not returned or returned incomplete it may result in delay of payment of any funds to which you may be entitled.

SECTION A:
ALL ITEMS IN THIS SECTION MUST BE COMPLETED (WHERE INAPPLICABLE PLEASE STATE "N/A")
CONTRIBUTOR DETAILS

SURNAME | FIRST NAME | MIDDLE NAME | EMPLOYEE NO. | EMPLOYEE NO.

MAIDEN NAME(S) | DATE OF BIRTH (DAY MTH YR) | NATIONAL INSURANCE NO. | TRN/SOCIAL SECURITY NO. | INCOME TAX REF NO. (Pre TRN)

PRESENT HOME ADDRESS
STREET | CITY/STATE/PROVINCE | POSTAL/ZIP CODE | COUNTRY | HOW LONG AT THIS ADDRESS

MAIL ADDRESS (IF DIFFERENT FROM ABOVE) | TELEPHONE NO. | FAX NO. | EMAIL ADDRESS

LAST ADDRESS WHILE EMPLOYED AT AIR JAMAICA
STREET | CITY/STATE/PROVINCE | POSTAL/ZIP CODE | COUNTRY

NAME OF NOMINATED BENEFICIARY

DATE OF JOINING (DAY MONTH YEAR) | DATE OF TERMINATION (DAY MONTH YEAR)

DATE OF JOINING (DAY MONTH YEAR) | DATE OF TERMINATION (DAY MONTH YEAR)

DID YOU MAKE CONTRIBUTIONS AT ANY TIME BETWEEN APRIL 1969 AND JUNE 1994 TO THE AIR JAMAICA PENSION SCHEME? | YES | NO

SECTION B:
TO BE COMPLETED ONLY BY EXECUTORS / ADMINISTRATORS OF ESTATES OF DECEASED CONTRIBUTORS OR ATTORNEYS
DETAILS

SURNAME | FIRST NAME | MIDDLE NAME | DATE OF BIRTH (DAY MONTH YEAR) | TRN/SOCIAL SECURITY NO.

HOME ADDRESS
STREET | CITY/STATE/PROVINCE | POSTAL/ZIP CODE | COUNTRY

MAIL ADDRESS (IF DIFFERENT FROM ABOVE) | TELEPHONE NO. | FAX NO. | EMAIL ADDRESS

RELATIONSHIP TO CONTRIBUTOR | DATE OF DEATH OF CONTRIBUTOR (DAY MONTH YEAR) | DATE OF YOUR APPOINTMENT AS EXECUTOR/ADMINISTRATOR/POWER OF ATTORNEY (DAY MONTH YEAR)

If there are any funds payable to me (or to the above estate, as the case may be) this serves as my authorisation and request to the Trustees of the Defunct Air Jamaica Pension Fund to open an account in my name at CIBC JAMAICA and at its branch stated on the reverse.

[*Source*: http://www.airjpension.com/pdf/Air%20Jamaica%20Pension%20Scheme%20Registration%20Form.pdf]

In giving his judgment in the case, Lord Millett said:

Prima facie the surplus is held on a resulting trust for those who provided it. This sometimes creates a problem of some perplexity. In the present case, however, it does not. Contributions were payable by the members with matching contributions by the company. In the absence of any evidence that this is not what happened in practice, the surplus must be treated as provided as to one half by the company and as to one half by the members.

The Attorney-General contended that neither the company nor the members can take any part in the surplus, which has reverted to the Crown as *bona vacantia*. He argued that clause 4 of the trust deed precludes any claim by the company, while the members cannot claim any part of the surplus because they have received all that they are entitled to . . . This is wrong in principle. Like a constructive trust, a resulting trust arises by operation of law, though unlike a constructive trust it gives effect to intention. But it arises whether or not the transferor intended to retain a beneficial interest – he almost always does not – since it responds to the absence of any intention on his part to pass a beneficial interest to the recipient. It may arise even where the transferor positively wished to part with the beneficial interest, as in [*Re Vandervell's*]. In that case the retention of a beneficial interest by the transferor destroyed the effectiveness of a tax avoidance scheme which the transferor was seeking to implement. The House of Lords affirmed the principle that a resulting trust is not defeated by evidence that the transferor intended to part with the beneficial interest if he has not in fact succeeded in doing so. As Plowman J had said in the same case at first instance: 'As I see it, a man does not cease to own property simply by saying "I don't want it". If he tries to give it away the question must always be, has he succeeded in doing so or not?'

It is evident from his statement that Lord Millett's feeling was more sympathetic to Mr Justice Megarry's original categorisation of resulting trusts than to Lord Browne-Wilkinson's revised categorisation. In any event, on the facts of the case itself, it is clear that Lord Browne-Wilkinson's alternative assessment of the second category of resulting trusts, whilst logical to a certain point, is nevertheless flawed if applied to such circumstances. How the law will resolve itself in this area remains to be seen; but it is certainly going to continue to be a moot point for some time to come.

Summary

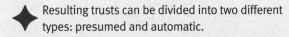 Resulting trusts can be divided into two different types: presumed and automatic.

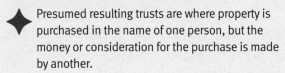 Presumed resulting trusts are where property is purchased in the name of one person, but the money or consideration for the purchase is made by another.

Automatic resulting trusts occur where a trust has failed, either because it has only partially been declared, or because there is a surplus remaining when the purpose of a trust has been completed.

In the case of presumed resulting trusts, only those contributions made towards the actual purchase of the property, and not any subsequent payments, will go to form the interest of the contributing party.

'Subsequent payments' include even substantial payments, such as the erection of an extension to the property. However, for married couples only, provision is made for this eventuality with section 37 of the Matrimonial Proceedings and Property Act 1970.

 Wherever a gift of property is made, the presumption will be made in equity that the gift is to be held on resulting trust for the person making that gift, in the absence of clear evidence to the contrary.

 However, there will be a 'presumption of advancement' (in other words, the presumption of an outright gift) in cases of transfers of property from father to child or husband to wife. This does not apply to transfers between mothers and children or wives and husbands.

 Evidence that a gift was made for an improper or illegal purpose will not be sufficient to rebut the 'presumption of advancement' of a gift made from husband to wife or father to child. However, illegal purposes will not necessarily defeat the presumption of a resulting trust altogether if the illegal purpose has no direct relationship to the contributions to the property claimed by the person claiming a stake in the property (see *Tinsley* v. *Milligan*).

 There has been criticism of Mr Justice Megarry's categorisation of automatic resulting trusts, but a satisfactory alternative has yet to be found to the problem of defining trusts which result from a failure of the fund under the various circumstances which can arise.

Question and answer*

Problem: Ten years ago Clyde asked Shenice to marry him, presenting her with a beautiful diamond solitaire engagement ring. Shenice accepted Clyde's proposal and they started making plans for their future together, first buying a car, which they paid for equally in instalments out of their joint bank account, and then a small house in the Bayswater area of London for £200,000. Both the car and the house were registered in the sole name of Clyde. Clyde obtained a mortgage of £150,000 to buy the property and Shenice contributed the other £50,000 from her savings.

Two years later Shenice's mother, Doretta, had a stroke and the couple decided she should come to live with them so they could keep a closer eye on her. Doretta paid for a large extension, costing £30,000, to the rear of the property to create a 'granny annexe'. Some time later it was agreed that Doretta should have a 10 per cent share in the house on account of the work that had been done.

Since they have been there Clyde has made all the payments on the mortgage out of his own money, but Shenice has decorated the house throughout and put in a new kitchen out of her savings. Doretta has also helped out with the household expenses since moving in, although her money was not required to make the mortgage payments.

Shenice has now become impatient with Clyde's empty promises of a wedding commitment and has decided to break off the engagement and move out of the house. She plans to buy somewhere new for her and her mother to live in and wants to know what her entitlement is in respect of the engagement ring, the car and the Bayswater house (if any), and how much Doretta will be able to claim in respect of the granny annexe.

Advise Shenice as to her rights under the doctrine of resulting trusts *only*.

You should allow yourself no more than 40 minutes to complete this task.

Essay: Should the presumption of advancement be abandoned and, if so, why?

This question should be answered in 40 minutes.

✱ Answer guidance is provided at the end of the chapter.

Further reading and references

Kodilinye, S. (1990) 'Resulting trusts, advancement and fraudulent transfers', Conv 213.

This article presents some interesting case comment on *Sekhon* v. *Alissa*, the case on which the Writing and drafting exercise in this chapter is based.

Law Commission Consultation Paper 154 (1999) *Illegal Transactions: The Effect of Illegality on Contracts and Trusts*, London: The Stationery Office.

The Law Commission's consultation paper recommending the giving to the judiciary of a discretion to decide when illegality should prevent a resulting trust from being asserted. Gives a useful overview and comment on the current state of the law in this area.

Law Commission Discussion Paper 278 (2002) *Sharing Homes*, Lodon: The Stationery Office.

Provides a useful overview of the law relating to cohabitation generally, including brief comment on the presumption of advancement.

Rickett, C.E.F. and Grantham, R. (2000) 'Resulting trusts – the nature of the failing trust cases', 116 LQR 15.

Commentary on the *Air Jamaica* case and in-depth discussion and suggested possible solutions to the difficulties with the Megarry categorisation of resulting trusts.

Stowe, H. (1994) 'The "Unruly Horse" has bolted', 56 MLR 441.

Another article providing useful case comment – this time on *Tinsley* v. *Milligan*.

Swadling, W. (2008) 'Explaining resulting trusts', 124 LQR 72–102.

A really excellent article discussing the problems in defining the different categories of resulting trusts, looking at the problems with both Mr Justice Megarry's and Lord Brown-Wilkinson's categorisations. Definitely worth a read.

Question and answer guidance

Problem:

The engagement ring

Under section 3(2) of the Law Reform (Miscellaneous Provisions) Act 1970, the gift of an engagement ring shall be presumed to be an absolute gift. This presumption may be rebutted by proving that the ring was given on the condition (express or implied) that it should be returned if the marriage did not take place for any reason, but there is no evidence of that here. In the case of *Cox* v. *Jones* the claimant failed to secure the return of a £10,000 engagement ring because he could not prove that the ring had been given on the basis that he would want it back if the engagement ended. Shenice should therefore be able to keep the ring.

The car

The purchase of the car would result in the creation of a presumed resulting trust in favour of Clyde and Shenice equally, as the couple paid for the car equally in instalments out of their joint bank account (*Dyer* v. *Dyer*). Note: presumably payment for the car in instalments would be considered payment towards the purchase price of the property, albeit the purchase of a car and not the payment of a mortgage (*Cowcher* v. *Cowcher*).

The house

Shenice would have an interest in the property under a resulting trust, on the basis of the principle in *Dyer* v. *Dyer*, above. In terms of the share she would have in the property, this will be dependent on the amount paid by Shenice towards the purchase price of the property. On resulting trust principles she would thus initially be entitled to a quarter share in the property, having paid £50,000 towards the purchase of a £200,000 house. In terms of Shenice's redecoration of the house and putting in of a new kitchen, neither of these matters relate to the acquisition of the property and so will not give her any further interest under a resulting trust, despite the fact that they may have added value (*Pettitt* v. *Pettitt*; *Gissing* v. *Gissing*; *Burns* v. *Burns*). If they had been married, she could have made a claim for improvements to the property under the section 37 of the Matrimonial Proceedings and Property Act 1970. However, they are not married. Note that Shenice may be entitled to more than a quarter share under the doctrine of constructive trusts.

Doretta paid for a large extension to the rear of the property to create a 'granny annexe', costing £30,000. The property had already been acquired by Shenice and Clyde when Doretta put money into the house, so this would suggest she is not entitled to an interest under a resulting trust. Distinguish from *Bull* v. *Bull*, where a mother put money into the purchase of the property. However, could the creation of a granny annexe be construed as the creation of a new property, and therefore that Doretta had paid for it, albeit that the couple owned the property from which it was formed?

Note that there can be no presumption of advancement in respect of the £30,000, as it would be between mother and daughter/son-in-law, and not father and child or husband and wife (*Bennet* v. *Bennet*).

Some time later it was agreed that Doretta should have a 10 per cent share in the house on account of the work that had been done. The timing in the creation of a resulting trust is important: such trusts are based on the presumed intention of the parties at the time the property is acquired, so any subsequent agreement between the parties would be irrelevant (although Doretta may have an interest under a constructive trust or proprietary estoppel). Doretta has also helped out with the household expenses since moving in. As with Shenice, helping out with household expenses would not be sufficient to create any interest under a resulting trust, as this does not relate to the acquisition of the property.

Essay: The question asks whether the presumption of advancement should be abandoned and, if so, why. A good answer to this question will start by explaining what the presumption of advancement is in resulting trusts: i.e. that it is the presumption that when a transfer is made of property by a father to a child or by a husband to his wife, the usual presumption of a resulting trust (*Fowkes* v. *Pascoe*; *Re Vinogradoff*) will be effectively reversed and instead the presumption will be made (in the absence of evidence to the contrary) that the transfer was intended to be an outright gift (*Dyer* v. *Dyer*).

The question is asking the student to comment on the suitability of this presumption in the current social climate. As the presumption only runs between father and child (and not mother and child, for example – see *Bennet* v. *Bennet*) or husband and wife (but not a gift from wife to husband) it is arguably very old-fashioned in its remit. Mention that the Law Commission in its discussion paper, *Sharing Homes*, has described the presumption as 'somewhat anachronistic'.

It is worth noting, however, that there have been exceptions made in situations where the person making the transfer has been acting in the place of a father by taking on the financial support of the child: see *Ebrand* v. *Dancer*, which concerned a grandfather who had taken on a parental role in respect of his grandson, the father having died. Could there be scope to extend the presumption, then, to anyone in a parental role, and to gifts from wives to husbands, or should the presumption be abandoned altogether?

Conclude by giving your views on the presumption and advancing some comment on where you think the law in this area should go.

Visit **www.mylawchamber.co.uk/warner-reed** to access study support resources including practice exam questions with guidance, interactive 'You be the judge' multiple choice questions, annotated weblinks, glossary and key case flashcards and audio legal updates all linked to the **Pearson eText** version of *Equity and Trusts* which you can **search**, **highlight** and **personalise** with your **own notes** and **bookmarks**.

Use Case Navigator to read in full some of the key cases referenced in this chapter with commentary and questions:

Gissing v. ***Gissing*** [1970] 2 All ER 780

Chapter 8
Constructive trusts

Key points In this chapter we will be looking at:

- ✦ The imposition of constructive trusts
- ✦ Defining unconscionability in constructive trusts
- ✦ Express and implied agreement constructive trusts
- ✦ The changing nature of implied trusts
- ✦ What is meant by proprietary estoppel
- ✦ The criteria required for the doctrine of proprietary estoppel to arise
- ✦ Remedies available in proprietary estoppel
- ✦ Differences between proprietary estoppel and constructive trusts

Introduction

In Chapter 7 we established that wherever a person makes contributions to the purchase price of a property, whether they are registered as the legal owner of the property or not, they will acquire an **equitable interest** in the property in the form of a **resulting trust**, proportionate to the amount of their contribution. We also learnt that if a person does not make a financial contribution to the purchase price, but they subsequently spend money on that property, perhaps by paying for repairs or maintenance to the property, or even by carrying out substantial works such as an extension to the property, under the doctrine of resulting trusts they will nevertheless gain no entitlement to any proportion of the property because they have not contributed towards the purchase price. Equally a person who makes no direct financial contribution to the property itself, but who stays at home and runs the household or brings up the children of the family over a number of years, will be entitled to nothing under the doctrine of resulting trusts.

It may come as a relief to know that the rather harsh results meted out by the doctrine of resulting trusts in such situations do find a solution in the doctrine of **constructive trusts**, however; and this is what we are going to be looking at in this chapter. This is not to say, of course, that resulting trusts do not have their place in the law (the doctrine of constructive trusts does not consider the situation of a partially created, or failed **trust**, for example). It is simply that the doctrine of constructive trusts has evolved to deal specifically with such situations as the family break-up, and is therefore more suited to the needs of persons who find themselves in this position.

What is a constructive trust?

Constructive trusts are fundamentally different from resulting trusts, not only in what they are designed to achieve (although perhaps because of this) but also in the basis on which they operate. Although we have seen that a resulting trust will be imposed, whether **presumed** or **automatic**, irrespective of the legal owner's conduct, the assumption being that the **settlor** does not intend to benefit the person to whom legal title is given or transferred, a constructive trust, on the other hand, is said to arise by operation of law, specifically *on account of* the legal owner's conduct. With a constructive trust, it is all about finding the just, or equitable, outcome, based on the circumstances of the case, and the conduct of the parties plays a huge part in this.

To give you a flavour of where a constructive trust will be imposed, let us have a look at an example: say Nadia and Tomas set up home together. Tomas pays the deposit on the house from some savings and pays the mortgage. The property is registered in Tomas's sole name. However, Nadia subsequently buys a new central heating system for the property, pays for repairs to the roof and redecorates and furnishes the property throughout on the understanding that the house is going to be her home together with Tomas and in the expectation that she will therefore have an interest in it. This is a situation we have come across before in the context of resulting trusts and we have seen that Nadia's entitlement would be nothing in that context. However, in the context of a constructive trust, we must ask: 'Would it be fair for Tomas to deny Nadia a beneficial entitlement to the property, knowing that she has spent many thousands of pounds on improving it and turning it into a comfortable home for the couple?' If, on considering this, your answer would be no, it would not be fair, then you are likely to have a constructive trust.

Lord Justice Chadwick in the case of *Banner Homes Group* v. *Luff Developments Ltd* [2000] 2 WLR 772 said that, with constructive trusts, it was a matter of **unconscionability**. The facts of this case were quite different from those of Nadia and Tomas, above. Here, the parties in question were companies, not individuals, and the disputed property consisted of a 4.8-acre development site, which the companies had agreed to buy and develop as a joint venture, for a purchase price of £3.4 million. Luff Developments Ltd had agreed to enter into a joint project to purchase the land, but had subsequently changed their minds, deciding to go ahead with the purchase without the **claimant**. However, they chose not to tell the claimant, Banner Homes, of their change of heart, for fear that the company would make a rival bid for the land. The court held in the event that Luff Developments had purchased the land on a constructive trust in favour of themselves and Banner Homes, in equal shares, and that all profits made from the site should be split equally between them. Quoting Lord Justice Millett from an earlier case, Lord Justice Chadwick said of constructive trusts:

Case Summary

> A constructive trust arises by operation of law wherever the circumstances are such that it would be **unconscionable** for the owner of property (usually but not necessarily the [owner]) to assert his own **beneficial interest** in the property and deny the beneficial interests of another.

The facts of this case may be quite different from the traditional view of constructive trusts set out in our earlier example of Nadia and Tomas; however, the principle is the same: that the legal owner of the property is deemed to have acted in an unconscionable manner in seeking to deny the claimant a beneficial interest in the property. The question to be asked here, then, with reference to Lord Justice Chadwick's judgment, is: when exactly will the circumstances be such that it would be unconscionable for the owner of the property to assert his beneficial interest over that of the claimant?

Defining unconscionability

Case Navigator

Case Summary

The House of Lords were first given the opportunity to consider this question in **Gissing v. Gissing** [1971] AC 886, a case which we have already come across in the previous chapter. You may remember that the case concerned a claim by a wife to a beneficial interest in the family home. The couple lived together in the family home which had been paid for by Mr Gissing. The house was in Mr Gissing's sole name. After 25 years of marriage, Mr Gissing left his wife for a younger woman. Mrs Gissing made an application to the court for an order in respect of her beneficial interest in the house.

The judges in the case did not consider the issue of constructive trusts in the context of 'unconscionability'; this expression was a much later description of the general equitable principles surrounding the imposition of the constructive trust, and the law concerning constructive trusts was still very much in its infancy at this point. Rather, the judges' focus was that the imposition of a constructive trust should be reliant on some evidence of a **common intention** between the parties that they would share the beneficial ownership in the property in question. Whilst Lord Diplock's judgment is the most frequently quoted in respect of this case, the words of Viscount Dilhorne perhaps provide the simplest analysis of the position in equity. Viscount Dilhorne said that:

> a claim to a beneficial interest in land made by a person in whom the legal **estate** is not **vested** and whether made by a stranger, a spouse or a former spouse must depend for its success on establishing that it is held on a trust to give effect to the beneficial interest of the claimant . . . Where there was a common intention at the time of the acquisition of the house that the beneficial interest in it should be shared, it would be a breach of faith by the spouse in whose name the legal estate was vested to fail to give effect to that intention and the other spouse will be held entitled to a share in the beneficial interest.

So, in effect, what Viscount Dilhorne is saying here is that it would be unconscionable for the legal owner of the property to deny a person an equitable interest in the property wherever there was a common intention between the parties that they should share the beneficial interest in it.

> There will rarely have been an explicit agreement between the couple

Of course, the problem with common intention, particularly in disputes between couples in the process of a relationship break-up, is proof. There will rarely have been an explicit agreement between the couple as to how the property is to be shared at the time of the purchase and any agreement, such as it was, is likely to have been oral. Viscount Dilhorne was quick to acknowledge this difficulty, stating that an absence of common intention could not be filled with inferences as to what the parties might have done if they had thought about it at the time, thus 'imputing' their intention: the common intention must have been a real one. However, in the absence of evidence of a specific agreement or discussion on the subject, Viscount Dilhorne did concede that reference could be made to the conduct of the parties and inference be made from that conduct. He said that:

in determining whether or not there was such a common intention, regard can of course be had to the conduct of the parties. If the wife provided part of the purchase price of the house, either initially or subsequently by paying or sharing in the mortgage payments, the inference may well arise that it was the common intention that she should have an interest in the house . . . Payment for a lawn and provision of some furniture and equipment for the house does not of itself point to the conclusion that there was such an intention.

The suggestion is, then, that in the absence of express agreement common intention can be inferred from conduct under certain circumstances, although it would appear that where common intention is implied by conduct and not specifically expressed only **direct contributions** to the purchase of the house, such as contributions towards the mortgage payments, will be considered sufficient to conclude that this is what the parties intended. On the facts of *Gissing* v. *Gissing*, the decision of the judges was in fact that the contributions made by Mrs Gissing were not sufficient to conclude that there was a common intention between the parties. The appeal was therefore allowed, and Mr Gissing was thus declared to retain the sole beneficial interest in the property.

But what about situations in which the agreement is express? In the 1975 case of *Eves* v. *Eves* [1975] 1 WLR 1338 the court took a somewhat more relaxed approach to the issue of **indirect contributions**. The case concerned a couple, Janet and Stuart Eves. Janet and Stuart were not married (in fact, they were both married to other people), but Janet changed her surname to Eves when they had a child together. Stuart bought a house for them to live in with the aid of a mortgage, which he registered in his sole name. He told Janet this was because Janet was under the age of 21 and therefore unable to go on the **title deeds**. However, Stuart said he would rectify this when she reached the age of majority. As a result of this, whilst Janet did not contribute to the mortgage payments, she did a lot of renovation work on the house and maintained the house and garden. Stuart subsequently left Janet and married another woman, named Gloria, and Janet made an application to the court claiming an equitable interest in the house.

Unlike the case of *Gissing* v. *Gissing*, in which common intention was implied, in this case there was an express agreement between the parties regarding beneficial ownership of the property, Stuart telling Janet that the house would be transferred into their joint names when she reached the age of 21. As a result of this, the court held that Janet's contributions to the renovation of the property and maintenance of the house and garden were sufficient by way of indirect contribution to confer a beneficial interest on her. The Court of Appeal held that Janet should be entitled to a quarter share in the property.

The later case of *Grant* v. *Edwards* [1986] Ch 638 (CA) turned on similar facts. The claimant, Linda Grant, who was separated from her husband, set up home with a man named George Edwards. In 1969 George bought a house and moved into it with Linda, their child and the two children of Linda's previous marriage. The house was purchased in the joint names of George and his brother, Arthur, who had no beneficial interest in the property and had been joined solely for the purpose of assisting in obtaining a mortgage. George told Linda that the reason her name was not included on the title was because it would prejudice the matrimonial proceedings which were pending against her husband. George paid the deposit and the mortgage instalments, while Linda made substantial contributions to the general household expenses. The couple lived in the house until it was damaged by fire, when they moved into council accommodation. Part of the insurance money received was used to repair the house and the property was subsequently let. The money left over was placed in the couple's joint account. In 1980 Linda and Stuart separated and Linda claimed a beneficial interest in the house.

As with *Eves* v. *Eves*, the court was happy to infer in *Grant* v. *Edwards* that there was a common intention between the parties that Linda was to have a beneficial interest in the property. The lack of formality was purely, in this case, to avoid complications in Linda's divorce proceedings. Again, indirect contributions, of a financial nature this time, were therefore held to be sufficient to confer a beneficial interest on the claimant. Lord Justice Nourse explained his reasoning:

> From the . . . facts and figures it is in my view an inevitable inference that the very substantial contribution which the **plaintiff** made out of her earnings after August 1972 to the housekeeping and to the feeding and to the bringing up of the children enabled the **defendant** to keep down the instalments payable under both mortgages out of his own income and, moreover, that he could not have done that if he had had to bear the whole of the other expenses as well. For example, in 1973, when he and the plaintiff were earning about £1,200 each, the defendant had to find a total of about £643 between the two mortgages. I do not see how he would have been able to do that had it not been for the plaintiff's very substantial contribution to the other expenses . . . In the circumstances, it seems that it may properly be inferred that the plaintiff did make substantial indirect contributions to the instalments payable under both mortgages.

Case Summary

One question to ask here is whether there are any circumstances in which indirect contributions will not be sufficient, in the case of an express agreement, to confer an interest on the contributing party. The case of *Burns* v. *Burns* [1984] Ch 317, which we came across in Chapter 7, answers this question. As you may remember, the case concerned a couple, Valerie and Patrick Burns. The house they lived in was bought and paid for by Patrick, with Valerie staying at home to look after the house and children. She also bought furniture, fixtures and fittings for the house and did some painting and redecoration. Unlike the situation in *Grant* v. *Edwards*, however, Valerie's money was not needed to pay for any of the household expenses. The Court of Appeal held that Valerie had no interest in the house because she had made no contributions referable to the acquisition of an interest in the property. Lord Justice Fox said:

> So far as housekeeping expenses are concerned, I do not doubt that (the house being bought in the man's name) if the woman goes out to work in order to provide money for the family expenses, as a result of which she spends her earnings on the housekeeping and the man is thus able to pay the mortgage instalments and other expenses out of his earnings, it can be inferred that there was a common intention that the woman should have an interest in the house – since she will have made an indirect financial contributions to the mortgage instalments. But that is not this case.

The suggestion here is therefore that, even in the case of indirect contributions, nothing short of substantial contributions enabling the legal owner to pay mortgage instalments which they could not otherwise have afforded will suffice. How this sits against the outcome in *Eves* v. *Eves*, in which Janet Eves had carried out renovation works to the property but did not contribute substantially from a financial perspective, is unclear. However, it should perhaps be noted that, on the facts of the two cases, Valerie Burns had made no contribution of her own money to the property, her only contribution being out of housekeeping money given to her by her husband, whereas Janet Eves had made a substantial contribution of her own time and effort.

Case Summary

The House of Lords were given the opportunity, some twenty years after *Gissing* v. *Gissing*, to consider for a second time the issue of common intention in constructive trusts. In the case of *Lloyds Bank plc* v. *Rosset* [1991] 1 AC 107 a husband and wife, Mr and Mrs Rosset, planned on buying a semi-derelict property together as a home for themselves and their two children. The house was to be paid for with money from Mr Rosset's family trust in Switzerland and the **trustees** insisted on the house being registered in Mr Rosset's sole name. The purchase was to be made without the assistance of a mortgage but, unbeknown to Mrs Rosset, shortly before the purchase was completed Mr Rosset acquired a loan from Lloyds Bank plc for £15,000 to meet the cost of the renovation, which he secured against the property. Mrs Rosset made no financial contribution either to the purchase of the property or to the cost of renovation. However she project-managed the renovation and personally carried out much of the decorating work. Mr Rosset left the following year, after matrimonial difficulties, leaving Mrs Rosset and their children at the property. After a formal demand for repayment of the loan had not been met, the bank claimed possession and applied for a court order for the sale of the property. Mr Rosset did not resist the claim, but Mrs Rosset said that she had a beneficial interest in the property under a constructive trust.

Whilst the Court of Appeal had found that, on the facts of the case, the wife's activities in relation to the renovation of the property were sufficient to justify an inference of a common intention, the House of Lords disagreed, reversing the Court of Appeal decision. In a dramatic departure from the mood of previous judgments, the Lords found against Mrs Rosset, stating that her contributions were insufficient to create a resulting trust. The Lords were keen to stress that, in their opinion, there was a fundamental distinction between cases in which there was evidence of an express discussion between the parties or representation from the legal owner regarding the beneficial interests the contributor would have in the property, and the inference of a common intention through conduct alone. They said that, where common intention was to be inferred by the parties' conduct, nothing less than direct contributions to the purchase price by the non-owning party would be sufficient evidence of such an intention, and Mrs Rosset had not provided this. Accordingly, the husband was declared to be the sole **beneficiary** of the property and the bank was allowed to repossess the house.

Using the opportunity to restate the law as applied by the House of Lords in *Gissing* v. *Gissing*, Lord Bridge said:

> The first and fundamental question which must always be resolved is whether, independently of any inference to be drawn from the conduct of the parties in the course of sharing the house as their home and managing their joint affairs, there has at any time prior to acquisition, or exceptionally at some later date, been any agreement, arrangement or understanding reached between them that the property is to be shared beneficially. The finding of an agreement or arrangement to share in this sense can only, I think, be based on evidence of express discussions between the partners, however imperfectly remembered and however imprecise their terms may have been. Once a finding to this effect is made it will only be necessary for the partner asserting a claim to a beneficial interest against the partner entitled to the legal estate to show that he or she has acted to his or her detriment or significantly altered his or her position in reliance on the agreement in order to give rise to a constructive trust . . .
>
> In sharp contrast with this situation is the very different one where there is no evidence to support a finding of an agreement or arrangement to share . . . and where the court must rely entirely on the conduct of the parties . . . as the basis from which to infer a common intention to share the property beneficially . . . In this situation direct contributions to the purchase price by the partner who is not the legal owner, whether initially or by payment of mortgage instalments, will readily justify the inference necessary to the creation of a constructive trust. But, as I read the authorities, it is at least extremely doubtful whether anything less will do.

In Lord Bridge's view, therefore, only direct contributions would suffice in cases of common intention based on the conduct of the parties alone.

Writing and drafting

An associate at your firm comes to see you in what can only be described as 'a bit of a flap'. He has been asked by the partner in the family law department to see a client at short notice, who apparently has a dispute over the ownership of their family home. The associate is a bit rusty on the subject, though (he usually deals with childcare matters), and cannot remember which contributions are sufficient to infer an agreement under a constructive trust. Can you help him by making a note of the circumstances (if any) under which the court will regard the following contributions as sufficient to infer an agreement that the property is to be held on trust?

✦ cash contribution to deposit;

✦ payment of stamp duty and legal fees;

✦ payment of mortgage instalments;

✦ payment of other household expenses;

✦ improvements to the property;

✦ payment for furniture and decorations;

✦ looking after the house and children;

✦ helping in the family business.

✦ **Handy tip:** Try drawing up a list with express agreements on one side and implied agreements on the other. This may help you in deciphering which contributions the associate can take note of.

In essence, the judgment in *Lloyds Bank* v. *Rosset* can be seen to have significantly tightened up the category of indirect contributions, restricting it to incorporate financial contributions which assisted in the payment of the mortgage instalments only (in other words, only situations such as those described in *Grant* v. *Edwards*). What is interesting to note from the wording of Lord Bridge's judgment is that, whilst it has the effect of cutting back significantly on the type of contribution which will amount to an indirect contribution for the purposes of gaining a beneficial interest in property, the Lords in *Lloyds Bank* v. *Rosset* have at the same time chosen to add not one, but two, new facets to the requirement for common intention. In Lord Bridge's view, common intention alone will now not be sufficient for a constructive trust to be imposed: there is also a need for the contributing party to have:

1. relied on the agreement between the parties; and

2. acted to their detriment or significantly altered their position as a result of that reliance.

Of course, Lord Bridge did not pull these 'new' requirements out of thin air. Although *Lloyds Bank* v. *Rosset* was the first House of Lords case to consider the issue of constructive trusts in the context of the family home since *Gissing* v. *Gissing*, as we have seen there had been a long line of Court of Appeal cases running from the judgment in *Gissing* v. *Gissing* up until the House of Lords hearing of *Lloyds Bank* v. *Rosset* and Lord Bridge was simply responding to, and consolidating, the various results of these. Nevertheless, this still leaves us with the question of how to show proof of reliance and how to define 'detriment'. Lord Bridge is quite clear that, in cases of financial contribution, whether direct or indirect, proof of the contributions will in itself be proof enough of detrimental reliance. But will any other kind of detriment suffice? If one chooses to stick slavishly to the judgment in *Lloyds Bank* v. *Rosset* itself, the answer of course would be no: absolutely not. But judgments which were being made in other contemporary cases, and certainly a number of judgments which have followed the decision in *Lloyds Bank* v. *Rosset*, would appear to suggest otherwise.

What amounts to detrimental reliance?

If we look at case law prior to *Lloyds Bank* v. *Rosset*, the interpretation of the facts in *Grant* v. *Edwards* stands out as supporting Lord Bridge's view. Here the evidence of detrimental reliance is clear: Linda Grant relied on George Edwards's representation to her that the only reason she didn't appear on the title deeds to the property was because of her marital situation and, as a result, acted severely to her detriment by making significant financial contributions to the running of the house, in turn allowing her partner to afford to make the mortgage instalments. Lord Justice Nourse in making his judgment in *Grant* v. *Edwards* gave the following, very logical, analysis of the facts:

> The defendant told the plaintiff that her name was not going onto the title because it would cause some prejudice in the matrimonial proceedings between her and her husband. The defendant never had any real intention of replacing his brother with the plaintiff when those proceedings were at an end. Just as in *Eves* v. *Eves*, these facts appear to me to raise a clear inference that there was an understanding between the plaintiff and the defendant of a common intention, that the plaintiff was to have some sort of **proprietary interest** in the house, otherwise no excuse for not putting her name onto the title would have been needed . . . Was the conduct of the plaintiff in making substantial indirect contributions to the instalments payable under both mortgages conduct upon which she could not reasonably have been expected to embark unless she was to have an interest in the house? I answer that question in the affirmative. I cannot see upon what other basis she could reasonably have been expected to give the defendant such substantial assistance in paying off mortgages on his house. I therefore conclude that the plaintiff did act to her detriment on the faith of the common intention between her and the defendant that she was to have some sort of proprietary interest in the house . . .

Having established a common intention a finding of detrimental reliance was easy. Linda had clearly gone over and above what she would have been expected to do as a member of the family under circumstances in which she did not expect to receive an entitlement: in short, a person quite simply would not go to such great lengths whilst expecting nothing in return. Later cases have proved less straightforward, however. The concept of 'detriment' has never been given a legal definition in the context of constructive trusts and there is therefore any number of situations to which the term might conceivably be applied. The only question this leaves is whether such examples of detriment tie in with the stipulation of an indirect financial contribution as set out in *Lloyds Bank* v. *Rosset*.

In the case of *Ungurian* v. *Lesnoff* [1990] Ch 206, the alleged detriment was of an altogether different nature. Kamilla Lesnoff was of Polish nationality. When the couple set up home together in London, Kamilla gave up her flat in Poland, which she could have

Case
Summary

stayed in for the rest of her life, and a promising university career. She also had to enter into a marriage of convenience with a French man to enable her and her two children to get out of the country. Having severed ties with Poland, which was as the time under Communist rule, both parties knew it would not be possible for her to go back. Ungurian bought a house for the couple to live in together in London, which he paid for and which they lived in together for four years, after which Ungurian left. Kamilla did not contribute financially to the property at all, but she carried out significant improvement works to the property herself, including putting in a new central heating system and various other renovations. The court held that Kamilla had a beneficial interest in the property under a constructive trust, based on the couple's agreement that Kamilla would be entitled to live in the property with her children for the rest of her life. The cumulative effect of the detriment she had suffered by leaving her position and family in Communist Poland was sufficient in terms of detrimental reliance.

Case Summary

This is obviously a case of very unusual circumstances. The case of *Hammond* v. *Mitchell* [1991] 1 WLR 1127 is perhaps easier to align with everyday family break-ups, although in its way it was no less out of the ordinary. The case concerned a love affair between a second-hand car dealer named Tom Hammond and a Playboy Club Bunny, Vicky Mitchell. Tom met Vicky in a chance encounter when Vicky stopped Tom to ask for directions. The couple hit it off and within a very short time had moved in together. The couple were an item for 11 years, during which time Vicky bore Tom two children. The house in which they lived together was bought and paid for by Tom. However, Vicky ran the household and helped out with Tom's business on a day-to-day basis. When the house was purchased, Tom had told Vicky that the house was being put into his name to save complications because he was going through a divorce at the time. However, he told her not to worry because they would soon be married and half of everything would be hers anyway. The subject was never discussed again. When the couple finally split, the joint assets of the house and business were worth £450,000. Tom claimed the whole of the assets belonged to him, but Vicky claimed a share. The court agreed with Vicky and held that she should have a half interest in the house under a constructive trust.

Clearly in the case of *Hammond* v. *Mitchell* there had been an express discussion between the parties as to the beneficial interest that Vicky would, albeit eventually, have in the property. The question was one of detriment. Had Vicky acted to her detriment in reliance on the agreement? The court believed that yes, she had. Vicky had given up a highly paid job as a croupier at the Playboy Club in Mayfair in order to set up home with Mr Hammond. In embarking with Mr Hammond on his various business ventures and in giving her support, on two occasions by waiving her occupational rights to the house with the bank so that he could take out mortgages to fund business deals, she had acted to her detriment and was therefore entitled to a half share of the house under a constructive trust.

Reflective practice

Take another look at the Writing and drafting exercise above. Would your answers still be the same, in the light of what you now know?

It is clear from these cases that, in cases of an express oral agreement, financial contribution is not essential to establish a beneficial interest in the property, provided a genuine detriment can be shown. Following Lord Bridge's judgment in *Rosset*, whilst financial contributions are fundamental in cases of **implied common intention**, it is detriment which is key to making a claim in cases where an oral agreement between the parties can be proved.

It may be a good idea at this point to have a little recap of the law that we have learnt so far in relation to constructive trusts. Take a moment to look at the recap of the law in the box.

Recap: constructive trusts

Following Lord Bridge's judgment in *Lloyds Bank* v. *Rosset*, there are three requirements for the finding of a constructive trust:

1. *Common intention*: there must have been some form of agreement, understanding or common intention that the person making the claim will have a beneficial interest in the property;

2. *Reliance*: the person making the claim must have acted or changed their position in reliance on that agreement; and

3. *Detriment*: it must be shown that the person will suffer a detriment if the legal owner of the property then tries to deny them an interest in it.

Common intention can be shown in one of two ways:

a. *Express agreement*: where there have been express discussions between the parties pointing to an agreement that the person making the claim is to have a beneficial interest in the property; or

b. *Implied agreement*: where such an agreement is implied from the conduct of the parties.

Where there is an express agreement, the detrimental reliance may consist of either direct or indirect contributions to the purchase of the property as well as, it would appear, non-financial contributions – provided they are sufficient in nature that the contributing party will suffer a genuine detriment on account of having made such contributions were they then denied an interest in the property.

Where the agreement is implied by conduct, nothing less than direct contributions (including the making of mortgage payments) to the purchase of the property will be sufficient. The contributions themselves will provide evidence of the required detriment.

Now that we have reminded ourselves of how to establish a beneficial interest in the property under a constructive trust, the only thing left to do is to quantify the share. And this is what we are going to look at in the next part of the chapter.

Calculating the share

With a resulting trust, the size of the contributing party's share is directly proportionate to the amount of their contribution. So if a person pays the 10 per cent deposit on the purchase of the property, they will be entitled to a 10 per cent share of the property when it is subsequently sold. With a constructive trust, calculating the size of the share is not quite so straightforward, however, especially in light of the fact that, in cases of express agreement constructive trusts, the party claiming an interest may succeed in doing so by virtue of a non-financial contribution or detriment which may be hard to quantify in terms of a cash share in the property. Unfortunately in the case of *Lloyds Bank* v. *Rosset*, there was no discussion as to how the share under a constructive trust should be calculated: because Mrs Rosset failed in her claim such discussion was simply not necessary.

So we must look to later case law for guidance on the best approach to take in such situations.

Case Summary

The Court of Appeal case of *Midland Bank plc* v. *Cooke* (1995) 27 HLR 733 is a useful starting point. The case concerned a married couple, Mr and Mrs Cooke, who were facing repossession proceedings from the Midland Bank. The house was in Mr Cooke's sole name and had been paid for out of a mixture of Mr Cooke's personal savings and a mortgage in his sole name. In addition, part of the deposit on the property had been funded out of a wedding gift which had been made to the couple by Mr Cooke's parents. When the bank sought repossession of the property following non-payment of the mortgage, Mrs Cooke resisted the application on the grounds that half the house belonged to her. The court at first instance agreed that Mrs Cooke had a beneficial interest in the property, but limited this to a 6.47 per cent share, representing her half of the wedding present from Mr Cooke's parents. However, the Court of Appeal disagreed with the decision and gave her a half share in the house in support of her initial application.

So what was the reasoning behind this? Clearly, the Court of Appeal did not believe that the quantification of shares in a constructive trust situation should be done by reference purely to the size of financial contribution (what you might call a 'resulting trust' calculation). How, then, did the Court of Appeal reach their conclusion that Mrs Cooke was entitled to half of the property? Lord Justice Waite explained the court's reasoning:

> When the court is proceeding, in cases like the present where the partner without legal title has successfully asserted an equitable interest through direct contribution, to determine (in the absence of express evidence of intention) what proportions the parties must be assumed to have intended for their beneficial ownership, the duty of the judge is to undertake a survey of the whole course of dealing between the parties relevant to their ownership and occupation of the property and their sharing of its burdens and advantages. That scrutiny will not confine itself to the limited range of acts of direct contribution of the sort that are needed to found a beneficial interest in the first place. It will take into consideration all conduct which throws light on the question what shares were intended. Only if that search proves inconclusive does the court fall back on the **maxim** that 'equality is equity'.

the court will look at the 'whole course of dealing between the parties'

According to *Midland Bank* v. *Cooke*, therefore, once a beneficial interest under a constructive trust has been established, although the interest may have been established by virtue of direct contributions by the person making the claim, the calculation of that person's interest will not be limited to those direct contributions. Rather, the court will look at the 'whole course of dealing between the parties' and make their decision based on what appears to have been the parties' intention in light of those dealings. In *Midland Bank* v. *Cooke*, Mrs Cooke had always been treated as an equal partner in the marriage, in terms of paying household expenses from her wages as a teacher, signing a waiver when a first, and then a second mortgage was taken out over the property, and generally in keeping house and bringing up the children. The court therefore concluded that the actions of the parties were such as to imply an intention that they intended to share everything equally, and Mrs Cooke was given a half share in the property. The Documenting the law feature contains an extract from the transcript in the court case, in which the barrister tries to establish the common intention of the parties.

Documenting the law

Extract from *Midland Bank* v. *Cooke* (evidence given by Mr Cooke)

Q: **Can you help me with this then? What were the source or sources of the cash deposit?**
A: I put in about £900 or £1,000 from my savings and my mother and father gave us a wedding gift of £1,000 towards the house.

Q: **You say that it was given by your parents to 'us'. By 'us' you mean . . . ?**
A: Well, my dad gave it to me, yes.

Q: **For what purpose?**
A: Well, to buy the house, help me with the deposit.

Q: **You referred to it being in the context of the wedding. What do you mean by that?**
A: Well, we were getting married in July and he gave it towards the deposit. Because the house was quite old the maximum mortgage we could get was £6,000.

Q: **You have referred to it earlier in the context of it being a wedding – the money from your father being a wedding gift.**
A: Well, I mean, he didn't wrap it up or anything but . . .

Q: **Well?**
A: It was their way of – because Jane's did the wedding and everything.

Q: **What, Jane's parents paid for the wedding?**
A: Yes.

Q: **And your parents . . . ?**
A: Put, yes, £1,000 towards the house.

Q: **Right. So far as the actual purchase is concerned, we see that it was taken in your sole name – your wife does not appear on the title deeds?**
A: No.

Q: **So far as you were concerned, at the time you were signing the conveyance, going through the legalities with the solicitors, whose house did you think this was to be once the transaction was completed?**
A: Well, it was very similar to sort of recalling what was happening 10 or 12 years ago. To be truthful, I can't actually remember, but I always thought of it as 'our house'. It was just because I did . . . Jane was at teacher training college in Eastbourne.

Q: **Do you remember anything in relation to the building society and obtaining the mortgage – any problems which arose there?**
A: Only in respect of when I told them that Jane was a student and they said they didn't want that on the form, basically, because she had no income, you see, so . . .

Q: **Do you now have any recollection of discussing before acquisition or at the time of acquisition or at the time you actually got married with your wife the precise arrangements in relation to the house?**
A: Not really, no. We were just happy, I suppose, you know.

For a full transcript of the case go to: *Midland Bank* v. *Cooke* (1995) 27 HLR 733.

We can see from the transcript just how difficult proving a common intention can be, in the absence of an express agreement.

A decade later the Court of Appeal saw fit to make comment on the finding in *Midland Bank* v. *Cooke*, in the case of *Oxley* v. *Hiscock* [2004] 3 All ER 703. The case concerned an unmarried couple, Elayne Oxley and Allan Hiscock. Elayne was living in a council house with her children when she met Allan, who owned his own house. In September 1987 Elayne exercised her right to buy her council house for £25,200 using funds provided by Allan from the sale of his property. In 1991 the couple bought a bigger house for £127,000, which was funded by the proceeds of sale of Elayne's house at £61,500 (of which £25,200 was attributable to Allan's original contribution and £36,300 to Elayne), by a further £35,500 from Allan's savings and by a mortgage loan of £30,000. The property was registered in the sole name of Allan.

After the purchase both Elayne and Allan contributed towards the maintenance and improvement of the property from pooled resources in the belief that each had a beneficial interest. By 2001 the couple had paid the mortgage off. Elayne and Allan separated and the property was then sold, each buying separate houses. Elayne applied for a declaration that the proceeds of sale of the property were held on trust for both parties in equal shares, which she was given. Allan appealed, contending that since there had been no discussion between the parties as to the extent of their respective beneficial shares at the time of purchase, the property should be held on resulting trust for both parties in beneficial shares proportionate to their contributions.

Following the reasoning in *Midland Bank* v. *Cooke*, the Court of Appeal held that, where there was no evidence of any discussion between the parties as to the amount of the share each was to have, each was entitled to that share which the court considered fair having regard to the whole course of dealing between them in relation to the property, including any arrangements made to meet the various outgoings required to be met in order to live in the property as their home. However, whilst the court was keen to state that:

(a) they were not required to make a finding that the property was held on trusts in proportion to the couple's respective financial contributions; and that

(b) regard should be had to the whole course of dealings between the parties;

they nevertheless found that a fair division of the proceeds of sale would be 60 per cent to the defendant (Allan) and 40 per cent to the claimant (Elayne). Taking a purely mathematical division of the parties' various contributions they therefore had, in fact, based their finding on a 'resulting trust' calculation, in proportion to the financial contributions the parties had made to the property and not taking into account any other factors. The following illustration summarises the parties' financial contributions:

			Percentage of purchase price
Elayne's equity	£36,300		
Half share in mortgage	£15,000		
Elayne's total share		£51,300	40
Allan's sale proceeds	£25,200		
Allan's savings	£35,500		
Half share in mortgage	£15,000		
Allan's total share		£75,700	60
Total (purchase price of property):		£127,000	100

Lord Justice Chadwick justified the Court of Appeal's approach to the case by stating that it would simply be unfair to ignore the different sizes of their respective financial contributions. However, the decision rests uneasily alongside that of *Midland Bank* v. *Cooke*. Exactly how much weight is supposed to be given to financial contributions when the amount of the beneficial interest is being calculated? According to *Midland Bank* v. *Cooke*, financial contributions should be given no more than a cursory glance; but according to *Oxley* v. *Hiscock*, it would appear that financial contributions are of paramount importance in deciding how the beneficial interest in a property is to be divided. The key distinction between the two decisions would appear to be the fact that in *Midland Bank* v. *Cooke* the couple were married, whereas in *Oxley* v. *Hiscock*, they were not. In *Midland Bank* v. *Cooke* the couple had made a legal commitment to one another, in the form of their marriage vows, whereas in *Oxley* v. *Hiscock* there was no such commitment, albeit they had set up home together. Perhaps if Elayne Oxley and Allan Hiscock had been married their share would have been calculated on a 50/50 basis as well.

Stack v. Dowden

In 2007 the House of Lords was, once more, given the opportunity to consider the issue when it heard the case of *Stack* v. *Dowden* [2007] UKHL 17. The facts of the case were as follows:

Barry Stack and Dehra Dowden met and began a relationship in 1975. In 1983 Dehra Dowden bought a house in her sole name in which the couple lived together and brought up their four children. Dehra, who earned considerably more than Barry, made all the mortgage payments and paid the household bills. The couple made substantial improvements to the property and in 1993 sold it for three times the amount Dehra had originally paid for it. Dehra and Barry then bought another property, which was purchased in their joint names. Over 65 per cent of the purchase price was paid out of funds from a building society account held in Dehra's sole name and which included the money made on the sale of the previous house. The balance of the purchase price was provided by a mortgage in the parties' joint names and two endowment policies (a type of life insurance policy which pays out at the end of a specified period or on the death of the policyholder), one in their joint names and one in Dehra's sole name. Barry paid the mortgage interest and the premiums due under the endowment policy in the couple's joint names and Dehra paid the premiums due under the endowment policy in her sole name. The parties kept separate bank accounts and made separate savings and investments. Over the course of their years in the house together the mortgage was paid off by a series of lump sum payments, of which Dehra provided just under 60 per cent. The couple separated in 2002 and Barry left the property while Dehra remained there with the children. Barry then successfully applied for an order for sale of the property and an equal division of the proceeds. However, on appeal the Court of Appeal found in Dehra's favour, ordering that the net proceeds of sale should be divided 65 per cent to 35 per cent in Dehra's favour. The House of Lords upheld this judgment in favour of Dehra.

So what was the reasoning of the Lords in upholding the decision? The facts of the case were of course different from the previous cases upon which the Court of Appeal had deliberated, in that the house in *Stack* v. *Dowden* was purchased in joint names. There was therefore no question as to whether or not Barry Stack had a beneficial interest in the property; the only question was as to the size of his share in it. The court took the view that, as the property had been purchased in joint names without any declaration as to shares, the initial presumption would be that the couple owned the house equally because

Case
Summary

of equity following the law, with the burden of proof lying with the party wishing to establish that they should have a greater beneficial interest in the property. It was therefore for Dehra Dowden to show the court that she was entitled to more than a 50 per cent share in the property. In claiming a constructive trust in her favour, Dehra would have to show a common intention between the parties that she would hold a greater interest in the property. Baroness Hale said that, in order to determine the exact amount of that share, the court would have to undertake 'a survey of the whole course of dealing between the parties . . . taking account of all conduct which throws light on the question what shares were intended'. As with previous cases, this would include whether or not the couple were married.

In divining the amount of Dehra's share in the property the Lords therefore took the following factors into account:

1. The couple were unmarried.

2. Dehra had contributed far more to the acquisition of the house than Barry.

3. The parties had never pooled their separate financial resources for the common good.

4. Everything, apart from the house and associated endowment policy, had been kept strictly separate.

They found that the case was highly unusual, as most couples did not put their finances on such a separate footing. On the facts of this particular case, therefore, the evidence was strongly indicative that the parties had *not* intended their shares in the property to be equal and, accordingly, Dehra should be entitled to a 65 per cent share of the beneficial interest in the house. In making their decision, the Lords stressed that each case would turn on its own facts and that many more factors than financial contributions may be relevant in divining the parties' true intentions. Here, the particular fact that the couple had kept their financial affairs so separate over a number of years was clearly indicative of their intent. Perhaps because of the unique facts in this particular case, we have been left in a slightly contradictory position, however. Whilst Lord Walker in his judgment in *Stack* v. *Dowden* said quite clearly that the use of resulting trusts should not operate as a legal presumption in a domestic context, the outcome on the facts of this case show that the reality of the situation is quite the opposite. Using *Midland Bank* v. *Cooke*, the result would have been a 50/50 split of the property but, under the new regime, it would appear that the outcome of any case in respect of unmarried couples is always going to be made on an arithmetical basis.

This dilemma is not helped by the **dissenting judgment** given in this case by Lord Neuberger. Whilst he agreed with the overall decision of the Lords, he believed that the reasoning behind their decision was made on the wrong footing. In his own words:

> where the resulting trust presumption (or indeed any other basis of apportionment) applies at the date of acquisition, I am unpersuaded that (save perhaps in a most unusual case) anything other than subsequent discussions, statements or actions, which can fairly be said to imply a positive intention to depart from that apportionment, will do to justify a change in the way in which the beneficial interest is owned. To say that factors such as a long relationship, children, a joint bank account, and sharing daily outgoings of themselves are enough, or even of potential central importance, appears to me not merely wrong in principle, but a recipe for uncertainty, subjectivity, and a long and expensive examination of facts. It could also be said to be arbitrary, as, if such factors of themselves justify a departure from the original apportionment, I find it hard to see how it could be to anything other than equality. If a departure from the original apportionment was solely

based on such factors, it seems to me that the judge would almost always have to reach an 'all or nothing' decision. Thus, in this case, he would have to ask whether, viewed in the round, the personal and financial characteristics of the relationship between Mr Stack and Ms Dowden, after they acquired the house, justified a change in ownership of the beneficial interest from 35–65 to 50–50, even though nothing they did or said related to the ownership of that interest (save, perhaps, the repayments of the mortgage). In my view, that involves approaching the question in the wrong way. Subject, perhaps, to exceptional cases, whose possibility it would be unrealistic not to acknowledge, an argument for an alteration in the way in which the beneficial interest is held cannot, in my opinion, succeed, unless it can be shown that there was a discussion, statement or action which, viewed in its context, namely the parties' relationship, implied an actual agreement or understanding to effect such an alteration.

It is clear, then, from Lord Neuberger's comments that he favours a more traditional resulting trust approach of initial contributions to the purchase price to be applied to such cases, and feels that, except in a small number of exceptional circumstances, the later actions of the parties will have no bearing on the size of the respective parties' shares. In any event, regardless of the reasoning, the outcome was the same: Dehra Dowden got her 65 per cent share in the property.

In the People in the law feature, barrister Caroline Wigin comments on the difficulties encountered where cohabiting couples separate.

People in the law

Name and Position: Caroline Wigin, barrister at Park Court Chambers, Leeds.

What kind of work do you do at Park Court Chambers? I deal with high value **ancillary relief** and care cases, specialising in ancillary relief in small companies or farms, where there tends to be a lot of money at stake. [Ancillary relief is a payment of money awarded by the court by way of a final settlement to either party in cases of divorce or judicial separation.]

Source: Caroline Wigin, Park Court Chambers (*text and photo*)

Is there still a high proportion of claims between husbands and wives where one party does not appear on the title deeds to the family home? Yes. You tend to find the woman not on the title deeds far more often in cohabitation cases. You do often find wives not on title deeds where the matrimonial home is a farm, in which case it may have been gifted to the son prior to his marriage. You also commonly find the wife not on title deeds in Asian family divorces, where a house has been gifted to the husband, pursuant to him marrying a wife from abroad and sponsoring her into this country. The other circumstance in which the matrimonial home tends not to be in joint names (and under these circumstances will usually be in the wife's name) is in second marriages, particularly where the wife has received the former matrimonial home in her first divorce and second husband is not on title deeds.

Do you deal with many claims between unmarried couples? Yes. This is becoming more and more common all the time.

Does this make matters more complicated, when staking your client's claim? Yes, it makes matters much more complicated. This is because the court still analyses the entire financial background of the couple in the case of cohabitation, whereas in a matrimonial case, the court seeks to be fair in the light of the parties' current financial circumstances. So in a matrimonial case, the court can take account of the parties' age, which of course affects mortgage capacity, and more importantly, with whom the children reside. In cohabitation cases on the other hand, you are essentially doing a forensic examination of the circumstances of the relationship, including any alterations and improvements to the property.

Do you feel that recent case law has blurred the line between resulting and constructive trusts, in terms of calculating the award given? Yes, I do.

Do you think the finding in *Stack* v. *Dowden* went far enough in clarifying the law in this area? The problem with *Stack* v. *Dowden* is the differing views of the judges. The judgments don't all dovetail into each other, meaning that you really have to read all of it to get anything out of the case. Overall, I do feel the case could have gone further to assist practitioners.

Do you believe there is a case for further reform? If so, what would you advocate, from a lawyer's perspective? Yes, although I don't think there is sufficient parliamentary interest in the subject for there to be legislation in this area. Certainly with the current law, where you are doing cohabitation cases and you are picking through bank statements which may be 10 or 15 years old, you feel fairly restricted, as opposed to matrimonial cases, which tend to be dealt with in fairly broad brush strokes. If there were to be reforms, I think the law would benefit from a more defined, but still separate, law of resulting and constructive trusts, rather than putting the two systems into one. A '*Stack* v. *Dowden* 2' would be of great assistance!

Overall, the decision in *Stack* v. *Dowden* could be described as a little disappointing. The Lords' opportunity in presiding over this case was twofold: first, to deal with the issue of calculating the share, which they duly did, albeit with Lord Neuberger dissenting, but also to clarify the issue of indirect contributions, which are still sitting in somewhat muddy waters following the previous line of case law and, in particular, the ruling in *Lloyds Bank* v. *Rosset*. Having said that the proof of Dehra Dowden's larger share in the property turned on an implied common intention of the parties, it is unfortunate that the Lords did not consider the facts in *Stack* v. *Dowden* warranted any in-depth discussion of exactly what, in the manner of indirect contributions to the purchase of the property, might be included, and indeed whether non-financial contributions should be taken into account at all, following the previous case law. In reality, the issue was effectively sidestepped and the Lords did not take the opportunity to focus on this difficulty at all. Baroness Hale's only comment on the issue of indirect financial contributions was that she felt that Lord Bridge's view in *Lloyds Bank* v. *Rosset* was unnecessarily restrictive, and that she thought the rather softer approach of the court taken in previous cases was perhaps the better course to take when deciding on the issue of indirect contributions.

The outcome? The House of Lords decision in *Stack* v. *Dowden*, despite being heralded as a landmark case, really leaves us no further forward in terms of which contributions, whether direct or indirect, will count in imposing a constructive trust, and what other matters should be considered when making a decision as to share. The Lords have chosen to restate the wording of the judgment in *Oxley* v. *Hiscock*, in that 'the whole course of dealings' should be taken into account, but this is extremely wide and more guidance would certainly not have gone amiss. As it is, the Lords have simply given the courts an ever-wider discretion to decide what they think is equitable under the circumstances. Where calculating the share under a constructive trust is concerned and, seemingly, in contradiction to the idea of taking into account a whole course of dealings, the outcome in *Stack* v. *Dowden* has merely mirrored the more restrictive approach of *Oxley* v. *Hiscock*.

Whatever their reasoning, the undeniable finding of the court was that Dehra Dowden's share should be proportionate to her contributions to the purchase price of the property, which leads us straight back to square one: the 'resulting trust' arithmetical method of share calculation. With shares being calculated on this basis, it makes it very difficult to tell the difference between the implied common intention constructive trust and a simple resulting trust itself. After all, why bother proving a common intention and detrimental reliance through the payment of direct contributions to the property, when the outcome of the case will still be that the contributing party is given no greater a share than that directly proportionate to their financial contribution? The argument would surely be that, taking into account the whole course of dealings between the parties, the beneficial interest could theoretically be adjudged to be considerably greater under the guise of a constructive trust. However, the reality of the decisions in *Oxley* v. *Hiscock* and now *Stack* v. *Dowden* would appear to show otherwise.

Other uses for constructive trusts

The focus of this chapter has been on constructive trusts in so far as they relate to private individuals and, in particular, the family home situation. However, although the spotlight has very much been on this area of constructive trusts in recent years, it is important to remember that this is not the only situation in which constructive trusts are used. In fact, the imposition of constructive trusts is commonplace in many situations, both individual and commercial. If we go back to the beginning of the chapter, you will remember that we looked at the case of *Banner Homes Group* v. *Luff Developments Ltd*, which concerned an agreement between two developers which had gone sour. In that case, Banner Homes were awarded a beneficial interest in a piece of development land owned

> the imposition of constructive trusts is commonplace in many situations

by Luff Developments Ltd because of the reliance they had placed on Luff Developments' representations that the companies were going to buy the property together by way of a joint venture.

Another situation in which constructive trusts are used, and one which is particularly relevant in the context of a book on trusts, is where a trustee has acted in breach of their **fiduciary duties**. The most common example of this might be in the case of an unauthorised profit made by a trustee. If you wish to know more on the topic of unauthorised profits, or of the duties of trustees in general, you may wish to refer to Chapter 10 at this point. But, just to give the briefest of overviews for the purposes of this chapter, it is a rule of equity that a trustee will be in breach of their duty to the trust if they make any form of profit from the trust. This includes, amongst other things, the taking of commissions or any other form of unauthorised payment, taking the benefit of a lease formerly in the ownership of the trust, and the purchase of trust property (even at market value). In all of these situations, the result of the trustee's actions will be that a constructive trust is imposed in favour of the beneficiaries, in respect of the 'profit' the trustee has made, in whatever form that may take.

So, take the example of a trustee who has taken a £1,000 commission from an insurance company for recommending their products to the board of trustees. A trustee is not allowed to benefit financially from his position as a trustee. On discovery of the unauthorised profit, therefore, that money would be deemed to be held by the trustee in breach on a constructive trust in favour of the beneficiaries. There are many examples of such situations occurring in case law, some of which you will come across again in Chapter 10. But to give you a flavour of the diverse situations in which a constructive trust will be held by a defaulting trustee, here are a few instances of decisions in which constructive trusts have been imposed.

The case of **Boardman v. Phipps** [1967] 2 AC 46 is a landmark judgment in this area. The case concerned a trust fund consisting of a large shareholding in a textile company. The trustees were unhappy with the way the company was performing but one of the trustees, Mr Boardman, suggested that if they could buy more shares in the company, it would give them a majority shareholding and they could then make changes to the company and improve its performance. The trustees would not take Mr Boardman's advice and so, believing this to be the only way to bring profit to the trust fund, he decided to buy the shares in his own name and restructure the company himself. Mr Boardman's actions made him a huge personal profit, as well as a large profit for the trust. However, one of the beneficiaries then claimed that Mr Boardman's personal profits should belong to the trust because he only benefited from the business deal due to the knowledge he had gained as a trustee of the fund. The court held that Mr Boardman, even though he had acted in good faith and in the best interests of the trust, had no right to profit personally from his actions. Therefore he should hold the profit he had made on a constructive trust in favour of the beneficiaries.

An example of a trustee with less innocent motives is that of **Attorney-General for Hong Kong v. Reid** [1994] 1 All ER 1. In this case a solicitor, Mr Reid, had accepted bribes in order to obstruct the prosecution of certain criminals, over a period of years. When Mr Reid's actions were discovered he was arrested and later sentenced to eight years imprisonment. The Hong Kong government was also successful in making a claim against Mr Reid for the sum of HK$12.43 million, which represented the amount Mr Reid was proved to have received in bribes. The money was held by the court to be held on a constructive trust by Mr Reid in favour of his employer, the Crown, to whom he had a fiduciary duty. To date, no part of this money has ever been repaid.

It should be noted that in cases of breach of trust the imposition of constructive trusts is not restricted to trustees alone. A person guilty of receiving trust property in the knowledge that the property is the product of a breach of trust can also have a constructive trust imposed upon them, with the effect that they will hold the misappropriated trust property on trust for the beneficiaries. (The receipt of trust property by a third party in breach of trust is known as '**knowing receipt**' and will be dealt with in detail in Chapter 14.)

A case in point is that of *Bank of Credit and Commerce International (Overseas) Ltd and Another* v. *Akindele* [2000] 3 WLR 1423. In this case the claimants were the liquidators of a banking company, BCCI. In 1985 the defendant, Chief Akindele, who was a prominent Nigerian businessman, entered into an agreement with BCCI to buy shares in the company for a guaranteed 15 per cent annual return. Chief Akindele paid US$10 million in exchange for 250,000 shares and received payments in return of some US$16.679 million. It transpired that the business deal was part of a fraud by some employees of BCCI, which the employees had entered into in fraudulent breach of their fiduciary duties to the company. On BCCI going into liquidation, the liquidators claimed that Chief Akindele was liable to account to the company for the sum of US$6.679 million, which they claimed he had received in knowledge of a breach. If Chief Akindele had been found to have received the money with knowledge of the breach, he would have been deemed to be holding any sums received by him under a constructive trust in favour of the company. However, the court held that the Chief did not have any knowledge of the fraud at the time he entered into the business arrangement and he was therefore cleared of any claim against his personal assets.

The defendant in this example was innocent of the allegations made against him by the liquidators; however, it is easy to see how, as a matter of **public policy** alone, a constructive trust could be imposed in cases of persons seeking to profit from their crimes. It would clearly be inequitable for a person receiving stolen goods, in full knowledge that they had been acquired illegally, to be allowed to keep the product of the crime, for example. Thus, in cases of fraud, the property is held by the fraudster on constructive trust for the original owner. One final, and rather more unusual, example of a situation in which a constructive trust will be imposed is in the case of a person who has received money as a product of murder. In *Cleaver* v. *Mutual Reserve Fund Life Association* [1892] 1 QB 147, the Court of Appeal allowed the **executors** of a man who had been murdered by his wife to claim a constructive trust in favour of the man's estate as against the wife, who was the sole beneficiary under an insurance policy. It was held that the wife should hold the proceeds of the policy on a constructive trust on the basis that she should not be entitled to benefit from her crime. Put simply, murder will make the killer a constructive trustee of whatever property they acquire as a result. If you want to find out more about this aspect of constructive trusts, take a look at the Out and about feature.

Case Summary

Out and about Fact-finding mission: the infamous case of Dr Crippen

Do you have the stomach for a murder investigation? See what you can find out about the infamous case of Dr Crippen. Put on your investigative hat and try to find answers to the following questions:

+ When did the infamous events take place?
+ Who were the parties involved?
+ What were the facts of the case?
+ Why was there a civil case and what was the outcome?
+ Why was the claimant unable to stake her claim?
+ What is the twist in the tale?

You should take no more than 40 minutes on this task.

 Handy tip: There is plenty on the internet about the murder case, but if you are struggling to find details of the civil case, try looking on Westlaw for *Re Crippen* [1911] P 108.

So, as we have seen, constructive trusts can be imposed in a number of situations, not just in relation to the family home but also in the case of businesses and in order to protect trust property where there has been a breach of trust by a trustee. More unusually, a constructive trust may also be imposed in cases of murder, on the basis that a person should not be allowed to profit from their crime. You can look out for examples of constructive trusts being imposed throughout the rest of the book.

Proprietary estoppel

You may be thinking: what is **proprietary estoppel** and why does it feature in a chapter on constructive trusts? The doctrine of proprietary estoppel is an old-established equitable principle, which shares a number of the features of constructive trusts. Indeed, a finding of proprietary estoppel can often result in the same outcome as a finding of a constructive trust. The idea behind proprietary estoppel is that, if the legal owner of a property induces a third party, either through misinformation or by allowing that party to continue in a belief the legal owner knows to be wrong, to act to their detriment in the mistaken belief that they will gain a beneficial interest in that property, then the legal owner will be 'estopped' from asserting their legal rights over the property and denying the third party their equitable interest. In order to gain a better understanding of the concept, it may help to take a look at a couple of examples of successful claims for proprietary estoppel.

Case Summary

In the case of *Inwards* v. *Baker* [1965] 2 QB 29, a father, John Baker, allowed his son to build a bungalow on the father's land. On the father's death the father's mistress, Miss Inwards, and their children sought possession of the bungalow. The Court of Appeal held that the son had built the bungalow on the father's land with the father's encouragement. He was entitled to remain in possession as a licensee so long as he wished to use it as his home, and the father's mistress was estopped from claiming the father's legal right to possession on the father's behalf.

Case Summary

To give another example, let us look at the case of *Pascoe* v. *Turner* [1979] 1 WLR 431, which concerned an argument over a family home. Mr Pascoe bought a house in his sole name, which he lived in with Ms Turner. Mr Pascoe told Ms Turner 'the house is yours and everything in it'. Ms Turner spent a considerable amount on repairs and improvements to the property, such as plumbing, repairs to the roof, putting in new carpets and the general redecoration of the house. However, when the couple later split up, Mr Pascoe sought to have Ms Turner removed from the house, saying she had no interest in it. The court held that the house belonged to Ms Turner and ordered the transfer of the property to her. Mr Pascoe was estopped from asserting his legal right over the property because he had promised Ms Turner the house and because she had believed his promise and acted to her detriment as a result of that promise.

Case Summary

A third example of proprietary estoppel in action is the case of *Greasley* v. *Cooke* [1980] 1 WLR 1306. This case, rather unusually, concerned a maid in service to a large house. Doris Cooke began to work at the age of 16 as a maid in a widower's house, and to look after his four children. The widower, Mr Greasley, died in 1948 leaving the house to two of his sons, who were now grown up. Doris looked after the eldest son and his mentally ill sister without receiving any payments and on the basis of assurances by the two sons who owned the house that she could remain in the house as long as she wished. On the death of the eldest son **intestate**, his share in the house passed to his three remaining siblings. Doris sought a declaration that she was entitled to remain in the house rent-free for the rest of her life. The Court of Appeal held that the two sons had made assurances to Doris and that she had acted on those assurances. Her application was therefore granted.

The above cases should give you a flavour of proprietary estoppel. Now let us consider in more detail how a claim is established.

Establishing a claim in proprietary estoppel

In order to establish proprietary estoppel a number of requirements need to be fulfilled. Traditionally there were five separate requirements, which were first set out by Mr Justice Fry in the case of *Willmott* v. *Barber* (1880) 15 Ch D 96. The case concerned an agreement to buy a piece of land. Joseph Willmott owned a timber yard which adjoined land belonging to William Bowyer. William let part of his land to Joseph, giving him an **option to purchase** the land at any time within the following five years. Unbeknown to Joseph the land, which was itself held by William on a long lease, was subject to a **covenant** not to sub-let or **assign** (that is, to transfer) the property without the written consent of the landlord, and William had not obtained this consent. Joseph spent a considerable amount of money improving the land by levelling it and incorporating it into his existing business premises. He then served notice on William that he wished to exercise his option to purchase the land. However, William was unable to go through with the sale because the landlord refused to give his consent to the assignment of the lease. Joseph brought an **action** against both William and the landlord, claiming **specific performance** of the agreement between William and Joseph, and to compel the landlord to give his agreement to the transfer. Joseph claimed that the landlord had acquiesced in his, Joseph's, expenditure because he knew that Joseph was acting in the mistaken belief that William was able to assign the property to him.

Case Summary

The court found that William could not be compelled to perform his agreement. The evidence in the case showed that the landlord was unaware of the covenant at the time of the agreement. He could not therefore be compelled to give his consent to assign to Joseph. In explaining his reasoning for the judgment, Mr Justice Fry said:

> A man is not to be deprived of his strict legal rights unless he has acted in such a way as would make it fraudulent for him to set up those rights.

As the landlord had been unaware of his right to withhold his consent to the assignment of the lease, it was impossible for him to have misled Joseph Willmott in the manner suggested.

In making his judgment, Mr Justice Fry said that, in order for a claim of proprietary estoppel to be established:

1. the claimant must have made a mistake as to their legal rights;

2. the claimant must have expended some money or must have done some act (not necessarily on the defendant's land) in the faith of their mistaken belief;

3. the defendant must know that their own right is inconsistent with the right claimed by the claimant;

4. the defendant must know of the claimant's mistaken belief in their rights;

5. the defendant must have encouraged the claimant in their expenditure of money or in the other acts which they have done, either directly or by abstaining from asserting their legal right.

Whilst these foundations laid down in *Willmott* v. *Barber* have stood the test of time, the attitude of the courts towards proprietary estoppel has tended to be rather more flexible over recent years. In the case of *Taylor Fashions Ltd* v. *Liverpool Victoria Trustees Co. Ltd* [1982] QB 133, Mr Justice Oliver said that the courts should adopt a broad approach to the five elements set out in *Wilmott* v. *Barber*, and that it was not necessarily essential for each element to be fully present in every case.

Case Summary

The case of *Taylor Fashions* itself concerned applications by the tenants of two adjoining shops for specific performance of options to renew in their leases, which the landlord was refusing to honour. The landlord said that the options were invalid because they had not been registered at the Land Charges Registry, which was a requirement under the Land Charges Act 1925. However, both tenants had carried out substantial improvements in reliance on their options. The case is interesting because the court found differently in respect of each tenant. Whilst the court acknowledged that options to renew are registrable, they found that, under the doctrine of proprietary estoppel, the landlord would nevertheless be bound by them if it would be 'dishonest or unconscionable' for him to argue otherwise. In the case of *Taylor Fashions* specific performance was refused on the basis that the landlord had arrived on the scene after the work had been done to the premises. It was therefore not possible to say that the tenant would not have carried out the works if he had known that the option to renew was invalid. However, in the case of the second tenant, Old & Campbell Ltd, the landlord had encouraged the tenant to carry out works, to take another lease of adjoining premises and had fixed the value of the freehold taking into account the option over it. Specific performance was granted therefore and Old & Campbell were allowed to renew their lease.

In making his judgments, Mr Justice Oliver said:

> the more recent cases indicate, in my judgment, that the application of . . . proprietary estoppel . . . requires a very much broader approach which is directed rather at ascertaining whether, in particular individual circumstances, it would be unconscionable for a party to be permitted to deny that which, knowingly or unknowingly, he has allowed or encouraged another to assume to his detriment than to inquiring whether the circumstances can be fitted within the confines of some preconceived formula serving as a universal yardstick for every form of unconscionable behaviour.

Unconscionability, then, would now appear to be the key element in proprietary estoppel. *Sledmore* v. *Dalby* (1996) 72 P & CR 196 (CA) is an interesting case in point. Although the facts of the case showed that there had been detrimental reliance on a statement by the legal owner, no finding of proprietary estoppel was made because no unconscionability on the part of the legal owner could be established. The facts of the case were that Mr Dalby had carried out repairs on the house in the belief that he and his family would have a licence to live there until the children left home. This undertaking had been given by the owner of the property, Mr Dalby's father-in-law, at a time when Mr Dalby was unemployed and his wife was seriously ill. The father-in-law died and the property passed to his widow, Mrs Sledmore. Mr Dalby was by this time employed and the children were grown up, although one still lived at home. Mrs Sledmore made an application to gain possession of the property, on account of the fact that she wished to live there herself. Her own home was in a state of some disrepair and she was behind on the mortgage payments. The court found in favour of Mrs Sledmore. There had been a change in circumstances of both parties and, as the legal owner of the property, she was entitled to assert her right to possession of the house. In addition, the court found that, as Mr Dalby had already lived in the property rent-free for 20 years, it was arguable in any event that he had already received the benefit of any proprietary interest he might have been entitled to by virtue of the repairs he had carried out at the property.

It should be remembered here that the fact that the legal owner of the property has acted in an unconscionable fashion will not in itself create the estoppel: there must also be detrimental reliance on the legal owner's assurances.

What constitutes detriment?

As with detrimental reliance in constructive trusts, detriment in proprietary estoppel can take many forms, not necessarily financial. In the case of *Re Basham* [1986] 1 WLR 1498 the claimant, Joan Bird, acted to her detriment by working in her stepfather's businesses without payment for many years and caring for him and his home. She did this on the understanding that she would inherit his estate on his death; however, the stepfather died intestate and his estate went to his children under the rules of intestacy, leaving Joan with nothing. Joan made a claim against the stepfather's **next of kin** and the court held that she was entitled to the estate as she had successfully established a case in proprietary estoppel in the circumstances. The Law in action feature illustrates a case in which the claimant made an altogether less successful claim of detriment.

Case Summary

Law in action
Judas Priest guitarist, K.K. Downing, in legal wrangle over country estate

The case of *Lissimore* v. *Downing* [2003] 2 FLR 308 provides a good illustration of what will *not* constitute detriment. The case concerned a claim by the former lover of the founder member, Kenneth 'K.K.' Downing, of heavy metal band, Judas Priest. Sarah Lissimore tried to claim half of Kenneth's 380-acre country estate in Shropshire, Astbury Hall. The couple had embarked on an eight-year relationship, with Miss Lissimore giving up her job as a pharmacist's assistant and moving in with Kenneth, but the couple did not marry. When the couple split up, Miss Lissimore made a claim for half the estate on grounds of proprietary estoppel. She said that she was entitled under the doctrine because Kenneth had promised to support her, based on his assertion, 'I'd bet you'd love to be lady of this manor, wouldn't you?' However, the court found that there had been no representation or assurance made by Kenneth and that there had been no action by Miss Lissimore which would be construed as detrimental above and beyond actions which would have constituted the ordinary course of such a relationship. Miss Lissimore's claim therefore failed and she received no part of the estate. It would appear that Mr Downing was luckier than many in his celebrity break-up.

To read the full facts of this case go to *Lissimore* v. *Downing* [2003] 2 FLR 308.

Source: Eyewire

In the recent Court of Appeal case of *Powell* v. *Benney* [2008] P & CR D 31, the claimants also failed to give sufficient evidence of detriment to gain the award they requested, albeit they were still given a sum of money in lieu of their expenditure. Mr Hobday owned several properties. He became friendly with a local pastor, Mr Powell, and his wife who, when Mr Hobday became incapable of looking after himself, took care of him and managed his affairs. Mr Hobday told the Powells several times that he was going to leave his properties to them and even signed a document purporting to leave them the properties, although this was not a valid will. He also invited them to use the properties. Powell and his wife spent time tidying and improving the properties and adapting one for the giving of music and Bible lessons. Mr Hobday died intestate and the properties passed to his cousins. The Powells claimed the properties on the grounds of estoppel, but their claim was rejected. They were nevertheless given a £20,000 award in lieu of their expenditure on the properties.

A similar outcome was reached in the case of *Cobbe* v. *Yeoman's Row Management Ltd* [2008] 1 WLR 1752, although for different reasons. The case concerned a block of flats in Yeoman's Row, London. Mr Cobbe, who was a property developer, claimed that in August 2002 he had reached an oral agreement with the owners of the flats, Yeoman's Row Management Ltd, that he would apply for planning permission for the residential development of the property. On such permission and consent being obtained, the block of flats would be sold to Mr Cobbe for the sum of £12 million plus 50 per cent of the gross proceeds of sale of the new homes, totalling in excess of £24 million. Mr Cobbe alleged that, pursuant to the agreement, he spent considerable time and money securing planning permission, which was granted in March 2004. Yeoman's Row denied that any legally enforceable agreement had been entered into and asserted that the expense incurred by Mr Cobbe was entirely at his own risk. Mr Cobbe claimed a lump sum payment under the doctrine of estoppel.

The judge at first instance, Mr Justice Etherton, found in favour of Mr Cobbe, awarding Mr Cobbe a one-half share in the increased value of the property as a result of the planning permission. The Court of Appeal also favoured this decision. However, the House of Lords overturned their findings. In their view, this was not a case of proprietary estoppel at all. Mr Cobbe was an experienced businessman who had carried out the work in the knowledge that the oral agreement which had been reached was not legally binding, and therefore his expenditure had been purely speculative. The property deal had never been a venture and so the outcome of the case should not be to treat it as one by giving Mr Cobbe a share of the increase in value on obtaining the planning permission. Mr Cobbe's only entitlement should therefore be the reimbursement of his outgoings and a fee for services rendered to the company. In the eyes of the House of Lords, therefore, detrimental reliance on a promise by Yeoman's had simply not been proved. This case has been heavily criticised by academics because of its purportedly restrictive approach to what will create a proprietary estoppel, as we shall see shortly. However, it is a very useful case for students to read because the court in giving its judgment has analysed the variety of remedies that might have been available to Mr Cobbe in the circumstances. It therefore gives a very good practical overview of the law in this area.

> his expenditure had been purely speculative

The problem with wills

One particular problem area with proprietary estoppel claims is that of wills purported to be written by the legal owners of the property. Many claims for proprietary estoppel have been based on promises made by the legal owners of property that the claimant will inherit on their death. You might think that this would make for a fairly straightforward claim: the legal owner promises the claimant will inherit; the claimant acts to their detriment in reliance on the promise, and a claim for proprietary estoppel is established. However, the view of the courts is clearly that the position is not altogether as straightforward as this. There have been a number of seemingly conflicting judgments on the issue of promises of inheritance, resulting in a rather subtle distinction being made between different wills cases.

A good starting point is the Court of Appeal case of *Wayling* v. *Jones* [1995] 2 FLR 1029. The background for this case was not that of a family, but rather the running of a business. Paul Wayling met Daniel Jones when he was 21 and Daniel was 56, and they entered into a relationship together. From the time they met in 1971 until Daniel's death in 1982, Daniel had bought and run various businesses, primarily hotels and guest houses. Paul acted throughout this time as Daniel's companion and chauffeur and gave substantial help in running the businesses. In return for his services Paul received pocket money, living and clothing expenses. Daniel also promised Paul on several occasions that he would leave him the business in his will, making provision first for Paul to inherit Daniel's café premises and later another hotel owned by Daniel, the Glen-y-Mor Hotel in Aberystwyth. In 1985 Daniel sold the Glen-y-Mor Hotel and bought the Hotel Royal, Barmouth, which he told Paul was for Paul to run and to inherit after Daniel's death. Daniel told Paul that he would alter his will to substitute the Hotel Royal, Barmouth for the Glen-y-Mor Hotel, but he had not done so by the time of his death in 1987. Upon Daniel's death, Paul claimed that he was entitled to the proceeds of the sale of the Hotel Royal, Barmouth on the principles of proprietary estoppel. The Court of Appeal held that Paul had relied on the promises made by Daniel to leave Paul property under his will, to his detriment. Daniel's executors should pay the proceeds of sale of the hotel to Paul out of Daniel's estate.

Case Summary

Three years later the outcome in the case of *Taylor* v. *Dickens* [1998] 1 FLR 806 came in complete contrast to *Wayling* v. *Jones*, with a finding at first instance that proprietary estoppel could not apply in the case of a promised **legacy**. Upon being told by the defendant that she would leave him her house in her will, Mr Taylor, the defendant's part-time gardener, stated that he would work without pay from then on. The defendant executed at least three wills leaving the house to Mr Taylor, but then made another will leaving it someone else, without telling Mr Taylor. Throughout this period Mr Taylor had provided care for the defendant without pay in the expectation that he would inherit the defendant's house. When the defendant died, Mr Taylor claimed to be entitled to the house on grounds of proprietary estoppel. However, the court held that Mr Taylor should not inherit the house. They said that it was not enough for Mr Taylor to believe that he was going to be left property by the defendant, if he knew that the defendant had the right to change her mind. Mr Taylor would also have to establish that the defendant had created or encouraged a belief that she would not revoke her will and that Mr Taylor had relied on that belief. As Mr Taylor had admitted in evidence that this was not the case, his claim for proprietary estoppel failed.

Case Summary

The findings in *Taylor* v. *Dickens* suggested that the cases in which a will could be relied upon would be almost negligible. After all, anyone can change their will at any time up until death: surely, then, there is never a situation in which a claimant could be absolutely sure the legal owner of the property would not revoke it. However, in the case of *Gillett* v. *Holt* [2001] Ch 210, which was heard at first instance not six months after *Taylor* v. *Dickens*, the findings in *Taylor* v. *Dickens* were disapproved. The facts of *Gillett* v. *Holt*

Case Summary

were as follows: Mr Gillett spent his working life as farm manager for Ken Holt, a land-owner of substantial means, who made repeated promises and assurances over many years, usually on special family occasions, that Mr Gillett would be the successor to his farming business, including the farmhouse in which Mr Gillett and his family had lived for over 25 years. However, after a falling out between the two men Mr Gillett was dismissed from Holt's service and subsequently cut out of his will. On Mr Holt's death, Mr Gillett made a claim against his estate under the doctrine of proprietary estoppel. The judge at first instance, following *Taylor* v. *Dickens*, dismissed Mr Gillett's claim, stating that there had been no irrevocable promise that the plaintiff would inherit. However, on appeal, the Court of Appeal said that Mr Holt's assurances had been made irrevocable by Mr Gillett's reliance on them over a period of years. Mr Gillett was therefore awarded the farmhouse in which he and his family lived, together with sum of money to compensate him for his exclusion from the rest of the farming business. In commenting on Mr Gillett's reliance on the will, Lord Justice Walker said:

> it is notorious that some elderly persons of means derive enjoyment from the possession of testamentary power, and from dropping hints as to their intentions, without any question of an estoppel arising. But in this case Mr Holt's assurances were repeated over a long period, usually before the assembled company on special family occasions . . . Mr Gillett, after discussing the matter with his wife and his parents, decided to rely on Mr Holt's assurances because 'Ken was a man of his word'. Plainly the assurances given . . . were intended to be relied on, and were in fact relied on.

Despite the finding in *Taylor* v. *Dickens* being disapproved, therefore, it is clear from the wording of the judgment that promises of inheritance should be substantial and repeated in order for a claim of proprietary estoppel to succeed in reliance on them. A simple, one-off statement or hints at an inheritance would not do. In the case of *Gillett* v. *Holt*, particular emphasis was placed by the Court of Appeal on the fact that Mr Holt was a dour man of few words and that such statements by him, such as were made from time to time, were therefore not to be taken lightly.

There are two recent House of Lords cases which have really thrown the issue of proprietary estoppel into the limelight. The first is that of *Cobbe* v. *Yeoman's Row Management Ltd*, and the second is *Thorner* v. *Major* [2009] 1 WLR 776 (see below). We have already considered the facts of *Cobbe* v. *Yeoman's Row* earlier in the chapter, and you will remember that it concerned a purported agreement between a developer and a management company. What, then, does all this have to do with wills? It is Lord Walker's speech in this case that we must look to for an answer to this question. Although the context of the case was vastly different from those listed above concerning wills, or the promise of them, Lord Walker in his speech went to some pains to talk about the issue of the revocability of promises of future events, something which, as we have seen, is particularly pertinent in the context of wills. Lord Walker, in discussing the issue of promises to do something at a future date, said that:

> Mr Cobbe's case seems to me to fail on the simple but fundamental point that, as persons experienced in the property world, both parties knew that there was no legally binding contract, and that either was therefore free to discontinue the negotiations without legal liability . . . Mr Cobbe . . . stood to make a handsome profit if the deal went ahead . . . the fact is that he ran a commercial risk, with his eyes open, and the outcome has proved unfortunate for him.

Reading this extract from Lord Walker's judgment out of context, it might appear that Lord Walker is suggesting that a finding of proprietary estoppel cannot be made unless the reliance of the third party is on a legally binding contract (something which would not apply to a will, which can be revoked at any time before death). Legal commentators and academics were up in arms about the judgment, believing it to signify a severe curtailment of the use of proprietary estoppel as an equitable remedy in the future. However, Lord Walker was in actual fact at great pains to differentiate the case of *Cobbe* v. *Yeoman's Row* from domestic cases. He said that, in his view and clearly in the general view of the courts from judgments before him, there was a marked difference between cases in which families had relied on promises of, in the most part, security of family life in the provision of a home, and a commercial case such as *Cobbe* v. *Yeoman's Row*. In this case, despite being a very experienced businessman, Mr Cobbe had decided to take a commercial risk without putting the agreement on a formal footing. Mr Cobbe was well aware that there was no legally binding contract and that therefore the management company could pull out of the deal at any time, without legal consequence. All Lord Walker was suggesting was that it would be unrealistic to impose a remedy under proprietary estoppel based on the suggestion that an experienced man of business would be naive enough to rely on another company's word that a £12 million business deal would go ahead without further negotiation.

In any event, the fears brought about by the outcome of this case appear now to have been allayed by a further House of Lords decision, that of *Thorner* v. *Major*. This most recent case concerned a promise of testamentary gift, and therefore put the discussion appertaining to promises of future action back in familiar territory, in terms of the subject matter of the promise or assertion. The facts of the case are very similar to the facts of *Gillett* v. *Holt*, in that they concern promises to inherit a farm. Peter Thorner and the claimant, David Thorner's father, were cousins who each had farms in Cheddar, in Somerset. Throughout his life David lived at home with his parents and helped his father and subsequently Peter, who had no children of his own, to farm their land. From 1986, after David's father gave up farming, David worked full time on Peter's farm and he continued to do so until Peter's death in 2005. David was never paid for his work and his only income was pocket money from his father. However, various remarks were made by Peter that led David to expect that he would inherit the farm on Peter's death. In particular, on one occasion Peter handed David a life insurance policy bonus notice, saying 'That's for my death duties' (by this he meant the payment of inheritance tax). Peter also made a will in which he left the whole of his **residuary estate** to David, but he later destroyed it after falling out with someone to whom he had left a smaller legacy in the will. Peter never made a new will and died intestate. David made a claim for the whole of Peter's estate under the doctrine of proprietary estoppel. The judge at first instance found in David's favour. However, the Court of Appeal reversed the decision on the grounds that Peter's statement regarding the payment of inheritance tax was not sufficient to show a clear and unequivocal representation by Peter upon which he had intended the claimant to rely. David appealed to the House of Lords.

Case Summary

Lord Neuberger's judgment is particularly valuable and worth reading in full for a detailed explanation of what will be sufficient in terms of assurances in cases of proprietary estoppel. In overturning the decision of the Court of Appeal, Lord Neuberger said that the meaning ascribed to words passing between parties will often depend on their factual context. He did not agree with the Court of Appeal's suggestion that the statements made by Peter Thorner were not of a

the meaning ascribed to words will often depend on their factual context sufficiently unequivocal nature to provide the basis for a claim in proprietary estoppel. In his view, the fact that the judge at first instance had found that the statements made by Peter were reasonably relied upon by David as indicating that Peter was committing himself to leaving the farm to David, should not be tampered with. The judge at first instance had heard a great deal of evidence on this point and the Court of Appeal had no right to question his judgment on that point. Lord Neuberger stated that:

> It may be that there could be exceptional cases where, even though a person reasonably relied on a statement, it might be wrong to conclude that the statement-maker was estopped, because he could not reasonably have expected the person so to rely. However, such cases would be rare, and, in the light of the facts found by the deputy judge, it has not been, and could not be, suggested that this was such a case.

He then went on further to say that:

> even if Peter's 'implicit statement' may have been revocable . . . it would [not] necessarily follow that, once the statement had been maintained by Peter and acted on by David for a substantial period, it would have been open to Peter freely to go back on it. It may be that he could not have done so, at least without paying David appropriate compensation, unless the change of mind was attributable to, and could be justified by, a change of circumstances. It seems to me that it would be arguable that, even assuming that the 'implicit statement' was not irrevocable, if, say in 2004, Peter had changed his mind, David would nonetheless have been entitled to equitable relief, in the light of his 14 or more years of unpaid work on the farm.

It is therefore clear from Lord Neuberger's judgment that in cases of proprietary estoppel:

1. the quality of the assurance made will depend on the individual facts of the case;
2. a promise to leave a gift of property in a will *can* be a sufficient assurance on which a party can rely, if taken in context;
3. it is the reliance of the claimant on the property owner's assurances which makes the assurance irrevocable, not the contractual (or otherwise) nature of the assurance itself.

It should be noted that Lord Scott, whilst agreeing with the outcome of the case, said that he would prefer to see the outcome of the case founded on the basis of a constructive trust, rather than proprietary estoppel. However, this was not a view shared by the other judges in the House and commentators have suggested that his comments were erroneous. For a further discussion of these two important House of Lords decisions, and commentary on the issues raised in relation to the use of testamentary promises in establishing a case for proprietary estoppel, see McFarlane and Robertson (2009).

The effect of proprietary estoppel

So far in this chapter we have explored the nature of proprietary estoppel and we have examined in detail what will be sufficient to constitute a claim in equity under the doctrine of proprietary estoppel. What remains is for us to consider what the effect of establishing such a claim is, in practice. In order to get a feel for this let us look at the case of *Crabb* v. *Arun District Council* [1976] Ch 179, which had a rather different outcome from those we have come across so far in this chapter. The case concerned neighbouring landowners, Mr Crabb and Arun District Council. Mr Crabb sold part of his land to a third party, without reserving a right of way over his remaining land to the public highway. This was because he had been led by the Council to believe that they would give him a right of way over their adjoining land, and so the reservation of a right of way over his own land was not necessary. However, after Mr Crabb's land had been sold, the Council then refused to give him a right of way over their land unless he paid them the sum of £3,000. The Court of Appeal held that Mr Crabb should be given the right of way under the doctrine of proprietary estoppel and that he did not have to pay the Council for it. He had sold his own land without reserving a right of way through it, based on the assurances of the Council, and they were estopped from denying him a right of way as a result of this. Lord Justice Scarman said that estoppel cases involved three questions:

Case Summary

1. *Has an equity been established?* In other words, has there been an assurance by the legal owner on which the claimant has relied to their detriment and is the legal owner's behaviour unconscionable in all the circumstances? (In brief, the prerequisites set out in *Wilmott* v. *Barber* as modified by *Taylor Fashions*.)

2. *What is the extent of the equity?* The extent of the equity will be a matter to be decided on the facts of each case, dependent on the extent to which the claimant acted to their detriment, on the basis of the assurances made to them. The court's decision as to the extent of the claimant's equity will have a direct bearing on the relief granted (below).

3. *What relief should be granted to satisfy it?* In other words, what remedy will the courts grant to the claimant? Again, this will be dependent on the facts of each case. In *Pascoe* v. *Turner*, Lord Justice Cumming-Bruce said that, in deciding what remedy to provide in cases of proprietary estoppel:

> the court must decide what is the minimum equity to do justice . . . having regard to the way in which [the claimant] changed [their] position for the worse by reason of the acquiescence and encouragement of the legal owner.

It is therefore not necessarily the case that the claimant, if successful, will be awarded the house or other property, or a share in that property, in every single case. If a claim for proprietary estoppel is established, the court has a broad equitable jurisdiction to prescribe whatever remedy they deem appropriate under the circumstances. It is particularly important to note that the remedy given cannot be punitive in nature. The 'minimum equity to do justice' in essence means that the claimant will be given, at most, the interest in the property which they believed they would receive on account of the assurances made to them. They cannot be given an award based simply on the unconscionability of the legal owner's actions, however morally reprehensible they might be.

The remedy given by the courts will be tailored to the facts of the individual case, the court doing whatever they consider necessary to reverse the detriment which has been suffered by the claimant. Such remedies are therefore many and varied in nature, and can range from a simple transfer of the legal estate from the legal owner to the claimant outright, to something more modest, such as the grant of a licence to occupy the land for a period of time. The You be the judge exercise will serve as a reminder of the many different remedies we have come across throughout the course of the chapter.

You be the judge

Q: Take another look through the chapter and find examples of the following remedies:

(a) a transfer of the legal estate;

(b) the grant of a right of way over land;

(c) the grant of a licence to occupy land for life;

(d) the grant of a licence to occupy for as long as the claimant wishes to use the land as a home;

(e) the payment of cash compensation.

A: (a) *Pascoe* v. *Turner*; (b) *Crabb* v. *Arun District Council*; (c) *Gillett* v. *Holt*; (d) *Inwards* v. *Baker*; (e) *Gillett* v. *Holt*.

Case Summary

A really interesting illustration of the court's attitude towards remedies in proprietary estoppel is that of *Jennings* v. *Rice* [2002] EWCA Civ 159. The case concerned a man named Jennings and an elderly widow, Mrs Royle. Jennings had worked for Mrs Royle on a part time basis, doing gardening, running errands and taking Mrs Royle shopping, since around 1970. In the late 1980s Mrs Royle stopped paying Jennings, telling him he need not worry about that since 'he would be all right' and that 'this will all be yours one day'. Mrs Royle subsequently became more and more dependent on Jennings, who helped her wash, dress and go to the bathroom, did her shopping, and even slept overnight at her house to provide her with security after a break-in at the house. When Mrs Royle died intestate in 1997, Jennings made a proprietary estoppel claim on the basis of Mrs Royle's assurances to him. The house was then worth £435,000. Mrs Royle's total estate was worth some £1.285 million.

The court found in favour of Mr Jennings but, rather than giving him the house or estate, instead gave him a monetary award of £200,000 which, the judge said, represented the estimated cost of full-time nursing care for Mrs Royle. Jennings appealed, contending that he was entitled under the doctrine of proprietary estoppel either to the whole of Mrs Royle's estate, or alternatively to the value of the house, on the basis that that was his expectation. However, the court held, dismissing the appeal, that to have awarded Jennings the value of the house would have been excessive. In the court's view, the value of the equity will depend upon all the circumstances, including not only the expectation of the claimant but also the detriment actually suffered by them. The task of the court was to do whatever is necessary to avoid an unconscionable result, but in doing so there had to be proportionality between the expectation and the detriment. On this basis if the claimant's expectations were extravagant, or out of all proportion to the detriment which the claimant had suffered, the court felt that the claimant's equity should be satisfied in another more limited way.

The 2008 Court of Appeal case of *Powell* v. *Benney*, which we came across earlier in the chapter, also provides some useful commentary on this point. Here the Court of Appeal said that estoppel could be broken down into two different kinds: bargain and non-bargain. In the 'bargain' variety of estoppel it would have to be shown that there was some bargain or agreement between the parties. On the facts of *Powell* v. *Benney*, Mr Hobday had said he would leave the properties to Mr and Mrs Powell but he had not required them to undertake the improvements, which they had done entirely at their own discretion, albeit that Mr Hobday had known about them. This was 'non-bargain' estoppel. Whilst this form of estoppel nevertheless required the judge to satisfy the equity which had arisen on the basis of the Powells' expenditure, the value of the properties was out of all proportion to their expenditure. Therefore the judge ordered a payment of £20,000 which he considered reasonable in order to meet the Powells' expectations.

It would thus appear that, regardless of the circumstances of the estoppel, the detriment suffered must be proportionate to the award claimed in order for 'the minimum equity to do justice' to be satisfied. As with the two cases above, and even the outcome in *Cobbe* v. *Yeoman's Row*, the court will look to the extent of the expenditure made or other detriment suffered by the claimant before making the appropriate award.

Similarities to constructive trusts

The two doctrines of constructive trusts and proprietary estoppel, as we have seen throughout the course of this chapter, are capable of producing very similar, or even identical, results for the claimant. However, they can also produce very different results. One only has to look at the preceding paragraphs to see how much wider the range of remedies available to a claimant of proprietary estoppel is and how much greater the court's discretion can be, than in cases of constructive trust. This does not mean that the remedies available in proprietary estoppel are superior to those available to the constructive trustee, of course. A wider discretion, as we have seen, does not necessarily equate to a more substantial reward: in fact, proprietary estoppel claims can often produce a financially lesser remedy for the claimant.

Nevertheless, owing to what has been traditionally perceived as the very similar natures of the two equitable doctrines, it has often happened that cases have been pleaded in the alternative, claiming the benefit of one doctrine if the other fails, and the courts have been happy to treat the two doctrines as overlapping if not synonymous in some circumstances. We have already come across a very recent case of this happening at House of Lords level, in the judgment of Lord Scott in *Thorner* v. *Major*. The willingness of the court to lump the two doctrines together in this way, however, is perhaps somewhat surprising, given their very different natures. In the case of *Yaxley* v. *Gotts* [2000] 1 All ER 711 (CA), the court again seemed to suggest that the doctrines of constructive trusts and proprietary estoppel were one and the same. The facts of the case were as follows: Mr Yaxley entered into an agreement with Mr Gotts, that Mr Gotts would buy a particular house requiring refurbishment. Mr Yaxley would then carry out repair works and convert the property into three flats, in return for which Mr Gotts agreed to transfer the ground floor flat to Mr Yaxley. In fact, unbeknown to Mr Yaxley, the house was purchased by Mr Gott's son, Alan. Mr Yaxley carried out the renovation work and, when the flats were let, acted as agent in collecting the rents and so on. After an argument with Mr Gotts's son, Mr Yaxley was locked out of the property, the son telling Mr Yaxley that he had no interest in it. Mr Yaxley sought the grant of a long lease of the ground-floor flat, on grounds of proprietary estoppel.

Case Summary

The outcome of the case was that, based upon the facts of the case, it was not possible to infer a common intention constructive trust, because the agreement was not with the legal owner of the property. For a constructive trust to be imposed, you will remember that there must be a common intention, whether actual or implied, between the legal owner of the property and the person making the claim. This is unlike the remedy of proprietary estoppel in which, according to the prerequisites in *Wilmott* v. *Barber*, the person making the representations need not be the legal owner of the property in question. The only possible outcome was therefore one of proprietary estoppel. However, Lord Justice Walker confused the issue by stating that, having established a case for proprietary estoppel, the award to be given was that of a constructive trust over the property. Thus, the remedy under the doctrine of proprietary estoppel was the imposition of a constructive trust. Such a statement has only served to muddy the waters in an area that is already fraught with difficulty.

Case Summary

In the subsequent case of *Van Laethem* v. *Brooker* (2005) WL 1767595, the issue of a possible overlap between constructive trusts and proprietary estoppel was again discussed. The claimant in this case, Penelope van Laethem, sought a declaration against the defendant, Kim Brooker, that she was entitled to an interest in a large Grade II listed house called Caradoc Court. The couple had bought the property together in a dilapidated state with a view to turning the house into 20 luxury apartments and building six new houses in the grounds. The legal title to the property was split between Mr Brooker, as to the house, and a company owned by Mr Brooker, as to the grounds, which the court referred to in their judgment as 'the development land'. Mrs van Laethem had made financial contributions to the purchase of Caradoc and assisted with its physical restoration. Mrs van Laethem argued that she was entitled to a half share in the house and the development land, either by virtue of a common intention constructive trust or by proprietary estoppel. Mr Brooker denied that Mrs van Laethem had any interest in the properties and submitted that he had bought Mrs van Laethem another property in full and final settlement of her claims.

The court held that Mrs van Laethem had acted to her detriment by relying on Mr Brooker's assurances. In particular, Mrs van Laethem had mortgaged her home and later invested her share of the proceeds from the sale of her home in the restoration of the house. By mortgaging her home, Mrs van Laethem had placed herself at substantial and very real risk as there was no obvious source of funds for Mr Brooker to service the loan. Mrs van Laethem's sale of her home in her middle age and her investment of the proceeds in the house were indicative of the fact that she thought she would ultimately have a home in which she would share her interest with Mr Brooker. Mrs van Laethem would not otherwise have rendered herself virtually homeless by trading in her home and capital. Mrs van Laethem had contributed a large amount of time by her physical contribution to the restoration of the grounds. Mr Brooker's unconscionable behaviour, as was required for proprietary estoppel, was his denial of her interest. In respect of the development land, the court also found that Mrs van Laethem held an interest. Mrs van Laethem had already received £280,000 from the sale of another property held in her sole name, and was entitled to a further £420,000 in addition in respect of her claim. As regards whether the claim was proved on grounds of proprietary estoppel or constructive trust, Mr Justice Collins had the following to say on the matter:

> the modern authorities . . . show that there is no substantial difference in the remedy as between constructive trust and proprietary estoppel. My primary holding is that Mrs van Laethem is entitled to an interest by way of proprietary estoppel in relation to Caradoc Court and by way of constructive trust in relation to the Development Land. My alternative holding is that Mrs van Laethem is entitled to an interest by way of proprietary estoppel in relation to both properties. I do not consider that it makes a difference as regards the remedy.

What remains unclear from his judgment is on what basis he differentiates between the two, if at all, and why he has chosen one possible remedy over the other. Whatever the reasons, it is clear that Mr Justice Collins views the degree of separation between the two equitable remedies as being very slim indeed. It remains to be seen where the courts will decide to go in light of these findings.

Table 8.1 shows the differences between resulting and constructive trusts and proprietary estoppel.

Table 8.1 Differences between resulting and constructive trusts and proprietary estoppel

	Resulting (presumed only)	Constructive	Proprietary estoppel
Requirements	Direct financial contribution to purchase price	Common intention (express or implied) + detrimental reliance	Assurance + reliance + detriment + unconscionability
Remedy	Share in property proportionate to contribution to purchase price	Share in property based on whole course of dealings between parties	Various: whatever will provide 'the minimum equity to do justice'

Summary

♦ A constructive trust arises by operation of law wherever the circumstances are such that it would be unconscionable for the owner of property to assert his own beneficial interest in the property and deny the beneficial interests of another.

♦ Such unconscionability exists wherever there is a common intention between the parties that they should share the beneficial interest in the property.

♦ Common intention can be express or inferred from conduct under certain circumstances, in the absence of express agreement.

♦ Where common intention is inferred by the parties' conduct, nothing less than direct contributions to the purchase price by the non-owning party will be sufficient evidence of such an intention.

♦ In cases of an express oral agreement, financial contribution is not essential to establish a beneficial interest in the property; rather it is proof of genuine detriment which is the key to making a claim.

♦ In calculating the amount of the claimant's interest under a constructive trust, the court will not look simply at direct contributions to the property; rather they will consider the 'whole course of dealing between the parties' and make their decision based on what appears to have been the parties' intention in light of those dealings (*Midland Bank* v. *Cooke*).

Proprietary estoppel is an equitable remedy available where the legal owner of a property has induced a third party to act to their detriment in the mistaken belief that they will gain a beneficial interest in it.

 In order to establish proprietary estoppel a number of requirements need to be fulfilled. Traditionally there were five separate requirements, which were first set out *Willmott* v. *Barber*. However, the attitude of the courts has become more flexible over recent years, and unconscionability would now appear to be a key element in deciding estoppel claims (*Taylor Fashions* v. *Liverpool Victoria Trustees*). The requirements for proprietary estoppel could now more easily be summarised as: assurance, reliance and detriment and unconscionability.

 Detriment, whilst it does not need to be financial, must be real and substantial in order to form the basis of proprietary estoppel.

 In cases of wills, promises of inheritance should be consistent and repeated in order for a claim of proprietary estoppel to succeed in reliance on them. A simple, one-off statement or hints at an inheritance will not be sufficient.

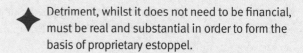 The remedy provided in cases of proprietary estoppel will be 'the minimum equity to do justice'. The court therefore has a broad equitable jurisdiction to prescribe whatever remedy they deem appropriate under the circumstances, whilst ensuring that the remedy remains proportionate to the detriment suffered.

Question and answer*

Problem: Duraid met Lynda in his local pub, the Flying Duck, where she was working as a bar-maid. The couple got on well and soon Duraid asked Lynda to move in with him. She was reluctant at first, as it would mean giving up her council flat, which she had been living in for 10 years. Duraid also said Lynda would have to give up her bar job, which she really enjoyed, because he did not want the other punters 'gawping at his missis'. Duraid told Lynda, however, that it would be for the best. He had a large detached house with a swimming pool and she could be his 'lady of the manor'.

For all the time she was living at the house, Lynda did not work (as it was against Duraid's wishes). However, Duraid expected Lynda to keep house for him, and he paid her an allowance for doing so. Duraid often brought businessmen to the house and on these occasions Lynda was expected to play the hostess, serving the men drinks and chauffering them home when they were unable to drive. When Lynda complained to Duraid about his treatment of her, he simply said that it would all be hers one day anyway and that he didn't know what she was worrying about. After a particularly big argument one day, he even made a will, leaving the house to Lynda, which he showed to her, saying 'there's your security, if you want it'.

Duraid came home last week and said that there was a new barmaid at the Flying Duck, and that he had asked her to come and live with him. He said that he would give Lynda until the end of the week to find somewhere else to live, but that it was over between them. Lynda has nowhere to go. She has lost the tenancy on her council flat and has no money with which to pay for a deposit on a new flat. She also has no job with which to support herself. Lynda has been unable to find the will.

Will Lynda be likely to succeed in a claim against the property and, if so, on what basis? What share or other remedy is she likely to get?

You should allow yourself no more than 40 minutes to complete this task.

Essay: 'The broadening scope of constructive trusts has rendered resulting trusts redundant in the context of trusts of the family home.' Discuss

This question should be answered in 40 minutes.

✱ Answer guidance is provided at the end of the chapter.

Further reading and references

Cullen, E. (2008) 'Stack v. Dowden: an end to uncertainty?', Insolvency Intelligence, 21(3), 43–6.
This article discusses the judgment in *Stack* v. *Dowden* and considers whether the case has assisted at all in determining how shares are quantified in the constructive trusts arena.

Ferguson, P. (1993) 'Constructive trusts – a note of caution', 109 LQR 114–31.
Despite this article dating back to 1993, it gives a really thorough and well-argued insight into the fundamental differences between constructive trusts and proprietary estoppel and is really worth taking a look at to gain an understanding of the issues involved in this area.

Law Commission Consultation Paper 179 (2006) Cohabitation: The Financial

Consequences of Relationship Breakdown, London: The Stationery Office.
Gives a broad overview of the law in this area, detailing the practical implications of relationship break-up in cases of unmarried couples.

McFarlane, B. and Robertson, A. (2009) 'Apocalypse averted: proprietary estoppel in the House of Lords', 125 LQR 535–42.
An article setting out the contrasting decisions in *Cobbe* v. *Yeoman's Row* and *Thorner* v. *Major*. Well worth a read for a really up-to-date understanding of proprietary estoppel, particularly in the context of testamentary promises.

Stack v. Dowden [2007] UKHL 17.
Essential reading for anyone studying constructive trusts. In particular, Baroness Hale's judgment is useful in restating the current legal position (if not clarifying it).

Question and answer guidance

Problem:

Constructive trust

In order to establish a claim under a constructive trust, Lynda will need to show that there was a common intention between the parties that she would have an interest in the property (*Gissing* v. *Gissing*). This common intention can be shown either by evidence of an express agreement between the parties, plus detriment on the part of the claimant (in this instance Lynda), or by the inference of such an agreement based on the conduct of the parties. In the case of an implied agreement, Lynda must also show that she has made direct contributions towards the purchase of the property.

Lynda has made no direct contributions towards the purchase of the property. She has simply kept house for Duraid and played hostess to his business clients. Compare with *Hammond* v. *Mitchell*. This is not sufficient to establish a claim under a constructive trust (*Burns* v. *Burns*). In order to make a claim on this basis she would therefore have to show evidence of an express agreement, plus detriment. The detriment need not be financial in this case, although it must be substantial (*Ungurian* v. *Lesnoff*). There is plenty of evidence of Duraid making assurances or statements to Lynda about her status within the household: she could be his 'lady of the manor'; that it would all be hers one day; the showing of his will. However, none of these things suggest a common intention, i.e. an agreement between the two parties. Lynda is moving into a house already owned by Duraid and he is simply stating, unilaterally, that he will leave it to her in his will. In *Eves* v. *Eves*, the man's statement that he would put her on the title deeds once she came of age was taken to be evidence of common intention; however, this was specifically an excuse as to why she wasn't put on the title deeds, rather than promises of future benefit, as here. More likely, then, this is going to be a claim for proprietary estoppel.

Proprietary estoppel

The five requirements of proprietary estoppel are set out in *Wilmott* v. *Barber*. However, it is not necessary to show all five elements in every case (*Taylor Fashions*) and the court will take more of a broad brush approach in a domestic context. The key elements would now seem to be assurance, reliance and detriment, plus an element of unconscionability (*Sledmore* v. *Dalby*). Assurances in the form of promises of inheritance are difficult. The simple promise of a legacy will not usually be sufficient, because a will can easily be revoked (*Taylor* v. *Dickens*; *Wayling* v. *Jones*). Such promises must be consistent and repeated (*Gillett* v. *Holt*). Equally, the statement that Lynda can be the 'lady of the manor' is weak (see *Lissimore* v. *Downing*). However, these two things, together with statements that it will all be hers one day, would probably collectively be sufficient to establish evidence of assurance on which she could rely (see in this respect the HL decision in *Thorner* v. *Major*), particularly as Duraid insisted she give up her job to live with him. In terms of detriment, this is clear from Lynda's giving up of her council flat, and arguably her job – although the job was simply something she enjoyed and not a professional position. Nevertheless, the fact that she no longer has a job has meant that she now has no means of financing herself independently, which is significant.

If Lynda can establish a claim in proprietary estoppel she will be entitled to 'the minimum equity to do justice'. She may not therefore be entitled to a beneficial interest in the house (which is what she would have received if she could establish an interest under a constructive trust). Rather she may be given financial compensation (as in *Gillett* v. *Holt*) equating to the loss she has suffered in giving up her council flat. Whatever the means of compensation given to her, it must be in proportion to her loss, and not punitive (*Jennings* v. *Rice*; *Powell* v. *Benney*).

Essay:

This question requires comments on two points:

1. the lack of availability of a remedy under the doctrine of resulting trusts in respect of indirect contributions made to the property; and

2. the arithmetical basis of calculation of the beneficial interest in resulting trusts.

On the first point, a good answer would set out the basis of making a claim under a resulting trust and the requirement of direct contributions to the purchase price of the property. Any subsequent contribution will not count in the case of resulting trusts, and this makes it impractical in cases of trusts of the family home, where a party may have contributed indirectly over a number of years by making improvements to the property, for example. It would be worth mentioning the difference here between married and unmarried couples, in that improvements made in the case of married couples are covered by section 37 of the Matrimonial Proceedings and Property Act 1970. The non-acceptance of indirect contributions in the resulting trusts scenario makes this a very limiting remedy in domestic situations.

Constructive trusts, on the other hand, do allow indirect contributions, where an express agreement common intention can be shown. However, exactly what will be included by way of indirect contributions is unclear (see *Gissing* v. *Gissing*; *Stack* v. *Dowden*). Where the common intention is implied by conduct only, nothing less than direct contributions will suffice. This suggests, at first instance, that where there is no express declaration of common intention a resulting trust might as well be used as a constructive trust. However, the two differ significantly in terms of the calculation of the beneficial interest.

With a resulting trust, the share in the beneficial interest is calculated on a purely arithmetical basis, based on the respective amounts that the parties put into the purchase of the property. With a constructive trust, the basis of calculation is more fluid, the court taking into account the 'whole course of dealings between the parties'. Nevertheless, there still seems to be a distinct difference in what will be considered in looking at the whole course of dealings, based loosely upon the couple's marital status. Whereas the court in the case of a married couple tends to look more at the position of the parties in the round, in the case of cohabitees the court still tends to focus on a consideration of the various financial contributions the parties have made throughout the course of the relationship. Reference should be made to the judgments in *Stack* v. *Dowden* here. In particular, the point should be made that, with constructive trusts, where a property is purchased in joint names the starting point will be equal shares ('equity follows the law') unless the parties can prove otherwise. Reference could also be made to Cullen 2008, which comments on this particular point.

It is worth noting that there will always be situations in which the contributions to the purchase are such that the claimant will want their claim calculated on a resulting trust basis, and not on a constructive trust basis. These cases will tend to be clear-cut, however.

Conclude by giving an opinion as to whether resulting trusts are redundant in the context of the family home, possibly with a call for further reform in the area.

Visit **www.mylawchamber.co.uk/warner-reed** to access study support resources including practice exam questions with guidance, interactive 'You be the judge' multiple choice questions, annotated weblinks, glossary and key case flashcards and audio legal updates all linked to the **Pearson eText** version of *Equity and Trusts* which you can **search**, **highlight** and **personalise** with your **own notes** and **bookmarks**.

Use Case Navigator to read in full some of the key cases referenced in this chapter with commentary and questions:

Attorney-General for Hong Kong v. *Reid* [1994] 1 All ER 1

Boardman v. *Phipps* [1966] 3 All ER 721

Gissing v. *Gissing* [1970] 2 All ER 780

Part 2
Management of Trusts

Chapter 9
Trusteeship and the appointment, retirement and removal of trustees

Key points In this chapter we will be looking at:

- ✦ What trustees do
- ✦ Who can be a trustee
- ✦ The number of trustees required in a trust
- ✦ The appointment of the first trustees to the trust

- ✦ The appointment of new or additional trustees
- ✦ The retirement or removal of trustees
- ✦ The ability of the court to appoint and remove trustees
- ✦ The ability of beneficiaries to appoint or remove trustees

Introduction

In Chapters 1 to 8 of the book we focused on the creation of **trusts** in their various forms and the difficulties inherent in the formation of certain types of trust. In the second section of the book we will be looking at how those trusts are administered: who looks after the trusts; who manages them; the rights and duties of the various parties to the trust; and what should happen if the trust is not administered properly or correctly.

In this chapter, we will be considering the nature of trusteeship: in other words, what **trustees** are and

what they are there for, and how those trustees are appointed or removed from their position as trustee. In Chapter 10 we will be looking at duties of trustees, and in Chapters 11 and 12 we will be considering the powers trustees have to deal with the trust. Chapters 13 to 16 deal with breaches of trust and the consequences that flow from a breach. But for now, let us start with the nature of trusteeship – how does someone become a trustee and what do they do, once appointed?

The nature of trusteeship

As we discovered in Chapter 1, the trustees are the people who are in charge of running the trust. They are the people who manage or administer the trust on a day-to-day basis. Trustees are in a quite unenviable position in that they are the legal owners of the trust property, but not the **beneficial owners** of it. This means that whilst they carry all the burdens and responsibilities of ownership of the trust assets, they have no right to benefit from or to enjoy those assets, or any income which they might produce: this privilege is reserved exclusively for the **beneficiaries**.

In addition to this, the trustees of a trust have a duty to act in the best interests of the beneficiaries of the trust and, as we will see in Chapter 10, this is a duty which is quite onerous and far-reaching in terms of its requirements of the trustee as an individual. As we shall also see in the next chapter, the trustees are not even allowed to receive payment for their role, however onerous and time-consuming it might be. The office of trusteeship is thus, one might say, a 'dubious honour' and it is not surprising that many trusts are run not by individuals at all but professionally by trust corporations. Having said this, being a trustee clearly isn't all bad. Take a look at the figures in the Key stats feature.

Key stats Being a trustee isn't all bad – the Charity Trustee Network survey results

Concerned that many people are being put off becoming trustees because the majority of what they hear about the role is negative, the Charity Trustee Network (CTN) has been running a survey seeking to explore some of the more positive aspects of being a trustee.

Over 200 trustees responded to a range of questions about their experience of being a trustee, the results of which are below.

CTN asked respondents, 'Since becoming a trustee, do you believe that . . .'

	Yes definitely %	Quite a lot %	A little %	Not at all %
You have acquired new skills	57.4	17.2	20.6	4.9
You have developed existing skills	52.5	30.7	15.3	1.5
Your skills and experiences have been valued by the charity of which you are a trustee	67.8	22.8	6.93	2.5
You have met people with different backgrounds that you might otherwise not have met	54.7	26.1	15.3	3.9

	Yes definitely %	Quite a lot %	A little %	Not at all %
You have found ways of managing the time commitment involved in trusteeship	36.0	38.9	23.6	1.5
It has helped you with your personal or career development	26.1	30.7	32.7	10.6
You have met people who have become good friends	33.8	25.9	32.3	8
You have enjoyed the experience	55.2	28.6	13.3	3

The results of this survey have been reproduced with the kind permission of the Charity Trustee Network. Further details can be viewed on their website: **http://www.trusteenet.org.uk/news/theres-lot-be-said-being-trustee**.

Who can be a trustee?

So that is a little about the nature of trusteeship. But who can actually become a trustee, and how? Sam de Silva from the charity the Terrence Higgins Trust reports his experience of trusteeship in the People in the law feature.

People in the law

Name and position: Sam de Silva, trustee of the Terrence Higgins Trust.

What attracted you to becoming a trustee? I wanted to broaden my skill set in addition to my City career. After seeing my father recover from cancer, I wanted to do something in the voluntary sector. That led to my first trustee role, on a cancer charity.

Which organisation do you represent? I'm currently a trustee of the Terrence Higgins Trust (THT), an HIV/AIDS charity.

What particularly attracted you to this organisation? I felt there was a real lack of support and understanding of people with HIV/AIDS.

Source: Sam de Silva, Terrence Higgins Trust (*text and photo*)

Is there anything that would make you an even more effective trustee? I think when you become a trustee at 30, you haven't had a long career, so your skill set is very specific.

Some comprehensive training course would have better prepared me for the role. Currently, I would say having more of a network to share ideas and learn from one another would help me become more effective.

What's the biggest challenge you have faced in your role? Being asked to take the role as chair of the audit committee within six months of becoming a trustee. The hardest thing about being a non-executive director is to stay out of the day-to-day management of the organisation, which is the executive's role.

What do you consider the most satisfying aspect of your role? Contributing to ideas and business plans that come to fruition. Being able to connect people especially around fundraising.

Do you think there is enough general recognition of the value of the trustee role? I think companies are seeing the value in having their employees take on non-executive roles outside their organisation, as part of the shift towards corporate social responsibility. There is now much more awareness of the importance of good governance and having capable people.

Do you feel that the demands made on trustees have grown over time? I think every time the economy sees an event like Enron, or the recent credit crunch we all wake up. So yes, higher governance standards require trustees to ask more difficult questions, understand more complex problems, dedicate more time, and build a larger network of resources.

What do you think is the ideal term of office that a trustee should serve? I think it depends on the size of the charity and how many roles you get through. In my first trustee role I served one term (4 years). I personally would look to do 1–2 terms, then open the door and let a fresh pair of eyes into the boardroom.

What tip would you give to a new trustee? Find a mentor and listen to their experiences. Read as much as possible about the charity and visit its services.

If you weren't a trustee, what would you do with that time? Windsurf! I do dedicate much time and energy to my trustee role. I block out weekends before a board meeting so that I allow enough time to read the papers.

What steps do you take to increase/retain your organisation's membership? I think every trustee has a broader responsibility to be a patron for the charity, whether fundraising or through awareness. I tend to use fundraising as a way to introduce people to the charities I've worked with, and hopefully that leads to others being inspired to become a member.

For more information on the Terrence Higgins Trust, go to: http://www.tht.org.uk.

We looked in Chapter 2 at who can be a **settlor** or a beneficiary and we thought about the **capacity** requirements for those parties to the trust. So, are the requirements for a trustee the same?

As in the case of settlors, generally any person able to hold property can be a trustee. Accordingly, under section 20 of the Law of Property Act 1925, a **minor** (that is, someone under the age of 18) cannot be appointed a trustee of land as they do not have the legal ability to own land.

Companies can also be trustees, either on their own or together with other individuals or companies. The management of large trusts, for example pension trusts, is often by companies who run the trusts on a professional basis. These specialist companies are commonly referred to as '**trust corporations**'. In accordance with the Public Trustee Act 1906 (as amended), such companies are authorised to act as trustees provided:

1. the company is constituted under the law of the United Kingdom or any other state of the EU;

2. the company's constitution authorises it to undertake trust business in England and Wales; and

3. the company has either been incorporated by special Act or Royal Charter, or has at least £250,000 of issued shares, with a minimum of £100,000 of those shares having been paid for in cash (effectively, the company must not be below a certain size).

The number of trustees

There is no minimum number of trustees required by law; so, it is possible for a sole trustee to act properly on behalf of a trust, either because that was the intention of the settlor, or because the other trustees have stopped acting for whatever reason. Neither is there any limit on the maximum number of trustees of **personal property** (as opposed to **real property**, or land). However, in the case of trusts which include land there can be a maximum of four trustees, section 34(2) of the Trustee Act 1925 stating that, where more than four persons are named as trustees of land, the first four named in the trust **deed** who are able and willing to act shall be the trustees, and the others shall only become trustees when they are appointed in the event of a vacancy occurring. It should be noted that this limit on the number of trustees applies only to **private trusts** of land and not to land held by trustees of charitable, or **public, trusts**.

Despite there being no legal minimum number of trustees, it is nevertheless sensible to ensure that there are not less than two trustees of land at any one time. There are two reasons for this:

1. Under section 27(2) of the Law of Property Act 1925 a sole trustee of land (with the exception of a trust corporation) is unable to give a valid receipt for the proceeds of sale of that land. This means that, in the case of a trust of land managed by a sole trustee, if ever the land contained within the trust needed to be sold, a second trustee would have to be appointed in order to complete the sale.

2. The process of '**overreaching**' under section 2 of the Law of Property Act 1925 cannot occur unless there are two trustees of land. This is the process whereby the beneficial, or **equitable**, **interest** on a sale of land is transferred from the land and attaches itself to the purchase monies during the conveyancing process. The effect of this is that the equitable interest of the beneficiaries will now be in the purchase money itself, and that the purchaser can take the property free from any equitable interest the beneficiaries have in it. A further discussion of the principles of overreaching is unnecessary for the study of trust law and is outside the scope of this book.

Appointment of the first trustees

The settlor will usually be the person to choose the first trustees of the trust, and this will be done in the **trust instrument**: that is, the document creating the trust. Consequently the first trustees will usually be people known to the settlor and will often be family members or trusted friends or business advisers; the first trustee may even be the settlor him or herself! Should the settlor fail to appoint any trustees, this will not be the end of the trust. Instead, the court has the ability to appoint trustees on behalf of the settlor to manage the trust, under the provisions of section 41 of the Trustee Act 1925, and we will be looking at this section in more detail a little later in the chapter.

> **the first trustees will usually be people known to the settlor**

So the appointment of the first trustees of the trust is pretty straightforward. And once these first trustees have been appointed they will, quite simply, remain trustees until their death, retirement, or removal from their position. But what happens after such an event occurs? Who will act in place of the original trustees and how will that person or persons be appointed?

Writing and drafting

You are a trainee solicitor at the firm of Ward Peake, Solicitors. Your client, Mr Addyman, is setting up a charitable trust for the care and rehoming of ex-battery hens. He intends to sit on the board of trustees himself but is concerned that the role will be too great for him to deal with on his own. He is also getting on in years and would like some younger trustees to continue his work.

Write a letter advising him on his choice of trustees. In particular, he would like to know how many additional trustees he should appoint and what qualities he should look for in a trustee.

You should take no more than 30 minutes on this task.

Source: Digital Vision

 Handy tip: this task is designed to get you thinking about the practical implications of becoming a trustee. Put yourself in Mr Addyman's shoes: what qualities would you want your trustees to have? Remember, as a member of the board you are going to be working closely with them! It may help to look back at the People in the law feature, which records an interview with a real-life trustee.

Appointment, retirement or removal under an express power

Occasionally, where a settlor has created the trust expressly or intentionally, the settlor may have thought to include provisions within the trust instrument either for new trustees to be appointed or current trustees to be removed or replaced. But in the majority of cases the trust instrument will be silent on the issue. In the absence of directions being contained within the trust instrument as to how to proceed in these circumstances, we must look to statute for guidance.

Death of a trustee

As we have seen above there is no minimum number of trustees. Where there are multiple trustees, as each trustee dies the surviving trustees can simply continue to act on behalf of the trust. On the death of the last remaining trustee, the **personal representatives** of that trustee become responsible for the trust (personal representatives are the people managing the administration of a person's **estate**). At this point, if the personal representatives wish to take up the reins as trustees, they may do so under section 18(2) of the Trustee Act 1925. But if they choose not to act they may instead appoint new trustees in place of the deceased trustee, under section 36(1) of the Trustee Act 1925. The appointment of new trustees under this section must be in writing, and new appointments must bring the total number of trustees acting under the trust to not more than four. This is regardless of the type of property comprised in the trust (whether land or personal property).

The provisions of section 36(1) are not restricted to personal representatives of the last remaining trustee. The section may also be used by any trustees remaining after the death of a trustee to appoint replacement trustees. They may wish to do this either if there is a trust of land, which really needs a minimum of two trustees to act, or even if the surviving trustees simply feel that they need more trustees to be appointed in place of the deceased trustee to help with the workload of managing the trust.

You should note that, for the purposes of section 36, it does not matter whether the trustee in question dies before or after their appointment has been formalised. This means that if a person is named as a trustee in a will but they die before the **testator**, section 36 can be used to appoint someone else in their place when that trust comes into being on the testator's death.

Retirement of a trustee

> the simplest way to do this is by asking to be discharged

Of course, death is not the only circumstance under which a trustee may cease to act under a trust. He or she may simply wish to retire from the trust. If a trustee wishes to retire, the simplest way to do this is by asking to be discharged under the provisions of section 39 of the Trustee Act 1925. This section of the Act authorises retirement if there will be two trustees or a single trust corporation remaining after his or her retirement from the trust *and* the decision to retire is approved by the remaining trustees. Such retirement from the trust must be made by deed in order to be valid.

Alternatively, a trustee wishing to retire may use section 36(1) of the Trustee Act 1925, provided another person will be appointed to replace them. Section 36(1) of the Trustee Act 1925 states that a new trustee may be appointed where the existing trustee has asked to be discharged on the basis that they longer wish to act as a trustee. If you are having trouble remembering the various different methods of retirement or removal at this point, don't worry! There is a handy reference table at the end of this section. In the meantime, take a look at the sample **deed of appointment and retirement** of a trustee in the Documenting the law feature.

Documenting the law

Deed of retirement of a trustee, with simultaneous appointment

THIS DEED OF APPOINTMENT AND RETIREMENT OF TRUSTEES is made the   day of   20[ ]

PARTIES:

(1) [ ] (the **'Retiring Trustees'**); and

(2) [ ] (the **'New Trustees'**).

RECITALS

(A) This Deed is supplemental to the trust (the **'Trust'**) specified in the First Schedule.

(B) The statutory power of appointment applies to the Trust and is exercisable by the Retiring Trustees.

(C) The Retiring Trustees are the present trustees of the Trust.

(D) The Retiring Trustees wish to appoint the New Trustees as trustees of the Trust in place of the Retiring Trustees.

(E) It is intended that the property now in the Trust, details of which are set out in the Second Schedule, shall be transferred to, or under the control of, the New Trustees.

OPERATIVE PROVISIONS

Appointment and retirement of trustees

In exercise of the power of appointment conferred by the Trustee Act 1925 and of all other powers (if any), the Retiring Trustees hereby appoint the New Trustees as trustees of the Trust in place of the Retiring Trustees who hereby retire and are discharged from the provisions of the Trust.

Declaration as to residence

It is hereby declared that, at the date hereof, there is no proposal that the trustees of the Trust might become neither resident nor ordinarily resident in the United Kingdom.

FIRST SCHEDULE

Date	Document or Event creating the Trust	Parties

SECOND SCHEDULE

[details of property contained within the trust]

Signed as a deed and delivered   )

by [   ]   )

in the presence of:)

Witness

Signature:

Name:

Address:

Occupation:

Removal of a trustee

A trustee may also be prevented from acting for other reasons. Section 36(1) of the Trustee Act 1925 states that a new trustee may be appointed where the existing trustee has been:

(a) out of the country for a continuous period of more than 12 months; or

(b) found to be unfit or incapable of carrying out the office of trusteeship.

The term 'unfit' in this context means that the trustee has either been convicted of a crime of dishonesty or has been made bankrupt. 'Incapable' means that the trustee is no longer able to act because of some mental or physical incapacity. It should be noted that a trustee who is a minor may also be replaced under this section.

Appointment of additional trustees

If the trustees or other nominated persons wish to appoint additional trustees they can use section 36(6) of the Act to do so, provided the appointment would not bring the total number of trustees beyond four. Appointment under section 36 must be in writing.

Law in action Heather Mills's fight over Stella McCartney's trustee appointment

It would appear that the highly controversial divorce settlement of Paul McCartney and Heather Mills in spring of 2008 was not the last of their legal wrangling.

According to the press, another bone of contention between the couple sprang from Paul's decision to appoint his eldest daughter, Stella McCartney, onto the board of trustees which takes care of the financial assets of Paul and Heather's daughter, Beatrice (now aged seven). Heather was very much against the idea, having never seen eye to eye with fashion designer Stella.

Heather is reported to have fought frequently with Stella during Heather's four-year marriage to former Beatle, Paul, and is said to have told her ex-husband that she would oppose any role given to Stella in Beatrice's life – in court, if she had to. From a legal standpoint she has little say in the matter, however.

On the other hand, as the settlor of the trust fund and chairman of the board of trustees, Paul's word is rule. An unverified source reported that Paul wanted to make the appointment to have someone represent his views should anything happen to him before Beatrice's 18th birthday.

Heather received a significant lump sum in the notoriously acrimonious divorce, in addition to a yearly child support payment of around £2.5 million until Beatrice turns 18.

[*Sources*: http://fametastic.co.uk/archive/20080224/9953/heather-mills-to-fight-over-stella-mccartney-trustee-appointment/; http://www.timesonline.co.uk/tol/news/uk/article3575582.ece. (Please note that this feature is intended for illustrative purposes only and is in no way authoritative on matters of law. Any references included in it should not therefore be used as a basis for serious legal research.)]

Ability of the court to appoint or remove trustees

The court can appoint or remove trustees under the power given to it by section 41 of the Trustee Act 1925. The County Court has jurisdiction where the value of the trust fund is up to £30,000, and thereafter the High Court has jurisdiction to act. The wording of section 41 states that the court may appoint new trustees in addition to, or in substitution for, the existing trustees, 'where it is expedient to do so and it is inexpedient, difficult or impracticable to do so without the assistance of the court'. This means that, essentially, the court may be used as a point of last resort to remove and replace trustees where the remaining trustees are unable to resolve the matter between them. This would be most useful where it was necessary to remove a trustee against his or her will (an eventuality sections 36 and 39 of the Trustee Act 1925 do not provide for). Hence, the discretion will be most often used where a trustee is guilty of misconduct of the trust, or if for any reason the trust will otherwise not be able to function properly if the trustee

> the court may be used as a point of last resort to remove and replace trustees

remains in office. An example of this can be seen in the case of *Letterstedt* v. *Broers* (1884) 9 App Cas 371, which concerned the will of a Mr Jacob Letterstedt who resided in Cape Town, South Africa. One of the beneficiaries under the will claimed that there had been misconduct by the trustees and said he wanted them to be removed on the basis that they were unfit to act on behalf of the trust. The allegations were never substantiated but there was a complete breakdown of confidence between the trustees and the beneficiaries as a result of the claims. The matter went to court and the **Privy Council** decided to remove the trustees on the basis that the best interests of the beneficiaries could not continue to be met in the light of the evident hostility between the parties.

Case Summary

The court also has an inherent jurisdiction to permit a trustee to retire, although this is rarely used.

Table 9.1 overleaf serves to recap the statutory provisions available to assist trustees in the appointment and retirement of trustees to a trust.

Appointment and removal by beneficiaries

Traditionally the position was always that beneficiaries had no power either to appoint or remove trustees, unless the trust instrument allowed this. In the case of *Re Brockbank* [1948] Ch 206, Joseph Brockbank set up a trust for the benefit of his wife and five children. The trustees were a Mr Ward and a Mr Bates. Mr Ward, with the support of the beneficiaries to the trust, wished to replace both trustees to the trust with a trust corporation, Lloyds Bank Ltd. However, Mr Bates opposed the change. The court held that the beneficiaries had no authority to demand the replacement of the trustees in this way. To allow this would interfere with the trustees' ability to act in the best interests of the trust, regardless of the views of the beneficiaries. The only way in which such a change could therefore be made would be for the trustees to end the trust under the rule in **Saunders v. Vautier** and resettle the trust fund under the care of the trust corporation. However, this could only be done if all the beneficiaries were of full age and capacity.

Case Summary

More recently under the Trusts of Land and Appointment of Trustees Act 1996, the general rule against the appointment of trustees by beneficiaries has been reversed.

Table 9.1 Dealing with the appointment, retirement and removal of trustees

Event	Action	Authority
Death of a trustee	Trustees can appoint replacement trustee(s) subject to a maximum of 4	s.36(6) Trustee Act 1925 ('TA 1925')
Trustee wishes to retire	Retire by deed with consent of other trustees, provided 2 trustees or a trust corporation remain	s.39 TA 1925
Trustee wishes to retire	Request in writing provided a new trustee is appointed in their place	s.36(6) TA 1925
Trustee is made bankrupt	Trustees can remove provided a replacement is appointed	s.36(1) TA 1925
Trustee can no longer act due to illness	Trustees can remove provided a replacement is appointed	s.36(1) TA 1925
Trustee is out of the country for more than 12 months	Trustees can remove provided a replacement is appointed	s.36(1) TA 1925
Trustee is under 18	Trustees can remove provided a replacement is appointed	s.36(1) TA 1925
Appointment of additional trustees	In writing provided the total number of trustees does not go beyond 4	s.36(6) TA 1925
Removal or appointment of a trustee in any other circumstances	Court can appoint or remove wherever expedient	s.41 TA 1925

Under sections 19(2) and (3) of the Act, beneficiaries are now able either to appoint additional trustees to the trust or to direct trustees to retire from the trust, provided that there will be at least two individual trustees or a trust corporation remaining and *either* a new trustee is appointed in their place *or* the continuing trustees consent to their retirement.

There are a number of provisos. In order to take such action, the beneficiaries must be of full age and capacity and absolutely entitled to the trust property, and must act unanimously (section 19(1)(b)). In this way, the provision mirrors the ability of beneficiaries to make the same changes under the rule in *Saunders* v. *Vautier*, but without the need to end the existing trust and set up a new one. The beneficiaries must also make 'reasonable arrangements' for the protection of any rights the trustee had in relation to the trust (section 19(3)(b)).

The new rules apply to all trusts, whenever created, but the settlor can exclude them, either by making specific provision for this in the trust instrument under section 21(5) or by nominating a person in the trust instrument for the purpose of appointing new trustees under section 19(1)(a). In the case of pre-Act trusts, the settlor can also execute a deed excluding any of these provisions under section 21(6)–(8).

Reflective practice

Take a look at Table 9.1. Did you find this easy to follow? What do you think about the statutory powers given to trustees to appoint and remove? What are the inconsistencies? What improvement (if any) would you make to the current provisions?

You be the judge

Q: Under section 19, do you think beneficiaries under a **discretionary trust** have the power to add or remove a trustee?

A: No (although they can resettle the trust on different terms under the rule in *Saunders* v. *Vautier*).
You will remember from the explanation given in Chapter 1 that the trustees under a discretionary trust have the final say over who will benefit under the terms of the trust and in what shares. Thus, the beneficiaries under a discretionary trust do not have any right to claim any portion of the trust fund until the trustees have made the decision to give the fund (or a part of it) to them. This means that the beneficiaries under a discretionary trust are not absolutely entitled to the trust property and thus cannot benefit from section 19. In fact, discretionary **objects** (that is, beneficiaries) are specifically excluded from the provisions of section 19 under section 22(1) of the Act.

What if nobody is willing to act?

One final point to note in this chapter is what occurs when there is no one either willing or available to act as a trustee in the administration of the trust fund.

Disclaimer

Just because someone is appointed trustee by the settlor, this does not mean they have to take up the position, of course. The person named as a trustee in the trust deed is free to '**disclaim**' their trusteeship at any time before accepting the post. This is usually done by deed; however it could be done orally or simply inferred from the conduct of the named person in certain instances. In the case of *Re Clout and Frewer's Contract* [1924] 2 Ch 230, a man left his estate in trust for his wife, Emma, naming her and two gentlemen, Mr Honton and Mr Crick, as his executors. The wife applied for a grant of probate and administered the trust in accordance with the terms of the will, Mr Honton and Mr Crick doing nothing to assist. Some thirty years later, on the wife's death, the question arose

Case
Summary

as to whether Mr Crick could be replaced as a trustee (Mr Honton had also died). The court held that Mr Crick had, by his inaction, disclaimed his trusteeship and that therefore is was possible to replace him.

When a trustee disclaims they are considered never to have been a trustee and so it is not possible to disclaim after they have taken up their position. In this case, therefore, the trustee in question would need to take steps to retire from the trust.

Disclaimer is final and a named trustee who has disclaimed their position is not able later to demand reinstatement as a trustee. In the case of *Holder* v. *Holder* [1968] Ch 353, a farmer, Frank Holder, left his estate by will. He appointed as **executors** his wife, daughter Barbara, and son Victor. When Frank Holder died, a bank account was set up in the names of all three executors for the payment of the funeral expenses. A year later, however, when the farm property came up for auction, Victor decided to renounce his executorship on the basis that he wished to buy the farm and his position as trustee prevented him from doing so. The courts held, however, that he was unable to disclaim his trusteeship as he had already acted as an executor in the administration of the estate. He was therefore unable to buy the land.

The Charity Commission is trying to encourage more people to take up the role of trustee on the board of charitable trusts. To get a feel for this, why not try the exercise outlined in the Out and about feature.

Out and about

Take a look at the appointments section of any national newspaper. How many advertisements can you find for trustee appointments? What do you think of them? Do they make you want to become a trustee? If not, how would you change them?

Now try writing your own advertisement to appoint a charity trustee. Don't forget to make it punchy!

This task should take no more than 30 minutes.

 Handy tip: If you do not have access to a national newspaper at home, try looking at the appointments section online.

If there really is no one available to administer the trust, whatever the reason might be for this, the courts have statutory powers to step in and appoint either the **Public Trustee** or a **judicial trustee** to act on behalf of the trust. The Public Trustee is an office established under section 1 of the Public Trustee Act 1906 and their official role is to administer any private trusts where there is no one else available to act in the capacity of trustee. Judicial trustees are usually appointed where the existing trustees have administered the trust poorly and the courts are forced to step in. They have all the usual powers of trustees but in their capacity as officers of the court are also able to seek the court's directions as to how best to administer the trust. Their appointment is authorised under the Judicial Trustees Act 1896.

> Judicial trustees are usually appointed where the existing trustees have administered the trust poorly

The court may also, under certain circumstances, act as a trustee itself where this is required on a particular matter, although they would not do so on an ongoing basis.

Summary

- Any person who can hold property can be a trustee.

- There is no minimum or maximum number of trustees in the case of personal property, but there can be no more than four trustees of land (section 34(2) Trustee Act 1925).

- The first trustees will usually be appointed by the settlor. After this, if the settlor has not made specific provision for the appointment of new trustees in the trust instrument, the appointment and removal of further trustees will be governed by statute.

- Section 36(1) of the Trustee Act 1925 allows trustees to be appointed to replace those who have become unable or unwilling to act by virtue of their death or other incapacity.

- Section 36(6) of the Trustee Act 1925 allows for the appointment of additional trustees, provided that the total number of trustees will not be more than four after the appointment.

- Trustees can retire under the provisions of section 36(1), provided someone is appointed to replace them. Alternatively, trustees can retire by deed

under section 39 of the Trustee Act 1925, with the consent of the other trustees, if there will be two trustees remaining after their retirement.

- The court has the authority to appoint or remove trustees under section 41 of the Trustee Act 1925. It also has an inherent jurisdiction to permit trustees to retire.

- As a general rule, beneficiaries cannot have trustees appointed or removed. However, under section 19 of the Trusts of Land and Appointment of Trustees Act 1996, they may do so, provided they are acting unanimously and provision is made to protect any rights the retiring trustees may have under the trust.

- Beneficiaries who are all of age and have the required mental capacity may nevertheless choose to bring an end to the trust under the rule in *Saunders* v. *Vautier*, and set up a new trust on new terms and with new trustees.

- If there is no one available or willing to act, the court may, as a last resort, appoint the Public Trustee or a judicial trustee to administer the trust fund.

Question and answer*

Problem: Aunt Annie died leaving her substantial fortune, including a large country estate in Shropshire, to her infant nieces and nephew, Annabelle (aged 3), Chloe (aged 5) and Tarquin (aged 7). She appointed as the executors and trustees of her will her brother James (the children's father), together with her elder brother Hamish and her youngest sister Yvette. Unfortunately, Hamish and James have never seen eye to eye, having fallen out over a mutual love interest some years ago (whom Hamish has since married and divorced). In addition, James's struggling event management business has finally gone under, leaving James threatened with bankruptcy. Yvette suffers from a nervous disorder and is less than reliable.

The children's mother, Maggie, is concerned that with all the infighting her children's best interests are not being protected. She has tried to speak to James about it but they are recently estranged and the relationship is somewhat strained. Maggie has also asked Hamish to step down from his position as trustee but he refuses to do so, saying that Annie would have wanted him to be involved. She has been unable to contact Yvette. Advise Maggie on the best course of action.

You should allow yourself no more than 40 minutes to complete this task.

Essay:

Trustees are the keepers of a charity's soul.

(Tom Levitt, MP)

What do you think the minister meant by this? Give a critical analysis of the role of a trustee in light of this statement.

This question should be answered in 30 minutes.

✱ Answer guidance is provided at the end of the chapter.

Further reading

Barlow, F. (2003) 'The appointment of trustees: a disappointing decision', Conv 15.
This article gives a case commentary on the recent decision in *Adam & Co. International Trustees Ltd* v. *Theodore Goddard (a firm)* [2000] WTLR 249, together with a very useful critique of the current statutory provisions on the appointment and removal of trustees. A very helpful summary of the law in this area.

Bell, C. (1988) 'Some reflections on choosing trustees', *Trust Law & Practice*, 2(3), 86–8.
More interesting reading on considerations to make when appointing trustees. Useful to read in conjunction with the Writing and drafting task, earlier in the chapter.

Keppel-Palmer, M. (1996) 'Discretion no more?', 146 NLJ 1779.
This article highlights potential problems arising from section 19 of the Trusts of Land and

Appointment of Trustees Act 1996, which gives more power to beneficiaries to appoint new trustees.

Kirkland, K. (2002) 'Recruiting, selecting and inducting charity trustees', *Private Client Business*, 4, 253.
An interesting article incorporating the results of surveys on the appointment of trustees onto the boards of charities, with suggestions for improvement in the recruitment process.

Website

http://www.trusteenet.org.uk
This website is well worth a look at. It contains some really useful resources and articles including information on the duties and responsibilities of trustees, recruitment of trustees and a whole host of other matters.

Question and answer guidance

Problem:

Maggie has no interest in the trust herself, other than a personal interest as the children's mother. She does not have any authority to require changes in the trust (unless the terms of the trust specify this, but we are not told that this is the case). The children are all under the age of 18 and so have no authority to make changes under section 19 of the Trusts of Land and Appointment of Trustees Act 1996 either.

It may be that, if Hamish will not step down, the infighting would stop if James was no longer a trustee of the trust. If he is made bankrupt, he can be removed by the other trustees under section 36(1) of the Trustee Act 1925, on the basis that he is 'unfit' to continue in his position as a trustee. However, a new trustee must be appointed in his place when removing him under this provision. From a practical viewpoint, James's removal from the trust would mean that neither parent was acting as trustee for their children's fund. Perhaps Maggie should volunteer to be appointed in his place.

If Yvette is mentally incapable she can also be removed as a trustee under section 36(1), provided that she is replaced by a new trustee. It should be noted that this provision allows for the replacement of trustees by the other trustees; therefore Maggie would need to get Hamish on board (as Maggie is not a trustee herself) to execute either of these replacements.

The court has the ability to do this under section 41 Trustee Act 1925, wherever 'it is expedient to do so and it is inexpedient, difficult or impracticable to do so without the assistance of the court'. In particular, it can remove a trustee against their will, which the other statutory provisions do not account for. This may be particularly useful in the case of Hamish, who has refused to stand down from the trust (assuming Maggie still wishes to see his removal in the event of James's retirement). However, it will have to be proved that Hamish is not fit to stand as a trustee before the court will remove him. Compare and contrast with the case of *Letterstedt* v. *Broers*, under which one of the beneficiaries claimed misconduct by the trustees. In *Letterstedt* there was a complete breakdown of confidence between the trustees and the beneficiaries as a result of the claims and the Privy Council decided to remove the trustees on the basis that the best interests of the beneficiaries could not continue to be met in the light of the evident hostility between the parties. Could this be the case here, given Maggie's concern over the siblings' infighting and her concern that the interests of the beneficiaries were not being served because of this?

Essay:
The question requires a discussion on what it means to be a trustee and the importance of the role. A good answer will talk about who trustees are and how important it is to have good trustees in the light of their position as guardians of the trust property and the interests of the beneficiaries.

The quote is actually taken from a parliamentary debate, and it would be worth taking a look at this to gain an insight into Mr Levitt's views on the matter. This can be seen at: **http://www.theyworkforyou.com/debates/?id=2010-01-18b.130.0**.

However, there is plenty in the comments of Sam de Silva in the People in the law feature, earlier in the chapter, and in the main body of the chapter, to make sound comment on the role of trustees, albeit in a general fashion given that the duties of trustees are not dealt in detail with until Chapter 10.

One point upon which the student would do well to comment is the use of lay trustees and professional trustees. If trustees are 'the keepers of a charity's soul', is it really the best course of action to hand over the running of the trust to professionals, or would it be better to keep its administration in the hands of individuals who know and care about the beneficiaries and the issues involved on a personal level. Or would a mixture of lay people and professional trustees provide the perfect balance?

Either way, do not forget to conclude your answer to the question by giving your views on Mr Levitt's statement.

Chapter 10
Duties of trustees

Key points In this chapter we will be looking at:

✦ The duties of trustees on appointment

✦ What is a fiduciary and what are fiduciary duties?

✦ A trustee's duty to act in the best interests of the beneficiaries

✦ The duty of a trustee to act impartially between the beneficiaries

✦ The payment of trustees

✦ 'Secret profits'

✦ Rules against the purchase of trust property by trustees

✦ Other basic duties of trustees

✦ The standard of care required of a trustee

Introduction

In the last chapter we looked at how **trustees** are appointed and the different methods of bringing that trusteeship to an end, whether because the trustees wish to retire from the trust, or because they need to be removed for some reason. Chapter 9 also considered the nature of trusteeship, and this chapter builds on that: considering in more detail the duties of trustees in carrying out their role.

Duties on appointment

So what exactly are the duties of trustees? What is required of trustees once they have been appointed? This may seem a question with an obvious answer: they are required quite simply to look after the **trust**. However, there are a number of restrictions and guidelines detailing how they do so, both statutory and otherwise, and these are what we are now going to consider. First of all, though, why not take a look at the Out and about feature and see if you can think of all the things you need to do on taking up your position as a new trustee of a trust fund or charity.

Out and about

You have been newly appointed as a trustee to the Green Men and Women of Yorkshire Benevolent Fund. You understand your predecessor took his role rather less seriously than both the beneficiaries and the other trustees would have liked and you are determined to do a better job.

Bearing in mind what you have learned about the nature of trusteeship from Chapter 9, try making a list of what immediate action you should take as a new trustee and of the information you will require to acquaint yourself fully with your role. Don't worry if you find it is a short list, you will have the opportunity to revisit it later in the chapter.

You should take no more than 20 minutes on this task.

 Handy tip: This exercise is designed to get you thinking about the practical implications of being a trustee. What would you need to be sure of in order to carry out your role effectively?

So, what action does a new trustee need to take upon appointment? As you may have put in your list, the first thing is to make sure that the property which makes up the **subject matter** of the trust has been properly transferred into the legal ownership of the trustees (and that includes you too, as a new trustee!).

To get the trust property into the trust

Remember, it is the trustees, not the **beneficiaries**, who hold the **legal title** to the trust property. In Chapter 2 we looked at the **formalities** required for transferring the property forming the subject matter of the trust over to the trustees. Bearing this in mind it makes sense then, when a new trust is formed, that it should be one of the first duties of the new trustees to make sure that the trust property is transferred over into the trust in accordance with those formalities. What happens, though, when a new trustee is appointed to an already existing trust, or when a current trustee ceases to act? Is it necessary to repeat all the formalities required when a new trust is created, for example by drafting a **deed** of transfer from the trustee who is ceasing to act into the name of the incoming trustee? The answer to this question is, no, not necessarily. Under section 40 of the Trustee Act 1925 all the property contained in the trust will automatically '**vest**' in (or 'be transferred to') the incoming trustee, provided the appointment of that trustee is made by deed. The same document would also serve to remove any outgoing trustees as legal owners of the property. You have already seen an example deed of retirement and appointment in the Documenting the law feature in Chapter 9.

To have a deed of appointment sounds ideal and, potentially, it can save a lot of work when new trustees are appointed or old ones retire; but there are a number of limitations to the provision.

You be the judge

Q: Due to his increasing work commitments, Jack Bundles decides to retire from the Pendle Heritage Trust. The trustees have a replacement for Jack in the form of Jack's son, Henry, and so they use their power under section 36 of the Trustee Act 1925 to allow Jack to retire and for Henry to be appointed as a new trustee. They draw up a document to this effect, which Henry and Jack both sign.

Will the trust property automatically vest in Henry upon his appointment?

A: No. Automatic vesting happens only on an appointment made by deed. A simple signed document will not be sufficient.

You will remember from Chapter 9, that the appointment of trustees made under section 36 of the Trustee Act 1925 does not have to be made by deed: the section only requires that the appointment be made in writing. Unfortunately, as we have seen in the You be the judge feature, this means that a simple appointment in writing will not, on its own, be sufficient to vest the trust property in the new trustees. Using the example of Henry and Jack, therefore, a separate additional document, in the form of a deed, would need to be drawn up to complete the transfer of legal ownership of the trust property to Henry, and to ensure Jack's removal as an owner of it. The usefulness of section 36 as a method of transferring the trust property is therefore limited, unless the appointment has specifically been made by deed. Having said this, it is easy to get around this problem simply by ensuring that any section 36 appointment is made by deed, and not simply in writing. That way, any property in the trust will automatically vest in the new trustees and the need for an additional transfer document will be removed.

As well as the slight awkwardness caused by the requirements of section 36 of the Trustee Act 1925, there may be additional requirements in any event which need to be fulfilled in order for the trust property to be formally transferred to the new trustees. This means that the simple transfer by deed envisaged by the terms of section 40 will not always be enough to transfer legal ownership in the trust property. For example, shares in limited companies will always have to be transferred formally using a **stock transfer form** and registration at Companies House. This is because of the risk of fraud, and the necessity for Companies House to keep an accurate and up-to-date record of who holds shares in a company at any one time. In addition, property which is mortgaged must be formally transferred by deed. Again, this is to minimise the risk of fraud for the benefit of the lender, who ideally should be kept informed of the parties holding the property which forms the **security** for their lending. Leasehold property containing a restriction in the lease on any transfer without the landlord's permission must, again, be transferred formally to ensure the landlord knows who is in possession of his property. And finally, a further limitation is that a change in ownership of the legal title to **registered land** must be registered at the Land Registry. Thus, a new trustee must go through the additional process of **registration** in order to ensure that they appear on the **register of title** to the trust property. We can see, therefore, that what at first seems a simple solution to the problem of the transfer of ownership of trust property in section 40 is not altogether as helpful as it might at first appear.

> property which is mortgaged must be formally transferred by deed

To familiarise themselves with the trust on appointment

As well as making sure the trust property is properly vested in them on their appointment, a new trustee has a number of other issues to check. The trustee should ideally look through the trust deed and any other documents relating to the trust to make sure they know all about the trust they are going to be looking after. They should also look at any investments which have been made by the trust to ensure these have been made correctly and in the names of all the trustees. Remember, certain types of property require special treatment to transfer them to the new trustees.

Another thing any new trustee should check is that there have been no breaches of trust and that they will not become liable for any breaches that have occurred on taking up their position as trustee. You may be thinking: 'How would a new trustee know what to look for in this respect?' It should be noted, however, that a new trustee will only be liable for such breaches if there are suspicious circumstances surrounding the breach which were evident to the trustee

> a new trustee will only be liable for breaches if there are suspicious circumstances

before they were appointed. Without any such indications a new trustee can assume there have been no breaches of trust; thus, this requirement on new trustees is not unduly onerous or unrealistic. This is illustrated by the case of *Re Strahan* (1856) 8 De GM & G 291, which considered whether a new trustee to a trust should be liable for the breaches of existing trustees who had misapplied the trust fund and subsequently been made bankrupt. It was held that the new trustee should not be liable, even though he had not enquired about the whereabouts of the trust monies on his appointment. There had been nothing to lead to a suspicion that any default had been made by the old trustees. Trustee liability on a breach of trust is discussed in more detail in Chapter 13.

Case Summary

Reflective practice

Now that you know a little more about the duties of trustees on appointment, take another look at your answer to the Out and about feature, above. Did you cover all the issues mentioned here? Is there anything you missed? Can you think of anything else you might do as a new trustee?

What is a fiduciary?

You will often come across the term '**fiduciary**' in the context of trusts; but what exactly is a fiduciary and how is it applicable to trustees? There is no definitive answer to the question of what makes a relationship between two people a fiduciary one, although the Courts have held a fiduciary relationship to exist in many circumstances. One could define the term 'fiduciary relationship' quite simply by saying that it exists wherever either person in that relationship has a duty to act in the best interests of the other; but what is it, exactly, that imposes that duty upon them in the first place?

What we can say is that, as a general rule of thumb, a fiduciary relationship will be created wherever one person puts the other in a position of trust or confidence. This is the accepted general definition of Lord Justice Millett in the case of *Bristol and West Building Society* v. *Mothew* [1998] Ch 1, which concerned an alleged breach of trust by a solicitor.

Case Summary

The solicitor had failed to mention to the building society for which he was acting that his client planned to take out a second charge over the property on which the building society was lending money. Lord Justice Millett said:

> a fiduciary is someone who has undertaken to act for or on behalf of another in a particular manner . . . which gives rise to a relationship of trust and confidence . . . [an] obligation of loyalty . . .

The relationship of trustee and beneficiary is one of the most obvious fiduciary relationships, the trustee being relied upon by the beneficiaries of the trust to manage and administer the trust fund on their behalf and for their benefit. However, the Courts have also commonly held the relationship between a director and his company to be a fiduciary one, as a director is expected to put the company's interests before his own. This also applies to business partners, who have the same fiduciary relationship with each other. In an **agency** agreement, the relationship of **principal** and **agent** also imposes fiduciary duties on the agent. You will remember that the concept of agency was defined and compared with the concept of the trust in Chapter 1.

The list is by no means exhaustive and fiduciary relationships can arise in almost any situation. Take the example of Naveen, who enters into an agreement with contractor Jerry to build a swimming pool for him. Naveen has never owned or built a swimming pool before and is ignorant of what is required to create one. He is therefore reliant on Jerry, who is a specialist in the field and who has 25 years' experience in building swimming pools, to act in his best interests. Naveen's inexperience, coupled with Jerry's years of experience and specialism, would be enough to create a fiduciary relationship.

Case Summary

In the Court of Appeal case of *Re Coomber* [1911] 1 Ch 723, which concerned a claim by a son that a fiduciary relationship existed between him and his mother (both worked together in the father's business), Mr Justice Fletcher Moulton said:

> Fiduciary relations are of many different types; they extend from the relation of myself to an errand boy who is bound to bring me back my change up to the most intimate and confidential relations which can possibly exist between one party and another where one is wholly in the hands of another because of his infinite trust in him. All these are cases of fiduciary relation, and the Courts have again and again, in cases where there has been a fiduciary relation, interfered and **set aside** acts which, between persons in a wholly independent position, would have been perfectly valid.

On the facts of the case, the son's claim was denied. The mother's relationship with the son was one of natural love and affection, and not a fiduciary one. Perhaps the most important point to take from Mr Justice Fletcher Moulton's judgment is that the acts or omissions which may create a fiduciary relationship will quite often be very simple ones, made without any formality. This is particularly well illustrated by the imposition of the **Quistclose trust**, which we looked at in Chapter 1. In this case (*Barclays Bank* v. *Quistclose Investments* [1970] AC 567) you may remember that a loan, which would usually be classed as a simple 'arm's length' business transaction (that is, a transaction between two unconnected parties), was deemed sufficient by the House of Lords to create a fiduciary relationship between the parties, because the loan was given for a specific purpose.

Fiduciary duties

Any person who finds themselves in a fiduciary position will, as a matter of course, have certain duties imposed upon them. These fiduciary duties flow from or are the embodiment, if you like, of the general principle that fiduciaries should always act in the best interests of the person they are bound to protect. This means that the fiduciary should do nothing which puts their own personal interests in the matter first; nor should they receive any personal benefit from the relationship. This general fiduciary duty can be broken down into a number of elements, and these will be discussed in turn throughout the remainder of the chapter. Note that for the purposes of equity and trusts it is the fiduciary relationship of trustee and beneficiary which is the focus of our primary interest. For the remainder of this chapter we will therefore refer to the fiduciary as the trustee and the person in reliance as the beneficiary.

Acting in the best interests of the beneficiaries

It is the duty of the trustees acting on behalf of a trust to act in the best interests of their beneficiaries in any matter relating to it, even if this means acting to the trustees' own detriment. Failure to put the beneficiaries first in this way would result in a breach of the trustees' fiduciary duties and consequently would be viewed as a breach of trust.

A famous example of this is the highly controversial case of *Cowan* v. *Scargill* [1985] Ch 270, which was held against the backdrop of the 1984 miners' strike. The bitter feud between the miners and the government-run National Coal Board followed the announcement of the Coal Board that they intended to close 20 coal mines, meaning the loss of 20,000 jobs and the primary source of employment for many communities in the north of England, Scotland and Wales. The case itself concerned the pension trust fund set up by the National Union of Mineworkers. Five trustees of the fund had tried to further the interests of the coal mining industry in England and Wales by influencing the investment of the trust fund, estimated at the time to be valued at the staggering figure of some £200 million. The trustees had refused to give their approval to the investment plan for the fund, unless new foreign investment was capped, existing foreign investment withdrawn wherever expedient and investment into competing fuel industries vetoed altogether.

The trustees' plan was thwarted, however. It was found by the court that the trustees' agenda was altogether political and not in the best interests of the beneficiaries of the trust, who consisted of retired miners and the families of ex-miners, none of whom were currently engaged in mining. The five trustees were therefore held to be in breach of their fiduciary duty to act in the best interests of their beneficiaries. In judging the case, Vice-Chancellor Megarry said:

> In considering what investments to make trustees must put on one side their own personal interests and views. Trustees may have strongly held social or political views. They may be firmly opposed to any investment in South Africa or other countries, or they may object to any form of investment in companies concerned with alcohol, tobacco, armaments or many other things. In the conduct of their own affairs, of course, they are free to abstain from making any such investments. Yet under a trust, if investments of this type would be more beneficial to the beneficiaries than other investments, the trustees must not refrain from making the investments by reason of the views that they hold.

It should be noted that, whereas the best interests of the beneficiaries under a trust will usually be their best financial interests, this is not always the case. In *Harries and Others* v. *Church Commissioners for England and Another* [1992] 1 WLR 1241, Vice-Chancellor Nicholls considered the question of whether the trustees of church funds could exclude certain types of investments from their portfolio for moral or ethical reasons. In this case the Bishop of Oxford, who was one of the trustees for the Church Commissioners for

Case Summary

Case Summary

England, claimed that the church should not be making investments in companies whose activities were incompatible with the aim of promoting the Christian faith, even if this meant producing a lower financial return for the trust. The bishop's claim failed.

However, Vice-Chancellor Nicholls conceded that there could be cases where the investment policy of a trust might well need to be tempered if investment in certain companies, products or activities would result in:

1. loss of sponsorship (in the case of charities); or

2. the refusal by the beneficiaries to accept benefits from that trust for moral or ethical reasons; or

3. there being a clear conflict between the investment policy and the purpose of the trust (such as in the case of *Harries* v. *Church Commissioners* itself).

Nevertheless, the Vice-Chancellor stressed that trustees must be careful to ensure that a policy abstaining from certain types of investment did not in turn create significant financial risk to the trust. However, it should be noted that if the trust instrument specifically allows for, or contemplates, ethical investments then these will be permitted.

Acting impartially between the beneficiaries

As well as acting in the best interests of the beneficiaries, trustees also have a duty to act impartially between the beneficiaries. A classic example of this would be where the trustees would have to weigh up the competing interests of, say, a **life tenant** and a beneficiary with an interest in **remainder**, in respect of their duties to distribute or accumulate trust funds. This is something we will touch upon again in Chapter 11 on **maintenance** and **advancement**. However, in the meantime, a better understanding of the concept could be gained by reference to an example. Imagine that a **testator** leaves in his will £100,000 on trust to his wife for life, and then to his daughter on the wife's death. The trustees will have a duty to balance the needs of the wife, who will want to receive a good income from the trust fund during her lifetime, with the needs of the daughter, who will wish to ensure that the **capital** sum comprised in the fund (that is, the £100,000) is maintained. It should be noted that in the case of *Nestlé* v. *National Westminster Bank* [1993] 1 WLR 1260, which concerned a claim against a bank who were acting as the trustees of a family trust, the court stated **obiter** (that is, as an aside) that if the life tenant (our wife, in this example), is known to the **settlor** (or, as in our case, the testator) then the trustees can pay more attention to income-producing investments (thus benefiting the wife) rather than investments which provide capital growth for the benefit of the ultimate beneficiary (in our case, the daughter). Investments are dealt with in more detail in Chapter 12.

Case Summary

The rule in *Keech* v. *Sandford*

Case Summary

This very specific rule concerns the renewal of leases. In the case of *Keech* v. *Sandford* (1726) Sel Cas Ch 61, a lease of a market stall was left on trust under the terms of a will for the benefit of a child. Before the lease expired the trustee applied for the lease to be renewed on behalf of the trust, but was refused, the landlord saying that he would only renew the lease if the trustee held the lease in his own name. The trustee therefore reapplied for, and was granted, a renewal of the lease for his own benefit but the Court subsequently ruled that the trustee nevertheless held the lease on the child's behalf and therefore that he was liable to account to the trust for all the profits made on it. It may seem a harsh outcome that a trustee cannot be permitted to take the benefit of the lease when the beneficiary would not have been allowed to renew that same lease in any event. However, the rule is intended to prevent a possible conflict of interests on the part of the trustee on the basis that if a trustee felt he might be able to renew a lease for himself he might not do his best for the trust.

The outcome in **Keech v. Sandford** can be contrasted with the facts of the later case of *Re Biss* [1903] 2 Ch 40 CA. In this case a man had the lease of a business, in which he employed his wife and son. The man died and his wife was appointed as the **administrator** of his **estate**. The lease came up for renewal and the person who owned the **freehold** of the property granted the lease to the son alone. The mother claimed that under the rule in *Keech* v. *Sandford* the son now held the lease on trust for her and himself jointly. The Court of Appeal disagreed, however. The son was not in a fiduciary position to the mother and did not owe her any duty of trust and confidence. Therefore the rule in *Keech* v. *Sandford* did not apply. Had the lease been taken by the mother, on the other hand, the rule in *Keech* v. *Sandford* would have applied, on the basis that she was acting as the administrator of the father's estate and therefore in a fiduciary position to the son as a beneficiary of it.

The rule in *Keech* v. *Sandford* applied in a more modern context can be seen in the case of *Protheroe* v. *Protheroe* [1968] 1 WLR 519. The lease in this case was of the matrimonial home which the husband held on a lease for the benefit of him and his wife. After the couple separated the husband was offered the opportunity to purchase the freehold of the house. The wife claimed that the freehold should be held upon the same trusts as the lease had been; however the husband claimed that the wife's interest applied only to the lease. Lord Denning, Master of the Rolls, said:

> although the house was in the husband's name, he was a trustee of it for both. It was a family asset which the husband and wife owned in equal shares. Being a trustee, he had an especial advantage in getting the freehold. There is a long established rule of equity from *Keech* v. *Sandford* downwards that if a trustee, who owns the **leasehold**, gets in the freehold, that freehold belongs to the trust and he cannot take the property for himself.

The husband was therefore held by the court to be holding the freehold of the property on a **constructive trust** for the benefit of himself and his wife equally.

Payment of trustees

a trustee should not profit financially from their position in any way

As we have seen above, the general rule is that a fiduciary is not allowed to receive any personal benefit from his position. It therefore follows that a trustee should not profit financially from their position in any way. This would naturally include the payment of a fee or wage for their services. The position of an ordinary or **lay trustee** (being someone acting as an individual and not in a professional capacity) is thus usually an unpaid one, albeit a trustee is entitled to make a claim for the reimbursement of their expenses, as long as those expenses have been properly incurred by them in the course of their acting on behalf of the trust. This is a statutory entitlement, under section 31(1) of the Trustee Act 2000. Trustees acting in their professional capacity, such as solicitors or financial advisers (**professional trustees**), are also allowed to be remunerated for their services under certain circumstances: primarily where a **charging clause** entitling the trustees to payment is put in the trust deed by the settlor, but also under statute, as we shall see below.

In the meantime, take a look at the Key stats feature from the charity the Directory of Social Change, which undertook an interesting survey on people's views towards the payment of trustees.

Key stats

In November 2007, the Directory of Social Change ('DSC'), a charity focused on providing information and training to the voluntary sectors, ran a survey aimed at gauging public opinion on whether the position of trustee should come with a wage attached. The DSC posed the following to a total of 932 people:

Source: Imagestate/John Foxx Collection

> **The DSC has long maintained that unpaid trusteeship is a fundamental characteristic of the voluntary sector, and that trustees should not receive remuneration either for their contribution as trustees, or for other services delivered to the charities they govern. Do you agree with us?**

A staggering 82 per cent of the people asked agreed with DSC that trustees should not receive remuneration for their services, although a number of those people qualified their answer, dependent on the kind of remuneration on offer. The payment of trustees was divided into three broad categories:

1. paying trustees to be trustees;
2. reimbursing trustees for legitimate expenses;
3. paying trustees for services rendered to the organisation.

The general consensus was that, whilst reimbursing trustees for their legitimate expenses was perfectly in order, paying trustees simply for being trustees was completely unacceptable, regardless of the reasons given for doing so. As to the third category of paying trustees for services rendered, opinion was divided. Here are some of the comments:

For

'There are occasions when it is more economic for smaller charities to pay for the expertise of one of their trustees to complete a discrete piece of work than having to tender for it or pay an outside contractor.'

'Depending on how trustees have been selected some may have skills and unique knowledge which makes them the right person to carry out a particular piece of work as a consultant.'

Against

'Too often we see trustees benefiting from their role, especially those who provide services through their company.'

'It would be wrong for trustees to receive financial or any other kind of reward for services rendered. Dodgy characters would become trustees just to make financial gain.'

'If you want to pay for advice, get a consultant!'

For full details of the survey, go to: **http://www.dsc.org.uk/NewsandInformation/PolicyandCampaigning/Policypositions/Paymentoftrustees**.

So, as we have seen, the general position is that trustees are not allowed to be paid for their services. The court does nevertheless have an **inherent jurisdiction** to authorise the payment of trustees for services carried out by them, which applies not only to payment for services already rendered but also for the carrying out of future services on behalf of the trust. Thus, in *Re Duke of Norfolk's Settlement Trusts* [1981] 3 WLR 455 the court awarded both:

Case Summary

1. payment for work undertaken by the trustees which went beyond the scope of their duties; and
2. an increase in the general level of payment to which the professional trustees were entitled under the charging clauses which entitled them to payment under the terms of the trust deed.

The work which had already been undertaken by the trustees was a scheme of redevelopment carried out to some property which the trust owned in London. The court found in that instance that the work involved in carrying out the redevelopment was mainly beyond the scope of the trustees' duties; however, they rejected an additional £50,000 claim by the trustees for services in rearranging the affairs of the trust so as to minimise its tax liability, on the basis that the trustees were under a duty to review the trust investments regularly in any event.

Under the inherent jurisdiction a further important example is the case of *Gray* v. *Richards Butler* [2001] WTLR 625. In this case the testator's will included a charging clause for the trustee's firm of solicitors. The solicitors charged the sum of £25,000 to administer the estate. However, the will was later declared **void**, due to the witnesses apparently not seeing each other sign the will, which meant that the charging clause contained within the will was also void. It also meant that an earlier will of the testator, which had been drawn up in the 1980s, was valid instead. The relevant beneficiary claimed successfully the return of the £25,000 on the grounds of the invalid charging clause in the later will, but the court nevertheless made an award of payment to the solicitors under its inherent jurisdiction. This was based on what the solicitors would have charged had they administered the earlier will, rather than the actual work they did under a void document.

Case Summary

In addition to the inherent jurisdiction of the courts to pay trustees, the Trustee Act 2000 has also made a recent change to the law to allow trustees acting in their professional capacity to be paid for their services (under sections 28 to 33). This means that, unless the trust deed specifically disallows this, professional trustees acting in the course of their business now have a right to receive payment for work carried out on the trust. It is interesting to note that under the Act it is irrelevant that a lay trustee would be capable of providing the services for which the professional trustee has charged. The provisions of the Act mean that professional trustees are no longer reliant on the settlor or testator putting a charging clause in the trust instrument to allow them to receive payment. The provisions of the act are retrospective, which means that professional trustees can make a claim for payment of their costs regardless of whether the trust was created before or after the Act came into force. It should be noted that non-professional or lay trustees are still subject to the old rules, however, and so will have to apply to the court if they want to be paid for any work they carry out.

Despite the changes made by the Trustee Act 2000, many people are still very much against the payment of trustees, in any capacity. In the People in the law feature, Ben Wittenberg, from the charity Directory of Social Change, gives his views on the ability of charities to pay their trustees.

People in the law

Source: Ben Wittenberg (*text and photo*)

Name and position: Ben Wittenberg, Director of Policy & Research, Directory of Social Change.

So, Ben, what is the Charity Commission's position on the payment of charity trustees? The Commission's *Guidance on Payment of Trustees* (CC11) states that trustees cannot receive any benefit from their charity in return for any service they provide to it unless they have express legal authority to do so. 'Benefit' includes any property, goods, or services which have a monetary value, as well as money.

And how does this differ from the DSC's position? It is our belief that trustees of charities should not be paid, either for their trusteeship or for the commercial services they provide to their charities outside of that role.

Why not? It is a matter of principle, really. We believe that paying trustees erodes one of the fundamental characteristics of the sector, and also calls into question the objectivity (and legality) of those governing with a financial interest. There are also some considerable practical impacts that the payment of trustees would have; it would increase problems of trustee recruitment for those that could not afford to pay, while adding to the core costs of those that could.

Are there no benefits to the payment of trustees? There are a number of arguments in favour of paying trustees for the fulfilment of their trusteeship: recruitment, lack of diversity, lack of appraisals and standards of governance are often cited as solvable through payment.

Would these benefits not outweigh the more negative issues? No. Even if governance is improved as a result, even if recruitment and diversity issues are addressed, and ignoring the significant principled objections, the financial impact on the sector would be devastating. For starters, of the 190,000 registered charities, half of them would have to increase their income by 30 per cent or more in order to offer that level of payment to their board members. Raising money for core costs is not an easy job at the best of times, but across the whole sector the amount of additional money required would be in the region of £450 million.

And the outcome of such payments continuing to be made? It will create a financial crisis in which the largest charities are able to offer benefits at the expense of smaller charities' boards. Quite simply, if the number of larger charities paying their trustees continues to increase, the smaller organisations that cannot afford to compete will suffer – and this is a game that no one should be playing.

For those who approve of the changes in the law, the Trustee Act 2000 has been useful in assisting the payment of professional trustees. Many settlors still prefer to set out the provisions as to the payment of professional trustees explicitly in the trust documentation, however. The Documenting the law feature shows an excerpt from the Charity Commission's model trust deed, which contains at Clause 25 a number of suggested options for specific clauses relating to the payment of trustees.

Documenting the law

23. Registered particulars

The Trustees must notify the Commission promptly of any changes to the Charity's entry on the Central Register of Charities.

24. Bank account

Any bank or building society account in which any of the funds of the Charity are deposited must be operated by the Trustees and held in the name of the Charity. Unless the regulations of the Trustees make other provision, all cheques and orders for the payment of money from such an account shall be signed by at least two Trustees.

25. Trustees not to benefit financially from their Trusteeship

Option 1

(i) Unless expressly authorised in writing in advance by the Commission to do so, no Trustee may buy goods or services from the Charity, or sell goods or services to the Charity or receive remuneration, or receive any other financial benefit from the Charity or from any trading company owned by the Charity.

Option 2

(i) (a) Subject to paragraph (b) of sub clause (i) of this clause, no Trustee may receive remuneration for any service provided to the Charity and no Trustee may acquire any interest in property belonging to the Charity or be interested in any contract entered into by the Trustee otherwise than as a Trustee of the Charity unless expressly authorised in writing in advance by the Commission to do so.

(b) Any Trustee who is a solicitor, accountant or engaged in any profession may charge and be paid all the usual professional charges for business done by him or her or his or her firm, when instructed by the other Trustees to act in a professional capacity on behalf of the Charity. However, at no time may a majority of the Trustees benefit under this provision and a Trustee must withdraw from any meeting of the Trustees at which his or her own instruction or remuneration or performance, or that of his or her firm, is under discussion.

Option 3

(i) (a) No Trustee may buy goods or services from the Charity, or sell goods or services to the Charity, or receive remuneration, or receive any other financial benefit from the Charity or from any trading company owned by the Charity, except in accordance with this deed or with the prior written approval of the Commission and any conditions it prescribes.

Notes

(b) The Trustees may employ, or enter into a contract for the supply of goods or services with, one of their number. Before doing so, the Trustees must be satisfied that it is in the best interests of the Charity to employ, or contract with, that Trustee rather than someone who has no connection with the Charity. In reaching that decision, they must balance the advantage of employing a Trustee against the disadvantages of doing so (especially the loss of the Trustee's services as a result of dealing with the Trustee's conflict of interest as required by the next sub-clause). The remuneration or other sums paid to the Trustee must not exceed an amount that is reasonable in all the circumstances. The Trustees must record the reason for their decision in their minute book.

(c) A Trustee must be absent from the part of any meeting at which his or her employment or remuneration, or any matter concerning the contract, are discussed. He or she must also be absent from the part of any meeting at which his or her performance in that employment, or his or her performance of the contract, is considered. He or she must not vote on any matter relating to his employment or the contract and must not be counted when calculating whether a quorum of Trustees is present at the meeting.

(d) At no time may a majority of the Trustees benefit under this provision.

(ii) This clause applies to a firm or company of which a Trustee is:

(a) a partner;

(b) an employee;

(c) a consultant;

(d) a director; or

(e) a shareholder, unless the shares of the company are listed on a recognised stock exchange and the Trustee holds less than 1% of the issued capital, as it applies to a Trustee personally.

(iii) In this clause:

(a) "Charity" shall include any company in which the Charity:

• holds more than 50% of the shares; or

• controls more than 50% of the voting rights attached to the shares; or

• has the right to appoint one or more directors to the Board of the company.

(b) "Trustee" shall include any child, parent, grandchild, grandparent, brother, sister or spouse of the Trustee or any person living with the Trustee as his or her partner.

November 2007

Source: http://www.charity-commission.gov.uk/Library/guidance/gd2text.pdf

Secret profits

In the same way that a trustee must not receive any payment or fees for work carried out on behalf of the trust, a trustee must also not receive any other form of profit from it unless this has been authorised by either the trust deed, the beneficiaries (provided they are of age) or the court. To do so otherwise would be classed as making a '**secret profit**' out of the trust, and would be in breach of the trustee's fiduciary duties. A trustee may profit from a trust in a number of different ways. We are only going to consider the more important ones in this chapter.

Directors' fees

If the trust comprises a large shareholding in a company, the trust may decide to appoint one of the trustees as a director of the company in order to better protect the interests of the trust. Any trustee who becomes a director, however, must do so in the knowledge that any fees received by them for acting in their capacity as a director of the company will be subject to the usual rule that a trustee must not profit from his trust and will therefore have to be surrendered to the trust for the use and benefit of the trust fund.

This is subject to certain exceptions, as follows:

1. Where the trust deed authorises the trustee to keep them (*Re Llewellin's Will Trusts* [1949] Ch 225).

2. Where the trustee became a director of the company before becoming a trustee (*Re Dover Coalfield Extension* [1908] 1 Ch 65).

3. Where the trustee secures his directorship by virtue of his own personal shareholding in the company, as opposed to that of the trust (*Re Gee* [1948] Ch 284).

4. Where the court exercises its inherent jurisdiction to permit directors' fees to be kept by the individual director (*Re Keeler's Settlement Trusts* [1981] 1 All ER 888).

Competition

In the same way, if a trustee makes a profit by entering into competition with a business belonging to the trust, he will also be liable to the trust for whatever profit he makes in doing so. This is clearly stated in the case of *Re Thompson* [1930] 1 Ch 203, which concerned an executor who purported to set up a business which directly competed with the business of the trust, which was, in that case, the very specialised business of yacht broking.

The more recent case of *IDC* v. *Cooley* [1972] 1 WLR 443, concerned the director of a firm of architects. Thus the fiduciary duty in question was one between a director and his company, as opposed to that which exists between a trustee and beneficiary of a trust fund. The architect, who had worked on behalf of his firm very closely with the gas board over the years, tried to win a contract with the gas board for the firm's services on a particular project, but was unsuccessful in doing so. Later, however, the gas board contacted him directly and engaged his services on a private basis. The court held that the architect was liable to account to the company for his profits on the contract. This was because, in his capacity as a director, the architect had a duty to obtain such contracts strictly on behalf of the company rather than for himself.

Case
Summary

This finding should be contrasted with the Commonwealth case of *Queensland Mines* v. *Hudson* (1978) 18 ALR 1 in which the company director of a mining company resigned in order to develop mines for which the company was unable to obtain the licences to mine itself. The company director in this case was held not to be liable to the trust for his actions. The difference between these two cases, however, is that the company director of Queensland Mines acted in the full knowledge of the company, and with their consent, whereas the architect had gone behind the backs of his fellow directors in taking up the contract for himself.

Misuse of confidential information

A trustee may not use information acquired in his capacity as trustee for his own personal profit. For example, if a trustee is given the opportunity to purchase land or shares for the benefit of the trust at less than market value, but instead buys that land or shares for himself, he will be required to deliver that property which he has bought at an undervalue over into the hands of the trust, and to account to the trust for any profits he has made in doing the deal.

Case
Navigator

Case
Summary

This was what happened in the case of ***Boardman v. Phipps*** [1967] 2 AC 46. A husband had left his estate on trust for the benefit of his wife for life and then to his children. Part of the trust fund consisted of a large shareholding in a textile company, Lester & Harris Ltd. The trustees were unhappy with the way the shares in Lester & Harris were performing and the trustees' solicitor advised them that if they could buy more shares in the company, it would give them a majority shareholding and the opportunity to control and influence any future decisions of the board of directors. Unfortunately the trustees could not be persuaded to take this course of action as they could not see the benefit in buying yet more shares in an already ailing company; but the solicitor, Mr Boardman, believed this to be the only way to bring profit to the trust fund. He therefore decided to buy the shares in his own name and restructure the company himself.

Mr Boardman's hunch was right and, having bought the required number of shares, he then went on successfully to sell off a number of the company's assets, making a substantial personal profit for himself, as well as a large profit for the trust, who still had a large stake in the company. One of the beneficiaries then claimed that Mr Boardman's personal profits should belong to the trust because he only benefited from the business deal due to the knowledge he had gained as the trust's solicitor. The House of Lords agreed by a majority decision of 3:2, and made Mr Boardman account to the trust for the profit he had made, in doing so taking a '**strict liability**' approach to the breach of trust. In recognition of the skill with which Mr Boardman had carried out the transaction, however, the court also used its inherent jurisdiction to award the solicitor a large fee for his services.

The minority judgment of Lords Upjohn and Dilhorne in *Boardman* v. *Phipps* went against the strict liability approach, stating that the test for misuses of confidential information by directors (or other fiduciaries) should be whether 'a reasonable person would believe that there was a real sensible possibility of conflict'. They were therefore advocating a more lenient approach than the stance taken by the majority of the Lords. However, it is significant that, in *Boardman* v. *Phipps,* the trustees could not have bought the shares on behalf of the trust anyway: the trust did not have the funds, nor did it have the power in its trust instrument to do. The trust would therefore have had to apply to court to vary the trust to allow it to buy the shares, and it is unlikely the court would have granted permission due to the lack of funds. In this particular case, then, there was actually no way in which there could have been a conflict of interest.

Whether the minority approach will be taken up in future cases remains to be seen. In the meantime, it is still the case that the majority decision of the House of Lords stands. This means that, as we have seen, the requirement on a trustee not to profit from the trust remains an extremely strict one. The sometimes rather contrary result of taking such an approach can be seen in the case of *Barrett* v. *Hartley* (1866) LR 2 Eq 789, in which a trustee was made to account to the trust for profits made by him from selling alcoholic drinks to a public house which was owned by the trust, even though the drinks were sold independently through the trustee's own wine merchant's business at his usual rates! Now test your understanding of the principle by taking a look at the Writing and drafting exercise.

Case Summary

Writing and drafting

Take a look at the case of *Guinness plc* v. *Saunders* [1990] 1 All ER 652. Now answer the following questions:

1. Which famous company takeover did this case involve?

2. Who were the judges presiding over the case?

3. How much money was Ward claiming and on what basis?

4. What was the decision of the House of Lords?

5. Name two cases relied upon by Lord Templeman in his judgment.

6. Which fiduciary duty or duties had Ward breached?

7. What happened to the money?

Handy tip: If you find reading the paper judgment a little hard going, try looking at the electronic version on Westlaw UK or LexisNexis UK. In particular, Westlaw has some very useful features on the left-hand side of the page, including a 'case digest', 'cases cited' and references to a number of journal articles discussing the case.

Purchase of trust property by trustees

Another possible source of benefit to trustees is where a trustee purchases property or other interests of the trust. This can be divided into two categories: **self-dealing** and **fair dealing**. We shall consider each of these in turn.

Self-dealing

As a general rule, a trustee will be in breach of trust if they purchase property out of the trust. This rule is often referred to as the 'self-dealing' rule. The rule applies regardless of whether the other trustees or beneficiaries were aware of the purchase. The self-dealing rule is therefore a strict liability offence and breach of it will result in a breach of trust by the purchasing trustee, regardless of their motives

> The self-dealing rule is a strict liability offence

in making the purchase. The rule also applies regardless of the price the trustee has paid for the property, even where the trustee paid the full market price for it. It may seem strange not to allow a trustee to purchase trust property, if everyone knows about it and a fair price is paid; however, the act of self-dealing actually creates a fundamental conflict of interests between the trustee and the trust. The reason for this is that the purchasing trustee would have to act in the transaction both as seller (on behalf of the trust) and buyer (in their own personal capacity). As the seller of the property and a trustee of the fund they would be under a duty to obtain the highest possible price for it; but as the buyer they would want to achieve the lowest price. This would make it almost impossible for them to act impartially and in the best interests of the trust.

Case Summary

A leading modern case on self-dealing is *Kane* v. *Radley Kane* [1999] Ch 274. Here the deceased man, who died **intestate**, left a widow and two sons from a previous marriage. His wife was the administrator of the estate. Under the intestacy rules she was entitled to a statutory **legacy** of £125,000. The estate was comprised primarily of shares worth about £50,000. She therefore kept the shares for herself in part payment of the legacy, thinking that the price of the shares was equivalent to money. The wife sold the shares about two years later for about £1.1 million. The court stated that the shares were not the same as money. The wife had therefore breached the self-dealing rule by purchasing or appropriating trust property for herself. It was therefore held that the wife should hold the profit made from the shares for the benefit of the two sons.

The self-dealing rule is strictly applied and will stand regardless of whether the trustee is purchasing the trust property in their own name, or in that of their spouse or children (these were the facts of the case in *Re Sherman* [1954] Ch 653), or even in the name of a company in which they have a majority shareholding (as in *Re Thompson* [1985] 2 All ER 720). If the trustee owns only a small number of shares in the company buying the trust property, the rule will not apply, however, unless it can be shown that the purchase of the trust property was not carried out in a fair and honest fashion (see *Farrar* v. *Farrars Ltd* (1888) 40 Ch D 395).

The rule against self-dealing will also not apply in the following circumstances:

1. Where the trust deed permits the trustee to purchase trust property (*Sargeant* v. *National Westminster Bank* [1990] EGCS 62).

2. Where the trustee has already entered into a contract to purchase the trust property before becoming a trustee (*Re Mulholland's WT* [1949] 1 All ER 460).

3. Where the trustee had retired from the trust a long time before the purchase takes place (see *Re Boles* [1902] 1 Ch 244, in which the trustee had retired some twelve years before purchasing the property). It should be noted this will not be the case with trustees who have only recently retired. See the **Privy Council** case of *Wright* v. *Morgan* [1926] AC 788, in which the trustee in question had technically retired from the trust in the year of his purchase of the trust property, but had put arrangements in place to purchase the trust property prior to his retirement.

4. Where the trustee has disclaimed the trust or has no active duties to perform in it (*Clark* v. *Clark* (1884) 9 App Cas 733).

The effect of the self-dealing rule is that any purchase of trust property by a trustee is **voidable** at the option of the beneficiaries and can be set aside by the court. This means that, if a trustee is found to have participated in self-dealing and the beneficiaries are unhappy about the purchase, they are entitled to have the property bought by that trustee returned to the trust, in return for the repayment of the purchase price to them out of the trust fund. If, on the other hand, the beneficiaries are happy about the purchase, they can choose to let it stand. However, it should be noted that this does not mean that the trustee is consequently deemed not to have breached the trust; only that the beneficiaries have effectively consented to the breach.

Fair dealing

Fair dealing is different from self-dealing in that it involves the purchase by a trustee not of trust property but of the **beneficial interests** of any of the beneficiaries under the trust. Unlike self-dealing, fair dealing is not a strict liability offence; rather it is open to the beneficiary whose interest has been purchased to prove that the trustee took advantage of his position by not providing full information or by abusing his position in some other way. The case of *Dougan* v. *MacPherson* [1902] AC 197 concerned the purchase of a beneficial interest made by a trustee from his brother, who was a beneficiary under the trust. The evidence in the case showed that the trustee had concealed the true value of the beneficial interest from his brother and the House of Lords set the transaction aside. However, it should be noted that whether the purchase by a trustee of a beneficial interest will stand is very much dependent on the facts of each individual case.

Case Summary

The rule in *Keech* v. *Sandford*

We have already seen how the renewal of a lease in the name of the trustees is not permitted as this would cause a conflict between the interests of the trustees and the interests of the beneficiaries. In the same way it would also breach the rule against a trustee profiting from a trust.

Other basic duties

There are a number of other basic duties of trustees, which can be listed as follows:

To adhere to the terms of the trust

It goes without saying that the trustees have a duty to adhere to the terms of the trust and that any departure from the requirements of the trust deed would result in a breach of trust on the part of the offending trustees. Breaches of trust will be discussed in more detail in Chapter 13.

To act personally

The general rule is that a trustee has a duty to act in their own personal capacity and it is therefore not permitted for a trustee to delegate their responsibilities to others. However, the Trustee Act 2000 does allow delegation under certain circumstances, particularly in the context of investment. Delegation under the Trustee Act 2000 is discussed in detail in Chapter 12.

To act unanimously

Trustees are obliged to act unanimously when exercising their duties and powers under the terms of the trust. It is therefore not possible for trustees to make decisions on behalf of a private trust fund by way of a majority vote. Such a rule may seem like an unnecessary burden on trustees, but in actual fact is exists for the trustees' protection. The case of *Re Flower* (1884) 27 Ch D 592 concerned the sale of trust property by trustees. Some of the trustees lived outside the country and they had consequently not given a receipt for the purchase monies. The court held that this was in breach of trust. Mr Justice Kay said in making his judgment in the case, that the whole point of a rule which prevents action being taken on behalf of the trust without the authority of all the trustees is to ensure that at no point will the trust property find itself in the hands of just one or a few of the trustees. In other words, the rule was there for a good reason: to discourage breaches of trust by leaving trust property unsupervised in the hands of a sole trustee. Having said this, there are clearly circumstances where such a rule would become impractical (such as one of the trustees being out of the country for an extended period, or where there are a large number of trustees). In any event, this potential difficulty is alleviated by the fact that the duty to act unanimously can either be overridden by the settlor putting a clause in the trust deed allowing for a majority vote, should they have the foresight to do so, or otherwise by court order, where necessary.

It should be noted that this limitation does not apply to charitable trusts, which often have a large number of trustees and for whom such a rule could lead to indecision and in the worst cases to the trust being unable to function fully and effectively. This was the outcome in the case of *Wilkinson* v. *Malin* (1832) 149 ER 268, in which the appointment of a schoolmaster by a majority of trustees of a charity was held to be valid, despite the later protestations of the minority.

To maintain the fund

Trustees have an overriding duty to preserve the trust property which, in the case of trust funds comprising cash or cash equivalents, usually means they have to invest it. The investment of trust funds will be considered in depth in Chapter 12.

To distribute the fund

Trustees may be required either to make distributions of income or capital out of the trust fund during the administration of the trust, or they may be required to distribute the whole of the trust fund on its completion and winding up. Whichever situation applies, the trustees are under a duty to distribute the contents of the trust fund (or the appropriate share of it) to the beneficiaries and a failure to do so will constitute a breach of trust.

If the trustees are unsure as to whom the distribution should be made, they should first make enquiries and try to find out themselves. In the case of gifts to a **class of beneficiaries**, the trustees should make enquiries of the family of the settlor or look at relevant records to draw up a list of persons included within the class. This would be relevant where the gift was to cousins of the settlor, for example, or classmates from the settlor's school. Of course, it may not always be possible to obtain a complete picture of who should be included in the list of beneficiaries in this way. Nevertheless, an approach to the court for directions should only be used as a matter of last resort and an unnecessary application to court may result in the trustees being ordered to pay the costs of the application out of their own monies.

There are some helpful measures which can provide assistance to trustees in such circumstances, however. Under section 27 of the Trustee Act 1925, trustees are protected from liability for the incorrect distribution of trust funds provided they have followed the correct requirements for advertising as set out in the Act. Section 27 requires the trustees to advertise in the *London Gazette*, where land or property is included in the fund, in a newspaper local to the area in which the property is situated, and also to place any other advertisements or notices 'as a court would direct in an action for administration'. The advertisements should take the form of a notice to the general public of the trustees' intention to distribute the trust fund, and require any person interested to send to them particulars of their claim. The trustees are then entitled after a period of two months to distribute the trust fund to whoever has come forward (provided, of course, that they are eligible beneficiaries) and they will not be liable for non-distribution to anyone of whom the trustees were not aware.

In the case of a named individual the more likely problem is going to be a difficulty in tracing that person, rather than in confirming their identity. In this instance again an advertisement under section 27 may help to find them. But if the beneficiary does not come forward and cannot otherwise be found the court may make what is known as a '**Benjamin order**'. The Benjamin order is so called because it comes from the 1902 case of *Re Benjamin* 1 Ch 723 in which a testator had left his estate to be divided between such of his children as were living at his death in equal shares. The testator had a large family, including 12 children, one of whom had not been seen in the 10 months prior to his father's death. The court allowed the distribution of the estate to the remaining 11 children in equal shares, on the assumption that the twelfth child was dead. The effect of a Benjamin order is that the trustees are released from any liability to the missing beneficiary who, if they turned up at a later date, would have to look to the remaining beneficiaries for the recuperation of their share.

Case Summary

Law in action

Source: Corel Corporation

A rather poignant example of the use of Benjamin orders is the case of *Re Green's Will Trusts* [1985] 3 All ER 455. Mrs Green had died in 1976 leaving a will in which she left the whole of her estate, worth in the region of £700,000 at the time, to her son. Sadly, Mrs Green's son had been a tail gunner in the Royal Air Force during the Second World War and had not been seen since January 1943, when he had gone out with his squadron on a bombing mission to Berlin. Mrs Green still believed her son to be alive, however, and had specified in the will that her executors should hold the estate on trust until the year 2020, at which time if he had not come forward to claim her estate the money should be applied for charitable purposes. The trustees of the will applied to the court for a Benjamin order and the court granted their application. Mr Justice Nourse said the fact that Mrs Green had believed her son to be alive for all those years should not prevent the order being granted as, on the balance of probabilities, her son had most likely died in action during the bombing raid.

Full details of the case can be read in the transcript at *Re Green's Will Trusts* [1985] 3 All ER 455.

To keep the beneficiaries informed

As you might imagine, the trustees are duty-bound to keep their beneficiaries informed about the state of the trust. For this reason the trustees should keep adequate written records of the day-to-day administration of the trust, which they can then make available to the beneficiaries.

It is interesting to note that the beneficiaries are not entitled to see every single document belonging to the trust. For example, they are not entitled to see the minutes of trustee meetings; nor are they entitled to see any correspondence between the trustees which might provide an explanation for the choices made by the trustees in the exercise of their discretion under the terms of the trust. The reason for this is that if beneficiaries were provided with this information they would be likely to challenge the decisions made by the trustees under their discretion, and this may not be in the interests of the trust.

Case Summary

This issue was considered in the case of *Re Londonderry's Settlement* [1965] Ch 918. The case concerned a family trust created by the 7th Marquess of Londonderry. The trustees decided, quite legitimately, to bring the trust to an end and distribute the trust fund amongst the beneficiaries in accordance with the discretion given to them to do so by the Marquess. The daughter of the Marquess, however, was unhappy with their decision and asked to see the minutes of trustee meetings and all correspondence which had passed between the trustees themselves and between the trustees and their advisers. The decision of the Court of Appeal was that, whilst the daughter was entitled to see the title deeds and any other documents which related to the trust, she was not entitled to see any correspondence or other document which contained confidential information as to the exercise of the trustees' discretion. This was because the court believed that the trouble caused within the family by the disclosure of such documents was likely be out of all proportion to any benefit which the daughter might gain from their inspection.

To produce accounts

The trustees have a duty to keep accounts for the trust and to produce them to the beneficiaries on request. Interestingly, however, whilst the beneficiaries are entitled to inspect the accounts and demand information about them and an explanation of the figures, they are not entitled to demand a copy of the accounts for free and can be expected to be charged a reasonable sum for their production! (See the case of *Re Watson* (1904) 49 Sol Jo 54.)

The standard of care required of trustees

Case Summary

There is a general **common law** duty of care imposed on trustees to exercise reasonable care in the management of the trust and to carry out their duties in a prudent manner. This was set out in the case of *Speight* v. *Gaunt* (1883) 9 App Cas 1, which concerned a trustee under the will of Mr Speight, who was accused of dereliction of his duties as a trustee by delegating his power to invest the trust property to a professional firm of stockbrokers which had been used by the testator during his lifetime. The trustee was held by the court not to be liable under the terms of the trust, Sir George Jessel, Master of the Rolls, stating that:

> a trustee ought to conduct the business of the trust in the same manner that an ordinary prudent man of business would conduct his own . . .

In other words, the general duty is to conduct the affairs of the trust with the same care as you would conduct your own personal business. On the facts of the case, the trustee had acted as any person without knowledge of investments would have done by handing over the investment decisions to a professional. The trustee was therefore not liable for losses to the estate caused by the firm of stockbrokers.

A more rigorous standard of care has now been imposed under section 1 of the Trustee Act 2000 as regards the investment of trust funds, albeit the common law duty of care still applies to trustees in the general conduct of their duties. The duty of care in investment will be discussed in further detail in Chapter 12.

Summary

- With the exception of mortgaged or leasehold property and stocks and shares, all property contained within the trust fund will automatically vest in any new trustees on their appointment, provided that appointment is made by deed (section 40 Trustee Act 1925).

- A fiduciary relationship exists wherever either person in that relationship has a duty to act in the best interests of the other.

- Fiduciaries should always act in the best interests of the person they are bound to protect, which means never putting their own personal interests first and never receiving any personal benefit from the relationship.

- The position of trustee is usually unpaid, although trustees can claim the reimbursement of any properly incurred expenses (section 31(1) Trustee Act 2000).

- The court has an inherent jurisdiction to authorise the payment of trustees for services carried out on behalf of the trust (*Re Duke of Norfolk's Settlement Trusts* [1981] 3 WLR 455).

- The Trustee Act 2000 also allows professional trustees to be paid for their services unless the trust deed specifically disallows this.

- A trustee must not receive any other form of profit from the trust unless these have been authorised by either the trust deed, the beneficiaries (provided they are of age) or the court. The receipt of such monies is known as 'secret profits' and includes the payment of director's fees to a trustee director, entering into competition with the business of the trust and the misuse of confidential information.

- Any purchase of trust property by a trustee is voidable at the option of the beneficiaries, even if the beneficiaries were aware of the purchase and a fair price is paid for the property. This is known as 'self-dealing'.

- A trustee is not allowed to buy the beneficial interest of a beneficiary, unless the deal is fair and done 'at arm's length'. This is known as 'fair dealing'.

A trustee is also not allowed to renew a lease held by the trust in his own name (*Keech* v. *Sandford*).

 There are a number of other trustee duties, which can be summarised as follows:

+ To act impartially between the beneficiaries
+ To adhere to the terms of the trust
+ To act personally
+ To act unanimously
+ To maintain the trust fund

+ To distribute the fund
+ To keep the beneficiaries informed
+ To produce accounts

 Trustees must exercise reasonable care in the management of the trust. A more stringent duty of care is imposed on trustees with regard to investment on behalf of the trust under section 1 of the Trustee Act 2000. The duty of care imposed upon trustees in respect of investment is discussed further in Chapter 12 on investment.

Question and answer*

Problem: Derek dies leaving the whole of his estate, which includes his thriving market stall business in Camden and a substantial number of shares in Pigling Industries Ltd, a company which produces pork scratchings, on trust for his infant son, Damien. Unfortunately the lease of the pitch from which the market stall is run is due to expire and Camden Borough Council refuses to transfer the lease to the trustees on the basis that each pitch must be let to an individual only. They will, however, agree to rent the pitch to one of the trustees, Albert, as long as he takes the pitch in his own name.

Albert is also concerned about the performance of the shares in Pigling Industries, which has been consistently losing money for 18 months now. Albert believes the dire performance of the company is due to its poor marketing strategy and is convinced that if they used the remaining capital in the trust fund to buy more shares in the company Albert could take a place on the board of directors of the company and make the necessary changes to turn the company around. The other trustees have their reservations, however.

Advise Albert as to how he should proceed.

You should allow yourself no more than 40 minutes to complete this task.

Essay: 'Is there scope within a trustee's duty to act in the best interests of their beneficiaries to operate an ethical policy on investment?' Discuss.

This question should be answered in 40 minutes.

✱ Answer guidance is provided at the end of the chapter.

Further reading and references

Hochberg, D.A. and Norris, W.V.W. (1999) 'The rights of beneficiaries to information concerning a trust', *Private Client Business,* **5, 292–9.**

Interesting article discussing the duty of disclosure of information by trustees to their beneficiaries.

Lee, R. (2009) 'Rethinking the content of fiduciary obligation', Conv, 3, 236–53.

This article gives an account of the development and operation of the no-profit rule in relation to fiduciary duties. A worthwhile read.

Ramjohn, M.A. (2003) 'Remuneration of express trustees', *Student Law Review,* **39, 30–1.**

This clear and useful article by author Mohamed Ramjohn uses case law to illustrate the rule against trustees deriving personal benefit from their

position and examines the exceptions to this rule, including authorisation in the trust instrument and payment of professional trustees under the Trustee Act 2000.

Smith, P. (2007) 'Harsh but fair?', *Trusts and Estates Law & Tax Journal,* **86, 17.**

This recent article reviews case law on fiduciary duty and conflicts of interest between trustees and beneficiaries. It considers the duty of trustees not to profit from their trust and the statutory powers of professional trustees to charge.

Thornton, R. (2008) 'Ethical investments: a case of disjointed thinking', CLJ, 67(2), 396–422.

Excellent article examining the rights and wrongs of the ethical investment of trust funds and the ability of trustees to make socially directed investments.

Question and answer guidance

Problem: A trustee is not allowed to renew a lease in their own name under the rule in *Keech* v. *Sandford*. If Albert goes ahead and renews the lease, he will be in breach of trust for doing so, despite his motives in taking the pitch. He cannot therefore do this.

In respect of Albert's wish to take a place on the board of directors of Pigling Industries, this brings up a couple of separate issues. The first is that Albert must be prepared to take up the position without payment if he wishes to do this, as he is not allowed to benefit personally from his position as a trustee. He cannot therefore accept any directors' fees which may come out of his appointment. These should belong to the trust, unless the trust deed authorises him to keep them (we are not told this is the case).

Secondly, we are told that the other trustees have reservations about the idea. Whilst there is nothing against placing a trustee on the board of directors of a company in which the trust has an interest, Albert must have the full permission of the other trustees in order to take up a place on the board (trustees must act unanimously). If he does this in his personal capacity, and he then manages to turn the company around, he will be liable for breach of the trust on the basis that he has benefited from confidential information which he has only by virtue of his position as a trustee. This is a strict liability breach, so will apply regardless of his motives in taking up the appointment. Any profit he makes in turning the business around will therefore be held by him on a constructive trust in favour of the beneficiaries (*Boardman* v. *Phipps*).

Essay:
If the trust instrument specifically allows for the making of ethical investments, then these will be permitted. However, where the trust deed is silent on the matter, it will be up to the trustees to decide whether any such investment is appropriate to the trust.

It is the duty of the trustees acting on behalf of a trust to act in the best interests of their beneficiaries in any matter relating to it. Failure to put the beneficiaries first in this way will result in breach of trust. This was set out in the case of *Cowan* v. *Scargill*, in which trustees who had tried to influence the investment strategy of a pension fund for political reasons were held to be in breach of trust, on the basis that their agenda was not in the best interests of the beneficiaries.

On the subject of ethical investments, Vice-Chancellor Megarry specifically said in this case: 'trustees must not refrain from making the investments by reason of the views that they hold'.

The question is, then, whether a trustee can ever be in a position whereby they are acting in the best interests of the beneficiaries and yet still maintaining a policy of ethical investment. The answer may be found in the case of *Harries and Others* v. *Church Commissioners for England and Another*, in which the making of ethical investments was further discussed.

In this case, a trustee of the Church of England wanted to refrain from making certain investments on the basis that they were not compatible with the beliefs of the Christian faith, even if this meant producing a lower financial return for the trust. The trustee's claim failed in this instance. However, the court said that there could be cases, nevertheless, where a scheme of ethical investment would be in the best interests of the beneficiaries. These cases were:

+ in the case of charitable trusts, where the investment in certain products would result in a loss of public support in the trust;

+ where the beneficiaries under the trust refused to receive benefits from the trust because of the way in which those benefits had been produced;

+ where there was a clear conflict between the investment policy and the purpose of the trust.

This is subject to the caveat that the making of ethical investments for any of these reasons did not have the resultant effect of causing significant financial risk to the trust.

Mention could be made here of Thornton 2008, which looks at the ability of trustees to make ethical investments in trust funds and comments on the rights and wrongs of doing so.

Students should conclude by giving their opinion on whether there is scope for the making of ethical investments within trust schemes.

Visit **www.mylawchamber.co.uk/warner-reed** to access study support resources including practice exam questions with guidance, interactive 'You be the judge' multiple choice questions, annotated weblinks, glossary and key case flashcards and audio legal updates all linked to the **Pearson eText** version of *Equity and Trusts* which you can **search**, **highlight** and **personalise** with your **own notes** and **bookmarks**.

Use Case Navigator to read in full some of the key cases referenced in this chapter with commentary and questions:

Boardman v. *Phipps* [1966] 3 All ER 721

Chapter 11
Trustees' powers: Maintenance and advancement

Key points In this chapter we will be looking at:

✦ The statutory power to maintain a beneficiary and how it is exercised

✦ The concept of 'intermediate income' and what it means for the trust

✦ How maintenance should be paid

✦ Overriding the power of maintenance

✦ The statutory power to advance money out of the trust fund to the beneficiaries

✦ Limitations on the statutory powers

✦ The discretionary nature of advancement

Introduction

You should now be starting to build up a picture of the role of a **trustee,** from a trustee's appointment right up until the point at which they retire. In Chapter 10 we considered the duties of trustees: in essence, what behaviour is expected of a trustee during their administration of the trust and what they are required to do in terms of the provision of information, accounts and so on.

In Chapters 11 and 12 we will be taking a look at the powers of trustees: what they are able to do in their role as trustees and what action they have the power to take on behalf of the **beneficiaries**. In this chapter we will be considering trustees' powers of **maintenance** and **advancement** (both of which are explained below); and in the next chapter we will be thinking about trustees' powers to invest the trust fund. First, let us turn to consider the power of maintenance.

Power of maintenance

Any substantial **trust** fund will naturally produce some form of income, whether the fund comprises commercial or residential property which is rented out or whether it comprises a lump sum of money which is invested for profit or simply sits in an interest-bearing bank account. So what do the trustees do with this income?

In the case of an adult beneficiary (that is, any beneficiary aged 18 or above), unless the **trust instrument** states to the contrary the trustees are required to pay to that beneficiary the whole of the income earned by the portion of the trust fund to which the beneficiary is entitled, as and when it is produced. This is simple; but the situation is somewhat different if the beneficiary in question is still a child. In the case of an **infant** beneficiary (that is, any child beneficiary under the age of 18), there is no general power on the part of the trustees to give the income from the fund to that child, unless the wording of the trust deed expressly allows this. Equally, the child has no right to receive the income until they reach the age of **majority**. The trustees will usually, therefore, retain any income made by the fund and simply keep adding it to the bulk of the trust fund on a cumulative basis until the child reaches the age of 18.

There is, of course, a certain element of logic to this. But what if the child requires money for clothing, food, or for his or her accommodation or education? It would not really make sense if the trustees were unable to provide payments out of the fund for such purposes. Trustees are therefore given a statutory power under section 31 of the Trustee Act 1925 to use the income from the trust fund for the maintenance of any beneficiary under the age of 18. The wording of section 31(1) of the Act is as follows:

Where any property is held by trustees in trust for any person for any interest whatsoever, whether vested or contingent, then, subject to any prior interests or charges affecting that property –

(i) during the infancy of any such person, if his interest so long continues, the trustees may, at their sole discretion, pay to his parent or guardian, if any, or otherwise apply for or towards his maintenance, education or benefit, the whole or such part if any, of the income of that property as may, in all the circumstances, be reasonable, whether or not there is –

   (a) any other fund applicable to the same purpose; or
   (b) any person bound by law to provide for his maintenance or education;

(You will remember that a **vested interest** is an interest to which the beneficiary is certain they will be entitled, albeit possibly at some point in the future, whereas a **contingent interest** is where there are conditions the beneficiary cannot be certain that they will fulfil, such as reaching a certain age. For further discussion of vested and contingent interests take another look at the explanation in Chapter 1.)

So, under the provisions of section 31, a trustee can pay the income of the trust fund to the parents or guardians of a **minor** to be used for their 'maintenance, education or benefit'. This is regardless of whether there are other funds available to the child to be used for this purpose, and regardless of the fact that there is someone (usually the parent) existing who has a legal requirement to pay for that child's maintenance. The Key stats feature gives you a flavour of the world of some children who are due to inherit substantial sums from their parents.

Key stats The Ten Richest Babies in the World

The following is a list of lucky infants set to inherit more money than they can count . . .

10 **Infanta Leonor of Spain**
Leonor is the eldest child of Crown Prince Felipe of Spain and second in line of succession to the Spanish throne. Already wealthy in their own right, Leonor's parents have recently been left a surprise **legacy** estimated to be worth in the region of $40 million by Spanish tycoon, Juan Ignacio Balada Llabrés, who died recently. The couple says they had never met their benefactor.

9 **Jayden James Spears-Federline**
Youngest son of pop princess Britney Spears and would-be rapper Kevin Federline, lucky Jayden stands to inherit half of his mother's estimated $100 million fortune.

Source: Ingram Publishing

8 **Dannielynn Hope Marshall Birkhead**
Dannielynn Hope Marshall Birkhead is the daughter of the late Anna Nicole Smith and is the sole **heir** of the estate of her mother's late husband, Texas oil tycoon J. Howard Marshall II. The estate is estimated to be worth in the region of $1.6 billion.

7 **Barron William Trump**
The son of Donald Trump could end up inheriting his father's vast personal fortune, estimated currently to be worth in the region of $2.7 billion. He is already amassing his own personal fortune, having been given his own gold pram just before he was born, by close family friend, American television chat show host Ellen Degeneres.

6 **Indigo Packer**
Indigo Packer is the daughter of the richest man in Australia, media tycoon James Packer. James is worth an estimated $5.2 billion. James is the son of the late media mogul Kerry Packer and inherited Consolidated Press Holdings Ltd from his father.

5 **Princess Catharina-Amalia**
Catharina-Amalia is the first child of Crown Prince Willem-Alexander and Crown Princess Maxima, a former investment banker formerly named Maxima Zorreguieta. Queen Beatrix, Prince Willem-Alexander's mother, has a personal wealth which is now estimated to exceed $5.5 billion. As well as being second in line to the Dutch throne, baby Catharina-Amalia can expect to inherit a considerable fortune herself.

4 **Alceo Bertarelli**
Swiss biotechnology company owner Ernesto Bertarelli is the 77th wealthiest person in the world. Bertarelli inherited the company, whose business was then pharmaceuticals, from his father Fabio in 1998. If, like his father, Ernesto passes on his own wealth to his son, then baby Alceo is set to inherit an estimated personal fortune of $8.2 billion.

3 **Valentina Paloma Pinault**
Valentina is the daughter of actress Selma Hayek and self-made French retail billionaire François-Henri Pinault. As well as being lucky enough to inherit her mother's looks, Valentina stands to inherit her father's $14.5 billion fortune.

2 Benji Brin
Benji Brin is the son of Moscow-born Google billionaire Sergey Brin and biotech entrepreneur Anne Wojcicki. It looks like Sergey might be preparing the world for the next internet mogul. **www.benjibrin.com** has already been snapped up by his dad! President and head of Google's technology division, Sergey is worth a staggering $18.7 billion.

1 Abdul Muntaqim
HRH Crown Prince Al-Muhtadee Billah is the eldest of eleven children and heir to the Sultan of Brunei, which makes his son, Abdul Muntaqim, one of the richest babies in the world. When Abdul Muntaqim was born in 2007 a 19-gun salute was fired from the sultan's grand palace. Abdul looks set to inherit a sizeable fortune, the sultan's estate being worth an estimated $22 billion.

[*Source*: based on information taken from **http://styleandlife.nl/lifestyle/rich-famous/10-rijkste-babys-de-wereld.htm**. Please note that this feature is intended for illustrative purposes only and is in no way authoritative on matters of law. Any references included in it should not therefore be used as a basis for serious legal research.]

Section 31 is straightforward. However, you should note that the power given under the statute is subject to a couple of provisos.

The first is that the power of maintenance applies to all trusts with the exception of those which have excluded the provisions of the Act in the terms of the trust document.

This means that it is possible for a **settlor**, who does not wish a child beneficiary to benefit from the income during the lifetime of the trust, to exclude the provisions of section 31 from the trust in question simply by putting a clause to that effect in the trust deed. Alternatively, a settlor would be equally at liberty to modify the provisions of section 31, rather than remove them altogether. So, for example, if the settlor wished to limit payments of maintenance to the funding of education only, or to put a cap on the amount paid to a particular child out of the income from the fund, they could do so by specifying this in the trust deed.

> a settlor would be equally at liberty to modify the provisions

The second point is that income can only be paid out of the fund if it carries, or is entitled to receive or keep, the income produced by the fund for itself.

In most circumstances the income produced by any particular fund will belong to that fund and will therefore be available for distribution in accordance with the terms of the trust. However, it may be that the settlor provides that the income from a fund should be applied for the benefit of a third party, and not the beneficiary of the capital sum. This would be the case with a **life interest**. Take the example of mother and daughter, Esther and Lesley. A husband might create a lifetime interest for the benefit of Esther and Lesley in the following terms:

1. I give £100,000 to be held on trust for my wife Esther for life, the remainder to go to my daughter Lesley, on Esther's death.

Under the terms of the trust, Esther, as the person with the life interest, would be entitled to receive any income produced by the £100,000 fund during her lifetime, but she would not be entitled to touch the £100,000 itself, this **capital** bulk of the fund being reserved for the ultimate beneficiary, or **remainderman**, Lesley, on Esther's death. Equally, however, the ultimate beneficiary, Lesley, whilst she is entitled ultimately to receive the capital sum of the trust fund (that is, the £100,000), would not be entitled to receive any income from the fund during the lifetime of her mother. This would belong to Esther. Take a look at the Documenting the law feature, for an example of how this might happen in a real-life scenario.

Documenting the law

The following is an excerpt from the will of a hotel keeper, James Fiddaman (the **testator**), made in 1884. The will creates a number of life interests for the testator's wife, with an interest in remainder to his nephews and nieces. Note in particular the specific power given to the trustees to use the income from the trust for the maintenance of the children (text in bold italic):

'I give devise and **bequeath** unto my said Trustees All that my Messuage or Dwellinghouse with the appurtenances thereof belonging situate in Norfolk Street King's Lynn aforesaid known as "Fiddaman's Hotel" my Dwellinghouse with its appurtenances in High Street King's Lynn aforesaid known as "The Restaurant" now occupied by the said James Wenn and all other my Real Estate not hereinbefore devised Also all my Stocks and Utensils in trade Household Furniture not hereinbefore bequeathed Stores and effects monies securities for money book and other debts and all other my personal estate not hereinbefore specifically bequeathed unto my said Trustees Upon trust as to my Real Estate to pay to my said Wife the rents of my estate in Norfolk Street King's Lynn and the profits arising from my business carried thereon until the same is let pursuant to the directions herein contained for the term of her natural life for her own absolute use and benefit and out of the rents of my said estate in High Street King's Lynn aforesaid to pay to the said Elizabeth Hollingsworth the sum of Twenty five pounds per annum for her life for her absolute use and benefit and to pay the residue of such rents to my said Wife for her life and after the decease of my said Wife to pay the whole of the rent of my said last mentioned estate to the said Elizabeth Hollingsworth during her life for her use and benefit but in case my said Wife shall survive the said Elizabeth Hollingsworth then I direct that the whole of such rent shall be paid to her for her life And after the death of my said Wife as to all my said Real Estate other than the estate in High Street King's Lynn aforesaid And after the death of the survivor of them my said Wife and the said Elizabeth Hollingsworth as to the said last mentioned **estate** I direct my said Trustees to sell the same either by public auction or private contract and to stand possessed of the monies to arise from such sale after defraying the expenses thereof Upon the trusts hereinafter declared concerning my residuary personal estate And as the **residue** of my personal estate Upon trust as soon as conveniently may be after my decease to call in collect and convert the same into money and after payment thereout of my funeral and testamentary expenses and debts and the legacies bequeathed by this my Will or any Codicil thereto to invest the proceeds to arise from such sale collection and conversion in the names of my said Trustees in or upon any Stocks funds or securities authorized by law as investments for trust funds or the debentures or debenture stocks or the guaranteed or preference stocks or shares of British or Indian Railway Companies such a sum of money as shall be sufficient to realize an Annuity of Fifty pounds per annum which I hereby give to my said Wife and I direct my said Trustees to pay the same to her during her life for her own absolute use and benefit by equal half yearly payments the first of such payments to be made at the expiration of six calendar months from the time of my decease And to invest the residue thereof in manner hereinbefore directed and to stand possessed of the stocks funds or securities in or upon which the same shall be invested together with the proceeds to arise from the sale of my said Real Estate and also the trust fund set apart for the annuity of my said Wife after her decease Upon trust for my Niece Susan the Wife of I.T. Dunning the daughter of my deceased Sister Fanny Fiddaman and for all such of my Nephews and Nieces the children of my said Brother and Sister Francis Fiddaman and Ann Flegg as shall be living at my decease to be divided between all my said Nephews and Nieces in equal shares and proportions . . . ***And I direct that it shall be lawful for my said Trustees to pay and apply the whole or such part as they in their discretion shall think fit of the interest dividends and annual produce arising from the shares of such of my said Nephews and Nieces whose interest shall not have become vested in or towards their maintenance education and advancement until they shall respectively attain the age of twenty one years***'

[*Source*: http://www.thornburypump.myby.co.uk/KingsLynn/will.html]

This is the position with a life interest. However, the settlor could easily set up an ordinary trust with the same effect: the beneficiary being entitled to the capital sum, but the interest on that capital going to a third party. Using the examples of Esther and Lesley again, the wording of such a gift might look as follows:

2. I give £100,000 to my daughter Lesley when she attains 18, the income to my wife Esther until then.

So, if the fund does not 'carry interest' – that is, if the income from the fund is not available to the trustees to use for the beneficiaries because it is reserved for the use of a third party – there will clearly be no money available over which the trustees can exercise their power of maintenance. In the case of a **lifetime trust**, such as that given in example number 2 above, the interest produced by a trust from the date the fund is created until the beneficiary reaches the age of majority is referred to as '**intermediate income**'.

When does the fund not carry intermediate income?

As we have already seen, in most circumstances, unless the terms of the trust deed state otherwise, any income produced by a trust fund will belong to that fund and will therefore be available for distribution under the maintenance provisions of section 31 of the Trustee Act 1925. This is the case with trusts created by a settlor during their lifetime regardless of whether the interests of the beneficiaries under the trust are vested and thus certain, or whether contingent upon the beneficiaries reaching a certain age or on some other event, such as marriage.

Trusts created by will are slightly different, however. With a vested interest created by will, the income from the fund will be available for the trustees to distribute in the same way as with a trust created during the settlor's lifetime, provided that interest vests immediately in the beneficiary. If the gift is a **deferred gift**, however (that is, a gift which will take effect on the occurrence of some future event, for example, 'to my daughter Lesley, on the death of my wife'), it will carry intermediate income only in the cases of gifts of **real property** (or land) or a specific gift of **personal property**, such as 'my MG sports car'. This means that, in the case of a **future interest**, any income received in the interim period on a gift of money or on a gift of the residue of the estate will not be available for distribution by the trustees. If you think about it this does make sense. After all, the whole point of a deferred gift is that the testator is delaying the beneficiary receiving the gift until some point in the future. If the income from that gift were made available to them immediately it could be said that it was defeating the terms of the gift.

The right to intermediate income from contingent gifts made under the terms of a will is also dependent on the type of gift being made, but the rules relating to them are slightly different again. Whilst both contingent gifts of specific items, such as a house or car, for example, and also contingent gifts of residue, *do* carry intermediate income, a contingent *general* gift, such as a gift of 'my jewellery' or a gift of money, will not. There are exceptions in certain cases, as follows:

1. Where the testator is the father of the beneficiary or is acting in the father's place, and the beneficiary is a child at the time the gift is made and there is no further provision in the will for the child's maintenance. Here the assumption is that the testator intended to make

the gift with a view to the maintenance of the child (*Harvey* v. *Harvey* (1722) 2 P Wms 21). Note that this same rule does not apply where the testator is the mother of the child.

2. Where the gift is to a child and the will shows an intention that the gift should be used for the child's benefit or maintenance. This was the case in both *Re Churchill* [1909] 2 Ch 431 and *Re Selby-Walker* [1949] 2 All ER 178, where the gift in each case was specified as being made for the child's education.

3. Where the gift is set aside from the rest of the property in the estate (see *Re Medlock* (1886) 54 LT 828).

It should be noted that, where the intermediate income from a contingent gift does not attach to the gift, it will fall into the residue of the estate and thus go to whoever is entitled to the residue under the terms of the will.

The rules relating to intermediate income are not straightforward, but the recap of the rules in the box should assist as a reminder of how it all fits together.

Recap: availability of intermediate income to the trustees for distribution

Lifetime trusts:

✦ Check the terms of the trust deed. If the settlor has not specified otherwise, the intermediate income will be available to the trustees to distribute under their powers of maintenance (section 31), regardless of whether the interest is vested (which includes future interests) or contingent.

Trusts created by will:

✦ The intermediate income from *current* vested interests is available for the trustees to distribute in the usual manner, unless otherwise specified by the testator (as with lifetime interests).

✦ *Future* vested interests (such as a gift taking effect on the death of another person) carry intermediate income only in the case of real property and specific gifts.

✦ Specific gifts of real property ('my house') contingent upon the happening of a future event (such as age or marriage) carry intermediate income.

✦ Specific gifts of personal property ('my car') contingent upon the happening of a future event carry intermediate income.

✦ Gifts of residue contingent upon the happening of a future event carry intermediate income.

✦ General gifts ('my jewellery') contingent upon the happening of a future event *do not* carry intermediate income, unless one of the exceptions apply.

✦ Gifts of money contingent upon the happening of a future event *do not* carry intermediate income, unless one of the exceptions apply.

general gifts will tend not to provide an income in any event

Basically, it is only future vested interests and contingent interests in wills that you have to be careful of. With future interests, whilst only specific gifts and real property carry intermediate income, it pays to remember the rationale behind the rule: that it was the intention of the testator to delay the gift. With contingent interests, remember that general gifts ('my jewellery') will tend not to provide an income in any event, so this will not have any practical effect on the beneficiaries. It is therefore only contingent gifts of money ('£100,000 to Lesley on her attaining the age of 18') that pose a problem. Again, it is worth considering the motives of the testator here. With a contingent gift of money presumably the intention of the testator was simply to give the beneficiary a lump sum at some point in the future. It is unlikely that the maintenance of that beneficiary was on their mind. Even then, where maintenance is an issue in most cases one of the exceptions will apply, thus sidestepping the problem.

One final point to note is that, under section 69(2) of the Trustee Act 1925, the above rules relating to intermediate income will apply only where there is nothing to the contrary stated in the will. Any solicitor worth their salt would therefore simply draft a provision in the will to the effect that any legacies made under it will carry intermediate income.

How should the power of maintenance be exercised?

Let us now turn back to the wording of section 31 and look a little more at how the general power of maintenance works. An important point to note from the wording of the section (at 31(1)(i)) is that, whenever it is available, the statutory power of maintenance given to trustees is a discretionary power. It is therefore entirely at the discretion of the trustees as to whether or not they make such payments out of the fund. Consequently, a child who is to benefit from any payment of maintenance has neither influence over their decisions nor any form of recourse. Neither do their parents or guardians, who are usually the persons who will make a request for maintenance on the child's behalf.

Nevertheless, trustees must think carefully about any payments of maintenance they do make, as monies paid out of a trust fund indiscriminately may end up having to be returned to the trust fund at the trustees' own personal expense. This is what happened in the case of *Wilson* v. *Turner* (1883) 22 Ch D 521, where the trustees were ordered by the court to replace with their own money payments of income which had been made automatically out of the trust fund to the father of a child beneficiary, without the trustees questioning what the money was to be used for and whether it was genuinely for the maintenance of the child. Any decision made by a trustee to give money to a beneficiary under their statutory power of maintenance is therefore not to be taken lightly, although the court will generally not interfere with a decision as to maintenance made by the trustees in good faith, regardless of the court's view of the wisdom of that decision. For an illustration of this point see the case of *Bryant* v. *Hickley* [1894] 1 Ch 324, in which the mother of infant beneficiaries made an application for an allowance for the maintenance of the children out of the trust fund. The trustees had refused the mother's request because they did not believe it to be necessary at that time, and the court upheld the decision on the basis that the trustees had been within their rights in exercising their discretion over the use of the fund.

Case Summary

Case Summary

Trustees are not completely without guidance in the matter of exercising their discretion as to maintenance, however. Brief guidance is given to trustees in section 31 as to the matters they should take into account. These are:

1. the age of the child;

2. the requirements of the child;

3. the general circumstances of the case; and

4. any other income available for the child's maintenance.

financial need is not a prerequisite for making a maintenance payment

With regard to matter 4, we can therefore see that, whilst financial need is not a prerequisite for making a maintenance payment under the terms of the statute, such matters can be taken into account. Thus, whether there may be another fund available to the child for the payment of that child's maintenance or education, or whether there is a parent or guardian in existence at the time who is bound by law to provide for the child and who has the financial wherewithal to do so, should be considered by the trustees, along with the general circumstances of the case in the decision-making process. In particular, in the Court of Appeal case of *Jones* v. *Jones and Another* (1989) *The Independent* 27 January, the court held that the trustees should not normally give the child in excess of their needs, if they have other financial resources available.

Case Summary

How maintenance is to be paid

Payments of maintenance out of the trust fund are to be paid, in accordance with section 31, either to the child's parents or guardians or should otherwise be applied directly by the trustees; so, for example, school fees might be paid direct to the school on production of an invoice. Any surplus income left after the payment of any maintenance will go back into the trust fund, but can be used for future payments of maintenance by the trustees in addition to any new amounts of trust income earned on the fund. Take a look at the Law in action feature, which shows how the trustees of one rather famous trust fund have earned a significant amount to add to the fund in this way.

Law in action Shrewd management by parents of Harry Potter star leave him Britain's richest teen

Daniel Radcliffe, the actor who plays the famous boy wizard from J.K. Rowling's novels, is one of Britain's richest youngsters.

Records at Companies House show that Gilmore Jacobs, a firm set up in 2000 by Daniel's parents to manage him, earned a staggering £10 million from the first three Harry Potter films.

Daniel's parents understand the entertainment industry better than most: his father Alan is a literary agent and his mother Marcia, a casting director. The couple set up Gilmore Jacobs shortly after the making of Daniel's first film, to maximise his earnings.

Daniel's parents own £1,000 of shares in the company but have stipulated that if Gilmore Jacobs is wound up they would expect only the return of their original investment.

Daniel, at the age of 11, was paid about £150,000 for the first Potter film, which took 11 months to make, mixing shooting scenes with his schooling. Since then, his fees have increased tenfold, with the last two films in the series reportedly earning him somewhere in the region of £25 million. Daniel, is now said to be worth in the region of £42 million.

Philip Beresford, compiler of The Sunday Times Rich List, who studied the Gilmore Jacobs accounts, said in 2007: 'I've never seen such profitable accounts for someone so young. He has left his teenage rivals struggling in the slipstream of his broomstick.'

[*Source*: http://www.timesonline.co.uk/tol/news/uk/article592193.ece.]

Overriding the terms of the trust

Despite the general rule, you may remember from Chapter 6 on the variation of trusts that, where the settlor has excluded the terms of section 31 from the trust, the court can nevertheless use its **inherent jurisdiction** to override the terms of the trust and allow payments of maintenance to be made out of the income from the trust fund. This is a useful tool where the child's welfare is at issue and the fund makes no provision for their care during infancy. The rationale for giving the courts such a jurisdiction, albeit against the wishes of the settlor, was explained by Mr Justice Pearson in the case of *Re Collins* (1886) 32 Ch D 229, which concerned an application to provide an annual sum to the beneficiary under a will to provide for the maintenance of her children. The application was granted, even though it had been the testator's wish that the income of the estate should be accumulated for 21 years. Mr Justice Pearson said:

> Where a testator has made provision for a family but has postponed the enjoyment, either for a particular purpose or generally for the increase of the estate, it is assumed that he did not intend that these children should be left unprovided for or in a state of such moderate means that they should not be educated properly for the position and fortune which he designs them to have, and the Court has accordingly found from the earliest time that where an heir-at-law is unprovided for, maintenance ought to be provided for him.

It is interesting to note from the judge's comments that grants of maintenance by the courts will not be restricted purely to cases of financial necessity, although this should be read in the light of the later case of *Jones* v. *Jones and Another*, above.

You may also remember from Chapter 6 that the court has an additional statutory power under section 53 of the Trustee Act 1925 to allow the trustees to use the capital element of a child's trust fund for his or her maintenance, should they deem it necessary to do so.

Power of advancement

The above discusses the use of any *income* produced by the trust fund to provide for the maintenance of a child beneficiary. It is also possible, however, to use up to a maximum of half of the *capital* sum of the fund under the terms of section 32 of the Trustee Act 1925 for the benefit of the child, under certain specified circumstances. The wording of section 32 is as follows:

> Trustees may at any time or times pay or apply any capital money subject to a trust, for the advancement or benefit, in such manner as they may, in their absolute discretion, think fit, of any person entitled to the capital of the trust property or of any share thereof, whether absolutely or contingently on his attaining any specified age or on the occurrence of any other event, or subject to a gift over on his death under any specified age or on the occurrence of any other event, and whether in possession or in remainder or reversion, and such payment or application may be made notwithstanding that the interest of such person is liable to be defeated by the exercise of a power of appointment or revocation, or to be diminished by the increase of the class to which he belongs.

We can thus see from the wording of the section that the trustees have the discretion to be able to advance monies out of the capital of the trust fund for the 'advancement or benefit' of the beneficiaries. Unlike the power of maintenance, however, we can see that the power of advancement given in the section gives trustees the right to advance payments of capital to the beneficiaries under the trust regardless of the type of interest the beneficiaries hold. So whether the interest of a beneficiary to whom the trustees wish to advance money is current, future, vested or contingent, and whether it is made during the settlor's lifetime or by will, the trustees are able to advance money out of the fund under the terms of the section.

As with section 31, although the power given under section 32 is very wide, there are nevertheless a number of provisos on the exercise of the trustees' discretion when making advancements out of the fund:

1. The first of these is that the trustees must not advance any more than half of the beneficiary's share of the capital fund under the terms of the statute. This means that, in the case of a trust fund of £100,000 for the benefit of Leila and Shadiv equally, the maximum the trustees could advance to either child under the terms of the statute would be £25,000, representing half of their share of the fund.

2. The second proviso is that the trustees cannot make an advancement of capital which would work to the detriment of any person entitled with a prior interest, unless that person is in existence and of full age and consents in writing to the advancement. This covers the situation where a mother with the benefit of a life interest in property might wish to allow an advancement out of the capital of the fund to her children, who have the benefit of the fund on her death. Under the terms of the section, the trustees could not diminish the capital sum of the trust fund, as this would have the knock-on effect of decreasing any income produced by the fund to which the mother is entitled. However, with the mother's consent in writing, the trustees could make an advancement of capital for the benefit of the children.

3. And the third proviso is that, if the full 50 per cent advance is made to a beneficiary under the section, then no further advances can be made to that beneficiary, even if the fund subsequently increases in value. Thus, in the case of *Marquess of Abergavenny* v. *Ram* [1981] 2 ALL ER 643, a request for additional advancements out of a trust fund was denied on the basis that the beneficiary had already received the maximum advancement allowed to them under statute, despite the remainder of the fund having increased significantly in value following the date of the advancement.

Case Summary

> **the settlor can expressly exclude the provisions of the section in the trust deed**

One further limitation on the provisions of section 32 is that, as with the power of maintenance, the power of advancement applies to all trusts unless the trust deed expressly disallows it. Thus, the settlor can, if they wish, expressly exclude the provisions of the section in the trust deed to prevent advancements from being made out of the fund. A settlor could theoretically also either limit or increase the amount of the fund which the trustees can advance to the beneficiaries, so that advancements of capital were, for example, limited to 25 per cent of the beneficiary's share (as opposed to the statutory 50 per cent limit); or alternatively advancements of capital could be increased to the whole of that beneficiary's share.

Now take a look at the You be the judge feature to assess your understanding of advancement under section 32.

You be the judge

Q: Valerie puts £90,000 into trust equally for her three children, Sean, Justine and Elliott, until they attain the age of 25. How much can be given to each child under the trustees' statutory powers of advancement? You can assume there are no specific clauses dealing with this issue in the trust deed.

A: The children will be entitled to half of their share of the fund each, meaning they can be advanced up to £15,000 each under the statutory power of advancement.

Q: The sum of £6,000 is advanced to Justine for her to go travelling in her gap year before she starts university in 2012. How much will she be entitled to when she reaches the age of 25?

A: Justine will be entitled to her share of the trust fund, minus the amount of any advancement which has been made to her previously. This would entitle her to receive £24,000 on her 25th birthday.

What can the power be used for?

So, we now know how advancements of capital can be made under section 32 of the Trustee Act 1925, but for what purposes, exactly, can such advancements of capital be made? The power of advancement does not give trustees the power simply to advance money to the beneficiaries for anything they wish. Advancements of capital from the trust fund are strictly limited to payments which are going to be 'for the advancement or benefit' of the beneficiary in question.

The wording of the statute is very wide and, as a consequence, has been subject to a great deal of conjecture in the courts over the years; however, the meaning of 'advancement or benefit' of the beneficiary is generally thought to be advancements for those purposes which would serve to set the beneficiary up in life: so that would include an advancement of money to buy or pay a deposit on a first home, a lump sum to set the beneficiary up in business, or other similar matters.

Perhaps somewhat surprisingly, monies given for the 'advancement or benefit' of a beneficiary can also include monies to pay off a beneficiary's debts, as in the case of *Lowther* v. *Bentinck* (1874) LR 19 Eq 166, or even for the benefit of the beneficiary's spouse (see *Re Kershaw* (1868) LR 6 Eq 322). It is clear from case law on the issue that what is important when the trustees are making an advancement is that the beneficiary derives a genuine benefit from it. As Lord Radcliffe said in the House of Lords case of *Pilkington* v. *IRC* [1964] AC 612, which concerned an application to make advancements of capital out of a trust fund to be placed in a separate fund for the beneficiary and others together for the purposes of tax avoidance, the fact that other persons (in this case the children of the beneficiary) benefited incidentally as a result of the advancement was irrelevant, provided the advancement was made for the benefit of the beneficiary in the first instance.

Case Summary

Case Summary

Writing and drafting

You work for a firm of solicitors who act for the trustees of the William Hensman Children's Trust Fund. The million pound fund was set up by the testator last year for the equal benefit of his four children on their attaining the age of 25. The children's current ages are 13, 17, 18 and 20. The trustees have contacted you recently as they have been approached by the children with a number of requests for payments of capital out of the fund. The trustees are unsure what payments they are able to make out of the fund and what matters, if any, they should take into account when making their decisions. You should write a letter of advice to the trustees, detailing the circumstances under which an advancement of capital should be made to a beneficiary.

You should spend no more than 40 minutes on this task.

◆ **Handy tip:** Think about the meaning of 'advancement' under the statute. What might be included within this term?

Reflective practice

Do you think it is easy to make decisions as a trustee? How easy would you find it to remain impartial in making your decisions? How would you ensure balancing the maintenance of the fund against the immediate needs of the children?

Case Summary

Trustees should be vigilant in ensuring trust monies advanced to beneficiaries are used only for the purpose for which it was intended the advancement should be made. In the Court of Appeal case of *Re Pauling's Settlement Trusts* [1964] Ch 303, the trustees were held personally liable for advancements of monies made from a trust fund to the parents of the beneficiaries, which they had allowed over a period of years. The rather shocking facts of the case were as follows:

The trust fund comprised a life interest for the wife with the remainder going to her four children. The trust deed contained a clause which gave the trustees the power to advance up to half of the capital comprising each child's share for that child's benefit, with the written consent of the wife. The wife and her husband led a rather lavish existence which led them into a great deal of debt. Over the course of more than a decade, the trustees advanced a little under £30,000 to the wife (which would equate to around £600,000 in today's money), which she used both to fund her extravagant lifestyle and to stem her spiralling debts. Eventually, realising what had been going on, the children brought an action against the trustees of the trust fund on the basis that the advances of capital made to their mother had been done on an improper basis. The court made the following findings:

1. A trustee could properly make an advance to a beneficiary for a stated purpose as long as they reasonably believed that the beneficiary in question could be trusted to carry out the purpose stated for the advance. However, the trustee had a responsibility to enquire if that money had been applied for the purpose it was given and could not freely advance money to be used by a beneficiary in any way he or she chose.

2. A beneficiary had a duty to use money advanced to them for the purpose for which it was given. If the trustee became aware of any misapplication of funds they should not make any further advances to that beneficiary unless they could be sure that the funds were going to be applied for the correct purpose.

It was held that the trustees were liable for the losses incurred in respect of all the advances they had made to the wife.

Out and about Coogan's Law

Not every child actor is lucky enough to have parents as prudent as Daniel Radcliffe's. Child actor Jackie Coogan may be better known to you in his adult role as Uncle Fester in the Addams Family television series. However, as a child actor, Jackie was a sensation in his time, having originally been catapulted to stardom in 1921 following his role alongside Charlie Chaplin as the 'Kid', aged 7.

As a child star, Jackie earned between $3 and $4 million (in today's money, estimated to be worth somewhere between $40 million and $100 million), but the money was taken by his mother, Lillian, and stepfather, Arthur Bernstein, for extravagances such as fur coats, diamonds and cars. Jackie eventually sued them for the loss to the trust fund in 1938, but after legal expenses, he received only $126,000, approximately half of what remained in the fund.

In a groundbreaking turn of events at the time, the court case resulted in the passing of what is now known as '**Coogan's Law**', a law designed to protect child stars' earnings. Take a look on the internet and see what you can find out about 'Coogan's Law'. Do you think child actors in the UK would benefit from such a system?

You should take no more than 30 minutes on this task.

Handy tip: Having difficulty finding it? Here's a starter for ten: the official title for 'Coogan's Law' is the California Child Actors' Bill. The bill was originally introduced in 1939, but has been amended a few times since then, most recently in 2004.

[*Source*: http://www.goldensilents.com/kids/jackiecoogan.html. Please note that this feature is intended for illustrative purposes only and is in no way authoritative on matters of law. Any references included in it should not therefore be used as a basis for serious legal research.]

Limitations on the power of advancement

As was previously stated, the amount of capital which can be advanced to a beneficiary under the statutory power of advancement is one half of the relevant beneficiary's share of the fund. However, settlors are free to increase or even remove this limit by specifying the same in the trust deed.

The courts also have the power under the Variation of Trusts Act 1958 to vary the terms of the trust to allow for an advancement of more than half of the trust fund for the benefit of an infant beneficiary. This was the case in *D (a child)* v. *O* [2004] 3 All ER 780, in which the court allowed a variation to the trust to allow the whole capital of the trust fund to pay the school fees of a child beneficiary. Such cases are unusual, however, and whether such a variation would be allowed would depend on the facts of each individual case.

Case Summary

Discretionary nature of advancement

One final point to make about the power of advancement is that, unlike payments of income out of the trust fund, which can only be made to child beneficiaries, trustees under their statutory powers of advancement have complete discretion as to whether or not to advance monies to the beneficiaries of the fund, regardless of whether the beneficiary has reached the age of majority or not. Thus, a beneficiary has no right to payments of capital irrespective of the nature of their claim.

Table 11.1 compares the statutory powers of maintenance and advancement.

Table 11.1 Comparison of the statutory powers of maintenance and advancement

Maintenance	Advancement
Section 31 Trustee Act 1925	Section 32 Trustee Act 1925
for maintenance, education or benefit	for advancement or benefit
from the income of the trust fund	from the capital of the fund
at the discretion of the trustees	at the discretion of the trustees
limited to child beneficiaries (under 18)	available to all beneficiaries, regardless of age
only beneficiaries entitled to intermediate income can benefit	available to all beneficiaries regardless of type of interest
not available where there is a prior life interest	available if person with life interest gives consent in writing and is over 18
no limit on the amount of income payable	limited to half the beneficiary's share, unless otherwise specified in the trust deed
payment is to the child's parent, guardian or directly to the source of maintenance	payment can be made to beneficiary direct, where an adult

Summary

◆ Adult beneficiaries are entitled to receive any income earned on that portion of the trust fund to which they are entitled, as and when it is produced.

◆ For beneficiaries under the age of 18, trustees have the discretion to use the income from the trust fund for their maintenance, education or benefit (section 31 Trustee Act 1925).

◆ Income can only be paid out of the trust fund if it carries intermediate income.

◆ Intermediate income attaches to capital in the case of all lifetime trusts and all current vested interests created by will. Future vested interests created by will, will only carry intermediate income in the case of specific gifts of real and personal property; contingent interests created by will, will only carry intermediate income in the case of specific gifts of real and personal property, and gifts of residue, although this can be overridden under certain circumstances.

◆ In making payments of maintenance the trustees should take into account the age of the child, the

requirements of the child, the general circumstances of the case and any other income available for the child's maintenance.

◆ Payments of income must either be made to the parent or guardian of the beneficiary, or be directly applied for the child's maintenance.

◆ Trustees can also use up to a maximum of half of the capital of a trust fund for the advancement or benefit of their beneficiaries (section 32 Trustee Act 1925).

◆ Trustees cannot make any payment to a beneficiary that might prejudice any person with a prior life interest or any other interest, unless that person is of full age and consents in writing to the advancement.

◆ The statutory power of advancement is solely at the discretion of the trustees, regardless of the age of the beneficiaries.

◆ The provisions of both sections 31 and 32 of the Trustee Act 1925 can be either excluded or modified by the settlor in the trust deed.

Question and answer*

Problem:
Priscilla died in 2008, leaving the residue of her estate in trust for her grandchildren, Isla and Elvis, on attaining the age of 25. Isla is now 15 and Elvis is 19. The trust fund is currently worth in the region of £300,000.

Elvis has written to the trustees of the fund requesting £100,000 for the purpose of setting up a recording studio and rehearsal space for him and his band. He is a talented vocalist, having come second in a television programme *Who Wants to be a Singer?* two years ago and believes he has a promising career in the pop music industry. The band currently rehearses in his parents' basement and he is under some pressure from them to find somewhere else to practise.

Isla's parents have also written to the trustees requesting that they forward all the income of the fund to them for the next six years, until Isla reaches the age of 21. They say this is to pay for Isla's school and university fees, but Isla's most recent school report shows that she is not particularly academically gifted and suggests Isla would be better turning her attentions to her real talent, which is contemporary dance. The trustees have also heard that Isla's father's business is struggling and that he is having some difficulty in meeting the mortgage payments on the family home. Isla's mother has quite openly told the trustees that they would welcome 'an injection of cash' from the trust fund to help them make ends meet.

    Advise the trustees as to whether they can forward the monies to Isla and Elvis and their parents.

You should allow yourself no more than 40 minutes to complete this task.

Essay: Is the statutory power of maintenance under section 31 of the Trustee Act 1925 simple for trustees to understand and implement? Explain the process trustees must follow and evaluate the pitfalls.

This question should be answered in 40 minutes.

✱ Answer guidance is provided at the end of the chapter.

Further reading and references

Denker, J. (2006) 'Contingent gifts: who receives the income?', *Private Client Business,* **6, 372–5.**
Concise but clear article dealing with the issue of intermediate income on contingent gifts in wills, with some practical advice on drafting.

Ker, B.S. (1953) 'Trustees' powers of maintenance', 17 Conv 273.
Although this is a very old article it gives a very clear and thorough explanation of the issues surrounding maintenance and advancement and, in particular, of when intermediate income attaches to capital.

Legge, H. (2000) 'Giving up an interest before death', *Trusts and Estates Law Journal,* **15, 10–13.**
This article deals with, amongst other things, the break-up of lifetime interest trusts through the power of advancement.

Ramjohn, M.A. (2005) 'Variation of the statutory power of advancement', *Student Law Review,* **44, 35–6.**
Interesting case commentary on the case of *D (a child)* v. *O*, questioning the court's jurisdiction to make the variation.

Question and answer guidance

Problem: Elvis is entitled to the income from his half share of the trust fund, as he is over the age of 18 (unless the trust instrument states otherwise).

    He can also request up to 50 per cent of his share of the fund as an advancement of capital, under section 32 of the Trustee Act 1925. But it is entirely at the discretion of the trustees as to whether they give him this money. His share in the fund is £150,000 and therefore the maximum the trustees could give him is £75,000, not the £100,000 he is requesting. 'Advancement' under the terms of the act includes setting up the beneficiary in business or for their future in general, and Elvis's request would appear to come within this requirement. However, it will be up to the trustees as to whether they think this would be a suitable use of the monies. They may feel it more appropriate to use the income from the fund to rent recording space. In any event, it will be their decision.

    In respect of Isla, she is under the age of 18, and so can make a request (although not a demand – this is at the discretion of the trustees) for maintenance out of the income from the fund, under section 31 of the Trustee

Act 1925. The payment of Isla's school fees would be a suitable use for the income from the fund; however, the trustees should take into account whether this would be in Isla's best interests, given her other talents. The trustees must be careful about how they pay the monies out. They can pay it direct to the parents but, given their clear ulterior motives, it might be better if they paid the fees direct to the school rather than giving the money to them. Any monies paid out under the provisions for maintenance must genuinely be for the benefit of the child, and not her parents. The trustees would be in blatant breach of trust if they simply forwarded the income to the parents for the next six years, as the parents have requested (*Wilson* v. *Turner*). In any event, maintenance is only payable to minors, so will only be available under the terms of section 31 for the next 3 years, when Isla reaches the age of 18. After this date, Isla has the right to receive the trust income for herself.

Essay:

The essay should begin by saying that trustees are given a discretionary power under the section to advance payments of income from the trust to the parent or guardian of a minor beneficiary, for the purposes of their maintenance or benefit. As the power is discretionary, there is no recourse for the beneficiaries or their parents or guardians for decisions made by the trustees, unless money has been advanced indiscriminately, without any thought of whether the money is genuinely being advanced for the beneficiary's own benefit (*Wilson* v. *Turner*). In addition, trustees are given guidance as to how they should exercise their discretion within the wording of the section, in the form of a list of matters they should take into account in exercising their discretion. We can see, therefore, that the power of maintenance is in this respect straightforward.

Students should go on to say that the problem with the statutory power of maintenance is therefore not in the interpretation of the Act, but in the difficulty in deciphering whether or not income is available to the trustees to pay out of the fund in the first place. In other words, 'does the trust carry intermediate income?'

Students should explain the meaning of intermediate income, and then go on to explain the difficulties encountered in divining whether or not trusts created by will carry such income. There are two main areas of discussion here: deferred gifts of vested interests, and contingent interests.

Both deferred and contingent gifts only carry intermediate income if they are of land, or if they are of a specific item; contingent gifts of residue will also carry intermediate income, but deferred gifts of residue will not. Deferred and contingent general gifts do not carry intermediate income, unless (in the case of contingent gifts only) the testator is the father of the beneficiary and there is no further provision in the will for the child's maintenance; the gift is to a child and the will shows an intention that the gift is to be used for benefit or maintenance; or the gift has been set aside from the rest of the property in the estate.

Students need to explain why this might be so complicated by answering the question 'what is the point of the testator making a deferred or contingent gift?' Comment on this point has been made within the chapter (that is, the intention of the testator to delay the making of the gift in the first place).

Reference could be made to Ker 1953 and Denker 2006, both of which comment on the issue of intermediate income. In particular, Denker 2006 adds an interesting practical overview to the question.

The essay should conclude by restating the law relating to section 31, recapping on the pitfalls of the intermediate income system, and perhaps giving an opinion as to whether they feel that change of law in this area is necessary.

Chapter 12
Trustees' powers: investment

Key points In this chapter we will be looking at:

✦ What do we mean by investment in the context of trusts?

✦ The trustees' duty to invest

✦ The statutory duty of care imposed upon trustees when making investments

✦ The 'standard investment criteria' imposed by the Trustee Act 2000

✦ Obtaining advice and reviewing investments

✦ The purchase of land as an investment

✦ Delegating investment decisions and the liability of trustees for their agents

Introduction

In the first of our chapters on **trustee** powers (Chapter 11) we considered the powers given to trustees to advance monies out of the trust fund for the **maintenance** and **advancement** of its **beneficiaries**. As we saw, these powers of maintenance and advancement give trustees the ability to carry out their duty to act in their beneficiaries' best interests: in this case by taking care of their financial needs, as and when they arise.

The second of our chapters on trustee powers deals with a different aspect of a trustee's duties: the duty to *maintain* the trust fund. One of the fundamental duties of a trustee, as we saw in Chapter 10, is to maintain the trust fund, in the first instance by maintaining its initial value, but also by ensuring that its value increases, as a minimum in line with inflation, to maintain its relative value over a period of time. In order to do this, a trustee will necessarily be required to invest the monies or property contained in the fund in order to produce the best return on the fund for the beneficiaries. Thus the power to invest is

a power which is vital to trustees for the successful running of any trust fund.

Prior to the Trustee Act 2000, the powers of investment given to trustees were subject to a large number of restrictions, which made the making of investments by trustees something of a legal minefield. The Act has widened trustees' investment-making powers considerably, to the extent that they now have the freedom to treat trust property to all intents and purposes as if it were their own when making investments of it. This freedom is, however, subject to the basic safeguard of a duty to take reasonable skill and care in making those investments. We shall be looking at this duty of care in more detail throughout the course of this chapter.

This chapter will also deal with the issue of the delegation of investment powers by trustees, which it is essential for any non-professional trustee (that is, any trustee not acting in the professional capacity of a financial adviser) to be able to do in order to ensure the efficient running of the trust fund's investments.

The Trustee Act 2000

The Trustee Act 2000 was brought in to replace the Trustee Investments Act 1961, which had been subject to criticism since its inception. The 1961 Act was unduly complicated and restrictive, requiring trustees to divide any investment made on behalf of the trust into two parts, one containing 'safe' investments, such as bank and building society savings and government-backed bonds, and the other containing more 'risky' investments such as shares in private companies. To complicate things further, Schedule 1 of the Act contained a list of investments trustees were allowed to make, broken down into four separate categories, two of which required the trustees to obtain advice in writing before they invested in them, and two of which did not. The types of investment listed within these categories were subject to change by statutory instrument from time to time. Aside from the rather convoluted procedure for deciding which investment to make, the requirement for written advice made investment an expensive and time-consuming business and unpopular with trustees. The outcome was that it had become standard practice to include clauses within trust deeds to widen the powers of investment given to trustees under the terms of the 1961 Act. This unsatisfactory state

> the requirement for written advice made investment expensive and time-consuming

of affairs was ended by the Trustee Act 2000, however. Following the changes brought in by the Act, the only reason now to include clauses relating to powers of investment in a trust deed is if the **settlor** wishes to *restrict* what the trustees can do. This is regarded as a far more satisfactory position.

The meaning of investment

The 2000 Act has very helpfully given trustees wide powers to make investments on behalf of the trust, but what is actually included within the meaning of the word 'investment'? The Trustee Act 2000 does not actually provide a statutory meaning for the term investment, so we are obliged to look to elsewhere for an answer. The common, or one might say wider, meaning of the term investment is where a person deposits money in a scheme or asset with a view to making a profit, whether that profit is achieved by way of interest received on a **capital** sum of money, income produced by the asset itself or by an appreciation in capital (due to the asset going up in value). The case law on the subject is somewhat more restrictive, however. In terms of investments of trust fund monies the courts have traditionally viewed investment as including only investments of cash or assets which provided either simple interest payments or an income for the trust fund (in other words, money placed in an interest-bearing bank account or in an investment scheme). They did not include investments which provided purely capital growth, however. This would mean that a speculative investment in property in an up-and-coming residential area, which was likely to go up in value and therefore yield a considerable growth in capital, but which would not produce a rental income, would not be considered an investment.

Equally, the purchase of a house for beneficiaries to live in was also not considered an investment, because the property would not produce any income, although it would naturally increase in value. In the case of *Re Power's Will Trusts* [1947] Ch 572, a will gave directions that all money in the deceased's **estate** should be:

Case Summary

301

invested by the trustee in any manner which he may in his absolute discretion think fit in all respects as if he were the sole **beneficial owner** of such monies including the purchase of . . . properties in England and Wales.

The trustee asked for directions from the court as to whether this wording permitted him to buy a house for the beneficiaries to live in, free of rent. The court held that the clause did not authorise the trustee to take such action. According to Mr Justice Jenkins, the use of the word 'investment' dictated that any purchases made under this clause should yield an income and the purchase of a house for the beneficiaries to live in rent free would not produce any such income.

This limitation on the meaning of investment did not just apply to property or land either. Speculative investments in fine art or other collectable items which might traditionally be considered investments on the basis of their incremental value were also not termed as investments for the purposes of trustee investment on this basis.

Together with the Trustee Investments Act 1961, this strict interpretation of investment by the courts was another area in which the law in relation to the investment of trust funds was unduly restrictive and one might say archaic, particularly in light of the current market trend to purchase property primarily on account of its value as a long-term investment. Judges in more modern cases, such as *Cowan* v. *Scurgill* [1985] Ch 270, which we first came across in Chapter 10, have now referred to investment as including both income and capital growth. However, the judiciary has nevertheless remained cautious in expressing their views regarding capital growth, stating that trustees must be careful to maintain a balance in their investments between income and capital growth. There has still been no categorical statement from the courts as to whether an investment which produced capital growth alone would be considered a sufficient form of investment for trustee investment purposes, albeit that Vice-Chancellor Nicholls in *Harries* v. *Church Commissioners* [1992] 1 WLR 1241 (the full facts of which, again, can be found in Chapter 10) would appear to suggest that capital growth and income could be considered as alternative forms of investment when he stated that:

> modern cases have referred to investment as including both income and capital growth

the purposes of the trust will be best served by the trustees seeking to obtain therefrom the maximum return, whether by way of income or capital growth . . .

Current views on investment would seem to suggest that this is a sensible step forward, however. Take a moment to look at the Out and about feature and formulate your views on the matter.

Out and about

Think about the general rule against investment in items which will accrue in value – and property in particular. Then answer the following questions:

1. Do you agree with the traditional view of the judiciary that, as far as trustees are concerned, investment should mean only the making of those investments which yield an income?

2. Do you think that investing in capital growth alone is more risky than investing in things which produce an income?

3. Why do you think the judiciary has traditionally been against non-income producing investments in land?

4. Do you think their view is outdated?

5. What might be the benefits of allowing investments in appreciating assets such as land?

6. Do you think there should be a change in the law to this effect?

 Handy tip: Consider the recent crash in the property market. This may help you to get a perspective on the judiciary's reticence (or maybe not . . .).

One area in which the Trustee Act 2000 has been able to help is in respect of the purchase of land. Under section 8(1) of the Act a trustee is now able to acquire land in the UK for any reason, including that of investment and for occupation of a beneficiary. As stated above, the law still remains unclear as regards other types of capital investment, however.

The standard of care

We have seen, above, that the Trustee Act 2000 gives trustees very wide powers of investment. However, these powers are not given without any safeguard. In fact, the first thing the Trustee Act 2000 does is to impose upon all trustees a duty of care which will apply to them whenever they make an investment. This is different from the **common law** duty of care, which applies to trustees in their management of the trust generally and which we came across in Chapter 10. The duty of care contained in section 1(1) of the Trustee Act 2000 applies specifically to investments of trust property, and is set out as follows:

Whenever the duty under this subsection applies to a trustee, he must exercise such care and skill as is reasonable in all the circumstances, having regard in particular –

(a) to any special knowledge or experience that he has or holds himself out as having, and

(b) if he acts as a trustee in the course of a business or profession, to any special knowledge or experience that it is reasonable to expect of a person acting in the course of that kind of business or profession.

Having read the section above, now have a look at the You be the judge feature and see if you can answer the question.

You be the judge

Q: Under the provisions of the Trustee Act 2000, are **professional trustees** subject to a higher standard of care than ordinary trustees?

A: Yes. The standard of care will differ depending on whether the trustee either has or holds themselves out as having any special knowledge about the investment in question. In addition, trustees acting in their professional capacity are singled out as being subject to a higher standard of care than ordinary trustees with no specialist knowledge. For a more detailed explanation, see the main text.

We can see from the wording of section 1, then, that the standard of care imposed by the statute is twofold: under section 1(1)(a), all trustees are subject to a duty to exercise reasonable skill and care, having regard to any specialist knowledge or experience they hold themselves out as having in the field of investment (thus, this is a **subjective** test, based upon the trustee's own belief in their individual capabilities); and, under section 1(1)(b), professional trustees acting in the course of their business are subject to an additional, **objective** standard, that standard being that of their profession. This means that professional trustees are subject to a higher standard of care because they have to comply with both the general, subjective standard imposed by section 1(1)(a) and the objective standard imposed on them by virtue of their professional status, under section 1(1)(b).

According to Schedule 1 of the Act, the duty of care applies to a trustee wherever they are exercising their power of investment, 'however conferred'. This means that the duty will apply to them regardless of whether they are exercising the general power of investment which has been conferred on them by the Act, or whether they are exercising a power to invest trust property which has been given to them by some other means, for example by the settlor under the provisions of the **trust instrument** itself.

Express powers of investment

As was mentioned earlier in the chapter, due to the restrictive nature of the Trustee Investments Act 1961 it has become standard practice to include investment powers in professionally drafted trust deeds and so many existing trust deeds will certainly include wide powers of investment. Even with the advent of the Trustee Act 2000, many law firms still include powers of investment when drafting the trust deed, for the sake of clarity.

Wherever a trust deed does contain such powers of investment, if there is any question as to the scope of the powers given the court will not be restrictive in their interpretation. Clearly, to do so would go against what the statute has meant to achieve; however, this has been the case since before the 1961 Act came into force in any event. In the case of *Re Harari's Settlement Trusts* [1949] 1 All ER 430 the trustees had been given the power within a trust deed to invest 'in or upon such investments as to them may seem fit'. When the trustees questioned whether this meant they could invest beyond the ordinary scope of trustee investments, Mr Justice Jenkins held that the wording should be construed in accordance with what should be considered 'the natural and proper meaning of the words used in their context'. On this basis, he said:

Case Summary

> I see no justification for implying any restriction. I think the trustees have power . . . to invest in any investments which . . . they honestly think are desirable investments.

So that deals with specific powers of investment given by the settlor to the trustees in terms of the trust instrument. But what power of investment is actually given to trustees under the Trustee Act 2000?

The general power of investment

Section 6(1) of the Trustee Act 2000 tells us that the power of investment conferred on trustees by the Act will apply to trustees in the absence of any powers contained within the trust instrument. Where a trust instrument does contain investment provisions, on the other hand, the statutory power will be subject to those provisions. This means that any provisions in the trust instrument restricting the investment powers of the trustees will take precedence over the trustees' ability to invest under the general power conferred by the Trustee Act 2000.

Where the general power of investment does apply, section 3 of the Trustee Act 2000 states that:

> a trustee may make any kind of investment that he could make if he were absolutely entitled to the assets of the trust.

As you can see, this gives trustees a very wide power of investment indeed – basically, in making investments on behalf of the trust they can treat the property as if it were their own (albeit subject to any limitations as may still exist on making investments which provide purely capital growth, as outlined above). However, whilst the general power to invest is very wide, any investments actually made must be made within the 'standard investment criteria' set out at section 4 of the 2000 Act. These state that the trustees must have regard to:

(3) . . .

(a) the suitability to the trust of investments of the same kind as any particular investment proposed to be made or retained and of that particular investment as an investment of that kind, and

(b) the need for diversification of investments of the trust, in so far as is appropriate to the circumstances of the trust.

In respect of subsection (a), this is simply a common-sense requirement that trustees should take time to consider the suitability of the type of investment they are considering making to the trust, and the suitability of the specific investment as an investment of its type: in other words, 'will this particular investment provide a good return for my money?' The second requirement, that trustees consider the need for diversification in their investments, still means in essence that the trustees must invest in more than one type of product or investment, much as the requirements of the 1961 Act did. However, the wording of the 2000 Act is far less prescriptive, giving trustees the freedom to choose such investments as they feel are appropriate in any particular case.

Bearing in mind the guidance given above, now have a go at the exercise contained in the Key stats feature and see what kind of investor you are.

Key stats How averse are you to investment risk?

Investment is a booming business, even in the current financial climate. The total net investment by insurance companies, pension funds and trusts alone was provisionally estimated to have been £5 billion in the first quarter of 2010.* Why not take this quick risk-profiling questionnaire and see what your attitude to risk is.

Instructions

1. Answer each question A, B or C.

2. At the end of the questionnaire count up the number of As, Bs and Cs you got. Now add up your scores, giving yourself no points for an A, 1 point for a B and 2 points for a C.

3. Check your overall score on the investment scale.

Questions

1 Your employer offers you a bonus, which you can take as cash, shares or a mixture of both. The shares have a 50:50 chance of doubling in value, or becoming worthless over the next year. What would you do?

 A. Take it all in cash
 B. Take half cash and half shares
 C. Take it all in shares

2 If you were investing in the UK stock market and it suddenly fell by 40 per cent, what would you do?

 A. Get out quickly
 B. Sell some of my investment
 C. Stay put

3 You are appearing on the hit game show *Win a Million!* but you don't know the answer to the next question. What would you do?

 A. Not answer and take the £50,000
 B. Eliminate 2 wrong answers, leaving a choice of 2. If you guess right you'll have £75,000. If not, you'll get only £25,000
 C. Guess the answer. If you are right, you'll have £100,000. If not, you'll get nothing

4 You're offered a new sales job with a choice of three pay options. Which one would you take?

 A. £30,000 per year
 B. £20,000 per year, plus a performance bonus of £0 to £20,000
 C. £10,000 per year, plus a 'sky's the limit' performance bonus

5 Two years ago you invested £100,000 in a stock market fund. But the value recently fell to £85,000. What would you do?

 A. Switch what's left into something safer
 B. Stay where you are, in the hope of recouping your losses when the market picks up again
 C. Stay where you are and invest more money while prices are low in the hope of making more money when the market picks up again

My total score is:

* National Office of Statistics: http://www.statistics.gov.uk/cci/nugget.asp?id=396

Your risk profile

0–2	3–4	5	6–7	8–10
Secure	Cautious	Balanced	Progressive	Adventurous

Risk profile definitions

Secure

Investments in this category provide a high degree of safety and can be expected to offer relatively low growth over the medium to long term.

Cautious

These investments are expected to have a relatively modest risk to the capital and/or income. They have the potential to provide income over the medium to long term, or relatively modest capital growth.

Balanced

These investments carry a risk of loss to capital value but have the potential for capital growth and/or income over the medium to long term.

Progressive

These investments are expected to have a relatively significant risk of loss to capital value, but with the potential of relatively more growth over the medium to long term.

Adventurous

These investments carry relatively a much higher risk of capital loss but with the potential for relatively higher capital growth over the medium to long term.

These questions are a sample taken from a longer questionnaire written by BHP Financial Services Ltd. To find out more about the company go to: **http://www.bhpfs.ifanetsite.com/**.

[*Source*: **http://preview.bhpfs.ifanetsite.com/companyData/490/resources/Risk%20Profile%20Questionnaire.pdf**]

Reflective practice

Take a moment to consider your results in the above exercise. What kind of investor are you? What kind of investor do you think you need to be in order to make investments on behalf of a trust fund?

Whilst the terms of the Trustee Act 2000 have, to all intents and purposes, given trustees an entirely free rein as to the types of income-producing investments they can make, it should nevertheless be borne in mind, as we have seen in Chapter 10, that trustees are also subject to the overarching common law duties of trustees when making investments, in particular the duty to act in the best interests of the trust, as illustrated by the case of *Cowan* v. *Scargill*. This includes trustees avoiding restricting their choice of investment on the grounds of moral, religious or ethical reasons, unless they can be sure that their proposal will not in any way prejudice the financial security or return on the trust fund.

As we saw in Chapter 10 trustees also have a duty properly to balance the needs of the respective beneficiaries. In terms of investment, this is an important consideration: whereas a beneficiary with a **life interest** would most likely prefer income-producing investments, the person with the benefit of the interest in **remainder** (that is, the person who gets the benefit of the trust on the death of the person with the life interest, the **life tenant**) would be more interested in investments which preserved and grew the capital sum forming the body of the trust fund. However, subject to these considerations the trustees are really given an extremely wide discretion to make whatever choice of investment they decide would be in the best interests of the trust.

Purchase of land as an investment

One of the biggest problems with the Trustee Investment Act 1961 was that it did not authorise the purchase of land by trustees. However, as stated above, section 8(1) of the Trustee Act 2000 now allows land to be acquired by the trustees of a trust fund for any purpose, including the purchase of investment property.

Requirement to obtain advice

In addition to the requirement that trustees make their investments within the boundaries of the standard investment criteria, trustees are also bound to 'obtain and consider' proper advice about the investments they are planning to make under section 5 of the 2000 Act. According to the section, proper advice means advice:

> from a person who is reasonably believed to be qualified to give it by his ability in and practical experience of financial and other matters relating to the proposed investment.

Who such a qualified person is will depend on the nature of the investment involved: in all usual cases one would expect this to be a qualified financial adviser, but if it were a specialised investment, such as the purchase of shares in a football club, you may prefer to base your advice on someone who knows more about the performance of the team in the league tables!

There is no requirement that such advice is in writing, although it may be sensible for the trustees to ensure any advice they take is made in writing, in order to protect themselves against the risk of future liability should the investments not turn out to be sound. For a further discussion on the liability of trustees for the action of their **agents**, see below.

It should be noted that trustees are not required to obtain advice if they reasonably conclude that in all the circumstances it is unnecessary or inappropriate to do so (section 5(3)). Therefore if they have some financial expertise themselves and are confident in their decision-making they need not obtain additional advice from a professional. Equally, if the investment risk is so small or the sums involved so little the trustees may consider that it is not worth going to the time (and possibly expense) of instructing a third party. In the People in the law feature, financial expert Jonathan Sapier gives his opinion on the use of professional advisers.

People in the law

Name and position: Jonathan Sapier, financial adviser.

What is your role as a financial adviser?

My role is to ensure that my clients are fully aware of the products and services that can benefit their short-term to long-term financial planning. I meet the clients, explain simply what I do, identify a need and facilitate that requirement. This is followed up with review meetings at least once a year to ensure that the client is kept up to date with planning their own finances as well as changes in legislation giving them further opportunities to enhance their financial situation.

Source: Jonathan Sapier (*text and photo*)

So (amongst other things) you advise people on the best way to invest their money?

I advise people of their most effective way of investing, yes. I cater for people with varying attitudes to risk and differing investment strategies. Tax efficiency, goals and monitoring are essential to a successful client relationship which is hoped can be long term.

How often do you advise your clients to review their investments? Why is this necessary?

It is necessary to review clients' investments for a few reasons. Their own circumstances may change whether they like it or not, for the good and sometimes for the not so good. We are living in an era that demands change, is changing rapidly and flexibility is absolutely essential in this changing and challenging environment.

New thresholds, tax and trust rules can change and it is absolutely vital that the clients are kept informed of these changes to ensure they are not being disadvantaged by any new legislation. Legitimate ways of tax avoidance are often looked upon and reviewed by the government, usually to their advantage, so it is increasingly important to be ahead of the game, aware and prepared to face such legislative changes as and when they occur.

It is important to review a client's portfolio to ensure that their goals are being achieved through their own strategy which may change. An investor who, say, was brave through the bull market [a rising market] and prepared to take a risk with a more adventurous fund, may not be so prepared in a bear market [a declining

market] to have the same courage of their conviction. In addition to that, an investment which seemed right at the time may not, retrospectively, seem so exciting so it is important to ensure that the client's goals and investment objectives are current, again in this ever-changing market. A client may wish to move money from fund to fund depending on their own attitude to risk, which tends to reflect the prevailing market. No one wants to be left behind or out of kilter with changes and a review can ensure that the client feels that they are being looked after with the backing of a reputable adviser and company.

Is this more frequent than was previously the case, say, since the recession?

The regularity at which clients should review their investments has not really changed much in my view. I think that it is important to keep apace with things but reviewing too regularly can be counter-productive as a change of strategy needs to have time to establish and develop. It can be a waste of time reviewing an investment only to have a change of heart a month or so later after reading an article in the press. Whilst this is possible to effect, it may be deemed to be acting too much on a whim or hearsay.

Trustees are given powers under the Trustee Act 2000 to delegate their powers to an agent. Do you think it would be necessary to review the investments of agents at the same intervals as if you had made the investments yourselves, or even more

frequently? With regard to agents, if investing is what they do full time, then surely they have the experience to be more aware of imminent changes, fund profiles and more aware of imminent opportunities so I would say that a more regular review of agents on behalf of their clients would be preferred.

Anything you would like to add about reviewing your finances (any handy tips or hints)? Don't 'do it yourself'. You may be tempted to talk to your usual financial adviser at the pub (who for a real job is an accountant, tradesman, private sector worker, builder, nurse, brother-in-law or old schoolmate) but do seek professional financial advice. When you have a toothache, you wouldn't let your bank manager look inside your mouth. Conversely, if you have some money that you're not sure where to invest, you wouldn't ask your dentist.

Don't follow the fashion. Ensure that you are investing for 'you'. We are all individuals with differing needs and priorities. Someone's idea of Heaven is someone else's idea of Hell. Have courage to take advice tailored specifically for your needs and not the needs of your neighbour or friend.

Requirement to review investments

So the trustees have made their investment decisions, perhaps with the benefit of advice from a professional. But their responsibility does not just end there. There is a further requirement placed upon trustees under section 4(2) of the Trustee Act 2000 to review the investments of the trust from time to time, and to consider whether they should be revised. This must be done with regard, again, to the standard investment criteria. It is interesting to note that the Trustee Act 2000 gives no specific guidance to trustees as to how often trustees should review their investments, other than to say that they should be reviewed 'from time to time'. As can be seen from Jonathan Sapier's comments in the People in the law feature, the time period which should ideally elapse between reviews will necessarily depend on the nature of the investment and the individual needs of the investor, however.

> the Act gives no specific guidance as to how often trustees should review their investments

The power to delegate

Many trustees may feel that, whilst obtaining advice on individual investment matters may be prudent, they would be happier if they were able to delegate this part of their duties altogether and employ a professional to deal with the investment of the trust fund as a whole. The Trustee Act 2000 now allows trustees to do this, stating at section 11(1) that:

> The trustees of a trust may authorise any person to exercise any or all of their delegable functions as their agent.

Such delegable functions would naturally include their investment decisions. However, the Act is quite clear about what trustees are not allowed to delegate too; in particular any decision relating to the distribution of trust assets to the beneficiaries under the terms of the trust, or to the payment of maintenance or advancement, must remain strictly with the trustees. In addition, the appointment of new trustees and the appointment of agents themselves cannot be delegated under section 11.

Who can be an agent?

It should be noted that, whilst a single trustee with the requisite set of skills can be authorised to act as an agent on behalf of the trustees, a beneficiary cannot act as an agent, even if that beneficiary is also already a trustee of the trust. This is presumably because to employ a beneficiary as an agent would be a conflict of interests too far. How the trustees choose their agent is up to them. The Law in action feature may act as a note of caution in making a careful choice, however.

Law in action Is it safe to delegate? Lessons to be learnt from the biggest investment fraud in history

In what is set to become known as one of the biggest frauds in history, in December 2008 Bernard Madoff was arrested for cheating his investment banking businesses out of a record $65 billion.

It transpires that former NASDAQ* chairman and powerful Wall Street figure Mr Madoff had been operating a '**Ponzi scheme**'. Named after Italian-American fraudster Charles Ponzi, a Ponzi scheme is where someone promises fantastic returns to his investors, but, instead of investing the money, simply uses the money of new investors to pay the original investors their 'returns'. Relying on his cast-iron business reputation for cover, Mr Madoff had been taking money from would-be investors in this way since 2005 (some say it may be even earlier), promising – and it would seem delivering – returns of up to 12 per cent annually.

Source: Photodisc/Steve Cole

Unfortunately, the recession hit everyone, however, and when the stream of new investors in the fund dried up to a trickle in the middle of 2008, Mr Madoff found he was able to give smaller and smaller returns to his original investors and people started wanting to take their money out of the 'fund'.

Knowing the game was up, Mr Madoff confessed – but not before writing out a series of cheques worth a total of $137 million to close family and friends, which were found stashed in his desk drawer shortly after his arrest.

Is there anything would-be investors can learn from this incident? Deborah Hargreaves, financial correspondent for the *Guardian* newspaper, offers a couple of sound points of advice on this:

1. If it appears too good to be true, it almost certainly is. There is no magical formula of

investment that allows you to outperform your rivals consistently.

2. Don't put all your eggs in one basket. Investments should be put into a range of funds to spread risk.

'We all need to take greater responsibility for our finances and try to manage them properly,' says Deborah. 'It takes time, commitment and some financial nous. But we can't afford not to.'

Prosecutors in the United States have charged Mr Madoff, 70, with a single count of securities fraud, for which he faces up to 20 years in prison and a fine of up to $5 million if convicted.

[*Source*: **http://www.guardian.co.uk/commentisfree/cifamerica/2009/jun/29/investment-bernard-madoff-finances**]

*NASDAQ – National Association of Securities Dealers Automated Quotation Systems – is a US stock exchange, the fourth largest in the world.

We can see that choosing an agent is not a task to be taken lightly, then. Nor is it without its risks and consequences. There are additional provisions put in place by the Trustee Act 2000 to assist trustees in ensuring the right choice is made, however.

Terms of agency

Whoever is chosen to be an agent of the trustees, if the agent is involved in the investment or management of trust property the trustees must enter into a written agreement with their agent, including a '**policy statement**' giving the agent guidance on how to act in the best interests of the trust. This is under section 15 of the Trustee Act 2000. Such a statement would cover such matters as the types of investment the agent is to make, the required projected income, any requirement for capital growth, any balance required between life interests and interests in remainder, and so on. The Act also allows for the payment of such agents within the terms of the agreement.

There is an example of a real policy statement in the Documenting the Law feature that follows. But before that, why not have a go at drafting your own in the Writing and drafting exercise.

Writing and drafting

Consider the case of Bernie Madoff in the Law in action feature, above. His investors, trusting him implicitly, obviously did not monitor the investments he made on their behalf as carefully as they might have done.

Unlike those investors, however, you have the benefit of hindsight! Imagine you are employing Bernie Madoff as your investment agent. Now draft a policy statement for him to follow in line with the requirements of the Trustee Act 2000.

You should take no longer than 30 minutes on this task.

 Handy tip: Try putting yourself in the investor's shoes. What would you want to know about the investments you were going to make on behalf of your client. Feeling really stuck? You could always cheat and take a sneaky peek at the example below in the Documenting the law feature.

How did you get on? Did you manage to draft something without referring to the sample policy statement? The Documenting the law feature provides a comprehensive example produced by investment management company Williams de Broë of an investment policy statement for a charity.

Documenting the law

An example of a policy statement

Company Name: The Example Charity
Charity Number: 1234 56789
HM Revenue and Customs Number: 123 456 789

i) General background

The charity was set up in 1850 by way of a legacy of farmland in the St. Mary's church parish. Where possible the vicar and at least one church warden of St David's church, Rufford, Lancashire should be appointed trustees, with any other trustees being chosen from those closely associated with the church's activities. The income from the trust's assets is to be used solely for the purpose of supporting the activities of the church, but specifically not for the maintenance of its fabric.

ii) Financial profile

The charity still owns land and property in the church parish of a value of approximately £6 million, from which annual rental income is achieved of the order of £200,000. An additional £2 million or so is held in investments from which annual income is derived of approximately £60,000. The total income generated at present is more than sufficient to meet the charity's normal outgoings.

iii) Investment powers

The charity's assets must be invested in accordance with the Trustee Act 2000 and the trust instrument.

iv) Investment policy

a) General objectives

The investments must be managed in such a way as to provide sufficient income to enable the charity to carry out its purposes effectively both in the short term and over the longer term. Where possible, the value of the assets should be enhanced so as to at least keep pace with inflation over the longer term.

The charity's capital constitutes a permanent endowment, and only the income from the charity's investments is to be used for furthering the charity's aims.

b) Balance between intended capital growth and immediate income requirements

An approximate balance is to be maintained between the enhancement of capital and the generation of income.

c) Acceptable risk

A 'medium risk' approach is to be adopted in the management of the charity's assets. Refer to 'investment parameters and exclusions'.

d) Functions delegated to the trustees' agent (investment manager)

The investments are to be managed on a 'discretionary' basis.

e) Cashflow

Working capital might constitute up to 5 per cent of the charity's assets, and reserves a further 5 per cent. This proportion of the overall assets will be retained by the trustees, although in this regard advice may be sought from time to time on cash deposits and short dated bonds. The remainder of the portfolio will be subject to the guidelines detailed in 'investment parameters and exclusions'.

f) Investment parameters and exclusions

Any bonds held in the portfolio should be of 'investment grade', and all should be denominated in sterling.

The trustees should be consulted in the event of the average yield on the portfolio falling below 2 per cent. No investment at the time of its acquisition should exceed 10 per cent of the overall value of the portfolio, and those investments that each account for more than 5 per cent of the total portfolio value should not combined exceed 40 per cent of the total funds under management.

The geographical and asset class constitution of the portfolio is to be based on that of the WM 'unconstrained' asset mix which, as at 28 September 2007, was as follows: –

WM 'unconstrained' average asset allocation 28/09/07

%
UK Equities 53.9
Overseas Equities 25.0
Bonds 10.5
Property 3.2
Other 3.3
Cash 4.1
Total 100

The investment manager has discretion to vary the UK equity element of the portfolio by up to 15 per cent either side of the current WM position, the bond and overseas equity element by up to 10 per cent of the WM positions and property, other and cash elements by up to 5 per cent of the respective WM positions. In the case of cash, additional leeway may be allowed after consultation with the trustees.

'Derivatives' may not be used without prior consultation with the trustees.

The objects of the charity are to be met by way of a prudent investment strategy based on a diversified range of bonds and equities which are quoted on a recognised investment exchange, and unit trusts and Open Ended Investment Companies (OEICs) which are authorised under the Financial Services and Markets Act 2000. The 'type' of each investment and the individual investments themselves should be suitable to meet the charity's purposes.

g) Ethical Restrictions

The portfolio should not include any investments in companies where more than 25 per cent of total turnover is accounted for by tobacco products.

No further ethical restrictions apply, although the trustees reserve the right to exclude from the portfolio any investments in companies whose representation might prove damaging, directly or indirectly, to the purposes or reputation of the charity.

v) Investment performance benchmarking

The performance of the overall portfolio is to be monitored against the quarterly returns reported by WM Performance Services in respect of the 'unconstrained' charities under their review.

vi) Income

Income that has accrued in each quarter is to be transferred to the charity's bank account within 30 days of the respective quarter end. The trustees may, at their discretion, re-credit all or part of these payments to the portfolio's cash account.

vii) Funds held on deposit

Cash retained on deposit by Williams de Broë as part of the ongoing management of the portfolio should be held in accordance with the terms of the contract between Williams de Broë and the charity. It is understood that interest earned on cash deposits will be not less than 0.5 per cent below the Bank of England's base rate; the trustees are to be advised in the event of any changes to these arrangements.

As already stated, the trustees may, from time to time, seek advice from Williams de Broë concerning cash balances held outside the portfolio.

viii) Use of nominee facilities

The investments are to be held by Williams de Broë's nominee company.

ix) Appointment of the charity's investment 'agent' (investment manager)

Williams de Broë, a suitably authorised person within the meaning of the Financial Services and Markets Act 2000, is the appointed investment manager, subject to the terms of both this investment policy statement and subsequent amendments to the statement, and the contract entered into between the charity and Williams de Broë relating to the latter's appointment.

x) Remuneration

The basis of Williams de Broë's remuneration will be that detailed at the time of their being appointed investment manager. One month notice should be provided to the trustees in the event of Williams de Broë intending to amend its fee and commission regime.

xi) FRAG 21/Insurance cover

Williams de Broë will provide on request both evidence of the company's insurance cover and a copy of its FRAG 21 document or its equivalent.

xii) Reporting requirements

A contract note and detailed explanatory letter is to be provided at the time that each transaction is undertaken. At the end of each calendar quarter a valuation and accompanying report is to be provided encompassing the following: –

✦ A list of all investments held together with their respective book costs, current market value, and estimated income and yield.

✦ A performance analysis for the period covered by the report (quarterly) providing the statistics necessary to comply with the performance requirements detailed in the investment policy statement.

✦ A transaction schedule detailing both purchases and sales.

✦ Details of any non-market transactions and rights issues, capitalisations or other corporate actions.

✦ A detailed review of the market environment for the period including specific comment on the individual holdings in the portfolio and any other economic considerations that are relevant.

✦ A separate report will be prepared at the end of the charity's financial year, 31 March, providing such information as is required by the trustees to meet their reporting obligations.

✦ The trustees will require the nominated investment manager to attend meetings at the offices of either Williams de Broë or the charity, as dictated by the trustees, as frequently as is required but, in any event, at least every 12 months.

xiii) Required periodic reviews of both the written investment policy statement and the provision of investment management services

The investment policy statement will be subject to reviews as required by the trustees, and amendments will be advised in writing to Williams de Broë. In any event, the investment policy statement will be reviewed at least once a year to ensure that it remains compatible with the charity's objects and requirements.

It is anticipated that the investment management services provided to the charity by Williams de Broë will be formally reviewed every two years, or at such time as deemed appropriate by the trustees. No notice period will be given by the trustees in respect of termination of the services provided to the charity by Williams de Broë.

xiv) Exercising delegated investment functions

In addition to complying with the specific requirements detailed in the investment policy statement the appointed investment manager must pay heed to the general power of investment embodied in Section 3 of

The Charity Act 2000. All investments should be suitable and, overall, constitute a degree of diversification as required by Section 4 of The Charity Act 2000.

xv) Powers delegated to an investment sub committee

While the charity's investment policy has been set by the Board of trustees as a whole responsibility for ongoing investment issues has been delegated to an investment sub committee whose members are listed below. The minute relating to this delegated authority is enclosed.

[*Source*: www.wdebroe.com/.../WDBCharitiesInvestmentPolicyStatement-TemplateForCharities07-08.doc]

Reflective practice

As you can see the policy statement is really quite comprehensive. How does it compare with the one you created for Bernie Madoff? Is there anything you missed from your statement that you think you should have included? Are there things that you thought of from which you think this policy statement would benefit?

Supervision of agents

Whilst trustees are allowed to delegate their investment powers this does not absolve them of all responsibility for investments made under the trust. They cannot simply sit back and allow their appointed agent to deal with the trust funds in whatever manner they see fit. Of course, the contract with the agent and the policy statement set out within it does go some way towards protecting the trustees as it sets out the limits within which the agent should be working. However, this should not be the end of the matter for the trustees. According to section 22 of the Trustee Act 2000 trustees should continue to monitor the work of their agent on a regular basis and to check that they are carrying out the terms of the agreement. They are also required, as and when necessary, to revise the policy statement. If the trustees feel that there is a need to do so, they should also take action to intervene in the making of decisions by the agent by giving their specific instructions to the agent or, where necessary, by revoking their appointment.

> trustees should monitor the work of their agent on a regular basis

However, as long as the trustees carry out the delegation of their duties and the subsequent monitoring of their agents with the required level of care (being the general duty of care imposed on them under section 1 of the Trustee Act 2000) under section 23 of the Act they will not be liable for any act or default of any agent they have employed.

Summary

◆ The Trustee Act 2000 imposes a duty of care on trustees when making investments. A trustee must exercise such care and skill as is reasonable in all the circumstances paying regard in particular to any special knowledge or experience that they may have. Professional trustees are subject to a higher standard of care than ordinary trustees, being judged by the standard of their profession.

◆ The Trustee Act 2000 does not give any statutory meaning for the term investment, but the courts have traditionally interpreted the term strictly, to include only investments yielding income rather than those providing purely capital growth. More modern cases have interpreted investment to include capital growth, but there has been no definitive decision on the point to date.

◆ Under the general power of investment set out in the Trustee Act 2000, a trustee can make any investment on behalf of the trust that they would make with their own money (section 3), including investments in land. This is subject to the trustees' general common law duties to act in the best interests of the trust and to balance the interests of the beneficiaries.

◆ The statutory power of investment applies wherever the trust instrument is silent in respect of investment. Where there are provisions governing investment contained in the trust instrument, the statutory power is subject to those provisions.

◆ In making investments, trustees must have regard to the standard investment criteria, however, which are the suitability of the investment to the trust and the need for diversification of investments within it (section 4).

◆ Trustees are also required to review the investments of the trust from time to time and consider whether they should be renewed (section 4(2)).

◆ Trustees must obtain and consider proper advice about the investments they are planning to make (section 5) wherever it is appropriate. There is no requirement for the advice to be in writing.

◆ Trustees can appoint an agent to make investment decisions on their behalf (section 11).

◆ On appointing an agent, the trustees must enter into a written agreement with them, including a detailed 'policy statement' giving the agent guidance on how to act in the best interests of the trust (section 15).

◆ Trustees must monitor the work of their agents, intervening wherever appropriate (section 22).

Question and answer*

Problem: A concerned beneficiary of a family trust fund comes to see you at your solicitors' offices. The trust, which contains the family home and somewhere in the region of a further £1 million in cash, stocks and shares, was set up by the beneficiary's late father in 2008. There are no clauses in the trust deed relating to investment. The beneficiaries under the trust are the beneficiary who has come to see you, Anna, her mother Nadège, and brother Felix.

Anna explains to you that the trustees named under the trust deed are the three beneficiaries and an old friend of Anna's father, Gregory Barr. Anna believes that her father envisaged Gregory running the day-to-day administration of the fund, with the family's input; but Gregory fell into a state of ill health 18 months ago, leaving Anna, her bother and mother to manage the fund alone. Anna and her mother know nothing about investments, but Felix, a mortgage adviser by trade, professes to know quite a lot and last month persuaded Anna's mother to delegate the task of looking after the trust fund investments to him, although nothing was put into writing to formalise this.

Anna felt uncomfortable about it at the time, but went along with her mother and brother's wishes, not wishing to rock the boat. However, she is now becoming increasingly concerned about how the trust fund is being invested by Felix. Alarm bells started ringing when Felix told her a month ago that he had bought a share in a racehorse, Old Sally, which he had received a tip-off from a drinking buddy is set to win the Grand National. And, to make matters worse, last week when she went round to Felix's house to discuss the situation, she found him in the garage with a large pile of 'Beanie Babies', which he said he was collecting on behalf of the trust as they are collectors items and will be worth a lot of money in a few years time.

Advise Anna.

You should allow yourself no more than 40 minutes to complete this task.

Essay: 'The Trustee Act 2000 does not provide enough guidance for non-professional trustees who know nothing about investment.' Discuss.

This question should be answered in 40 minutes.

✱ Answer guidance is provided at the end of the chapter.

Further reading

Clifford, J. (2009) 'Investment: can private trustees learn anything from pension scheme trustees?', *Trusts and Trustees*, 15(7), 611–18.
This useful article compares the statutory regime for pension scheme investment under the Pensions Act 1995 with the scheme for investment of private trusts under the Trustee Act 2000. The author suggests the adoption of a pensions law-style statement of investment principles to provide trustees with a benchmark by which to operate.

Le Poidevin, N. (2009) 'The worried trustee', *Trusts and Trustees*, 15(7), 596–601.
This recent article considers the liability of trustees under the Trustee Act 2000 for poorly-performing trust investments. The article also examines the duty of care owed by investment managers at common law and under the Supply of Goods and Services Act and looks at the trustee's obligation to claim for breach of this duty.

Wain, M. and Shenkin, M. (2009) 'Trustee investment powers and the use of asset managers', *Trusts and Trustees*, 15(2), 72–9.
This useful article outlines the power of investment for trustees under the Trustee Act 2000, focusing on the issue of delegation. The article contains useful guidance on the writing of investment policy statements, noting matters for trustees to consider when drafting their statement.

Question and answer guidance

Problem:

Meaning of investment

There is no statutory definition of the term investment, but it is generally thought to mean the laying out of money in return for an income or return. Presumably, the purchase of Old Sally would bring in a return in terms of cup winnings, if it is a truly talented racehorse, as well as going up in value as a result of the races it wins. It is a highly speculative investment, however, based on a tip-off which is far from scientific, and one could question the suitability of such an investment to the trust.

As regards the Beanie Babies, these would accumulate in value, but not make any income. Traditional views of investment in trust funds have been that assets acquired on the basis that they will increase in value, but which will not produce an income, cannot be classed as investments. However, newer cases have suggested that such assets would now qualify as an investment.

Power to invest

Trustees have a power to invest under the Trustee Act 2000. The power is very wide, allowing trustees to invest in personal and real property as if it were their own (section 3). In making such investments, the trustees nevertheless are subject to a statutory duty of care, under section 1 of the Trustee Act 2000. Trustees have a duty to exercise reasonable care and skill, bearing in mind any special knowledge or experience they profess to have. Felix says he is knowledgeable on the subject, and this will be taken into account when deciding on whether he has exercised reasonable care and skill. The trustees also have to take into account the standard investment criteria in making their investment choices, under section 4 of the Act. These require that the trustees consider the suitability of the investments to the trust and the diversification of investments. It is questionable whether either of the investments made are suitable. In addition, both are high-risk investments which does not show an even spread of investment for the fund.

Regarding the liability of the trustees for their delegation of the investment to trustee, Felix, the trustees have a power to delegate their investment functions under section 11 of the Act. However, they should have entered into a written agreement with their agent, including a 'policy statement' directing him how best to act in the interests of the trust. As they have not done so they are likely to be unable to escape all accountability for Felix's actions.

Essay: The question is expecting students to give an overview of the power to invest as contained within the Act, with reference to the guidance it gives to ordinary trustees.

The Trustee Act 2000 gives trustees a very wide discretion to invest, to the point that trustees can invest trust property as if it were their own. But does this give those without investment knowledge too wide a discretion? Arguably not, because of the safeguards put in place by the act to protect trust funds from trustees who make poor investment decisions. The guidance given to trustees is threefold:

1. They are given a wide discretion to invest trust property as if it were their own.
2. They must nevertheless exercise that discretion in the light of the standard investment criteria. These say that a trustee must take into account the suitability of the investment to the trust and consider the diversification of investments under the trust when making investments.
3. In addition, trustees are required to reach the necessary standard of care in making investments. The statutory duty of care which applies is that trustees should exercise reasonable skill and care in making investments on behalf of the trust (section 1). This is measured against any particular skill the investing trustee may profess themselves to have in the area of investment.

If this guidance isn't specific enough for a trustee who wishes to make investments on behalf of the trust, they have the option (and duty) of obtaining and considering proper advice (section 5). If they aren't sure about which investments to make, therefore, the Act clearly tells them to seek advice about it.

In addition, if the trustees wish to delegate their investment powers altogether to a professional, they can do so under section 11. Trustees are then required to review any investments made on behalf of the trust on a regular basis, under section 4(2).

The student should conclude by stating whether or not they believe this gives trustees enough guidance on how to invest trust funds, or whether they feel the Act could go further.

Chapter 13
Breach of trust

Key Points In this chapter we will be looking at:

- ◆ The definition of breach of trust
- ◆ The extent of liability
- ◆ Liability for breaches by other trustees
- ◆ Defences available to trustees in breach of trust

- ◆ The limitation periods which apply to actions for breach of trust
- ◆ The availability of relief from liability under section 61 Trustee Act 1925
- ◆ Exclusion from liability for breach of trust

Introduction

Having considered, in Chapters 1 to 8, the nature and creation of **trusts** and, in Chapters 9 to 12, how those trusts are administered, we have now reached what must be viewed, from a student perspective at least, as the really meaty and interesting part of this text – which is what happens when trustees misbehave! In these final four chapters we will be dealing with:

- ◆ breaches of trust: that is, when a **trustee** breaches his duties under the terms of the trust (Chapter 13);
- ◆ liability of **strangers** to the trust: that is, liability of people who receive trust funds or property from a rogue trustee (Chapter 14);
- ◆ **tracing** trust property: this is the real detective work of following and finding trust funds or

property which have been illegally removed from the trust (Chapter 15); and

- ◆ remedies available to the **beneficiaries** of a trust fund for a breach of trust (Chapter 16).

Whether you realise it or not, you will undoubtedly have come across countless instances of abuses of trust, from the investment manager who spends his clients' investment monies, as we saw in the celebrated Bernie Madoff fraud in Chapter 12, to the film stereotype of the company secretary who flies off to South America with millions of pounds of stolen company money, to the real-life case of reckless market trader Nick Leeson, who lost millions of pounds of client money trading speculatively on the stock market (see Law in action).

Law in action Nick Leeson: the 'rogue trader'

Nick Leeson began working as a stock market trader in the City of London in 1982. Starting in a modest role, he quickly worked his way up the ranks, soon becoming the star trader for the Singapore office of the UK's oldest merchant bank, Barings, and bringing in substantial profits.

By 1993, Leeson had made more than £10 million, which was about 10 per cent of Barings's total profit for that year, and Leeson earned a bonus of a staggering £130,000 on his £50,000 salary (a bonus of around £235,000 in today's money).

But in 1994 his luck began to run out, the final straw being the economic crisis caused when the Kobe earthquake hit Japan on 17 January 1995, killing an estimated 6,500 people and causing $102 billion in damage. Leeson attempted to make up his losses by making ever more speculative deals, requesting and receiving additional funds from the bank in order to continue trading. However, his bosses became suspicious and carried out a spot audit in February 1995, in doing so discovering losses amounting to more than £800 million: almost the entire assets of the bank.

When he was discovered, Leeson went on the run, first to Borneo, then to Frankfurt, but he was arrested and then extradited from Germany back to Singapore.

Source: Photodisc/Photolink

Leeson pleaded guilty to fraud and was sentenced to six and a half years in prison.

Dozens of Barings executives who were implicated in the failure to control Leeson either resigned or were sacked.

Barings Bank collapsed as a direct result of Leeson's dealings and was eventually bought for £1 by the Dutch banking and insurance group ING.

[*Sources*: based on information from http://news.bbc.co.uk/1/hi/business/375259.stm; http://www.nickleeson.com/biography/full_biography.html.]

As a stockbroker, Nick Leeson was in a **fiduciary** position in respect of his clients' money. By trading speculatively he was in clear breach of trust. Of course, not all cases of breach of trust are as excessive, or indeed as serious in their implications, as the instances cited here, however. There are plenty of examples of breaches of trust which have little or no impact on the beneficiaries, or which are both easy and painless to remedy, for example where the trustees fail to appoint or remove trustees in the correct manner. In this first chapter on breaches of trust, we will be taking a look both at some of the more serious breaches of trust and at some of the more innocent mistakes a trustee can make in the course of their duties.

> plenty of breaches of trust have little or no impact on the beneficiaries

One point that you should note before reading this chapter is that it is closely linked with Chapter 10, on duties of trustees. It would therefore be sensible to refresh yourself of the main points in Chapter 10 before you commence your reading on breach of trust. As a brief reminder, you will remember that whilst the duties of a trustee are numerous, the most important and fundamental duties appertaining to their role are these:

✦ First, the basic duty to act in the best interests of the beneficiaries, which includes the duty not to compete with the interests of the trust.

✦ Second, the duty not to profit from the trust, either by receiving payment for their role or by receiving benefits of any other kind by virtue of their position.

It should also be noted that only the civil liability for trustees in breach will be considered in this chapter, criminal liability being outside the scope of this book. It is interesting to note, however, that under sections 2(1)(c) and 4(2)(a) of the Theft Act 1968, fraudulent criminal activity can bring with it a sentence of up to a maximum of 10 years per offence, plus a further year if the breach also involved breaching court directions, this being equated to contempt of court. In many of the examples given in the chapter, such as that of Nick Leeson above, the person in breach of trust was tried on criminal charges, as well as having a civil action brought against them for recovery of the monies.

How do we define a breach of trust?

A breach of trust can be defined as any act or omission by a trustee that takes that trustee outside the terms of the trust or outside of their duties as a trustee. This means that a trustee will be in breach of trust not only for doing something which is beyond the scope of his powers as a trustee, but also for failing to act in accordance with his duties. Take, by way of example, the duty of a trustee to invest the trust fund. A trustee who makes an investment they are not authorised to make under the terms of the trust deed, for example, will be in breach of trust. This might be the case if they were to invest in a company outside the UK, when the trust deed specified that the trustees should invest in UK-based companies only. Equally, a trustee who failed altogether to invest trust monies with which they were entrusted would also be in breach of their duty to invest because of their failure to take any action.

You be the judge

Q: Which of the following do you think amount to breaches of trust?

(a) Danyl, following a top tip from a reliable source at his local pub, invests half of the trust fund of which he is trustee on a horse named Diamond Duke in the 3.30 at Aintree Racecourse.

(b) Trustee Simon invests trust monies with White Horse Insurance. In return he receives a commission (that is, a cash payment) from the insurance broker for giving them the business.

(c) Mika wishes to retire as a trustee. He enters into a **deed of retirement** from the trust under section 39 of the Trustee Act 1925, leaving Elana as sole trustee.

(d) Trustee Chelsea buys a house owned by the trust which the trustees no longer have any use for. She pays full market value for the property.

(e) Trustees Alice and Cheryl distribute half the trust fund to Horace, an imposter, believing him to be Charles, one of the beneficiaries of the fund.

A: They all are. Did you remember the answer to (c) – Mika's retirement? If not, you may wish to refer back to Chapter 9 on the appointment and retirement of trustees. There must be two trustees remaining on the retirement of a trustee under section 39. It may surprise you to know that even Alice and Cheryl, who have acted in good faith by distributing the funds to someone they believe is the correct person, and who are themselves the victims of a fraud, are still technically in breach of trust because they have failed in their duty to distribute to those entitled to the trust monies. This is because of the **strict liability** of trustees, which we will look at further on in the chapter.

The remedies available to beneficiaries for a trustee's breach are various and will be dealt with in detail at Chapter 16. However, the measure of liability in each instance will be the same. The general rule is that a trustee in breach of trust will be required to put the trust fund back to the position it would have been in, had the breach not occurred: so any monies or property which have been removed from the fund must be replaced, any profits made by trustees should be paid into the fund and any losses reimbursed. This will be explored further in the later chapter on remedies.

How many civil fraud cases do you think pass through the courts every year (fraud being the most common breach of trust, as we have seen above)? It may be more than you imagine! Forensic accountancy firm KPMG have been keeping records on their 'Fraud Barometer' of major fraud cases being heard in the UK's Crown Courts for some 22 years, keeping records of cases where the charges are in excess of £100,000. Take a look at the results in the Key stats feature for some shocking statistics.

Key stats KPMG Fraud Barometer

Fraud by perpetrator (Jan–Dec 2009)

Perpetrator	Total (£)	Number of cases
Management	335,610,686	65
Customer	26,426,554	40
Professional criminals	718,758,413	101
Employee	232,626,170	58
Other	1,004,312	7
Total	**1,314,426,135**	**271**

Well – was it more than you thought?

For more information on KPMG's Fraud Barometer, go to: **http://www.yhff.co.uk/KPMG%20FB%20Jan%20 2010.pdf.**

Strict liability of trustees

As we saw in the You be the judge feature, above, the liability of a trustee in breach of trust is strict. This means that the trustee will be liable for a breach regardless of their motives for committing that breach, and even a trustee acting in good faith will still be liable for a breach of trust if one is committed.

Case Summary

The example of Alice and Cheryl in the You be the judge feature mirrors the facts of a real case, which was heard in 1861. In the case of *Eaves* v. *Hickson* 30 Beav 136, the trustees mistakenly paid over an entire trust fund to the illegitimate children of William Knibb. The trustees had believed the children to be legitimate because of a forged marriage certificate produced to them by the children's father. However, despite the forged nature of the document on which they had relied and despite the fact that the trustees had acted honestly, the trustees were nevertheless liable of breach of trust. The presiding judge in the case, Mr Justice Romilly, Master of the Rolls, said that it was a very hard case on the trustees, who had been deceived by a forgery 'which would have deceived anyone who was not looking out for forgery or fraud'. In recognition of this the judge ruled that William Knibb should be liable to replace the trust, to the extent that the fund could not be recovered from the children. Only when those sources of cash had been exhausted should the trustees face liability to top up the remainder of the misappropriated fund.

Case Summary

Another example of the strict liability of trustees is that of *Re Diplock* [1948] Ch 465. The case concerned the interpretation of the will of a Mr Caleb Diplock. The will directed Mr Diplock's **executors** to distribute the **residue** of his **estate** to 'such charitable . . . or benevolent . . . **objects**' as they should select. Mr Diplock's solicitors did exactly this, dividing a total sum of over £200,000 between various charities chosen by them. However, Mr Diplock's **next of kin** subsequently challenged the solicitors' actions on the grounds that the gift was not exclusively charitable and was therefore invalid. (You will remember from Chapter 5 on charities that the gift must be exclusively charitable in order to be valid. This gift was for charitable *or* benevolent objects and therefore not exclusively for charitable purposes.) The outcome of the case was that the trustees were, despite the fact that they had acted in good faith, held to be in breach of trust. An interesting point to note about this case is that it was in fact ultimately the charities that were required to pay the money back into the trust fund, despite being entirely innocent parties to the breach. The fact that the charities were '**innocent volunteers**', having received the money as a gift from the trustees, did not entitle them to keep the money which had been given to them in error by the trustees. This could be interpreted as the court's adherence to one of the **equitable maxims**, that '**equity** will not assist a volunteer'.

Extent of trustee liability

We have seen that the liability of a trustee is strict, so that they will be liable for a breach even if that breach is committed innocently, but how far does that liability extend?

Personal liability of the trustee

The general rule is that a trustee's liability for breach of trust is limited to breaches which the trustee has themselves committed; in other words, a trustee is not liable for the breaches of their fellow trustees. The authority for this lies in a very old case, that of

Case Summary

Townley v. *Sherborne* (1620) Bridg J 35 which concerned a single trustee receiving rents on a trust property. The question arose as to whether the other trustees were responsible for giving a receipt for the rents received by their co-trustee. The judge held that:

1. Where lands are conveyed to two or more upon trust, and one receives the rents, his co-trustees shall not be liable unless some purchase, fraud, or evil dealing seems to have been in them to prejudice the trust, for them being by law **joint tenants**, every one of them may receive either all or as much of the rents as he can come by.

2. That it is no breach of trust to permit one of the trustees to receive the rents, it happening many times that some of the trustees live far from the lands, and it is inconvenient for them all to receive them.

3. That if, however, a trustee, having allowed his co-trustee to receive rents, subsequently leaves in the co-trustee's hands the money that has been received, he is liable therefor.

So the outcome was one in which practicality and common sense prevailed. The judgment is obviously very specific to the issue of the receipt of rents on trust property; however, there are a couple of important points that we can take from the decision. First, it is plain from the judgment that a trustee does not simply have a blanket **indemnity** against any breach which their fellow trustees may commit. What the case says, rather, is that a trustee will not be **vicariously liable** for the acts of their co-trustee (in other words, that they will not be held personally responsible for acts carried out by others). So if Joel and Simon are trustees and Joel runs off with the trust money, Simon will not be liable to replace that money unless he had allowed that loss to occur, either by turning a blind eye to the theft or by assisting or facilitating Joel's misappropriation of the funds in some other way.

> a trustee will not be vicariously liable for the acts of their co-trustee

And this is the second point, that if a trustee chooses to willfully ignore or even to condone the acts or omissions of his counterparts, that trustee cannot rely on this case as an escape from liability for his actions. Hence, we can see in the third part of the judgment that a trustee who allows his co-trustee to collect trust monies will nevertheless be responsible if he then stands idly by while his co-trustee goes on to commit a breach. Even more pertinent is that the wording of the judgment suggests that a failure to supervise the actions of co-trustees would also be sufficient to constitute a breach in this case.

That a trustee will be as liable for their failure to act as they are for an act in breach of trust has been confirmed in many subsequent cases. A particularly notable case is that of *Bahin* v. *Hughes* (1886) 31 Ch D 390. In that case a father, Robert Hughes, had left in his will the sum of £2,000 on trust to Mrs Bahin for life and then to her children. Mr Hughes's three daughters were named as trustees of the trust. One of the daughters, Miss Eliza Hughes, who was a spinster, was left by the other two married sisters to manage the trust affairs alone, however. Eliza made the decision to reinvest the trust funds in a mortgage which, unbeknown to Eliza, was an unauthorised investment. Unfortunately, the investment proved a poor one and some of the trust money was lost. Mrs Bahin then sued all three sisters as co-trustees for the loss to the fund. The two sisters who had taken no part in the management of the trust tried to absolve themselves from responsibility for the loss by saying that they had had no dealings as trustees. However, the Court of Appeal held that no indemnity would be given to them. All three sisters were trustees of the trust and the fact that two of them had wilfully neglected their duties in failing to manage the trust together with their sister made them equally, if not more, responsible than the sister that had tried to carry out her duties diligently.

Case Summary

Out and about

There are many other cases of trustees being held liable in the face of inaction, some of which show the trustees to be more actively to blame than others. Here's a chance for you to do a bit of paper research. Take a trip to your university law library and have a go at finding the following old cases:

✦ *Boardman* v. *Mosman* (1779) 1 Bro CC 68

✦ *Booth* v. *Booth* (1838) 1 Beav 125

✦ *Styles* v. *Guy* (1849) 1 Mac & G 422

Now try answering the following questions:

1. What are the facts of each case?
2. Who are the trustees in each case?
3. What was the nature of the failure of each of the inactive trustees?
4. Do you think that all the trustees should have been liable in each case?
5. Was any trustee's conduct worse than the others?

This task should take no more than 45 minutes.

Handy tip: Remember, this is a paper exercise, so no cheating on this one! Ask your librarian if you are struggling with the citations – they should be happy to help.

Reflective practice

How useful did you find that exercise? Did it help to improve your understanding of trustee liability? Did you find it difficult to find the cases in the library or was this easy for you? You will not always have access to cases and articles online, especially those that are older or more obscure, so this is a skill which may be worth brushing up on!

Liability before or after appointment

Case Summary

A trustee is not normally liable for breaches taking place before his appointment or after his retirement. In the case of a newly appointed trustee, *Re Strahan* (1856) 8 De GM & G 291 tells us that the new trustee is entitled to assume the other trustees have performed their duties properly, as long as there is nothing present in the documentation which might arouse the new trustee's suspicion. The case was the first in a series of groundbreaking court applications concerning trust monies being misapplied by Victorian bankers, only then to become bankrupt and unable to return the monies to the trust fund. In *Re Strahan*, Mr Strahan had been appointed a trustee to the trust fund after the misappropriation of part of the fund had taken place. He failed to make enquiries as to the whereabouts of certain trust monies but it was held that he was not liable, there being nothing suspicious to lead him to question the previous running of the trust. Unfortunately, Mr Strahan was not so lucky in his criminal trial. Take a look at the following abstract from a contemporary newspaper article to see what sentence he was given.

Documenting the law

THE AGE, SATURDAY, JANUARY 26, 1856.

TRIAL OF STRAHAN, PAUL AND BATES.

Sir John Dean Paul, Mr Bates and Mr Strahan were placed in the dock, on the 26th, at the Central Criminal Court, on a series of indictments for misdemeanour. The prisoners pleaded not guilty.

On Saturday, the 27th, the jury, after deliberating about twenty minutes, returned a verdict of guilty against all the defendants.

Mr Baron Alderson, after a short pause, proceeded to pronounce the judgment of the Court upon the prisoners in the following terms: – William Strahan, Sir John Dean Paul and Robert Makin Bates, the jury have now found you guilty of the offences charged upon you in this indictment – the offence of disposing of securities which were intrusted by your customers to you as bankers, for the purpose of being kept safe for their use, and which you appropriated, under circumstances of temptation, to your own. A greater and more serious offence can hardly be imagined in a great commercial city like this. It tends to shake confidence in all persons in the position you occupied, and it has shaken the public confidence in establishments like that you for a long period honourably conducted. I do very, very much regret, that it falls to my lot to pass any sentence on persons in your situation; but yet the public interests and public justice require it; and it is not for me to shrink from the discharge of any duty, however painful, which properly belongs to my office. I should have been very glad if it had pleased God that some one else now had to discharge that duty. I have seen (continued the learned judge, with deep emotion) at least one of you under very different circumstances, sitting at my side in high office, instead of being where you now are, and I would scarcely then have fancied to myself that it would ever come to me to pass sentence on you. But so it is, and this is a proof therefore, that we all ought to pray not to be led into temptation. You have been well educated, and held a high position in life, and the punishment which must fall on you will consequently be the more seriously and severely felt by you, and will also greatly affect those connected with you, who will most sensitively feel the disgrace of your position. All that I have to say is, that I cannot conceive any worse case of the sort arising under the Act of Parliament applicable to your offence. Therefore, as I cannot conceive any worse case under the Act, I can do nothing else but impose the sentence therein provided for the worst case – namely, the most severe punishment, which is, that you be severally transported for 14 years.

The rev. prosecutor, Dr. Griffiths, was observed to shed tears when the sentence was pronounced, but the judgment appeared to give satisfaction to a crowded court.

It is stated that Paul, Strahan and Bates will appeal against their sentences.

It is stated that these prisoners will remain in Newgate or the Milbank prison until a complete investigation of the affairs is made and a balance sheet in bankruptcy filed; and that afterwards they will be removed to Gibraltar for the remaining period of their sentence.

[*Source*: http://news.google.com/newspapers?nid=1300&dat=18560126&id=BkIQAAAAIBAJ&sjid=AJEDAAAAIBAJ&pg=3018,3467127]

If there is a lesson to be learned from the *Strahan* case, then, it is just how vital it is for a new trustee to familiarise themselves with the trust documentation immediately on their appointment to the trust, and to check that there have been no breaches. If the new trustee does then discover any breaches in the course of doing their checks they can take immediate steps to remedy them.

As with breaches committed before a new trustee takes up their appointment, trustees are also not usually responsible for breaches committed after their retirement from the post. Similar provisos to those applying to newly appointed trustees also apply to retiring trustees, however, and these are again based on the knowledge of or expectation of the trustee as to how the trust is going to be managed after their retirement. Thus, if a trustee retires knowing full well that as soon as they are gone the continuing trustees will commit a breach of trust, the retiring trustee will still find themselves in breach of trust. A trustee has a clear duty to act in the best interests of the trust and to protect trust property and if, by retiring, he knowingly facilitates a breach of trust by the other trustees he is just as liable as those actually committing the breach.

It should be noted that, in order to be liable, a retiring trustee must do so in the knowledge that a specific breach is going to be committed, however; it is not sufficient simply that they were aware that the continuing trustees might more generally act in breach of trust at some point in the future. An example of this in practice is the case of

Case Summary

Head v. *Gould* [1898] 2 Ch 250. The case concerned a trust which gave a **life interest** in the trust property to Mrs Head, with the property going to her three children on her death. Mrs Head was struggling financially and so her daughter, Adelaide Head, who was also a trustee of the fund, asked her fellow trustees if they would help by agreeing to give Mrs Head an advance of **capital** out of the daughter's share of the fund. The trustees agreed to this but the money was not enough and, although Adelaide's share had been depleted, she asked if more money could be advanced out of the remaining children's shares.

The trustees said that they were unable to give Adelaide more money and, feeling their position to be compromised, suggested that they should retire from the trust, leaving Adelaide to find new co-trustees who might be more willing to comply with her requests. Adelaide then appointed in their place a solicitor, Mr Gould. The solicitor made a number of further advances to the mother, with the result that the share of the trust fund belonging to one of the other children was spent. Adelaide's younger brother then brought an action for breach of trust, seeking to make both the old and the new trustees liable for the loss. The presiding judge in the case, Mr Justice Kekewich, found that the retiring trustees were not liable for the breaches, stating that:

> in order to make a retiring trustee liable for a breach of trust committed by his successor you must show, and show clearly, that the very breach of trust which was in fact committed, was not merely the outcome of the retirement and new appointment, but was contemplated by the former trustee when such retirement and appointment took place . . . it will not suffice to prove that the former trustees rendered easy or even intended, a breach of trust, if it was not in fact committed. They must be proved to have been guilty as accessories before the fact of the impropriety actually perpetrated.

Thus, because the retiring trustees in *Head* v. *Gould* had not retired specifically to allow a breach to take place, but rather because they felt unable to commit a breach of trust on behalf of the beneficiaries, the court said they should not be held liable.

The examples given above relate to breaches committed by other trustees after the retirement of an innocent trustee. It should be remembered, however, that a trustee will still continue to be liable for breaches of trust committed by them during the period of their trusteeship notwithstanding their retirement from the trust, bankruptcy or even

Case Summary

their death! This is shown in the case of *Dixon* v. *Dixon* (1879) 9 Ch D 587, where a claim for losses caused by a breach of trust succeeded against the estate of a trustee who had subsequently died.

Joint and several liability

We have so far looked at the extent of a trustee's liability for their own actions and the actions of their fellow trustees, and we have established when a trustee will be liable for the actions of their co-trustees and when they will not. The next point to look at is what the extent of that trustee's liability will be, once it has been established that they are liable for a breach. So what we want to know then is if it is established that all three trustees of a trust are liable for breach of trust in a particular matter, how will that liability be shared? And the answer to this question is that the trustees' liability will be **joint and several**. This means that if three trustees, let

> the trustees' liability will be joint and several

us call them Steve, Jayden and Anil, are all liable for a breach of trust, the beneficiaries can choose to sue any one or all of them for the whole of the amount for which they are liable. So if Steve has no money and Jayden has disappeared, it may fall to Anil to reimburse the full amount that has been lost to the trust. Alternatively, the beneficiaries may simply sue all three of them equally for the monies. It should be noted that this does not mean the trustees could theoretically claim the full amount from all three trustees, thus ending up with a trust fund of three times its original size! If the full amount of the fund is recovered from one trustee this will bring an end to the beneficiaries' claim.

But is this a fair way of apportioning liability? There will almost undoubtedly be many cases where one trustee is more or less to blame than the others, as we saw in *Re Strahan*. The rules of equity have traditionally dictated that all the trustees should share responsibility for paying monies back into the trust equally, although the court did concede the point that allowances should be made in the severest of cases. In *Bahin* v. *Hughes*, Lord Justice Cotton said that only in a situation where the trustee had taken all the trust property for themselves, should that trustee be held solely responsible for the breach. Another situation in which the court has been minded to apportion more blame to one party than the others is where one of the trustees is a solicitor and the others had relied very heavily upon their advice. This was the situation in the 1897 case of *Re Turner* 1 Ch 536, in which the trustees participated in a breach of trust solely on account of advice given them by a solicitor co-trustee who had been very controlling in the administration of the trust from the beginning. It should be stressed that this does not give non-professional trustees an automatic release from liability wherever a professional solicitor is involved. As Mr Justice Kekewich said of Adelaide Head in the case of *Head* v. *Gould*:

Case Summary

> I do not . . . think that . . . any . . . judge ever intended to hold that a man is bound to indemnify his co-trustee against loss merely because he was a solicitor, when that co-trustee was an active participator in the breach of trust complained of, and is not proved to have participated merely in consequence of the advice and control of the solicitor.

In any event, the position has now been modified by section 2(1) of the Civil Liability (Contribution) Act 1978, which says that contribution between the trustees will be 'such as may be found by the court to be just and equitable having regard to the extent of that person's responsibility for the damage in question'.

The Act also allows the court to give a full or partial indemnity (that is, exemption from liability) to any person whom they consider to be an innocent party in the committing of the breach. This is a much fairer system, allowing the courts to apportion financial responsibility in line with the level of blame which attaches to any one party.

Impounding a beneficiary's interest

In the case of *Head* v. *Gould*, of course, Adelaide Head had already depleted her interest in the trust fund and moved on to spend that of her brother. But under more usual circumstances, if a trustee is also a beneficiary of the trust, as Adelaide Head was, then the court will allocate that beneficiary's interest or as much as is needed of it to cover the loss to the trust. This is known as '**impounding**' the beneficiary's interest. Impounding does not just apply to trustee beneficiaries either: if a trustee has committed a breach of trust either at the instruction of, or with the consent of a beneficiary, that beneficiary's interest may also be impounded to rectify the breach. The Court of Appeal case of *Chillingworth* v. *Chambers* [1896] 1 Ch 685 concerned a claim made by a trustee beneficiary against his co-trustee in respect of poor investments made by the trustees on behalf of a family trust. However, the trustee beneficiary did not receive any reimbursement in respect of his share. The judge, speaking of trustee beneficiaries, said:

> as a general rule defaulting trustees cannot claim any **beneficial** entitlement in a trust estate until they have made good their default, as they are deemed to have received their share already.

The right to impound a beneficiary's interest exists both in equity and under statute at section 62 Trustee Act 1925. The equitable right to impound is available where the beneficiary has agreed or consented to the breach only if that agreement has resulted in some personal benefit to the beneficiary. However, where the beneficiary has been the instigator of the breach, as in *Head* v. *Gould*, there is no requirement that benefit to the beneficiary be proved. The right to impound under section 62 is wider than the equitable right in that it is not dependent on showing some benefit to the beneficiary. But the statutory provisions contain the additional proviso that consent given by a beneficiary under section 62 to a breach must be in writing in order for impounding to take place.

Table 13.1 shows the differences between the two methods of impounding, in equity and by statute.

It should be noted that, whether impounding takes place by an equitable or statutory route, the beneficiary's interest will only be impounded where it is clear that the beneficiary was

Table 13.1 Impounding a beneficiary's interests in law and in equity

Right to impound	Agreement or consent by beneficiary	Instigation or request of beneficiary
In equity	Yes, provided personal benefit to the beneficiary can be proved	Yes, regardless of benefit
Section 62 Trustee Act 1925	Yes, provided consent is in writing	Yes, regardless of benefit

Case Summary

aware that they were requesting or consenting to a breach of trust. If the beneficiary agreed to something or even instructed the trustees to take certain action, unaware that what they were agreeing to or requesting would amount to a breach of trust, they will not be liable to lose their interest. This is illustrated in the case of *Re Somerset* [1894] 1 Ch 231, in which a beneficiary wrote to the trustees suggesting they sell some of the trust property and invest it in a mortgage. The trustees did this, but the property proved to be inadequate **security** for the loan and the money was lost. The beneficiary then sued the trustees for the loss to the trust fund. The trustees applied to the court to impound the interest of the beneficiary on the basis that he had instigated the breach, but it was held that, whilst the beneficiary had clearly requested the investment, it was still the responsibility of the trustees to ensure that the investment was sound. The beneficiary's interest was therefore not impounded. Lord Justice Lindley said:

> If a [beneficiary] instigates, requests or consents in writing to an investment . . . [he] has a right to expect that the trustees will act with proper care in making the investment, and if they do not they cannot throw the consequences on him unless they can show that he instigated, requested or consented in writing to their non-performance of their duty in this respect.

Liability on delegation of powers

As we saw in Chapter 12, trustees have wide powers of delegation under the Trustee Act 2000. However, you will remember that, under section 22 of the Act, trustees remain liable for their **agents**' actions only in so far as they have a duty to monitor and review their agents' work regularly and to take immediate action if any agent is found to be acting inappropriately. Thus, they are not, in the first instance, liable for the actions of a rogue agent, such as Nick Leeson, who acted without the authority of his employers or his clients.

Trustee defences

We have so far considered the extent of trustee liability for breaches of trust, both individually and as between co-trustees where there is more than one trustee in breach. We have also looked at ways of reducing an individual trustee's liability, both under the Civil Liability (Contribution) Act 1978 and through the medium of impounding a trustee beneficiary's interest. But are there any other defences available to a trustee who has acted in breach of trust? The short answer to this question is, yes, there are various ways in which a trustee can reduce or escape liability for breach of trust, and the first of these ways is by claiming that the breach of duty was carried out with the consent of the beneficiaries themselves.

Consent of beneficiary

If a trustee commits a breach of trust with the full knowledge and consent of an adult beneficiary, that beneficiary cannot then make a claim against the trustees for breach of trust. This makes perfect logical sense if we look again at the example of our trustee Danyl, from the You be the judge feature, above. You will remember that Danyl has used half of the trust money to put a bet on a horse in the 3.30 at Aintree. Imagine he did so, not because of a tip he received at the pub, but because he has been asked to by beneficiary Stuart, who is 21. Stuart, fully comprehending the unauthorised nature of the transaction he is asking Danyl to carry out, cannot then make a claim when the horse comes fourth in the race and the trust money is lost. This does not mean, of course, that the other beneficiaries cannot make a claim against Danyl for the loss, and the likely outcome of the case is that Stuart's share of the trust fund will be impounded to cover the loss to the trust. Stuart himself, however, is in no position, either morally or legally, to blame Danyl for something that he has consented to with full knowledge of the possible consequences.

Another example of a consenting beneficiary being unable to make a claim for breach of trust can be seen in the case of *Fletcher* v. *Collis* [1905] 2 Ch 24. In this case the claim was made by the **trustee in bankruptcy** of a beneficiary who had become **insolvent**. The trust fund had been dissipated with the consent of the bankrupt beneficiary, who had asked the trustees of the trust fund to sell off the trust fund property and give the proceeds to his wife (who then spent it). However, the court held that, as the husband had clearly consented to the breach, the trustee in bankruptcy could not then, acting on the husband's behalf, seek to require the trustees to make good the loss to the fund.

It is important to note that, for a trustee to claim this defence, they must be able to prove that the beneficiary was of not only over the age of 18, but also that they fully understood the nature of the breach to which they were agreeing at the time of giving their consent. Two contrasting cases serve to illustrate this point. First, in the case of *Re Garnett* (1885) 31 Ch D 1 the court set aside a **deed of release**, the purpose of which was to release the trustees from liability for a breach of trust, on the basis that the beneficiaries had executed it at a time when they did not sufficiently understand the nature of what they were giving up by signing it. The case concerned the will of Jeremiah Garnett. In his will, Jeremiah left half of his estate to his sister, Henrietta, and the other half to be shared between his two nieces, Mary and Frances. Henrietta was also a trustee of the will. The estate, which consisted mostly of railway stocks and shares, was valued in 1855 at £42,000. In 1859, the nieces signed a deed of release in favour of their aunt in return for payments of £10,500 each, which was the sum the nieces understood their half share of the fund to be worth. However, the aunt had not taken into account in calculating the amount due to the nieces the fact that the shares had increased considerably in value since 1855 and that the nieces were in fact owed in the region of £5,000 to £6,000 more than they had been given. The outcome of the case was that the deed of release was held to be invalid and a claim for further monies by the nieces was allowed.

In the contrasting case of *Farrant* v. *Blanchford* (1863) 1 De GJ & Sm 107, a similar deed of release was held to stand; so what was the difference here? The facts were that a father was trustee of a trust fund together with another man, Mr Bidwill. The father had been permitted by his co-trustee to use the property comprised in the trust fund in breach of trust as security for a loan, which he never repaid. The father subsequently asked his son, who was one of the beneficiaries of the trust, not to hold Mr Bidwill responsible for the breach and to give him a release. The father was at this time dangerously ill and the son duly signed the release and sent it to Mr Bidwill. However, six months after the subsequent death of his father, the son sought to make a claim against Mr Bidwill for the breach of trust. The court held, however, that the son was an adult and had been fully aware of the actions of the trustees for quite some time before signing the release. The release was therefore held to be valid and no action was taken against Mr Bidwill for the loss to the trust.

The suggestion in *Farrant* v. *Blanchford* is that the son had **acquiesced** to the breach through his inaction, long before he signed the release of Mr Bidwell. However, it is suggested that a beneficiary's knowledge of a breach will not, by itself, be sufficient to establish a defence of acquiescence, even if the beneficiary was aware of the breach for a number of years before making a claim. Nevertheless, if there is a long delay by the beneficiaries in pursuing a claim, the court will presume acquiescence in the absence of an explanation for it: see *Sleeman* v. *Wilson* (1871) LR 13 Eq 36, in which beneficiaries, who had waited 38 years until the death of the trustee in breach before making a claim against his estate on the grounds that they were 'not desirous of interrupting the friendly relations they had enjoyed with [the trustee]', were held by the court to be unable to make a claim on the grounds of acquiescence.

Case Summary

A rather more recent case in the area of beneficiary consent is the 1964 case of *Re Pauling's Settlement Trusts* [1964] Ch 303, a case which we came across earlier in the book, in Chapter 11 on **maintenance** and **advancement**. The facts of the case were as follows: Miss Pauling, who was a wealthy heiress, married a naval officer with very little money. As a protective measure, her considerable fortune was put into trust for Miss Pauling for life and then to her children. The trust contained a provision allowing the trustee to advance the children up to half of their share of the fund in advance of them becoming entitled. Miss Pauling requested and received a number of advancements on the children's shares of the trust fund, using the money not solely for the children's benefit but for the benefit of the family as a whole, purchasing not one but two houses (one in Chelsea and one in the Isle of Man) and paying off various debts and loans to finance the family's rather extravagant lifestyle. When the children became aware that breaches of trust had been committed, they made a claim against the trustees for the depletion of the fund. However, they were only partially successful in their claim. The children had been over 21 and had consented to the advancements (the legal age of majority in 1964 was still 21; it was not reduced to the age of 18 until 1 January 1970). The outcome was that, whilst during the earlier advances the children were adjudged by the court to be under parental control, and therefore incapable of giving their consent freely, they were held to have freely consented to the later advances and therefore they could not make a claim on these. Lord Justice Willmer said:

Case Summary

> the question is one of fact and degree. One begins with a strong presumption in the case of a child just 21 living at home, and this will grow less and less as the child goes out in the world and leaves the shelter of the home. Nevertheless, the presumption only lasts a 'short' time after the child has attained 21.

One final interesting point to note relating to the age of the beneficiaries in giving their consent to a breach is the case of *Overton* v. *Banister* (1884) 3 Hare 503. Here a beneficiary who had consented to a breach but who had fraudulently misstated his age at the time of consenting, was held to be bound by the release despite the fact that he turned out to have been a minor when his agreement was given.

Case Summary

Relief by the court

A claim of beneficiary consent is a good defence to trustee breaches where there has been some form of beneficiary involvement; but where a trustee is guilty of nothing more than an honest mistake, by far and away the best defence to a breach of trust is the application for a grant of **relief** by the court under section 61 of the Trustee Act 1925. The section stipulates that, if it appears to the court that in committing a breach of trust a trustee:

✦ has acted honestly; and

✦ reasonably; and

✦ ought fairly to be excused for a breach of trust or for omitting to obtain the directions of the court,

then the court may relieve them either wholly or partly from personal liability for that breach.

The important point to note about this provision is that it is not enough for a trustee to act honestly to be granted relief: they must also have acted reasonably. *Re Turner* [1897] 1 Ch 536 concerned a breach of trust resulting in significant loss to a trust fund, carried out by two trustees, Mr Ivimey and Mr Turner. Ivimey was a solicitor and Turner a linen draper. Mr Turner sought to claim relief from the court under section 3 of the Judicial Trustee Act 1896 (this section preceded section 3 of the Trustee Act 1925, but was in exactly the same terms), on the grounds that he had acted honestly in reliance on his professional co-trustee. However, the court did not accept Mr Turner's argument, saying that in order to claim relief under the act the trustee must be able to prove not only that he had acted honestly but also that he had acted reasonably. In this case that meant proving that he was 'as prudent in his actions as he would have been in relation to his own affairs'. It should be noted from this case that the fact that the trustees have acted on legal advice does not necessarily mean that they will be granted relief under section 61.

A more successful claim for relief was made in the case of *Re Evans (Deceased)* [1999] 2 All ER 777. David Evans died in 1987 without leaving a will. His daughter, Lillian Westcombe, acted as the **administrator** in his estate. Lillian and her brother David were next of kin and stood to inherit equally under the **intestacy** rules, but Lillian thought her brother was dead because she had not heard from him for 30 years. After taking legal advice on the matter, Lillian purchased a missing person insurance policy which would pay out half the value of the estate in the event that her brother ever reappeared. Her brother did in fact resurface four years later and sought to claim his share of the estate, plus interest. The insurance policy only covered the amount of David's share of the estate at the time of distribution, not interest. However, in spite of David's claim for the balance, the court held that Lillian had done everything she reasonably could in the circumstances and she was therefore excused from further liability under the section.

Even if the trustee satisfies all of the conditions in section 61, it should be remembered that it is still completely at the discretion of the court as to whether they grant relief. Whether the court decides that a trustee has acted reasonably will very much turn on the facts of each particular case and, in exercising discretion, the court may take into account a number of factors, including:

✦ the size of the trust fund in question;

✦ the amount of the loss;

✦ what advice the trustees have taken; and

✦ whether trustees are paid for their role.

The court can also take into account the effect that a grant of relief might have on the beneficiaries and if granting the trustees relief would cause the beneficiaries significant hardship the court will be less inclined to be lenient.

Case Summary

Case Summary

Limitation of actions

Another way in which a trustee might escape liability for breach of trust is through a simple lapse of time. Under section 21(3) of the Limitation Act 1980, the general rule is that beneficiaries cannot bring an action in respect of breach of trust any more than six years after the date of the breach. This period is doubled to 12 years in the case of actions taken to recover losses from a deceased person's estate.

So, the usual time limit for a beneficiary bringing an action is six years. However, there are two situations in which the **limitation** period does not apply. These are:

1. where the trustee in breach has committed a fraud (section 21(1)(a)); and
2. where the trustee is still in possession of the trust property or the proceeds of its sale (section 21(1)(b)).

One question which arises from the wording of the Act is: what is the date on which the action accrued? In other words, when exactly does the six-year limitation period start to run? The answer is different depending on the circumstances of the breach. The most basic scenario is where a simple breach is committed and in this case the six years will start to run immediately following the breach. However, if the breach of trust has been covered up by the trustees, time does not begin to run until the beneficiaries discover the breach. This is under section 32(1) of the Limitation Act 1980. In addition, section 28 of the act states that, where the beneficiary is 'under a disability', in other words where the beneficiary is either under the age of 18 or is mentally incapable, the limitation period will not begin until that disability has ended. So what this is saying is that the clock does not start ticking for child beneficiaries until they reach the age of majority. In the case of those suffering from a mental incapacity, the limitation period will start either when their disability ends or from the date of their death. And lastly it should be noted that in the case of a life interest, the limitation period will not begin to run for the ultimate beneficiaries until the person with the life interest dies.

Writing and drafting

There are so many provisos which apply to the limitation period that it can be difficult to know exactly when to apply it! Why not try drawing up a flow chart indicating the circumstances under which the limitation act will apply and when the limitation period starts to run.

You should take no longer than 20 minutes on this task.

 Handy tip: A suggested answer can be found on the website at **http://www. mylawchamber.co.uk/warner-reed**. How does it compare to your flow chart?

One final point to mention is the equitable **doctrine of laches**, which is the rule which states that a beneficiary may be prevented from making a claim because there has been a substantial delay in taking action. This may, of course, be used in any situation where the Limitation Act does not apply (for example, in cases of fraud under section 21(1)(a) of the Limitation Act 1980, as stated above). As the doctrine is an equitable one, there is no specific time period after which a beneficiary will be prevented from making a claim; rather the court will consider whether it would be inequitable under the circumstances of each particular case to give a remedy to the beneficiaries. However, as a general rule of thumb, Lord Justice Lawrence stated in the 1929 case of *Weld* v. *Petre* [1929] 1 Ch 33, citing a number of earlier cases, that a period of over 20 years is generally thought to be the maximum delay allowed before laches will be invoked. As it happened this was of little help to the claimant in the case, who had waited exactly 20 years before making his claim to redeem a mortgage.

Exemption clauses

The last of the trustee defences to be listed in this chapter is that of the **exemption clause**. Provided that such a clause exists within the trust deed, an exemption clause is the ultimate 'get out of jail free' card available to a trustee. Perhaps surprisingly, exemption clauses are generally not considered to be contrary to **public policy** and so an appropriately drafted clause can give a trustee a complete exemption from any breach of trust short of actual fraud. In the case of ***Armitage v. Nurse*** [1997] 2 All ER 705, a trust contained the following clause:

> No trustee shall be liable for any loss or damage which may happen to [the] fund or any part thereof at any time or from any cause whatsoever unless such loss or damage shall be caused by his own actual fraud . . .

The beneficiary of a trust of agricultural land, Paula Armitage, brought an action against the trustees on the grounds of poor management of the land, leading ultimately to the sale of the trust property at a time when it was severely depressed in value. The trustees, however, were exonerated by the court and the exemption clause upheld. Lord Justice Millett somewhat controversially said:

> In my judgment [the exemption] clause . . . exempts the trustee from liability for loss or damage to the trust property no matter how indolent, imprudent, lacking in diligence, negligent or wilful he may have been, so long as he has not acted dishonestly.

The practice of including exemption clauses in trust deeds continues to be heavily criticised. The Law Commission published a consultation paper in 2003 on *Trustee Exemption Clauses*, and in 2006 a Law Commission report (No. 301) was published recommending reform. The Law Commission has shied away from any move to legislate in the area, believing that legislative restrictions on trustee exemption clauses would serve only to deter people from taking up appointments as trustees. Instead, the report calls for the introduction of a 'best practice' rule across the professions which could be adapted as appropriate, depending on the nature of the trusts dealt with by any particular professional body. The wording of the best practice rule that the Law Commission suggests is as follows:

> Any paid trustee who causes a settlor to include a clause in a trust instrument which has the effect of excluding or limiting liability for negligence must before the creation of the trust take such steps as are reasonable to ensure that the settlor is aware of the meaning and effect of the clause.

The basic effect of the clause is that a paid trustee will not be able to avoid liability for breach of trust where they have been negligent. This sounds good in theory, but as there is no central register of trusts or trustees in the UK at the moment, there is currently no way of ensuring that the best practice rule is taken up or followed. Thus, one could argue that, in its current form, the Law Commission's suggestions amount to no more than sticking plaster where a bandage is quite obviously required.

Summary

- A breach of trust is any act or omission by a trustee that takes that trustee outside the terms of the trust or outside of their duties as a trustee.

- Liability for breach of trust is strict. This means that the trustee will be liable for a breach of trust even where they acted honestly and in good faith.

- A trustee is not liable for the breaches of their fellow trustees unless they have intentionally allowed or facilitated those breaches.

- A trustee is not usually liable for breaches committed before their appointment or after their retirement, unless the trustee retired in contemplation of a particular breach taking place.

- The court can apportion liability between co-trustees in any manner they consider to be just and equitable taking into account the circumstances of the case (section 2(1) Civil Liability (Contribution) Act 1978).

- If a trustee has, in committing a breach of trust, acted honestly and reasonably and ought fairly to be excused then the court may grant them full or partial relief from the breach (section 61 Trustee Act 1925).

- A beneficiary cannot bring an action in respect of breach of trust after a period of six years has elapsed from the date on which the action accrued (section 21 Limitation Act 1980). The limitation period starts to run at the time the breach occurs, unless the breach was concealed, in which case it runs from the time when it is discovered by the beneficiaries.

- An exemption clause in a trust deed will give a trustee a complete protection against any action for breach of trust, provided that breach was not dishonest.

Question and answer*

Problem: Husband and wife, Christopher and Delia, die tragically in a car accident, leaving behind them three children: Quentin, Harriet and Daisy. Quentin is the child of Christopher's first marriage and is 24 at the time of Christopher and Delia's deaths; Harriet and Daisy are 3 and 9 respectively. Christopher and Delia's will leaves the family home, Red Gables, to Quentin for life and then to Harriet and Daisy, and everything else to the three children equally in trust on their attaining the age of 30. The will names Quentin and Delia's brother Gareth, who is a solicitor, as trustees. Quentin is also named in the will as the legal guardian of the two smaller children.

As Quentin is in charge of the day-to-day care of the children, Gareth leaves Quentin pretty much well alone, leaving him to make decisions as to when he needs advancements from the trust for the children's maintenance. Quentin, struggling to cope on his own with the responsibility of two young children, soon develops a drinking and gambling habit and, within five years, has dissipated the children's fortune. In addition, he has mortgaged Red Gables and is now unable to make the mortgage payments. The house is repossessed and Quentin is declared bankrupt.

No longer able to cope and with nowhere else to turn, Quentin asks Gareth if he will give the girls a home and, as Gareth and his wife have no children, Gareth agrees. Quentin begs Gareth not to tell the girls about the dissipated fortune and Gareth, feeling somewhat guilty for not getting the measure of the situation earlier, agrees to say nothing.

A dozen years later, Daisy is going through some papers at home when she comes across a copy of her parents' will. She takes the will to her sister and asks her if she knew about the trust. Harriet says that she did know about it, but that she had not said anything about it to Uncle Gareth because he had taken them in and she felt it would be ungrateful to take action against him. Daisy feels quite differently about the matter, however, and says that she intends to take legal advice the very next morning, with a view to suing both Gareth and her brother for the lost trust monies. She urges Harriet to join her in making a claim.

Assuming both girls decide to make a claim, what are their chances of success against Quentin and Gareth?

You should allow yourself no more than 40 minutes to complete this task.

Essay: The New Zealand Law Commission has recommended an outright ban on trustee exemption clauses. Could preventative legislation in this area work for us?

This question should be answered in 40 minutes.

✱ Answer guidance is provided at the end of the chapter.

Further reading and references

Dal Point, G.E. (2006) 'Wilful default revisited – liability for a co-trustee's defaults', Conv (Sept/Oct) 376–86.
An interesting discussion on the meaning and usefulness of the term 'wilful default' in apportioning blame between trustees.

Harris, D. (2005) 'Investments by professional trustees in private companies and partnerships', *Private Client Business*, 3, 167–75.
A practical discussion of what trustees should consider when being asked by their beneficiaries to invest in private companies. Really brings to life some of the dilemmas and conflicts faced by trustees in making investment decisions on behalf of the trust.

Law Commission Consultation Paper 171 (2003) *Trustee Exemption Clauses*, London: The Stationery Office.
Consultation paper preceding the 2006 Law Commission Report.

Law Commission Report 301 (2006) *Trustee Exemption Clauses*, London: The Stationery Office.
Law Commission Report in which the introduction of a 'best practice' rule is called for in respect of exemption clauses.

Reed, E. (2007) 'Trustee exemption clauses: the Law Commission pronounces', *Private Client Business*, 3, 196–204.
Excellent article summarising the proposals of the Law Commission for reform in the area of trustee exemption clauses. Not too long, clear and easy to follow.

Sheridan, L. (1955) 'Excusable breaches of trust', 19 Conv (NS) 420.
Whilst this is an old article, it provides a useful summary on a number of the authoritative cases on section 61 of the Trustee Act 1925. Worth taking a look at.

Question and answer guidance

Problem: Generally, a trustee is not liable for breaches of their fellow trustees (*Townley* v. *Sherborne*). But in this case, Gareth has left the running of the trust to Quentin, which he should not have done. He should have played an active part in the running of the trust, and there is therefore some liability on his part (see in particular *Bahin* v. *Hughes* on this point). If Gareth is found liable for breach of trust, his liability will be joint and several together with Quentin. This means the beneficiaries can sue either one of them for the full amount. As Quentin is bankrupt, the girls' only recourse will be to Gareth.

Under section 2(1) of the Civil Liability (Contribution) Act 1978 a full or partial indemnity may be given to any trustee who may be considered innocent of the breach. Obviously Gareth did not misappropriate the trust money himself, but he did stand by and let the Quentin take the money. Presumably, then, he should shoulder some responsibility for his actions (or lack of them) in this respect. In any event, as a solicitor, Gareth would be expected to exercise a higher standard of care.

Impounding Quentin's interest is pointless, because he has no money.

As far as trustee defences are concerned, Daisy knew nothing about the breach, but Harriet did. Harriet could be accused of acquiescing to the breach; however, knowledge of a breach alone will not be enough to amount to a claim of acquiescence, particularly given her age and situation (see *Sleeman* v. *Wilson*; *Re Pauling's Settlement Trusts*).

Gareth is unlikely to be granted relief by the court under section 61 Trustee Act 1925 because, although he did not know about the breaches being committed by Quentin until some time afterwards, he was in dereliction of his duties by not supervising the actions of his fellow trustee and could not therefore be said to be in a position whereby he ought to be fairly excused from liability.

The limitation period is 6 years under the Limitation Act 1980. However, this does not apply in cases of fraud (and Quentin stole the money). In addition, the period does not start to run until the trustee found out about the breach if it has been concealed. This is certainly the case for Daisy (section 32(1)). In addition, if the beneficiaries are minors the time period will not start to run until they reach the age of majority (section 28). Harriet was 9 when her parents died. The fund was dissipated within 5 years, making her 14. It is now a dozen years later, making her 26. For her, the limitation period will have run out, therefore, as she knew about the breach at the time and has been over 18 for 8 years. Daisy was 3 when her parents died. When they moved in with Gareth she would have been 8; and she is now 20. She has only been over 18 for two years and, in any event, time will not have started to run until she found out about the breach, so she can sue Gareth (there is no point suing Quentin because he is bankrupt).

Essay: A good essay will start by explaining what exemption clauses are and the current legal position in this country as it relates to them. Exemption clauses are generally not considered to be contrary to public policy and so an appropriately drafted clause can give a trustee a complete exemption from any breach of trust short of actual fraud. Provided there is an exemption clause in the trust deed, this will be sufficient to exempt a trustee from liability for any breach of trust, therefore.

A discussion of the case of *Armitage* v. *Nurse*, which concerned a claim against trustees for bad management of the trust fund, and which resulted in substantial losses to the fund, would be a useful point of reference to show the views of the judiciary on the use of exemption clauses. In particular, mention Lord Justice Millett's judgment, in which he said that an exemption clause would be valid 'no matter how indolent, imprudent, lacking in diligence, negligent or wilful he may have been, so long as he has not acted dishonestly'.

Students should go on to discuss the current criticism which has been levelled at the practice of including exemption clauses in trust deeds. Reference should be made to the findings of the Law Commission's consultation paper in 2003 and report in 2006. An overview should be given of the 'best practice' rule put forward as a protective measure by the report. Give reasons as to why this may not be enough in the current legal framework, i.e. there is no central register of trusts or trustees in the UK at the moment, and therefore no way of ensuring that the best practice rule is taken up or followed.

A balanced essay should also give the reasons for avoiding legislation in this area: that is, the fear that legislative restrictions on trustee exemption clauses would deter people from taking up appointments as trustees.

Students should conclude by saying whether they think the current position is acceptable and whether exemption clauses should be banned (and if so, why).

Visit **www.mylawchamber.co.uk/warner-reed** to access study support resources including practice exam questions with guidance, interactive 'You be the judge' multiple choice questions, annotated weblinks, glossary and key case flashcards and audio legal updates all linked to the **Pearson eText** version of *Equity and Trusts* which you can **search**, **highlight** and **personalise** with your **own notes** and **bookmarks**.

Use Case Navigator to read in full some of the key cases referenced in this chapter with commentary and questions:

Armitage* v. *Nurse [1997] 2 All ER 705

Chapter 14
Liability of strangers

Key points In this chapter we will be looking at:

✦ How a third party can become liable for a breach of trust

✦ Assistance by a third party to a breach of trust

✦ The meaning of 'dishonesty' in dishonest assistance

✦ Receipt of misappropriated trust funds by third parties

✦ Knowing receipt: 'guilty knowledge' and 'innocent knowledge'

✦ The 'change of position' defence

Introduction

Imagine the following scenario: Bob has been skimming money from a **trust** fund for 18 months, and depositing the money in his current account to clear his overdraft. Finally, he cashes a large trust cheque at the local branch of the bank and uses the money to purchase a lifetime club membership for himself and his wife at a very exclusive golf club in Portugal where they have a holiday home. Bob is clearly in breach of trust, but what about the bank and what about Bob's wife: are they liable in any way and, if they are, how can the beneficiaries make a claim against them?

In the last chapter we examined the liability of **trustees** for breaches of trust. We considered the extent of liability of a defaulting trustee as against co-trustees and we considered the defences available to a defaulting trustee against a claim made against them by the **beneficiaries**. In such scenarios the relationship between the parties is very straightforward: there is a **fiduciary** relationship, or relationship of trust, between the trustee and the beneficiary

and when that trust is breached there is a clear action against the trustee for that breach. What this chapter is going to examine, however, is a little more complex, in that we are going to be considering the liability to beneficiaries of third parties, or '**strangers**', as they are legally termed, to the trust. So, this might encompass the situation where trust property is received by a third party, say a bank or building society receiving misapplied trust monies as in our scenario above, or where a third party such as a solicitor assists a trustee in committing a breach of trust.

There are a couple of immediate problems which spring to mind when we start discussing the liability of strangers. The first is: how can a third party be liable for a breach of trust if they have no connection with the trust itself, either as a trustee or in any other capacity? And the other is: how is a beneficiary able to make a claim against a stranger to the trust with whom they have no relationship, either fiduciary, contractually or otherwise? The answer to these questions, put simply, is that **equity** steps in and, if the third party is found guilty either of knowingly receiving trust property or of giving **dishonest assistance** to a trustee in the breach of a trust, that third party will be considered, by their actions, to have made themselves a **constructive trustee**, thereby becoming liable to the beneficiaries in addition to the trustees themselves for the breach of trust committed.

So, to summarise, a third party, or stranger to the trust, who either dishonestly assists in committing a breach of trust or who takes possession of trust property knowing that it is the product of a breach of trust, will be held in equity to be guilty of a breach of trust as if that person had been a trustee of the trust and can be sued in equity by the beneficiaries as such. We will deal in turn with each of the two separate areas of 'dishonest assistance' in the committing of a breach of trust and the '**knowing receipt**' of misappropriated trust property.

It should be noted that there exists a huge amount of commentary and discussion surrounding this area of the law and it would be well worth you taking some time to read around the subject. As with the other subjects covered in this book, there is a list of additional reading at the end of the chapter, but there is a plethora of other equally good reading matter in existence on the topic and it is worth dipping into at least some of it to give you a really clear insight into the problems and issues which surround this area of law.

Dishonest assistance

So what exactly is dishonest assistance? Somewhat unhelpfully the courts have, over a period of years, struggled considerably with the concept of dishonest assistance and with how it should be defined. The difficulty is understandable. If you think about it, the courts have taken a very serious step in saying that someone who has no connection whatsoever with the trust itself and more than likely no detailed knowledge of the trust can, through their actions, find themselves liable to the beneficiaries for breaching that trust. It is natural therefore that there should have been, and that there continues to be, a considerable amount of discussion and even disagreement over what exact approach should be taken in deciding whether or not a person should be guilty of dishonest assistance. It is a huge responsibility and the courts have been traditionally very nervous of labelling third parties to the trust 'dishonest', especially when nine times out of ten these people are lawyers, accountants, bankers or other professionals acting in the course of their business.

> the courts have struggled with the concept of dishonest assistance

What can we say, then, about dishonest assistance? The first important point to note is that dishonest assistance is just that: assistance. Unlike its counterpart, knowing receipt, dishonest assistance does not require the party in breach to receive, or even to handle, the trust property; all that is required is that the third party plays some part in assisting the trustee to commit the breach.

The second point, and that which has caused all the controversy, is the question of whether the person assisting in the breach of trust must actually do so dishonestly.

Out and about

Are you an honest person? Do you think your friends and family are honest? Here's your chance to find out. Why not carry out a little survey of your family and friends by asking them whether they consider the following actions to be honest or dishonest?

1. A man is walking along the street and sees a £20 note on the pavement. He picks it up and puts it in his pocket.
2. A woman samples the grapes in the supermarket before buying them.
3. A woman takes a DVD off the supermarket shelf and leaves without paying for it.
4. The security guard sees the theft but, feeling sorry for the woman, turns a blind eye to the crime.
5. A man downloads a yet-to-be released film off the internet.
6. A woman accesses her partner's text messages and reads them.
7. A man takes stationery home from work.
8. A woman makes personal telephone calls from her work telephone.
9. A man buys a jacket from Marks & Spencer to wear for a job interview, then returns it the following day.
10. A woman persuades an elderly relative whom she cares for to change her will in her favour.

Reflective practice

Now take a little time to reflect on the answers you have been given. Do you agree with all the responses given? Are you surprised at any of the results? Are any of these things that you have done yourself? Have your views of dishonesty changed as a result of answering these questions?

Case Summary

The first case to deal with the issue of dishonest assistance was that of *Barnes* v. *Addy* (1874) 9 Ch App 244. This case concerned the family trust funds of two sisters, Ann Barnes and Susan Addy. Susan's husband was sole trustee of the trusts following the deaths of his co-trustees. Diagrammatically, the fund would have looked as shown in Figure 14.1.

Following a falling-out with his brother in law, Mr Barnes accused Mr Addy of a breach of trust. It was proposed that Mr Barnes should be appointed in place of Mr Addy as sole trustee of Ann's half-share of the trust. This would have meant that the trust fund would have been split into two, as shown in Figure 14.2.

Mr Addy's solicitor, Mr Duffield, advised against this course of action because of the obvious risk of misapplication of trust funds by a sole trustee, but Mr Addy was insistent and Mr Duffield eventually agreed to prepare the **deed of appointment** for Mr Barnes. In the meantime, Mr Barnes's solicitor, Mr Preston, wrote to Ann expressing his concerns about the appointment, but she instructed him to proceed in any event. He therefore approved the draft deed and the appointment was completed. On 31 March 1857 Ann's share was transferred to Mr Barnes, and by the next day he had placed her share of the trust fund directly into his own business in an outright breach of trust. Mr Barnes was bankrupt a year later.

Ann's children sued Mr Addy and the two solicitors for breach of trust (there was no point suing Mr Barnes due to his bankrupt status). Mr Addy was held liable for making

Figure 14.1 The Barnes and Addy family trust fund

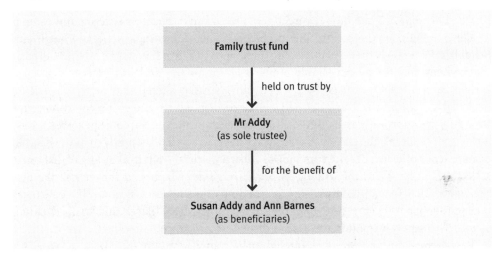

Figure 14.2 Proposed division of the trust fund

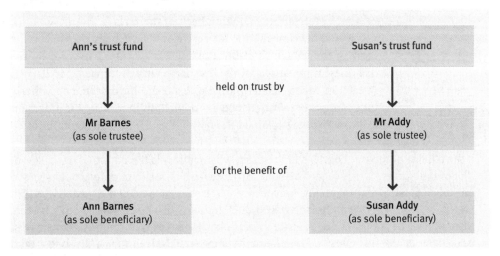

the appointment, albeit that he did not do so fraudulently. However, the solicitors were held not liable for the breaches of trust, the judge in the case, Lord Selborne, saying that: 'strangers are not to be made [liable] . . . unless they assist with knowledge in a dishonest and fraudulent design on the part of the trustees'.

The solicitors to the trust were not aware that Mr Barnes had acted with dishonest or fraudulent intent: they did not assist him in his 'fraudulent design', and they were therefore not held responsible for the breach he committed. It is interesting to note that the solicitors' own intentions were irrelevant, only their knowledge of the trustee's breach was important.

Lord Selborne's statement was considered to be good law for more than a century until the 1995 **Privy Council** case of *Royal Brunei Airlines* **v.** *Tan* [1995] 3 WLR 64. The case considered a rather different set of facts in that the party accused of dishonest assistance was not a solicitor, who might be expected to have a full knowledge and understanding of the trust, but rather was the managing director of a travel company. The facts of the case were as follows: Royal Brunei Airlines had appointed Borneo Leisure Travel ('BLT') to act as its agent. BLT was required to account to the airline within 30 days for all monies received

Case Summary

Case Navigator

on ticket sales and, in return, would receive a commission. However, rather than keeping a separate account of the monies and forwarding the ticket sale proceeds to the airline, BLT had been paying the money directly into its ordinary business account and using it to alleviate the company's cash flow problems. When the company became insolvent, Royal Brunei Airlines sued the managing director of BLT, Mr Tan, personally, on the basis that he knew that the money should not be used in this way and was guilty of dishonest assistance in a breach of trust by the company. Mr Tan argued that he should not be responsible because the company had not acted dishonestly and so he could not have been guilty of knowingly assisting a dishonest breach. However, the court held that, whilst it was clear that both the company and the trustee had acted dishonestly in any event, the dishonesty or otherwise of the company as trustee was irrelevant to a finding of dishonest assistance. Contrary to the finding in *Barnes* v. *Addy*, which said that it was the dishonesty of the trustee which was key to a finding of dishonest assistance, the court was now stating that it was the motives of the stranger to the trust that should be the deciding factor in determining guilt in the case of dishonest assistance.

The outcome in *Royal Brunei* v. *Tan* signifies a complete shift in the emphasis placed on the requirement for dishonesty in cases of dishonest assistance. Whereas before, a finding of dishonest assistance was entirely reliant on the dishonest behaviour of the trustees to the trust, now a third party could be liable based solely on their own personal motivations. Looking back at the facts of *Barnes* v. *Addy*, this would have meant that the case would have been decided on the basis of the solicitor's motivations in varying the trust, not on the dishonest motivations of the dishonest trustee himself, Mr Barnes. In fact, in such a scenario Mr Barnes could have been a completely innocent party to the change. Lord Nicholls in making his judgment in *Royal Brunei* explained the reason for this change in emphasis:

> now a third party could be liable based solely on their own personal motivations

> If the liability of the third party is fault-based, what matters is the nature of his fault, not that of the trustee. In this regard dishonesty on the part of the third party would seem to be sufficient basis for his liability, irrespective of the state of mind of the trustee who is in breach of trust. It is difficult to see why, if the third party dishonestly assisted in breach, there should be a further prerequisite to his liability, namely that the trustee also must have been acting dishonestly. The alternative view would mean that a dishonest third party is liable if the trustee is dishonest, but if the trustee did not act dishonestly that of itself would excuse the dishonest party. That would make no sense.

Lord Nicholls went on to set out four prerequisites which now form the requirement of liability in cases of dishonest assistance. These can be summarised as follows:

1. there must be a trust;
2. there must be a breach of trust;
3. the third party must have assisted in the breach; and
4. the third party must have been acting dishonestly when they assisted.

There must be a trust

There is no requirement for a formally documented trust to be in existence; rather there must be a clear position of trust or fiduciary relationship. This means that, as with

Royal Brunei Airlines v. *Tan*, we are not necessarily always dealing with a trust fund in the most narrow and traditional sense of the word; but we might also be dealing with companies and directors, bank, building society, solicitor and client relationships or any other relationship of trust.

There must be a breach of trust

That there must be a breach of trust is clear. In a complete departure from *Barnes* v. *Addy*, however, *Royal Brunei Airlines* v. *Tan* has confirmed that there is no need for the breach of trust to have been committed dishonestly by the trustees (although the company had in fact been dishonest in *Royal Brunei*). An innocent breach of trust of the types we have seen in the previous chapter, such as a failure to appoint or remove directors in the correct manner, would be sufficient to satisfy this requirement of dishonest assistance.

> there is no need for the breach to have been committed dishonestly by the trustees

The third party must have assisted in the breach

It should be noted that the third party must have taken some active part in assisting the breach in order to be found liable for dishonest assistance. This means that the third party must have been actually involved in committing the breach, not just have been on the sidelines when the breach happened. A recent illustration of what may or may not constitute assistance can be seen in the case of *Brinks Ltd* v. *Abu-Saleh (No. 3)* [1996] CLC 133. You may not recognise the name of the case, but in fact this involves one of the most famous gold bullion heists which have ever taken place in Britain. Take a look at the Law in action article for details.

Law in action The Brinks Mat bullion heist

This is the story of the largest gold heist in British history. At 6.30 am on 26 November 1983, a gang of six armed robbers, led by Brian Robinson and Mickey McAvoy and with the help of a Brinks Mat security guard, Anthony Black, broke into the Brinks Mat warehouse at Heathrow Airport. They expected to make off with about £3 million in cash; however, when the safe was finally opened the cash they had expected to see was in fact no less than a hoard of 6,800 gold bars, together with £100,000 worth of cut and uncut diamonds, all of which had been bound for the Far East. With a little bit of a rethink and two hours of heavy lifting, Robinson and McAvoy's team of robbers made off with a staggering £26 million worth of gold bullion.

What at first had seemed a dream come true for the robbers soon proved a major headache for the

Source: Photodisc

gang. The conversion of £26 million worth of bullion into cash was far from being an easy task and they were forced to approach a senior underworld figure, known only as 'The Fox', for help. He had the necessary gangland connections to smelt down the gold, specifically with the assistance of the Adams family, one of London's most notorious crime syndicates. They then recruited a jeweller named Solly Nahome, who agreed to sell on the smelted down goods.

As is often the case in these matters, however, things did not go to plan, and eventually Robinson and McAvoy were caught and each sentenced to 25 years in prison. Brinks Mat has vowed to trace and reclaim the whole of the £26 million stolen from its warehouse.

[*Sources*: based on information from http://news.bbc.co.uk/1/hi/uk/714289.stm; http://www.crime and investigation.co.uk/crime-files/brinks-mat-bullion-heist/crime.html]

Case Summary

The case of *Brinks Ltd* v. *Abu-Saleh* was actually one in a number of civil **actions** brought by the security company to recover the stolen money. The case in point concerned a Mr and Mrs Elcombe, who were accused of smuggling £3 million in cash from England to Switzerland by car on behalf of the gang, in return for a pay-off of £30,000 plus expenses. Mr Elcombe settled the matter out of court but Mrs Elcombe denied all charges made against her, stating that she had been unaware of the nature of her husband's activities and that she was therefore unable to be guilty of the dishonest assistance of Mr Elcombe in moving the money abroad. Mr Justice Rimer agreed with her submissions, concluding that:

> the couriering arrangement was made exclusively between Mr Parry and Mr Elcombe and that Mrs Elcombe was not a party to it . . . Mrs Elcombe knew that the various trips on which she went to Zurich were in pursuance of this arrangement. However . . . she provided no encouragement to her husband and provided no material assistance or played any material part in its execution. I do not consider that it is sufficient to fix her with participation in the alleged conspiracy that she knew the essence of what her husband was doing and acquiesced in it by accompanying him on four of the trips he made.

A particularly interesting point to make about the outcome of this case is the judge's **obiter** remark that Mrs Elcombe's claim that, whilst she was unaware that she was assisting in a breach of trust, she believed that she was assisting in some completely different type of crime (to assist in a tax evasion scam), was nevertheless irrelevant in making a finding of dishonest assistance.

The third party must have been acting dishonestly when they assisted

In making his judgment in *Royal Brunei Airlines* v. *Tan*, Lord Nicholls said that the question of whether or not a third party had acted dishonestly should by measured **objectively**: in other words, the question should be asked whether any honest person would act in that manner under the circumstances. But what is an honest person? The Key stats feature may help you to decide.

Key stats

A little earlier in the chapter, in the Out and about feature, you carried out a small survey on people's attitudes to dishonesty. The questions you asked were actually a small sample of the types of questions asked in a much bigger survey recently carried out by criminal lawyers at Brunel University, which asked over 15,000 participants to give their opinion on varying degrees of dishonest behaviour.

The study, which was intended to discover whether objective tests for dishonesty in the law were in need of review, has revealed some surprising results. Whereas the law assumes that the majority of people in any particular society hold the same views about what conduct is dishonest, the survey shows that quite the opposite is in fact the case. Definitions of dishonesty tend to vary from person to person and situation to situation.

The study found that, whilst, women are more likely than men to categorise some behaviour as dishonest, a person is more likely to be convicted of a dishonest crime in a court of law if they are being judged by men. Dr Emily Finch, who worked on the Brunel honesty project, said 'female participants are more likely to excuse conduct by reference to the circumstances or character of the person involved'.

The study also found disparity between the views of older and younger generations of people, older people being more quick to judge someone dishonest than younger people. However, dishonest actions such as cheating in exams or reading someone else's email were considered more serious offences by younger people.

Here are some more interesting statistics from the survey:

1. 31 per cent of people thought it dishonest for someone to keep money found in the street, but only 8 per cent would convict someone of theft for doing so.

2. 82 per cent thought it dishonest to take stationery home from work, yet as many as 65 per cent of people said that they had actually done this.

3. 96 per cent said taking a DVD from a shop was dishonest, but only 49 per cent though it was dishonest to buy a pirate copy of a DVD.

Perhaps the most shocking result of the survey was that only 43 per cent of people thought it was dishonest for a carer to try to persuade an elderly person to change their will in their favour (twice as many people actually thought it was dishonest to wear a dress before returning it to the shop), and only 21 per cent said that they would convict a carer of such a crime.

For more information about the work of Brunel University, visit their website at: **http://www.honestylab.com/**.

Lord Nicholls, in his interpretation of what would be classed as 'honest', then went on to say that in making their judgment the court would look at the circumstances known to the third party at the time of giving the assistance, together with their experience and intelligence and the reason why they acted as they did. In saying this Lord Nicholls appeared to introduce some **subjective** elements into the equation, and this has led necessarily to further debate as to how dishonesty should be adjudged in cases of dishonest assistance.

The House of Lords was given the opportunity to consider the issue further in 2002, in the case of ***Twinsectra* v. *Yardley*** [2002] 2 All ER 377. The case concerned a loan of £1 million, which Twinsectra Ltd had made to a Mr Yardley. One of the terms of the loan was that the money should only be used for the purchase of property. The loan money was forwarded to Mr Yardley's solicitor, Mr Sims, who undertook to hold the money on trust for Mr Yardley and only to use the money on Mr Yardley's behalf for the purchase of

Case Summary

Case Navigator

property. However, Mr Sims instead forwarded the money to another solicitor, Mr Leach, who allowed Mr Yardley to use the money for his own purposes. Mr Yardley spent the money and defaulted on the loan. Twinsectra brought a claim against all the parties to the transaction, including Mr Leach, on the basis that he had dishonestly assisted Mr Yardley by allowing him to use the money for his own purposes. Mr Leach argued, however, that he had not entered into any undertakings with Twinsectra and therefore was entitled to allow Mr Yardley to use the money for whatever purposes he chose. He had therefore not acted dishonestly. The House of Lords allowed Mr Leach's appeal against the decision of dishonesty and Mr Leach escaped liability from the claim.

The decision of the House of Lords was a majority decision, with Lord Millett dissenting. Lord Hutton, who led the majority, gave the following helpful definitions of both subjective and objective tests:

> Whilst in discussing the term 'dishonesty' the courts often draw a distinction between subjective dishonesty and objective dishonesty, there are three possible standards which can be applied to determine whether a person has acted dishonestly. There is a purely subjective standard, whereby a person is only regarded as dishonest if he transgresses his own standard of honesty, even if that standard is contrary to that of reasonable and honest people. This has been termed the 'Robin Hood test' and has been rejected by the courts . . . Secondly, there is a purely objective standard whereby a person acts dishonestly if his conduct is dishonest by the ordinary standards of reasonable and honest people, even if he does not realize this. Thirdly, there is a standard which combines an objective test and a subjective test, and which requires that before there can be a finding of dishonesty it must be established that the defendant's conduct was dishonest by the ordinary standards of reasonable and honest people and that he himself realized that by those standards his conduct was dishonest. I will term this 'the combined test'.

Lord Hutton then went on to approve the combined test as the method for determining whether or not dishonest assistance had taken place. Lord Millett disagreed with the majority decision, however, favouring the more objective approach that had been taken by Lord Nicholls in *Royal Brunei Airlines* v. *Tan*. In his opinion, there was no necessity for the third party to have actually appreciated that they were acting dishonestly; it was sufficient simply that they were doing so.

Case Summary

A still more recent Privy Council case, *Barlow Clowes International Ltd (in Liquidation)* v. *Eurotrust International Ltd* (2005) UKPC 37 would appear also to favour the call by Lord Millett for a reversion to Lord Nicholl's more objective test. The case concerned a fraudulent offshore investment scheme operated by Mr Clowes of Barlow Clowes International Ltd during the mid 1980s. The scheme made in the region of £140 million during this time, the money being spent by Mr Clowes and his associates. Mr Clowes was convicted of fraud and sentenced in the criminal courts to a prison sentence. Some of the funds were paid to Mr Clowes and his associates through bank accounts maintained by the International Trust Corporation (Isle of Man) Ltd ('ITC'). A claim was subsequently brought against ITC for the dishonest assistance of Mr Clowes in the misappropriation of his investors' funds. The court held that ITC were liable for dishonest assistance, commenting that:

> it was not necessary to know the 'precise involvement' of Mr Cramer in the group's affairs in order to suspect that neither he nor anyone else had the right to use Barlow Clowes' money for speculative investments of their own.

This case has been closely followed by a Court of Appeal case, *Abou-Rahmah* v. *Abacha* [2006] All ER (Comm) 247, in which the judge laid down guidelines to follow when determining whether or not a third party had been dishonest in assisting a breach. These are as follows:

1. A dishonest state of mind on the part of the person assisting is required in the sense that that person's knowledge of the relevant transaction had to be such as to render his participation contrary to normally acceptable standards of honest conduct.

2. Such a state of mind may involve knowledge that the transaction is one in which they cannot honestly participate (i.e. a misappropriation of other people's money), or it may involve suspicions combined with a conscious decision not to make enquiries which might result in knowledge.

3. It is not necessary for the claimant to show that the person assisting knew of the existence of a trust or fiduciary relationship . . . or that the transfer of the claimant's money . . . involved a breach of that trust or fiduciary relationship. It is sufficient that they should have entertained a clear suspicion that this was the case.

The facts of *Abou-Rahmah* v. *Abacha* actually centre around what is commonly referred to as a 'Nigerian Letter' scam (if you don't know what one of these is, take a look at the Documenting the law feature). In this particular case, the **claimants**, Kuwaiti solicitor Mr Abou-Rhamah and his client, a Kuwaiti trading company, were offered a 40 per cent share in a $65 million trust fund which, they were told by the **defendant**, Mr Abacha, was stuck in the republic of Benin in West Africa. The claimants were told by Mr Abacha and his associates that, in order to get access to this money, they needed to make a number of payments, totalling $1.375 million, to various government agencies, purportedly to acquire regulatory permission to move the money out of the republic and to pay VAT. The claimants made all the payments and the defendants absconded with the money. Unable to find the perpetrators of the crime, the claimants tried to recover their losses from a variety of third parties who had been involved in the scam, including a Nigerian bank, the City Express Bank, which had taken two payments totalling $625,000 from the claimants. However, the Court of Appeal found, upholding the decision at first instance, that the bank was not liable for dishonest assistance, having had no particular knowledge of a scam going on at the time at which the payments were made.

Case
Summary

Documenting the law
The 'Nigerian Scam' letter

The Nigerian Scam has been running for decades: in fact, many of you have probably received such a letter via email or through the post yourselves.

How does the scam work? Basically, a letter is sent to you from Nigeria begging for help to get large sums of money out of the country and offering you a slice of the money in return. However, there is a catch – the scam artist needs money from you up front to cut through red tape and bribe corrupt officials (the list is endless) to get the money out of the country. The scam artists keep asking you for ever greater sums of money and, when eventually you can't or won't pay any more, they simply disappear. When you report the crime, you find that, as the scam is not operated on UK soil there is no one to catch – at least no one who can be found. Take a look at the following example of a Nigerian Scam letter. Would you fall for the promise of a slice of $80 million?

CONFIDENTIAL

Dear Sir,

Good day and compliments. This letter will definitely come to you as a huge surprise, but I implore you to take the time to go through it carefully as the decision you make will go off a long way to determine the future and continued existence of the entire members of my family.

Please allow me to introduce myself. My name is Dr. (Mrs.) Mariam Abacha, the wife of the late head of state and commander in chief of the armed forces of the federal republic of Nigeria who died on the 8th of June 1998.

My ordeal started immediately after my husband's death on the morning of 8th June 1998, and the subsequent take over of government by the last administration. The present democratic government is determined to portray all the good work of my late husband in a bad light and have gone as far as confiscating all my late husband's assets, properties, freezing our accounts both within and outside Nigeria. As I am writing this letter to you, my son Mohammed Abacha is undergoing questioning with the government. All these measures taken by past/present government is just to gain international recognition.

I and the entire members of my family have been held incommunicado since the death of my husband, hence I seek your indulgence to assist us in securing these funds. We are not allowed to see or discuss with anybody. Few occasions I have tried traveling abroad through alternative means all failed.

It is in view of this I have mandated DR GALADIMA HASSAN, who has been assisting the family to run around on so many issues to act on behalf of the family concerning the substance of this letter. He has the full power of attorney to execute this transaction with you.

My late husband had/has Eighty Million USD ($80,000,000.00) specially preserved and well packed in trunk boxes of which only my husband and I knew about. It is packed in such a way to forestall just anybody having access to it. It is this sum that I seek your assistance to get out of Nigeria as soon as possible before the present civilian government finds out about it and confiscate it just like they have done to all our assets.

I implore you to please give consideration to my predicament and help a widow in need.

May Allah show you mercy as you do so?

Your faithfully,

Dr (Mrs.) Mariam Abacha (M.O.N)

N/B: Please contact Dr Galadima Hassan on this e-mail address for further briefing and modalities

For more examples of Nigerian Scam letters go to: **http://www.quatloos.com/cm-niger/abacha.htm.**

It would seem in the light of these cases that the meaning of dishonesty will continue to be judged for the foreseeable future on the objective test set down by Lord Nicholls in *Royal Brunei Airlines* v. *Tan*, the honesty of third parties being judged by the standards of the ordinary man, rather than by the standards by which the third party judges themselves. However, it is certainly likely that the meaning of 'dishonesty' in the arena of dishonest assistance will continue to be a hot topic for debate.

Knowing receipt

Let us move on, then, to the topic of knowing receipt. As the name suggests, knowing receipt differs from dishonest assistance in that it involves the actual receipt by the third party of trust property. Knowing receipt also differs from dishonest assistance in that the remedy available to the beneficiaries against someone who is in knowing receipt of trust property is a personal one. So, whereas with dishonest assistance the offending third party will be held in the place of a trustee on constructive trust and can be sued for the breach of trust, with knowing receipt the beneficiary is able to claim either return of the goods from the offending party or, if they have since disposed of them, can make a personal claim against them for the value of the property received. This makes the equitable remedy of knowing receipt a very potent one for a wronged beneficiary.

The basic definition of knowing receipt is a simple one: it is the receipt by a third party of trust property, either by way of purchase or through the receipt of a gift; but what about the element of 'knowing'? How do we define that? The answer may seem straightforward: if a person receives trust property in the knowledge that it has been misappropriated from the trust, they will be guilty of knowing receipt. But the courts have found it less than simple to come to a consensus on what will be sufficient to prove that the receiving party had the requisite amount of knowledge.

A first attempt to measure exactly what level of knowledge would be required before a person could be held guilty of knowing receipt was made by Mr Justice Gibson in the case of *Baden* v. *Société Générale pour Favouriser le Développement du Commerce et de l'Industrie en France SA* in 1983 (BCLC 325). The case concerned a large financial consortium, Investors Overseas Services, which managed offshore funds. Money was misappropriated from the funds and deposited into various trust accounts, one of which was the well-known French bank, Société Générale. Société Générale then received instructions to transfer the $4 million to a Panama bank. After making enquiries, the bank complied with their instructions and transferred the money. A writ was issued by Mr Baden and a number of other investors against Société Générale claiming that, by transferring the money, the bank had become a constructive trustee and was liable to account for it. It was held, however, that Société Générale was not liable because it was not aware at the time of the fraudulent design it was assisting. In giving his judgment, Mr Justice Gibson stated that the knowledge in knowing assistance could be of five different kinds:

Case Summary

1. Actual knowledge.

2. Wilfully shutting one's eyes to the obvious.

3. Wilfully and recklessly failing to make such enquiries as an honest and reasonable man would make.

4. Knowledge of circumstances which would indicate the facts to an honest or reasonable man.

5. Knowledge of circumstances which would have put an honest and reasonable man on enquiry (in other words, they would have been made naturally suspicious by what they had learnt).

Of these five kinds of knowledge, the first three were considered to be 'guilty knowledge', whilst the fourth and fifth kinds of knowledge were considered to have more of a constructive element and thus to be more innocent in nature – although still amounting to knowledge, nonetheless. Indeed, Mr Justice Gibson's original intention in setting out the five types of knowledge was that a third party would be guilty of knowing receipt whichever of the five types applied to them.

Case
Navigator

Case
Summary

This comprehensive approach to knowing receipt was subsequently criticised, however, later case law favouring a more restrictive interpretation. Four years after the *Baden* case, further opportunity to comment came with the case of ***Re Montagu's Settlement Trusts*** [1987] Ch 264, which concerned the transfer of **chattels** under the terms of a family **settlement**. A settlement was drawn up by the 9th Duke of Manchester in which trustees were supposed to draw up an inventory of the Duke's chattels, those of value being held in the family trust (for the benefit of the 11th Duke and his successors), the remainder being given to the 10th Duke absolutely. However, on the death of the 9th Duke no inventory was drawn up and the chattels were simply given to the 10th Duke to dispose of at will. Many of the items were subsequently sold. On the death of the 10th Duke, the 11th Duke then claimed that the trustees had acted in breach of trust and that the widow of the 10th Duke was holding the remaining chattels on a constructive trust by virtue of her husband having received the chattels dishonestly out of the trust. However, it was held that, whilst the chattels had been transferred to the 10th Duke in breach of trust, the 10th Duke was not guilty of knowing receipt because he did not have the requisite knowledge of the terms of the settlement.

Referring to *Baden* in the case, Vice-Chancellor Megarry said of the fourth and fifth constructive kinds of knowledge, those of 'knowledge of circumstances which would indicate the facts to an honest or reasonable man' and 'knowledge of circumstances which would have put an honest and reasonable man on enquiry':

> In considering whether a constructive trust has arisen in a case of the knowing receipt of trust property, the basic question is whether the conscience of the recipient is sufficiently affected to justify the imposition of such a trust . . . Whether knowledge of the Baden types (iv) and (v) suffices for this purpose is at best doubtful; in my view, it does not, for I cannot see that the carelessness involved will normally amount to a want of probity.

the fourth and fifth kinds of knowledge lacked the element of bad faith

In his view, then, only the first three categories of knowledge should be sufficient to prove knowing receipt, because the fourth and fifth kinds of knowledge lacked the element of bad faith required to impute knowledge on a third party in receipt of trust monies. Certainly in the case of *Re Montagu's*, the 10th Duke of Manchester lacked the requisite element of **unconscionability** because he did not have a thorough understanding of the legal implications of the settlement when the property was transferred to him.

Case
Summary

In 1992 the *Baden* categories of knowledge came under yet further attack in the case of *Polly Peck International plc* v. *Nadir (No. 2)* [1992] 4 All ER 769, which again concerned the purported knowing receipt of trust funds. The funds had been stolen by Asil Nadir from the company of which he was a director, Polly Peck International plc, and paid into Mr Nadir's bank, the Central Bank of Northern Cyprus. In giving his judgment in the case Lord Justice Scott criticised Vice-Chancellor Megarry's reasoning in *Re Montagu's*, stating that 'the *Re Baden* categories are not rigid categories with clear and precise boundaries. One category may merge imperceptibly into another'. His feeling was that the five categories should be used more as a guideline, with the bottom line being whether the third party in receipt should have been suspicious of the transaction.

This less rigid approach seems also to have found favour with the Court of Appeal, who followed the dictum of Lord Justice Scott in *Polly Peck* in *Bank of Credit and Commerce*

International (Overseas) Ltd v. *Akindele* [2001] Ch 437. Lord Justice Nourse held that it was not necessary to establish that a third party had acted dishonestly in receiving the trust property, only that his conscience should have been pricked by what he knew. He referred to this as the 'conscionability test', stating that 'all that is necessary is that the recipient's state of mind should be such as to make it unconscionable for him to retain the benefit of the receipt'. The case of *Bank of Credit and Commerce International (Overseas) Ltd* v. *Akindele* concerned an agreement which the defendant, Chief Akindele, had entered into with a company controlled by the claimant, 'BCCI'. The agreement, which was for the purchase of shares in the BCCI group's holding company, guaranteed Chief Akindele a return of 15 per cent per year on his holding of $10 million. However, it turned out that the agreement was in reality simply a front for BCCI's holding company to conceal the purchase of its own shares in an attempt to boost its share capital. When the company went into administration, the liquidators made a claim against Chief Akindele for knowing receipt for the sums paid to him under the agreement. However, applying Lord Justice Nourse's conscionability test, Chief Akindele was found innocent of the charge, on the basis that there was no reason for anybody outside of the company at the time of the transactions to doubt the integrity of its management.

Case Summary

Writing and drafting

It may be that you are struggling at this point to remember exactly how the definition of knowledge has evolved: it certainly has changed a lot over a relatively short space of time. A helpful way to remember the changes in attitudes of the judges is to draw up a timeline of the cases as they were heard and the comments of the judges in each case. Why not draw your own timeline showing the evolution of knowing receipt. There is a really useful article on how to create a timeline in Microsoft Word at: **http://www.microsoft.com/education/TimelinesWord.mspx.**

You should take no longer than 40 minutes on this task.

 Handy tip: If you really don't know where to start, try drawing yourself a simple table, stating for each case the year, the judge, and the comments that judge made, and create the timeline out of this.

The debate about what constitutes 'knowledge' in knowing receipt continues to rumble on, the latest controversy having been stirred up by an obiter comment made by Lord Nicholls of Birkenhead in the 2004 case of *Criterion Properties* v. *Stratford UK Properties LLC* [2004] 1 WLR 1846, HL. The case concerned an agreement entered into between the directors of Criterion Properties and a company called Oaktree, who were in partnership together. The purpose of the agreement was to oblige Criterion to buy Oaktree out of the partnership if Criterion was subject to a hostile takeover: something of which Criterion was fearful at the time. As it happened, the threat of hostile takeover subsided (perhaps because of the existence of the agreement) and there was no need for the agreement, often referred to as a 'poison-pill device', to be put into effect. However, when the managing director of Criterion was later dismissed Oaktree sought to exercise its right to be bought

Case Summary

out under the terms of the agreement. Criterion applied to court to have the agreement set aside on the basis that it had not been properly authorised by the board of directors, but their application was unsuccessful. But what is the relevance of all this to the issue of knowing receipt? Barrister Bajul Shah explains in the People in the law article.

People in the law

Name and position: Bajul Shah, barrister at a leading commercial barristers' chambers XXIV Old Buildings in London. Bajul specialises in civil fraud, trusts and probate.

So, Bajul, how does the issue of knowing receipt relate to this case? *Criterion* was not actually a knowing receipt case; instead, the issue was whether the directors of Criterion had actual or ostensible authority to enter into the contract with Oaktree. However, Lord Nicholls went on to state, obiter, what consequences would follow if the agreement was set aside and it is these obiter remarks that impact upon knowing receipt.

He said (taking the example of A, who enters into a contract with B under which B acquires benefits from A):

> If, however, the agreement *is* set aside, B will be accountable for any benefits he may have received from A under the agreement. A will have a proprietary claim, if B still has the assets. Additionally, and irrespective of whether B still has the assets in question, A will have a personal claim against B for unjust enrichment, subject always to a defence of change of position [see below]. B's personal accountability will not be dependent upon proof of fault or 'unconscionable' conduct on his part. B's accountability, in this regard, will be 'strict'.

What is the significance of Lord Nicholls's statement? The significance of Lord Nicholls's comments is that he advocated replacing fault-based knowing receipt liability with a strict liability personal restitutionary claim, which operated irrespective of whether the claimant also had a proprietary claim, and which was subject to a change of position defence.

Source: Bajul Shah (*text and photo*)

What are your views on the introduction of a strict liability offence for knowing receipt? This is a very significant departure from existing principles. Whilst the principles are clearly stated and would assimilate knowing receipt with common law restitutionary claims, it could work real injustice. In the example he posed, money received by B under the agreement may have been used by it in the ordinary course of its business in the belief that it was entitled to that money. If the agreement is subsequently set aside, B would be strictly liable to return it despite its belief. This does not seem just. The formulation shifts the burden on B to show why it would be unjust to return the money, when arguably the burden should be on A to show why it would be unjust (or unconscionable) for B to retain it. His formulation appears to put the risk of loss on B who may be an innocent recipient. Certainty of receipt in commercial transactions could also be undermined if innocent recipients could be liable to return them even when they longer have them.

Do you think the change of position defence will be a sufficient foil to such claims in the case of banks and building societies? A change of position defence may not be a sufficient foil to such claims because this defence does not generally apply to payments made in the ordinary course of business, or for ordinary expenses, or which one is already otherwise liable to make. Thus, in the example, if the money has been utilised in the ordinary course of business, B may not be able to rely on the defence of change of position. This does not seem just.

Do you think it will make the banks and other large financial institutions easy targets for claimants? It may make it easier to bring claims against banks or building societies,

although they may be able to argue that if they received the money as agents for their customers rather than as principals they are not liable in any event.

How do you see the law unfolding from here? What would you like to see happen? Lord Nicholls's remarks had the potential to bring about a momentous change in this area of the law. But so far no reported case has followed them. My own view is that orthodox principles will continue to apply. Knowing receipt is basically about making third party recipients of trust property liable *when they no longer have the property*. The case for making innocent recipients *strictly* liable does not seem as just as making an unconscionable recipient liable and the common law is generally cautious about imposing strict liability.

How the law will evolve following *Criterion* remains to be seen. However, it seems likely, as Bajul Shah states in his case comment, that despite Lord Nicholls's suggestion, the law will continue to follow the *Re Baden* categories in the traditional manner, albeit with the focus remaining firmly on unconscionability, for the foreseeable future.

Defences against knowing receipt

There are two defences available to a third party accused of knowing receipt:

✦ the first is that they were a **bona fide purchaser for value without notice** of the breach of trust: in other words, that they bought the trust property without knowing that it was the product of a breach; and

✦ secondly, the change of position defence.

The defence of bona fide purchaser for value without notice is self-explanatory. However, the change of position defence works on the basis that the third party changed their position in good faith in reliance on receipt of the trust property. The leading case in this area is that of *Lipkin Gorman* v. *Karpnale* [1991] 3 WLR 10. The facts of the case are interesting, in that they concern a corrupt solicitor, Norman Barry Cass. Mr Cass was a partner in the firm of Lipkin Gorman. He was an authorised signatory of the firm's bank account. Mr Cass was having a mid-life crisis. Over a period of eight months Mr Cass withdrew £220,000 from his firm's account and spent it at the gambling tables at the Playboy Club in London, which was owned by the defendants, Karpnale Ltd. Of the money gambled, the club retained £154,695, the rest being paid out to Mr Cass in winnings. When the theft was discovered by Lipkin Gorman, Mr Cass fled to Israel, but he was brought back and sentenced to three years in prison for theft. Lipkin Gorman then brought a civil action against Karpnale Ltd, for the return of the stolen monies they had received from Mr Cass. Whilst the claim was dismissed both at first instance and by the Court of Appeal, the House of Lords held that the company should pay back the solicitors, having been unjustly enriched by the proceeds of a theft. Karpnale were given

Case Summary

a partial defence, however, on the basis of a change of position, for the money which had been paid out to Mr Cass in winnings. This was on the basis that they would not have paid out winnings to Mr Cass had they not received money from him at the gambling tables. They were therefore only liable to pay their profit of £154,695 back to Lipkin Gorman.

Obviously these facts are very specific and the change of position defence has to be available in circumstances other than these to have credibility as a method of defence for those accused of knowing receipt. So how might it work with a different set of facts? Effectively, the court in the case of a change of a position defence is giving the third party relief from liability on the basis that they have 'changed their position' specifically in reliance on receipt of the property which has been misappropriated. So, another example of change of position might be a scenario in which a fraudulent trustee misappropriates money from a trust fund and gives some of that money to a favourite nephew. The nephew, unaware of the source of the money, then spends a proportion of it on a luxury holiday which they never could have otherwise afforded. In a subsequent claim by the beneficiaries of the trust against the nephew for return of the monies, the nephew could claim change of position as a defence in respect of the monies spent on the luxury holiday: something he would never have contemplated if he had not received the gift from his uncle. A further example might be where the Inland Revenue gives a tax rebate which has been incorrectly calculated. Believing the overpayment to be genuine, the person in receipt of the rebate then spends the money on a slap-up meal for themselves and their family at their favourite restaurant. The Inland Revenue then asks for the money back, but the person in receipt of the rebate claims that they have spent it, on account of a change of position caused by the receipt of the overpayment.

It should be noted that the defence of change of position is not available where the third party is proved to have had knowledge of the breach or to have acted dishonestly. So if the same person receiving the overpayment of tax realises that they should not have received the money, but goes ahead and spends it anyway, they will not be able to rely on the change of position defence.

You be the judge

Q: In which of the following examples do you think the defendant could claim a change of position defence:

✦ Defendant A is given money by her husband that, unbeknown to her, the husband has embezzled from their business. The defendant spends the money making home improvements.

✦ The bank make a credit into defendant B's bank account and, not noticing the overpayment, the defendant spends the money on groceries.

✦ Defendant C receives an overpayment of insurance and, believing the payment to be correct, spends the money in paying off his mortgage.

✦ Defendant D receives money from her husband which she knows he has come across by illegal means. She spends the money on a fur coat.

A: Only A could claim a change of position. Whereas it could be argued that A has spent money on improvements to the home which she would not otherwise have done or have been able to afford, B and C are both spending money on things they would have had to pay for in any event: B is paying for groceries – an everyday necessity, and C is repaying a debt which would be payable in any event. D knows the money has been acquired dishonestly and so will not be eligible to rely on the defence.

Summary

◆ Dishonest assistance does not require the party in breach to receive, or even to handle, the trust property; all that is required is that the third party plays some part in assisting the trustee to commit the breach.

◆ The requirements for dishonest assistance are that:

   ◆ there must be a trust;

   ◆ there must be a breach of trust;

   ◆ the third party must have assisted in the breach; and

   ◆ the third party must have been acting dishonestly when they assisted (*Royal Brunei Airlines* v. *Tan*).

◆ There is no requirement for a formally documented trust to be in existence; rather there must be a clear position of trust or fiduciary relationship.

◆ There is no need for the breach of trust to have been committed dishonestly for dishonest assistance to apply.

◆ In order to assist dishonestly, the third party must have been actually involved in committing the breach, not just have been on the sidelines when the breach happened.

◆ The measure for dishonesty is objective: so a person acts dishonestly if his conduct is dishonest by the ordinary standards of reasonable and honest people. However, this is subject to consideration of the person's individual circumstances and knowledge.

◆ Knowing receipt requires the third party actually to receive property which has been misappropriated from the trust.

◆ Originally, knowledge was thought to consist of five types of differing severity; however, later case law has moved towards a more fluid approach to the meaning of knowledge, based on the unconscionability of the third party in receiving the property.

◆ There has been some call for a strict liability offence of knowing receipt to be created, subject to defences (as per Lord Nicholls's dictum in *Criterion Properties* v. *Stratford Properties*).

◆ Knowing receipt can be defended either if the third party is a bona fide purchaser for value of the trust property or if they have 'changed their position'.

◆ The change of position defence will apply wherever the third party expends all or some of the money received in honest reliance on that receipt.

Question and answer*

Problem: Gerald, who is a partner at Greed & Co. Solicitors, steals a total of £2 million from the firm's client account over a period of two years. He spends some of the money himself, giving the rest to his wife and three children. Gerald's wife, Cynthia, believing business is booming, spends the money in paying off their credit card debts and on a replacement diamond engagement ring (Gerald had always promised her a better one. He had bought her original ring when he was an impoverished trainee solicitor and the stone was cubic zirconia). Gerald's elder son, Tom, is aware of his father's dealings, but spends the money anyway to pay off his bar bill. Gerald's younger son, James, is best friends with Gerald's business partner in Greed & Co., Archie. James is aware, from spending a lot of time at Archie's house, that they are not as well off as his own family, and he often hears Archie complaining that business is bad. He begins to suspect that everything is not as it should be. By this time, he has already spent the money received from his father on a new state-of-the-art home cinema system and a cruise off the Canaries. Gerald's daughter is unaware of the theft. She spends the money on riding lessons and a new pony.

Archie discovers the theft and Gerald disappears. Determined to see the return of his clients' money, Archie brings actions against Gerald's wife and three children. Comment on the extent of each party's liability for knowing receipt and any defences they may have.

You should allow yourself no more than 40 minutes to complete this task.

Essay: 'The precise meaning of dishonesty in dishonest assistance has been a source of some confusion since the decision in *Royal Brunei Airlines* v. *Tan*.' Discuss.

This question should be answered in 40 minutes.

✱ Answer guidance is provided at the end of the chapter.

Further reading

Andrews, G. (2003) 'The redundancy of dishonest assistance', Conv (Sep/Oct), 398–410.
An interesting article suggesting that the remedy of dishonest assistance is outdated and no longer required by equity.

Kiri, N. (2006) 'Recipient and accessory liability – where do we stand now?', *Journal of International Banking Law and Regulation*, 21(11), 611–20.
Another well-written article from Nikunj Kiri on changes in the law of knowing receipt and discussing the notion of a strict liability offence based on unjust enrichment.

Kiri, N. (2007) 'Dishonest assistance: the latest perspective from the Court of Appeal', *Journal of International Banking Law and Regulation*, 22(6), 305–17.
Nice clear article tracking the development of dishonest assistance since *Twinsectra* v. *Yardley* and commenting on the change in direction indicated by the recent case of *Abou-Rahmah* v. *Abacha*.

Nolan, R. (2000) 'How knowing is knowing receipt?', CLJ, 59(3), 447–50.
Case comment on *Houghton* v. *Fayers* [2000] 1 BCLC 511 highlighting the differences between knowledge and dishonesty in knowing receipt and advocating the adoption of a strict liability offence.

Question and answer guidance

Problem: All the parties have received trust property, having been given money by Gerald. The question is whether they are guilty of knowing receipt. Look back at the definition in *Baden*: five categories of knowing: actual knowledge; wilfully shutting one's eyes; failing to make enquiries; knowledge of circumstances which would indicate the facts; knowledge of circumstances which would put a person on enquiry. Note, however, the more general unconscionability test which has found favour in later cases (see *Polly Peck* v. *Nadir*; *BCCI* v. *Akindele*).

✦ We are told that Gerald's wife, Cynthia, believed that the money came out of the business because it was doing well. She is therefore innocent of any knowledge of the fraud. Whether she could be accused of wilfully shutting her eyes to the obvious, or even of failing to make enquiries where she reasonably should have done, would depend on the production of more evidence, and whether her actions amounted to the required level of unconscionability overall. If Gerald has been lying to her about how the business has been doing, however, arguably she could not be expected to know any better.

✦ Gerald's elder son, Tom, is aware of his father's dealings, but spends the money anyway to pay off his bar bill. He clearly has actual knowledge and so is guilty of knowing receipt.

✦ James is aware, from spending a lot of time at Archie's house, that they are not as well off as his own family, and he often hears Archie complaining that business is bad. He begins to suspect that everything is not as it should be. By this time, he has already spent the money. James is therefore suspicious but does not have actual knowledge. Whether he is guilty of failing to make enquiries or the lesser guilt of having knowledge of circumstances which would either indicate the facts or put him on enquiry would be a matter of fact and degree. In any event, it is unlikely that at the time he received the money he did so with the required level of unconscionability. He did not start to realise there might have been a problem until after the event.

✦ Gerald's daughter is unaware of the theft. She has no knowledge and is innocent of the theft. She cannot therefore be guilty of knowing receipt.

As for defences, either Cynthia or James could possibly argue the change of position defence (*Lipkin Gorman* v. *Karpnale*). That is, that they received the money quite innocently and then spent it, relying on their change in position in terms of their wealth. James has spent the money on a home cinema system and a cruise. If these were things he would not otherwise have been able to afford he could claim change of position in respect of these. With regard to Cynthia, she would not be able to claim change of position in respect of the payment of her overdraft, as this is a debt she would have been liable to pay in any event. She could, however, claim change of position in respect of the replacement engagement ring if she was proved to be innocent of guilty knowledge in respect of the receipt.

Essay:

If you have already had a go at doing the timeline in the Writing and drafting exercise above, you will find it an invaluable tool in answering this question.

Although the question asks students to comment on the meaning of dishonesty since *Royal Brunei* v. *Tan*, it may be worth setting the scene by mentioning that, prior to *Royal Brunei*, a finding of dishonest assistance hinged, not on the motivations of the third party, but of the trustee committing the breach (*Barnes* v. *Addy*). There has therefore been a complete shift in emphasis since *Royal Brunei* on the requirement of dishonesty in dishonest assistance, from the dishonest trustee to the assisting party themselves.

Students should then go on to say that there has been some confusion over whether the measure of dishonesty applicable to third parties should be gauged subjectively or objectively.

In *Royal Brunei* v. *Tan*, Lord Nicholls said that the question of whether or not a third party had acted dishonestly should be measured objectively: in other words, the question should be asked whether any honest person would act in that manner under the circumstances. However, he then went on to say that, in making their judgment, the court would look at the circumstances known to the third party at the time of giving the assistance, together with their experience and intelligence and the reason why they acted as they did. This would appear to introduce a subjective element to the test of dishonesty.

Lord Hutton attempted to resolve this riddle in *Twinsectra* v. *Yardley*. He said that the method for determining whether or not dishonest assistance had taken place was indeed a combined test, incorporating a mixture of both subjective and objective standards. This combined approach was not agreed with by Lord Millett, however, who said that, in his opinion, there was no necessity for the third party to have actually appreciated that they were acting dishonestly; it was sufficient simply that they were doing so. He favoured a more objective test, therefore.

Later cases have appeared to favour Lord Millett's approach (see Privy Council case *Barlow Clowes* v. *Eurotrust International* and Court of Appeal case *Abou-Rhamah* v. *Abacha*), but a definitive answer is yet to be given on the matter. Students might conclude by saying that a definitive answer to the problem may be found when the issue once again reaches the House of Lords for discussion.

Visit **www.mylawchamber.co.uk/warner-reed** to access study support resources including practice exam questions with guidance, interactive 'You be the judge' multiple choice questions, annotated weblinks, glossary and key case flashcards and audio legal updates all linked to the **Pearson eText** version of *Equity and Trusts* which you can **search**, **highlight** and **personalise** with your **own notes** and **bookmarks**.

Use Case Navigator to read in full some of the key cases referenced in this chapter with commentary and questions:

Re Montagu's Settlement Trusts [1992] 4 All ER 308
Royal Brunei Airlines Sdn Bhd **v.** *Tan* [1995] 3 All ER 97
Twinsectra Ltd **v.** *Yardley* [2002] 2 All ER 377

Chapter 15
Tracing

Key points · In this chapter we will be looking at:

+ What is tracing?
+ How property can be traced at common law
+ Limitations with common law tracing: tracing into mixed accounts
+ The tracing of property in equity
+ The need for a fiduciary relationship before tracing in equity can take place
+ The rules for tracing into an asset in equity
+ The rules for tracing into bank accounts in equity
+ Bars to tracing: bona fide purchasers, dissipated funds and inequitable outcomes
+ The call for a unified law of tracing

Introduction

In the previous two chapters we have talked about the liability both of **trustees** and of **strangers** to the **trust** for breaches of trust. Establishing such liability is important and will obviously form the basis of any court claim for breach of trust; but for the **beneficiaries** the bottom line is that, if a trustee misappropriates or otherwise loses or misdirects money out of the trust fund, the beneficiaries want to see that money returned. Of course, nine times out of ten the offending trustee will either have spent the money they have taken or, still worse, will have gone bankrupt. So how can the bene-ficiaries go about getting their money back, if at all? This is where the process of **tracing** comes in.

Case Navigator

Case Summary

Probably the most famous example of a tracing claim is that in the case of ***Attorney-General for Hong Kong v. Reid*** [1994] 1 AC 324, [1994] 1 NZLR 1 (PC). Mr Reid, who was at that time the solicitor-general for Hong Kong, had received substantial bribes for passing information to organised crime syndicates in Hong Kong. Mr Reid then invested the proceeds of the bribes in land in New Zealand, and the land increased substantially in value. When he was caught, it was held that, under the law of Hong Kong, the proceeds of those bribes were held on **constructive trusts** for the Hong Kong government. Mr Reid accepted this, but argued that he should only be liable to repay the amount of the bribes. However, the **Privy Council** held that the government of Hong Kong's claim to the money could be traced into the land, and so the **claimant** was entitled to the full value of the land. Mr Reid would never have made a profit on the land without having taken the bribes and it would therefore be inequitable for him to keep them.

So it can be seen that through the process of tracing it may be possible for beneficiaries to see the return of their trust property, albeit that it has since been converted into other forms. There are two forms of tracing, one applicable to the **common law** and one applicable in **equity**; this chapter deals with both in turn.

What is tracing?

Despite often being referred to as a remedy, tracing is not a remedy at all – it is simply the process through which trust property is traced from its source into whatever form it may take at the point at which the claim for return of the monies is made. As Lord Millett explained in the leading case in the field of tracing, *Foskett* v. *McKeown* [2000] 3 All ER 97, which concerned the tracing of misappropriated investors' monies:

> Tracing is . . . neither a claim nor a remedy. It is merely the process by which a claimant demonstrates what has happened to his property, identifies its proceeds and the persons who have handled or received them, and justifies his claim that the proceeds can properly be regarded as representing his property.

The full facts of this case are given later on in the chapter.

So how does it all work? The idea behind tracing is that, by following the money from the point at which it is removed from the trust, a claimant can bring an **action** not necessarily against the original trust property (which will often have been spent) but against whatever property into which that trust money has been converted. This has the distinct benefit that it allows the beneficiaries to see monies returned which, in the case of a penniless or bankrupt trustee, would have otherwise been impossible. The interview in the People in the Law feature with David Sowden of the Grant Thornton accountancy practice gives us a flavour of tracing in practice.

People in the law

Name and position: David Sowden, Director in Forensic & Investigation Services, Grant Thornton, Leeds.

What is your role at Grant Thornton? I have been involved in forensic accounting since the 1990s, and actually started out doing work on the Maxwell pension scheme. Since then I have concentrated on large-scale fraud and money laundering investigations, often based in Jersey.

Source: David Sowden (*text and photo*)

How do you go about the tracing process? The tracing of funds is generally a common-sense process, but is driven by a lot of complex case law, particularly if you are trying to recover them. The area I am often involved in covers multi-jurisdictional money flows. The implication of this is that differing rules may apply in differing jurisdictions. For example, whilst Clayton's Rule (or First In First Out) is often used in the UK where there is no other obvious way to match monies flows, in Jersey the presumption is to use the apportionment method. These two approaches can result in different answers to the question of how the funds ought to be matched. [An explanation of Clayton's Rule is given further on in the chapter.]

I tend to be more involved in the criminal side of tracing than the civil side, which by its nature is less focused on recovery of the money per se: rather we tend to concentrate more on proving the source of stolen or defrauded funds and how they have been dealt with. In some instances this involves using the matching principle followed in civil tracing. In others, such as money laundering, the case is that the launderer has deliberately moved the funds in such a way that they cannot be traced and as a result have been 'cleaned'. In such cases the approach is to show what really happened to the funds in the mind of the launderer rather than the strict explanation of each money flow. For example, in one case the use of two apparently unrelated bank accounts allowed funds to be received into one and paid out of another. Other than a paper reconciling note these transactions could not be matched when in fact they did represent the same funds.

In criminal cases, on conviction the defendant can be ordered to pay a confiscation order or a compensation order based on the benefit obtained from the funds stolen. Whilst this may result in restitution, it is up to the defendant how he pays such orders and as such the actually stolen funds may not be the actual funds returned to the victim.

How many tracing claims/cases does your firm deal with in a year? It is difficult to say because cases can run for a considerable length of time, particularly if they involve complex money laundering investigations, and can span a number of different jurisdictions. For example, one case which I have been currently working on involving a Nigerian business man and frauds of an estimated £185 million has been ongoing for 6 years now.

How much stolen money do you chase and what proportion do you find? We do not think of it as recovering 'stolen' money as such in civil matters, just that the person is recovering their own money. In the Robert Maxwell case we recovered all the monies which had been taken and were able to return them to the pension schemes. In criminal matters, we take a different approach in proving what percentage the money represents of the proceeds of criminal conduct. For example, in a recent case $45 million was withdrawn from six bank accounts by way of bank drafts. Of this total we were able to prove that about 78 per cent could be traced back to funds which had been stolen from the Nigerian Treasury.

What's the biggest/strangest tracing claim your firm has had to deal with? In some of the bigger cases funds can run into the billions. One of the biggest cases we have worked on is the BCCI scandal in the 1990s. That involved huge sums of money. [The BCCI scandal was a huge banking scandal involving the Bank of Credit and Commerce International, a huge global bank, which went into administration in 1991 amidst multiple money laundering and regulatory claims.]

What are your thoughts on the differing rules on tracing at law and in equity? Should there be just one system? As forensic accountants we need to be aware of the different systems of tracing. However, we are accountants and not lawyers and as such we seek guidance from our legal advisers. This is essential as much of tracing is case law driven and as such can be constantly changing. We keep abreast of these changes, but essentially our job is more to try to work out what has happened and then we rely on the lawyers to guide us on whether the monies can be followed or how they want to approach a particular matter for the purposes of the court hearing.

Are there any other comments you would like to make? From the perspective of the criminal investigations the access to information, although still difficult to obtain, is assisted by the investigative powers available to the prosecuting authorities. These include the powers to compel banks and individuals to produce documents and explanations of transactions. They also include the mutual assistance provisions whereby one jurisdiction can seek that similar actions to those outlined above be executed on their behalf by another jurisdiction.

Whilst civil applications also exist, the criminal investigator enjoys the powers of compulsion to a greater extent.

As in all legal proceedings the extent of knowledge is paramount and such tools are essential in piecing together often extensive and complex webs of trust structures and money flows, often involving many jurisdictions and currencies.

Finally I often get involved in investigating what has gone on within offshore trusts including those set up by Politically Exposed Persons. Whilst some of these are set up with the intention of concealing criminal conduct, the majority are not. Consequently we are often engaged to untangle the complex web and then to succinctly present the real picture behind the trust which may or may not involve wrongdoing. [Politically Exposed Persons (often referred to as PEPs) are those who have a prominent public function with a great deal of sway or influence and who are therefore more likely to be targets for bribes or other forms of corruption.]

As you will have gathered from the interview, tracing can be separated into two separate categories: common law tracing and tracing in equity. Whilst both follow the same aim – to follow property as it changes hands in order to be able to recover that property (or its value) – the principles under which the two types of tracing operate are really quite different. Let us take a look at common law tracing, first of all.

Common law tracing

At common law, the principle is very much that it is the physical item itself that is being traced: the item to which the claimant has **legal title**, or ownership. So if an item, let us say a gold pocket watch, is misappropriated, common law tracing can be used to recover that pocket watch, or its value, from any person who takes physical possession of it. With common law tracing it is all about the recovery of the physical item: in order for the owner of property to assert their rights at common law, they must be able to identify that thing over which they claim ownership. Thus, in common law tracing, it is of paramount importance that the item to be recovered remains recognisable, or distinct, in whatever form it may take, from other property of the **defendant**. As Lord Ellenborough said in *Taylor* v. *Plumer* (1815) 3 M & S 562, which concerned money misappropriated by a stock-broking agent:

> common law tracing is all about the recovery of the physical item

Case Summary

> It makes no difference in reason or law into what other form, different from the original, the change may have been made, whether it be into that of promissory notes for the security of the money which was produced by the sale of the goods of the **principal** . . . or into other merchandise, for the product of or substitute for the original thing still follows the nature of the thing itself, as long as it can be ascertained as such, and the right only ceases when the means of ascertainment fail, which is the case when the subject is turned into money, and mixed and confounded in a general mass of the same description.

As can be seen from Lord Ellenborough's quote, the need for an ability to identify the property makes it impossible to trace money at common law once it has been mixed with other money in a bank account. The effect is that common law tracing is of limited practical application. Imagine the difficulty this presents: it is highly unlikely that a fraudulent trustee who misappropriates money from a trust fund will deposit that money in a separate account, labelled 'the stolen trust fund account' and use that money only for specified purchases. The more likely scenario is that the trustee will deposit the money in their current bank account, which has money from different sources coming into it at different times, and money constantly going out. It will, almost from the moment of deposit, become impossible to tell which money is being used for which purchases – the trust money or the trustee's own money – and hence common law tracing cannot work.

To make matters worse, the courts have held that it is not even necessary for the trust money to be mixed with other money of the trustee in order to become unidentifiable: the simple placing of the money in a bank account can be enough to prevent common law tracing. This was the outcome in the case of *Agip (Africa) Ltd* v. *Jackson* [1992] 4 All ER 385. The case concerned an Italian mining company, Agip, which was drilling for oil in Tunisia. Over a period of years, Agip was systematically defrauded of millions of dollars by its chief accountant, Mr Zdiri. Mr Zdiri was neither a director of Agip, nor

Case Summary

an authorised signatory of the company; his job was to give the completed payment orders to an authorised signatory for their signature and then take them to the bank. From time to time, Mr Zdiri fraudulently altered the name on the payment orders so that the money was diverted to one of his criminal associates in London. Between 1983 and 1985 alone, Mr Zdiri had stolen over £6.5 million using this method.

The court case of *Agip (Africa) Ltd* v. *Jackson* actually concerned the last fraudulent transfer to be made, which was for $518,822.92. Agip sought to reclaim the lost funds by tracing them from their bank account through the telegraphic transfer system and onwards, once they reached their destination in London. However, the court rejected their claim at common law, stating that it was impossible to identify the money received by the defendant as Agip's money, because of the process it had been through. In the words of Mr Justice Millett at first instance, 'nothing passed between Tunisia and London but a stream of electrons'. At the Court of Appeal hearing the outcome was the same, the court stressing that the very process of putting money in at one branch of a bank and taking it out at another would result in a mixing of funds, the money having being put with other money in the bank's internal clearance system.

One final limitation of common law tracing is the necessity of the claimant retaining the legal title to the property. This means that:

1. if the defendant successfully transfers the legal title to the trust property to a third party, it will not be able to be traced any further than the transfer (although it may be possible to recover that property from the third party under circumstances, which will be discussed below); and

2. because a beneficiary under a trust has only an *equitable* title to the trust property (you will remember that the legal title to the trust property is held by the trustee), common law tracing is completely inaccessible as a process to beneficiaries under a trust.

This latter point was confirmed in the case of *MCC* v. *Lehman Brothers* [1998] 4 All ER 675, when the Court of Appeal refused to allow the beneficiaries under a trust to pursue a claim at common law on the basis that they had no legal title – only an equitable one. Of course, the beneficiaries could always force the trustees to assert their legal title and follow the property at common law, but such a ploy would only be achievable in cases where only some of the trustees were guilty of the misappropriation, the innocent trustees being left to reclaim the money on behalf of the beneficiaries.

Tracing in equity

Tracing in equity has a much wider application

We have seen that, whilst common law tracing is useful in tracking down money misappropriated by an impecunious trustee, it is subject to a number of quite heavy restrictions which limit its practical use. Tracing in equity has a much wider application, however. This is because, in equity, the process of tracing follows the claimant's **beneficial**, or equitable, **interest** in the property, rather than the claimant's legal title to the property. This opens up the process of tracing to beneficiaries under a trust, and also allows monies to be traced further than at common law, despite a possible legal transfer of the property into a third party's hands.

Another distinct benefit of tracing in equity, and one which gives it a real edge as against common law tracing, is that if the trust property is converted into something

Figure 15.1 Diversion of funds into life insurance policy

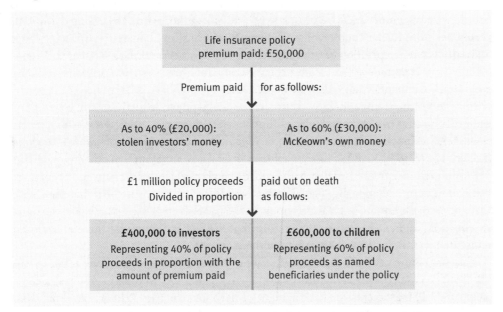

Life insurance policy
premium paid: £50,000

Premium paid | for as follows:

As to 40% (£20,000):
stolen investors' money

As to 60% (£30,000):
McKeown's own money

£1 million policy proceeds
Divided in proportion | paid out on death
as follows:

£400,000 to investors
Representing 40% of policy
proceeds in proportion with the
amount of premium paid

£600,000 to children
Representing 60% of policy
proceeds as named
beneficiaries under the policy

which then increases in value, the beneficiaries will get back not only the value of the misappropriated money but any 'profit' which was made on that money as well. This might be the case where a trustee used trust money to buy land which has gone up in value, such as in the case of *Attorney-General for Hong Kong* v. *Reid*, or more commonly where the trustee has used the money to purchase shares.

The leading case of *Foskett* v. *McKeown* centred on this very issue. Mr McKeown obtained money from a number of investors for a property development in the Algarve in Portugal. The development was never commenced, however; Mr McKeown simply spent the money and then, in a rather dramatic turn of events, committed suicide. On investigation it was discovered that, prior to his death, Mr McKeown had fraudulently used a little over £20,000 of the money to pay two out of five £10,000 premiums on a life insurance policy, which would pay out the sum of £1 million to his three children on his death. The remaining three premiums he paid out of his own money. The investors made a claim against the children for 40 per cent of the policy proceeds, which equated to the proportion of premiums the investors had paid. Diagrammatically, the situation might look as shown in Figure 15.1.

The children argued that the investors should only be entitled to a return of the amount of the premiums, plus interest; however, the House of Lords found in favour of the investors, allowing them 40 per cent of the policy proceeds on the basis that the equitable interests of the investors in the money was directly traceable into the policy proceeds. Mr McKeown had held the money on trust for the investors. In using that money to buy an insurance policy, he was deemed to have invested the money in the policy on behalf of the investors, transferring the investor's beneficial interests from the cash into the policy.

Case Summary

There must be a fiduciary relationship

There are various rules to apply with equitable tracing, depending on the route of the money being traced. However, the one common aspect of every equitable tracing case is the requirement that the claimant has a beneficial, or equitable, interest in the property being traced. In order to prove the existence of this beneficial interest, it is not necessary to show the existence of a formal trust, but rather that there is a **fiduciary** relationship between the claimant and the person who has misappropriated the money. You will remember from earlier chapters that a fiduciary relationship is any relationship in which one party is put in a position of trust and reliance by another; as well as trustees and beneficiaries, it will include solicitors and clients, company directors and their shareholders, and so on (for further examples see Chapter 10).

Case Summary

It is interesting to note that the courts have been happy to infer the creation of a fiduciary relationship in cases of misplaced funds, where no such relationship has previously existed. An example of this is the case of *Chase Manhattan Bank* v. *Israel-British Bank (London) Ltd* [1979] 3 All ER 1025, in which the Chase Manhattan Bank made a payment of $2 million twice to the Israel-British Bank through clerical error. There had previously been no fiduciary relationship between the two banks, but the court held that the Chase Manhattan Bank, having made the payment to the Israel-British Bank by mistake, retained an equitable interest in that payment; and that a fiduciary duty was thereby imposed upon the Israel-British Bank on receipt of the payment.

Case Summary

This was confirmed in the subsequent case of *Neste Oy* v. *Lloyds Bank plc* [1983] Com LR 185. The case concerned a Finnish ship owner, Neste Oy, who had employed a company called PSL as agents for the payment of harbour expenses (Lloyds Bank plc were appointed **official receivers** of PSL on its becoming **insolvent**). Unaware that PSL had ceased trading, Neste Oy continued to make payments to them. Lord Bingham said:

> the receiving of money which consistently with conscience cannot be retained is, in equity, sufficient to raise a trust in favour of the party for whom or on whose account it was received.

Case Summary

These rulings, in which payments have been made to the defendants by mistake, should be distinguished, however, from cases in which payments are made on the basis of an invalid agreement. In *Westdeutsche Landesbank* v. *Islington London Borough Council* [1996] 2 All ER 961, where payments made to the Council by the Westdeutsche Landesbank on the basis of agreements which were subsequently ruled (in a different case) to be beyond the powers of local authorities to make, those payments were held not to be recoverable by the bank. According to the court in this case, the payments were simply the product of a contract which was null and void and no trust had been imposed in relation to them. Therefore any claim made in respect of the monies paid should come under the law of contract and not the law of equity.

So, provided there is a fiduciary relationship between the person who has misappropriated the property and the person making the claim against them, tracing in equity can be used to follow it. Now we have covered what tracing is we can take a look at how it works in different scenarios.

Tracing into an asset

Perhaps the simplest example of when tracing will be put into use is where a trustee misappropriates money from the trust and uses it to buy a specific asset: a house, for example. Under the rules of tracing this gives the beneficiaries two choices. They can either claim the house itself, as this now represents the trust money, albeit converted into bricks and mortar, or they can claim a charge over the house as security in lieu of the trust monies being returned to the fund. Whether the beneficiaries choose to claim the asset or choose to take a charge over the asset in lieu of the return of their funds is entirely at the discretion of the beneficiaries and they are at liberty to choose which route best serves their purposes. So, for example, if the house purchased in our example above has gone up in value, the beneficiaries would most likely claim the house; but if it has decreased in value they are more likely to hold the house as security for payment of the debt to the trust fund. Lord Millett explains the reasoning behind this in *Foskett* v. *McKeown*:

> where a trustee wrongfully misappropriates trust property and uses it exclusively to acquire other property for his own benefit . . . the beneficiary is entitled at his option either to assert his beneficial ownership of the proceeds or to bring a personal claim against the trustee for breach of trust and enforce an equitable lien or charge on the proceeds to secure the restoration of the trust fund. He will normally exercise the option in the way most advantageous to himself. If the traceable proceeds have increased in value and are worth more than the original asset, he will assert his beneficial ownership and obtain the profit for himself. There is nothing unfair in this. The trustee cannot be permitted to keep any profit resulting from his misappropriation for himself . . .

If you think about it this makes sense: if the trustee were allowed to keep the appreciating asset and simply return the value which had originally been taken from the fund, this would be effectively allowing the trustee to profit from the trust, and this is a clear breach of their obligations as a trustee.

Writing and drafting

You are a solicitor at Markham Hinds Solicitors. A client comes to see you for some advice. It would appear that the sum of £30,000 has been misappropriated from their trust fund by one of the trustees. The beneficiaries have done a little detective work and it would appear that the money has been used to purchase the following items:

(a) A brand new Volkswagen Polo for £9,470.

(b) 5000 shares in British Telecommunications plc.

(c) £10,000 worth of premium bonds.

Write a letter to the beneficiaries explaining which, if any of the assets they should claim on behalf of the trust.

You should take no more than 25 minutes on this task.

 Handy tip: Consider what each item might be worth in the future: will they be worth more or less than the trustee paid for them?

So far we have looked at the situation where the trust monies are used to purchase the whole of an asset. But what would happen if the monies were used to buy part of an asset, the rest of the purchase price being made up out of the trustee's own funds? In this case, clearly the beneficiaries would not be able to claim the whole of the asset for themselves, because some of it had been bought with the trustee's own funds. However, *Foskett* v. *McKeown* would still apply in that the beneficiaries could take a charge over the asset purchased for the proportion of the asset actually purchased with trust monies.

If you remember, the facts of *Foskett* v. *McKeown* dealt with this exact situation, the fraudulent trustee having made five equal payments into a life insurance policy: two out of the trust money and three out of his own money. It was held on this basis that the beneficiaries should be entitled to 40 per cent of the policy, this having been the proportion of trust monies which had been paid into the policy.

To give another example of how this might work, imagine Maria has misappropriated £1,000 from a trust fund. She uses the whole of this money, together with a further £3,000 of her own money, to buy a greyhound. As she has used some of her own money to buy the greyhound, the beneficiaries will not be able to claim the animal for themselves. However, they will be able to take a charge over the greyhound to the value of £1,000, in order to replenish the monies which have been taken from the fund. Now, imagine the greyhound wins a number of races over the course of the racing season. The dog may now be worth £5,000, which means the beneficiaries can claim a £1,250 share in the dog, this being the proportionate amount of their investment. If, on the other hand, the dog falls during the last race and becomes lame, it may now only be good for breeding and its value is reduced to £400. However, the beneficiaries will in this event be entitled to claim the *full* value of the dog by way of an equitable charge over the asset, in part payment of the debt of £1,000 which is owed to them. Consequently, the beneficiaries would have the benefit of the full £400 value of the dog, although they would be out of pocket as to the remaining £600. However, this is still better than the £100 quarter share of the dog they would be entitled to if they could only claim a proportionate share of it.

Let us take this one step further. Now imagine that the fraudulent trustee has used your trust money to buy the greyhound together, not with their own funds, but with the funds of another innocent party. In this scenario it would clearly be inequitable if you were allowed to take a charge over the whole of the asset to cover your debts, if the asset had decreased in value; after all, why should you have a greater claim in equity than the other innocent person? In this case, therefore, if the value of the asset remains the same or increases, the rules of proportionate contribution as set out in *Foskett* v. *McKeown* would apply in the same way. However, if the asset decreased in value, you would be able to make a claim on the asset only to the value of your proportionate share of it. This means that in the case of the greyhound, above, you would only be able to claim £100 as your proportionate quarter share of the lame dog, the remaining share being given to the other innocent party.

Case Summary This was the outcome of the case of *Re Diplock* [1948] Ch 465, which concerned monies paid out to a number of charities incorrectly by the executors of the will of Caleb Diplock. In the case Lord Greene, Master of the Rolls, commented on the issue of the mixing of funds of innocent parties, stating that:

> Where the contest is between two claimants to a mixed fund made up entirely of moneys held on behalf of the two of them respectively and mixed together . . . they share **pari passu** [that is, proportionate to their contributions], each being innocent.

Following trust money which has been converted into an asset then, it would seem, is in most cases relatively straightforward:

1. If the trust money is used exclusively to buy an asset, the beneficiaries can either claim the asset or take a charge over it to the value of that asset.

2. If the trust money is mixed with monies belonging to the trustee in order to purchase the asset, the beneficiaries can take a charge over the asset to the value of their contribution, plus a proportion of any profits made on it.

3. If the trust money is mixed with monies belonging to another innocent party, the beneficiaries are entitled to a proportionate share of the asset in accordance with the amount of their contribution. This will be the case even if the asset decreases in value, so any loss will be in proportion to their share, as well as any gain.

But what if that money is paid into a bank account? This is where matters become a little more complicated, as we shall now see.

Tracing into bank accounts

If a trustee steals money from a trust fund and either opens up a new bank account or uses an empty bank account to put the money in, it will be easy to see where that money went and it will be easy to trace it should it then leave that account. More problematic is where a trustee places money into a bank account which already has money in it, or into which the trustee subsequently deposits their own money. Whereas in the case of common law tracing this would prevent the money from being traced any further, with equitable tracing, fortunately, the money can still be followed. The courts have developed a strict set of rules to deal with this, which can be summarised as follows:

1. *If a trustee mixes money stolen from the trust with money of their own, the beneficiaries are entitled to take first charge over the bank account which holds the money.*

This is the first fundamental rule of tracing into a mixed account: that the beneficiaries get to take the first charge, or claim, over the money. The rule was established in the case of ***Re Hallett's Estate*** (1879) LR 13 Ch D 696, the facts of which are given below. To give an example of how this would work: if a trustee, Gulfraz, steals £5,000 from a trust fund and places it into his current bank account, which already has a balance of £1,500, the beneficiaries can place a charge over the whole £6,500 as security for the £5,000 which has been stolen. It does not matter whether the £5,000 was put into an account with a standing balance of £1,500, or whether the £1,500 was paid in later; neither does it matter if there was £750 in the account already, and then the £5,000 was placed in the account, followed by another £750 of Gulfraz's own money: as long as the account contains a mixture of trust monies and personal monies, this rule will take effect.

So this deals with money being placed in a 'mixed account'. Where matters become a little more interesting is when Gulfraz then withdraws money from the account. And this is where the second rule comes in.

Case Navigator

2. *Where a trustee withdraws money from a bank account containing a mixture of trust monies and his own money, he is assumed to be withdrawing his own money first.*

This was the finding in the case of *Re Hallett's Estate*, mentioned above. The case concerned the misappropriation of trust funds by a solicitor. The solicitor had mixed the money taken from the trust fund with his own money in a bank account, subsequently making various payments out of the account. At the date of the claim, the solicitor's bank account contained sufficient monies to replace the trust monies which had been taken, but did not contain enough to clear the solicitor's other debts; nevertheless, the court held that what remained in the bank account was the trust money: the solicitor was assumed to have spent his own money first, leaving the trust monies safe in the account. Explaining the reasoning behind this in the case, Sir George Jessel, Master of the Rolls, said:

Case Summary

When . . . a trustee . . . has blended trust moneys with his own, it seems to me perfectly plain that he cannot be heard to say that he took away the trust money when he had a right to take away his own money. The simplest case put is the mingling of trust moneys in a bag with money of the trustee's own. Suppose he has a hundred sovereigns in a bag, and he adds to them another hundred sovereigns of his own, so that they are commingled in such a way that they cannot be distinguished, and the next day he draws out for his own purposes £100, is it tolerable for anybody to allege that what he drew out was the first £100, the trust money, and that he misappropriated it, and left his own £100 in the bag? It is obvious he must have taken away that which he had a right to take away, his own £100.

Putting it simply, then, if our rogue trustee, Gulfraz, withdraws money from a bank account containing both his own money and money belonging to the trust, it will be assumed in the first instance that Gulfraz acted honestly, spending only his own money and leaving the trust money safely in the account. But what if, rather than simply withdrawing cash to spend, Gulfraz uses the money to buy something specific, like a painting, for example. This would be quite a different story, as demonstrated by the third rule.

3. *Where a trustee uses money from a mixed account to purchase an asset, the trustee is assumed to have used trust monies to have bought the asset.*

Case Summary

This third rule of equitable tracing, which was established in the case of *Re Oatway* [1903] 2 Ch 356, reverses the presumption of the honest trustee in *Re Hallett's Estate*, then, by allowing the beneficiaries of the trust fund to claim any asset which has been purchased with stolen trust monies and, consequentially, claim any profit which may have come from that purchase. The facts of *Re Oatway* were as follows: a claim was again made against a solicitor, Mr Lewis John Oatway, for misappropriation of trust funds. Mr Oatway was a trustee of a trust fund created by the will of Charles Skipper, deceased. Between 1899 and 1900 Mr Oatway misappropriated in the region of £3,000 from the trust, placing the funds into his personal bank account, which also contained his own monies. Mr Oatway then proceeded to spend all of the monies in the account, leaving nothing to show for his spending but 1,000 shares in the Oceana Company, which he paid for with a cheque out of the account. The beneficiaries of Charles Skipper's trust fund then made a claim for the shares, which were then valued at £2,137. The court held that the shares were the property of the trust, having been deemed to have been purchased with the trust money.

Particularly relevant here is the fact that the rest of the monies in the bank account were subsequently dissipated. It is arguable that, if sufficient monies had remained in the bank account the beneficiaries would have chosen to make a claim on the account instead, especially as the value of the shares was not at that time sufficient to cover the amount of the debt owing to the trust fund.

So, let us now consider our scenario on slightly different facts. In this instance, our rogue trustee, Gulfraz, has placed the stolen £5,000 of trust money into his bank account, together with £1,500 of his own money. Gulfraz then withdraws and spends £6,000 of the money, leaving £500 in his account. Gulfraz later pays a further £3,500 of his own money into the account, leaving a balance of £4,000.

You be the judge

Q: Using the rogue trustee scenario under rule 3, how much do you think the beneficiaries can claim out of Gulfraz's account? (Note: the £6,000 has not been used to buy any assets.)

A: You may think that the logical answer to this question is that the beneficiaries can claim the whole of the remaining £4,000, but this is not the case. Perhaps surprisingly, the ruling of the courts is that there is no presumption that money added to an account which had previously contained misappropriated trust money is intended to replace that trust money, unless the trustee has specifically shown this to be their intention.

This is the fourth rule to be considered.

4. *There is no presumption that money added later to the account by the trustee is intended to replace the trust money, unless a contrary intention is shown.*

This rule is often referred to as the 'lowest intermediate balance' rule, and was first held in the case of *James Roscoe (Bolton) Ltd* v. *Winder* [1915] 1 Ch 62. The case concerned the sale of a company, James Roscoe (Bolton) Ltd, to a Mr Wigham. As part of the sale agreement Mr Wigham agreed to collect in all the debts of the company and to forward the monies received in respect of them to the company on or before a certain date. Mr Wigham did collect in the debts, but rather than forwarding the money to the company he put £455 of it into his own personal bank account. Mr Wigham then withdrew all of the money in the account, except for £25, applying the money for his own purposes and not paying the company as agreed. He subsequently paid money of his own into the account, and made further withdrawals, with the result that on his death there was a credit balance of £358. The company made a claim for this sum in lieu of the £455 owing to them. However, the court held that, whilst the defendant was liable to the company for the £455 he had taken, the company's charge could extend only to the intermediate balance in the account, of £25. But what did the court mean by this, exactly? Put plainly, if someone puts trust money into their own bank account and then spends it, any money they subsequently paid into the account cannot be claimed in lieu of the spent trust monies. Rather, the largest sum which can be claimed is the lowest amount remaining in the account before it was replenished: the 'lowest intermediate balance'. Now check your understanding of this by taking a look at the Reflective practice exercise.

Case Summary

Reflective practice

Take another look at the scenario from the You be the judge question. What is the lowest intermediate balance?

You will remember that, in the scenario, Gulfraz has placed £5,000 of stolen trust money into his bank account, together with £1,500 of his own money. This equates to a total in the bank account of £6,500. He then withdraws and spends £6,000 of the money, leaving £500 in his account. Gulfraz later pays a further £3,500 of his own money into the account, leaving a final balance of £4,000.

The lowest intermediate balance was therefore £500, because this was the lowest balance showing in the account before it was replenished with the trustee's own funds. Did you get this?

What do you think about it? Do you think it is fair, and if so, to whom?

Whilst at first sight the rule may seem inequitable, it is certainly logical. Mr Justice Sargant in his judgment in *James Roscoe* v. *Winder* explains why:

> although **prima facie** under the second rule in *Re Hallett's Estate* any drawings out by the debtor ought to be attributed to the private moneys which he had at the bank and not to the trust moneys, yet, when the drawings out had reached such an amount that the whole of his private money part had been exhausted, it necessarily followed that the rest of the drawings must have been against trust moneys. There being on May 21, 1913, only 25 [pounds] and 18 [shillings] in all, standing to the credit of the debtor's account, it is quite clear that on that day he must have denuded his account of all the trust moneys there – the whole 455 [pounds] – except to the extent of 25 [pounds and] 18 [shillings].

This judgment was followed in the more recent case of *Bishopsgate Investment Management Ltd (in liquidation)* v. *Homan* [1995] 1 All ER 347. The case was actually one of the many court cases resultant from the notorious Robert Maxwell pension scandal. Take a look at the Law in action feature to find out what the scandal was all about.

Law in action The Robert Maxwell scandal

Probably the most famous media mogul of the 1980s, Robert Maxwell was the notorious owner of the Mirror Newspaper Group. Plagued with financial scandals throughout his career, Mr Maxwell drowned in November 1991 under mysterious circumstances whilst cruising off the Canary Islands in his luxury super yacht, the *Lady Ghislaine*.

It was soon after his death that it was discovered that Mr Maxwell, in a clear breach of his fiduciary duties to his employees, had been secretly diverting hundreds of millions of pounds from his companies' employee pension scheme funds in an effort to keep the Mirror Group solvent. However, ultimately his efforts failed and following his death the Maxwell companies went into insolvency. As the heir to the Maxwell estate, Mr Maxwell's son Kevin was declared bankrupt with debts of a staggering £400 million. In 1995 Mr Maxwell's two sons Kevin and Ian, and two other former directors of the Maxwell companies, were tried by jury for conspiracy to defraud but they were unanimously acquitted.

The pension funds were eventually replaced with monies from investment banks Shearson Lehman and Goldman Sachs, as well as the British government.

Source: Photodisc/Photolink

The *Lady Ghislaine*, which sports a gymnasium and a discotheque, was sold to a private buyer in 1992 for in excess of £12 million.

[*Source*: Based on http://news.bbc.co.uk/onthisday/hi/dates/stories/november/5/newsid_2514000/2514649.stm; http://www.encyclopedia.com/topic/Robert_Maxwell.aspx]

Case Summary

Bishopsgate Investment Management Ltd was a trustee of one of Robert Maxwell's employee pension schemes. In the case of *Bishopsgate* v. *Homan* (cited above), the company tried to claim the right to trace monies which had been misappropriated from the pension scheme into the account of one of Mr Maxwell's insolvent companies: the

Maxwell Communications Corporation (of which the defendant, Mr Homan, was an **administrator**). They asserted their right to do this in priority over the other creditors of the insolvent company, saying that they had an equitable **charge** over the stolen monies which should take precedence over any **unsecured debts** of the company. However, the Court of Appeal rejected Bishopsgate's argument, finding that, because the accounts of the Maxwell Communications Corporation had been overdrawn when the monies had been paid into them, or had become overdrawn shortly afterwards, no tracing could take place. In applying *James Roscoe (Bolton) Ltd* v. *Winder*, on the basis of the 'lowest intermediate balance' rule, it was impossible to trace funds into an overdrawn account.

5. *Where the funds of two innocent parties are mixed, the first monies put in will be presumed to have been the first monies taken out, unless this would result in unfairness to the parties.*

The final rule which applies to the tracing of funds into mixed bank accounts applies to the situation where monies have been misappropriated from more than one fund. In the first instance, the common sense 'first in first out' rule will apply, unless this would be inconvenient or would otherwise promote injustice between the parties.

The authority for the general rule is an old one, that of *Devaynes* v. *Noble* (*Clayton's Case*) (1816) 1 Mer 572. The case concerned a claim made by Mr Clayton, who was a client of the banking house of Devaynes, Dawes, Noble, & Co. One of the partners of the banking house, Mr Devaynes, died. The surviving partners of the firm subsequently went bankrupt, and Mr Clayton claimed that the estate of the deceased partner of the firm was liable to him for debts owing to him by the banking house. However, the banking house was held to have paid off the debt to Mr Clayton in payments which had been made to him subsequent to Mr Devayne's death. The somewhat complicated facts of the case disguise the rather more simple outcome: where monies are being paid in and withdrawn from an account with no reference as to which payment out was in respect of which payment in, debits and credits will be set off against one another in order of their dates, in a 'first in, first out' format.

The principle may be better explained by way of an illustration. Take a look at the fictitious example account shown below. Imagine that our rogue trustee, Gulfraz, is a trustee for several trusts. He deposits £20,000 belonging to the Frog Trust into his bank account. One week later, he deposits £10,000 belonging to the Newt Trust into the same account. A further two months later, Gulfraz makes a final deposit of £5,000 belonging to the Toad Trust into the same account. The week after that, Gulfraz withdraws £25,000 from the account, leaving £10,000 remaining in the account. The account would look as follows:

The rule in *Clayton's Case*

		Credit
Frog Trust		£20,000
Newt Trust		£10,000
Toad Trust		£ 5,000
Total credit		£35,000
Debit of £25,000 attributed as follows:		
To the Frog Trust	(£20,000)	
To the Newt Trust	(£ 5,000)	
Balance payable to the Frog Trust		£ 0
Balance payable to the Newt Trust		£ 5,000
Balance payable to the Toad Trust		£ 5,000
Total balance		£10,000

According to the rule in *Clayton's Case*, the first £20,000 debited by Gulfraz would be accounted to the Frog Trust, so they would get nothing; and the remaining £5,000 debited would be accounted to the Newt Trust, as they were the second in time to have their money deposited in the account. The balance of £10,000 would thus be shared between the Newt Trust as to £5,000 and the Toad Trust for the remaining £5,000. The outcome of this, of course, is that only the Toad Trust would get the whole of the money deposited back out of the account which may seem a little unfair on the other two innocent parties. But remember that the rule in *Clayton's Case* is only a presumption, which the court need not follow if the result would result in an outcome which they consider to be unfair in all the circumstances.

The application of the rule was more recently addressed in the case of *Barlow Clowes International Ltd* v. *Vaughan* [1992] 4 All ER 22. In this case, money had been paid by a large number of investors into various investment plans, which had then been misappropriated by the investment company. Considering the rule in *Clayton's Case*, the court concluded that, where the application of the rule would be impractical or would result in injustice between the innocent parties, or would otherwise be contrary to the parties' intentions, the rule could be displaced if a preferable alternative method of distribution of the monies was available. The problem with *Barlow Clowes* v. *Vaughan* was that the court was dealing with such a huge number of investors (around 11,000 in total) that it would have been impracticable to have tried to work out each individual transaction on a 'first in, first out' basis. In addition the investors had bought into a collective investment scheme with the intention that their monies would be mixed with the monies of other investors in a larger investment fund. It therefore made sense that the investors should share their losses as a collective on the same basis '*pari passu*', in other words that the remaining monies should be distributed between them proportionately in accordance with their respective contributions to the fund.

This approach has been followed in several more recent cases, including that of *The Russell Cooke Trust Company* v. *Prentis* [2002] All ER (D) 22 which involved the misappropriation of monies from a property investment plan by Sheffield solicitor, Richard

Prentis, and *Commerzbank AG* v. *IMB Morgan Plc* [2005] 2 All ER (Comm) 564 which involved a claim for monies which had been obtained fraudulently from a number of innocent parties and mixed in a number of bank accounts. In both cases it was held that it would be impractical to follow the rule in *Clayton's Case*. In particular, in the case of *Commerzbank* v. *IMB Morgan* Mr Justice Collins said that it would be both impractical and unjust to apply the rule. Not only did the amount of the claims far exceed the sums left in the accounts to be divided, but because of the complicated nature of the fraud it would be extremely onerous, and perhaps impossible, to determine what sums the defendant had paid out in date order. Mr Justice Collins concluded that in that particular case, to adopt the fiction of 'first in, first out' would be 'to apportion a common misfortune' through a test that 'bore no relation to the justice of the case', and that need only be applied when it was convenient and 'could do broad justice'.

> It seems likely that the rule in *Clayton's Case* will be used less frequently

It seems likely that the rule in *Clayton's Case* will be used less and less frequently in tracing cases and that the courts will continue to favour a more practical and, one might say, fairer approach wherever possible. One very telling comment of Mr Justice Lindsay in the *Russell Cooke* v. *Prentis* case, that 'the rule in *Clayton's Case* may be fast becoming more the exception than the rule', would seem to point to a definite cooling of the judiciary against a rule which is approaching its bicentenary.

Tracing into the hands of a third party

This chapter has so far seen the tracing of trust monies limited to the trustee who has misappropriated them; but what happens when that trust money is passed on to a third party: can the trust property continue to be traced? The answer to this question is, in most cases yes: a beneficiary can trace misappropriated trust property into the hands of a third party. As we have seen in the previous chapter, if the third party knew that the monies they were receiving were the proceeds of a misappropriation of trust funds then they would be guilty of **knowing receipt** and would have no defence against the claims of the beneficiaries. However, even if the third party is an innocent recipient of the property, there is usually no bar to the beneficiaries claiming the property from them. This may seem unfair, that the innocent recipient of a gift of money should be required to return that money, even though they had no knowledge that the money had been obtained dishonestly. However, it is a fundamental rule of law that persons should not be unjustly enriched by the proceeds of crime. Thus, as we have seen in the case of *Re Diplock* [1948], above, the courts allowed the beneficiaries to trace the misapplied trust funds into the hands of the charities who had received them.

> persons should not be unjustly enriched by the proceeds of crime

Situations in which trust property cannot be traced

What we have covered under equitable tracing so far might seem to suggest that there are no bars to tracing at all and that there are no limitations on the right to trace, either into the hands of the trustee themselves, or into the hands of innocent third parties. However, this is not entirely the case. There are a number of situations which will halt the tracing process, preventing the beneficiaries from following their misappropriated trust property any further. These can be listed as follows:

✦ When it has become inequitable to trace.

✦ When the change of position defence can be claimed.

✦ When the property is bought by a bona fide purchaser for value without notice.

✦ When the trust property has been dissipated.

When it has become inequitable to trace

Despite the ruling in *Re Diplock* that the misapplied trust monies could be traced into the hands of the innocent recipients of the fund, the court nevertheless did make comment that there could be some situations where it would simply become inequitable to trace into the hands of an innocent third party. In giving his judgment Lord Green, Master of the Rolls, cited as particular examples cases where the innocent recipient had used the money either to make home improvements or in paying off debts. On the matter of home improvements, he said:

> The owner of a house who, as an innocent volunteer [that is, an innocent recipient of trust property], has trust money in his hands given to him by a trustee uses that money in making an alteration to his house so as to fit it better to his own personal needs. The result may add not one penny to the value of the house. Indeed, the alteration may well lower its value; for the alteration, though convenient to the owner, may be highly inconvenient in the eyes of a purchaser. Can it be said in such cases that the trust money can be traced and extracted from the altered asset? Clearly not, for the money will have disappeared leaving no monetary trace behind: the asset will not have increased (or may even have depreciated) in value through its use.

It is therefore possible that the inequity of certain scenarios may result in the court declining to make a finding that results in the tracing of trust property into the hands of an innocent third party (although presumably in the scenario cited by Lord Green the outcome would be different if the home improvements succeeded in adding value to the house). Very closely allied to this issue, is the change of position defence.

Using the change of position defence

You will remember from Chapter 14 that the change of position defence can be used by recipients of stolen trust monies against a claim of knowing receipt. As a quick reminder, the defence works as follows: Imagine a person is the innocent receiver of trust money. Perceiving the receipt of that money as an unexpected windfall, they spend some of the money on something which otherwise they would not have been able to afford or do. When approached for the return of that money, the innocent receiver is then able to claim that they effected a change of position in their lifestyle so significant, as a result of their receipt of the monies, that it would be inequitable for the court to find them liable for those monies which they have spent.

You should note that although the judgment in the leading case in this area, that of *Lipkin Gorman* v. *Karpnale*, related to a common law claim, Lord Goff made it clear that the defence should also apply to claims made in equity.

Purchase by a bona fide purchaser for value without notice

It is a long-established principle of the law of equity that equity will protect a **bona fide purchaser for value** of property **without notice**. This means that a beneficiary will have no claim against a third party who purchases trust property in good faith (in Latin: '*bona fide*'), without any knowledge that the property in question was acquired through a breach of trust (in other words, they had *no notice* of the breach). The law was restated succinctly by Lord Browne-Wilkinson in the case of *Westdeutsche Landesbank* v. *Islington LBC*, in which he said that:

once a trust is established, as from the date of its establishment the beneficiary has, in equity, a **proprietary interest** in the trust property, which proprietary interest will be enforceable in equity against any subsequent holder of the property (whether the original property or substituted property into which it can be traced) other than a purchaser for value of the legal interest without notice.

It is worth noting from the bracketed part of Lord Browne-Wilkinson's statement that, whilst the purchase of trust property by a bona fide purchaser for value without notice will be a bar to further tracing into the purchaser's hands, the beneficiaries are nevertheless able to trace into the purchase price paid by the third party to the trustee, and thus reclaim the value of the misappropriated property in that way. Effectively this means that the beneficiary would have a claim on the sum paid for the property but not the property itself.

Dissipation of trust property

The final bar to tracing is that, if the trust monies have been dissipated (that is, that they have been spent or otherwise lost), tracing cannot occur: quite simply because there is no longer anything which can be traced. Most obviously, dissipation of the trust property could mean that the money has been spent on something like a holiday from which, once the holiday has been taken, the money cannot be recovered, or consumables, such as food or drink. But it could also refer either to the fact that the trust property has been destroyed, or that it has been used to pay off debts or an overdraft. You will remember from reading about the *Bishopsgate Investments* v. *Homan* case earlier in the chapter, which concerned the Robert Maxwell scandal, the ruling that it is not possible to trace into overdrawn accounts. This is because, upon payment of the debt, the trust monies are deemed to have been spent or dissipated and, from the moment the debt is discharged, are therefore no longer recoverable.

Out and about

So now, having almost completed the chapter, you should know everything there is to know about the rules of tracing. Time to do a little tracing of your own. Think about the next £50 you spend. If possible take this out of your bank account now. The sum can be more or less if you would like. If you are unable to get hold of cash, try doing the exercise in retrospect, with money you have had before.

Now, having acquired your £50 by whatever means, your next task is to trace, over a period of four days, where that money goes. Then, using the rules of tracing, you should document where that money can be traced to, and whether any of it can be recovered, either in equity or in law.

 Handy tip: Remember, if you pay the money into your bank account, you will need to follow the relevant rules when any money is drawn out, or again if you use your bank card to pay for anything directly.

Why the need for a difference between tracing at common law and in equity?

One final point which should perhaps be addressed about the tracing process is the question of whether there is any continued need to maintain separate systems of tracing at common law and tracing in equity. Each method of tracing by itself has significant flaws:

✦ Common law tracing is limited to the contractual parties to an action and is therefore unavailable to beneficiaries under a trust fund.

✦ In addition there is the problem of not being able to trace into mixed funds at common law, which makes the process very limited in its application.

✦ On the other hand, whilst much broader in its application, equitable tracing is limited to cases where a fiduciary connection between the parties can be proved, albeit that the courts have been eager to find such a connection even where no such relationship existed before the misappropriation of funds.

✦ In addition, tracing in equity is subject to equitable restraints which mean that very often the property which has been traced will be found to be unrecoverable, either through having been dissipated or through some sense of injustice on the part of the courts should a remedy be sought against the person in receipt of the funds. The effect of this is that the tracing process is rendered immaterial as the claimant will be left with no choice but to sue the defaulting trustee for the money – a remedy which is useless if the defendant is insolvent.

The courts have been quite scathing of the continued existence of separate systems of tracing in law and in equity, Lord Millett stating as recently as 2001 in the House of Lords case of *Foskett* v. *McKeown* that:

> Given its nature, there is nothing inherently legal or equitable about the tracing exercise. There is thus no sense in maintaining different rules from tracing at law and in equity. One set of tracing rules is enough.

Lord Millett went on to say that the case in question was not the place to explore the issue further. However, in the wake of such strongly felt comment on the part of the House of Lords (Lord Millett's view was echoed by Lord Steyn in the same case) it is likely that, whilst change in the law in this area is yet to be seen, this is an issue which will return to the spotlight just as soon as another opportunity arises to consider it at **Supreme Court** level. In the meantime, Table 15.1 should serve as a reminder of the differences between the two systems currently.

Table 15.1 Differences between tracing at common law and in equity

Common law	Equity
The claimant must have a legal claim to the misappropriated property	The claimant must have a fiduciary relationship with the person who misappropriated the funds
Tracing is not available to beneficiaries under a trust	Tracing is available to beneficiaries under a trust
Money cannot be traced into mixed accounts	Money can be traced into mixed accounts
Tracing is for the money which has been stolen or its equivalent asset, if converted	Tracing is allowed to incorporate the profit made on any investment
Tracing will cease if the legal title to the property is successfully transferred to a third party	Tracing will cease when the trust property is bought by a bona fide purchaser for value without notice

Summary

◆ Tracing is the process through which trust property is traced from its source into whatever form it may take at the point of claim.

◆ There are two types of tracing: common law tracing and tracing in equity.

◆ In order to trace property at common law, the claimant must be able to identify the item over which they claim ownership, albeit that it has been converted into another form.

◆ Tracing at common law cannot take place where the money has been mixed with other funds.

◆ Common law tracing is not accessible to beneficiaries under a trust.

◆ Tracing in equity requires the presence of a fiduciary relationship between the parties, although the courts have in the past been happy to infer the creation of such a relationship where necessary.

◆ Where trust property is traced into an asset, the beneficiaries can claim either the asset, or take a charge over the asset to the value of the money taken.

◆ Tracing in equity allows the beneficiaries to claim any profit made on assets bought with trust property, as well as the asset itself.

◆ If an asset is bought with part trust property and part the trustee's property, the beneficiaries can take a charge over that property proportionate to their contribution to its purchase.

◆ If an asset is bought with part trust property and part the property of an innocent third party, the same rule applies, save that if the asset drops in value, the beneficiaries' claim will be shared *pari passu* with the third party.

 If a trustee mixes money stolen from the trust with money of their own, the beneficiaries are entitled to take first charge over the bank account which holds the money.

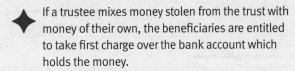 Where a trustee withdraws money from a bank account containing a mixture of trust monies and his own money, he is assumed to be withdrawing his own money first (*Re Hallett's*).

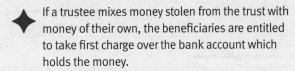 Where a trustee uses money from a mixed account to purchase an asset, the trustee is assumed to have used trust monies to have bought the asset (*Re Oatway*).

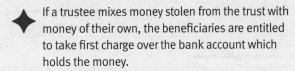 There is no presumption that money added later to the account by the trustee is intended to replace the trust money, unless a contrary intention is shown.

 Where the funds of two innocent parties are mixed, the first monies put in will be presumed to have been the first monies taken out, unless this would result in unfairness to the parties (*Clayton's Case*).

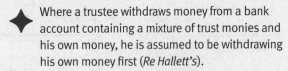 Tracing will come to an end:

- ✦ when it has become inequitable to trace;
- ✦ when the change of position defence can be claimed;
- ✦ when the property is bought by a bona fide purchaser for value without notice;
- ✦ when the trust property has been dissipated.

Question and answer*

Problem:

Bruce is the trustee for two trusts: the Hincklemeyer Family Trust and the Rani Family Trust. Over the course of the last year, the following events have occurred:

- ✦ In January Bruce paid a cheque for £5,000, representing income from the Hincklemeyer Family Trust, into his personal current bank account. At the time of the deposit, the account had a debit balance of £1,000.
- ✦ In February, Bruce transferred a further £5,000 to his current account from the Rani Family Trust.
- ✦ In March, Bruce invested £3,000 in two bronze statues from an up-and-coming local sculptor, paying for the statues out of his current account. He also withdrew £1,000 which he gave to his son, Gilbert, to help out with his student debts.
- ✦ In May, Bruce paid for two meals for himself and his family at his favourite restaurant, Hosterios Romanos, both with his current account debit card. The meals cost £300 and £200 respectively. He also spent a further £3,000 on a second-hand car for his daughter, Thalia, who had just passed her driving test.
- ✦ In May Bruce wrote a cheque for £1,000 which he gave to the local children's hospice, Happy Days.
- ✦ Finally, in June, Bruce paid £2,500 into his current account, which he had received as payment for some consultancy work he had carried out.

Bruce has now gone bankrupt. His only assets are the sculptures, which due to a drop in the artist's popularity are now worth £2,000, and the money remaining in his bank account. Gilbert has spent his money clearing his student loan. Happy Days have spent the money given to them on toys and a new outside play area for the children. Thalia still has the car.

Advise the beneficiaries of the two trusts what principles the court will apply to trace the assets and what they are likely to recover from the various recipients of the monies.

You should allow yourself no more than 50 minutes to complete this task.

Essay: Tracing runs into problems when it encounters mixing.
(P. Birks, 'Mixing and tracing' (1992) *Current Legal Problems* 69)

Explain the difficulties faced in the tracing of funds into mixed bank accounts at common law, in contrast with the equitable tracing system.

This question should be answered in 30 minutes.

✻ Answer guidance is provided at the end of the chapter.

Further reading and references

Birks, P. (1997) 'The necessity of a unitary law of tracing', in *Making Commercial Law: Essays in Honour of Roy Goode*, Oxford: Clarendon Press, 239.
An excellent essay by the eminent academic, Professor Peter Birks, calling for an end to separate systems of common law and equitable tracing.

Breslin, J. (1995) 'Tracing into an overdrawn bank account: when does money cease to exist?' *Company Lawyer* 16(10), 307–11.
An interesting article giving an overview of the rules of tracing into bank accounts and discussing the extent to which money paid into overdrawn accounts can be traced.

Millett, P.J. (1991) 'Tracing the proceeds of fraud', 107 LQR 71–85.
Good practical explanation of how funds are traced both at common law and in equity, drawing together the threads of the process along with the issue of knowing receipt in the case of third party recipients.

Pawlowski, M. (2003) 'The demise of the rule in Clayton's Case', Conv (Jul/Aug), 339–45.
Really nice clear article discussing the rule in *Clayton's Case* in the light of recent cases, in particular the Court of Appeal decision in *Barlow Clowes International Ltd (In Liquidation)* v. *Vaughan.*

Question and answer guidance

Problem: Bruce has stolen £10,000 from the two trusts. The funds are mixed and so the principles of equitable tracing will have to apply (plus, common law tracing cannot be used to benefit beneficiaries under a trust fund).

When the money from the Hincklemeyer Trust was put into Bruce's bank account, the account was overdrawn by £1,000, so this money will have been immediately lost (it having been dissipated).

Following the deposit of the Rani Trust money to the account, the fund is now mixed, and totals £9,000. When Bruce withdraws money to pay for the statues and to give to Gilbert, there are two possible ways in which the withdrawals can be viewed:

1. *Clayton's Case* – the rule of 'first in, first out'. This way, the first money to be deposited (that of the Hincklemeyer Trust) will be assumed to be the first money used. The full amount of the £4,000 withdrawal will therefore be taken out of the Hincklemeyer deposit – thus reducing the amount in the account to £5,000.

2. *'Pari passu'* – if imposing the rule in *Clayton's Case* would be seen as unfair, the money of each fund could be reduced proportionately, so that each would share equally in the loss (see *Barlow Clowes*, but distinguish as only two parties here – to use *Clayton's Case* in Barlow Clowes would have been impractical).

Assuming, therefore, that the rules in *Clayton's Case* apply:

Of the £5,000 taken from the Hincklemeyer Trust, the first £1,000 was paid into an overdrawn account, and is therefore unrecoverable (as seen above).

£3,000 was spent on sculptures. These are now worth only £2,000. The trust can either claim the sculptures themselves and hope they go back up in value, or use them to secure up to £2,000-worth of the debt owed to them.

The final £1,000 has been used by Gilbert to pay off a loan and is therefore dissipated and unrecoverable.

The maximum the beneficiaries can recover is therefore £2,000 (or the statues themselves).

Of the £5,000 taken from the Rani Trust, there is £3,000 remaining in Bruce's bank account. But the Rani Trust will only be entitled to the lowest intermediate balance of the account, which was the amount in the account immediately before Bruce paid in the money received from his consultancy. This balance was only £500. The remainder of the monies will therefore have to be traced through his other assets/third parties.

The first £500 was spent on restaurant meals and is therefore dissipated.

The next £3,000 was given to Thalia to buy a car. She still has the car, but it will have depreciated in value. The trust can choose to claim return of the car or to take a lien over it in part payment of the debt. They would be more sensible to choose the latter option as the car will not go back up in value (unlike the statues, which may do).

A further £1,000 has been given to the charity, Happy Days. They have spent the money given to them on toys and a new outside play area for the children. The money spent on the creation of the play area will be considered dissipated, unless it consists of movable items which have a residual value. The works themselves have no value to the trust. In terms of the toys, would it really be equitable to recover those from the hands of the charity (*Re Diplock*)? In any event, the charity, as an innocent receiver of the moneys, may be able to claim the change of position defence (*Lipkin Gorman* v. *Karpnale*).

The final £500 remains in Bruce's bank account (as seen above).

The maximum amount recoverable by the Rani Trust is therefore the value of the car, plus £500.

Essay:

A good essay will start by explaining what tracing is: that it is a method by which money is 'followed' from the source of its misappropriation into its conversion into other assets or money, or into the hands of a third party.

There are two types of tracing: tracing at common law and tracing in equity. The student should list the problems which can be encountered with common law tracing, focusing on the difficulty with tracing into mixed bank accounts. The main point is that the need for the ability to identify the physical property in common law tracing makes it impossible to trace that money at common law once it has been mixed with other monies in a bank account. Discussion should be made of *Agip (Africa) Ltd* v. *Jackson*, and Mr Justice Millett's comment that, 'nothing passed between Tunisia and London but a stream of electrons'.

Students should then go on to explain the significance of this, in view of the fact that it is highly unlikely that a person who has misappropriated money will keep that money separate from other funds. It is more likely to go into their current account, which is likely to have a balance when the stolen funds are credited to it, and which will probably have other sources of income going into it after the stolen money has been deposited. Students should conclude from this that common law tracing is of limited practical application.

In equity, the practical application of tracing is much wider, because it is not the physical item which is being traced, but the beneficial, or equitable, interest in it which is being followed. This not only allows the stolen property to be transferred from one form into another, but the lack of need for a physical item to follow also allows for the interest to be followed into a mixed bank account. An explanation of how this might work in a practical context might work well here. There are several examples given within the chapter to refer to.

Students should conclude by commenting on the usefulness of the equitable tracing system in contrast to the common law system, and perhaps by commenting on the perceived need to unite the two systems to provide for one single tracing system that applies in both law and equity. Reference could be made to Birks 1997, in which Professor Birks calls for an end to separate systems of common law and equitable tracing.

Visit **www.mylawchamber.co.uk/warner-reed** to access study support resources including practice exam questions with guidance, interactive 'You be the judge' multiple choice questions, annotated weblinks, glossary and key case flashcards and audio legal updates all linked to the **Pearson eText** version of *Equity and Trusts* which you can **search**, **highlight** and **personalise** with your **own notes** and **bookmarks**.

Use Case Navigator to read in full some of the key cases referenced in this chapter with commentary and questions:

Attorney-General for Hong Kong **v. Reid** [1994] 1 All ER 1
Re Hallett's Estate (1880) 13 Ch D 696

Chapter 16
Remedies

Key points In this chapter we will be looking at:

- ✦ The use of common law and equitable remedies in breach of trust
- ✦ The discretionary nature of equitable remedies
- ✦ How an equitable claim for compensation is calculated
- ✦ The equitable remedy of account

- ✦ The equitable remedy of specific performance
- ✦ Declarations of the court and how they differ from specific performance
- ✦ Interim and final injunctions, and the use of search and freezing orders
- ✦ The equitable remedies of rescission, rectification and subrogation

Introduction

Throughout this second part of the book on the administration of **trusts** we have sought to establish: first, what are the duties of a **trustee**; and then, over the last three chapters, what is the extent of liability of a trustee who commits a breach of trust and when an accessory to that breach will be held liable. This might be because they have assisted the trustee in committing the breach, or because they have actually received trust property. We have also looked, in Chapter 15, at the process of **tracing**, which enables trustees or **beneficiaries** to follow money

which has been removed from the trust into whatever forms it may have been converted. So, to put it simply, we have caught the thief and found the stolen trust property. The last thing we need to know now is exactly what we can do to see the return of that trust property into the trust fund. In other words: what remedies are available to us?

The focus of this chapter is on remedies available to a beneficiary in **equity**. But why is this? Why not look at **common law** remedies? Let us explore this for a moment.

The use of common law remedies

Traditionally the remedy available through the common law is that of **damages**. So if a trustee is found liable at common law for perpetrating a breach of trust which resulted in the loss of the trust fund, the beneficiaries will be entitled, *as of right*, to damages equalling the amount of the loss. This is a **personal claim** against the trustee and the trustee would be liable personally for the loss, meaning that they would have to find the monies out of their own funds or assets.

Why not make the claim at common law, then? It seems straightforward: the remedy is available as of right. The trustee breaches the trust; the trustee loses or misappropriates the trust money: if the trustee no longer has those trust monies they are required to replace the trust monies through their own personal means. However, on closer inspection, this simple reasoning falls down on a number of levels. These are the problems:

1. What if the trustee, having spent the trust money, is declared bankrupt? The claim at common law is a personal claim only as against the trustee themselves. If the trustee has no money or assets, this leaves nothing to claim from them. Even if the trustee does have some assets, the beneficiaries would have to fall in line with the other creditors of the trustee for a share in those assets, and would have to share any monies which could be found with those other creditors in proportion with the amount of their claim.

2. At common law, the process of tracing is little additional help. Even if the trustee is not declared bankrupt, which would in itself defeat the common law tracing process, as soon as the money goes into a mixed bank account it is to all intents and purposes lost to the beneficiaries. Given that the majority of misappropriated trust funds end up in bank accounts, this is a particularly limiting factor. In addition, tracing at common law is unavailable to the beneficiaries in any case and so the beneficiaries would be reliant on the other trustees (if there were any) to make a claim for the missing trust property on their behalf.

3. Damages alone may not be an appropriate remedy. What if the trust property was a family dowry of antique gold jewellery which had been passed down through generations of the beneficiaries' family? Not only would the jewellery consist of unique, one-off pieces which would prove impossible to replace, but there would be a sentimental attachment to the jewellery itself for which hard cash could never be a sufficient replacement. In such a situation a personal claim for damages against the person who had committed the breach would not be enough. What would be more effective in this scenario would be if the beneficiaries could make a proprietary claim for the stolen jewellery: a claim which would enable the family to recover the actual jewellery itself, and only in the worst case scenario rely on the payment of money for its replacement.

For all these reasons beneficiaries are altogether better placed to rely on equitable remedies when a breach of trust has been committed. After all, the trust itself is a creation of equity and it seems therefore logical that its remedies should be found in equity too. In terms of tracing alone, the ability of the equitable tracing process to follow trust property through mixed accounts and onwards into whatever form it is converted gives a far better chance to beneficiaries of their monies being returned, even in the event of the trustee's bankruptcy. And, in terms of the assets themselves, it means that the beneficiaries have an altogether better chance of seeing the return of that family heirloom, rather than just compensation in cash for their loss.

The discretionary nature of equitable remedies

There has traditionally been a perceived disadvantage in the seeking of equitable remedies in that, unlike remedies available at common law, they are only available at the discretion of the court, and not as of right. However, the discretion is not a completely arbitrary one: the judiciary is very much bound by the rules and **maxims of equity** in making their decisions and they will be loath to allow a claim in equity to be defeated on any grounds other than those which have been previously laid down in **precedent**. On balance, therefore, the advantages far outweigh the disadvantages of following the equitable route.

Let us now move on to talk about the equitable remedies themselves: what is available to a beneficiary who has lost their trust money through the incompetence or dishonesty of a trustee, and, equally importantly, how far does their claim extend?

Equitable compensation

The basis of a claim in equity for loss to a trust fund is to put the beneficiaries back in the position in which they would have been, had the breach of trust not occurred. If trust property has been stolen, the best possible outcome would be for the beneficiaries to see the return of that property. However, it may be that this is not possible, in which case the beneficiaries will have to rely on compensation to cover their loss. Historically, the court of equity was unable to give monetary compensation as a remedy: the common law remedy of damages was put in place for the making of such payments, and the role of equity was simply to step in with an alternative or additional remedy, where damages did not form an adequate solution to the particular case. However, advances in the law of equity now allow for the payment, not of damages, but of equitable compensation in addition to the other remedies equity can provide. Lord Browne-Wilkinson summarised the position of equity in the following statement from *Target Holdings Ltd* v. *Redferns* [1996] AC 421, a case which concerned the payment of mortgage monies held by a firm of solicitors to a borrower prior to completion of a property purchase, which was an act in breach of trust to the lender:

Case Summary

> the basic rule is that a trustee in breach of trust must restore or pay to the trust estate either the assets which have been lost to the estate by reason of the breach or compensation for such loss. Courts of Equity did not award damages but . . . ordered the defaulting trustee to restore the trust estate . . . If specific restitution of the trust property [that is, the return of the trust property to the trust] is not possible, then the liability of the trustee is to pay sufficient compensation to the trust estate to put it back to what it would have been had the breach not been committed . . .

The payment of compensation in equity may seem very similar, at first glance, to the payment of damages at common law: both are seeking to put the **claimants** back into the position they would have been in if the breach had not occurred, after all.

However, there are some subtle differences between the two. In the first instance, common law damages allow for payments to be made over and above the amount of the monetary loss – so they allow a punitive element, which equitable compensation does not do. On the other hand, equitable compensation allows not just for the return of property or monies taken from the trust, but it also requires the

> common law damages allow a punitive element

defaulting party to account for any profit made on that trust property – either by way of unauthorised payments or commissions received by the trustee or by way of actual profit made on the sale of trust property, or even profits made on any investment made with the money. So if a trustee in default made an illegal transfer of shares in a company into their own name, for example, the trustee would be liable not just for the value of the shares at the time the transfer was made but also for any rise in value in the shares and any dividends declared on those shares whilst in the trustee's possession. In addition, it should be said that, whilst compensation in equity does not allow for a punitive element, the courts will always be quick to overcompensate beneficiaries who have lost trust monies, purely because they are afraid of allowing the trustee to make even the smallest profit from the breach. The You be the judge exercise should help to illustrate this.

You be the judge

Q: In which of the following circumstances do you think the beneficiaries will be entitled to equitable compensation?

   (a) The trustees have stolen £100,000 from the trust fund.

   (b) The trustees have sold trust property, making a profit of £20,000.

   (c) A trustee has been receiving unauthorised commissions on his investment of trust property.

   (d) The trustees have bought shares with the trust property which have now fallen in value.

   (e) The trustees have misappropriated a gold watch from the fund, which is of great sentimental value to the beneficiary.

A: The beneficiaries will be entitled to equitable compensation in all of the above examples. However, whilst compensation may be given for the value of the lost watch in (e), the beneficiary will not be able to make any claim for their disappointment or upset at the loss, as this would be punitive.

As can be seen from (d) in You be the judge, equitable compensation allows not just for the return to the fund of profits made on misappropriated trust funds but also for any loss made. So if, for example, a trustee were to make an unauthorised investment of trust property which resulted in a loss to the fund, equitable compensation would ensure that the trustee would be liable to account for that loss to the fund by requiring the return of the full amount of the original investment.

To summarise, then, the initial position of the trustees is that their trust property will be returned to them or, if this is not possible, they will be compensated financially for the loss to the fund. Now let us turn to what other remedies might be required or useful when a breach of trust has been committed.

Account

You will remember from your reading on the duties of trustees in Chapter 10 that it is a fundamental duty of trustees to provide an adequate account to their beneficiaries of their management of the trust. This duty to account necessitates not only that the trustees keep full and accurate records of all their dealings with trust assets but also that they provide any relevant information relating to those dealings to the beneficiaries at their request. Probably the first thing the beneficiaries are going to do, then, if they suspect a breach of trust, particularly if they think it has resulted in the loss of trust monies, is to request the trustees to account for the use of the trust monies.

Accounting is both an equitable process and a remedy, the court's **order to account** typically being combined with an order to pay any sums found to be due once the accounts have been completed back into the trust fund. There are three different bases on which a beneficiary can request from the court an order to account:

1. Common account.
2. Account on the basis of wilful default.
3. Request for account of profits.

Each request for an account is made for a different reason: a **common account** is designed simply to compel the trustees to fulfil their basic duty to account to the beneficiaries; so, in other words, if the trustees have failed to produce accounts for whatever reason, the beneficiaries can apply to the court for an order to common account to force the trustees to provide them. The request for an **account on the basis of wilful default** is quite different from common account in that it is used when the beneficiaries suspect foul play or, at the very least, extreme negligence on the part of the trustees. An order to account on the basis of wilful default will often therefore be used as the basis for obtaining equitable compensation in respect of any losses uncovered by the process of accounting. And the final method of account is the request for an **account of profits**. This is used when a trustee is suspected of making a **secret profit** or other unauthorised gain from the trust, so it will require the trustees not simply to show the workings of the trust account itself but also to account for any personal transactions the trustees may have entered into on the strength of their trusteeship.

Regardless of whichever basis of accounting is requested, if the trustees are ordered to account by the court they must provide the court with a full account of all payments and receipts which have been made in and out of the trust fund. If the trustees are asked by the court to account for their actions in this way, the onus is on the trustees to justify their treatment of the fund: if they have failed to keep adequate records, the court will presume that there has been some wrongdoing and the court will require the trustees to replenish any gaps discovered in the fund.

It should be mentioned here that the term 'accounting' does not necessarily require the provision of documentary evidence. In the very early case of *Morley* v. *Morley* (1678) 22 ER 817, a trustee was robbed by his servant, who stole from him £40-worth of gold which he was holding in trust for a third party. There was obviously no written account of how the trust money had been spent, but the court accepted the trustee's oath as sufficient evidence of the robbery. The court can also make the ruling that no account is required under certain circumstances. In the case of *Campbell* v. *Gillespie* [1900] 1 Ch 225, the beneficiary told the trustee that the terms of the trust had been fulfilled and that no further account would therefore be required of him. The trustee consequently destroyed the trust records, believing there was no longer any use for them. When the beneficiary later made an application for the trustee to account on the basis of an alleged wilful default, the court dismissed the beneficiary's claim and said that under the circumstances no account could be demanded of the trustee.

An order to account will never require a trustee to replenish trust funds out of their own pocket, unless any holes in the fund are shown to have been caused by the trustee's own breach; this is the case even where the account shows that there has been a substantial loss to the fund. In *Re Chapman* (1896) 2 Ch 763 the claimants brought an action requiring the **defendant** trustees to account for losses to the trust fund on the basis that the defendants had retained within the fund a number of mortgage investments which had lost the fund a considerable amount of money. Lord Justice Lindley said in defence of the trustees:

Case Summary

> There is no rule of law which compels the Court to hold that an honest trustee is liable to make good loss sustained by retaining an authorised security in a falling market, if he did so honestly and prudently, in the belief that it was the best course to take in the interest of all parties. Trustees acting honestly, with ordinary prudence and within the limits of their trust, are not liable for mere errors of judgment. Any loss sustained by the trust estate under such circumstances falls upon and must be borne by the owners of the property . . . and cannot be thrown by them on their trustees, who have done no wrong, though the result may prove that they possibly might have done better.

What kind of losses will trustees actually be required to reimburse, then? Apart from the obvious situation in which a trustee has dishonestly misappropriated the fund or a part of it, here are some examples of when trustees might be held liable to account for a loss in the fund:

✦ Where the trustees make an unauthorised profit from the fund.

✦ Where trustees fail to keep adequate records and are therefore unable to verify otherwise legitimate expenses paid for out of the fund.

✦ Where a trustee incurs expenses on behalf of the trust which are unreasonable.

The list is by no means exhaustive but should give you a flavour of the types of things a trustee may be responsible for following an order to account.

The remedies of compensation and account both provide some form of financial recompense for a wronged beneficiary. However, this may not always be the remedy the beneficiaries need. Sometimes the best remedy for the beneficiaries is that the trustees are required to carry out their duties correctly. This is where the remedy of **specific performance** comes in.

Specific performance

As we have seen in previous chapters, a decree of specific performance is an order made by the court requiring the defendant to comply with their obligations to the claimant. As with all equitable remedies, there is no absolute right to an order for specific performance: the remedy is given at the discretion of the court. Once granted, however, an order for specific performance packs quite a punch, refusal to comply with such an order being subject to the criminal sanctions of **contempt of court**, which can bring with it a sentence of a fine and up to two years imprisonment. It is therefore not a remedy to be sniffed at.

> there is no absolute right to an order for specific performance

You will most commonly come across orders for specific performance in actions for **breach of contract**. So, for example, the court might give an order for specific performance where a buyer has failed to complete on their purchase of a house, despite having previously entered into a contract to do so. The Law in action box features a recent example of such a case.

Law in action Apartment buyers sued for specific performance

In the latest of a series of actions taken by development companies seeking to compel customers to honour their contracts, on Friday 30 April 2010 a prominent Northern Ireland property development firm, Abey Developments Ltd, made no less than ten applications to the High Court to force its customers to complete the purchase of apartments at its Custom House Square complex in Belfast.

Abey Developments is taking action against all those who have failed to complete their purchases of flats in the complex, which consists of around 85 apartments. The developer has applied in each case for an order of specific performance, which obliges the buyer to perform their part of the contract and complete the purchase of the flats, some of which carry with them a purchase price of up to £315,000.

Purchasers have been caught out by the property price crash, which has meant that in more than a few unlucky cases people have contracted to buy properties, only to find that they are unable to get a mortgage for the full purchase price of the property, which was agreed when property prices were elevated. Since the peak of the housing boom when work on many of these city centre developments began, property prices have dropped by more than 30 per cent, making them worth far less than the original price agreed between the developer and purchasers, and the banks are simply not willing to accept the properties as security for the inflated purchase prices originally agreed.

The result is that some prospective buyers face losing large deposits and, in the worst case scenario, being held liable for the total cost of their apartment. This is the outcome with which the purchasers of the Custom House Square development are faced, and their chances of a reprieve do not look good: until now the majority of similar cases which have come before the courts have been settled in favour of the developer.

[*Source:* Based on http://news.bbc.co.uk/1/hi/northern_ireland/ 8653714.stm; http://liammacuaid.wordpress.com/2010/04/30/justice-for-property-developers]

It can be seen, then, that the remedy of specific performance can be a useful tool in forcing a party in breach to perform their contractual obligations. Remember that if the orders are granted and the purchasers still fail to complete they will be liable to a fine and perhaps even imprisonment.

Reflective practice

Take a look at the Law in action article again. It seems likely that the buyers of the flats will be required to complete their purchases. Do you think this is equitable? Remember, in the case of breaches of contract, the equitable remedy of specific performance can only be granted where the legal remedy of damages would not be adequate compensation for the claimant's loss. Why do you think damages would not be sufficient in this case?

We have looked so far at the remedy of specific performance in the context of a breach of contract. The remedy is not just available to enforce contractual obligations, though; it can also be used to compel a trustee to perform their obligations under a trust. And there is a particular benefit to the remedy of specific performance as granted in relation to trusts as opposed to the performance of contractual obligations, too: whilst an order for specific performance of a contract will only be granted in situations where common law damages are not an adequate remedy, there are no preconditions for the use of specific performance as a remedy in cases of breach of trust.

So, when might you need to apply for an order of specific performance in relation to a trust fund? In the case of *Re Tillott* [1892] 1 Ch 86, the beneficiaries wished to obtain documents, information and accounts relating to certain trust properties which had been withheld from them by the trustees. A request to account would have provided some of this information, but not everything they required. They therefore applied to the court for an order requiring the trustees to give the bank in which the trust monies were invested authorisation to allow the beneficiaries to enquire directly with them about the investment. The order was granted.

To give another example of the use of specific performance as a remedy in a trust scenario, it might be used where trustees have failed to distribute the trust fund in accordance with its terms; and there are many more examples. Whatever the reason for the order, an order for specific performance when granted will usually take the form of a direction to the trustees to carry out a specific task or action. There are limitations on this, however. If the trust has a discretionary element the court will not force the trustees to exercise their discretion in any particular way, as this would take away the powers given to them by the settlor as trustees. So in the case of *Re Blake* (1885) 29 Ch D 913, the beneficiaries under the terms of the will of Susanna Blake applied to the court for an order forcing her executors to sell the property comprised in the estate. However, the will gave the executors discretion to postpone the sale of the property. The court therefore held that it would be improper for them to interfere with the discretion given to the trustees and force them to sell.

Having said this, the court can in exceptional cases make an order overruling the trustees' discretion if the trustees fail to exercise that discretion in the proper manner. This was the case in *Re Hodges* (1877–78) LR 7 ChD 754. The case concerned the will of Richard Hodges, who had left in his will a **legacy** of £3,000 to three children, Catherine, Teresa and Mary Davey, on their attaining the age of 21. The will contained a direction to the trustees to apply the whole or such parts of the income from the legacy as they thought fit for the maintenance and education of the children; however, no such payments had ever been made by the trustees. The court ordered, in opposition to the trustees' wishes, that payments of maintenance should be made to the children's father, who was a man of little means, in order that their education could be continued (something the father could no longer afford to do out of his own funds). A similar case is that of *Klug* v. *Klug* [1918] 2 Ch 67, in which the trustees were ordered to advance monies to a beneficiary in order to assist them in making payments of inheritance tax on the £10,000 trust fund. As it turned out in this particular instance the trustee who was refusing to give financial assistance to the beneficiary in question was actually the beneficiary's mother, who was angry with her daughter for marrying without her mother's consent!

It is worth mentioning here, briefly, that the court can also make an order preventing the trustees from exercising their discretion improperly by way of **injunction** (injunctions are discussed in further detail below), or to remove or replace the trustees if they refuse to exercise their discretion at all.

Case
Summary

Case
Summary

Case
Summary

Case
Summary

Declarations

As an alternative to making an order for specific performance, the court can also enforce trustees' duties by making a **declaration** that the trustees should or should not behave in a particular way. An example of this is the 1984 case of *Cowan* v. *Scargill* [1985] Ch 270, in which Vice-Chancellor Megarry declared that half of the trustees of a pension fund were in breach of trust by refusing to agree with the other half in the adoption of an investment strategy and business plan.

The case concerned a dispute over the management of the Mineworkers' Pension Scheme. An investment plan was submitted to the trustees for their approval, but the defendants refused to agree to the adoption of the plan unless it was amended so that there would be no increase in the percentage of overseas investment, that overseas investments already made would be withdrawn at the first appropriate opportunity and that there would be no investment in energy companies which directly competed with the coal industry. The claimants applied to the court, hoping to bring an end to the deadlock, and claiming that the defendants were acting in breach of their duty as trustees by failing to agree to the investment plan. The court held that it was the duty of the trustees to exercise their powers in the best interest of the beneficiaries without regard to their own personal interests or views and that, where the trust is required to provide financial benefits, maximising those benefits on behalf of the beneficiaries should be the paramount concern of the trustees, unless there are exceptional reasons not to do so. As the restrictions to the investment plan, which were sought by the defendants, would not benefit the beneficiaries in any way but rather were the product of union policy, the court made a declaration that the defendants were in breach of their duty in refusing to agree with the adoption of the plan.

Whilst the making of declarations by the court is often considered to be a lesser form of enforcement than an order for specific performance, declarations nevertheless have the effect of requiring the trustees to do their duty under the terms of the trust. Vice-Chancellor Megarry in *Cowan* v. *Scargill* said, in choosing to make a declaration rather than ordering specific performance, that:

> I think . . . it would be more appropriate for me to make declarations, and leave it to the defendants to carry out their duties as trustees in accordance with those declarations. I am ready to assume that they will comply with the law once the court has declared what it is . . . I shall not assume that the defendants intend to demonstrate their unfitness to continue as trustees by refusing to comply with the law as declared by the court.

It could therefore be said that, whilst an order for specific performance requires the trustees of a trust fund to carry out certain actions in compliance with the law as stated by the court, a declaration makes a statement as to what the law is and leaves it to the trustees to use their discretion in complying with it.

Injunctions

Like the remedy of specific performance, an injunction is also a type of court order, punishable with a fine or imprisonment for contempt of court in the event of non-compliance. However, whereas an order for specific performance requires the defendant to carry out certain specific acts which they have failed to do in their position as a trustee, an injunction on the other hand will usually be used as a preventive measure: either ordering the defendant to stop doing something in breach of trust (commonly known as a '**prohibitory injunction**') or, more rarely, to do some positive act (a '**mandatory injunction**'). A good illustration of a mandatory injunction is the case of *A.G. Man* v. *Campbell* (1983) 26 CCLT 168, in which a farmer was required to dismantle a tower on his land which was disrupting flights from an adjoining airport.

Case Summary

In the context of breaches of trust specifically, an injunction might be used, for example, to prevent trustees from selling trust property at an undervalue, or perhaps from transferring trust property to the wrong person. In the case of *Buttle* v. *Saunders* [1950] 2 All ER 193, trustees under a will had entered into negotiations with Mrs Simpson for the sale of some trust property at a sale price of £6,000. Draft contracts had been prepared and passed to Mrs Simpson's solicitors, but she had been unwilling to pay the seller's costs, which amounted to £142. A beneficiary of the trust then offered to purchase the property for the sum of £6,142, but the trustees felt honour-bound not to withdraw from their negotiations with Mrs Simpson. A week later, just before exchange of contracts, the same beneficiary made a further offer to pay £6,500 for the property; however the trustees refused to accept this, still feeling obliged to continue with Mrs Simpson. The beneficiary applied for an injunction to prevent the sale to Mrs Simpson, on the grounds that the trustees had a duty on behalf of the trust to obtain the highest price for the property. The court agreed with the claimant and granted the injunction.

Case Summary

A rather more unusual case was that heard by the **Privy Council** in *Wylde* v. *Attorney-General for New South Wales* (1948) 78 CLR 224. The case concerned the use of an order of service book compiled by Anglican bishop, Arnold Lomas Wylde. The book, commonly known as the 'Red Book' because of its red cover, caused a huge amount of controversy when it was introduced by the bishop into the diocese of Bathurst in New South Wales, Australia. Such was the outrage by some of Bathurst's parishioners, that in 1944 a number of complainants instituted legal proceedings against Bishop Wylde, on the grounds that the bishop was guilty of heresy in his deviation from the *Book of Common Prayer* and that the mandatory use of the sign of the cross and the sanctus bell during the service were 'in direct conflict with the doctrines of the Church of England'. The bishop claimed in the first instance that a secular court had no jurisdiction to hear an ecclesiastical case, but said in any event that he had the right as a bishop to authorise deviations from the *Book of Common Prayer*. The charge of heresy was eventually withdrawn but the case proceeded on grounds of breach of trust by the bishop to his parishioners. The somewhat shocking result was that an injunction was granted against the use of the Red Book anywhere within the diocese. On appeal to the High Court of Australia, the bishop's case was dismissed and the judgment upheld; however, it was limited to a small number of parishes and the Red Book continued to be widely used within the diocese.

Case Summary

Out and about

We have been focusing here on injunctions for breaches of trust, but there are many different reasons for an injunction to be granted: they are more common than you might think. Here's a challenge for you: take a look through any national newspaper and see how many examples of injunctive action (threatened or actual) you can find.

 Handy tip: If the pickings are looking slim, don't forget to look through the sports pages! Footballers and other sports professionals are often the subject of injunctions.

You should by now have a good idea of the reasons why people apply for injunctions. Now let us look at the different kinds of injunctions which might be available to a wronged beneficiary under the terms of a trust. Generally speaking, there are two different types of injunctions:

✦ **interim injunctions**; and

✦ **final injunctions**.

An interim injunction is granted as a holding measure pending a full court hearing, whereas a final injunction is given at the end of an action as part of the judge's final decision. The cases mentioned above are all examples of final injunctions: in each case the order granted has provided a final solution to the problem at hand – the use of an offensive book has been prevented; the sale of trust property has been halted; the distribution of trust monies to the wrong parties has been stopped. Interim injunctions tend to be used more as a last-minute emergency procedure where there is imminent danger to the trust: for example, to prevent a dishonest trustee from moving trust funds out of the country. Because of the urgency of interim injunctions and because of the nature of the breaches of trust which are often involved in them, applications for an interim injunction are commonly held '***ex parte***', meaning that the defendant is not involved in the application and will not usually be aware of the order being granted until it is served on them by the court.

> Interim injunctions tend to be used more as a last-minute emergency procedure

As with all equitable remedies, the grant of an injunction by the court is discretionary. However, due to the serious nature and consequences of the grant of an injunction, the courts tend to be cautious in granting them, particularly interim injunctions where a case has not yet been heard or proved, and especially where the grant of an injunction would result in undue financial hardship on the defendant. For this reason, the court will commonly request an undertaking from the claimant on the grant of an interim injunction to pay damages in respect of any financial loss caused to the defendant by the grant of the order. This makes the application for an interim injunction an expensive process for claimants and serves as a deterrent to all but the most serious of cases. In addition to this, Lord Diplock in the House of Lords case of *American Cyanamid Co.* v. *Ethicon Ltd* [1975] 2 WLR 316, a case which concerned an application for an interim injunction to prevent the release of a pharmaceutical product to the British market which the claimants believed infringed their patent, set out a number of guidelines designed to aid the court's discretion in the granting of interim injunctions. These are set out below:

Case Summary

1. The court must be satisfied that the claim is not frivolous or vexatious.

2. The material available to the court at the hearing must show that the claimant has a real prospect of succeeding in his claim for a permanent injunction at the trial.

3. The court should consider whether the balance of convenience lies in favour of granting or refusing the interim injunction.

With reference to the third point, Lord Diplock went on to say that if common law damages would be an adequate remedy no interim injunction should normally be granted, however strong the claimant's claim appeared to be at that stage. However, it should be noted that, as with orders for the specific performance of trust duties, an injunction restraining a threatened breach of trust is available regardless of the adequacy of other remedies. The point to be taken from Lord Diplock's comment about the 'balance of convenience' is really just that the idea behind the grant of an interim injunction is that it is a holding measure: an emergency tactic designed to maintain the status quo between the parties until such time as the matter is given a full hearing. Therefore if the granting of an injunction will be severely prejudicial to the defendant it is unlikely to be granted, unless there is a truly compelling reason to do so. This can be illustrated by the case in *Jaggard* v. *Sawyer* [1995] 2 All ER 189, in which the court refused to grant an injunction to prevent the defendants from completing the building of a house in their back garden in breach of a restrictive covenant on the property. The claimants, who owned the property adjoining that of the defendants, had not started proceedings until the building of the house was well under way. The court felt that, if the defendants were ordered to pull the house down, the detriment to them would be well out of proportion to the detriment the building of the house would cause to the neighbouring property.

Case Summary

Having now explored in brief the nature of interim and final injunctions, let us take a look at some of the more well-known types of injunction used by the courts.

Search orders

Search orders are a special type of mandatory injunction which orders the defendant to permit the claimant's representatives to inspect the defendant's premises in search of, in the case of a breach of trust, items such as either the stolen trust property itself or evidence of its removal. A search order will also usually give the claimant's representative authority to seize or make copies of any items or documents of relevance found during the search. Originally named **Anton Piller orders** after the case of *Anton Piller KG* v. *Manufacturing Process Ltd* [1976] Ch 55, search orders now have a statutory basis under section 7 of the Civil Procedure Act 1997. The Act provides that a search order may be made for the purpose of:

(a) the preservation of evidence which is or may be relevant to the main court action; or
(b) the preservation of property which is or may be the subject matter of the proceedings or as to which any question may arise in the proceedings.

It is clear from the wording of the Act, then, that this is an order which is designed to prevent the defendant from concealing, removing or destroying vital evidence before the main action is heard. Owing to the nature of the search order, applications for this type of interim injunction tend to be made *ex parte*, without the knowledge of the defendant, in order that the defendant is not 'tipped off' about a possible search of premises and given the opportunity to remove incriminating evidence before the order is granted. The *Anton Piller* case itself was an action requesting an injunction to prevent the defendants from providing confidential information about computer parts manufactured by the claimants to rival companies, and to obtain an order to allow the claimants to search the defendants' premises and remove any documents containing confidential information about the products from their possession. The action was dismissed at first instance, but on appeal the court held that an order to search and confiscate such any such information from the defendants' premises would be allowed.

Case Summary

Nevertheless, because of the invasive nature of this type of injunction, the Court of Appeal was eager to lay down strict preconditions for the granting of search orders in the future, albeit that the equitable remedy of the grant of an injunction is still technically a discretionary one. These requirements, as stated by Lord Justice Ormrod in the *Anton Piller* case, are that:

1. the claimant must have an extremely strong case at first instance;
2. the actual or potential damage to the claimant must be very serious;
3. there must be clear evidence that the defendants have in their possession incriminating documents or things, and that there is a real possibility that they may destroy such material before the matter is given a full hearing.

In addition to these preconditions, the claimants also have a duty to disclose fully any information of which they are aware that the defendant might raise against their application. Failure to do so may result in any order made being overturned if the claimant is found to have suppressed or concealed material evidence. It is the court's decision whether or not information held by the claimant is relevant; therefore the claimant has no excuse for withholding information on the grounds that they did not believe it to be material to the case. Furthermore, a search order cannot be used as a method of obtaining information to further the claimant's claim. In *Hytrac Conveyors* v. *Conveyors International* [1983] FSR 63, a number of search orders which had been made in favour of the claimants were overturned on the basis that the claimants did not have a sufficiently proven case and were simply using the search orders to seek additional evidence against the defendants.

Case
Summary

Key stats

In England, it has been reported that approximately 500 Anton Piller orders were granted per year between 1975 and 1980. During the 1990s this rate had dropped tenfold. Why do you think this might be?

[*Source:* http://en.academic.ru/dic.nsf/enwiki/256073]

Looking at the Key stats feature, were you able to guess why the rate of Anton Piller orders granted has dropped so significantly? One reason might be that they were considered open to abuse by claimants. Despite the extensive provisions which have been put into place for the protection of defendants in the grant of search orders, this type of injunction has nevertheless been the butt of a continuous stream of criticism and there are those who would even go as far as to say that search orders represent a basic infringement of human rights. In an attempt to minimise the perceived risks to defendants in receipt of search orders, yet further statutory safeguards have been put into place, in the form of a requirement that the search of the defendant's premises must be conducted by an independent **supervising solicitor**, and not by the claimants themselves. In the People in the law interview, supervising solicitor Ian Coupland considers the merits of such a system.

People in the law

Name and position: Ian Coupland, supervising solicitor, Lupton Fawcett.

So, Ian, what does a supervising solicitor do? A supervising solicitor is an independent solicitor who 'supervises' the enforcement of search and seizure orders. The supervising solicitor's role is to read and explain the terms of the order to the defendant and then to watch the claimants do the search and make sure they comply with the terms of the order in respect of how they go about the search and what they are looking for.

Source: Ian Coupland (*text and photo*)

Why do we need supervising solicitors? For independence and so that there are ground rules for the carrying out of the search and seizure order. Guidelines were drawn up by the court in the case of *Universal Thermosensors Ltd* v. *Hibben* [1992] 1 WLR 840. [A full explanation of the procedure outlined by the case is given in J. Hull's 1992 article, 'Anton Piller orders', referenced at the end of the chapter.]

Is it true that there was a lot of abuse of the system before the advent of supervising solicitors? Not abuse, just that it was recognised that this area of the law needed to be developed. For example, a representative of the defendant should be present at the search and have the right to obtain their own legal advice before the search is carried out.

Do you think there are now adequate safeguards in place to protect defendants from the negative effects of search and seizure orders or is still further restriction needed? I think the system works well. Search and seizure orders are commonly sought as a matter of great urgency in cases involving highly sensitive and valuable business information. The role of the independent solicitor is to give some protection to both parties whilst this order is being carried out.

It has been said that the grant of a search order is a potential violation of human rights. Would you agree with this? No, because usually the issue will be a commercial one, a court has to be satisfied that the appropriate criteria has been satisfied to make a search and seizure order in the first place and then if a party is not happy with the way it has been carried out, there is the right of recourse to the court as the independent solicitor has to lodge a full report to the court on the enforcement.

Would you say, then, that search and seizure orders in their current form provide both an adequate and fair form of justice? Yes, for the reasons mentioned above.

Is there anything else you would like to add? Search and seizure orders are very expensive as not only does a considerable amount of preparatory work need to be done before obtaining an order, the court will normally order a return date to consider the effect of the order and the rights of the defendant as the order will have been made without their knowledge in the first place. Also there is the cost of the independent supervising solicitor to pay. This means you are talking at least £30,000 for the search on one site and that's before the usual legal case starts – so to justify doing it, it either has to be business-critical, e.g. trade secrets, or the claim is worth a lot of money.

One final point that should be made is that a search order is not akin to a search warrant. As Lord Denning explained in the *Anton Piller* case, a search order:

> does not authorise the [claimant's] solicitors or anyone else to enter the defendant's premises against their will. It does not authorise the breaking down of any doors, nor the slipping in by a back door, not getting in by an open door or window. It only authorises entry and inspection by the permission of the defendants.

As with all injunctions, the damage which will be caused to the defendant on the granting of the order must not be out of proportion to the damage to the claimant against which the order is protecting them. So if the disruption caused by the grant of a search order is going to have the effect of putting the defendant out of business, for instance, it is unlikely to be granted unless the potential damage to the claimant is extremely severe.

Freezing injunctions

Whereas a search order is a mandatory form of injunction, one which forces the defendant to allow the search of his premises, a **freezing injunction** is prohibitive in nature. The purpose of a freezing injunction is to prevent the defendant from moving assets out of the reach of the claimants before the matter has a chance to come to final hearing. Freezing injunctions are also often referred to as '**Mareva injunctions**', because of the leading case of *Mareva Compania Naviera SA* v. *International Bulk Carriers SA* [1975] 2 Lloyd's Rep 509. The case concerned a ship, the *Mareva*. The claimants, the Mareva Shipping Company, had chartered (or leased) the ship to the defendants, International Bulk Carriers. International Bulk Carriers then sub-chartered the ship to the President of India for the sum of £174,000. Despite having sub-let the ship, however, and although they had made the first two payments due to the Mareva Shipping Company for the hire of the vessel on schedule, International Bulk Carriers then failed to make the third payment. The Mareva Shipping Company applied to the court for an order to freeze International Bulk Carriers' London bank account. By doing this they hoped to prevent International Bulk Carriers from spending the money received from their sub-letting of the vessel and thereby dissipating the balance of monies owing. The injunction was granted. It is easy to see from these facts how the same remedy could be applied in the case of a dishonest trustee who had misapplied trust funds.

It should be mentioned that, although the *Mareva* case is the leading case in this area, the freezing injunction has now received statutory force under the Civil Procedure Rules 1998, Part 25(1). The rule says that the court may grant a freezing injunction:

(i) restraining a party from removing from the jurisdiction assets located there; or
(ii) restraining a party from dealing with any assets whether located within the jurisdiction or not.

You may have noticed from the wording of the rule that, whilst the original 'Mareva' injunction was put into place to prevent assets from being moved out of the UK, freezing orders may now also be used to prevent the defendant from moving monies located in any other jurisdiction. This is possible because the injunction is made by the court against the person, not against their assets; thus the location of the assets is irrelevant.

In much the same way as with the grant of search orders, the courts have chosen to err on the side of caution in the grant of freezing injunctions. Thus, in *Third Chandris Shipping Corporation* v. *Unimarine SA (The Angelic Wings, The Genie and The Pythia)* [1979] 2 All ER 972, which was another shipping case, Lord Denning spelt out a number of basic guidelines that should be followed when applying for such an order, as follows:

Case Summary

1. The claimant should make a full and frank disclosure of all matters within their knowledge which are material to the judge's decision.

2. The claimant should give particulars of their claim against the defendant, stating the ground of their claim and the amount, and fairly stating the points made against them by the defendant.

3. The claimant should show that they have some grounds for believing that the defendant has assets within the jurisdiction. The existence of a bank account in the defendant's name will be sufficient proof of this, even if it is overdrawn.

4. The claimant should show that they have some grounds for believing that there is a risk of the assets being removed before the judgment order can be satisfied. The mere fact that the defendant is abroad will not by itself be sufficient evidence of this.

5. The claimants must give an undertaking in damages, in case their claim fails, or the injunction turns out to be unjustified. This should be supported by a bond or security where appropriate.

Whilst we can see that many of these guidelines are similar in nature to the prerequisites for the granting of search orders, the guidelines nevertheless send out a clear message to the courts and to any purported claimant: freezing injunctions will not be granted without due consideration and the provision of serious evidence.

Quia timet injunctions

One final type of injunction it is worth mentioning before we move on to consider the other equitable remedies you might use in a breach of trust situation, is the **quia timet injunction**. This type of injunction, which takes its name from the Latin, literally meaning 'because of fear', can be granted either as an interim or final measure. In either case it is only granted in the special situation of where the claimant is afraid that the defendant is going to do something in the future, rather than where the defendant has actually done something the claimant wishes to prevent from continuing or reoccurring. Naturally the courts will be quite reticent to grant such an injunction unless the claimant can prove that there is real and imminent danger of the action being carried out. After all, it has never been the place of the law either to punish or to restrict a person's movements simply because they have contemplated a wrongful act. However, a *quia timet* injunction will be granted in any situation where the claimant is able to show 'a strong case of probability that the apprehended mischief will, in fact, arise'. Such was the statement of Mr Justice

Documenting the law

If you were wondering what a freezing injunction looks like, Practice Direction 25A includes an example.

FREEZING INJUNCTION

IN THE HIGH COURT OF JUSTICE
[   ] **DIVISION**

Before The Honourable Mr Justice   [   ]

Claim No.

Dated

Applicant

Seal

Respondent

Name, address and reference of Respondent

PENAL NOTICE

IF YOU [   ]¹ DISOBEY THIS ORDER YOU MAY BE HELD TO BE IN CONTEMPT OF COURT AND MAY BE IMPRISONED, FINED OR HAVE YOUR ASSETS SEIZED.

ANY OTHER PERSON WHO KNOWS OF THIS ORDER AND DOES ANYTHING WHICH HELPS OR PERMITS THE RESPONDENT TO BREACH THE TERMS OF THIS ORDER MAY ALSO BE HELD TO BE IN CONTEMPT OF COURT AND MAY BE IMPRISONED, FINED OR HAVE THEIR ASSETS SEIZED.

1 Insert name of Respondent

THIS ORDER

[*Source*: http://www.justice.gov.uk/civil/procrules_fin/contents/practice_directions/pd_part25a.htm#IDANPKTB, Ministry of Justice.]

1. This is a Freezing Injunction made against [   ] ('the Respondent') on [   ] by Mr Justice [   ] on the application of [   ] ('the Applicant').

2. This order was made at a hearing without notice to the Respondent. The Respondent has a right to apply to the court to vary or discharge the order – see paragraph 13 below.

3. There will be a further hearing in respect of this order on [   ] ('the return date').

4. If there is more than one Respondent –
   (a) unless otherwise stated, references in this order to 'the Respondent' mean both or all of them; and
   (b) this order is effective against any Respondent on whom it is served or who is given notice of it.

FREEZING INJUNCTION

5. Until the return date or further order of the court, the Respondent must not –
   (1) remove from England and Wales any of his assets which are in England and Wales up to the value of £   ; or
   (2) in any way dispose of, deal with or diminish the value of any of his assets whether they are in or outside England and Wales up to the same value.

6. Paragraph 5 applies to all the Respondent's assets whether or not they are in his own name and whether they are solely or jointly owned. For the purpose of this order the Respondent's assets include any asset which he has the power, directly or indirectly, to dispose of or deal with as if it were his own. The Respondent is to be regarded as having such power if a third party holds or controls the asset in accordance with his direct or indirect instructions.

7. This prohibition includes the following assets in particular –
   (a) the property known as [address] or the net sale money after payment of any mortgages if it has been sold;
   (b) the property and assets of the Respondent's business [known as [name]] [carried on at [address]] or the sale money if any of them have been sold; and
   (c) any money standing to the credit of any bank account including the amount of any cheque drawn on such account which has not been cleared.

8. (1) If the total value free of charges or other securities ('unencumbered value') of the Respondent's assets in England and Wales exceeds £   , the Respondent may remove any of those assets from England and Wales or may dispose of or deal with them so long as the total unencumbered value of the Respondent's assets still in England and Wales remains above £   .
   (2) If the total unencumbered value of the Respondent's assets in England and Wales does not exceed £   , the Respondent must not remove any of those assets from England and Wales and must not dispose of or deal with any of them. If the Respondent has other assets outside England and Wales, he may dispose of or deal with those assets outside England and Wales so long as the total unencumbered value of all his assets whether in or outside England and Wales remains above £   .

You should note that the example above is only an extract: to see a full copy of a freezing order, including appendices, go to the Ministry of Justice website at: **http://www.justice.gov.uk/civil/procrules_fin/contents/ practice_directions/pd_part25a.htm#IDANPKTB.**

Case
Summary Chitty in the case of *Attorney-General* v. *Manchester Corporation* [1893] 2 Ch 87. The case concerned an application for an injunction by the claimant to prevent the defendant from building a smallpox hospital because they believed it would present a danger to the health of the people living in the surrounding area. The court held, though, that the risk of smallpox spreading from the hospital into the wider community was no more than a mere possibility and therefore the injunction was not granted.

Case
Summary Conversely, in the case of *Goodhart* v. *Hyatt* (1883) 25 Ch D 182, a *quia timet* injunction was granted. In this case the claimant had a right to repair water pipes that ran under the defendant's land. The defendant wanted to build a house over part of the pipes, but the claimant objected to his plans on the grounds that this would, in all likelihood, make any future repairs to the pipes both very difficult and expensive. Clearly in this case the 'strong probability' of danger to the claimant could be clearly shown.

Writing and drafting

You are a trainee solicitor at the firm of Reece & Co. Yesterday you attended a client interview with your training principal. The client, Mr Abu of 25 West Heights, Yorkfield, owns a business, the Traditional Egyptian Paper Company, which he runs from a converted water mill situated on the bank of a river. The water from the river is used in the process of manufacturing the paper. Mr Abu says that it is essential that the water should be very pure for the process to work correctly.

A manufacturing business had taken up residence further up the river and had started to accumulate a large heap of refuse from their works on the river bank. Whilst there had been no damage to the water as yet, Mr Abu was afraid that if any of the refuse should find its way into the river the water would be rendered unfit for the manufacturing process and his trade would be ruined.

Source: Photodisc/Photolink

Mr Abu had spoken to the manufacturing company and they had assured him that they intended to use all proper precautions to prevent the refuse from getting into the river, but Mr Abu was not satisfied with their promises and has asked you to apply for an injunction to prevent them from storing their rubbish on the site. Your training principal has now asked you to write a letter of advice to Mr Abu in response to his query.

You should take no longer than 30 minutes on this task.

 Handy tip: Think about the facts of the case: is there 'a strong case of probability that the apprehended mischief will, in fact, arise'?

The facts of Mr Abu's fictional case are almost identical to those from the case of *Fletcher* v. *Bealey*, which was heard in 1885 (LR 28 ChD 688). The result of the case was that an injunction was refused: the court held that it was quite possible that by careful management of the waste the defendants could prevent it from going into the river altogether; the feared damage might therefore never happen and an injunction could not be justified.

Case Summary

Reflective practice

Take another look at the letter of advice you wrote in the Writing and drafting exercise. Does the finding of the court accord with the advice you gave to Mr Abu?

In more recent years the 'strong probability' requirement laid down by Mr Justice Chitty has been criticised as being too prescriptive. In the case of *Hooper* v. *Rogers* [1974] 3 All ER 417 Lord Justice Russell said that 'It seems to me that the degree of probability of future injury is not an absolute standard: what is aimed at is justice between the parties, having regard to all the circumstances.' The facts of the case were that Mr Hooper and Mr Rogers were the owners of neighbouring farmhouses, owning the land separating the two houses in common between them. Mr Rogers decided to dig a path into the hillside, right across the steeply sloping common land. Unfortunately this had the effect of exposing the slope to soil erosion and putting the stability of the foundations of Mr Hooper's house at risk. Mr Hooper therefore applied for a mandatory injunction to have the path filled in and the slope restored to its former state. In the event, the court actually decided to award damages in lieu of an injunction as, although the danger to Mr Hooper's house was quite real, the likelihood of damage was far from imminent. Nevertheless, the judge defended Mr Hooper for making the application, stating that he was right to do so under the circumstances, being given no other choice than to apply for injunctive measures to be put into place.

Case Summary

It should be noted here that it is possible under section 50 of the Senior Courts Act 1981 for the court to grant damages in lieu of either an injunction or specific performance, where the outcome of the case is that either remedy would be desirable but is impracticable under the circumstances of the case. Such damages can be awarded even where damages at common law would not normally be available.

Rescission

The equitable remedy of **rescission** allows a contract or other transaction to be reversed or '**rescinded**' where that transaction has been carried out in an unconscionable, or morally reprehensible, manner. In the case of breaches of trust, any improper transfer of trust assets would qualify for rescission; so this might apply where the trust assets have been transferred to a third party either innocently or with that person's knowledge. As with all other equitable remedies the decision to rescind is at the discretion of the court. Because the point of rescission is to 'undo' the transaction and restore the parties to their original positions, if this becomes impossible to do the right to rescind is lost.

An example of how this might happen can be seen in the case of *Erlanger* v. *New Sombrero Phosphate Co.* (1878) 3 App Cas 1218. The case concerned a Parisian banker, Mr Erlanger. Mr Erlanger bought the lease of the Anguillan island of Sombrero for phosphate mining for £55,000. He then set up the New Sombrero Phosphate Company and sold the island to the company for £110,000 through an agent. After eight months of mining, the public investors in the company found out the fact that Erlanger had bought the island at half the price the company (with their money) had paid for it. The New Sombrero Phosphate Company sued for rescission because of non-disclosure by a director. The House of Lords held that Mr Erlanger was in a **fiduciary** relationship with the investors, and therefore had a duty of disclosure towards them. Rescission was granted. There was a question as to whether rescission was possible, since phosphate had already been taken from the mine and could not be replaced. The court held, however, that in this case adequate compensation could be paid and the removal of the phosphate was not considered a bar to rescission.

Rectification

Whereas rescission is the process of reversing the effects of a transaction or document, **rectification** is the equitable remedy which allows a **deed** or document to be corrected. In a trust situation, such a remedy could therefore prove useful where, for example, the trustees had incorrectly documented the removal or replacement of one of their number. Rectification cannot be used to improve the position of the parties over and above what was agreed between them, however, even if that position was more favourable to one party than the other; it can only be used to correct a document so that it gives an accurate reflection of the original agreement as made between the two parties. This means that if one party was mistaken as to what had been agreed between them, they would be unlikely to get the remedy of rectification because it would not be an accurate reflection of what the parties had jointly agreed. Lord Denning in the case of *Frederick E. Rose (London) Ltd* v. *William H. Pim & Co. Ltd* [1953] 2 QB 450 explained how this works in practice:

> ## Rectification cannot be used to improve the position of the parties

> In order to get rectification it is necessary to show that the parties were in complete agreement upon the terms of their contract, but by an error wrote them down wrongly . . . One looks at their outward acts, that is what they said and wrote to one another in coming to their agreement and then compares it with the document they have signed . . . if you can predict with certainty what their contract was, that it is, by common mistake, wrongly expressed in the document, then you may rectify the document.

The case of *Frederick E. Rose* v. *William H. Pim* actually concerned a contract for the purchase of horse beans (more commonly known today as broad beans). The claimants, a retail establishment, had been asked to supply some beans, described as 'Moroccan horse beans described here as feveroles' from their client in Egypt. Not knowing what 'feveroles' were, they contacted their suppliers, the defendants, who, after making some enquiries, confirmed that they were the same as horse beans, and that they could supply them. The beans were sent to the Egyptian client, but it turned out that they were not the correct type of bean. The client claimed damages from their suppliers for supplying the wrong bean. Despite the parties' common mistake as to the identity of the beans, the court refused to grant rectification of the document because the contract nevertheless did accurately reflect the parties' agreement. Lord Denning explained:

> Though both parties were under a fundamental mistake as to the nature of the subject-matter, the contract was not a nullity, for where parties to a contract were to all outward appearances in full and certain agreement, neither of them could set up his own mistake, or the mistake of both of them, to make it a nullity [from the outset].

Even though the beans supplied were not the beans requested by the claimants' client, both the company and their supplier had been in agreement as to the type of beans ordered. Thus, there had been no mistake in the terms of the contract; it was simply that both company and supplier had misunderstood the type of bean the client required.

Again, it should be stressed that this is a discretionary remedy and it is therefore at the discretion of the court whether to grant rectification or not.

Subrogation

The final equitable remedy of which we should give brief mention is that of subrogation. Subrogation is a rarely used remedy under which the rights of the claimant are transferred to another party, who is then entitled to enforce those rights for their own benefit. The most common situation in which subrogation will be used is when the claimant's insurer has already made payment to the claimant under the terms of their insurance policy for the loss incurred. It makes sense in such circumstances that the insurer should then have the right to take up the injured party's claim with a view to recouping their loss. An example might be in the case of a car accident. If Winnie's car is hit by another driver, Paul, her insurance company will pay her for the damage to her vehicle under the terms of her car insurance policy. However, the insurance company will then have the right to sue Paul, in place of Winnie, to be compensated in respect of the damage Paul has caused to Winnie's vehicle.

Summary

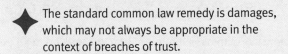 The standard common law remedy is damages, which may not always be appropriate in the context of breaches of trust.

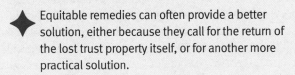 Equitable remedies can often provide a better solution, either because they call for the return of the lost trust property itself, or for another more practical solution.

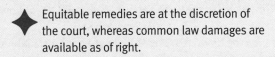 Equitable remedies are at the discretion of the court, whereas common law damages are available as of right.

If the trust property cannot be returned to the trust, the beneficiaries may be able to claim equitable compensation equal to their loss to the fund.

◆ A beneficiary can apply to the court for the remedy of account. This forces the trustees to account for all movement of trust funds: explaining what has been spent and why.

◆ Specific performance is where the court make an order requiring the trustees to perform their duties to the trust correctly.

◆ An alternative to an order of specific performance is where the court makes a declaration on a particular point of law. A declaration is a statement of position, which leaves the trustees to decide how to resolve it between them.

◆ Injunctions can be granted as an interim measure, where the action has not yet been brought to full hearing, or as a final remedy instead of, or in addition to, any other remedies available to the court.

◆ Search orders and freezing orders are particular types of injunction, both designed to prevent assets or evidence from being destroyed or hidden before the matter comes to full hearing.

◆ In rare circumstances, an injunction will be granted '*quia timet*', on the basis that the claimant is in fear of the defendant carrying out certain acts which will damage either their claim or the trust assets.

◆ Rescission allows a contract or other transaction to be reversed where the transaction has been carried out in an unconscionable manner.

◆ Rectification allows the amendment of a contract or other document to reflect the original agreement of the parties, if a mistake has been made in its translation onto paper.

◆ Subrogation allows for a third party, typically an insurer, to step into the shoes of the claimant and make a claim for their own benefit.

Question and answer*

Problem: Lenny Han is the curator of the Orton Parish Museum of Art and Culture. Sadly the museum building has fallen into quite a state of disrepair over the years and the small number of visitors to the museum has not provided sufficient revenue to pay for the repairs. Lenny has on a number of occasions drawn the declining condition of the building to the attention of the Orton Parish Museum Trust, which owns the museum. However, their interest is primarily in finding and purchasing new works to exhibit in the museum and they pay little attention to the plight of the building.

Eventually, after a leak in the museum roof causes damage to one of the museum's most valuable paintings, Lenny decides to take matters into his own hands and secretly starts selling off some of the more expensive museum pieces in order to pay for ongoing repairs. First he sells one of a matching pair of Chippendale console tables to a foreign private buyer; then he sells half the museum's collection of eighteenth-century snuff boxes to a local antiques dealer, who has been pestering him as to whether he can procure the boxes for quite some time; and finally he sells a collection of love letters reputed to be written by legendary highwayman Davey 'Blackheart' Haynes to his mistress. Lenny makes quite a profit on the sale of the letters, which are bought by an avid fan and collector of Blackheart Haynes ephemera.

By the time the trustees find out about his actions, Lenny has employed roofing contractors and spent all the money made on the sale of the exhibits on repairs to the roof. Lenny is not a rich man and has no assets of his own with which to reimburse the fund. To make matters worse, the trustees hear that the Chippendale console table has perished at sea whilst in transit to the buyer's home in Nova Scotia. In addition, the trustees learn that the snuff boxes were sold at a huge undervalue, Lenny relying on the valuation given to him by the dealer, which was adrift by an incredible £20,000. Talk in the village is that Lenny has made a deal with the local antiques dealer to sell the other half of the snuff box collection, and the trustees are keen to stop the sale.

What remedies are available to the trustees and what can they claim for?

You should allow yourself no more than 40 minutes to complete this task.

Essay: The Anton Piller order has often been described as 'an inequitable remedy'. Why is this and do you consider it a fair statement?

This question should be answered in 40 minutes.

✱ Answer guidance is provided at the end of the chapter.

Further reading and references

Conaglen, M.D.J. (2003) 'Equitable compensation for breach of fiduciary dealing rules', 119 LQR 246–71.
A really comprehensive article on the availability and merits of equitable compensation and other equitable remedies available in cases of self-dealing and unfair dealing in breaches of trust. Interesting and worth a read.

Hull, J. (1992) 'Anton Piller orders', International Banking and Financial Law, 11(2), 19–21.
A nice concise article and case comment on Anton Piller orders setting out the procedural guidance mentioned by Ian Coupland in the People in the law feature, which has been laid down by the court for

their execution in the case of *Universal Thermosensers* v. *Hibben* [1992] 1 WLR 840.

Martin, J.E. (1990/91) 'Equitable and inequitable remedies', *King's College Law Journal*, 1, 1–15.
Interesting article considering whether increasing use of Anton Piller orders and Mareva injunctions is causing remedies to become oppressive. Slightly dated now but still brings up some interesting points for discussion.

Wabwile, M. (2000) 'Anton Piller orders revisited', JBL, Sep, 387–404.
Excellent overview and explanation of search orders with comment on the dangers of abuse in their use and suggestions for reform.

Question and answer guidance

Problem:

The common law remedy available to the trustees is that of damages; however, suing Lenny for damages may be of little use to the trustees, as a claim for damages is a personal remedy and we have been told that Lenny has no money of his own. In addition, presumably the trustees want to see the trust property returned to the museum, if possible, and so a simple remedy of damages would not suffice.

There are various remedies available in equity. Where the return of the trust property to the fund is not possible, such as in the case of the console table, the trustees could claim equitable compensation to the trust fund.

The benefit of claiming equitable compensation over common law damages is that the trustees can claim for loss to the fund as a result of the sales, in addition to the price the items actually sold for. As the console table is one of a pair it is likely that the value of the remaining table will also have diminished, because the two together will be worth more than the value of the tables as individual items. This is something which a claim can be made for in equity and is therefore worth pursuing. The trustees could also claim for the loss to the fund caused by the sale of the snuff boxes at an undervalue; however, if the trustees are able to seek the return of the boxes equitable compensation may not be available as this is a measure of last resort and the courts prefer to explore other remedies first. In any event, as Lenny has no money where would the money come from to pay the equitable compensation?

In terms of tracing, the money has been spent on the roof and is therefore dissipated; the table has perished. Only the letters and snuff boxes remain. Assuming the letters were sold to a bona fide purchaser for value without notice, this will defeat any tracing claim. We have been told that all money received by Lenny from the sales has already been spent on the roof, and so the money itself cannot be recouped. It is possible that the antiques dealer did not have the necessary requirement of good faith, however, having purchased the snuff boxes at a significant undervalue. The trustees may therefore be able to claim the return of the boxes from the dealer under the rules of tracing.

In respect of the rumours of the sale of the remainder of the snuff box collection, the trustees could apply to the court for a prohibitory injunction to prevent the sale (*Buttle* v. *Saunders*). As Lenny hasn't actually done anything yet, the trustees merely fear that he may do, so the trustees would be best applying for a *quia timet* injunction. In order to be granted such an injunction, there must be 'a strong case of probability that the apprehended mischief will, in fact, arise' (*AG* v. *Manchester Corporation*). It is questionable whether the rumours in the village amount to a 'strong probability'. Thus, the trustees' success in getting an injunction may rely on the provision of further proof that Lenny plans to do this.

Essay:

A good essay should begin by explaining what an Anton Piller order is and how it works. In brief Anton Piller orders, or search orders as they are now known, are a special type of mandatory injunction (an equitable remedy) which orders the defendant to permit the claimant's representatives to inspect the defendant's premises in search of, in the case of a breach of trust, items such as either the stolen trust property itself or evidence of its removal. Originally named 'Anton Piller' orders after the case of *Anton Piller KG* v. *Manufacturing Process Ltd*, search orders now have a statutory basis under section 7 of the Civil Procedure Act 1997.

Students should then go on to list the requirements for Anton Piller orders, set out by Lord Justice Ormrod in the *Anton Piller* case, which are that:

✦ the claimant must have an extremely strong case at first instance;

✦ the actual or potential damage to the claimant must be very serious;

✦ there must be clear evidence that the defendants have in their possession incriminating documents or things, and that there is a real possibility that they may destroy such material before the matter is given a full hearing.

In addition to these preconditions, the claimants also have a duty to disclose fully any information of which they are aware that the defendant might raise against their application. Failure to do so may result in any order made being overturned if the claimant is found to have suppressed or concealed material evidence.

Given the prerequisites for the granting of an order, it is perhaps surprising that Anton Piller orders were considered open to abuse by claimants. However, they have nevertheless been subject to a great deal of criticism and some say these orders are an infringement of human rights. It would be worth referring to the People in the law interview with Ian Coupland at this point, who gives useful insight into the practicalities of carrying out search orders, and who comments on the perceived problems with the form of the orders as they stand.

The student should conclude by stating whether or not they agree with the statement that Anton Piller orders are inequitable, and if so, why. A good point to mention here is the additional prerequisite on granting search orders, that the damage which will be caused to the defendant on the granting of the order must not be out of proportion with the damage to the claimant against which the order is protecting them. So if the disruption caused by the grant of a search order is going to have the effect of putting the defendant out of business, for instance, it is unlikely to be granted unless the potential damage to the claimant is extremely severe.

Visit **www.mylawchamber.co.uk/warner-reed** to access study support resources including practice exam questions with guidance, interactive 'You be the judge' multiple choice questions, annotated weblinks, glossary and key case flashcards and audio legal updates all linked to the **Pearson eText** version of *Equity and Trusts* which you can **search**, **highlight** and **personalise** with your **own notes** and **bookmarks**.

Chapter 17
Lawyer's brief

Introduction

So you have reached the end of Chapter 16 and the substantive part of the textbook has finished – now for something a little different! This final chapter of the book gives you the opportunity to put into practice many of the skills and much of the knowledge that you have learned throughout the rest of the book. Aptly named the 'Lawyer's brief', what you will see in this chapter is a series of documents presented in much the same way as you would see them in the file of a working solicitor. In addition to these documents there are a number of questions and tasks, which have been designed both to test your understanding of the law of trusts and to give you a real flavour of how the law is applied in practice. We hope that you will find this a valuable and worthwhile learning tool as well as a fun exercise. You will play the part of an executor and trustee in the estate of the deceased – good luck in your task!

The brief

You are Nathan Soames, a junior partner at the firm of Wardell James, in Wakefield, West Yorkshire. A long-standing client of your firm, Country and Western singing sensation, Ricky Louden the Third, has recently died in an unfortunate shooting accident, and you have been asked to act as an executor and trustee in the administration of his estate. The other executor and trustee is the senior partner at Wardell James, Addy Wardell. Mr Wardell was a great personal friend of Ricky Louden and is godfather to two of Ricky's children. He therefore has a personal, as well as a professional, interest in the matter, so you must be seen to do a good job!

Although he was only 52 when he died, Ricky had been prudent enough to make a will, which was kept at Wardell James's offices. A copy of the will is represented in Document 1.

The wills and probate department have applied for a grant of probate and have collected in all of the assets belonging to Ricky's estate. Your job, as an executor and trustee, is now to distribute the monies in accordance with the terms of the will, and to administer any trusts arising from it.

Document 1

THIS IS THE LAST WILL AND TESTAMENT of me **RICHARD WAYNE LOUDEN** of Green Trees, Edge Hill, Ossett, Wakefield, West Yorkshire WF5 1DF
I revoke all previous wills.

1. **I APPOINT** the partners at the date of my death in the firm of Wardell James, Wakefield to be executors and trustees of my will (hereinafter called 'my Trustees') and I express the wish that two and only two of them shall prove my will and act initially in its trusts.

2. I wish my body to be cremated.

3. I GIVE my collection of silver collar tips and bola ties to my brother GERVAIS LOUDEN free of tax.

4. I GIVE to the Wakefield branch of the National Line Dancing Association the sum of ten thousand pounds in order that they might resurface their dance floor with Texan Redwood floor tiles.

5. I give the royalties from the sales of all of my music recordings to the British Arachnid Preservation Trust for its general charitable purposes absolutely.

6. I give forty thousand pounds to my brother Marshall for the maintenance of my beloved pet tarantula, Arabella, who has been a dearer friend to me than Marshall. I trust that Marshall will use the money to keep Arabella on the diet of live locusts which she so enjoys.

7. I give the sum of five hundred thousand pounds to my Trustees to hold on trust for such of my nephews and nieces as shall survive me, in equal shares absolutely subject to them attaining the age of 25 years.

8. I give the residue of my estate to my Trustees to distribute between any of my brothers Gervais Louden and Dewey Louden and my sister Hettie Louden as shall survive me in such shares as my Trustees shall at their absolute discretion decide.

AS WITNESS my hand this *fourth* day of *July* 2000

Signed by me **RICHARD WAYNE LOUDEN**

R W Louden III

Signed by the Testator in our presence and then by us in the presence of the Testator and of each other

	Witness 1	Witness 2
Signature:	A C Wardell	J Merriweather
Full Name:	Adrian Charles Wardell	June Merriweather
Address:	Wardell James, Wakefield	Wardell James, Wakefield
Occupation:	Solicitor	Secretary

Consider this

Take a look at the will of Ricky Louden the Third and prepare answers to the following questions:

1. Are you able to distribute the gifts listed in clauses 3, 4 and 5 of the will?

2. If you are not able to distribute the gifts, why not?

 Handy tip: Is the nature of each gift certain? Can you name the subject matter of the gift and the object to which it is being given?

A situation arises

A trainee solicitor from your department comes into your office. She is worried because she has received a telephone call from a rather hysterical Marshall Louden. Apparently there is some problem with the terms of the will and Mr Louden is insisting on a call back from somebody senior within the hour. You reassure her that you will deal with the matter and ask for details of the call. The trainee leaves you with her telephone attendance note and returns to her desk. The attendance note reads as follows:

Document 2

TELEPHONE ATTENDANCE

Name:	Mylee Shah
File Reference:	LOUDEN/LOU01458
Date:	16 February 2010
Time:	11.20 a.m.
Length of Call:	40 minutes

A Marshall Louden called. He is the brother of Ricky Louden III. He has seen a copy of the will and is very upset at the contents of one of the clauses. Apparently the will requires him to look after a spider, but he suffers from severe arachnophobia and breaks out into hives if he even hears mention of a spider. He is furious because his brother knew of his disability and feels he did this to spite him. He is also very annoyed that he has not been named with his brothers and sisters to receive a gift from the residue of the estate.

He wants to know if he can keep the money but not the spider, or whether he could give the spider away. Mr Louden says female tarantulas live for a really long time and that it would turn his life into a 'perpetual hell'. Mr Louden is even more upset that the spider is to be fed on a diet of live locusts, as this offends his strict vegetarian moral code. He wishes to know if he is forced to keep the spider, whether he can feed it a vegetarian diet. He also wondered whether he could use some of the money to treat his arachnophobia, given that he had been charged with its care.

He became very angry when I struggled to answer his questions and said that he wanted a call back from 'someone with clout' within the hour.

Consider this

You now have only 30 minutes to answer Mr Louden's call. Take a look at the telephone attendance note and consider how you are going to respond.

 Handy tip: Try thinking about what type of trust has been created here. What would prevent the trust from being valid? If the trust is invalid, where would the money go?

A piece of correspondence

Your secretary brings a letter in to you which relates to the Louden file. It is from the deceased's half-sister, Annabelle Holding. The letter reads as follows:

Document 3

Annabelle Holding
Crabapple Cottage
Orchard Lane
Arnoldswick
Lancashire

Wardell James Solicitors
Lamb Lane
Wakefield
West Yorkshire
WF2 4JP

14 February 2010

Dear Sirs,

My name is Annabelle Holding and I am the half-sister of Ricky Louden, who I believe is your client. We share the same father, although we have different mothers.

Ricky and I have always been close and Ricky has always gone out of his way to help me financially, especially by giving generous and regular donations to the Rainbow Days Donkey Sanctuary, which I founded in 1986 and which I run here in Arnoldswick. To be honest, without his financial input the sanctuary would never have survived as long as it has and me and the donkeys would have been home-less many years ago.

It is for this reason that I was rather surprised to see that Ricky had not left anything in his will, either to me, or to Rainbow Days. I was still more surprised to see that he had left a substantial sum to the British Arachnid Preservation Trust, a charity in which he has never previously expressed an interest.

I think I have found a solution to the problem, however. I learned from a local newspaper that the British Arachnid Preservation Trust has disbanded, and an old solicitor friend of mine mentioned that the money which had been set aside in the will for them might be able to be applied to another charitable use. I wondered if it would be possible to give the royalties from Ricky's records to Rainbow Days instead. As I said before, I know it is a cause which Ricky was a great supporter of, and I am sure he would be happy for the money to go to this good cause, given that his first choice of charity is no longer in existence.

I look forward to hearing from you.

Yours faithfully,

Annabelle Holding

Annabelle Holding

On reading the letter, you decide to carry out a quick check on the charitable status of the British Arachnid Preservation Trust and you discover that Annabelle is right – the charity has gone into administration. Armed with this knowledge you should now prepare the following:

Writing and drafting

Write a response to Ms Holding, advising her on whether the monies can be applied as she wishes, giving reasons for your answer. Remember to start and end your letter in the correct form.

You should take no more than 30 minutes on this task.

 Handy tip: Consider the doctrine of cy près. Can it be applied and, if so, how?

Reflective practice

What if no charity can be found with similar purposes to the British Arachnid Preservation Trust? Would this make any difference to your answer? If not, how would the money be applied and on what grounds?

Administering the trusts

Mr Wardell asks you to come and see him in his office. He wants an update on the work you have carried out so far on the Louden file. You apprise him of your progress to date and Mr Wardell seems pleased with what you have done. However, he says that it is now time for you to turn your attention to what he considers to be the main body of work on the file: the administration of the trusts contained in clauses 7 and 8 of the will. He tells you that he has arranged a first meeting of the trustees on Thursday 25 February to discuss matters further, but in the meantime he would like you to get the ball rolling by finding out the following:

Consider this

1. What are the nature of the trusts listed in clauses 7 and 8 of the will?

2. Is there any additional information you might need in order to administer these trusts effectively?

Handy tip: Think about what practical information you need to know to administer the will: are you able to name all of the beneficiaries? What is the entitlement of each individual beneficiary? Is there anything which might prevent you from distributing the money to them? Why not try drawing up a list of what you need to know before embarking on the management of the trust.

Realising that you need a significant amount of extra information to administer the trust, you set about doing some additional researches to find out the identities of the beneficiaries and to glean what information you can about each one. Your findings are as follows:

Document 4

Personal information on the beneficiaries to the Ricky Louden will

Brothers and sisters

Marshall Louden, brother. Age 54. Lives at 35 Rountree Gardens, Ossett. Humanitarian rights campaigner.

Gervais Louden, brother. Age 49. Lives at Mount House, Kirkella, East Yorkshire. House husband. Married to Tracey Louden who runs her own business making and selling designer bridalwear.

Dewey Louden, brother. Age 49. Twin brother of Gervais. Divorced with two children, Craig and Hannah Louden. Died last year in a canoeing incident off the North Yorkshire coast.

Hettie Louden, sister. Age 43. Suffers with Down syndrome. Lives in a special needs community at the Clear Horizons Village Trust, Scotton Village, Richmond, North Yorkshire.

Annabelle Holding, half-sister. Age 38. Lives at Crabapple Cottage, Orchard Lane, Arnoldswick, Lancashire. Runs the Rainbow Days Donkey Sanctuary. Long-standing financial dependence on the deceased. Not a beneficiary under the terms of the will.

Nephews and nieces

Sheena Louden, age 22. Daughter of Gervais and Tracey Louden. Works with mother in the family business. Lives with parents at Mount House.

Barry Louden, age 20. Son of Gervais and Tracey Louden. Currently studying mechanical engineering at the University of Northumbria. Living in student digs in Newbottle.

Cecily Louden, age 17. Daughter of Gervais and Tracey Louden. Living at home with parents whilst studying for A Levels at a local private school.

Craig Louden, age 12. Son of Dewey Louden. Lives with mother in Kirk Upton, Huddersfield. Currently attending local comprehensive school in Huddersfield.

Hannah Louden, age 12. Daughter of Dewey and twin sister of Craig Louden. Lives with mother in Kirk Upton, Huddersfield. Currently attending local comprehensive school in Huddersfield. Talented ballerina. Has been awarded a place at the Royal Ballet School in London.

Neither Marshall nor Hettie has any children.

Reflective practice

Compare the above with the list of additional information required that you compiled earlier. How does it compare? Does it include any information you had not thought to ask for? Is there any further information you think you need which is still missing?

Letters from the beneficiaries

In advance of the meeting, a number of letters start trickling into the office from the various beneficiaries under the will. The letters read as follows:

Document 5

3a Forth Street
Newbottle
NB1 2HA

16 February 2010

Wardell James Solicitors
Lamb Lane
Wakefield
West Yorkshire
WF2 4JP

Dear Trustees,

I understand you are acting in the matter of my late Uncle's will. My sister tells me that we have been left £100,000 each in trust until we reach the age of 25.

I am currently studying at the University of Northumbria and, as a student in my second year of study, times are pretty hard. I was therefore wondering if it would be possible to get an advance on some of the money. I do not need much: I have a student loan which I would like to clear plus an overdraft of around £4,000.

I also wondered whether I could get some money towards my living expenses. I have a small allowance from my mum and dad but it is not really enough and once I have paid my rent there is very little left to go around.

I do hope you can help and look forward to hearing from you.

Thanks.

Barry

Barry Louden

Document 6

Mount House
Kirkella
East Yorkshire
HU10 1SR

17 February 2010

Wardell James Solicitors
Lamb Lane
Wakefield
West Yorkshire
WF2 4JP

Dear Trustees,

Re: Ricky Louden, deceased

I am the brother of the deceased and one of the beneficiaries under his will, as are my children, Sheena, Barry and Cecily. I am writing to ask you when we will be entitled to our shares of the money and if it is possible to have some money for the children straightaway.

My eldest daughter, Sheena, works with my wife in the family business, Country (and Western) Brides. Sheena has some great ideas about how she would like to expand the business and would like to put the whole of her £100,000 share into product development and a marketing scheme covering a number of bridal fairs around the country over the next 12 months. She is really excited about working with her mother on this new project and is keen to do this as soon as possible.

My son and youngest daughter are still in full-time education: Barry is at university and Cecily is at the local independent girls' school, Newlane School for Girls. Until now, their mother and I have been funding their education, but I feel it only fair, given their substantial inheritances, that their school and university fees should come out of their own funds from now on.

In addition, Cecily has decided to take a gap year next year and has asked me if she can have some money to go travelling round Europe. Her mother and I cannot possibly afford such an extravagant trip, but presumably she can have some money out of her share of the trust fund for this. Cecily tells me the trip will cost around £3,000 for the air ticket, accommodation and spending money.

Please could you let me know as soon as possible when we will receive the money for these things and also when I am to receive my share of the inheritance.

Yours sincerely

Gervais Louden

Document 7

The Crow's Nest
Kirk Upton
Huddersfield

Wardell James Solicitors
Lamb Lane
Wakefield
West Yorkshire
WF2 4JP

18 February 2010

Dear Sirs,

Louden Estate Trust

My children, Craig and Hannah, are the nephew and niece of the late Ricky Louden. The children's father was my first husband, Dewey Louden, who was Ricky's brother.

The children, who are twins, both attend a local comprehensive school in Huddersfield. My daughter, Hannah, is a very talented ballerina and has recently won a place at the Royal Ballet School in London. Unfortunately the fees are way outside my league and her father left no money to provide for her so I was wondering whether any money might be forthcoming from the trust to pay for her school fees and boarding (given that we are too far from London to commute). It would be a pity to see such a talent go to waste but there is no way we could afford this on our own.

As far as Craig is concerned, he seems very happy at the local school but he is a lazy boy and a bit of a dreamer and I feel he would be better placed at an independent school, where he would receive more individual attention and better discipline. I would like to send him to Huddersbank Grammar, which is an excellent private school in the area. Please could you let me know if it would be possible to pay for this out of his share of the inheritance.

And finally, I should like £50,000 from each of the children's shares to go towards a larger family home for them to live in with me and their step-father, Alan. The house is very small and, whilst it was adequate when I was on my own with two small children, now that there are four of us and the children are getting so big, things are becoming rather fraught and I think more space would do us all good.

I do hope you can help and look forward to hearing from you.

Yours faithfully

Marcia M. Hughes

Consider this

Now that you have read through the letters, take some time to think about whether you would grant the various individuals' requests – you will be required as a trustee to make decisions on these matters and to respond in due course. In particular, you may wish to consider whether you will require any additional information from the beneficiaries before you are able to make a decision.

 Handy tip: You need to think about how, if at all, you are able to advance sums of money to these people. Have you considered the powers of advancement and maintenance under sections 31 and 32 of the Trustee Act 1925?

The memorandum

It is Monday 22 February and you arrive in the office to find an internal memo on your desk from the senior partner, Mr Wardell. The memo reads as follows:

Document 8

INTERNAL MEMORANDUM

To: Nathan Soames
From: Adrian Wardell
File Reference: LOUDEN/LOU01458
Date: 22 February 2010

Nathan,

I have been called away from the office all week on urgent business and so will be unable to make the first trustee meeting on the Louden file. With regard to the discretionary trust, my experience is that the best way to deal with such matters is simply to divide the money equally between the parties involved; I have written to Gervais and Hettie informing them of our intentions.

I have not had an opportunity to look at the nephews and nieces' correspondence, however. Please would you write to them in response to their various queries and requests. I am happy to go along with whatever you decide in relation to these.

Regards,

It seems you have no choice but to make the decisions by yourself and write to the beneficiaries with your findings!

Writing and drafting

You should have already considered your responses to the beneficiaries when you looked at their letters in the earlier exercise. Now it is time to put pen to paper. Write letters to Sheena, Barry, Cecily and the twins (or their parents, as appropriate) detailing your findings, remembering to start and end your letters correctly.

Handy tip: Remember, you may not be granting all of their requests at this stage – you may just be asking for additional information from some of them.

Reflective practice

Do you think there is anything wrong with the way in which you and Mr Wardell have conducted your trustee business? Have you both complied with your duties as trustees?

A summary of assets

You now realise that, in order to distribute the residue to Mr Louden's brother and sister, you need to know how much the residue of the estate amounts to, so you request a copy of the estate summary from the wills and probate department. The summary of assets reads as follows:

Document 9

RICHARD WAYNE LOUDEN DECEASED

Summary of assets

Assets:

Freehold house 'Green Trees', Ossett	£300,000
Personal chattels (incl. car)	£ 6,000
Barclays Bank plc current account	£ 3,000
Bradford & Bingley building society account	£ 250
National Savings certificates	£ 300
Shares in British Telecommunications plc	£ 450
Scottish Widows life insurance cover	£250,000
Annual income from royalties on record sales	£ 50,000
Total assets:	£610,000

Debts:

Goldfish credit card	(£ 7,600)
Yorkshire Water	(£ 200)
Sampson & Sons funeral directors	(£ 2,200)
Balance:	**£600,000**

Consider this

Take a look at the figures above. Can you work out how much the residue is? Look back through the information you have been given so far and the work you have done on the Louden file. Is there anything which might change the amount of the residue?

 Handy tip: Take another look at clauses 4, 5 and 6 of the Will. What did you decide about the validity of these clauses? Where would the money go if the clauses failed?

Investing the trust monies

Mr Wardell has now returned from his business trip and asks for a progress report. You bring him up to date on the file and show him copies of the letters you have written. Whilst he seems pleased with your conduct of the file, he is concerned that the trust monies have not yet been invested in any way – and in particular the nephews and nieces' fund, which will continue to run for a number of years. The funds are currently sitting in the firm's client bank account and Mr Wardell is keen that the money is invested as soon as possible.

Investment revision exercise

What can you remember about the rules of investment for trustees? Here is a little revision exercise. You should answer the following questions:

1. Why do trustees have a duty to invest?
2. Where does the power of investment come from, and what does it enable trustees to do?
3. What standard of care does a trustee have to abide by when making investments?
4. Does a higher standard of care apply to you as a solicitor?
5. What are the 'standard investment criteria'?
6. What is the requirement to obtain advice?
7. Can the duty to invest be delegated to a third party?
8. How often should you review your investments?

Hopefully the revision questions above will have jogged your memory about the rules of investment for trustees and, of course, you can always refer back to Chapter 12 of the book for more detail on the subject. Making decisions on how to invest trust property is one of the most important functions of a trustee where there is an ongoing trust, and these are very real considerations for anyone administering one.

Consider this

What steps would you take on the Louden file to ensure that the trust funds are properly invested?

 Handy tip: Remember, you are not an investment specialist – it may make sense to delegate your powers to someone who is!

Trouble on the horizon

It is the end of a long week and you are just switching off your computer ready to leave the office for the weekend, when Mr Wardell comes in and says he needs a 'quiet word'. Apparently he has just been on the telephone to his god-daughter, Hannah Louden. It appears that the child has just been told by her head teacher that she is being removed from the school because of non-payment of her school fees.

Mr Wardell goes on to explain that he had been making regular payments to Hannah's mother by standing order to cover the cost of Hannah's schooling, on the assumption that the mother would apply the funds in the correct way – little did he know that she would be using the money for altogether different purposes! Mr Wardell asks you to sort the mess out before it is too late and then leaves the office. With your vision of a quiet, work-free weekend vanishing before your eyes you sit back down at your desk and pick up the telephone . . .

Document 10

TELEPHONE ATTENDANCE

Name:	Nathan Soames
File Reference:	LOUDEN/LOU01458
Date:	21 May 2010
Time:	5.30 p.m.
Length of Call:	55 minutes

Spoke to the twins' mother, Marcia Hughes. I asked her what had happened to the money which had been sent to her to pay her daughter's school fees. After some initial resistance she broke down and said that she and her husband had spent the money. She blamed her husband for this, saying that he had always been jealous of the twins' money, and jealous of the fact that it had come from her uncle, who he considered a 'talentless individual'. He said that they needed the money more than the twins, persuading her first to use the money to pay off their £7,000 overdraft, and then for a new car costing £10,000, and a luxury cruise for the two of them, in lieu of the honeymoon they had never been able to take because of family commitments, costing a further £6,000. Marcia also said that they she had transferred some of the money into a savings account. A little of this remained, the rest she had given in several instalments to her 'sister-in-law' (Ricky's half-sister, Annabelle Holding) for whom Marcia felt sorry due to her financial circumstances. Annabelle has been spending the money on donkey food and her own upkeep. It would appear that, of the £25,000 taken, only £1,500 remains in the savings account, the rest having been spent as detailed.

Consider this

1. Make a list of the monies taken. What, if anything, can you recover from Marcia and Annabelle?

2. How might this situation have been avoided?

 Handy tip: You will need to use what you have learned about tracing and the liability of strangers to answer this question.

A few weeks later you receive the following internal memorandum from Mr Wardell:

Document 11

INTERNAL MEMORANDUM

To:	Nathan Soames
From:	Adrian Wardell
File Reference:	LOUDEN/LOU01458
Date:	8 June 2010

Nathan,

I am afraid my business is taking me out of the office more and more and, given my prolonged absence, I feel unable to continue to act in the best interests of the trust as a trustee.

I have asked the managing partner of the firm, Leslie James, to step into the breach and take up my place as the second trustee of the Louden trusts, whilst you remain at the helm as the other trustee. Please would you draft the documentation to make the necessary changes as soon as possible. I am leaving the office on Thursday afternoon and will not be returning for some weeks, so it is vital this is done before then.

Regards,

A ddy

You know what you must do!

Writing and drafting

Draft a deed of appointment and retirement to effect the changes detailed in Mr Wardell's memo.

 Handy tip: Don't know where to start? Try looking elsewhere in the book for a precedent . . .

A final blow

As if things are not already complicated enough, you receive the following letter in the post from Clear Horizons Village Trust:

Document 12

Clear Horizons Village Trust
Scotton Village
Richmond
North Yorkshire

Wardell James Solicitors
Lamb Lane
Wakefield
West Yorkshire
WF2 4JP

14 June 2010

Dear Sirs,

In the estate of Ricky Louden III, deceased

We act in the interests of the deceased's sister, Hettie Louden.

You may be aware that Hettie suffers with Down syndrome, and that she is quite severely disabled, both mentally and physically, as a result of this. Hattie lives with us in an assisted community at Scotton Village, North Yorkshire. The Village, which is especially designed to help people like Hattie, is run and financed through the charitable trust, the Clear Horizons Village Trust. Whilst we are a registered charity, we are still very much reliant on donations from our residents and their families for our survival and Mr Louden has been a regular and generous benefactor since 2003, when Hettie came to live with us.

It is our understanding that the residue of the estate, a proportion of which Hettie is entitled to receive, may amount to nothing once the payment of the other legacies and debts has been made. In the best interests of Hettie, therefore, it is our intention to make a claim against the estate under the Inheritance (Provision for Family and Dependants) Act 1975 in order to secure her long-term future within our community.

We will be writing to you further with full details in due course. However, you should take this letter as notice of our intention to proceed with a claim.

Yours faithfully

Jake Singleton

Clear Horizons Village Trust

It would appear that a claim is being made against the estate. You decide that you had better find out whether there is any basis to their claim – time for a bit of research:

Research

Go on line and find a copy of the Inheritance (Provision for Family and Dependants) Act 1975. Now answer the following questions:

1. Who is able to make a claim under the terms of the Act?

2. How and where is a 'dependant' defined within the Act?

3. What is 'reasonable financial provision'?

4. What matters should the court take into account when making an order under the terms of the Act?

5. Do you think Hettie is entitled to make a claim under the Act? If not, why not?

6. What kind of order could the court make in favour of Hettie?

 Handy tip: If you are struggling to find a copy of the Act, try going on to the website for the Office of Public Sector Information at **http://www.opsi.gov.uk** and searching for the Act there by reference to the year.

Consider this

Do you think that either of the following persons will be able to make a claim under the Inheritance (Provision for Family and Dependants) Act 1975? State reasons for your answers:

(a) Marshall Louden

(b) Annabelle Holding

Alas, the Clear Horizons Trust's threat to take court action against you under the Inheritance (Provision for Family and Dependants) Act 1975 has taken the matter beyond the scope of your department. You have no choice but to pass the file over to the litigation team.

File round-up

Before you pass your file over to the litigation department it might be helpful to have a look back through the chapter and reflect upon the various areas of law that you have considered. The key academic areas from the book that you have covered in this chapter are as follows:

First, you looked at the issue of certainty in respect of some of the gifts the testator purported to leave in his will, which we covered in detail in Chapter 3 of the book; and in particular you considered the issue of making gifts to unincorporated associations and some of the difficulties which can be encountered with purpose trusts, which were dealt with in Chapter 4. You also considered a gift made to a charity and looked into the issue of cy près, all of which were dealt with at Chapter 5 of the text.

Then you moved on to consider the administration of two trusts created under the terms of the will and you made some practical decisions on whether to advance monies under the trusts under the provisions for maintenance and advancement set out in sections 31 and 32 of the Trustee Act 1925. Maintenance and advancement, you will remember, were covered in Chapter 11 of the book. You were also given the opportunity to consider the conduct of the matter by the trustees and whether there might be a breach of trust in the way in which they had carried out their duties. Duties of trustees were dealt with at Chapter 10. There was a short exercise on the investment of trust funds, recapping on what you learned in Chapter 12 of the book, and then you were asked to consider breaches of trust and the liability of strangers to the trust, as well as a little bit of tracing; these matters were covered at Chapters 13, 14 and 15. And finally, you were asked to consider the appointment and retirement of trustees and to draft a deed of appointment, which recapped on Chapter 9.

The various writing and drafting exercises were designed to get you thinking practically as a lawyer would and to give you practice in some of the skills you will need to use as a solicitor or barrister. The little bit of academic research which took you outside the scope of the book at the end of this chapter was hopefully both a useful and interesting tool which should help to form the foundation of your practical legal research skills.

If you have been struggling with any of the areas covered in this chapter, the above summary should point you in the right direction in terms of the chapters you perhaps need to look back at or revise a little more. In addition, you will find guidance on the accompanying website to this book at **www.mylawchamber.co.uk/warner-reed**.

Visit **www.mylawchamber.co.uk/warner-reed** to access study support resources including practice exam questions with guidance, interactive 'You be the judge' multiple choice questions, annotated weblinks, glossary and key case flashcards and audio legal updates all linked to the **Pearson eText** version of *Equity and Trusts* which you can **search**, **highlight** and **personalise** with your **own notes** and **bookmarks**.

Glossary

Note: Glossary terms are highlighted in the text in **black bold**

Account of profits The equitable process or remedy whereby the court orders the trustees to account to the beneficiaries for monies going in and out of the trust account, in circumstances where the beneficiaries believe one or more trustees have made a secret profit from the trust.

Account on the basis of wilful default The equitable process or remedy whereby the court orders the trustees to account to the beneficiaries for monies going in and out of the trust account, in circumstances where one or more of the trustees is suspected either of foul play or extreme negligence in the administration of the trust.

Acquiesced/acquiescence A defence claimed by trustees in breach of trust whereby the trustees claim that the beneficiaries are unable to bring an action against them because they knew about the breach and either did nothing about it or otherwise allowed it to happen.

Action The legal term for a case or law suit brought in the civil courts.

Administrative unworkability The situation in which a trust is held invalid on the basis that it would be either impractical or impossible to administer, usually because of the enormity of the class of beneficiaries it is designed to benefit.

Administrator (in insolvency) An authorised insolvency practitioner who is appointed to manage the affairs, business and property of a company that has gone into administration (that is, it has gone bust).

Administrator (in probate) A person appointed by the court to collect in and distribute the assets and liabilities of a person who has died without making a valid will.

Administratrix A female administrator.

Ad valorem stamp duty The tax payable on the value of an instrument or document of transfer under the old stamp duty regime.

Advancement (power of) The power given to trustees to advance up to half of a beneficiary's share of the capital bulk of the trust fund for the beneficiary's benefit or advancement in life.

Agency A contractual arrangement whereby one person or business is authorised to act on another's behalf, either generally or to carry out a specific task (such as estate agency).

Agent A person authorised to act on behalf of another under a contractual arrangement.

Ancillary relief A payment of money awarded by the court by way of a final settlement to either party in cases of divorce or judicial separation.

Anton Piller order Also known as a search and seizure order, this is a type of court order that gives the holder the right to search premises and seize evidence without prior warning. The primary purpose of the order is to prevent the destruction of evidence against the defendant in a case.

'Arm's length' A transaction between two unrelated people or businesses that are not connected to each other in any way.

Assign/assignment The legal process whereby the remaining term of a lease is transferred from a seller to a buyer (or donor to donee).

Automatic resulting trust A trust created informally in favour of the settlor, on account of the fact that the settlor has tried to create a trust in favour of another but has somehow failed to transfer the beneficial interest in the property effectively.

Bailee The holder of property under a bailment agreement.

Bailment An agreement (usually contractual) under which the legal owner of property places that property under the physical control or possession of another for a specified period or pur

Bailor The legal owner of propert ferred possession or control of thei the terms of a bailment agreement.

Bare legal title Refers to the situation in which the legal owner of property holds the legal title of the property alone, but does not retain any beneficial interest in it, such as in the case of trustees of a trust.

Beneficial interest/ownership The right which a person has to enjoy property, regardless of whether they also have legal ownership of it. A beneficiary under a trust is the beneficial owner of the trust property. The term is interchangeable with that of 'equitable ownership'.

Beneficiary The person who is entitled to receive the benefit of a trust or a will. Also known as the object of the trust.

Beneficiary principle The legal doctrine which states that a trust must have a human beneficiary in order to be valid.

Benjamin order An order of the court which allows the trustees to distribute a trust fund or assets under a will where one of the beneficiaries cannot be traced.

Bequeath The act of giving or leaving property by will.

Bequest A gift made under the terms of a will.

Bona vacantia The common law doctrine under which property for which no owner can be found is claimed by the Crown.

Bona fide purchaser for value without notice A person who buys property in good faith, or innocently, without knowledge of any claim a third party might have to that property.

Breach of contract The simple failure of a party to a contract to adhere to its terms and conditions.

Capacity In the context of trust law, the ability of a person to create a trust or will, in terms both of mental capability and being of the required age.

Capital The money or property which forms the basis of a trust fund. Thus, if £100,000 was put into trust for Sue until she reached the age of 18, the capital of the trust fund would be the £100,000 itself.

Chancery (court of) The court which has jurisdiction to deal with matters of equity (as opposed to the common law). The court of equity.

Charge The process whereby a third party imposes an obligation or claim against property in respect of money owing to them by the owner. The charge entitles the person in possession of it to claim that property as against the loan, should the property owner fail to repay them.

Charging clause A clause in a trust deed or will which allows professional trustees or executors to receive payment for professional services carried out in connection with the trust or will.

Chattel Any article of personal, moveable property, for example a car or pocket watch.

Claimant The person who brings an action in a civil court of law. Formerly called plaintiff.

Class of beneficiaries A group of beneficiaries determined by reference to a common factor, such as nephews and nieces, or employees of a company.

Common account The equitable process or remedy whereby the court orders the trustees to account to the beneficiaries for monies going in and out of the trust account, in circumstances where the trustees have failed to do so.

Common intention constructive trust A constructive trust imposed in the situation where there is no evidence of an actual agreement between the parties, but where it can be shown that it was the intention of both parties that they would share the beneficial ownership of the property.

Common law The system of legal principles developed through the courts and by the decisions of judges. The system of law which runs parallel to the law of equity.

Completely constituted A trust can be said to be completely constituted when the legal ownership of the trust property has been formally conveyed to the trustees. A trust cannot function fully until it has been completely constituted.

Conceptual uncertainty A trust will fail on grounds of conceptual uncertainty if its terms are not sufficiently precise to allow the trustees to administer the trust. For example, a gift to 'my colleagues' would be conceptually uncertain, because the word 'colleagues' means different things to different people. Equally a gift of 'my gold ring' would be conceptually uncertain if the donor had more than one gold ring, because there would be no way for the trustees to establish to which ring the donor was referring.

Consideration A legal term for payment, either monetary or in the form of goods or reciprocal services. See also Marriage consideration.

Constructive trust An informal trust imposed by operation of law in any situation where the conduct of one party is so unconscionable that to allow any other outcome would be unjust.

Contempt of court An order declared by the court where one party to an action has either disobeyed the court or acted in a disrespectful manner towards it. Contempt of court can bring with it the criminal sanctions of a fine or imprisonment.

Contingent interest An interest which is dependent on the happening of some future event which is not certain, such as coming of age.

Conveyance A document effecting the legal transfer of property. The term is most commonly associated with transfers of land.

Coogan's Law The common name for the Child Actors Bill, which protects the rights of child actors in the USA and offers some measure of protection in respect of any earnings made during the child's infancy.

Co-ownership The situation in which two or more persons own property together. The term is most commonly associated with the ownership of land.

Covenant A promise made in a deed.

Covenant to settle A deed in which the settlor promises to create a trust of specified property.

Cy près The equitable doctrine which allows monies given to charity to be redirected to another charity with similar aims, if the named charity ceases to exist.

Damages The common law remedy under which a sum of money is paid by the defaulting party in respect of loss or injury, in an action for a breach of contract or tort.

Declaration (of the court) A declaration made by the court that the trustees should or should not behave in a particular way, thus requiring the trustees to do their duty under the terms of the trust.

Declaration of trust A statement made by a trustee (usually in writing) in which the trustee acknowledges that either they or a third party are to hold the legal title to property on behalf of someone else (the beneficiary of the trust).

Deed A legal document which is signed and witnessed. Unlike a contract, a deed does not require consideration in order to be valid. A deed is usually used for the transfer of property or the grant of a right.

Deed of appointment/retirement A deed which has the purpose of appointing a new trustee or effecting the retirement of an existing trustee.

Deed of family arrangement A document made between the beneficiaries under a will to vary the terms of the will after the testator has died.

Deed of gift A deed used to transfer property from one person to another by way of gift.

Deed of release A deed which has the purpose of releasing, or exempting, a person from liability under the terms of the trust.

Deed of retirement See Deed of appointment/retirement

Defendant The person against whom the claim is made in a legal action.

Deferred gift/interest A gift or interest which does not start immediately, but which is dependent upon the happening of a future event. This may simply be the arrival of a date in the future, or it may be the death of a third party, a marriage, and so on.

Direct contributions In the context of resulting and constructive trusts, means any payment representing a direct contribution to the purchase price of the property (including the making of mortgage payments).

Disclaim/disclaimer of trusteeship The situation where a trustee renounces their position as trustee. If a person disclaims their trusteeship they are considered never to have been a trustee.

Discretionary trust A trust in which the trustees are given a discretion as to how, or to whom (but not whether) to distribute the trust fund.

Dishonest assistance The situation in which a third party, or stranger, to the trust is held liable for assisting a trustee to commit a breach of trust.

Dissent/dissenting judgment A judgment given by one or more of the judges in a case which conflicts, or disagrees with, the decision of the majority.

Dividend A distribution of profits to the shareholders of a company, based on the number of shares owned.

Doctrine of laches See Laches, doctrine of

Doctrines of equity An accepted group of principles or rules, held by the court of equity.

Donatio mortis causa A gift made in contemplation of death.

Donee The legal term for the recipient of a gift.

Donor The legal term for the person making a gift.

Equitable interest An interest in the equitable, or beneficial, rights in property. The person with the equitable interest in property has the right to benefit from it, or enjoy it. A beneficiary under a trust is the holder of the beneficial interest in the trust property.

Equitable maxims See Maxims of equity

Equity The system of law in England and Wales designed to provide remedies for wrongs which were traditionally not legally recognised under the common law.

Equity (court of) see Chancery (court of).

Estate A term commonly used to describe the whole of a person's wealth, including property of all types owned by that person, at any particular time: usually on death.

Evidential uncertainty Refers to the inability of the trustees to administer the trust on account of difficulties in proving the identity of (usually) the beneficiaries under the trust. An example might be where a gift is made to 'the class of '89', but the class records have been destroyed.

Exchange of contracts On a sale of land, the point at which both parties become legally and contractually bound to complete the transfer of the property.

Executor The person who is appointed to administer the estate of someone who has died leaving a valid will.

Executorship The role of acting as an executor or executrix.

Executrix A female executor.

Exemption clause A clause in a contract or deed which excludes the liability of one or more of the parties either wholly or partially.

Ex parte Refers to the case where an application is made to court without the knowledge of the other party. Often done in the case of applications for an emergency injunction.

Exporting the trust This is where the administration of a trust is relocated to a foreign jurisdiction.

Express trust A trust created expressly, with the intention of the settlor.

Fair dealing The purchase by a trustee of the beneficial interests of any of the beneficiaries under the trust. Such a purchase can be set aside by the beneficiary if it can be proved that the trustee abused their position in making the purchase.

Fiduciary A person placed in a position of trust, such as a trustee to a beneficiary, a director to a company or a solicitor to a client.

Fiduciary duty In the context of trusts, the legal duty of a fiduciary to act in the best interests of the beneficiary.

Final injunction An injunction which forms part of the final judgment of the court in a case. See also Interim injunction.

Fixed trust A trust in which the trustees are given no discretion as to how the trust is to be administered.

Formality/formalities The formal steps which need to be taken to complete the trust (for example, the transfer of the trust property to the trustees).

Freehold The right to hold land in perpetuity. The nearest equivalent to absolute ownership of land as exists in England and Wales (ultimate ownership remaining with the Crown).

Freezing injunction An injunction preventing the defendant from moving property or assets out of the reach of the claimant before the matter gets to court, either by moving them out of the UK, or from one jurisdiction to another.

Fusion of common law and equity Refers to the administrative unification of the courts of law and equity, so that both arms of the law, whilst remaining separate, are now able to be administered out of the same court.

Future interest A claim on property which will come into being at some point in the future, usually on the happening of a future event.

General power A power to appoint which is not made subject to any restrictions.

Gift over In the context of life interests, a gift which comes into being on the expiration of the life interest. A gift over is what the remainderman will receive upon the death of the life tenant.

Grant of probate The legal document which authorises the executors under the will to administer the deceased person's estate.

Grantor/grantee The legal term for the person who grants a right or who is the recipient of a right.

Heirs Refers to those relatives who would inherit the estate of a deceased person under the laws of intestacy if the deceased died without a will.

Hybrid power In the context of a trust, a power given to the trustees to distribute the trust fund amongst anyone *except for* a specified class of beneficiaries. See also General power and Special power.

Imperfect gift A gift which fails, usually because the correct formalities have not been followed to complete its legal transfer.

Implied common intention In the context of constructive trusts, where the intention of the parties to share the beneficial ownership of the property is implied because there is no evidence of an express agreement between them.

Implied trusts Generic name for trusts which have been informally created, encompassing both resulting and constructive trusts.

Impounding (a beneficiary's interest) The situation in which a beneficiary's interest is claimed by the trustees or the court, in lieu of their liability under a breach of trust.

Incompletely constituted A trust will be incompletely constituted where it has not complied with all the required formalities to complete the trust, such as the transfer of legal ownership of the trust property to the trustees. An incompletely constituted trust cannot be enforced.

Incorporated/incorporated association A person or organisation which has been formed into a legal corporation with the ability to act as an independent legal entity. A company.

Indemnity Where a person or persons are given protection or immunity against damage or loss.

Independent person A person who is in no way related or connected with another. Not a family member of anyone who may benefit from the transaction in question.

Indirect contributions In the context of resulting and constructive trusts, contributions which do not relate directly to the purchase price of the property, such as payment for improvements to the property or household expenses.

Infant In legal terms, a child under the age of 18.

Inherent jurisdiction The overarching judicial power of the court to make judgment on any particular matter.

Injunction An order of the court requiring the person in question to do something, or refrain from doing something. An injunction is an equitable remedy.

Innocent volunteer Any person who receives trust property as a gift innocently, or without knowledge of any breach of trust.

In personam A claim made against an individual, as opposed to against a piece of property.

In rem A proprietary claim directed at a specific piece of property, rather than a claim being made against a person.

Insolvent The legal term for a person or more commonly a company that has insufficient funds to cover its debts. Bankrupt.

Intangible property Property which can be owned but which has no physical presence, such as stocks and shares, or intellectual property such as copyright.

Interim injunction An injunction made as a holding measure, whilst the final outcome of the case is still pending.

Intermediate income The income received on a trust fund in the period before the fund is distributed.

Inter vivos trusts Lifetime trusts. Trusts made during the lifetime of the settlor (as opposed to trusts created by will).

Intestate/intestacy The situation in which a person dies without having made a will.

Issue The descendants of a person, including children, grandchildren and so on.

Joint and several liability Where a number of persons are held equally liable for compensation or loss. In such circumstances, the claimant may claim the whole of the loss from any or all of those jointly and severally liable. This means that one person may become liable for the whole loss, if the others have no money or cannot be found, for example.

Joint tenants A method of co-ownership of property whereby the co-owners together own the whole as a single group, rather than having divisible quantified shares.

Judicial notice The ability of the court to recognise and accept the existence of a commonly known fact without the need for proof of that fact (for example, that Christmas Day is the 25 December).

Judicial trustee Trustees appointed by the court under the Judicial Trustees Act 1896 where the existing trustees have administered the trust badly.

***Keech* v. *Sandford*, rule in** The rule which prevents a trustee from renewing a lease in their own individual name that was formerly held by the trust. Any lease taken on in this way can be set aside by the beneficiaries of the trust.

Knowing receipt The receipt by a third party of trust property in breach of trust.

Laches, doctrine of The legal doctrine by which a person is prevented from bringing an action because they have delayed in making a claim.

Land Register/Registry See Register.

Lay person/lay trustee A person acting in their private or personal capacity, without the benefit of professional skills.

Leasehold Ownership of property which lasts for a limited period of time, in accordance with the terms of a lease.

Legacy A gift made in a will.

Legal title The legal basis on which a person is able to assert their ownership of property.

Life in being The human life against which the perpetuity period is measured at common law, in the context of trusts.

Life interest An interest in property which lasts for the duration of the life of the beneficiary. A person with a life interest will be entitled to the income or benefit from the trust property, but not to the trust property itself.

Life tenant A person with the benefit of a life interest.

Lifetime trust A trust which is created during the lifetime of the settlor (as opposed to a trust created by will).

Limitation The period defined by statute or common law, within which proceedings may be brought in a court of law.

Maintenance (power of) The power of trustees to advance all or part of the income of the trust fund to a child beneficiary for the purposes of their maintenance or education.

Majority (age of) Refers to a person who has reached the legal age of adulthood (currently 18 in England and Wales).

Mandatory injunction An injunction which requires the person against whom the order is made to carry out a particular action. See also Prohibitory injunction.

Mareva injunction The former name for a freezing order, a type of injunction designed to prevent the person against whom the order is made from moving assets out of the jurisdiction of the court.

Marriage consideration Refers to the recognition by the court of equity of marriage as a form of legal consideration, or payment. A trust can therefore be created 'in consideration of marriage'.

Marriage settlement A settlement or trust made in contemplation of marriage.

Maxims of equity/equitable maxims A set of guidelines or standards devised by the court of equity as an aid to deciding cases which come before them.

Mental capacity In the context of trust law, the ability of a person to create a valid trust or will, by reason of their mental capability.

Minor A child under the age of 18.

Next of kin Those relatives of the deceased entitled by law to inherit the property of a person who dies without leaving a will.

Obiter A remark or comment made by the judge in giving judgment, which is not relevant or necessary to deciding the case in question.

Object The object of the trust is the person who stands to benefit from it. Also known as the beneficiary.

Objective Where a person is judged on the basis of the ordinary standards of reasonable and honest people, irrespective of their own views of their actions. So, for example, a person would be judged dishonest in this instance if a reasonable and honest person considered their behaviour to be dishonest, even if the person themselves had believed themselves to be acting honestly at the time.

Official receiver An agent appointed by the court to manage the affairs of a person who had become bankrupt.

Option to purchase A contract giving a person the right to purchase an asset (usually land) within a set period of time at an agreed price, upon service of a notice to the seller.

Order to account An order of the court for the trustees to account to the beneficiaries for income and expenditure to the trust fund.

Overreaching The process by which the beneficial interest in property attaches to the purchase price of that property on its sale, so that the beneficiaries retain a beneficial interest in the purchase monies and the buyer is able to take the property free of the beneficiaries' interest.

Pari passu Legal term meaning 'in proportion' or 'equally'. For example recipients of dividends from a company would receive *pari passu*, each shareholder receiving an amount in proportion to their share-holding in the company.

Pecuniary legacy A gift of money left by will.

Perfect/perfected In the context of trust law, to do everything necessary to formalise the trust and make it enforceable.

Perpetuities' rule against The common law rule which says that a trust cannot be valid unless the trust property vests in the beneficiaries within 21 years plus a life in being from the creation of the trust.

Perpetuity period In the context of trusts, 21 years plus a life in being (or human life).

Personal nexus test The test for public benefit in the context of charitable trusts which says that a trust cannot be for the benefit of the public in general (and is therefore invalid) if the thing which connects a class of beneficiaries is their relationship with the settlor. So, for example, a trust for the benefit of employees of a company could not be for public benefit.

Personal property Any property which can be owned by a person, except land.

Personal remedy/claim A claim made against an individual for a sum of money, as opposed to a claim against a piece of property.

Personal representatives Generic term denoting the persons appointed to administer the deceased's estate, either under a will or on intestacy (and thus including both executors and administrators).

Per stirpes In the context of wills, where a child or children takes the share their parent would have done if the parent had survived them.

Plaintiff The term which used to be used for the person who brings an action in a civil court of law. Now called the claimant.

Policy statement (in respect of investment) Where a trustee appoints an agent to act on their behalf in the making of investments for the trust, a written statement advising the agent on how best to act on behalf of the trust.

Ponzi scheme A type of investment fraud whereby 'returns' on the investment are paid to existing investors from funds contributed by new investors to the scheme.

Power Authority given by the owner of property to a person to act in respect of certain property. In the case of a trust, this would be authority to act given by the settlor to the trustees.

Power of appointment In the context of trusts, authority given by the settlor to the trustees to pass property on to another person.

Precatory words Words which express a hope, wish or desire.

Precedent A legal authority created by the decision of the court which can be followed in later cases.

Presumed resulting trust A trust created informally in the situation where contributions are made to the purchase price of property by more than one person but the legal title is held by one of the parties only.

Presumption of advancement In the context of resulting trusts, the presumption that, where property is transferred from father to child or husband to wife, the transfer is intended to be a gift and that the property is not intended to be held on resulting trust for the father/husband.

Prima facie Literally meaning 'in the first instance'. Something which is presumed to be true unless it is disproved.

Principal In the context of agency, the principal is the legal owner of the property who instructs the agent to act on their behalf.

Private purpose trust A trust created for a private (as opposed to a public, or charitable) purpose.

Private trust A trust created for private, as opposed to public, or chartiable, purposes or persons.

Privy Council The court of final appeal for the UK overseas territories and Crown dependencies, and for those Commonwealth countries that have retained the appeal to the Crown, such as Australia.

Professional trustees Trustees acting in their professional capacity.

Prohibitory injunction An order of the court preventing the subject of the order from doing a particular action or thing.

Property adjustment order An order made by the court in divorce or separation proceedings transferring property belonging to one spouse to the other, either in whole or in part.

Proprietary estoppel The equitable doctrine which prevents the legal owner of property from asserting their legal rights in the property to the detriment of a third party (thereby preventing them from having an interest or benefit in the property), on account of the legal owner's unconscionable behaviour.

Proprietary interest A whole or partial interest in the ownership of property.

Proprietary remedy A proprietary remedy asserts that some property in the defendant's possession belongs to the claimant, either at common law or in equity. This is as opposed to a personal remedy, whereby the claimant asserts that the defendant must pay them a sum of money.

Protective trust A special kind of trust set up to protect the assets of the settlor, usually against bankruptcy.

Public policy The rule of law which states that the courts will not make a decision which acts against the public interest.

Public purpose trusts Trusts with a purpose that seeks to benefit the public in general. Charitable trusts are public purpose trusts.

Public trust A trust created for the benefit of the public and not for the benefit of certain private individuals. Charities are public trusts.

Public Trustee The role of Public Trustee is an official office established under section 1 of the Public Trustee Act 1906. The role of the Public Trustee is to administer any private trusts where there is no one else available to act in the capacity of trustee in the trust.

Purpose trusts A trust created for a specified purpose and not for the benefit of a person.

***Quia timet* injunction** An order of the court preventing the subject of the order from carrying out certain actions. Such orders are granted where the applicant is in fear of a particular action being carried out by the person against whom the order is made.

Quistclose trust A special form of trust imposed in the situation where a loan is made for a specific purpose and the lender requires the money to be held in a separate account and used only for the purpose specified for the lending.

Real property Property that includes land or buildings, and anything affixed to the land.

Receiver A person appointed by the court to take charge of the property or business of a business which has run into financial difficulty and is unable to pay its debts.

Rectification The equitable remedy which allows the content of a deed or document that has been drafted in error to be corrected.

Register/land register/register of title The central government register in which details of all registered land is kept.

Registered land/title The system of land ownership whereby ownership of land is proved by registration at the Land Registry, as opposed to by the production of title deeds (as with unregistered land).

Registration The process of registration of legal title of land at the Land Registry.

Relief Where the court exempts the defendant, either in whole or in part, from liability under a breach of trust.

Remainder In the context of wills, all the assets of a deceased person remaining after the payment of their debts and any gifts specified under the terms of their will. Also called the residue.

Remainderman The person who is entitled to inherit property upon the death of another. The beneficiary under the terms of a trust on the death of a person with a life interest.

Rescission/rescind The process of reversing the effects of a transaction or document where that transaction has been carried out in an unconscionable, or morally reprehensible, manner.

Resettlement Where the trust is brought to an end and the trust property is 'settled' or put into trust under new terms.

Residue/residuary estate In the context of wills, all the assets of a deceased person remaining after the payment of their debts and any gifts specified under the terms of their will. Also called the remainder.

Resulting trust An informal trust created in favour of the settlor, either where the settlor has tried to create a trust in favour of a third party but has failed to do so successfully, or in situations where it is presumed by the actions of the settlor that it was their intention to create a trust.

Ring-fence/fencing The placing of client assets by a company into a designated trust account to protect them from the hands of the company's creditors in the event of its liquidation.

Royal lives clause A clause in which the duration of the trust is measured by reference to the life or lives of the last descendant then living to survive of the current monarch. Used as a tool to prevent a purpose trust from being in breach of the perpetuity rule.

Rule against perpetuities See Perpetuities, rule against

***Saunders* v. *Vautier*, rule in** The rule which says that if all of the beneficiaries in the trust have reached the age of majority and have the required mental capacity to do so, they may require the trustees to transfer the legal estate in the trust property to them and terminate the trust.

Search order/search and seizure order An order of the court allowing the person with the benefit of the order to search premises and confiscate or seize evidence found during the search. Formerly called an Anton Piller order.

Secret profit Profit made by a trustee in breach of their trustee duties; for example, the receipt of undeclared commission on an investment of trust funds.

Security (for a loan) Collateral given to a lender in return for the loan of monies, in order to secure the provision of the loan. The lender will then be entitled to keep the security if the loan is not repaid.

Self-dealing The rule which states that a trustee will be in breach of trust if they purchase property belonging to the trust.

Set aside The process whereby the court orders a transaction to be cancelled, revoked or annulled.

Settlement A legal term denoting the formal creation of a trust.

Settlor The person who creates the trust.

Special power The authority given by one person to another to distribute property between a specified class of persons.

Specific performance An equitable remedy which forces the defaulting party to meet their obligations under the terms of an agreement or trust.

Standard investment criteria A set of requirements imposed on trustees under Trustee Act 2000 to which trustees must have regard when making investments of trust money.

Statutory trust A trust created by operation of law under the provisions of a statute.

Stock transfer form A form used to effect the legal transfer of shares in a company.

Strangers In the context of trusts, strangers are third parties with no connection to the trust – in other words, they are not the settlor, they are not a trustee and they are not a beneficiary of the trust.

Strict liability The situation in which a person will be liable for their actions regardless of fault or motive.

***Strong* v. *Bird*, rule in** The rule which says that if a testator appoints someone who owes them money to be their executor, the debt is cancelled when the testator dies.

Subjective Where a person is judged taking into account their own standards. So, for example, a person would only be judged dishonest in this instance if they considered their own behaviour to be dishonest at the time.

Subject matter The property or money of which the trust consists.

Sub-trust A trust created out of a beneficial interest.

Supervising solicitor A solicitor qualified to carry out search and seizure orders.

Supreme Court The highest court of authority in England and Wales (superseding the House of Lords).

Tangible property Property which has a physical existence and can therefore be touched, such as land or buildings, a car, a watch and so on.

Testator The legal term for a person creating a will.

Testatrix A female testator.

Title deeds The deeds and documents which form the basis of legal title to property in unregistered land.

Tracing The legal process of following money which has been misappropriated with a view to reclaiming it.

Trust A creation of the court of equity whereby a person gives property to another to hold for the benefit of a third person.

Trust corporation A professional body or company acting in the capacity of trustee under a trust.

Trustee The person who administers the trust fund on behalf of the beneficiaries and who has legal ownership of the trust property.

Trustee in bankruptcy A person appointed by the court to administer the affairs of a person who has been declared bankrupt.

Trust instrument Any deed or document (including a will) which has the effect of creating a trust.

Unclean hands Refers to a person who is not blameless. A person cannot claim the benefit of equity if they are in some way responsible for the fate which has befallen them: 'he who comes to equity must come with clean hands'.

Unconscionable/unconscionability To act in a way which is morally reprehensible, or which would prick the conscience of the ordinary reasonable man.

Unincorporated/unincorporated association An organisation or group which has not been formally incorporated to form its own legal personality, such as a sports club or political party.

Unregistered title The system of legal ownership of land in England and Wales which pre-dates Land Registration. Ownership proved by the production of title deeds, as opposed to registration on a central government register.

Unsecured debts Debts which do not have the backing of any collateral security. They are only as good as the personal worth and reputation of the debtor.

Use An ancient right held by one person to take the profits arising from a particular parcel of land which is owned and possessed by another.

Vest/vested/vesting The process by which a right is transferred to another person unconditionally. In the case of trusts this might refer to an interest vesting in a beneficiary, or to the legal title to the property vesting in the trustees.

Vested interest In the context of trusts, where the beneficiary has an interest in a trust fund which is certain. Can include future interests, as long as the future event is certain to occur and not dependent on an event that might not happen.

Vicarious liability This is the situation in which a person may be held liable for the actions of another, even though the person being held responsible may not have done anything wrong. For example, the liability of an employer for the actions of their employees.

Void Legal term meaning 'invalid'.

Voidable The situation in which a transaction is not automatically held to be invalid, but can be set aside at the instigation of the beneficiaries (in the case of a trust) or some other third party.

Volunteer Someone who receives a benefit without consideration.

Index